The Life and Times of THEODORE ROOSEVELT

The Life and Times of
Theodore Roosevelt

WILLIAM HENRY HARBAUGH

NEW, REVISED EDITION

COLLIER BOOKS   NEW YORK

Preface

THIS BIOGRAPHY is written for the general reader—for the man or woman with a broad interest in American history, and for the college student. I have based it partly on original sources, partly on memoirs and other works by Theodore Roosevelt's contemporaries, and partly on the collection of Roosevelt's letters and the numerous scholarly reappraisals of his turbulent career, published in the last fifteen years. Throughout, I have tried to keep Roosevelt in the context of his age while yet exercising the historian's heavy and sobering responsibility of judging his subject's deeds in the perspective of time.

Inevitably, I am heavily obligated—to my friend and professor, Arthur S. Link of Princeton, who urged me to undertake the project; to Elting E. Morison of M.I.T. for his thoughtful appraisal of the entire manuscript; to Hermann Hagedorn, director emeritus of the Theodore Roosevelt Association, for the generous gift of his time and for his many provocative and informative suggestions; to Alfred Young of Paterson State College for his numerous perceptive criticisms of the whole; and to Richard Lowitt of Connecticut College for Women, who was a source of intellectual sustenance throughout, criticizing, encouraging, and sharing always his own vast knowledge of the period.

I am also grateful to numerous other friends, colleagues, or graduate students for reading particular chapters or discussing special topics with me. Among them are Louis L. Gerson, Peter Schroeder, John Thorkelson, and Sam Witryol of the University of Connecticut; Norman Enhorning and Ronald Grele, formerly of that institution; Ernest Cawcroft of Jamestown, New York; Alexander M. Bickel and Ward S. Bowman, Jr. of the Yale Law School; Thomas N. Bonner of the University of Omaha; John Wells Davidson and David W. Hirst of The Papers of Woodrow Wilson; and Captain David Horner of the United States Military Academy.

Edmund A. Moore, my former chairman at the University of Connecticut, and Harrison W. Carter, dean of the college of arts and sciences, gave me the understanding without which books can hardly be written under the new dispensation of overcrowded classes and increased teaching schedules. Calvin Woodward read the galleys and caught a number of errors of fact and interpretation. Frances Stearns met my typing deadlines with skill and equanimity.

I am also indebted to Robert H. Haynes, curator of the Theodore Roosevelt Collection at Harvard University; to Leslie C. Stratton, formerly director of the Theodore Roosevelt Association, and to Helen MacLachlan, the Association's curator; to Roberta Smith, reference librarian at the University of Connecticut; and to the staff of the Manuscript Division of the Library of Congress.

I should like further to record my warm pleasure in the stimulating cooperation of John Farrar, friend, editor, and publisher, and of John Peck, associate editor of Farrar, Straus and Cudahy.

Finally, I am indebted to my wife, Wayne Talbot Harbaugh, for more than the usual reasons. She not only compiled the index, she made clear, logical, and penetrating criticisms of many parts of the manuscript. In a different way I am also grateful for the diversions afforded by the invasions of my study by Lyn, who has grown to learn that daddy was not really writing a story about her teddy bear; by her friend Clemency, who was always a little skeptical; and more recently by Billy, to whom teddy bear and Teddy Roosevelt are just becoming synonymous.

Out of personal affection, and in appreciation of his long and fruitful service to the scholarship and memory of a great and controversial man, I dedicate this book to Hermann Hagedorn.

A Note to the Collier Books Edition

Although this edition is somewhat shorter than the original, it has been tightened rather than abridged. At the most, three or four minor episodes have been cut out. Substantive revisions have also been minor. I have sharpened some criticisms of Roosevelt, softened one or two others, and changed a few interpretations in the light of the most recent scholarship. I have also brought the Chapter Notes up to date. But in the main I have held to the point of view of the original.

I am indebted to Warren I. Susman for textual criticisms and to Gail Talbot and Joseph W. DeMent for editorial suggestions.

W. H. H.

Bucknell University
Lewisburg, Pa.
October, 1962

Contents

Part Five / THE HIGH TIDE OF PROGRESSIVISM

Part Six / ONE LAST GREAT CAUSE

PART ONE

The Making of a Man

Chapter 1

The First Battle

> *When I went into politics at this time I was not conscious of going in with the set purpose to benefit other people, but of getting for myself a privilege to which I was entitled in common with other people.*
> —Theodore Roosevelt, *An Autobiography*

AN AIR of expectation fell over the New York Assembly in Albany on April 5, 1882, as Theodore Roosevelt, a twenty-three-year-old freshman, arose to speak.

Roosevelt was already a young man apart. He stood only five feet eight inches high and weighed perhaps 140 pounds; but his head was so large and distinctive that it made his muscular shoulders and heavy chest appear slight. It rested on a bull neck and was crowned by a shock of wavy yellow hair parted a little off center. Beneath a moderately low brow, blue-gray eyes squinted behind thick pince-nez and a full blond mustache set off a square face framed by extraordinarily small ears knit close to the head. Roosevelt's manner was at once engaging and disturbing. His clothes were conservative in cut; but he wore them with a flair that suggested affectation. He was cordial and courteous, yet unconsciously patronizing. And though he pronounced *A* with a broad accent and *R* with a soft roll, he spoke with a kind of suppressed vehemence. When excited his voice would shift involuntarily from a resonant tenor to a shrill falsetto.

"What on earth will New York send next?" an upstate newspaperman had mused on meeting him for the first time. "We almost shouted with laughter to think that the most veritable representative of the New York dude had come to the Chamber," a close friend recalled long afterward.

Roosevelt's remarks that April afternoon were exceptional even for him. In words the press described as "almost startling," he demanded that the Assembly investigate reports that T. R. Westbrook, a Republican-appointed justice of the State

Supreme Court, had colluded with Jay Gould, Russell Sage, and Cyrus Field in a "stock-jobbing" deal for control of the Manhattan Elevated Railway. The professionals were shocked, for neither the G.O.P. regulars nor the Tammany Democrats wished to cross the notorious Gould or to impugn state officials who owed their positions to behind-the-scenes arrangements by the leaders of both parties. But Roosevelt, who had obtained an unpublished letter in which Westbrook promised Gould that he would "go to the very verge of judicial discretion" to advance the financier's interests, insisted on an investigation.

Young Roosevelt's charges were temporarily buried as the Assembly recessed for the Easter holidays. They had so aroused civic leaders, however, that when the Assembly reconvened the Republican leader, Thomas Alvord, and his Tammany counterpart, John Kelly, lost control of their forces. In spite of Alvord's assertion that the only people upholding the attack on Westbrook were the "unnaturalized Englishmen who edited the *New York Times*" and the publisher of the *New York Herald* who "desired merely to get a strike at John Kelly," Roosevelt's resolution for an inquiry went through by 104 to 6.

The victory proved short-lived, the Judiciary Committee exonerating Westbrook late in May. "To you, members of the Legislature of the greatest Commonwealth in this great Federal Union," Roosevelt grandiloquently declared following this rebuff, "I say you cannot by your votes clear the Judge. He stands condemned by his own acts in the eyes of all honest people. All you can do is shame yourselves and give him a brief extension of his dishonored career. You cannot cleanse the leper. Beware lest you taint yourself with his leprosy."

The Westbrook affair was a political landmark for Theodore Roosevelt. For the first time he had tasted popular favor, and for the first time he had emerged as the leader of a faction. Although his brashness had incited resentment, especially among the regulars, his courage and persistence had also won respect. From then until the presidential campaign of 1884 his reputation as a reformer with the temerity to act on his principles rose; and from then until 1884 his influence on independent-minded men inside and outside the legislature burgeoned. "I think he grew faster than anybody I ever knew," Isaac Hunt, a taciturn farmer-lawyer-assemblyman from Jefferson County later reflected. "He increased in stature, in strength, mentally all the time. . . . I thought I knew more than he did, but before we got through he grew right away from me."

The way had been superficially easy for this scion of the old New York aristocracy. Theodore had enjoyed numerous advantages—a warm family circle, tutors, vacations in the country and travel abroad, a gentleman's education at Harvard, and a modest inheritance on reaching age. Had his background been different, in fact, had he not been known as an educated, high-minded gentleman of independent income, he would not have been nominated for the legislature in the autumn of 1881.

Yet the difference between outward appearances and inner pressures is often great. The courageous, fearless man whom the world eventually came to know—the crusader against crime and corruption, the heroic soldier, the assailant of big business, the creator of a national political party—was not always the man that Roosevelt himself knew or had known. His vaunted self-confidence derived more from experience and achievement than inherent security. Roosevelt's is the story of a man driven: of a man whose strength came from the conquest of fear, not from the lack of it; of a man compelled again and again to prove himself and possessed, happily, of the moral and physical stamina to do so.

Theodore had been asthmatic from birth. Rarely a day or a night passed during which the baby, the boy, or the adolescent did not suffer. One of his earliest recollections was of his father walking up and down the room at night holding him in his arms. Summers in the Hudson River country or the New Jersey highlands failed to induce a cure; nor did a tour of Europe help. "I was very sick last night and Mama was so kind telling me storys [sic] and rubbing me with her delicate fingers," Theodore wrote from abroad at the age of eleven. "I am here in Richfield now," he reported the next year, ". . . because I was sick."

By then, however, his health had already begun to change for the better. Told by his father that he would have to build himself up by his own efforts, the twelve-year-old youngster had thrown back his head, flashed his prominent teeth, and retorted, "I'll make my body." That fall he started daily workouts in a gymnasium and on apparatus on the back porch of his house; and by the following summer he had improved so markedly that asthma never again seriously interrupted his activities.

In spite of his infirmities, the child "Teedie" had early displayed a remarkable zest for life. His parents were partly responsible. So great was their affection and responsiveness, in fact, that he might have developed abnormal attachments had he been an only child. But fortunately there were brothers and sisters—Anna, the eldest, then Elliott and Corinne, both born after Theodore. There was also direction and discipline, perhaps in excess, from the father. In his *Autobiography* Roosevelt described his mother as "a sweet, gracious, beautiful Southern woman, a delightful companion . . . beloved by everybody" and "blessed with a strong sense of humor." But he lavished praise upon his father. "He combined strength and courage with gentleness, tenderness, and great unselfishness. . . . With great love and patience, and the most understanding sympathy and consideration, he combined insistence on discipline . . . he was the only man of whom I was ever really afraid."

Theodore's anguished diary entries following the senior Roosevelt's death in 1878, when Theodore was nineteen, offer even sharper insight into the relationship between father and son. "I feel that if it were not for the certainty, that . . . 'he is not dead but gone before,' I should almost perish," he wrote five days after his father died. A month later he said that it seemed as if his heart would break when he thought of his terrible loss. He added that his father had "shared all my joys, and in sharing doubled them, and soothed all the few sorrows I ever had." A later entry lamented the loss of "the only human being to whom I told *everything,* never failing to get loving advice and sweet sympathy in return; no one, but my wife, if ever I marry, will ever be able to take his place."

The number of references gradually declined, but the intensity remained. "O, Father, Father how bitterly I miss you, mourn you and long for you!" Theodore wrote several months afterward. "I realize more and more every day that I am as much inferior to Father morally and mentally as physically," he confessed a full half year after the senior Roosevelt died. "But," he added in a display of fatalism that would lose its religious cast as he grew older, " 'Trust in the Lord and do good!' "

Theodore Roosevelt, Sr. had been a large-framed, athletic man with a leonine head, a striking beard, and a buoyant, dominant manner. Born to the old Dutch mercantile tradition, he loved life and regarded business as merely a means to supply his family's considerable wants. After his main interest, the import glass trade, collapsed some years before his death, he never took up another, absorbing himself instead in social life and philanthropic and civic matters. His understanding of social and economic problems was restricted by his concern with character and morality; yet he felt obligated to aid the suffering and the oppressed, to work for reform without disturbing the existing social framework. To Theodore, Jr. he transmitted his sense of moral duty and habit of *noblesse oblige*.

Whatever the psychological nuances of their relationship, this distinguished gentleman failed his eldest son in only one overt respect: he remained a civilian throughout the Civil War, probably in deference to his Southern-born wife. To be sure, he gave abundantly of his energies and talents. He helped draft the bill establishing an Allotment Commission and then toured the camps in an exhaustive effort to persuade enlisted men to send home a portion of their monthly salaries. "I would never have felt satisfied with myself after this war is over if I had done nothing," he confided to his wife, "and that I do feel now that I am only doing my duty." But it was the duty of the civilian rather than that of the soldier.

After the war the Roosevelt family again enjoyed the perquisites of moderate wealth and social position. For the parents there were gracious entertainments, dinner parties and balls, fine wines, and small talk with relatives and friends, as well as civic activity. For the children there were exciting rides in the rig with their father, who loved to race; long hours reading with their mother, who was well read in a limited, genteel sense; most of the toys they chanced to want; and frequent visits with other youngsters of their background. On the whole, however, the children's activities centered in and around the four-story brownstone house and yard at 28 East 20th Street where Theodore had been born on October 27, 1858, and where the family lived until they moved into another brownstone on 57th Street.

Theodore's advantages softened the misery of his poor health somewhat; his effort to conquer it stands as a striking testament to his courage and determination. Yet to explain

Roosevelt the man in terms of his sickly childhood is to do injustice to other of his natural endowments. Even as a slender, almost spindly youngster, his surging physical and intellectual energy left little time either to brood or to suffer. From the beginning he used his keen intelligence, gave vent to his insatiable curiosity, and sought outlets for his burning desire to be recognized.

Of Theodore's youthful passions, nature was the most consuming. At the age of eight he started the practice of collecting live mice and reptiles which would later be emulated by his sons and would keep various Roosevelt family servants on edge for forty years. By the age of fourteen he had grasped the main tenets of Darwin. And when he entered Harvard in the autumn of 1876 he could probably have passed an examination in the works of the most renowned naturalists of the era. By then, too, he had built a collection of bird skins, writes the zoologist, Paul R. Cutright, "which for size, variety, and skill of preparation was doubtless unequalled by any boy his age in the United States." Based on the observation and study which always distinguished Roosevelt from the man of pure action, this interest later enabled him to discourse learnedly with eminent professional naturalists and to make modest contributions to scientific classification. It also formed the springboard for one of his greatest accomplishments, the vitalization of the conservation movement.

If nature was young Roosevelt's first great interest, books were his second. Even as a child he read omnivorously and with surprising catholicity. Works of maudlin sentimentality, pious morality, high adventure, and classic quality were all devoured by his restless mind. "I worshipped *Little Men* and *Little Women* and *An Old-Fashioned Girl*," he recalled. But "I disliked the Swiss Family Robinson because of the wholly impossible collection of animals met by that worthy family as they ambled inland from the wreck."

Theodore's travels in Europe, his fascination with nature, his reading, and his vacations with his sisters, cousins, and robust younger brother Elliott, who served as his protector for a while—these and the passage of time wrought their influence upon his personality. From a rather shy, retiring child he changed into an outgoing, uninhibited adolescent with a delightful sense of humor and a tendency toward mild exhibitionism.

"As a young girl," wrote one of the family friends, "I remember dreading to sit next him at any formal dinner lest I become so convulsed with laughter at his whispered sallies as to disgrace myself and be forced to leave the room." Or, as Theodore himself once wrote his mother, "I went to Miss Nelly Dean's wedding yesterday, and made myself so agreable [sic] that one old Lady paid me a compliment. She evidently had a great deal of discrimination." These traits did not escape his contemporaries. Theodore "always thought he could do things better than anyone else," his cousin, Maude Elliott, once wrote.

Actually, Theodore only *tried* to do things better than everyone else. His formidable powers of rationalization notwithstanding, he had a realistic insight into his own abilities; and neither as a boy nor as a man did he tend to overestimate them. If he indulged in self-praise, it was because of deserved pride in deeds performed and barriers surmounted. Life was an unrelieved, if joyous, struggle, and false modesty was not among its virtues. As Theodore wrote his father that same year, "I then had several rounds with Johnie and Edward, in which I kept my own, as Johnie is smaller, though more used to fighting, and Edward, although much larger does not know so much about boxing." A few years later he remarked that of his five closest friends, two overestimated him, two undervalued him, and only one gauged his true worth.

Young Roosevelt also abounded in warmth, sympathy, and affection. His letters repeatedly reveal him inquiring solicitously of his parents' health, writing fondly of "cunning" young children, and pouring out his love for "My own darling little Motherling" and "My dear Papa." The diary entries of his college years were similarly effusive: "Elliott is a noble fellow, wonderfully grown up in every way." "What a wonderful set of relations I have got—cousins and all, especially my own family." "I wonder if ever a man had two better sisters than I have!"

Roosevelt lost few, if any, of those qualities in maturity. They were modified or offset, however, by an extraordinary severity of judgment and by a strain of ruthlessness and capacity for passing hatred which so often mar the competitive personality.

If there was anything in Theodore's boyhood aside from the sense of duty and *noblesse oblige* he got from his father to suggest that he would someday become a social reformer, it was only his strident moralizing. "Did you hear that Percy Cushion was a failure?" he once wrote his father from Dresden. "He swore like a trooper and used disreputable language, so I gave him some pretty strong hints, which he at last took, and we do not see much more of him." As a green college freshman a few years later Theodore righteously reported that of the eleven other boys at his table, "no less than seven do not smoke and four drink nothing stronger than beer." As a more sophisticated sophomore, however, he conceded that although he got rather bored with the drunken brothers of D.K.E., he found an occasional fraternity social "good enough fun." In one of the few intimations in his diary of repressed aggressions, he also confessed that "Wine makes me awfully fighting."

Roosevelt had entered Harvard in 1876 after two years of intensive preparation under a private tutor. Because of his lingering asthma he took private rooms; and in spite of membership in the best clubs, success in athletics and studies, and an active social life in Cambridge, he remained always a little apart. William Roscoe Thayer remembered that he was "a good deal of a joke . . . active and enthusiastic and that was all." But Charles Washburn, who knew him more intimately, contended that he was "loved by many," was "in a class by himself," and was recognized as "a person *sui generis*" who was not to be judged by ordinary standards.

"What a royally good time I am having," Roosevelt exclaimed as a junior. "I can't conceive of a fellow *possibly* enjoying himself more." Academically, he did well in those subjects which interested him, notably natural history, literature, and political economy; only passably in those which did not. But his over-all performance was sufficiently high—he finished "second among the gentlemen" and twenty-first in a class of 158—to win election to Phi Beta Kappa. He also became an editor of *The Advocate,* one of the three undergraduate papers. He later complained, however, that "There was very little in my actual studies which helped me in after-life." In his *Autobiography,* written just after the Progressive campaign of 1912, he lamented that "there was almost no teaching of the need for collective action, and of the fact that in addition to, not as a substitute for, individual responsibility, there is a collective responsibility. Books such as Herbert Croly's *Promise of American Life* and Walter E. Weyl's *New Democracy* would generally at that time have been treated either as unintelligible or else as pure heresy."

Perhaps. Yet Roosevelt conceded that his readings at Harvard did reinforce that "self-reliance, energy, courage, the power of insisting on his own rights and the sympathy that makes him regardful of the rights of others" which had been his father's teaching as well as the lesson of *Our Young Folks*. He was also stimulated. As he wrote his mother in October, 1878, political economy and metaphysics "are even more interesting than my Natural History courses; and all the more so, from the fact that I radically disagree on many points with the men whose books we are reading (Mill and Ferrier)."

Roosevelt's extracurricular life at Harvard attests further to his intellectual awakening. He became a convert to free trade after reading John Stuart Mill and other laissez-faire economists. He served as head of the Natural History Society. He helped organize the Finance Club, under whose auspices two of the most celebrated economists in the nation, William Graham Sumner and Francis A. Walker of Yale, gave special lectures at Cambridge. And in a mock presidential election in 1880 he voted for the Democrat, Senator Thomas Bayard, out of contempt for the Republican candidates—Grant, Sherman, and Blaine. "The gentleman [Roosevelt] in charge of the polls," said *The Advocate*, "is a proof that the movement is not one of idle curiosity, but of earnest purpose."

Roosevelt was also a member of the Art Club, supported the Glee Club in a non-singing role, and belonged to a literary-political discussion group to which he submitted a paper, "The Machine in Politics." He was "forever at it," one of his classmates recalled, "and probably no man of his time read more extensively or deeply, especially in directions that did not count on the honor-list or marking-sheet. He had the happy power of abstraction, and nothing was more common than a noisy roomful of college mates with Roosevelt frowning with intense absorption over a book in the corner." Theodore himself was satisfied. "[My] *career* (both in and out of college) *has been more successful than that of any man I have known,*" he confided to his diary shortly after graduation.

Meanwhile Roosevelt's compulsion to exhort and admonish grew. "He used to stop men in the Yard, or call them to him," a classmate remembered. "Then he would block the narrow gravel path and soon make sparks from an argument fly. He was so enthusiastic and had such a startling array of deeply rooted interests that we all thought he would make a great journalist." His *Advocate* editorials suggest, however, that he was already more moralist than journalist. "Last year we had good individual players, but they did not work together nearly as well as the Princeton team, and were not in as good condition as the Yale men," he wrote in one. "The football season is short; and while it does last, the men ought to work faithfully, if they expect to win for Harvard the position she held three years ago." As President of the United States twenty years later, Roosevelt addressed the captain of the Harvard squad in the same vein.

Theodore also developed into a competent athlete at Harvard. After being soundly thrashed by a country bully as a youngster, he characteristically resolved to learn to box well enough to defend himself. Long after he fulfilled that purpose (he won one fight as an assemblyman) he continued to spar regularly, often with professionals. He became as proficient as his poor eyesight would permit—his right hand was said to have been powerful—and in his junior year he reached the finals in the lightweight class. Although he lost the championship bout, he won the plaudits of the spectators by commanding them to stop hissing his opponent for bloodying his nose after the referee had called the end of a round. "It's all right," he dramatically exclaimed with his arm upraised, "he didn't hear him." (He failed to mention the incident in his diaries.)

Roosevelt was too light for football; so besides rowing, tennis, and riding, he channeled his cascading energy into camping trips into the Maine wilderness where he fused the qualities of the hunter and naturalist. W. W. "Bill" Sewall, a brawny, bearded woodsman of thirty-three who served Roosevelt as guide, counselor, and companion for several years thereafter, recalled that "He was different from anybody that I had ever met," especially in that "he was fair-minded."

He and I agreed in our ideas of fair play and right and wrong. Besides, he was always good-natured and full of fun. I do not think I ever remember him being 'out of sorts.' He did not feel well sometimes, but he never would admit it. . . . Some folks said that he was headstrong and aggressive, but I never found him so except when necessary. . . . Of course he did not understand the woods, but on every other subject he was posted. The reason that he knew so much about everything, I found, was that wherever he went he got right in with the people . . . he was quick to find the real man in very simple men. He didn't look for a brilliant man when he found me; he valued me for what I was worth.

Theodore's contact with Sewall and other woodsmen was his one broadening influence during his undergraduate years; he otherwise consorted with his social peers. Although he gradually lost his blatant class-consciousness (as a freshman he had found the Yale undergraduates a "scrubby set" and had been reluctant to become intimate with the New York group at Harvard because he knew nothing of their "antecedents"), he always prided himself on his election to The Hasty Pudding and the Porcellian. As President of the United States, he was concerned lest his sons not receive the same distinctions. A letter to his "Darling Motherling" describes a normal round of social activities:

Last Monday I drove Jack Tebbets over to call on the Miss Bacons, who are very nice girls. Wednesday I dined at the Lees, and spent the loveliest kind of an evening with Rosy, Alice and Rose. The two girls must come on to Boston next month if only to see Chestnut Hill; and, by Jove, I shall be awfully disappointed if they do'n't like it. Mamie Saltonstalls birthday was on Friday; I gave her a small silver fan-chain. Saturday I spent all the morning playing tennis with the two Miss Lanes. . . .
. . . Wednesday Harry Shaw and I give a small opera party to Mr. and Mrs. Saltonstall, Rose and Alice.

One of those girls was Alice Hathaway Lee, a tall, graceful young lady of Brahmin lineage, classic features, and coquettish demeanor who resided on Chestnut Hill. Theodore had been courting her since early in his junior year and in February, 1880, their engagement was formally announced. "She is just the sweetest, prettiest sunniest little darling that ever lived, and with all her laughing, teasing ways, she is as loving and tender as she can be," he wrote his sister Corinne. Everything had been "subordinate to winning her," he confided to a friend, Henry Minot, "so you can perhaps understand a change in my ideas as regards science &c."

Not quite "everything" had been subordinated to romance during that final year. Roosevelt neglected his duties on *The Advocate* and failed to deliver the commencement "dissertation" his rank in the class entitled him ("I have always studied well . . . so I can afford to cut now," he explained in his diary shortly after his engagement). But he won honor grades in four of his five courses, wrote a senior thesis on "The Practicability of Equalizing Men and Women Before the Law," and drafted the first two chapters of his *Naval War of 1812*, which was published two years after his graduation. A work of limited scope, high technical competence, and considerable dramatic power, *The Naval War* was to win favorable reviews in the United States and be so well received in Great Britain that Roosevelt would be invited to do the section on the War of 1812 for Clowes's *History of the Royal Navy*.

Alice Lee was only eighteen years old when she became engaged to Theodore after a frenetic courtship of eight months. "See that girl?" he exclaimed to a friend at one point. "I am going to marry her. She won't have me, but I am going to have her." Alice resisted him, however, and in the fall of 1879 Theodore became so depressed that friends sent to New York for a relative to soothe him. "I have been pretty nearly crazy," he later confessed (night after night he had wandered through the woods). "But I do not think any outsider suspected it; I have not written a word about it in my diary since a year ago last Thanksgiving."

On January 25, 1880, Alice Lee had submitted. "I am so happy that I dare not trust in my own happiness," Theodore wrote in his diary that night. "How she, so pure and sweet and beautiful can think of marrying me I can not understand, but I praise and thank God it is so." He added that it was love at first sight. "Thank heaven I am absolutely pure," he wrote two weeks later. "I can tell Alice everything I have ever done."

Alice's parents had at first opposed an early marriage. But after what Theodore described as "a long but very peaceable argument," they acceded to his wishes. On October 27, 1880, his twenty-second birthday, Theodore and Alice Lee were married in the Unitarian Church of Brookline. A short honeymoon at Oyster Bay, Long Island, followed. "Our intense happiness is too sacred to be written about," was Theodore's terse diary entry. They drove in the buggy, played tennis, walked in the woods, and read aloud from the *Pickwick Papers, Quentin Durward*, and Keats. A few months later Roosevelt purchased the first of three deeds totalling 155 acres and including the hilltop overlooking the Long

Island Sound where Sagamore Mohannis and other Indian chieftains had held their councils of war in years long past.

At the end of their brief honeymoon Theodore and Alice returned to New York City to pass the winter in the house on West 57th Street with Mrs. Roosevelt, Sr. preparatory to a tour of Europe in the spring. Meanwhile Alice joined the Presbyterian Church. "Now we are one in *everything*," Theodore said in his diary. "My cup is almost running over."

Roosevelt had entered Harvard determined to prepare for a scientific career in spite of his father's warning that the financial remuneration would be small. In his sophomore year he and Henry Minot published a paper, "Summer Birds of the Adirondacks in Franklin County, N.Y.," which the zoologist, C. Hart Merriam, commended. (Merriam later termed Roosevelt the "world's authority on big game mammals.") The next year Roosevelt published on his own, "Notes on Some of the Birds of Oyster Bay." Meanwhile his name was listed in the *Naturalist's Directory*.

By the time of his engagement, however, Roosevelt had decided to forego science. He later blamed Harvard's teaching methods: "They treated biology as purely a science of the laboratory and the microscope. There was a total failure to understand the great variety of kinds of work that could be done by naturalists, including what could be done by outdoor naturalists." The charges may have been true, but there is no evidence that Roosevelt thought so at the time. Indeed, his diary reveals that although he enjoyed laboratory work, he was "perfectly blue" at the need to spend three years abroad completing his professional training.

A year before his engagement to Alice Lee, moreover, Roosevelt had stopped taking field notes. At almost the same time he severed connections with the Harvard Natural History Society because of the "press of other duties (in my studies and in outside societies)." Sometime later he sought the advice of J. Laurence Laughlin, then a young economics instructor. Should he continue in biology or turn, perhaps, to economics? Laughlin replied that the nation needed men who could think clearly on public questions.

Following his graduation and honeymoon, Roosevelt read law in the offices of his uncle, Robert Barnhill Roosevelt. He also attended the Columbia Law School where his egotism and energetic questioning of the lecturers set him off from his peers. He lacked the air of the professional student, a classmate recalled, but he was a "favorite" and was "one of the best men there, considered as a man." Theodore was already too moralistic to give his heart to the law, however, and though he professed to "like the law school work very much," he soon abandoned it. "Many of the big corporation lawyers, to whom the ordinary members of the bar then as now looked up, held certain standards which were difficult to recognize as compatible with the idealism I supposed every high-minded young man is apt to feel," he explained in his *Autobiography*. That statement rings too much with the progressivism of 1912 to be taken literally; yet it probably reflected Roosevelt's views of 1880-81 in some degree. As Putnam cogently phrases it, "He aligned the moral law and the common law and was shocked at the discrepancy."

Meanwhile Roosevelt had been nominated as the Republican candidate for assemblyman for the Twenty-first District. He had joined the District Club the year before because "I intended to be one of the governing class." And he had joined the Republican club in particular because "a young man of my bringing-up and convictions could join only the Republican party." For all its corruption and callous neglect of the public interest, the G.O.P. still loomed large as the preserver of national unity. Roosevelt had been an uncompromising Unionist since boyhood—he had once prayed to "divine Providence to grind the Southern troops to powder"— and a strident nationalist from his matriculation in college. So even if he had not been prompted by class-consciousness, he would have doubtless cast his lot with the Grand Old Party.

Roosevelt's baptism occurred at a District Club meeting during the winter of 1880–81 when he and a handful of idealistic compatriots stood against almost a hundred regulars in hopeless support of a movement for nonpartisan street cleaning. Otherwise he devoted his energies to breaking the barriers that separated him from the lower-class Republicans: "I went around there often enough to have the men get accustomed to me and to have me get accustomed to them, so that we began to speak the same language, and so that each could begin to live down, in the other's mind, what Bret Harte has called 'the defective moral quality of being a stranger.' " He succeeded. Although most of the professionals continued to regard Roosevelt as unique, many of them also liked him. By the spring of 1881 he was on fairly good terms with Jake Hess, the German-American district leader, and on quite close terms with Joe Murray, an Irish-born lieutenant who had been "raised as a barefoot boy on First Avenue," served in the Army of the Potomac, and was eventually appointed Deputy Commissioner of Immigration for New York by Roosevelt himself.

While Theodore and his bride were leisurely wandering through Europe in the summer of 1881, rumblings of revolt were disrupting the District Club's harmony. Riled by the failure of Hess's man to support the nonpartisan street-cleaning bill in the last legislative session, civic-minded Republicans were threatening defection, or at least a tightening of the purse strings. Other, less civic-minded Republicans were champing at Hess's inability to get a full measure of patronage from President Chester A. Arthur.

Roosevelt's new-found friend, Joe Murray, accordingly decided to break Hess's control by backing a candidate of his own for the Assembly. Fastening upon Roosevelt as most likely to appeal to the "better" elements—the Twenty-first District ran from the pretentious stone mansions of Fifth Avenue to the shabby brick tenements of the West Side—Murray prepared his ground well. When the nominating convention met on October 28 in the large, barn-like room over a saloon that served as Club headquarters, he mustered a 16–9 majority for Roosevelt, who had allowed his name to be entered with some reluctance. Roosevelt meanwhile announced that he was owned by no man, would go to Albany untrammeled and unpledged, and would vote independently on municipal and other public matters. He added upon formal notification of his nomination that he would vote with the Republican party on national issues.

Roosevelt's nomination struck a responsive chord except among a few close relatives. One Republican newspaper pointed out that the "substantial property owners" of the district needed a representative at Albany; Roosevelt was ideal because his "family has been long and honorably known as one of the foremost in this City." Another declared that "no better representative of the taxpayers of New York could have been selected." And a group of Republican gentlemen and lawyers of the type against which Theodore would later inveigh applauded him as "conspicuous for his honesty and integrity, and eminently qualified."

Meanwhile, Hess good-humoredly mustered the machine behind the young aristocrat who had been made the instrument of his own rebuke—but not until after he and Murray changed tactics following Roosevelt's first sally into the heart of the district.

"We started in a German lager-beer saloon on Sixth Avenue," Murray recalled:

The saloon keeper's name was Carl Fischer. Hess was well acquainted with him. I knew him slightly. We had a small beer and Hess introduces T. R. to Fischer and Fischer says, "By the way, Mr. Roosevelt, I hope you will do something for us when you get to Albany. We are taxed much out of proportion to grocers, etc., and we have to pay $200 for the privilege."

"Why that's not enough!" said T.R.

After we got out on the sidewalk we came to the conclusion that we had better stop the canvass right then and there. I says, "Mr. Roosevelt, you go see your personal friends. Hess and I will look after this end. You can reach your personal friends, we can't."

Roosevelt heeded their advice; on election day he led the entire Republican ticket by 600 votes. "Too True! Too True! I have come a 'political hack. . . .'" he wrote Washburn the day after his election. "But do'n't think I am going to go into politics after this year, for I am not." A little less than two months later he presented himself in pince-nez, gold fob, and evening dress to the Republican caucus at the Delavan House in Albany.

The outlook was not encouraging. The Republicans were bad, Roosevelt wrote in a diary he kept sporadically. But at least they had numbers of lawyers and farmers among them. The Democrats included "six liquor sellers, two bricklayers, a butcher, a tobacconist, a pawn broker, a compositer [sic] and a typesetter . . ." Worse yet, twenty-five were Irish, and "the average catholic Irishman of the first generation as represented in this Assembly, is a low, venal, corrupt and unintelligent brute." The Tammany men were "managed entirely by the commands of some of John Kelly's lieutenants who are always in the Assembly chamber"; the County Democrats by the Commissioner of Public Works, Hubert O. Thompson, "a gross, enormously fleshy man, with a full face and thick, sensual lips . . . " Still, there were a few who seemed "to be pretty good men." Two Republican farmers, O'Neil and Sheehy, were "among the best members of the house."

Roosevelt's strictures against first-generation Irish Catholics were grounded more on observation than deep-seated bias; before the end of the five-month session he formed strong friendships with several Irish Democrats of anti-Tammany persuasion. Nor did he then sympathize with those of his class who tended "to trace all evils, from the absence of rain to the fight with Arabi Pascha, to the presence of Roman Catholics in America." He recognized Tammany Hall for what it was—a sink of corruption dominated by Irish Catholics—and he saw among Republicans a somewhat better class of citizen. As he confided to his diary, "if the worst elements of all, the twenty low Irishmen, were subtracted, the Republican average would still be higher than the Democratic." It would be some time before Roosevelt realized that up-state Protestant Republicans could be as opposed to social justice in their avowedly moralistic way as Tammany Democrats in their blatantly unscrupulous way; that Democratic iniquity in low places had long been surpassed by Republican solicitude for private business interest in high places.

Roosevelt managed to conceal most of his views of his associates, but he proved unable to suppress his opinions on public matters. Every fiber of his being compelled him to speak out. "He was the most indiscreet guy I ever met . . . ," Isaac Hunt recalled. "George [Spinney], Billy O'Neil and I used to sit on his coat-tails. Billy O'Neil would say to him: 'What do you want to do that for, you damn fool; you will ruin yourself and everybody else!' . . . He was the most impulsive human being I ever knew."

Age and responsibility were to temper Roosevelt; only rarely would he make important decisions without careful deliberation in later years. Yet even as he matured he remained impulsive in his personal habits, especially his conversation. And to the end the quality endeared him to much of the American public.

Roosevelt's maiden speech on January 22, 1882, had been fatuous and patronizing. Protesting a move to overcome the factionalism that had prevented organization of the Assembly for three weeks, he declared: "While in New York I talked with several gentlemen who have large commercial interests at stake, and they do not seem to care whether the deadlock is broken or not. In fact, they felt rather relieved."

Within a few weeks, however, Roosevelt proved his real mettle. A group of Republican spoilsmen had agreed to support the Tammany legislative program in return for a division of appointive offices. The deal called for the transfer of a number of positions to the control of the Republican Clerk, and on February 21 the veteran war horses held a G.O.P. caucus preparatory to feeding at the Tammany trough. Roosevelt, Hunt, and a number of like-minded younger Republicans raised such a vigorous protest, however, that they carried the majority with them. "I did not believe the Republican party should degenerate and become a party scrambling for the spoils of office, and such action would certainly drive the best elements of the party from it," Roosevelt explained to a reporter as the caucus ended. "Rarely in the history of legislation here has the moral force of individual honor and political honesty been more forcibly displayed," the *New York Herald* asserted the next morning. Theodore's diary entry was less high blown. "I firmly and sweetly declined" the preferments offered for a change of position, he wrote.

Ten days after that first minor triumph Roosevelt spoke in support of a bill of his own to alter the procedure for electing aldermen in New York City. Contending that the nominating power was "largely divorced from the mass of voters of the same party" and that "every underhand expedient known to the lowest kind of trading politics" was called into play, he proposed to have each Assembly District elect its own alderman. This would have reduced the number of seats held by his own party and would have weakened the influence of the professionals in both parties. The bill died aborning.

Roosevelt's attitude toward labor showed few signs of the obsession with justice which otherwise characterized him. His social philosophy encompassed little more than the Republican predilection for low taxes and minimal social services, and when a measure to pay municipal laborers a minimum of two dollars a day was favorably reported, he had bolted from his seat to oppose it. "Why, Mr. Speaker, this bill will impose an expenditure of thousands of dollars upon the City of New York," he shouted. He also opposed salary increases for New York City's underpaid policemen and firemen.

However narrow his views, Roosevelt had not lacked

courage during this baptismal year. He alone of the representatives from New York City had spoken out against the popular salary-increase measures. And he alone, reported the militantly Democratic *New York World*, had "put a quietus upon a gigantic job which had been quietly reported" to grant monopolistic powers over the construction of bonded warehouses and grain elevators along the waterfronts to the Terminal Warehouse Elevated and Docking Company. He had capped those signal actions by forcing the investigation of Judge Westbrook.

The result was reward, and in certain places, approval. The *New York Evening Post* said at the end of the session that young Roosevelt "accomplished more good than any man of his age and experience has accomplished . . . in years." Carl Schurz, the German-American Civil War general and civil service reformer, declared that Roosevelt and two other assemblymen had "stemmed the tide of corruption in that fearful legislative gathering." And a group of his personal friends tendered him a testimonial dinner at Delmonico's. But most important of all, Isaac Hunt recollected, he was now "considered a full-fledged man worthy of any one's esteem."

Chapter 2

A Leader Emerges

But as yet I understood little of the effort which was already beginning . . . to secure a more genuine social and industrial justice.
—Theodore Roosevelt, *An Autobiography*

A MILD FLURRY of activity marked Roosevelt's campaign for re-election in the fall of 1882. He was commended for his "fearless, honest, and independent action" by a group of prominent constituents. Jake Hess and his regulars fell in behind him because they were stuck with him. And the *New York Times, Herald,* and *Evening Post* supported him on the grounds that he had been "self-sacrificing," "the leader of the younger and better element," and opposed to "corrupt jobs of all kinds." On November 7 Roosevelt led the entire ticket with a spectacular two-to-one majority even though Grover Cleveland, the Democratic candidate for governor, carried his district by 1,800 votes.

Roosevelt had made only one important campaign speech. To an overflow crowd of friends and party workers in Lyric Hall, he had forthrightly stated his own policies, called for party regularity, and lashed the Democrats with partisan fury.

"As long as the history . . . of our nation has lasted, the Democrats have been one and the same," he asserted. He then contemptuously dismissed Thomas Jefferson, "miscalled the Great," and James Buchanan, "the Little." The Republicans? Were they not the party of Hamilton, Webster, and Clay; the "great party which has produced a Lincoln . . . the party within whose ranks we now hold Schurz and Choate, and every other name almost that tends to make this city illustrious"? If re-elected, Roosevelt declared, he would endeavor to carry "honesty and courage" as well as "private morality" into public office. He would also tackle the issue of "great importance"—monopoly. "[There] is no question that there is a vital spirit underlying it; that we as a people are suffering from new dangers; that as our fathers fought with slavery and

32

crushed it, in order that it would not seize and crush them, so we are called on to fight new forces."

The young New Yorker kept well that faith. During his second term he again stood out as a fearless foe of corruption and an unfailing champion of governmental reform. He also started a campaign to control monopoly which was to carry into his governorship and on through his presidency. Halfway through the session he received national recognition in the pages of *Harper's Weekly* and by the end of the session he had emerged as the leader of a faction openly known as "The Roosevelt Republicans."

Roosevelt's near-meteoric rise was the result of a partial measure of good fortune and a full measure of initiative and daring. It was his fortune that those ignoble exemplars of easy political virtue, Roscoe Conkling and Thomas C. Platt, were without great power during his three years in the legislature. It was probably his fortune, too, that his last terms coincided with the governorship of Grover Cleveland. Several times during the sessions of 1883 and 1884 Cleveland and Roosevelt joined forces against their party machines, and in one graphic cartoon the stolid Democratic Governor and the ebullient Republican Assemblyman were portrayed with arms linked surveying a disintegrated Tammany tiger. But in the end the relationship between the two future Presidents, the one forty-six years old and increasingly conscious of his destiny, the other twenty-four and still uncertain of his life's work, was marred by recrimination.

The two men first formed common cause after Cleveland's veto of a bill, twice supported by Roosevelt, to reduce the fare on the elevated railways from ten to five cents. Always a popular issue, it had special significance at the time because of hostility toward Jay Gould. Many respectable citizens regarded the bill as a means of dealing that haughty buccaneer a heavy blow, and the city's Republican delegation at Albany prepared to support it almost to a man.

Roosevelt normally would have opposed such a radical measure. The laissez-faire teachings of Harvard had held that the regulation of business was not a legislative function. The social milieu in which he had been reared confirmed the tradition-ordained rights of property. And the experience of the previous year had convinced him that "corporations are more sinned against than sinning." Yet the Westbrook investigation had given him an insight into the machinations of Jay Gould and men like him. He allowed himself to be carried along by the swelling tide.

The tide failed to engulf the ultraconservative gentleman in the Executive Mansion, however. Convinced that the fare-reduction bill embodied a breach of contract, Governor Cleveland vetoed the measure in a magnificent display of courage. "The State should not only be strictly just," he solemnly affirmed, "but scrupulously fair."

Young Roosevelt took Cleveland's words to heart. No sooner was the veto message read to the Assembly on March 2, 1883, than he jumped to his feet (he had already been likened to a jack rabbit by Gould's *New York World*). He had risen to confess, he dramatically announced, that he had blundered grievously in supporting the bill originally. "I . . . weakly yielded, partly in a vindictive spirit toward the infernal thieves and conscienceless swindlers who have the elevated railroads in charge, and partly to the popular voice of New York." The measure "breaks the plighted faith of the state" and was therefore at root "a question of justice to ourselves." He would rather leave politics with the feeling "that I had done what was right than stay in with the approval of all men, knowing in my heart that I had acted as I ought not to."

Roosevelt's courageous sentiments were echoed by many of his colleagues, and on March 7 the veto was decisively sustained. Roosevelt was a gentleman "whose probity is as generally recognized as his ability," the *New York Tribune* said in a representative editorial; he had acted with "characteristic manliness" in reversing himself on the five-cent-fare bill.

That was not the only time Roosevelt made a manly change of front that spring. For some months he had been immaturely criticizing an aged assemblyman from Richmond, one Erastus Brooks. Finally, near the close of the session, Brooks delivered a full-dress defense of his actions; he also attacked Roosevelt sharply. When the Richmond Assemblyman had finished Roosevelt strode forward with tears in his eyes to shake his adversary's hand. "Mr. Brooks, I surrender," he contritely exclaimed. "I beg your pardon."

By then Roosevelt had mounted a new assault on Jay Gould. Within a week of his vote in support of Cleveland's veto he introduced a resolution directing the Attorney General to bring suit for the dissolution of Gould's Manhattan Elevated Railway Company. A few days after that he boldly charged that the *New York World* was "a local stock-jobbing sheet of limited circulation and versatile mendacity, owned by the arch thief of Wall Street, and edited by a rancorous kleptomaniac with a penchant for trousers."

The words were impetuous, but the theme was not. A year before Roosevelt had come to a personal crossroads. Some time after the Westbrook investigation an old family friend had taken Theodore to lunch. He remarked that it had been a good thing for Roosevelt to have made the "reform play," then advised him to leave politics and identify himself with "the right kind of people, the people who would always in the long run control others and obtain the real rewards." Theodore asked if this meant that he should yield to the "ring." The patronizing retort was that the so-called "ring" included "certain big business men, and the politicians, lawyers and judges who were in alliance with and to a certain extent dependent upon them, and that the successful man had to win his success by the backing of the same forces, whether in law, business, or politics."

Meanwhile, Roosevelt and Cleveland had come together in support of civil service reform, the bête noire of machine politicians in both parties. Early in the session Cleveland conferred in his office with Roosevelt and a few other Republicans in an effort to form a coalition of antimachine Republicans and anti-Tammany Democrats. Roosevelt was amenable, and the coalition was created. Several important measures followed, the most far-reaching of which created a Civil Service Commission. In addition, numerous bills conferring special privileges on corporations were killed. The Roosevelt Republicans, reported the *New York Times* correspondent at the close of the session, had been "as effective as any minority the writer has ever seen in the Assembly."

Governor Cleveland's refusal to compromise with Tammany had split the Democrats and provoked a Republican victory in the legislative elections of 1883. Roosevelt thereupon decided to bid for the speakership (he had received his party's complimentary nomination at the start of his second term). He threw himself into the contest with remarkable vigor. He went into remote rural regions to seek out assemblymen-elect. He requested his friends to work for him. And he wrote numerous letters soliciting support. Yet he apparently made no deals. "I am a Republican, pure and simple, neither a 'half breed' nor a 'stalwart'; and certainly no man, nor yet any ring or clique, can do my thinking for me," he wrote one wavering colleague.

As you say, I believe in treating all our business interests equitably and alike; in favoring no one interest or set of interests at the expense of others. In making up the committees I should pay attention, first, to the absolute integrity of the men, second, to their capacity to deal intelligently with the matters likely to come before them—for . . . honesty and common sense are the two prime requisites for a legislator.

Roosevelt concluded that he was much stronger than he had dared hope even though the lobby and the politicians had raised the free-trade scarecrow against him. Had not the *New York Times* remarked that the only thing against him was "the curable defect of being a young man"? When the Republican caucus met on New Year's Eve, however, Titus Sheard, a reputable, self-made manufacturer from Herkimer County was elected by 42 votes to 30. Theodore had suffered his first political defeat. He was, he conceded, "chagrined."

So great was Roosevelt's strength, however, that Sheard appointed him chairman of the Committee on Cities and then made him chairman of a special committee to investigate the Public Works Department. One of the most sensational investigations of municipal government to that time followed. Day after day Roosevelt and his colleagues relentlessly grilled minor and major officeholders in an effort to unravel the interlocking corruption of New York City. Finally, on March 14, the committee filed its report. "Appalling Condition of Affairs"; "Surrogate's Office a Place for Blackmailing"; "How the City is Robbed"; "Sweeping Changes Urged"; "Roosevelt's Blunderbuss"—so the newspapers heralded it.

The findings justified the headlines. The committee's report revealed that the county clerk had netted $250,000 through the fee system and that the register of deeds and mortgages had paid approximately $50,000 for his appointment. It showed that "a system of the grossest blackmail and extortion prevailed among the employees" in the surrogate's office. The Department of Taxes and Assessments was found to have "absolutely no system whatever in the assessing" of real estate. And the "grossest abuses" were discovered in the sheriff's office. The investigation also indicated that the real governing authorities of the City of New York were "outside parties who cannot be held responsible to the law."

Roosevelt thereupon introduced nine reform bills, seven of which were eventually enacted into law. The most important substituted salaries for fees, deprived the board of aldermen of the authority to confirm the mayor's appointments, and empowered the mayor to appoint city department heads and other municipal officials as well as to remove them for cause with the governor's approval.

Roosevelt's legislative lodestar was political reform. But his restless mind and sense of duty impelled him to speak out on a wide range of subjects. In 1883 he vigorously opposed a bill to tighten the newspaper libel law, contending that "it is a great deal better to err a little bit on the side of having too much discussion and having too virulent language used by the press, rather than to err on the side of having them not say what they ought to say, especially with reference to public men and measures." And in 1884 he opposed a prohibition bill on the grounds that it would play into the hands of the elements it was designed to repress.

Roosevelt also stood firmly for the absolute separation of church and state. Periodically, Catholic and Protestant charitable organizations solicited financial support from the legislature; and in his second term a bill to grant the Catholic Protectory at Elmira $25,000 for a new sewerage plant came up. Roosevelt at once interposed a forceful objection, asserting that the connection of church and state was "wholly wrong," that it brought religion into politics, and that it violated the Constitution. His brief proved unavailing, however, the bill passing by 99 to 17. He repeated his objections against a Protestant measure a few weeks later and was again resoundingly defeated. "Mr. ROOSEVELT," said the *New York Times,* "enjoys in the Assembly the distinction of having convictions and acting up to them."

Roosevelt's attitudes toward labor were even more revealing of his development. He was slow to grasp the changes brought about by the Industrial Revolution—the growing impersonality of relations between employer and employee, the wearying monotony of routine labor, the frequent intervals of unemployment, and the intense competition for jobs of the meanest sort. Nor did he then understand the function of unions. He attributed the deplorable conditions of labor to the workings of natural law rather than to the gross mismanagement of human resources. And natural law, in the prevailing view, was inviolable.

It is a tribute to Roosevelt's capacity for growth that his labor views changed at all. Unlike Henry Cabot Lodge, Elihu Root, and most leading Republicans of his generation, he gradually came into some comprehension of the labor problem. And though he failed to emerge suddenly as an advanced labor reformer, his three years as an assemblyman saw his first cautious wandering from the hallowed highway of laissez faire.

True, his course was inconsistent. As late as his third term Roosevelt opposed a bill to reduce to twelve hours the workday of 15,000 streetcar conductors. He first argued that to oppose the law of supply and demand because it was unfeeling was like trying to repeal the law of gravity because its results were sometimes brutal; he then charged that the twelve-hour legislation would tie labor to the apron strings of the state. To offer a worker such protection, he exclaimed, was both un-American and insulting! Had not Speaker of the Assembly Titus Sheard risen from laborer to manufacturer without such aid? The statement was correct, Sheard acknowledged. He added, however, that he had found working fourteen hours a day painful, brutalizing, and not in any way related to his subsequent success. Indeed, he believed that he would have been even more self-reliant if his hours of labor had been shorter and his wages higher!

Nevertheless, the still callow Roosevelt continued to oppose the bill. He raised the specter of communism and socialism and he inveighed against the Knights of Labor, who were then approaching the peak of their power. Every man should stand on his own bottom, he self-righteously declared, only to be reminded that his own bottom was his inheritance from his father, the laboring man's nothing. Yet Roosevelt won his point. Grover Cleveland, who proved far less sympathetic to labor than Theodore Roosevelt in the summing up, vetoed the bill on the grounds that it was "class legislation."

By then Roosevelt had several times flouted labor or its interests. He had recommended public whipping for some crimes. He had dismissed with thinly veiled contempt labor's charge that the convict-labor system "was a vital cobra which was swamping [sic] the lives of laboring men." He had supported an antiriot bill that labor realistically regarded as an antistrike measure. And he had once invited "a labor agitator from Brooklyn" to "step outside" to defend himself. The trouble with workingmen, he wrote in a patronizing magazine article the year after he retired from the Assembly, was that they had been instilled with false hopes by "professional agitators" who were "always promising to procure by legislation the advantages which can only come to workingmen . . . by their individual or united energy, intelligence, and forethought."

Years later Roosevelt regretted his manifest hostility toward unions and most labor legislation during this period. "One partial reason for my slowness in grasping the importance of action in these matters," he wrote in his *Autobiography,* "was the corrupt and unattractive nature of so many of the men who championed popular reforms, their insincerity, and the folly of so many of the actions which they advocated."

Samuel Gompers, the convivial, English-born Jew who gave the American labor movement its pragmatic character, was responsible for Roosevelt's first real insight into the degrading effects of his vaunted natural law. For years humanitarians had been denouncing the manufacture of cigars in New York tenements by unorganized immigrants who labored for wages that might have been termed subsistence had not their death rate belied it. Finally, in 1882, Gompers arranged the introduction of a bill to outlaw the manufacture of cigars in tenements. A three-man committee, including the freshman Roosevelt, was appointed to investigate.

Roosevelt believed that he was put on the committee in the cynical expectation that he would perfunctorily report against the tenement bill. Possibly he was. Neither the Democratic nor the Republican leadership wanted to strike against the status quo; nor did the two other members of the committee plan to act in full conscience. The Republican member confided to Roosevelt that he would support the measure because of labor strength in his district, and the Democrat, "a sporting Tammany man who afterward abandoned politics for the race-track," so Theodore remembered, admitted that he had to oppose the bill because of unnamed interests. But he suggested that Roosevelt look into the situation, adding that Roosevelt would probably favor the labor proposal on first-hand knowledge.

Impressed by Roosevelt's "aggressiveness and evident sincerity," Gompers meanwhile invited the young Assemblyman to tour the tenement area with him. Roosevelt accepted, though he then inclined to oppose the bill: "The respectable people I knew were against it; and it was contrary to the principles of political economy of the *laissez-faire* kind; the businessmen who spoke to me about it shook their heads and said that it was designed to prevent a man doing as he wished and as he had a right to do with what was his own." But his several inspections of tenements—he went once with Gompers and several union officials, once with the other members of the committee, and once or twice on his own—convinced him of the need for the legislation. "I have always remembered one room in which two families were living," he recalled. "There were several children, three men, and two women in this room. The tobacco was stowed about everywhere, alongside the foul bedding, and in a corner where there were scraps of food. The men, women, and children in this room worked by day and far on into the evening, and they slept and ate there. They were Bohemians, unable to speak English, except that one of the children knew enough to act as interpreter."

When the tenement bill was brought out of committee late that winter, Roosevelt supported it on the floor. The measure passed the Assembly but failed even to come up in the Senate, a lobbyist for the manufacturers stealing the official copy from the clerk's files. The next year a similar measure was approved by both houses only to have Cleveland balk. The Governor did agree, however, to hold a hearing. Roosevelt thereupon consented, as he phrased it, to act "as spokesman for the battered, undersized foreigners who represented the Union and the workers," and on the appointed day he argued convincingly for the bill's adoption. After listening impassively, the Governor surmounted his constitutional scruples and signed the measure into law.

Refusing to accept defeat, the manufacturers took the issue to the courts. Their able attorney, former Secretary of State William M. Evarts, argued that tobacco was "a disinfectant and a prophylactic," that socialism and communism were responsible for the bill's conception, and that home manufacture was actually conducive to "the proper culture of growing girls." Convinced by this reasoning, the New York Court of Appeals ruled the tenement law unconstitutional within less than a year of the bill's passage.

Three months after that shocking decision an indignant legislature overwhelmingly passed a slightly modified bill. Again, Roosevelt vigorously championed the measure in a speech that strayed far from the philosophical tenets of his youth. He conceded that the abolition of tenement workshops was not only a dangerous departure from prevailing doctrines, but was "in a certain sense a socialistic one." Nevertheless, the constantly increasing extremes of poverty and wealth demand that we "modify the principles or doctrines on which we manage our system of government." Otherwise, he continued, neither the cigar makers nor their children would ever be fit to perform the duties of American citizenship. He concluded that the bill merited passage as a "hygienic measure alone," and he emphasized that he was supporting the measure on the basis of his own findings rather than the union's recommendations.

Whatever his reservations about labor unions, the struggle over the tenement bill was a critically formative experience for Roosevelt. For the first time he had faced the bleak fact that the American economic system was cruelly denying social development to hundreds of thousands, and probably millions, of working people. Either their lot would be ameliorated or democratic capitalism would be destroyed. Those were the alternatives. Young Roosevelt was one of the few of his class or party to perceive them.

Thus he sponsored a bill to regulate the working conditions of women and children; he voted for bills instituting safety measures in factories and various trades; and he gave full support to the creation of a labor bureau. Only on the wage increases for firemen, policemen, and city laborers, which he regarded as politically inspired, did he stubbornly hold out.

Roosevelt's insight into the character of American society, and especially of the judiciary, continued to deepen after he left the legislature. In January, 1885 the New York State Court of Appeals found in the *In re Jacobs* case that the tenement law passed in 1884 was patently unconstitutional. How, the court asked, can the health and morals of the producer be improved "by forcing him from his home and its hallowed associations and beneficent influences, to ply his trade elsewhere?" The tenement law, the court continued, was an indisputable abridgment of the cigar makers' "fundamental rights of liberty."

Roosevelt's autobiographical reaction to the *Jacobs* decision is probably a fair statement of his attitude. "It was this case which first waked me to a dim and partial understanding of the fact that the courts were not necessarily the best judges of what should be done to better social and industrial conditions," he wrote. "Of course it took more than one experience such as this Tenement Cigar Case to shake me out of the attitude in which I was brought up," for "the people with whom I was most intimate were apt to praise the courts for just such decisions as this, and to speak of them as bulwarks against disorder and barriers against demagogic legislation." But as a result of numerous such decisions, he continued, "I grew to realize that all Abraham Lincoln had said about the Dred Scott decision could be said with equal truth and justice about the numerous decisions which in our own day were erected as bars across the path of social reform, and which brought to naught so much of the effort to secure justice and fair dealings for working men and working women, and for plain citizens generally."

Young Roosevelt's political horizons meanwhile broadened even more rapidly than his social insights deepened. Eighteen eighty-four was a presidential election year, and the Grand Old Party's ruling clique was determined to make James G. Blaine, of Maine and "Mulligan letters" fame, the Republican nominee. Repelled by Blaine's unsavory character, George W. Curtis, Carl Schurz, Henry Cabot Lodge, and other reform-minded Republicans decided to oppose the "Plumed Knight" with Senator George F. Edmunds of Vermont, an honest, conservative Yankee of no particular distinction. Roosevelt joined them. He announced for Edmunds in mid-January, though the Twenty-first District machine was for President Arthur, and in mid-April his slate of Edmunds men defeated Jake Hess's in the contest for delegates to the Republican State Convention.

Thereafter the story blurs. The *World* later charged that Roosevelt had compromised with John J. O'Brien, the city

Republican leader, in his battle against Hess. Roosevelt needed O'Brien's support to defeat Hess, the *World* said, and he failed to push a bill which would have removed O'Brien as Chief of the Bureau of Elections. Had Roosevelt worked as hard for passage of that bill as for the tenure-of-office bill, the *World* contended, it would have gone through.

No other evidence confirms those charges, and Putnam concludes they are groundless. Yet Roosevelt made this admission in his *Autobiography:*

I at one period began to believe that I had a future before me, and that it behooved me to be very far-sighted and scan each action carefully with a view to its possible effect on that future. This speedily made me useless to the public and an object of aversion to myself; and I then made up my mind that I would try not to think of the future at all, but would proceed on the assumption that each office I held would be the last I ever should hold, and that I would confine myself to trying to do my work as well as possible while I held that office.

The Republican party was torn with dissension as it prepared to convene in the Utica Opera House that spring. Most "stalwarts" lined up behind President Chester A. Arthur, who had drawn on theretofore untapped resources to give the country a competent administration. The "half-breeds" fell in behind Blaine as did a faction of stalwarts headed by State Senator Thomas C. Platt, who had come out of seclusion and was soon to build the machine that made him the dominant power in New York politics for almost two decades. The Oswego druggist was for Blaine because he thought he would win; also because he hated Arthur. Between the stalwarts and the half-breeds stood the independents. They numbered perhaps a seventh of the convention delegates and they were led by the twenty-five-year-old Roosevelt. At stake was the selection of four delegates-at-large to the national convention scheduled to convene in Chicago six weeks after the state meeting.

Fresh from his victory over Hess four days before, Roosevelt arrived in Utica on April 21. Perceiving the Arthur forces' implacable opposition to Blaine, he insisted that they support the entire Edmunds slate. The Arthur men bitterly resented his imperious demand; but they despised Blaine more. After a final conference in Roosevelt's hotel room at two A.M., April 22, they reluctantly submitted. Early that afternoon Roosevelt, Curtis, and President Andrew D. White of Cornell University were elected on the first ballot. Roosevelt then turned to ex-Governor Warner Miller, who had spearheaded his defeat for Speaker in January, and expostulated, "There, damn you, we beat you for last winter." Meanwhile a great cry went up for Roosevelt to appear on the platform. The *New York Times* described the scene:

Mr. Roosevelt disregarded the call for a moment, and then, amid enthusiastic cheers, made his way to the stage. His slender, erect form, bright young face and active ways have made him familiar within a few days to almost every one who took part in the convention, and his legislative work had won admiration and a respect for his industry, capacity, and judgment. He wisely curbed any natural desire he may have had to make a speech. Simply and frankly he said: "I have nothing to say except to thank you for the honor you have conferred upon me. I shall try to so behave myself as to serve the best interests of the Republican Party, and to make you feel no regret in selecting me."

All through his life, even in moments of triumph, Theodore Roosevelt had forebodings of disaster; the aftermath of Utica proved no exception. A week later he unburdened himself to a friendly Utica newspaper editor:

I have very little expectation of being able to keep on in politics; my success so far has only been won by absolute indifference to my future career; for I doubt if any man can realise [*sic*] the bitter and venomous hatred with which I am regarded by the very politicians who at Utica supported me, under dictation from masters who were influenced by political considerations that were national and not local in their scope. I realize very thoroughly the absolutely ephemeral nature of the hold I have upon the people, and a very real and positive hostility I have excited among the politicians. I will not stay in public life unless I can do so on my own terms; and my ideal, whether lived up to or not, is rather a high one.

What did he mean? That he had compromised once and was too conscience-ridden to do it again? That he sensed that he would have to support Blaine eventually or get out of Republican politics? That he was not yet ready to accept politics as the art of the possible?

Whatever he meant, he characteristically acted rather than

brooded. During the interim between the state convention at Utica and the national convention at Chicago, Roosevelt worked feverishly to bind the scattered Edmunds delegates, who never numbered a hundred. He hoped that they would again comprise the balance of power though he was far from sanguine. "Unquestionably, Blaine is our greatest danger," he warned Henry Cabot Lodge, "for I fear lest, if he come too near success, the bread-and-butter brigade from the south will leave Arthur and go over to him. We who stand against both *must* be organized."

At Chicago, however, the forces of emotionalism and materialism proved overpowering. Blaine's magnetic personality inspired loyalty and enthusiasm if not much else, and on the fourth ballot the Grand Old Party gave him its nomination. There followed a wildly climactic scene which saw William McKinley, then a relatively obscure Ohio congressman, push his way through to Roosevelt on the floor and ask him to make a unity speech for the "Plumed Knight." The New York leader refused.

The first of a long succession of Gethsemanes was now at hand. Roosevelt had been a center of attention throughout the convention. The press had treated him whimsically, commenting on his "nobby straw" hat, "jaunty" attire, "nervously forcible" gestures and "pugnacious" nose. The *New York Sun* had described him as "bubbling over with martial ardor" as he vainly sought to bolster the dampened spirits of the Edmunds men. And another paper related that "Roosevelt, Fish and Lodge applauded with the tips of their fingers held immediately in front of their noses."

Yet Roosevelt's remarkable capacity for leadership had come through. The *World* called his seconding speech for Thomas R. Lynch, a Mississippi Negro nominated for temporary chairman by Lodge in a successful maneuver against the Blaine delegates, blunt and manly. The *New York Times* reported that though he "scrambled to his perch on the chair with juvenile activity," he spoke with the authority of "a positive practical man" rather than a youth. And Joseph B. Foraker, an Ohio spoilsman with whom Roosevelt would clash bitterly when President, said that his conferences with Roosevelt had been "so taxing upon the strength and the mental operations . . . that I felt scarcely able to attend the evening session . . ." Obviously, McKinley would not have sought Roosevelt's support for Blaine had the convention as a whole regarded the young reformer as sensationalists portrayed him.

Roosevelt and the other independent-minded New Yorkers had "sat with troubled countenances biting their lips, crimson with vexation and dismay" as Blaine's fourth-ballot nomination impended. Now, in the agonizing aftermath of the "Plumed Knight's" victory, they had to decide whether they would support him in the campaign that fall. "I was at the birth of the Republican party, and I fear I am to witness its death," Curtis exclaimed as he awaited the final tally. The *Harper's* editor refused, however, to comment once the final result was announced. Roosevelt was less self-contained. He was reported as declining comment, advising reporters to see him the next week, and attributing Blaine's nomination to "mistaken public enthusiasm." The *New York Times* quoted him most fully:

To say that I am satisfied with the nomination of Mr. Blaine would be false. I have participated in a Republican convention, and by all the usages of the party, I would be expected to support its nominee. I could have given an earnest and enthusiastic support to a ticket headed by such a man as George F. Edmunds. . . . I should suppose, from what I have heard many independents say, that they would not give Mr. Blaine any support whatever; and I believe they will keep their promise.

Roosevelt's assertion was correct. Curtis, Carl Schurz, Henry Ward Beecher and a great host of reformers and plain, respectable citizens throughout the nation were going to bolt. That Roosevelt would fail to go along with them was unthinkable. William Roscoe Thayer, upon whom the nomination of Blaine weighed "like a nightmare," described the esteem in which he then held the young reformer. "I thought of him as of a paladin against whom the forces of evil would dash themselves to pieces," Thayer wrote. "I thought of him as the young and dauntless spokesman of righteousness whose words would silence the special pleaders of iniquity. I wrote him and besought him to stand firm." Others implored him to do the same.

When it became clear in July that Roosevelt would "stand firm," but with the Republican party instead of his reformer friends, it was as though a piece of Thayer's heart had been cut out. "I felt as Abolitionists felt after Webster's Seventh of March speech," he recalled. "My old acquaintance, our trusted leader, whose career in the New York Assembly we had watched with an almost holy satisfaction, seemed to have strangely abandoned the fundamental principles which we and he had believed in, and he had so nobly upheld. Whittier's poem, 'Ichabod,' seemed to have been aimed at him."

Not all the fundamental principles had been on the side of the poet; nor were they now all with the reformers. Roosevelt had gone to Chicago knowing that Blaine's nomination was probable. By the rules of politics he was bound to support the convention's choice. Moreover, he regarded the Republican party as a principle itself. Much as he gloried in the heroic exploits of Confederate soldiers, he deplored the states' rights philosophy upon which secession had been based and to which the Democratic party still adhered. He would write the next year that Jefferson Davis "enjoys the unique distinction of being the only American with whose public character that of Benedict Arnold need not fear comparison"; and when he himself stormed out of the G.O.P. in 1912 it was partly to create a more nationalistic party than the one he was abandoning. If ever a reformer was foreordained to swallow the bitterness of personal contempt with the sweetness of party loyalty, it was Theodore Roosevelt in 1884.

It is hard, even so, to explain the intensity of Roosevelt's activities that fall. He could have refused to issue a public statement, or he might have sat out the campaign on his ranch in Dakota, where he had sped at the close of the convention. Either course would have enabled him to retain his party standing. Either would have maintained his prized reputation for independence. But he chose instead to come out openly for the "decidedly mottled" Blaine, as he privately referred to his party's nominee, and to castigate the rock-ribbed Cleveland.

Roosevelt's public statement evoked a bitter outcry from the independents. The Boston banker, Colonel Henry Lee, growled at his cousin George, Roosevelt's father-in-law: "As for Cabot Lodge, nobody's surprised at *him;* but you can tell that young whipper-snapper in New York from me that his independence was the only thing in him we cared for." The *New York Evening Post* observed that "There is no ranch or other hiding place in the world in which a man can wait for

Blaine and the Mulligan letters to 'blow over.' " And others spared Roosevelt no less.

Roosevelt never forgave the mugwumps for their failure to accept his decision to support the Republican ticket in 1884. As that astute English observer, James Bryce, perceived, they had "impeached his own righteousness and classed him with the politicians." They had also abandoned the party of Union for that of secession. "I am glad I am not at home," Roosevelt wrote Lodge from Dakota just before he decided to enter the campaign actively. "I get so angry with the 'mugwumps,' and get to have such a scorn and contempt for them, that I know I would soon be betrayed into taking some step against them, and in favor of Blaine, much more decided than I really ought to take." That fall he lashed them almost as ferociously as he whipped the Democrats.

Roosevelt had returned on October 9 to New York where he told a reporter that "It is altogether contrary to my character to occupy a neutral position in so important and exciting a struggle." Then, in a series of speeches delivered in Massachusetts, New Jersey, and New York, he revealed the depth of his Republican convictions, discreditably capitalized on Cleveland's moral laxity, and conveniently dismissed Blaine's. "Now in 1864 nobody that I know of questioned the moral character of George B. McClellan, and yet no disaster . . . would have begun to equal in importance the terrible disaster that it would have been to have McClellan elected as President," he said at Malden, Massachusetts. Therefore, he continued, "everyone in his senses must recognize that the man is not everything, that the man is not even so much, but that the party is most of all." In Winchester he warned that the next President might appoint as many as four new justices to the Supreme Court:

Now I want to have a bench that will decide, should the question ever come before them, that the national banks are constitutional, that the law providing for the suppression of pleuro-pneumonia and of kindred [cattle] diseases by the National Government should be held constitutional. Issues like that are not decided in a day. They are not decided in 20 years. It is a question of national growth, and the same fight that has been going on for the last half century or more will continue to go on for some time longer.

Roosevelt was received well in Massachusetts. But his address to the Young Men's Republican Club in New York evoked the most enthusiastic response. "A gentleman told me recently he doubted if I would vote for the Angel Gabriel if found at the head of the Democratic party, to which I responded that the Angel Gabriel would never be found in such company," he remarked at the outset. He then rationalized his decision to remain with the G.O.P. "It may be right to bolt," he acknowledged, "but you must be certain that the time is right; that you are acting to reform, not to destroy the Republican party." He had opposed Blaine's nomination, he disingenuously added, "but then I saw, and every man who didn't view the scene with jaundiced eyes saw too that Mr. Blaine was nominated fairly and squarely because the bulk of Republicans in the Republican States wishes him to be their nominee." Adding that these were the men Abraham Lincoln used to call the "plain people," he concluded: "I am thankful that I am still, where by inheritance and education I feel that I belong, with the Republican party."

Chapter 3

The Westerner: Rancher, Hunter, and Historian

> *We knew toil and hardship and hunger and thirst; and we saw men die violent deaths as they worked among the horses and cattle; but we felt the best of hardy life in our veins, and ours was the glory of work and the joy of living.*
> —Theodore Roosevelt, *An Autobiography*

ROOSEVELT'S POLITICAL and social life had merged only infrequently during his three years in the legislature. His young bride, whom Isaac Hunt remembered as "a very charming woman . . . tall and willowy," had spent most of the first term and part of the second term with him in a suite at the Delavan House in Albany. But they had seen little of his colleagues except at official functions. When Theodore's third term started in January, 1884, Alice stayed in New York to wait for the birth of their first child.

Two or three weeks before Alice's baby was expected, she entertained three of her husband's colleagues, one an Irish-American Democrat, at lunch. "All of the men were perfectly enchanted with their visit," Theodore wrote after he returned to Albany. "They could hardly believe that mother was really our mother; and above all they praised my sweet little wife. I was very much amused by Welch, who said that he had never seen anyone look so pretty as you did when you were asking me not to tell the 'shaved lion' story; he said 'I would have felt just as badly as she would have if you had gone on to tell it.' So I felt very glad we had entertained the three 'pollys.' "

Seventeen days later Roosevelt's mother and Alice were dead.

Theodore and Alice's three years of marriage had been extraordinarily happy. Although she seems never to have ma-

tured—he deferred to her as to a child during the whole of
their brief life together—he was as enamored of her at the
end as he had been at the beginning. "How I did hate to leave
my bright, sunny little love yesterday afternoon," he had
written her from Albany the week before she died. "I love
you and long for you all the time, and oh *so* tenderly; doubly
tenderly now, my sweetest little wife."

Roosevelt's letters from Europe during a tour they had
made the first year of their marriage are similarly illuminating. "Really, Alice is an excellent traveller," he wrote his
sister Corinne. "When I reach a station I leave her in a chair
with the parcels, and there she stays, round eyed and solemn,
but perfectly happy, till I have extricated my luggage, had it
put on a hack and arranged everything." In other letters Theodore referred to Alice as "Baby," indulgently reported that
she resented being addressed in any other language than
"english" [*sic*], and described how she had been convulsed by
seasickness on the voyage over and had "requested me to wear
a mustard plaster *first*, to see if it hurts." Yet they also shared
many pleasures maturely, including art. Theodore freely conceded that her appreciation was "far keener" than his.

The idyl ended on February 14, 1884, the fourth anniversary of the announcement of their engagement. In Albany,
the day before, Theodore had reported fourteen bills out of
the Cities Committee and was planning to remain in the
Chamber until the vote on his Aldermanic Bill, though he had
received a telegram that morning reporting the birth of a
daughter. "I shall never forget when the news came and we
congratulated him . . . ," Hunt recalled. "He was full of life
and happiness." But then, Hunt added, "the news came of a
sudden turn and he took his departure."

After a depressingly slow trip through a dense fog then in
its tenth day, Roosevelt reached his mother's house on West
57th Street shortly before midnight. He found Alice stricken
by Bright's disease and barely able to recognize him. All that
night he held her in his arms, leaving only to spend a few
minutes with his mother who was dying of typhoid fever in
another room. At about three o'clock that morning Martha
Bulloch Roosevelt died. Standing by her bedside, Theodore
repeated the words his brother Elliott had greeted him with a
few hours earlier: "There *is* a curse on this house." He then
returned to Alice. Dawn came, but Alice continued to sink;

at two o'clock that afternoon, February 14, she also died. She was twenty-two and one-half years old.

The senior Mrs. Roosevelt, reported the *New York Herald* the next day, was the "widow of the distinguished philanthropist" who had founded the Roosevelt (Orthopedic) Hospital. "The devotion of her four children to her person was akin to chivalrous loyalty, and was remarked by all who came under her roof and under the spell of her hospitable manner and brilliant powers as the leader of a *salon.*" The junior Mrs. Roosevelt, the *Herald* continued, "was famed for her beauty as well as for many graces of the heart and head." The two ladies took an active interest in the late Mr. Roosevelt's many charities, the obituary concluded, and from "visiting hospital wards to dispensing ice cream at a newsboys' lodging house, both found pleasure in making this world less of a sorrow to the poor and more of a lesson to the rich."

In Albany, meanwhile, seven assemblymen, including two or three of Theodore's inveterate opponents, spoke movingly in support of a resolution to adjourn in the hope that Roosevelt might be fortified "in this moment of his agony and weakness." When finally the members arose to endorse the resolution unanimously, tears swelled many of their eyes. It was "an unusual compliment," the *New York Times* reported, one that reflected "the high position in the general esteem which Mr. Roosevelt has won by his straightforward and courageous course in the Legislature and in politics."

A little after 10 A.M. on Saturday, February 16, Theodore entered a front pew of the Fifth Avenue Presbyterian Church. The choir chanted "Jesus, Lover of My Soul" and a quartet sang "Rock of Ages." His mother's friend and pastor, the Rev. Dr. John Hall, then preached a short sermon under visible strain. Following the benediction the choir sang "Angels of Jesus, Angels of Light." Two rosewood coffins covered with roses and lilies of the valley were then borne down the center aisle to the muted organ tones of the funeral march from Beethoven's Third Symphony. Theodore and the immediate family walked behind. They entered waiting coaches and rode slowly behind twin hearses to Greenwood Cemetery.

Theodore was "in a dazed, stunned state" that day, his old tutor, Arthur Cutler, wrote Bill Sewall, "He does not know what he does or says." Sometime that day, however, Roosevelt noted in his diary that "we spent three years of happiness greater and more unalloyed than I have ever known fall to the lot of others." He added that "For joy or for sorrow my life has now been lived out."

Yet in death there was life. The four-day-old baby, Alice Lee, survived; and within less than a week her twenty-five-year-old father had returned to Albany and immersed himself in the investigation of corruption in New York City, the struggle for his reform bills, and the organization of the Edmunds forces. By every law of nature that Roosevelt had studied and by most of those he had superimposed on human history, life went on. Resolutely, he expressed his philosophy to Sewall three weeks later: "It was a grim and evil fate, but I have never believed it did any good to flinch or yield for any blow, nor does it lighten the blow to cease from working."

Nevertheless, Theodore suffered. Alice seems hardly to have influenced his basic personality; but she had touched the depths of his sensitivity. "You could not talk to him about it," Hunt recalled. "You could see at once that it was a grief too deep. . . . There was a sadness about his face that he never had before. . . . He did not want anybody to sympathize with him."

In Dakota that summer Roosevelt penned for private circulation a moving memorial to Alice Lee. "She was," her young widower wrote, "beautiful in face and form, and lovelier still in spirit; as a flower she grew, and as a fair young flower she died."

Her life had been always in the sunshine; there had never come to her a single great sorrow; and none ever knew her who did not love and revere her for her bright, sunny temper and her saintly unselfishness. Fair, pure, and joyous as a maiden; loving, tender, and happy as a young wife; when she had just become a mother, when her life seemed to be but just begun, and when the years seemed so bright before her—then, by a strange and terrible fate, death came to her.

"And when my heart's dearest died," the memorial concluded, "the light went from my life forever."

As Henry Pringle writes, a door then closed on Alice Lee. Roosevelt maintained cordial relations with her relatives. But that was all. Within three years he had married again; and in the crowded years that followed he never again mentioned her, not even to their daughter Alice. His silence, Putnam measuredly concludes, "seems pathologically rigorous" and suggests a "discipline approaching cruelty."

Fortunately, Roosevelt had entered the cattle business in the Bad Lands of the Dakota Territory the autumn before his double bereavement. Following the Republican Convention in Chicago in June, 1884, he went directly West to lose himself in the challenge—of the roundup, of exploration, of man-killing animals, and of near total isolation. He found that and more. His years in Dakota were one of the great formative experiences of his life, and in passing moments he even considered making a full-time career of ranching, hunting, and writing.

The spurs were not easily won. As Roosevelt half-seriously remarked, glasses were considered a sign of "defective moral character" in the Bad Lands; and when he first visited Dakota in 1883 he had been forced to use all his persuasive powers merely to hire a hunting guide. Only after he had several times proved his mettle did opinion change, and then but slowly.

Once, Roosevelt relates in his *Autobiography,* a drunken stranger accosted him in a hotel. "Four-eyes is going to treat," bellowed the inebriate, who had already shot up the face of the barroom clock. Waving two cocked pistols, he strode over to Roosevelt, who had quietly taken to a chair behind the stove. He repeated his demands in a stream of profanity. Roosevelt rose from his chair as if in obedience, then suddenly struck, first with a short right and left, then with another right. The guns discharged aimlessly as the stranger fell to the floor.

On another occasion Roosevelt brought "Hell-Roaring" Bill Jones, the sheriff of Billings County, to bay. Primitive, shiftless, and quick-tempered, "Hell-Roaring" Bill was "a thorough frontiersman, excellent in all kinds of emergencies, and a very game man," or so Roosevelt wrote. He was also "a thoroughly good citizen when sober." The brush occurred in the storefront office of the *Bad Lands Cowboy* where Jones had been telling off-color stories to several cowpunchers. Roosevelt had no taste for obscenity though he swore moderately; and he decided finally that he had heard enough.

"I can't tell why in the world I like you, for you're the nastiest talking man I ever heard," he blurted out. The cowpunchers froze in their seats, for "Hell-Roaring" Bill had been known to shoot on less provocation. But he had also developed a rough admiration for Roosevelt. Sheepishly, he replied: "I don't mind saying that mebbe I've been a little too free with my mouth."

These and similar incidents gradually earned Roosevelt acceptance in the Bad Lands. Nevertheless, his breeding, wealth, and mastery of men kept him apart; he was always a captain, never a private. He continued, moreover, to amuse the hard-bitten Dakotans. He once ordered a hand to "Hasten forward quickly there" when some cattle broke loose. He gave forth war whoops and went into ecstatic Indian dances after a successful shot. And he regularly stepped off the train at Little Missouri in a derby hat and rode the range in a buckskin suit. Yet even the Dakotans' laughter was respectful. "He was not a purty rider," one of Roosevelt's companions recalled, "but a hell of a good rider."

Roosevelt's hunting experiences also enhanced his stature. Stories of his pluck and courage, his insistence on taking the hard way, and his perseverance under adverse conditions soon spread. He himself captured the tension of his first kill in a letter to his sister Bamie:

Cocking my rifle and stepping quickly forward, I found myself face to face with the great bear, who was less than twenty-five feet off—not eight steps. He had been roused from his sleep by our approach; he sat up in his lair, and turned his huge head slowly towards us. At that distance and in such a place it was very necessary to kill or disable him at the first fire; doubtless my face was pretty white, but the blue barrel was as steady as a rock as I glanced along it until I could see the top of the bead fairly between his two sinister looking eyes; as I pulled the trigger I jumped aside out of the smoke, to be ready if he charged; but it was needless, for the great brute was struggling in the death agony. . . .

Drawing on that and other experiences, Roosevelt wrote *Hunting Trips of a Ranchman,* the first volume of a trilogy on hunting, ranching, and nature observation in 1885. Three years later the second, *Ranch Life and the Hunting Trail,* was published, and in 1893 the last, *The Wilderness Hunter,* came out. They set a new style in hunting books, embracing, in Cutright's words, "vivid pictures of windswept prairie and bald-face mountain, of lovely, sweet-smelling flowers and endless virgin forests; thumbnail sketches of birds and small mammals; and fascinating biographies of large game animals, from buffalo to bighorn."

All three books were warmly praised by critics in spite of serious deficiencies. They tended to be repetitious, to draw too heavily on unreliable sources, and to indulge in superlatives. Roosevelt himself was dissatisfied. "I wish I could make my writings touch a higher plane," he confided to the novelist Owen Wister, "but I don't well see how I can. . . . I go over them a good deal and recast, supply or omit, sentences and even paragraphs, but I don't make the reconstruction complete in the way that you do." Nevertheless, the chapter on the habits of the grizzly bear in *The Wilderness Hunter* was the most comprehensive to that time, and the essay on the Bighorn in *Ranch Life and the Hunting Trail* is still considered a classic. As Brander Matthews, the Columbia professor and arbiter of Arts and Letters, wrote years later, Roosevelt's writings were invariably "tinglingly alive, masculine and vascular."

Impressed with the rugged beauty of the Bad Lands, desirous of a hunting base of his own, and pleased by a financial investment in which he could be actively interested, Roosevelt meanwhile expanded his original stake of $14,000. Shortly after Alice died he invested $26,000 more; then, in April, 1885, he poured in an additional $12,500, all against the advice of his banker uncle, James Roosevelt, who termed him a visionary.

Roosevelt's original contract with two young and sinewy Canadians, Sylvane Ferris and Bill Merrifield, called for them to purchase cattle for him in the fall of 1883 and run them on government lands around their ranch, the Maltese Cross. But when Roosevelt returned in June, 1884, he bought another thousand head and established his own ranch, Elkhorn, thirty miles down the Little Missouri River. Bill Sewall and his nephew, Will Dow, came out to manage it under an arrangement that gave them specified salaries, a percentage of the profits, and no liability for losses. That summer they built a log ranch house which Roosevelt used as his Dakota headquarters until he sold out in 1897.

Roosevelt soon plunged into the region's turbulent affairs. Plagued by thieves, marauders, and inadequate range laws, the ranchers were ripe for organization; and when Roosevelt issued a call in November after riding through blizzards in temperatures of twenty below to sound out sentiment, they formed the Little Missouri Stockmen's Association. Roosevelt was elected chairman and was re-elected the next year. "The association can congratulate itself," the *Bad Lands Cowboy* commented. "Under his administration, everything moves quickly forward and there is none of that time-consuming, fruitless talk that so invariably characterizes a deliberative assembly without a good presiding officer."

In April, 1886, Roosevelt attended the convention of the much larger Eastern Montana Stockgrowers Association in Miles City, a thriving frontier town thronged, so he wrote, "with hundreds of rough-looking, broad-hatted men, numbering among them all the great cattle and horse raisers of the Northwest." Appointed to the committee charged to influence the establishment of stockyards in St. Paul, Minnesota, Roosevelt persuaded the convention to table a resolution criticizing the plans to create the Interstate Commerce Commission. He also got the incompetent livestock inspector at Medora discharged. "I took my position very well in the convention," he reported, "and indeed these Westerners have now pretty well accepted me as one of themselves, and as a representative stockman."

By the next year Roosevelt's interest had waned. A prolonged drought in the summer of 1886 was followed by an extraordinarily severe winter that wiped out much of his herd. He had committed himself to the East for personal reasons. Bill Sewall and Dow had returned to Maine in the late summer of 1886. A fire had destroyed the office and press of the *Bad Lands Cowboy*. And rancher after rancher had gone out of business in the aftermath of the disastrous winter of 1886–87. A brief item in the *Dickinson Press* summed it up: "D. O. Sweet and family have moved from Medora to Dickinson. Mr. Sweet desired to reside where there was some life and prospect of growth."

Roosevelt returned to the Bad Lands on hunting trips in 1888, 1890, 1892, 1893, and 1896; but he never again took an active part in running his cattle. When he finally sold out in 1897 he had lost more than $20,000. Yet the money had been well spent. In spite of arduous days in the saddle, almost sleepless nights on the roundup, and prolonged exposure to extreme heat and cold, his health had improved remarkably. "No longer was he the slight and somewhat delicate-looking young man whom we had entertained at the Cannonball camp less than two years before," one of his Western friends recalled. Roosevelt "got to be lookin' more like a rugged man," another added. Even more important, he had proved what he was constrained to prove again and again throughout his life— he was a man among men. He had held his own on the roundup, captured two thieves at gun point, and showed his mettle in dozens of other incidents. He had also comported himself with dignity, discretion, and bravery when threatened with a duel. What many men sublimated, Theodore Roosevelt had experienced.

Meanwhile, the young rancher-hunter-historian had written and published a biography of Thomas Hart Benton, was writing one of Gouverneur Morris, and was planning a multivolume history of the settlement of the West. Both biographies were superficial. *The Life of Thomas Hart Benton* represented not more than three months of scholarship and three months of intense, but spasmodic, writing in the ranch house at Elkhorn and over a store in Medora. But as Putnam suggests, "To produce such a work in a few months, with all its faults, required both basic knowledge and prior deliberation to which few men of his age and varied activities could aspire."

However serious the academic deficiencies of the lives of Benton and Morris, the books are invaluable for their insight into the future President's political philosophy. They showed Roosevelt grappling with currency problems, public morality, and land policy—with the great questions of the American past and the American future. They stamped him as a politician justifying his own support of Blaine in 1884 and visiting his resentment on the mugwumps with broad indictments of extremist reformers and spirited defenses of party regularity. And they revealed him as a young intellectual forging an interpretation of American history which was to influence his own actions until the end of his life.

Of the two books, *Benton* was the most complex. The magniloquent senator from Missouri represented much that Roosevelt admired. He was at once a sectionalist and a nationalist, a spokesman of the West and a staunch defender of the Union. He disdained the abolitionists and proslavery extremists alike. He championed the interests of individual Western settlers and he condemned out of hand the great land engrossers and speculators. He wanted no part of Mexico to the southwest, but he wanted a large part of Canada to the northwest. And he resisted at all times infringement by the states of the rights of the national government. Benton "had risen and grown steadily all through his long term of service," Roosevelt concluded. "Compare his stand against the slavery extremists and disunionists, such as Calhoun, with the position of Webster at the time of his famous 7th of March speech, or with that of Clay when he brought in his compromise bill! In fact, as the times grew more troublesome, he grew steadily better able to do good work in them."

Roosevelt's own value judgments were even more illuminating than his favorable appraisal of the broad sweep of Benton's career. He viewed the Missouri Senator's fight to dispose of the public lands to actual settlers at low cost as "a move of enormous importance to the whole West," one which encountered intense opposition, "especially from the shortsighted selfishness of many of the northeasterners." The drive toward Mexico was a "belligerent, or, more properly speaking, piratical way of looking at neighboring territory." But the land claimed by Canada in the old Northwest, so Roosevelt agreed with the vain and swaggering Missourian, "was by right our heritage."

Roosevelt regarded slavery as "a grossly anachronistic and un-American form of evil." He believed, however, that it might have been better to have allowed it to continue a century longer, "its ultimate extinction being certain." And he was sure that non-abolitionist political leaders such as Lincoln and Seward "did more than all the professional Abolitionists combined really to bring about its destruction." The abolitionists "belonged to that class of men that is always engaged in some agitation or other," he sharply asserted; "only it happened that in this particular agitation they were right."

Roosevelt's contempt for the abolitionists was matched by his disapproval of Andrew Jackson's wholesale removal of officeholders and destructive attack on the Second Bank of the United States. The former was a change "for the worse"; the latter an appeal "to the vague fear with which the poorer and more ignorant voters regard a powerful institution whose workings they do not understand." Conversely, Roosevelt extolled Jackson and Benton for standing by hard money; he also foreshadowed his own attitude toward the Populists and Free Silver Democrats in the 1890's:

A craze for "soft," or dishonest, money—a greenback movement, or one for short-weight silver dollars—works more to the disadvantage of the whole mass of the people than even to that of the capitalists; it is a move directly in the interest of "the money power," which its loud-mouthed advocates are ostensibly opposing in the interests of democracy.

The biography of Gouverneur Morris was poorer history than the life of Benton. But it also offered a penetrating insight into Roosevelt. Morris was a Federalist, one who "embodied to a peculiar degree both the qualities which made the Federalist party so brilliant and so useful, and those other qualities which finally brought about its downfall." He had those attributes "of generous daring and lofty disinterestedness which we like to associate with the name American. . . . He stood for order. He stood for the honest payment of debts." Yet—and here was Roosevelt's brief against the Federalists and eventually much of the Republican party as well—Morris "distrusted the mass of the people, and especially the mass of the people in other sections of the country."

Indeed, Roosevelt continued, "the force and subtlety of his reasoning were all marred by his incurable cynicism and deeprooted distrust of mankind." At the Constitutional Convention Morris "throughout appears as *advocatus diaboli*," frankly avowing "his disbelief in all generous and unselfish motives." The New York financier "championed a strong national government, wherein he was right; but he also championed a system of class representation, leaning toward aristocracy, wherein he was wrong." Moreover, he "feared and dreaded the growth of the Union in the West," actually desiring the Convention "to commit the criminal folly of attempting to provide that the West should always be kept subordinate to the East." And worst of all, he opposed the War of 1812, appearing as the "open champion of treason to the nation, of dishonesty to the nation's creditors, and of cringing subservience to a foreign power."

Roosevelt was not wont to brook intellectual confinement. In writing the work on Morris he had wandered through Hamilton to Abraham Lincoln, whose life he seems really to have wanted to write. Hamilton remained Roosevelt's intellectual hero, for he was the architect of the base. But Lincoln, who had both preserved and humanized the Federalist system, captured his heart.

Yet Roosevelt rarely admitted Lincoln's Jeffersonian strain. Nor would he concede that his own views reflected Jefferson's influence, though he repeatedly exhorted the Republican party to pursue policies that embodied Jefferson's humanism. Only after he had twice been President did Roosevelt conclude, and then but temporarily, that the marriage of government and business that Hamilton had fostered was beyond the power of high-minded men to direct in the public interest. Otherwise he never abandoned hope that the Republican leaders would rise above private interest and exert their great abilities for the good of all as they had, he believed, in Lincoln's time. The ennobled Civil War President, Roosevelt wrote, "was the first who showed how a strong people might have a strong government and yet remain the freest on earth."

He seized—half unwittingly—all that was best and wisest in the tradition of Federalism; he was the true successor of the Federalist leaders; but he grafted on their system a profound belief that the great heart of the nation beat for truth, honor, and liberty.

If the fame of the *Benton* and *Morris* rests on Roosevelt's political eminence, the four-volume *Winning of the West* endures for its merits. It stamped its author as a historian of genuine distinction: of brilliant, though uneven, literary power; of broad, and often acute, comprehension; and of extraordinary narrative force. As the foremost academic historian of the West, Frederick Jackson Turner, wrote in his review of the final volume, "Mr. Roosevelt has done a real service to our history" and "has rescued a whole movement in American development from the hands of unskillful annalists." With "graphic vigor," he continued, "he has portrayed the advance of the pioneer into the wastes of the continent" and yet "considered his subject broadly, in its relations to world-history." Roosevelt's work "will be to the general reader a revelation."

The Winning of the West failed, however, to fulfill Roosevelt's youthful ambition ("a mere dream," he called it) to write someday a book "that would really take rank as in the very first class." It lacked reflection and sobriety of judgment, and it was weak in analytical quality. It also abounded in partisanship and presentism. The failings were unfortunate, for Roosevelt could be forcefully objective. His later tendency

to offset the emphatic criticism with the emphatic commendation was even then apparent; and many of his appraisals of
controversial issues were scrupulously fair. But he could not
consistently hold the high ground. His obsessive contempt for
the Jeffersonians and their political descendants colored *The
Winning of the West* no less than his other writings, and with
grievous consequence. On the flimsiest circumstantial evidence
he accused Jefferson of engaging in a "characteristic . . .
tortuous intrigue" against President Washington. He further
failed, so Turner pointed out, to make a "detailed study of the
incompatibility of temperament between Federalism and the
West."

The work had other shortcomings. Roosevelt drew on many
theretofore unexamined manuscripts; but his heavy duties (he
wrote most of the four volumes while civil service or police
commissioner) precluded their proper exploitation. He also
neglected economic and institutional history. As he explained
to Turner, "I have always been more interested in the men
themselves than in the institutions through and under which
they worked." Nevertheless, *The Winning of the West* stands
as a pioneering account of the American people's westward
advance; one that justifies its author's reputation as a major
American historian of the narrative school.

Although the main focus was on the quarter century between 1765—when intrepid Daniel Boone, "a tall, spare, sinewy man with eyes like an eagle's and muscles that never
tired," made his first exploration—and 1796—when the British, who were "guilty of treachery to both friend and foe," at
last recognized America's conquest of the West—the intro-
ductory chapter's terse yet graphic description of the spread
of the English-speaking peoples is one of the classics of American historical literature. "They were led by no one commander," wrote Roosevelt of those who thronged across the
Alleghenies:

They acted under orders from neither king nor congress; they
were not carrying out the plans of any farsighted leader. In obedience to the instincts working half blindly within their breasts,
spurred ever onward by the fierce desires of their eager hearts, they
made in the wilderness homes for their children, and by so doing
wrought out the destinies of a continental nation. They warred and
settled from the high hill valleys of the French Broad and the upper
Cumberland to the half-tropical basin of the Rio Grande, and to
where the Golden Gate lets through the long-heaving waters of the

Pacific. . . . The fathers followed Boone or fought at King's Mountain; the sons marched south with Jackson to overcome the Creeks and beat back the British; the grandsons died at the Alamo or charged to victory at San Jacinto. They were doing their share of a work that began with the conquest of Britain, that entered on its second and wider period after the defeat of the Spanish Armada, that culminated in the marvelous growth of the United States.

Within those broad outlines Roosevelt wove his story, retracing the steps of the pioneers, superimposing chronology upon chronology, wallowing in tales of Indian massacres, swiping at the French, the British, the Indians—at all who stood in the way. Within that framework, too, he discoursed perceptively on the character of the frontiersmen and the social customs of those who settled in their wake; he waxed eloquent on the courage of friend and foe alike; and he gloried, always, in the ceaseless and terrifying advance to the West.

Roosevelt regarded the British effort to forestall the colonists' occupation of the trans-Appalachian regions as the main cause of the Revolution. Great Britain "wished the land to remain a wilderness, the home of the trapper and the fur trade, of the Indian hunter and the French *voyageur*," he asserted. "She desired it to be kept as a barrier against the growth of the seaboard colonies toward the interior. She regarded the new lands across the Atlantic as being won and settled, not for the benefit of the men who won and settled them, but for the benefit of the merchants and traders who stayed at home. It was this that rendered the Revolution inevitable." Roosevelt conceded that "the sins and shortcomings of the colonists had been many—but on the great underlying question they were wholly in the right, and their success was of vital consequence to the well-being of the race on this continent." It was no less true that Americans might have stirred up the Indians themselves under different circumstances. But, he concluded, "We have to deal, not with what . . . the Americans might have done, but with what the British actually did; and for this there can be many apologies, but no sufficient excuse."

Roosevelt saw no moral question in the engrossment of Indian lands by the American pioneers (his "courageous and virile" treatment, wrote Turner, "enables the reader to correct the . . . not altogether well-founded criticisms . . . by Eastern writers"):

There were a dozen tribes, all of whom hunted in Kentucky and fought each other there, all of whom had equally good titles to the soil, and not one of whom acknowledged the right of any other . . . save the right of the strongest. . . . The conquest and settlement by the Whites on the Indian lands was necessary to the greatness of the race and to the well-being of civilized mankind. It was as ultimately beneficial as it was inevitable . . . all that can be asked is that they shall be judged as other slayers and quellers of savage people are judged.

And so Theodore Roosevelt judged them, extolling their intrepidity and denouncing their regression to semibarbarity. The story of the white man's triumph over the redman, he wrote,

shows us a stern race of freemen who toiled hard, endured greatly, and fronted adversity bravely, who prized strength and courage and good faith, whose wives were chaste, who were generous and loyal to their friends. But it shows us also how they spurned at restraint, and fretted under it, how they would brook no wrong to themselves, and yet too often inflicted wrongs on others; their feats of terrible prowess are interspersed with deeds of the foulest and most wanton aggression, the darkest treachery, the most revolting cruelty . . . we see but little of such qualities as mercy for the fallen, the weak, and the helpless, or pity for a gallant and vanquished foe.

Roosevelt's sketches of frontier types were as sharp as his accounts of the long hunt, the pursuit of new lands, and the Homeric battles between Indians and whites. Among the best was that of the great Iroquois warrior, Logan:

He was a man of splendid appearance: over six feet high, straight as a spear-shaft, with a countenance as open as it was brave and manly, until the wrongs he endured stamped on it an expression of gloomy ferocity. He had always been the friend of the white man, and had been noted particularly for his kindness and gentleness to children. . . . A skilled marksman and mighty hunter, of commanding dignity, who treated all men with a grave courtesy that exacted the same treatment in return, he was greatly liked and respected by all the white hunters and frontiersmen whose friendship and respect were worth having; they admired him for his dexterity and prowess, and they loved him for his straightforward honesty, and his noble loyalty to his friend.

Of all the frontiersmen, Roosevelt most admired the Scotch-Irish. "These Irish representatives of the Covenanters were in the West almost what the Puritans were in the Northeast, and more than the Cavaliers were in the South," he wrote. "Mingled with the descendants of many other races, they nevertheless formed the kernel of the distinctively and intensely American stock who were the pioneers of our people in their march westward, the vanguard of the army of fighting settlers, who, with axe and rifle, won their way from the Alleghenies to the Rio Grande and the Pacific."

True, there were great numbers of others—English, German, Huguenots, and some Dutch and Swedish. But a single generation "was enough to weld together into one people the representatives of these numerous and widely different races." Long before the Revolution they had "lost all remembrance of Europe and all sympathy with things European," Roosevelt wrote in a passage that anticipated many of Turner's formal conclusions. "Their iron surroundings made a mould which turned out all alike in the same shape. They resembled one another, and they differed from the rest of the world—even the world of America, and infinitely more, the world of Europe —in dress, in customs, and in mode of life." Furthermore, he concluded, "the influence of heredity was no more plainly perceptible than was the extent of individual variation. . . . All qualities, good and bad, are intensified and accentuated in the life of the wilderness."

Similarly, Roosevelt maintained his faith in the uplifting influence of the battle hard-won, of manly physical combat, of the near-animal struggle for existence. "The first lesson the backwoodsman learnt was the necessity of self-help; the next, that such a community could only thrive if all joined in helping one another. . . . Their lives were harsh and narrow, they gained their bread by their blood and sweat, in the unending struggle with the wild ruggedness of nature. . . . They were relentless, revengeful, suspicious, knowing neither truth nor pity"; but, he continued, "they were also upright, resolute, and fearless, loyal to their friends, and devoted to their country." And so, it might be said of those last words, was Theodore Roosevelt. But his perspective was deeper, his stage of action wider, and his values more complex.

Roosevelt repeated those generalizations many times in *The Winning of the West*. He also touched upon the democratizing influence of the frontier, a thesis Turner was developing when the third and fourth volumes were published. And he particularly stressed the deterministic character of the mighty westward advance. Thus Boone proved more interesting as a type than as an individual, for the West was neither discovered, won, nor settled by any single man. Of George Rogers Clark alone, Roosevelt concluded, "can it be said that he did a particular piece of work which without him would have remained undone."

Such, then, was Theodore Roosevelt's literary and historical contribution to the epochal story of the American people. As the political leader of those people, he would soon project that epoch onto the world-wide stage.

The Winning of the West had been started shortly after and had been completed long after Roosevelt had shifted his base of operations back to the East in 1886–87. But his own experiences in the Bad Lands had made it richer. (Even Turner held that he had depicted the westward movement "as probably no other man of his time could have done.") Without them he could not have written so perceptively of Boone and his like; nor could he have understood so acutely the frontier's tendency to barbarize the weak and to make superior men of those who were already strong. "All qualities, good and bad, are intensified and accentuated in the life of the wilderness," he had written in a passage as applicable to the Bad Lands of the 1880's as to the black forests of Kentucky in the 1770's.

That was as true, probably, of Roosevelt himself as of Boone, Clark, and the others. Two years in the West had converted Roosevelt's iron resolve to one of steel. They had reinforced his high code of personal morality. They had developed his natural qualities of leadership. And they had encouraged his growing disposition to judge men on their merits. They had also intensified his intolerance of the weak, if not of the colorfully wicked. They had whetted his craving for hardship. And they had made his Darwinian concept of struggle more harsh and inclusive than ever.

With genuine regret Dakota bade him what it knew was good-by when he went East in the fall of 1886. "Theodore is a Dakota cowboy, and has spent a large share of his time in the Territory for a couple of years," the *Sioux Falls Press* said.

He is one of the finest thoroughbreds you ever met—a whole-souled, clear-headed, high-minded gentleman. When he first went on the range, the cowboys took him for a dude, but soon they realized the stuff of which the youngster was built, and there is no man now who inspires such enthusiastic regard among them as he.

PART TWO

The Road to the White House

Chapter 4

For the Good of the Nation

> *He is a young man still, with all the impulsiveness characteristic of youth, and occasionally this leads him to say or do zealous things which seem to older men imprudent; but . . . he is so honest and so courageous that he does not make the serious blunders resulting from dishonesty or timidity.*
>
> —The *Philadelphia Record*

WITHIN TWO and one-half years of his return to New York in the fall of 1886 Roosevelt had begun a flamboyantly creative six-year tenure on the Civil Service Commission in Washington. Before assuming this new charge, however, he had scored labor violence in a memorable personal letter, engaged in a "bully" campaign for the mayorship of New York, and made an eminently successful second marriage with a childhood playmate.

TR's epistolary foray against labor actually occurred five months before he left Dakota. On the evening of May 4, 1886, a seething crowd of strikers, socialists, and anarchists had gathered in Haymarket Square, Chicago, to protest police violence in particular and managerial repression in general. The meeting had been proceeding peaceably, though passions were high and words from the platform incendiary, when suddenly, on an ill-considered command from their captain, 180 policemen had moved to disperse the assemblage. Someone, identity unknown, had thereupon heaved a bomb into the officers' serried ranks, and in the ensuing melee eight policemen had been killed and sixty-seven wounded.

Eight known anarchists were subsequently arrested and tried. No one of them was ever proved to have thrown a bomb, but all eight were found guilty: first by an inflamed and vengeful public opinion, then by courts of law after one of the most injudicious trials in American legal annals. Seven were sentenced to death and one to life imprisonment.

Like most other vocal Americans, Roosevelt had been outraged when he read reports of the Haymarket tragedy at the
Chimney Butte ranch in Dakota; and like many of his countrymen, he had reacted instinctively in terms of counter-
violence. "My men are hard working, labouring men, who
work longer hours for no greater wages than many of the
strikers . . . ," he wrote his sister Bamie. "I believe nothing
would give them greater pleasure than a chance with their
rifles at one of the mobs. . . . I wish I had them with me
and a fair show at ten times our number of rioters; my men
shoot well and fear very little."

To this day that statement flaws Roosevelt's reputation
among sensitive men. Possibly they have exaggerated its importance. And surely they have failed to weigh it against TR's
signal services to labor during his long career. TR was only
twenty-seven years old when he made the statement and his
judgment had been formed by biased newspaper reports. Furthermore, even the noble humanist, Henry George, endorsed
the anarchists' death sentences.

Yet TR never softened the virulence of that first reaction.
Long after the evidence was in he continued to rail against
the "murderous rioters"; long after thoughtful Chicagoans
had conquered their own base instincts Roosevelt remained
vengeful. And when, seven years after the tragedy, Illinois's
German-born governor, John Peter Altgeld, responded to the
humane dictates of his own great conscience by pardoning
the three surviving victims, Roosevelt angrily relegated him
to the ranks of Robespierre and the Jacobins. The conclusion
is inescapable: TR's compulsion for order and a Hebraic-like
justice constrained him to give short shrift to the historic
safeguards of Anglo-American law.

Roosevelt's inability to fathom the wellspring of industrial
violence reflected his failure to frame the passing insights of
his legislative years into a mature philosophy of labor. At
times he perceived the near-controlling force of the external
environment; but he could not, or would not, generalize rationally on his perceptions. His campaign for mayor of New
York in the fall of 1886 bears further on this.

TR had entered the race with some reluctance. The real
contest was between Abram S. Hewitt, a Democratic indus-
trialist-philanthropist, and Henry George, running on the
United Labor party's ticket. George's classic indictment of

poverty and his imaginative proposals for tax reform in his epochal work, *Progress and Poverty,* had terrorized conservatives, and it was understood that thousands of Republicans would vote Democratic to assure his defeat. No prominent Republican wanted the nomination, so early in October Tom Platt had turned in desperation to young Roosevelt. "The simple fact is that I had to play Curtius and leap into the gulf that was yawning before the Republican party," TR explained. Had the party's chances of winning been better, he added, he would not have been asked.

During the whirling campaign that followed, Roosevelt acted as though he thought he could win. He tried to forestall a mass defection of Republicans to Hewitt, whose intemperate attack on George did his own reputation no honor, by treating George's advanced views lightly and playing on the Republicans' disdain for Tammany. He charged that Hewitt would not be a free man. And he promised again and again that he himself would "go to City Hall unpledged to any one."

Roosevelt also reaffirmed the views of his years as an assemblyman by flailing owners of slum properties. At the same time, however, he exposed his limitations by trying to redress a balance that had never been. Only through "steady, individual self-help" could industrial evils be stamped out, he told slum-imprisoned workers who were powerless even to form an effective union. He added that such evils could "no more be done away with by legislation than you could do away with the bruises which you receive when you tumble down, by passing an act to repeal the laws of gravitation." Not until TR became President did he finally realize that the repressive force of capital was so powerful, the enervating effect of subsistence wages so pervasive, that "individual self-help" was shamefully inadequate for all but the very strongest. Had he digested *Progress and Poverty* in 1886, he would have known it then.

Roosevelt's energetic campaigning availed him little; he ran third, 30,000 votes behind Hewitt and 8,000 behind George. "[In] the wild dread of the disaster that was [supposedly] coming," wrote Jacob Riis, "men forsook party, principles, everything, and threw themselves into the arms of Tammany." Young Roosevelt was hurt. "Am badly defeated," he wired Cabot Lodge. "Worse even than I feared."

A few days later Roosevelt sailed for England to be married again. For more than a year after Alice Lee's death in 1884 he had avoided meeting Edith Carow, his childhood sweetheart. Theodore and Edith's friends had assumed before he met Alice that they would be married; but they had drifted apart, perhaps because "Her ladyship," as he often referred to her, had her "bad days" as well as her "good days." Edith herself later held that she had rejected Theodore's proposals several times, but his diary offers no evidence.

Neither is there any record of Edith's thoughts when she attended Theodore and Alice's wedding in 1880. During the next five years, however, her disposition to remove herself from society increased. "I believe you could live in the same house with Edith for fifty years and never really know her," said a classmate at Miss Comstock's school. Nevertheless, Edith continued to see Theodore's sister Bamie, and about eighteen months after Alice's death she accidentally met Theodore himself. His romantic resolve to be true to the memory of Alice began at once to weaken and for days the letter "E" was his only diary entry. Finally, on November 17, 1885, they became secretly engaged. Although Theodore was later overheard murmuring fitfully to himself that he wished he could be constant to Alice, he and Edith were married in London in December, 1886. Cecil Spring-Rice, an urbane and witty young English diplomat, was best man.

Edith Carow Roosevelt was a woman of many moods and some paradoxes. She was kind, considerate, and tactful; she was also shrewd, calculating, and at times ruthless. She suffered from neuralgia, and neither Theodore nor the children knew quite what to expect of her. Her tongue was sharp, and for all her affection for her ebullient husband, she often silenced him with a rapier-like word or phrase. She is said to have been possessive and demanding; yet she tolerantly accepted her children as nature had variously endowed them. Her intelligence was wide-ranging and sensitive and her literary judgments were by all accounts penetrating. She read poetry aloud with quietly moving effect, and she was considered by her friends an authority on Shakespeare. She was also well read in philosophy and versed in current affairs. As Theodore observed many years after their marriage, she "is not only cultured but scholarly."

Down through the years Edith became as indispensable, probably, as any one person could to her many-sided and resilient husband. She raised Alice Lee's daughter and bore four sons and a daughter of her own. She suffered Theodore's myriad political acquaintances and she tolerated some and enjoyed others of the legions of intellectuals who crossed her threshold on his invitation. When she was bored or tired, as she often was, she absented herself from lunch or retired early after dinner. And though she was invariably gracious at official functions, she was to the end of her life more spectator than participant.

Edith wisely gave sparingly of her counsel on political affairs—she seems to have sensed intuitively when her advice would weigh—and she resignedly accepted many of Theodore's most disruptive decisions in the realization that they "were best for him." TR was aware that he often piqued her, and when Ted, Jr. became engaged in 1910 he commented revealingly on their quarter century together. "Greatly tho I loved Mother," he wrote his first-born son, "I was at times thoughtless and selfish, and if Mother had been a mere unhealthy Patient Griselda I might have grown set in selfish and inconsiderate ways." She was "always tender, gentle and considerate, and always loving, yet, when necessary pointed out where I was thoughtless, instead of submitting to it." Had she done otherwise, he concluded, her life would have been "very much harder, and mine very much less happy."

Nor was Edith uninfluenced by her gregarious husband. "One should not live to oneself," she warned Ted in her congratulatory letter. "It was a temptation to me, only Father would not allow it. Since I have grown older and realize that it is a great opportunity when one has a house that one can make pleasant for younger—and also older—people to come to, I have done better."

Following their wedding on December 2, 1886, Theodore and Edith had leisurely toured the Continent. Theodore was captivated by Venice. ". . . [The] architecture has a certain florid barbarism about it—Byzantine, dashed with something stronger—that appeals to some streak in my nature," he wrote. He was also impressed by the Dying Gladiator, Raphael, Michelangelo, and the Milan cathedral.

The lofty aisle, with its rows of towering columns, white and shadowy, and the fretted, delicate work above, all seen in the dim half light that comes through the stained glass windows, really awes me; it gives me a feeling I have never had elsewhere except among very wild, chasm-rent mountains, or in the vast pine forests where the trees are very tall and not too close together. I think I care more for breadth, vastness, grandeur, strength, than for technique or mere grace or the qualities that need artistic sense or training to appreciate.

After a short visit in Paris and an exciting whirl in high British social and intellectual circles, the Roosevelts embarked for the United States on March 19. They were to make their home at Sagamore Hill, the spacious gabled house which Theodore and Alice had planned and the architects Lamb and Rich had executed.

The house "was nothing to soothe the eye or melt the spirit with subtle harmonies of proportion or grace of line," Hagedorn writes in his engaging *Roosevelt Family of Sagamore Hill*. Roosevelt knew what he wanted in the interior—a library, great fireplaces, and a big parlor or drawing room—but he had slight conception of how the exterior should look. "So the architects gave him on the outside what self-respecting men of substance of the 1880's valued more than beauty, and what architects were summoned to express: solidity, first of all; dignity, hospitality, comfort, the social stability of the owner, and permanence. The foundations were twenty inches thick; joists, rafters and roof boards were in proportion. Long Island's gales were not going to shake this house. . . ."

At Sagamore, Theodore immersed himself in the pleasures of family life. Alice is "too sweet and good for anything," he wrote of his first wife's child. "Eleanor"—the shy and retiring niece who was to marry a distant cousin, Franklin Delano Roosevelt—"plays all the time with her." Theodore, Jr., born September 13, 1887, "crawls everywhere, does his best to stand and talk—but fails—and is too merry and happy for anything. I go in to play with them every morning; they are certainly the dearest children imaginable." And so it was over the years. Kermit came in 1889, Ethel in 1891, Archibald in 1894, and Quentin in 1897. Each was "the sweetest little fellow [or girl] in the world"; each received a surprising measure of the father's time and attention.

Meanwhile Roosevelt published his biography of Thomas Hart Benton, wrote his *Gouverneur Morris,* and started *The Winning of the West.* He rode to the hounds and he helped organize a polo club. He took a perverse pleasure in falls—

only the courageous rode hard enough to suffer mishap—and he once remounted with a broken arm and continued the chase to the kill. He talked glowingly of his triumphs and humorously of his foibles, especially in tennis, which he played with more energy than finesse. "I was given a first class partner who won in spite of me," he said after a tournament victory. "I have turned my share of the 'cup' into a new Winchester rifle that I have been longing for." He also went West to hunt during these years; and partly to replenish his ranching losses, but mainly because of his compulsion to express himself, he wrote numerous accounts of his experiences.

TR's circle of friends gradually became wider and more cosmopolitan. But it was with Henry Cabot Lodge, ten years his senior and his opposite in personality, that the deepest friendship developed. A moralist sans fervor, Lodge began his long career as a moderate reformer and ended it as the arch-partisan of his age. More intellectually agile and polished than Roosevelt, he lacked his friend's breadth and flexibility. Nor was he warm and spontaneous. His letters reveal a man as calculating in the small things as in the large things, a man predisposed to read the meanest motives into others. From his adolescence to his old age, moreover, there was about him a supercilious quality that his drooping eyelids sharply accentuated; and though his abilities were widely recognized, he was respected but neither liked nor generally admired. Never, not even in the United States Senate where he held the seat of Webster and Sumner for thirty years, was Lodge a leader in the classic mold; and never, for all his eminence, was he seriously considered for the presidency, except by Roosevelt in 1916. Yet his intellectual power was considerable, and he had an element of high-mindedness. His contributions to the civil service movement, to administrative reform, and to national defense were substantial and meritorious.

Roosevelt and Lodge's relationship had been forged on the political crucible of the Blaine campaign and tempered by common interests uncovered thereafter. No less than Roosevelt, Lodge loved history; and even more than Roosevelt, belles-lettres. Both men had been long interested in civil service reform; both were strident nationalists and budding imperialists. Until Roosevelt espoused the liberalism of Jefferson, or so he always insisted, of Lincoln, both were also conservative Hamiltonians. Notwithstanding his public hauteur, Lodge was affectionate and gracious in the security of his home. And though he lacked TR's bubbling zest, he was an impassioned horseman and polo player. His wife, Nannie, had a scintillating mind and surpassing charm as a hostess; Theodore admired and enjoyed her, and so, happily, did Edith.

From the outset Lodge recognized Roosevelt's extraordinary potential; through the three and one-half decades of their relationship he labored devotedly and at times almost selflessly to advance TR's political career. Roosevelt, who numbered few men among his friends although he had thousands of acquaintances, responded with his greatest gift. To Cabot Lodge more than to any other man, he gave his personal confidence. As TR once confessed, "I can't help writing you, for . . . there are only one or two people in the world, outside of my own family, whom I deem friends or for whom I really care." Such was the strength of the bond that bound them together that not even Roosevelt's bolt from the Grand Old Party in 1912 dissolved it completely.

Following his return from abroad in 1887 Roosevelt took a passing interest in politics. He engaged in a vendetta with the mugwump editor, E. L. Godkin of *The Nation*. He attacked Henry George's theories, which he misrepresented. And he supported Benjamin Harrison for the presidency in 1888, though he had again steeled himself to accept Blaine on the grounds that "his name alone wakens enthusiasm, and . . . he would poll the most votes." Even as he stamped himself as a partisan Republican, however, he worked sincerely and energetically to reform the G.O.P. from within.

After Benjamin Harrison's election, Roosevelt sought to stay the victorious G.O.P.'s gathering assault on the merit system in a speech to the Federal Club of New York City. Conceding that there was "an immediate necessity to remove a great number of Mr. Cleveland's more vicious and incompetent appointees," he urged that the classified system be substantially extended "on the lines of the excellent bill introduced in Congress by my friend Cabot Lodge." He was speaking, he pointedly exclaimed, "on behalf of very many tens of thousands of Republicans who belong to the party because they believe in it, not for what they can make of it. . . ."

For some time TR had yearned to play the larger role for which friends, newspapermen, and his own consciousness had told him he was destined. Neither his interests in the West nor his writing had absorbed his vaulting energies. And he had begun to doubt that he could write a great book. Almost three years before, in August, 1886, he had rejected overtures to serve as president of the New York Board of Health. That same month visions of military glory—visions that would never die—had brightened momentarily when an incident along the Mexican border precipitated a flurry of war talk. Eagerly, Roosevelt petitioned the Secretary of War for authority to raise an outfit of horse riflemen in the event of hostilities. "I haven't the least idea there will be any trouble," he explained to Lodge, "but as my chance of doing anything in the future worth doing seems to grow continually smaller I intend to grasp at every opportunity that turns up."

As the Harrison administration took shape in the spring of 1889, TR's political ambition flared anew. He would, he now confided to Lodge, "like above all things to go into politics." He feared, however, that he was *persona non grata*, and he resigned himself to a literary career, planning only to take the interest in politics "that a decent man should." The reaction of the new Secretary of State, James G. Blaine, to Mrs. Lodge's suggestion that he appoint Roosevelt Assistant Secretary of State suggests that his fears were warranted. "I do somehow fear that my sleep at Augusta or Bar Harbor would not be quite so easy and refreshing if so brilliant and aggressive a man had hold of the helm," Blaine wrote. "Matters are constantly occurring which require the most thoughtful concentration and the most stubborn inaction. Do *you* think that Mr. T.R.'s temperament would give guaranty of that course?"

Blaine knew his man. And so did Benjamin Harrison. The President was reluctant to give the thirty-year-old New Yorker any post in his administration; but under pressure from Lodge and others, he finally agreed to offer Roosevelt one of the four posts on the Civil Service Commission. To the President's subsequent dismay, Roosevelt accepted.

The civil service system was in a precarious state when Roosevelt breezed into office on May 13, 1889. Although Cleveland had strengthened the rules and extended the classified lists as he left Washington, he had made a partisan sweep of all positions not covered by the law during the preceding four years. Partly in retaliation, but mainly because they also accepted the spoils system, thousands of Republicans had swarmed into Washington or beseeched congressmen by mail for appointments in the weeks preceding Roosevelt's appointment. "Hundreds of Offices," "Places to Suit All Classes," "Take Your Choice," ran the headlines in one uninhibited Republican newspaper.

Unable to withstand the onslaught, President Harrison resignedly gave the job-hunger of the party stalwarts precedence over the moral fervor of the reformers. Under the benign dispensation of Postmaster-General John Wanamaker, pioneering merchant, Sunday school teacher, and G.O.P. "fat cat," 30,000 fourth-class postmasters were soon replaced by loyal, and presumably deserving, Republicans. Other cabinet officers were more restrained because their departments were smaller; but their comparative performances were as good, or bad. Harrison had been in office hardly a month before *Harper's Weekly* was angrily charging that "There was never in our history a grosser violation of distinct promises and pledges than the partisan devastation of the post offices under this administration."

The belated appointee of a skeptical President, Roosevelt was determined nonetheless to enforce the law with zeal. "I am a great believer in practical politics," he wrote Lodge a little later, "but when my duty is to enforce a law, that law is surely going to be enforced, without fear or favor. I am perfectly willing to be turned out—or be legislated out—but while in I mean business." In truth, the waters ran deeper. Civil service reform was at once the most confirmed and most sustained cause of Roosevelt's career; he read into it both the gospel of efficiency which is the conservative's creed and the open society which is the democrat's dream. As he and his colleagues wrote in their annual report of 1892–93, "a man enters the public service on his merits, after fair trial, in comparison with others of his fellow citizens, and is retained as long as he honorably serves the public." Roosevelt also regarded it as a prime preventive of moral degradation. The "spoils system," said that same report, "is a fruitful source of corruption in national life," one that prevents "decent men" from taking part in politics and that "degenerates into a mere corrupt scramble for plunder."

Young Roosevelt believed at first that President Harrison would approve his rigorous enforcement of the existing laws. "I have strengthened the administration by showing, in striking contrast to the facts under Cleveland, that there was no humbug in the law now," he wrote after six weeks in office. Two years later he was not so sanguine. On count after count Harrison, who privately complained that TR "wanted to put an end to all the evil in the world between sunrise and sunset," had failed him. "The President actually refuses to consider the changes in the rules . . . necessary to enable us to do our work effectively," Roosevelt wrote Lodge. "He has never given us one ounce of real backing. He won't see us, or consider any method for improving the service, even when it in no way touches a politician. It is horribly disheartening to work under such a Chief."

Nevertheless, Roosevelt and his colleagues accomplished much during those first two years. They issued critical reports on examination procedures, they relentlessly pursued reports of fraud, and they made a well-publicized inspection tour of government offices in the West. "We have to do two things," Roosevelt told reporters on the eve of their departure. "One is to make the officials themselves understand that the law is obligatory, not optional, and the other is to get the same idea into the heads of the people."

Roosevelt's dynamic exertions continued throughout the Harrison administration though he privately complained of inactivity. The annual reports "revealed the presence of a new vigor and administrative power, and of a mind appreciative at once of ideal ends and practicable possibilities," one of the historians of the movement wrote. Stories of Roosevelt's deeds "are handed down from generation to generation of Commission employees," the Chairman of the Commission reported sixty-two years after TR had resigned his post. And understandably so. Roosevelt lectured a recalcitrant Congress on means to improve the Pendleton Law. He called Southern Democratic congressmen into his office to explain how their constituents could win federal jobs by competitive examination. And he firmly refused to jump names on the lists. "You saw the . . . register when you were down here," he wrote a congressman who made inquiries for a constituent. "Her average was good . . . but it was not good enough." Or, as he bluntly admonished a job-seeker who had the temerity to discuss his connections: "No political influence will help you in the least. Not both your Senators and all your Representatives in Congress together could avail to have you certified from our registers."

That was not all. Roosevelt devised new and practical tests

for applicants. "When we hold an examination for assistant statistician our aim is to get . . . an assistant statistician, not . . . a Civil Service Commissioner or Cabinet Officer," he explained to one correspondent. "We make the examinations as simple as the duties of the places to be filled admit," he informed another. He also placed women on the same competitive plane with men in many positions. In addition, TR wrote numerous magazine articles, delivered uncounted speeches, and lobbied vigorously for increased appropriations for the Commission. "The last few years politically for me have been largely a balancing of evils," he confided revealingly to Brander Matthews, "and I am delighted to go in on a side where I have no doubt whatever."

One of the side effects of Roosevelt's relentless enforcement of the civil service laws was his restoration to grace by the mugwumps. The Old Guardsmen and their organs fumed over his refusal to play the party game, the *Washington Post* labeling him "The Rollicking Ranchman of Bogus Reform." But President Eliot of Harvard praised him as the "ideal citizen" and the *New York Evening Post* began again to refer to TR's "characteristic candor." Many Republican and Democratic newspapers also endorsed him warmly. He was, said the *Philadelphia Record,* a man who "believes rather in the principles than the practices of his party."

His colleagues were quiet men, who supported him to a considerable extent, but he did the fighting in the newspapers, before congress and everywhere else, and of course bore the brunt of the consequent attack which by and by came largely to be personal to himself, as he became recognized as the leading spirit of the Commission.

TR professed to resent the plaudits of the mugwumps and Democrats on the grounds that they would "discredit me with well-meaning but narrow Republicans." But it was his own actions that alienated him from the party warhorses. He not only cut their feed bags, he impugned the integrity of a cabinet officer and spread the charges on the record in the election year 1892.

The main fight centered on the Post Office Department. John Wanamaker's talents were those of a near administrative genius. Although the most imaginative of his proposals—

those for parcel-post deliveries, postal savings banks, and the decentralization of administration—were blocked by the indifference of Congress, he nevertheless pushed through such a spate of reforms as made his tenure the most distinguished since the Civil War. On the other hand, Wanamaker continued to promote the political interests of the Grand Old Party, partly because he hoped for congressional support of his legislative program but also because he was a thoroughgoing partisan. As his sympathetic biographer admits and his 30,000 removals of fourth-class postmasters prove, he had "no profound objection to the theory that to the victors belong the spoils." Nor did Wanamaker have any "profound" respect for certain laws of the land.

In the spring of 1891 Roosevelt investigated reports of maladministration in the Baltimore office. "We certainly struck pay gravel," he enthusiastically wrote Charles J. Bonaparte, the Baltimore patrician reformer who later served in his cabinet. Roosevelt found that the Baltimore postmaster had arbitrarily removed about half the employees in the classified service and had allowed the law banning compulsory political assessments of classified employees to be violated flagrantly. Roosevelt thereupon recommended to Wanamaker and the President that twenty-five Republican appointees in the Baltimore office be dismissed; but the report was pigeonholed. Unable to endure the agony of inaction, TR soon unburdened himself at a tempestuous meeting of the Civil Service Reform Association in New York. Then, following a melodramatic scene in which he exclaimed "damn John Wanamaker," he returned to Washington and demanded an investigation by the House Civil Service Committee.

The Democratic-controlled committee cheerfully complied. For days charges and counter-charges filled the air as Roosevelt and Wanamaker appeared before the committee. Finally, with just the slightest indirection, Roosevelt accused the Postmaster-General of "slanderous falsehoods." The episode constituted a heavy blow to Harrison's chances of reelection, and TR knew it. Contritely, yet resolutely, he wrote the President that he had "used every effort to avoid a conflict with the Post Office Department," but that it had "now become merely a question of maintaining my own self-respect and upholding the civil service law."

By then the damage was done. The "little grey man in

the White House," as Roosevelt called the cold and distant President, had to retain his maverick Civil Service Commissioner because his dismissal would have been construed as repudiation of the merit concept. To be sure, Roosevelt oiled the raging waters by speaking energetically for Harrison's re-election that fall. But the oil proved too thin or the waters too turbulent. The Wanamaker affair, the Populist movement, and numerous other factors combined to defeat the President and make Grover Cleveland the only man to serve two interrupted terms in the White House.

Roosevelt wished to continue as Commissioner under Cleveland, and with characteristic aggressiveness he encouraged Carl Schurz to intercede with the President-elect. He warned him, however, that he would stay on only if Cleveland agreed to stand by him and appoint a strong board. Schurz thereupon advised Cleveland that he was in a unique position to "deal a blow to the spoils system from which it will never recover"; he added that he could "hardly find a more faithful, courageous and effective aid than Mr. Roosevelt" for that purpose. Six weeks after his inauguration the President reappointed TR.

Many of the old problems now recurred, for the Democratic hosts proved as numerous and deserving as the Grand Old Party's. Indeed, an attorney-general's opinion that political parties could solicit contributions from government employees by mail resulted in more solicitation in the congressional campaign of 1894 than in any previous non-presidential canvass. Nevertheless, the merit principle advanced steadily. President Cleveland cooperated generously with Roosevelt and he encouraged high administration officials to do likewise. Early in his tenure he removed a Democratic commissioner who opposed TR's policies; and in the one instance that Roosevelt tangled publicly with a cabinet officer the President backed TR.

It was with deep satisfaction in his achievements, therefore, that TR resigned in April, 1895, to become a member of the Board of Police Commissioners of New York City. He had not, it is true, persuaded Congress to place a sufficiently large number of upper level positions under the civil service laws. Nor had he found a full solution to the perplexing problem of promotion for merit in a bureaucracy. Yet the classified lists had been more than doubled during his regime and the importance of civil service had become widely recognized.

Others shared in the achievement. The Civil Service Reform Association, major elements of the American press, and uncounted public-spirited citizens had contributed to the climate of opinion that made reform possible. President Cleveland's cooperation had been vital. As TR wrote in a letter of resignation that warmly commended the Chief Executive for his courtesy and cooperation, Cleveland's "sweeping reduction . . . of excepted places . . . worked a most valuable reform in the execution of the law itself." Roosevelt's colleagues had also borne a share of the load; and TR rejoiced when one of them, "high-minded and upright" John R. Proctor, ex-Confederate soldier and Democrat, was selected by the President as the new head of the Commission. But more than any other individual, Roosevelt had been responsible for the Commission's rejuvenation and for the marshaling of public sentiment behind its program. His imaginative and energetic enforcement of the laws had virtually institutionalized civil service; and had he never performed another service for the American nation, that alone would have perpetuated his memory as a secondary figure of substantial accomplishment.

Chapter 5

The Fight for the Right

> *It may be truthfully said that Theodore
> Roosevelt at no time in his career fought more
> effectively for the basic principles of free gov-
> ernment than he fought for them as New
> York Police Commissioner.*
> —Former Commissioner Avery D. Andrews

WHEN Roosevelt resigned his police commissionership two
years later he could also look back to reforms accomplished
and victories hard won. But the reforms were even more
intangible, the battles yet more bitter and controversial, than
those of his civil service years.

Not in all Roosevelt's career were the opponents of honest
government more widely and deeply entrenched than when
he accepted Fusion Mayor William L. Strong's appointment
in the spring of 1895. Their locus was Tammany Hall, or so
it seemed to the uninitiated. But Lincoln Steffens reported
that they included "parts of the Republican machine, the
saloons, gambling-houses, all vice interests, sportsmen generally, and to [Steffens'] . . . curious surprise many business
men—the ablest, biggest, richest business men in local business; gas, transportation, banks, and the great financiers."
Periodically, civic leaders like the fiery, bearded, Presbyterian
minister, Dr. Charles H. Parkhurst, would expose corruption
with such penetrating intensity that the citizenry would
become aroused. But the "system" described by Steffens was
too well organized, its tentacles too sharp and grasping, for
reform to have enduring impact. Roosevelt sensed the formidable nature of his new assignment. "I must make up my
mind to much criticism and disappointment," he confided
to Bamie, for conditions make it "absolutely impossible to
do what will be expected of me."

Having put his forebodings on the record, Roosevelt
bounded up the steps of Police Headquarters on May 6 in
his usual high spirits. "Where are our offices? Where is

the board room? What do we do first?" he asked Jacob Riis, who introduced him to Lincoln Steffens on the run. "It was all breathless and sudden," Steffens recalled. "It was just as if we three were the police board, T.R., Riis, and I, and as we got T.R. calmed down we made him promise to go a bit slow, to consult with his colleagues also. Then we went out into the hall, and there stood the three other commissioners together, waiting for us to go so that they could see T.R."

They at once elected Roosevelt president of the board. But only one of the three, Major Avery D. Andrews, supported him for long. A West Pointer and nominal Democrat, Andrews was soft-spoken and unobtrusively efficient. He had already started the reform program TR would shortly expand. The other two, Colonel Frederick D. Grant and Andrew D. Parker, were soon to break with Roosevelt. Grant was the son of the illustrious general and hapless President. Slow-moving, kindly, and weak, he was shortly compared to TR as "a freight train" to a "limited express." As his father had done under President Johnson, he would seek to advance his fortunes by joining a cabal against his superior. Parker was a handsome, strong-willed lawyer who had served three years as an assistant district attorney. He was affiliated with the County Democracy, though not because he opposed Tammany on ethical grounds. Steffens tolerantly described him as "the man that liked to sit back and pull wires just to see the puppets jump." But Andrews' insight into Parker was deeper; he recalled simply that he "lacked the moral character . . . essential to the post."

Buoyed up by the apparent quality of his colleagues, TR plunged into his new duties amidst the usual newspaper fanfare: "Roosevelt on Deck; Roosevelt on the Board for Business; He Wants to Know, and He Asks Some Pointed Questions; Trials are Trials Now; New Police Brooms Busy; Delinquent Policemen Get Short Shrift From Roosevelt."

Throughout the spring of 1895 TR's midnight prowls over patrolmen's beats, dramatic changes in personnel, and emphatic pronouncements kept him favorably in the news. As he histrionically exclaimed at the end of his second month in office, "Two years and eight months left to me on this Board and that is time enough to make matters very unpleasant for policemen who shirk their duty."

Many of the police reporters—Steffens, Arthur Brisbane,

and Joseph B. Bishop—meanwhile formed strong attachments to the effervescent Commissioner. They gravitated to TR because his every move and offhand remark were lively with human interest; but they supported him because they believed in what he was doing. "We have a real Police Commissioner," Brisbane wrote in the hostile *World*. "His teeth are big and white, his eyes are small and piercing, his voice is rasping. He makes our policemen feel as the . . . little froggies . . . [yet] he looks like a man of strength . . . a determined man, a fighting man, an honest, conscientious man, and like the man to reform the force."

Bishop was not less perceptive. "The peculiarity about . . . [Roosevelt] is that he has what is essentially a boy's mind," he wrote in the *Evening Post*. "What he thinks he says at once, thinks alive. It is his distinguishing characteristic." However, Bishop added, "with it he has great qualities which make him an invaluable public servant—inflexible honesty, absolute fearlessness, and devotion to good government which amounts to religion. We must let him work in his own way for nobody can induce him to change it." Furthermore, "he is talking to a purpose. He wishes the public to know what the Police Board is doing so that it will have popular support."

Roosevelt's "popular support" proved short-lived. It began to diminish when he forced out Superintendent Tom Byrnes, an extraordinarily able and popular officer who had long collaborated with the politicians, vice men, and businessmen who comprised the grand *mésalliance*. And it suffered a mortal blow when he persisted in enforcing a law against the sale of intoxicating beverages on Sunday. Put on the statute books by the Tammany Democrats and kept there by the votes of well-meaning Protestant legislators from upstate, the Raines, or Sunday closing law, was an open sesame of graft. Saloon-keepers by the hundreds regularly paid off the police for the privilege of opening their doors in defiance of its provisions.

Roosevelt realized that the Raines Law should have been repealed, and at one point he stated publicly that he would have opposed its enactment. But as he also explained, he had "to choose between closing all the saloons and violating my oath of office" as long as it remained on the books. More important, for TR was never as committed to a literal interpretation of his duties as that remark implied, he had to enforce the Raines Law in order to attain his pre-eminent objective—the creation of an honest police force. Not until all the saloons were closed on Sundays could bribery be stamped out; not until bribery was eliminated could the reforms he and Andrews were fostering become meaningful.

Unhappily, the Sunday closing law ran athwart the customs of New York's large and reputable German-American population. The German-Americans had always observed the Continental Sunday, and they bitterly resented the imputation that a Sunday afternoon spent in a beer garden with a string ensemble playing Strauss and children pattering around the tables was immoral. All that summer they grumbled over the forced closing of their neighborhood drinking places. Finally they organized a tremendous protest parade and invited Roosevelt to review it. Early in September thousands of marchers bearing placards emblazoned with remarks such as "Good Morning, Have You Seen Roosevelt's Name in Print?" "Liberty, Priceless Gem, Where Hast Thou Flown? To Hoboken!" streamed by the reviewing stand where TR responded with such good spirit that he changed their jeers to cheers.

Roosevelt's troubles were compounded meanwhile by misrepresentations in unfriendly newspapers. Actually, TR's patrolmen enforced the Raines Law broadly and effectively. The protest of the German-Americans and the complaints of the counsel for the Liquor Dealers' Association, who claimed that ninety per cent of the saloonkeepers had gone bankrupt from loss of revenue, attest to that. To discredit TR, however, newspapermen trailing Roosevelt and Andrews when they made Sunday inspections reported that saloons were doing a flourishing business by means of side or rear doors. " 'East Side, West Side, all around the town,' yesterday went King Roosevelt I, ruler of New York and patron saint of dry Sundays," William Randolph Hearst's *Evening Journal* commented a month before the German-Americans organized their demonstration. Even Mayor Strong, who understood Roosevelt's purpose, succumbed to a demagogic urge to ridicule his ubiquitous commissioner. "I found that the Dutchman whom I had appointed meant to turn all New Yorkers into Puritans," he said at a public dinner that fall.

Not all the criticism was humorous. The daily mail brought in anonymous denunciations, threats, and, at least once, a crudely designed bomb. TR was shadowed at night in a vain effort at blackmail. And the chairman of the Republican County Committee angrily read Roosevelt out of the G.O.P. in a desperate attempt to hold the German-American vote. Unmoved by these and other pressures, including an implied threat by Strong that he would remove him unless he relaxed his enforcement of the Raines Law, TR resolutely held his ground. "We have no right to consider the [political] results," he admonished the Republican Reform Club at the height of the campaign against enforcement.

The consequence was disaster for Roosevelt's party and vindication for his program. The Republicans suffered a crushing defeat at the polls that fall as 30,000 German-Americans reportedly bolted to the Democrats. But the Wine, Liquor and Beer Association resolved that it would expel any member who opened his shop on Sunday. "There has not been a more remarkable triumph of law in the municipal history of New York," the correspondent for the London *Times* reported. "The consensus is that to Theodore Roosevelt's courage and ability more than to any other single cause this victory is due."

Newspaper charges to the contrary, TR had enforced the law against the dining and drinking places of the rich as well as against the beer gardens and saloons of the middle and lower classes. One of the most sensational incidents of the enforcement campaign, in fact, had been a raid on Sherry's restaurant during a dinner attended by many prominent New Yorkers. Partly to forestall such inconveniences to gentlemen but largely to circumvent the Raines Law as a whole, the legislature then passed a measure permitting the sale of liquor with meals in hotels. The law was so loosely framed, however, that it spawned a host of fake hotels and ramshackle brothel-saloons. And though Roosevelt again took the offensive, it proved impossible to close most of the places legally.

Roosevelt's second year in office was even more tumultuous than his first, the Board of Commissioners being virtually paralyzed by internal dissension and deadlock. Steffens later blamed personalities:

> T.R. liked to lead cavalry charges with a whoop out in the open, Parker to direct his troops mysteriously from the rear unseen. He hated the way T.R. took command of the police from the first day and kept saying "I" and "my policy." . . . Parker enjoyed turn-

ing up at a meeting one day with Grant to block some proposition of the president. He tried to get Andrews, too, but the young West Pointer did not like the crafty conspirator; he did not approve of T.R.'s cowboy style either, but he stared Parker down and joined and stood by the president.

Steffens was partly right; Roosevelt was dominating if not domineering. Yet Steffens' statement was also misleading. Parker was later tried for maladministration, and if his trial did nothing else, it proved that he would have fought anyone who opposed his drive for control of the force.

As it happened, Parker found an ally in Tom Platt. The "Easy Boss" was angered by Roosevelt's support of Thomas B. Reed's presidential aspirations (Platt was for McKinley), by TR's removal of many of "his men" from the police force for incompetency and worse, and especially by his enforcement of the Sunday closing law. Platt could not offend the upstate "drys" by repealing the law; yet he had to win back the German-Americans. He decided, therefore, to deadlock the Board of Commissioners in the hope that the enforcement campaign would then break down. He used Grant as his instrument.

Roosevelt's response to Platt's diabolical scheme set a pattern he was to follow through his governorship and presidency. He avoided a personal break with Platt, and he continued to identify himself as a regular Republican. But on the main issue, the enforcement campaign, he held absolutely firm. "I work and fight from dawn until dark, almost," he wearily wrote his sister, "and the difficulties, the opposition, the lukewarm support I encounter give me hours of profound depression; but at bottom I know the work has been well worth doing."

. . . All day I strive to push matters along; to keep on good terms with the Mayor, while rejecting his advice and refusing to obey his orders; not to be drawn into a personal quarrel with Platt; not to let my colleagues split either among themselves or with me; to work with reformers like Dr. Parkhurst, and yet not let them run away with the Department; to keep weeding out the bad men. . . .

The deadlock lasted into the spring of 1897. "I cannot shoot . . . [Parker]," TR complained to Lodge, "or engage in a rough-and-tumble with him—I couldn't even as a private citizen, still less as the chief peace-officer of the city; and I hardly know what course to follow as he is utterly unabashed by exposure and repeats lie after lie with brazen effrontery." Finally, however, Roosevelt, Andrews, and the Parkhurst group forced Mayor Strong to hold the public hearing that exposed Parker, after which Strong ordered his dismissal. But at the instance of "Boss" Platt, the Republican Governor refused to approve the order. When Roosevelt left office Parker remained to feud with his successor.

One illuminating exchange highlighted the Parker hearing. After TR charged that Parker was "mendacious, treacherous, capable of double dealing and exercising a bad influence upon the force," he was asked if he would refuse to support Parker if he knew him to be right.

"No sir. I would be glad to yield to him if he was right."

"You enjoy yielding to a man, don't you?"

"By George, I do, and that's a fact."

Roosevelt understandably seized an opportunity to move gracefully out by accepting the assistant secretaryship of the Navy that April. Not until the last year of his presidency would he again be so frustrated; not until 1912 so embattled. The Rev. Dr. Parkhurst had stood by him until the end—he even blazed out at Platt, who attended his church, from the pulpit. Thousands of disinterested citizens and dozens of reporters and editors, especially from out of state, also continued to support him. A reporter for the *Chicago Times-Herald* termed him "undeniably the biggest man in New York"; others boomed him for the presidency. Yet his enemies had proved even more numerous and powerful than he had expected. They included not only Tammany and the Republican machine, not only the German-Americans, the saloonkeepers, and the vice lords generally, but clergymen who resented his refusal to ban a professional fight. ("I suffered a heavier punishment sparring at Harvard," he told newspapermen after witnessing the bout, "and I have been knocked out at polo twice for a ten times longer period.")

Roosevelt had also antagonized labor. Union leaders had lauded his enforcement of the Sunday law against the restaurants and hostelries of the rich. And they had warmly endorsed his condemnation of more than one hundred "wretched and crowded" tenements, as he described them. (Twice wrathful landlords had tried to sue TR.) But they deplored his terrifying remarks about striking mobs, and they felt that he had thrown the police force on the side of capital by giving protection to strikebreakers.

The raging controversies of Roosevelt's two years as president of the board have lent to easy sensationalism and facile generalization. As TR had foreseen, he proved unable to rid New York City of corruption; and as he had not wholly foreseen, the leaders of his own party actively opposed him. Only the moral support of the decent elements had prevented the machine from turning him out; only his extraordinary courage and self-esteem had kept him from resigning after three or four months in office. Yet he had compiled a peerless record. Never in the department's history had the law been so effectively and dramatically enforced; never had two years seen so many basic reforms. When Roosevelt took office the price of a captaincy was said to have been $10,000; when he left office it was nothing. When Roosevelt assumed his duties on May 5, 1895, the flow of dismissals from the force was but a trickle; when he resigned in April 1897 it had become a flood. Steffens described the scene at the height of the turnover:

"Hey, there," [Roosevelt] yelled to me from his window one day, "come up here." I ran upstairs to his outer office, which was filled with all sorts of respectable people, evidently business men, lawyers, doctors, women, and two priests. Waving his hand around the circle of them, he squeezed through his teeth aloud: "I just want you to see the kind of people that are coming here to intercede for proven crooks. Come on, come into my office and listen to the reasons they give for letting bribers, clubbers, and crime-protectors stay on the police force and go on grafting on the public."

There were other, more permanent reforms. An examining board was set up, religious and political affiliations were struck off the list of unwritten requirements for appointment, and examinations patterned on the federal civil service were instituted. The eligibility list was scrupulously observed, though TR often made spot promotions for heroism. And a probationary period was established.

Repeatedly, politicians tried to break down or get around the merit system. Owen Wister recalled visiting TR one day when a surgeon named Marvin Palmer came in bearing a letter of recommendation from the Surveyor of the Port. "I entirely agree that a Republican appointment would be timely," Roosevelt said after perusing the letter. "And I am quite sure, Dr. Palmer, that you are qualified for the position." Then, after a momentary pause, he added: "And here's the way you can get the position. . . . Stand first on the Civil Service list!"

The physician thereupon stalked out of the office, stopping at the door just long enough to exclaim, "You can go to hell!"

Meanwhile the force was partially modernized. A bicycle squad was formed, a telephonic system of communications was established, and recruits were given fairly intensive training before being assigned to beats.

But above everything else towered Roosevelt's inspirational power. As an obscure patrolman confided to Steffens when TR's resignation was announced in the spring of 1897, "It's tough on the force, for he was dead square, was Roosevelt, and we needed him in the business." Years later veteran officers affirmed the truth of the *New York Evening Post's* tribute when Roosevelt closed his desk in April:

The end of the reign of Mr. Roosevelt . . . is not the end of Rooseveltism. Mr. Roosevelt may disappear utterly . . . but his personality will persist as an active influence in the force for a generation at least, till the youngest 'reform cop' is retired, and then he will not 'go out of business' entirely. . . . He will furnish another example for the young policeman and though most of them may choose the majority ideal, all will remember Roosevelt.

Chapter 6

The Great Adventure

> *No qualities called out by a purely peaceful*
> *life stand on a level with those stern and virile*
> *virtues which move the men of stout heart and*
> *strong hand who uphold the honor of their flag*
> *in battle.*
>
> —Theodore Roosevelt*

THEODORE ROOSEVELT "will bring with him to Washington all that machinery of disturbance and upheaval which is as much a part of his entourage as the very air he breathes," the *Washington Post* said the day the Senate confirmed TR's appointment as Assistant Secretary of the Navy. "He is inspired by a passionate hatred of meanness, humbug, and cowardice. He is a fighter, a man of indomitable pluck and energy, a potent and forceful factor in any equation into which he may be introduced. A field of immeasurable usefulness awaits him—will he find it?"

The President of the United States had been reluctant to appoint Roosevelt to the Navy Department post. William McKinley had been eased into the White House to preserve the business civilization against William Jennings Bryan and his rampant agrarian legions, not to build up the battle fleet or to force Spain out of the New World. Would there be a clash of interests if TR became a member of his administration? "I hope he has no preconceived notion which he would wish to drive through the moment he got in," McKinley said to Lodge when the Massachusetts Senator pressed Roosevelt's case upon him in the winter of 1897. But Lodge, with what reservations we may never know, had assured him that he "need not give himself the slightest uneasiness on that score."

Besides, the President-elect owed a political debt to the New York Police Commissioner. Roosevelt had at first opposed McKinley's nomination for President in the belief

---

* In a review of Captain Alfred Mahan's *Life of Nelson* in *The Bookman,*
June 1897.

that he would not hold up in a crisis, whether "a soft-money craze, a gigantic labor riot, or danger of foreign conflict." But the confluence of Roosevelt's election-year regularity and his exaggerated fears of Bryan—he called the convention that pressed its highest accolade upon the broad, unfurrowed brow of the Boy Orator of the Platte a "Witches' Sabbath"— had altered his perspective. When Mark Hanna invited him to join his multimillion-dollar crusade for McKinley and the gold standard, TR signed on with a vengeance; during the late summer and fall of 1896 he had campaigned furiously for the Ohioan's election and the Great Commoner's defeat.

Furthermore, Tom Platt and other prominent Republicans had urged Roosevelt's appointment upon McKinley. Platt had been hesitant when TR first asked him to use his influence. But he was eager to have the righteous Police Commissioner out of his hair, and after concluding that TR would probably "do less harm to the organization as Assistant Secretary of the Navy than in any other office that could be named," he submitted Roosevelt's name. Thus pressed, the President also gave in.

TR's drive for the assistant secretaryship reflected more than a wish to ease out of his untenable situation in New York. The quality of destiny which newspapers, his friends, and even his political opponents read into his future was looming larger, and he could hardly have remained long as Police Commissioner under any circumstances. More than a decade earlier the editor of the *Bad Lands Cowboy* had suggested to Roosevelt that he might someday become President of the United States. Forthrightly TR replied: "If your prophecy comes true, I will do my part to make a good one." But that had been in Dakota where men were inclined to be direct. Rarely again did Roosevelt admit such a lofty ambition, and never quite so simply.

Once, during Roosevelt's police commissionership, Riis had asked him outright if he sought the presidency. Indignantly, TR responded that no friend would raise such a question. After regaining his composure he placed his arm over Riis's shoulder, screwed his face into a knot, and said softly: "I am going to do great things here, hard things that require all the courage, ability, work that I am capable of." He then added in a flash of self-revelation: "I must be wanting to be President. Every young man does. But I won't let myself think of it; I must not, because if I do, I will begin to work for it, I'll be careful, calculating, cautious in work and act, and so—I'll beat myself. See?"

Roosevelt also looked forward to his return to Washington because his new post gave him a seat on the fringe of power. He had chafed under the bipartisan restrictions of his civil service office. "I often have a regret that I am not in with you, Reed, and others in doing the *real* work," he had once written Lodge. Through all the years of his apprenticeship, moreover, TR had been interested in foreign policy and military preparedness. He had fretted over Cleveland's and Harrison's lack of concern for the Navy while taking heart at such assertiveness toward Germany, Spain, and Great Britain as they sometimes displayed. Cleveland's belligerence toward the British in the Venezuelan boundary dispute had won Roosevelt's warm endorsement, his refusal to annex Hawaii his unbridled contempt—"a colossal crime," he called it. Roosevelt had further deplored Cleveland's resistance to demands that he force the decadent Spanish government to grant independence to the Cubans. At times, also, Roosevelt had looked forward to American acquisition of Canada, half hoping for an incident with Great Britain as the means to effect that end. Finally, he was disgusted by the apathy toward construction of a canal across the Central American isthmus, for he had long foreseen the strategic and economic advantages of such an undertaking. TR had no illusions that his new post would give him a major voice in the formulation of such policies. But he did believe that it would give him access to some of the men who made the decisions.

As it turned out, Roosevelt exercised a far greater influence during his year as Assistant Secretary of the Navy than he had expected. Secretary John D. Long, an indulgent gentleman of declining energy, was often away from the department; and in any event, he delegated considerable authority to his energetic assistant. Roosevelt was able from the start to direct his energies toward the realization of three broad objectives: the improvement of morale, administration, and tactical efficiency; publicity of the case for increased naval power; and preparation of the battle fleet for war with Spain.

Soon after assuming office Roosevelt was detailed to investigate an accident involving a torpedo boat. Dutifully, he stated in his official report that commanders should take proper safety precautions. He added, however, that "it is more important that our officers should handle these boats with dash and daring than that the boats should be kept unscratched." Shortly afterward the new Assistant Secretary visited Newport News where the battleships *Kentucky* and *Kearsarge* were being built. He was enthusiastic about the quality of the ships, but he disapproved their double turrets because they made it necessary to train both light and heavy-caliber guns on the same target. In June, while Secretary Long was on vacation, Roosevelt lightened the paper work assigned torpedo-boat commanders. And in August, with Long again away, he reduced the load for battleship and battle-cruiser captains.

Meanwhile Roosevelt zealously guarded the civil service rights of Navy Department employees, bombarded Secretary Long with advice, and made numerous personal inspections of naval installations. At the Cramp shipyard in Philadelphia, where he inspected the *Iowa,* he reportedly "broke the record for asking questions" and surprised officers and shipbuilders with his "evident theoretical knowledge of the construction of ships of war down to the details of bolts and rivets."

During the fall of 1897 Roosevelt served as chairman of a board on naval personnel which recommended that the distinction between engineering and line officers be eliminated, that unfit officers be pensioned, and that the salaries of line officers be increased. Over the opposition of economy-minded critics, he then drew up a bill incorporating those recommendations. It passed in 1899. He continued to rail meanwhile against the advancement of officers on the basis of tenure rather than ability.

Roosevelt's administrative reforms were usually made in cooperation with Secretary Long. Nevertheless, TR's tendency to exert even more authority than Long had granted him and especially to make public statements on policy matters made conflict inevitable. The first major difference occurred in August, 1897, when Roosevelt told naval reservists in Ohio that the United States ought to decide whether it should annex Hawaii without regard to the attitude of Japan or any other power. The headlines, TR confided to Lodge, "nearly threw the Secretary into a fit, and he gave me as heavy a wigging as his invariable courtesy and kindness would permit." A few weeks after that Long deleted a passage urging an increase in the size of the Navy from an article the Assistant Secretary was preparing for publication. Other incidents followed. Although the two men were still on good terms when Roosevelt resigned, it was mainly because of the Secretary's easygoing temperament and his personal affection for his irrepressible subordinate. Assuredly, TR had transgressed. "My chief usefulness has arisen from the fact that when I was Acting Secretary I did not hesitate to take responsibilities," he wrote Lodge shortly before he resigned in the spring of 1898, "and from the further fact that I have continually meddled with what was not my business, because I was willing to jeopardize my position in a way that a naval officer could not." Nor did Roosevelt overestimate his services. During the years from 1897 to 1909, writes a recent naval historian, Roosevelt "was perhaps more responsible than any other individual . . . for the shaping of the Navy into an effective instrument of war and diplomacy."

Roosevelt was particularly exercised by Long's sensitivity to the economy bloc in Congress. He urged the Secretary to request funds for six battleships—four for the Atlantic, where he foresaw ultimate trouble with Germany, and two for the Pacific, where Japan's growing power was the catalyst —but the best he could get was a recommendation in December, 1897, for the construction of one new battleship. The result, concludes William R. Braisted, was that "American naval strategists, with but a one-ocean navy, were still studying the means to defend American possessions against Japan without opening the way for a German assault in the Atlantic" a decade later. As early as May, 1897, Roosevelt assigned the Naval War College the following problem:

Japan makes demands on Hawaiian Islands.
This country intervenes.
What force will be necessary to uphold the intervention and how shall it be employed?
Keeping in mind possible complications with another Power on the Atlantic Coast (Cuba).

While the war clouds over Cuba continued to darken, Roosevelt tried to persuade his superior to dispose the fleet in a way that would give it the greatest possible striking power in the shortest time span should war break out. But Long, who apparently lacked the power of bold decision, refused to act.

He even failed to move following the destruction of the *Maine* in Havana Harbor on February 15, 1898. Ten days after that tragic event, however, he unwittingly gave Roosevelt his opportunity by absenting himself from the Department for the day. He warned him not to take "any step affecting the policy of the administration without consulting the President or me." But Roosevelt ignored his instructions in a characteristic disregard of authority. That afternoon he dispatched to Commodore Dewey the fateful telegram which prepared the way for the defeat of the Spanish fleet in Manila Bay:

Dewey, Hong Kong: Order the squadron, except the *Monocacy* to Hong Kong. Keep full of coal. In the event of declaration of war Spain, your duty will be to see that the Spanish squadron does not leave the Asiatic coast, and then offensive operations in Philippine Islands. Keep *Olympia* until further orders.

Secretary Long was furious. TR had "gone at things like a bull in a china closet"; he lacked "a cool head and discrimination." Long failed, however, to countermand the order, perhaps because he was relieved that the Assistant Secretary had made the decision for him. When war was declared on April 19, Dewey set off in full steam for his rendezvous with destiny.

Although Roosevelt's breach of personal faith was unpardonable, the move was right from an internal point of view; nor was it lightly made. The dispatch of the telegram may have been impulsive, but the plan, which had been conceived by Mahan, was one that Roosevelt had long pressed upon his chief. As TR had written Secretary Long six weeks earlier, the nation might suffer "one or two bitter humiliations" and would "certainly be forced to spend the first three or four most important weeks not in striking, but in making those preparations to strike which we should have made long before."

The tactical wisdom of Assistant Secretary of the Navy Roosevelt's order to Dewey should not be confused with his unofficial war-mongering as war impended in the spring of 1898. For many years Roosevelt had been extolling the warlike virtues, writing contemptuously of those who opposed preparedness, and advocating American expansion as the manifest right of a superior people. Three years after he sought in 1886 to raise a troop of "as utterly reckless a set of desperadoes as ever sat in the saddle" for possible conflict with Mexico, TR was hoping for "a bit of a spar with Germany." To Spring-Rice he confided that "the burning of New York and a few other seacoast cities would be a good object lesson on the need of an adequate system of coast defences; and I think it would have a good effect on our large german [sic] population to force them to an ostentatiously patriotic display of anger against Germany." By 1895 he was requesting Governor Levi P. Morton of New York for a captaincy should war break out with Spain over Cuba. And late in the same year he was scorning "the bankers, brokers and Anglomaniacs generally" who opposed Cleveland's truculence toward the British in the Venezuelan crisis. Then, in the spring of 1897, less than two months after he became Assistant Secretary of the Navy, he declared in a prepared address at the Naval War College that "No triumph of peace is quite so great as the supreme triumph of war." Unquestionably, as Howard K. Beale concludes in his authoritative work on Roosevelt's foreign policies, TR "came close to seeking war for its own sake."

It is difficult and probably impossible to square many of Roosevelt's statements on war with Roosevelt the moral man. Doubtless, as many students of Roosevelt's life have concluded, his aggressiveness derived in part from his boyhood struggle against illness. But it is unlikely that the experience of his youth did more than determine the degree of his belligerence, for thousands of men of divergent psychological make-up held the same general theories. Cabot Lodge and John Hay shared TR's attitude toward war, though they were more circumspect in expressing it. Henry Adams' brilliant, introspective, younger brother, Brooks, was a philosophical militarist. And Oliver Wendell Holmes, Jr., whose militarism has curiously escaped the obloquy of historians, was quite convinced that war "was divine" and that "this snug, over-safe corner of the world" needed one in order that the people might "realize that our comfortable routine is no eternal necessity of things . . . and . . . that we may be ready for danger." Furthermore, the cult of military valor was world-wide. The commander in chief of the British forces merely expressed what hosts of Englishmen believed when he wrote in 1889 that "All other pleasures pale before the intense, the maddening delight of leading men into the midst of an enemy, or to the assault of some well-defended place." The generation that thrilled to Alfred Lord Tennyson's "Charge of the Light Brigade" was followed by one that took Rudyard Kipling's *Barrack-Room Ballads* to its heart; and the reception accorded the poet laureate of imperialism was even more uncritical in Great Britain than in the United States.

Had Roosevelt been born in a later era he might have released his primitive instincts on the athletic field. As it was, he thought of man-to-man combat, dashing cavalry charges, and brilliant tactical maneuvers; not of mass carnage, germ-infested prison camps, and endless, stultifying boredom. Perhaps his heroic visions should not have been. Many sensitive men, even in Roosevelt's time, cried out against them; among them his quondam friend, Carl Schurz, most of the other mug-wumps, and toughminded William James. It was James, in fact, who stripped the veneer of moral purpose from Roosevelt's exhortations. Not only is he "still mentally in the *Sturm und Drang* period of early adolescence," the Harvard philosopher wrote of his former student, he regards "one foe . . . as good as another," and "swamps everything together in one flood of abstract bellicose emotion."

For all who had eyes to see, moreover, the Civil War was the first of the great modern holocausts. But for reasons that cut to the core of the human experience, a generation of politicians, participants, and propagandists of a lost cause endowed it with an ultraromantic aura before Roosevelt reached adolescence; and to this day their creation survives. TR matured in that milieu. He despised Jefferson Davis, whom he once subjected to personal insult, as the symbol of disunion; but he esteemed Robert E. Lee, whose services to the Confederacy were far greater, as the exemplar of the soldierly virtues.

However base their instinctual force, the views of Roosevelt, Holmes, and the rest had an intellectual rationale. Their emphasis on preparedness and the will to fight reflected a reading of the grand sweep of human history from a social-Darwinian frame of reference. And if Roosevelt did not necessarily regard the race among individuals as invariably to the swift, he nevertheless believed that it was almost always so among nations. A country had to expand its influence by peaceful means if possible or by war if not. Otherwise it would lose place, power, and prestige; or at the least it would fail to fulfill its potential, of which there was no greater failing for individual or nation in Roosevelt's value system. This required strength, determination, and sacrifice. It also demanded the development of the soldierly virtues and the will to use them when challenged. "If our population decreases; if we lose the virile, manly qualities, and sink into a nation of mere hucksters, putting gain above national honor, and subordinating everything to mere ease of life; then we shall indeed reach a condition worse than that of the ancient civilizations in the years of their decay," Roosevelt wrote in his review of Brooks Adams' *The Law of Civilization and Decay.* Rome began to decline, he declared in one of those classic half truths of which he was sometimes a master, when the "Roman army became an army no longer of Roman citizens, but of barbarians trained in the Roman manner . . ."

Still, there were qualifications. TR was too buoyant, too much in love with life, to accept the Adams brothers' pessimism. Even as he regretted with Brooks the passing of the military man, he read his values into the new economic man. There were in the American capitalistic system, he also said in his review of *The Law of Civilization and Decay,* "great branches of industry which call forth in those that follow them more hardihood, manliness, and courage than any industry of ancient times. . . . As yet, while men are more gentle and more honest than before, it cannot be said that they are less brave." In 1917, when it seemed to Roosevelt that Western civilization stood on the brink of disaster, he earnestly sent forth his sons to war. But some years before, when it had been time for his first-born to choose a career, he urgently advised him against West Point and the enervating life of a regular army officer.

Meanwhile there was a war at hand. Two generations of American historians have deprecated McKinley's submission to the hysteria generated by the "yellow journalists," Hearst, Pulitzer and their imitators, to a Protestant clergy overcome with compassion for the oppressed Cubans, to statesmen obsessed with illusions of national grandeur, and to a public opinion bursting with ultrapatriotism. James Ford Rhodes, friend of McKinley, brother-in-law of Mark Hanna, and judicious defender of Republican policies, called the conflict with Spain "a needless war." The distinguished student of

American diplomacy, Samuel Flagg Bemis, termed its aftermath the "great aberration." And a great many others have poured forth condemnations that are harsher still. Not even the relatively exemplary administration of the colonial empire which arose in its wake and the perspective afforded by two world wars have substantially changed those judgments. The most that has been said in extenuation is that resort to the sword was perhaps the only way to cut the Gordian Knot of Spanish barbarities in Cuba and to meet the American people's humanitarian demand that they be ended; and that is hardly a tenable thesis. For Theodore Roosevelt, however, the war represented intellectual and emotional fulfillment.

Roosevelt believed that "every foot of American soil, including the nearest islands in both the Pacific and Atlantic, should be in the hands of independent American states," and he regarded the liberation of Cuba as a first step toward that end. He also believed that war with undermatched Spain would prove a rewarding tactical exercise for the fleet and would spur sentiment for a more powerful Navy. He argued that unless the United States had a strong navy, it had no justification for retaining Alaska and annexing Hawaii and little possibility of building up its Far Eastern trade. Repeatedly in 1897 and early 1898 he pointed out to Long and others that Japan threatened to surpass the United States as a naval power and that the Imperial German government showed a tendency "to stretch out for colonial possessions which may at any moment cause a conflict with us." We should beware, he warned, "of letting a foolish hatred of England blind us to our honor and interest." Germany, not England, was the power most likely to conflict with the United States over the Monroe Doctrine.

As war impended in the winter and early spring of 1898 Roosevelt's emotions came to rule him. Fearful that a joint inquiry with Spain would fail to impose responsibility for the *Maine* disaster on Spain, he urged Secretary Long to advise the President against such an investigation. Then, in a ratiocination that gives point to Arnold Toynbee's aphorism that patriotism is the last infirmity of noble minds, he concluded that Spain was in fact culpable, that the ill-fated battleship "was sunk by an act of dirty treachery on the part of the Spaniards." Again and again as the crisis heightened he pleaded for war. On the eve of conflict he revealed his frustrations to Brooks Adams, whose courageous great-grand-father, John, had won historical fame and contemporary condemnation by preventing another needless war just one hundred years before:

The blood of the Cubans, the blood of women and children who have perished by the hundred thousand in hideous misery, lies at our door; and the blood of the murdered men of the *Maine* calls not for indemnity but for the full measure of atonement which can only come by driving the Spaniard from the New World. I have said this to the President before his Cabinet; I have said it to Judge Day, the real head of the State Department; and to my own chief. I cannot say it publicly, for I am . . . merely a minor official in the administration.

Finally, on March 21, the naval court of inquiry reported that although the *Maine* had been destroyed by the explosion of a submarine mine, it had been "unable to obtain evidence fixing the responsibility. . . ." Nor has that responsibility ever been determined. Three weeks later, despite last-minute concessions by Spain, the President submitted a militant war message to a war-mad Congress. His action, write three recent historians, was "one of the most disastrous failures in the history of presidential leadership."

The pressures had been too overwhelming for McKinley, whom Roosevelt had characterized as having the backbone of a "chocolate eclair," to surmount. So great was the demand for war on all sides that there had been talk of Congress passing a war resolution over the President's veto. The talk was probably idle; but speculation that McKinley and the Republican party would be defeated in 1900 if he failed to take the country into the war may have been well founded. In any event, it was this threat that caused Mark Hanna, business leaders, and the President to decide for war despite their own reluctance and Spain's near total submission. Elihu Root's warning that "Fruitless attempts to hold back or retard the enormous momentum of the people bent upon war would result in the destruction of the President's power and influence, in depriving the country of its natural leader, in the elevation of the Silver Democracy to power" was but one of several such counsels. In the face of them McKinley lost the will to resist. "I think . . . possibly the President could have worked out the business without war," his friend and confidant, Senator John C. Spooner of Wisconsin, mused three weeks later, "but the current was too strong, the demagogues too numerous, the fall elections too near."

Theodore Roosevelt was not thinking of the congressional elections of 1898 nor of the presidential campaign of 1900. He was consumed as few men have ever been consumed by the role he would play in the war that at last had come; and he at once made plans to resign from the Navy Department and to organize a regiment of volunteer cavalry. His family, his friends, and his superiors wanted him to continue as Assistant Secretary. Edith had given birth to her fifth child, Quentin, the previous fall and was then convalescing after a major operation. She hoped that her husband would not go, though she knew that he must. President McKinley twice asked him to stay. And Secretary Long, who continued to treat TR with fatherly indulgence, implored him not to go. "His heart is right, and he means well," he wrote of Roosevelt in his diary, "but it is one of those cases of aberration-desertion-vain-glory; of which he is utterly unaware."

But the most ironic pressure came from Roosevelt's fellow warhawk, Cabot Lodge. A few years earlier Lodge had collaborated with TR on a book entitled *Hero Tales of American History*. Now, in the hour of trial, he sought to dissuade both his own spirited son and his dearest friend from volunteering. There was, he said, no need for them to go to war. He further warned Roosevelt that his resignation would spell the end of his political career.

Roosevelt himself professed to be torn by conflicting emotions. He claimed that he was not going to war "with any undue exhilaration of spirits or . . . recklessness or levity." And he protested that he was not seeking military glory. Yet his entire life had been a preparation for the test that was then to come. Few men ever went forth to war with greater zest and higher resolve to act gallantly than TR did in that turbulent spring of 1898; and when he wrote from the battlefield outside Santiago three months later that the charge up the heights had been his "crowded hour," he wrote in total emotional satisfaction. No other episode in Roosevelt's career, not even his election to the presidency in his own right in 1904, quite compared. As he confided to his military aide several years afterward, "I know now that I would have

turned from my wife's deathbed to have answered that call."
It was, he said, "my chance to cut my little notch on the stick
that stands as a measuring rod in every family."

Roosevelt's sense of duty was so compelling, however, that
he would have volunteered even if he had been unmoved by
the call of glory. "I want to go because I wouldn't feel that
I had been entirely true to my beliefs and convictions, and
to the ideal I had set for myself if I didn't go," he wrote Paul
Dana of the *New York Sun:*

> I don't want you to think that I am talking like a prig, for I know
> perfectly well that one never is able to analyze with entire accuracy
> all of one's motives. . . . For two years I have consistently preached
> the doctrine of a resolute foreign policy, and of readiness to accept
> the arbitrament of the sword if necessary; and I have always in-
> tended to act up to my preaching if occasion arose. Now the occa-
> sion has arisen, and I ought to meet it . . . if we who have preached
> the doctrine fail to put our words into effect when the time comes,
> our preaching will lose much of its force.

The announcement that Theodore Roosevelt had resigned
as Assistant Secretary of the Navy on May 6, 1898, to organize the First Volunteer Cavalry Regiment reverberated
throughout the United States. A flood of applications for
service—23,000 all told—poured in from men in all walks
of life and from all sections of the country. Several hundred
cowboys, a score of Indians, a handful of New York policemen, and a sizable number of athletes from the Ivy League
were finally accepted. The selection process was erratic and
personal, yet nonetheless effective:

> "My name is Dudley Deane," said a fine, athletic young man to
> Col. Theodore Roosevelt yesterday afternoon.
> A broad and cordial smile of welcome beamed on Col. Roose-
> velt's face. "Yes," he said, "I know you. You are the man who
> saved the day for Harvard in the great football game with Yale.
> You are one of the kind of men we want."

More of that "kind" were taken—even the chaplain had
played three years of varsity football at Wesleyan. "You've
got to perform without flinching whatever duty is assigned
you regardless of the difficulty or danger attending it," Lieu-

tenant Colonel Roosevelt told a batch of recruits in Washington. "If it is the closest kind of fighting you must be anxious for it. . . . No matter what comes you mustn't squeal."

At San Antonio that spring Roosevelt and the regiment's actual commander Colonel Leonard Wood, quickly molded their troops into a surprisingly efficient fighting force. Inevitably, minor problems arose. TR never mastered regular army formalities though he maintained a rough dignity, and when he detrained in San Antonio late in April he responded warmly to the thunderous cheers of troops who should have received him in a formal ceremony. A few weeks later Wood was forced to rebuke him for buying his men all the beer they could drink after a hot march in the saddle. "Sir, I consider myself the damnedest ass within ten miles of this camp," he contritely replied. And in Tampa, Florida, shortly before the Rough Riders, as they had been affectionately dubbed by the press, sailed in mid-June for Cuba, Roosevelt took two of his sergeants to dinner in a hotel where Wood was dining with the commanding general of the Army.

The Rough Riders' first engagement occurred at Las Guasimas, a small Cuban village, on June 24. Their point ran into a force of Spaniards and a sharp action ensued. The enemy mounted a strong resistance, but they eventually gave way. By the time American reinforcements arrived the fight had ended. Sixteen Rough Riders lay dead.

The supreme test came one week later after Wood had been advanced to brigade commander and Roosevelt had replaced him. On June 30 TR was ordered to move his regiment, which was without mounts, into position for an attack on the Spanish stronghold of Santiago. By nightfall the Rough Riders were bivouacked in a jungle at the foot of a series of hills flanking the east side of the city. The most prominent hill was San Juan, but there were entrenchments on all.

Morning came, but no further orders. Roosevelt champed. When the regulars moved out from cover to attack he was about to order his men to advance to the sound of the gunfire. But before he could give the command, he received a message directing him to advance through the bush toward the hill directly in front of his bivouac. It was the one next to San Juan, and it was called Kettle Hill. "The instant I received the order I sprang on my horse," TR later wrote, "and then my 'crowded hour' began."

It lasted most of the day. Through the whole time Roosevelt was a conspicuous figure as he exhorted his Rough Riders to charge against the Spanish, who maintained a destructive fire from behind their fortifications. "Are you afraid to stand up when I am on horseback?" he shouted at one terrified trooper. He said worse to others. His elbow was nicked by a bullet, a trooper was killed at his feet, and he had several other calls as close. Early that afternoon the Rough Riders and fragments of other regiments took the hill and held it under fire from the Spanish on San Juan. That night they dug in. More fights followed, but none matched the intensity of that charge. It was remarkable, wrote Richard Harding Davis, that anyone had survived.

The campaign had brought out Roosevelt's best and some of his worst. He took pride in his regiment's heavy casualties; they proved that he and his troops had been in the thick of action. He gloated that he had personally "doubled-up" a Spaniard. And in one of those desecrations of the human spirit that will forever bar him from the immortality of Jefferson, Lincoln, and Wilson, he invited post-battle visitors to "look at those damned Spanish dead." He had been as foolhardy as he had been brave and daring. And beyond a doubt he was boastful. "I do not want to be vain, but I do not think anyone else could have handled this regiment quite as I have," he wrote Lodge. "I rose over those regular army officers like a balloon," he told Hermann Hagedorn many years later. He also wrote as much in a book, *The Rough Riders*, the title of which Finley Peter Dunne's Mr. Dooley found misleading. "If I was him," said Dooley, "I'd call th' book 'Alone in Cubia!' or 'Th' Darin' Exploits iv a Brave Man be an Actual Eye-Witness.' "

The campaign had also proved what there had been no need to prove—Theodore Roosevelt was an inspiring leader of men. He had, Leonard Wood wrote, the all-important virtues of the soldier. He was courageous, solicitous of his troops' welfare, and accessible to those who bore complaints; he commanded in consequence the respect of both his men and his officers. Stephen Crane, who observed TR in the field hospitals between engagements, wrote at the time that he "worked like a cider press . . . let him be a politician if he likes, he was a gentleman down here."

It was perhaps inevitable that Roosevelt should mar this

hour of greatest glory by thrusting his bull neck into controversy with those who had power to honor him. Yellow fever raged through the camps after Santiago fell, and when a group of ranking regular officers asked TR to request Secretary of War Russell A. Alger to expedite the army's transfer north, the Rough Rider consented. With the tacit approval of the commanding general, W. R. Shafter, he wrote a letter that was given out to the press before it reached Washington.

President McKinley and Secretary Alger were understandably outraged. Roosevelt's letter, together with one which the regular officers had drawn up on reconsideration, was an indirect, but damning indictment of the administration. It also advertised to the Spaniards, who were then negotiating peace, that the American Army in Cuba was no longer a disciplined and effective fighting force. Furthermore, Alger had made the decision to evacuate the previous day.

On August 15, 1898, the disease-ridden but all-conquering Rough Riders disembarked from the transport *Miami* at Montauk Point, Long Island. A month later Roosevelt was called from his tent on the sands. The First Volunteer Cavalry Regiment was formed in a hollow square with the officers and color sergeant in the center. As Roosevelt strode into the square, one of the troopers stepped forward and presented him with a reproduction of Frederick Remington's famed bronze, "The Bronco-Buster." It was a gift from the enlisted men. TR now addressed his troops for the last time. "I am proud of this regiment beyond measure," he said, his voice throbbing with emotion. "It is primarily an American regiment, and it is American because it is composed of all the races which have made America their country by adoption and those who have claimed it as their country by inheritance." He closed with a tribute to the Negro soldiers who had fought with distinction beside the Rough Riders. Then, as the entire regiment, many of its members in tears, filed by him, he shook hands with each man and officer. The great adventure had ended.

There was an epilogue. Roosevelt had been recommended for the Medal of Honor. He wanted it painfully, partly because he believed it would help him in his political career, mainly because he craved the outward symbols of achievement. After the original recommendation had been drawn up, TR wrote numerous letters on his own behalf, sought affidavits from those who had been with him in battle, and beseeched Lodge to obtain the War Department's endorsement. But Secretary Alger refused to make the recommendation to Congress.

There was a pathetic quality about it, for most of the nation knew anyway that Colonel Theodore Roosevelt had been a hero. The medal finally came, forty-six years late, and to TR's oldest son, who by all accounts had kept his father's faith on a beachhead in Normandy where he died in 1944. For his own bravery under fire Congress posthumously awarded to Brigadier General Theodore Roosevelt, Jr. the medal which Colonel Theodore Roosevelt, Sr. had also earned but never received.

Chapter 7

The Final Preparation

An honest and fearless Governor—a combination of conscience and backbone—is a mighty good thing to have at Albany!
—The *New York World*

THE ROUGH RIDERS were still convalescing or frolicking on the wind-swept sands of Long Island when their Colonel plunged boldly into politics. His objective was the governorship of New York.

The administration of the incumbent, Republican Frank S. Black, had proved a grievous failure. Black had antagonized Tom Platt by his calculated independence and had offended respectable opinion by weakening the civil service and failing to rid the Erie Canal administration of graft and corruption. His defeat for re-election was a foregone conclusion. So Platt, who was no sentimentalist, began casting about for a new candidate. He wanted a man whom the people would elect and he could control.

Theodore Roosevelt fitted the first particular. His emergence as a military hero, coupled with his fifteen-year record as an incorruptible reformer, made him the only Republican who could possibly stave off a Democratic landslide in November. Even before his transport dropped anchor off Montauk Point many G.O.P. newspapers had nominated him and some had all but elected him.

Senator Platt sensed that Roosevelt, a minor irritant as police commissioner, would prove a major sufferance as governor. He also had a presentiment that the Colonel would move on to the presidency. An anti-imperialist, the "Easy Boss" was loath to place Roosevelt in a position to handle colonial problems. Yet Thomas Collier Platt was a practical politician to the marrow. As Chauncey M. Depew, the witty and jaded president of the New York Central Railroad, pointed out, the G.O.P.'s one chance of retaining the governorship lay in diverting attention from the Black administration's shortcomings. When questioned about the canal frauds during the campaign, Depew remarked, he could say with conviction:

We have nominated for governor a man who has demonstrated in public office and on the battlefield that he is a fighter for the right, and always victorious. If he is selected, you know and we all know from his demonstrated characteristics, courage and ability, that every thief will be caught and punished. . . . Then I will follow the colonel leading his Rough Riders up San Juan Hill and ask the band to play the "Star-Spangled Banner."

Platt saw Depew's point. But he feared Roosevelt would break with him once he had galloped triumphantly into office, so he refused to endorse the Colonel until he received assurances of cooperation. A protracted negotiation followed. "We buried past differences," Platt afterward wrote. The Colonel agreed to "consult with me and other party leaders about appointments and legislation in case he were elected."

The announcement that Roosevelt had visited Tom Platt provoked howls of anguish from reformers who had naïvely hoped that Roosevelt would head up an Independent party ticket. "By accepting Platt he becomes the standard bearer of corruption and demoralization," Fulton Cutting charged in the *New York Evening Post*. "The matter is a question of honor," John Jay Chapman, who convinced himself that Roosevelt had committed himself to their project, confided to his wife. "I do not believe that Teddy Roosevelt . . . has so far humbled himself as to go to Mr. Platt," TR's old ally, the Rev. Dr. Parkhurst, protested. It was 1884 and the fateful decision to support Blaine all over again, or so they believed.

The reformers should have known better. When Theodore Roosevelt made the supreme sacrifice it would be as a lion, not as a lamb. He knew, as the reformers did not, that he had to match power with power; that he had to have office or a good chance of getting it before he could act constructively. His flouting of Jay Gould, Benjamin Harrison, and even Tom Platt had proved that before; his leadership of the Bull Moose party in 1912 would prove it again. Resignedly, therefore, he adjusted to the realities of the situation.

The decision hurt. Had Roosevelt's ideals been lower his contemporary reputation might have been higher, for independent reformers would not have expected so much of him.

Repeatedly, however, he had shown that he was one of them in spirit; and when, accordingly, he failed to fulfill their every ideal, they inevitably visited upon him the self-righteous contempt of the true believer for the heretic.

The Colonel naturally returned their spleen. Only rarely thereafter would he concede that the ferment whipped up by these and other men of good hope—the mugwumps, the muckrakers, the social reformers Jane Addams and Ben Lindsey, and the humanistic politicians Bryan and La Follette—was all that saved America from being swallowed whole by the voracious materialism he himself so deplored. It was an irony that history later crowned. Theodore Roosevelt's greatest contribution to American life, historians now agree, was the awakening of the people to the need for even further reform.

Roosevelt spelled out the immediate political problem to Francis E. Leupp, a civil service reformer, just before he and Platt came to terms. "I should be one of the big party leaders if I should take it," he wrote, and "I should have to treat with and work with the organization."

I should see and consult the leaders—not once, but continuously —and earnestly try to come to an agreement on all important questions with them; and of course the mere fact of my doing so would alienate many of my friends whose friendship I value. On the other hand, when we come to a matter like the Canal, or Life Insurance, or anything touching the Eighth Commandment and general decency, I could not allow any consideration of party to come in. And this would alienate those who, if not friends, were supporters.

A few reformers accepted Roosevelt's logic. "Nobody who has followed his career can doubt that in him, as Governor, civil-service reform would have a champion whom nothing could intimidate or seduce," *The Nation* said editorially. But others, whom Roosevelt termed "the idiot variety of 'Goo-Goos,'" viewed his fall from grace with less tolerance ("That goose Parkhurst is giving me some trouble," the Colonel soon complained). And some, including Carl Schurz, came out against him because of their still-seething resentment of his imperialism.

The campaign that autumn confirmed the prescience of Chauncey Depew. The cheers at the Republican state convention had been louder for Platt than for Roosevelt; but it was the Colonel's show on the hustings. The canal frauds were all but ignored as the crowds partook of the Rough Rider's hard-won fame and succumbed to his vibrant personality. "Seven Rough Riders, wearing their uniforms of glory, were on the special train on which Roosevelt began a tour on October 17," writes Pringle. A bugler would sound the cavalry charge at each stop, and as the notes died the candidate would begin his address. " 'You have heard the trumpet that sounded to bring you here,' he exclaimed at Fort Henry. 'I have heard it tear the tropic dawn when it summoned us to fight at Santiago.' " Roosevelt would then urge his listeners to affirm the results of the war by electing a Republican Congress (also a Republican governor). At Port Jervis ex-Sergeant Buck Taylor, one of the seven glorious props, was permitted to speak. "I want to talk to you about mah Colonel," Taylor told the crowd. "He kept ev'y promise he made to us and he will to you. When he took us to Cuba he told us . . . we would have to lie out in the trenches with the rifle bullets climbing over us, and we done it. . . . He told us we might meet wounds and death and we done it, but he was thar in the midst of us, and when it came to the great day he led us up San Juan Hill like sheep to the slaughter and so he will lead you."

It was a remarkable performance; and neither the Colonel's infectious pride in his own and his Rough Riders' heroics nor the need to create a diversionary political issue quite explains it.

A possible explanation is that Roosevelt had no program. As he wrote James Bryce, he planned only to conduct an "honest administration." He also feared the anti-imperialistic Democrats. "Do you wish to keep or throw away the fruits of what we won in the war?" he asked the crowds that swarmed about his campaign train. "We cannot avoid facing the fact that we occupy a new place among the people of the world . . . Greatness means strife for nation and man alike. . . . We must dare to be great . . . We are face to face with our destiny and we must meet it with high and resolute courage."

But the most compelling explanation is Roosevelt's desperate desire to win. Even John Jay Chapman was willing to overlook the Fourth of July aura of the Colonel's canvass on the ground that he "really believes that he is the American flag." As he confided to his wife, however, when Roosevelt "endorses the administration of McKinley in words that are intended to cover and do cover Alger, I despise him, for I know him to be dishonest."

The Colonel's deft glossing over of Republican corruption contrasted sharply with his full-bodied criticisms of Democratic malfeasance. Confined at first to generalizations about Tammany, he got the issue he needed when it came out late in the campaign that Croker had refused to permit a state supreme court justice to be renominated because he would not appoint a Tammany hack as clerk of the court. Croker's action, Roosevelt wrote, enabled me to "fix the contest in the public mind as one between himself and myself." It paid off; and so probably did $60,000—$10,000 of it reportedly from J. P. Morgan—which Platt poured into Roosevelt's cause the last week or ten days. In any event, TR defeated his opponent, Augustus Van Wyck of Brooklyn, by 17,794 votes. He ran well ahead of his ticket and for the first time, perhaps, became fully conscious of his extraordinary power to move great masses of people.

Billy O'Neil, Roosevelt's old compatriot in the Assembly, described that power. "Just before I met him [TR] I received a letter from a friend in Albany saying 'For God's sake tell Roosevelt to stop his self-adulation and talking about himself so much,' " O'Neil wrote. After listening to the Colonel's speeches, however, O'Neil advised him to follow "his own instincts and inspiration."

At Carthage, in Jeff. County, there were three thousand people standing in the mud and rain. He spoke about ten minutes—the speech was nothing, but the man's presence was everything. It was electrical, magnetic. . . .

Some Democrats say it was only the idle curiosity of the crowd that always attends the entrance of a circus. . . . perhaps my own love and admiration for the man blinded me to the real facts. Perhaps I measured others by my own feelings, for as the train faded away and I saw him smiling, and waving his hat at the people, they in turn giving abundant evidence of their enthusiastic affection, my eyes filled with tears.

"Senator Platt," wrote Roosevelt when he was still Governor-elect "is to all intents and purposes a majority of the Legislature." The statement was accurate. Yet Roosevelt, armed with his own righteous enthusiasm and supported by a public opinion which he both formed and reflected, soon proved that Platt was not always an intractable "majority." By the end of Roosevelt's administration the "Easy Boss" had deferred more to the Colonel on major matters than Roosevelt had to him. The Governor regularly consulted him, after which he "frequently did just what he pleased," Platt ruefully recalled. "My desire was to achieve results, and not merely to issue manifestoes of virtue," Roosevelt explained in his *Autobiography.* "I had to work with the the tools at hand. . . . It was only after I had exhausted all the resources of my patience that I would finally, if he still proved obstinate, tell him that I intended to make the fight anyhow."

Tom Platt's first insight into the Governor's independence came hard on Roosevelt's inauguration on January 1, 1899. Determined to administer the canal system honestly, Roosevelt proposed to make former Comptroller James A. Roberts, who had clashed with the "canal ring" in the past, the new superintendent. But Roberts rejected the appointment for personal reasons. Platt thereupon offered the post to Francis J. Hendricks, a machine politician of integrity and ability. Hendricks accepted Platt's offer, and when the Senator next saw the Governor he informed him of his *fait accompli.*

Roosevelt was invariably polite and sometimes deferential to Platt; he replied simply that he was "sorry" he could not appoint the Senator's man. Platt then lost his temper. Roosevelt finally settled the matter with a constructive compromise: he drew up a list of four acceptable names and permitted Platt to select the one he preferred. A master at playing on men's weaknesses, Platt never understood their strength. As William Allen White perceived, the Republican boss "underestimated Roosevelt . . . because he had no sort of conception of that part of a man which is called the moral nature."

Roosevelt usually pursued the same course thereafter. The result was a minimum of friction and a generally high level of major appointments. On minor offices, however, the Governor gave the machine a relatively free choice, partly in order to build up support for his legislative program. Only when he had special knowledge or desired to appoint a personal friend did he intervene. Joe Murray received an appointment as did an occasional former Rough Rider. But in most instances

Roosevelt refused even his close friends. During his two years in office he handed out roughly a thousand dollars to needy acquaintances rather than put them on the public payroll.

It was in the legislative arena that Roosevelt and Platt clashed most significantly. The "Easy Boss" believed that government's function was to serve business, especially big business, and he tolerated no tampering with the foundations or even the superstructure of economic power. His machine drew its campaign funds from businessmen, and he prided himself openly on his ability to get contributions from J. P. Morgan and other titans. When, therefore, Roosevelt threw his weight behind measures to curtail corporate privileges in the spring of 1899, Platt became thoroughly alarmed:

> I had heard from a good many sources that you were a little loose on the relations of capital and labor, on trusts and combination . . . on those numerous questions . . . affecting the security of earnings and the right of a man to run his business in his own way, with due respect, of course, to the Ten Commandments and the Penal Code.

Actually, Roosevelt's first message to the legislature had given the status quo slight cause for uneasiness. Within a few months, however, the Governor became engaged in a full-scale battle over bills to establish stricter controls on the operations of gas and transportation companies and to impose taxes on their franchises or earnings. None was conceived by Roosevelt; but all received his considered support once he decided they were efficacious.

The most radical called for the taxation of the value and tangible assets of all street railway, gas, electric, and water franchises. It had been introduced by Senator John Ford, a Democratic lawyer and economist, and was approved by Roosevelt in principle. Over the remonstrations of Elihu Root, who was lobbying for the Astoria Gas Company and had written a bill responsive to that company's interests, Roosevelt also favored a specific tax on the earnings of franchises. "Ought there not be some arrangement by which, if the franchises prove very valuable, a portion of the gross earnings should be paid to the public treasury?" he wrote Platt at the time. "I have no sympathy whatsoever with the demagogic cry against corporations when those corporations render public service," he told a state senator the same day. "But where, by act of the legislature, and through taking possession of a part of the public domain, state or municipal, the corporation gets advantages, it should be taxed for them in some intelligent way."

Jolted by this threat to their privileged position, the corporations raised a tremendous outcry through their retainers in the legislature and elsewhere. But small property holders all over the state stood to gain relief in the amount the utilities corporations were taxed; they exerted such an effective counterpressure on the legislature that passage of a token tax bill became politically necessary.

Meanwhile, the Governor pondered over the state's over-all tax structure. His own knowledge was deficient, so he turned to experts—Professor Richard T. Ely of the University of Wisconsin; George Gunton, an independent labor economist; and Professor E. R. A. Seligman of Columbia University, the nation's foremost authority on public finance. Impressed by the complexity of their responses, Roosevelt on March 27 sent in a special message recommending creation of a joint committee to study the situation and report to the next legislature. The message pointed out that farmers, mechanics, and tradesmen bore a disproportionate share of the tax burden, and it pronounced the light taxation of corporations an "evident injustice."

Surprised and disappointed by the Governor's action, Senator Ford's supporters interpreted it as a shrewd maneuver to avoid a showdown with the corporations and Platt. Roosevelt vehemently denied that it was; yet he argued that the Ford bill might prove "so crude a measure as to provoke a revolt, or else be inoperative."

For reasons unexplained, Roosevelt reversed himself within the month. As the session drew to a close he threw the full force of his office and powerful personality behind the Ford bill. To ease the way for legislators beholden to the corporations—one such blandly explained that he had "received orders not to pass it"—he even sent a special emergency message to the Assembly which the speaker, a Platt man, refused to read. Meanwhile he was warned that he could not expect to run for office again because "no corporation would subscribe to a campaign fund" with him on the ticket. The result, Platt later conceded, was that Roosevelt "clinched his fist and gritted his teeth, and drove the franchise tax-law through the legislature."

At the time, however, Platt was enraged by this frontal assault on his power base. On May 6 he wrote the letter questioning Roosevelt's conception of the proper relations between capital and the public. "At the last moment, and to my very great surprise, you did a thing which has caused the business community of New York to wonder how far the notions of Populism, as laid down in Kansas and Nebraska, have taken hold upon the Republican party of the State of New York," the irate, sixty-five-year-old boss added. He then predicted that the Democrats would capture control of the state in 1900 unless Roosevelt changed his ways.

The Governor was now in command, the bill being his to sign or veto. He was alternately ingenuous and disingenuous. He wrote Platt that he would have preferred to take no action and that the bill was "forced upon" him. But he also wrote that his study of the problem had convinced him that the bill "was along the right" lines. He further responded to Platt's charge that he was fostering Populism:

I do not believe that it is wise . . . for us as a party to take refuge in mere negation and to say that there are no evils to be corrected. It seems to me that our attitude should be one of correcting the evils and thereby showing that . . . the Republicans hold the just balance and set our faces as resolutely against improper corporate influence on the one hand as against demagogy and mob rule on the other.

Until 1912 that remained Roosevelt's abiding hope.

Roosevelt was of no mind to veto the measure—he later termed it "the most important law passed in recent times by any American state legislature"—but he wanted to remedy its imperfections. So he decided to call a special session to amend the bill. Platt would then have to accept his constructive amendments or suffer the original measure's being signed into law during the thirty-day period authorized for that purpose. The machine was thus cornered. As Roosevelt confided to Lodge, many corporations preferred in the showdown "to be blackmailed by Tammany rather than to pay their just dues to an honest Board of Assessors." Meanwhile, so Roosevelt wrote, Platt's son, Frank, and the corporation attorneys tried to sell him "a gold brick, by putting in seemingly innocent provisions which would have made the taxation a nullity." He rejected them outright. "I told them that unless they passed the bill exactly as I wished it, I should sign the Ford bill."

Cowed by Roosevelt's threat, the machine swung resentfully behind his amendments. These empowered state officials to make the assessments and provided for evaluation of corporate property as realty rather than easily undervalued securities.

Conservatives reacted with near-hysteria to the Governor's triumph. The *New York Times* called the franchise tax "the robber baron science of taxation ruthlessly applied." Chauncey Depew dolefully predicted that every country trolley line in the state would be driven out of business. And the *Brooklyn Daily Eagle* first labeled the Ford bill "communistic," then castigated it as an "invasion of Bryan's vocabulary or an infringement of geographical rights of use and sale in Bryan's territory."

As the vehemence of the conservative reaction suggests, the franchise tax was indeed a milestone in the advance of economic justice in New York State and the nation. It also set Roosevelt off from the leaders of his own party—McKinley, Root, Platt, and virtually everyone else of importance—while nurturing his growing realization that many industrial problems were beyond the capacity of local authorities to resolve. Laissez-faire would have to be abandoned, he came more and more to see, if corporations were to serve responsibly the society that sustained them.

Roosevelt's insight into corporate amorality had been further deepened in his third month in office when Armour & Company offered to settle for $20,000 fines of $1,500,000 for violations of the law against selling oleomargarine as butter. Outraged by the packing company's effrontery, he flatly refused the offer. The Governor's action, Platt's son reported in awe, was "admirable, even if it was not what I wanted."

Roosevelt's labor record proved no less controversial. He now understood labor better than in earlier years, though the memory of the Haymarket Riot, the Homestead, the Pullman, and other violent strikes remained fresh. And even as he made measured contributions to workingmen's welfare, he was beset by fear that labor would once again march.

Thus Roosevelt once accepted a Board of Mediation report

that wrongly exonerated a traction company charged with violating the ten-hour law. On another occasion he alerted the state militia for strike duty without real cause. And on a third he called out the National Guard to forestall rioting by grossly underpaid Italian workmen on the Croton Dam project. A riot, one death, and suppression of a legitimate strike resulted. Roosevelt's precipitate action, like President Cleveland's in the Pullman Strike, was partly instinctual; but unlike Cleveland, Roosevelt perceived that constructive action was needed.

Roosevelt counseled with union officials more than any of his predecessors had done. And in his first message as governor he gave greater space to labor issues than to any other subject. The problem was not too few laws, he asserted, but "the lack of proper means of enforcing existing laws." He recommended that enforcement be placed under the board of factory inspectors, that the number of inspectors be raised to fifty, and that the governor be authorized to appoint ten unsalaried investigators, presumably social workers.

As the session unfolded, labor matters absorbed much of the Governor's energy. His first concrete achievement came on April 1, 1899, when he signed bills providing for more stringent regulation of working conditions in tenements, increases in the number and authority of factory inspectors, and limitations on the hours of women and minors. All three bills had been passed over the concerted opposition of employer representatives.

Roosevelt also won labor's approval by supporting a bill to strengthen the eight-hour-day law for state employees. It was the state's duty, he said in a memorandum released as he signed the bill, "to set a good example as an employer of labor, both as to the number of hours of labor exacted and as to paying a just and reasonable wage." Conversely, Roosevelt antagonized labor by vetoing a bill to reduce the long hours of drug clerks. "I am very much puzzled," he explained to Jacob Riis.

. . . You and Seth Low and Reynolds are for it and I have had some touching letters from drug clerks . . . while the smaller east and west side druggists who keep but one clerk say it would mean absolute ruin. . . . What I am anxious to do is whatever will really benefit the druggist clerks in the smaller shops. . . .

I wish you would take the bill . . . and . . . go to some small druggist anywhere . . . on the East Side, and find out if you can what some of the clerks and some of the small druggists really think about it, and what they believe its effects really would be.

But the labor issue which most excited Roosevelt was New York City's schoolteachers' fight for a minimum salary schedule. A bill embodying their demands had been vetoed by his predecessor on the grounds that teachers' salaries should be fixed by city officials. Roosevelt entertained similar views at first; but after conferring with Nicholas Murray Butler and the Superintendent of Schools he came out for state action in a ringing statement. The prevailing level of salaries inflicts "grinding injury on people who are more than any others responsible for the upbringing of the citizens of the next generation," he declared. The level must be raised.

Roosevelt was too firm an advocate of the merit principle to endorse increases based solely on length of service; he therefore opposed the bill then pending. But the measure sailed through both houses of the legislature over his objections. Caught between his conviction that a general increase was desirable and that superiority rather than mediocrity should be rewarded, Roosevelt finally compromised. He accepted the minimum-salary feature after persuading the teachers' representatives to agree to inclusion of a partial merit clause. He then combined "pleasure with duty" and signed the bill.

The action was characteristic of the mature Roosevelt. He deplored waste, and he moved relentlessly against it whenever feasible. But he was no longer obsessed, as he had been fifteen years before, by the need for low taxes. Only infrequently during his later career did he permit short-term considerations of economy to thwart programs he deemed in the public interest.

Those first four and one-half months in Albany had been the most sustained effort of all. From the colorful inaugural parade and reception for six thousand people on New Year's Day until the last bill was studied and signed into law in May, Roosevelt had been immersed in his duties. Veteran newspapermen were amazed at his energy and work habits. He maintained a rigorous schedule, conferred with numberless visitors—corporation lawyers, labor leaders, politicians, social workers, college professors—and usually held two press conferences a day. "With a disregard of precedent that puzzles the politicians," the *New York Times* observed, "he has torn down the curtain that shut in the Governor and taken the public into his confidence . . . beyond what was ever known before."

Roosevelt became friendly with Finley Peter Dunne at this time. "I regret to state that my family and intimate friends are delighted with your review of my book," he wrote Dunne shortly after Dunne's "Mr. Dooley" had retitled Roosevelt's *The Rough Riders* "Alone in Cubia." What's more, he informed Dunne, your work is full of "profound philosophy" even on points of disagreement. "I am an Expansionist, but your delicious phrase about 'take up the white man's burden and put it on the coon,' exactly hit off the weak spot in my own theory; though mind you, I am by no means willing to give up the theory yet."

One tragic incident marred the Governor's record. A month after he took office he had to decide if a Brooklyn woman who had killed her stepdaughter with an ax in a jealous frenzy should be executed. Humanitarians, women's organizations, and sensational newspapers subjected him to heavy pressure to commute the sentence. He was also warned that no governor who approved the execution of a woman could possibly be elected President (such a threat, he wrote, was "the last thing that will influence me"). Meanwhile his advanced views toward women pushed him the other way. Roosevelt had never abandoned completely the mild feminism of his college years; indeed, his first annual message had called for giving women the vote in school board elections. So when medical reports indicated the murderess was sane, he approved the sentence. Sex, he explained at a press conference, was not a valid reason for clemency.

Roosevelt's second year in office followed substantially the same pattern as his first. In December, Platt's lieutenant, Benjamin Odell, urged him to give up his drive for stronger employers' liability legislation and to modify his recommendation for increased publicity of corporate earnings. He also asked him to soften his remarks on the canal frauds. Roosevelt refused, though he replied in deferential, or at least conciliatory, tones.

The Governor also sent Platt the proofs of his annual message of January 3, 1900. "All the important parts I had gone over by various experts," he disarmingly explained. That was the point. The Platt forces bitterly resented his association with intellectuals or, as they called them, "visionary reformers"; but to little avail. Roosevelt was too astute to adopt Platt's ways as his own and he was too wise to devise a program without aid from specialists. "I have come to the conclusion that I have mighty little originality of my own," he wrote President Andrew White of Cornell at the time. "What I do is to try to get ideas from men whom I regard as experts along certain lines, and then try to work out those ideas." To Lemuel Quigg, another Platt lieutenant, he tried further to explain himself:

As for my impulsiveness and my alliance with labor agitators, social philosophers, taxation reformers and the like, I will also go over all these questions with you when we meet. I want to be perfectly sane in all of these matters, but I do have a good deal of fellow feeling for our less fortunate brother, and I am a good deal puzzled over some of the inequalities in life, as life now exists. I have a horror of hysterics or sentimentality, and I am about the last man in the world who sympathizes with revolutionary tactics, or with the effort to make the thrifty, the wise and the brave go down to the level of the unthrifty, the slothful and the cowardly. I would a great deal rather have no change than a change that would put a premium upon idleness and folly. All I want to do is cautiously to feel my way to see if we cannot make the general conditions of life a little easier,—a little better.

And so Roosevelt continued to govern by consultation with experts. It was a technique that Robert M. La Follette was to use more intensively, more creatively, and more dramatically the next year in Wisconsin where the forces of reaction and corruption were never as deeply entrenched as in New York, and it has come down in history as the Wisconsin Idea.

The trust section of Roosevelt's second annual message was written in collaboration with President Arthur T. Hadley of Yale, Professor Jeremiah W. Jenks of Cornell, and Professor Seligman as well as Elihu Root and James B. Dill, who had recently drafted the New Jersey statute on holding companies. It reflected Roosevelt's belief in the inevitability of corporate growth and his revulsion against corporate malpractices. And it came out forthrightly for government regulation. It advocated publicity of corporate earnings, proclaimed the right of the state to intervene against monopoly, and asserted that corporations should not be exempted from taxation because of their mismanagement of resources. "Our laws," the message stated in words that would become increasingly familiar during Roosevelt's presidential years, "should be so drawn as to protect and encourage corporations which do their honest duty by the public; and to discriminate sharply against those organized in a spirit of mere greed, for improper speculative purposes."

The legislature failed to act on the proposals, and Roosevelt went out of office with his program unfulfilled. Aside from bringing the trust problem into political focus, their chief value was the definition they gave Roosevelt's own thought.

The Governor's attitude toward public utilities also revealed his non-doctrinaire quality of mind. "There is grave danger in attempting to establish invariable rules," he said in a passage defending public ownership of the New York City water supply. "In one instance a private corporation may be able to do the work best. In another the State or city may do it best. In yet a third, it may be to the advantage of everybody to give free scope to the power of some individual captain of industry."

As the new session advanced Roosevelt's cold war with Platt again became momentarily hot. This time conflict centered on the reappointment of Superintendent of Insurance Louis F. Payn, an upstate spoilsman and one-time lobbyist for Jay Gould who had earlier abused civil service procedures. By October, 1899, Roosevelt had decided not to reappoint Payn when his term expired in February. Payn had the insurance industry's concerted support, however, and the Governor doubted that he could name a successor acceptable to the industry's henchmen in the Platt organization.

The conflict was still building up when a new scandal broke. Newspapers reported that the State Trust Company had made an unsupported loan of $435,000 to Payn though his salary was only $7,000 per year. They also pointed out that several of the bank's directors served on the boards of insurance companies under Payn's supervision. His resolve to displace Payn strengthened by these charges, Roosevelt informed Platt of his plan. The Senator accepted the decision at first; but when Payn told him that he would fight for his job, Platt changed his mind. An impasse loomed: Roosevelt could refuse to make the appointment; Platt could prevent the confirmation of Payn's successor. Bowing to the inevitable, the Governor prevailed on Platt's close friend, Francis J. Hendricks of Syracuse, to accept the position.

To Roosevelt the displacement of Payn was another hard-won victory for good government. But to many reformers the selection of Hendricks was a sellout to Platt; indignantly they labeled it such. Hurt and irritated, Roosevelt unburdened himself to Louisa Lee Schuyler. "I can say with all sincerity," he wrote, "that I do not believe that any Governor but myself could have put Mr. Payn out, backed as he was by the strongest political influences in the State, and in addition the entire enormous money power of the big insurance companies."

You can have no conception of the pressure, political, financial, and every other kind that has been brought to bear upon me to keep him in. . . . If I had done what the *Evening Post* and Dr. Parkhurst and Mr. Godkin and the smaller fry like Jack Chapman advised, I would not have had ten votes in the Senate to confirm my man and Payn would have stayed in permanently.

A secondary scandal further complicated the Payn affair. The banking superintendent's report criticized Elihu Root, the State Trust Company's legal counselor and one of its directors, for countenancing the nearly half-million-dollar loan to Payn. Roosevelt responded uncharacteristically. He buried the report, ostensibly to avert a run on the Trust Company, but also, one suspects, to protect Root, who was by then Secretary of War, from unfavorable publicity (Root and the other director's action was legally, if not morally, defensible). So at least the *World,* which charged that the Governor wanted "to shield a personal friend," contended.

It might be argued, though surely crudely, that Roosevelt was repaying a favor (when a technicality had threatened his eligibility to serve as governor, Root had devised an argument to offset it), or that he was reluctant to embarrass the McKinley administration. It is more likely, however, that uncritical admiration for Root was Roosevelt's controlling motive.

Incapable of panic, loyal yet curiously detached, a constructive adviser on programs that he would not himself have initiated, Elihu Root was to his intimates, and to many who were not, the embodiment of wise and incisive judgment. He was—and the comparison is not invidious—more analytical than creative, though his organizing intelligence was perhaps the finest of his era; and his mental cast was both sharpened and narrowed by a hard-tempered realism that blunted his resentments even as it dulled his enthusiasms. He was, as Morison puts it, "without illusion in his calculation of what had to be done or could be done by the human agency," and he had no conviction that "he or anyone else could remold the condition of things much closer to the heart's desire." Lacking the moral fervor that inspires men to supreme acts of the spirit, Root's appeal was to their instinct for order, as Roosevelt's, for all his own similar commitment, was to their puissant ideals and unfulfilled emotions. Such, indubitably, was Root's pull on Roosevelt himself.

Understanding intuitively the need to contain his rawer impulses as well as to refine his nobler ones, Roosevelt sought in this confident, matter-of-fact counselor, thirteen years his senior, the means of restraint. And Root, standing almost always firm in the turbulent backwash of Roosevelt's surging force, supplied the want. He saw as few men did the throbbing tension induced by Roosevelt's unconscious urge to love or to hate and even, at times, to rule or to ruin, and he strove in his quietly self-assured way to reduce it; and also, because he was at heart conservative, to keep Roosevelt's creative drives within bounds. Repeatedly, Root turned his biting, sardonic humor on his ebullient friend, and Roosevelt, seemingly sensing the need for his own deflation, delighted in its edge.

Yet the relationship was not without impact on Root. What this eminent public servant possessed in administrative ability, he lacked in boldness of imagination. More administrator than social philosopher, he recoiled from the possible ill consequences of change as other men were attracted by its potential liberating effect. He suffered especially the conservative's dependence on convention, and he actually opposed Roosevelt's corporate tax program with the classic half-truth that "the vast preponderance of the grand fortunes" had conferred "great benefits on the community." Still, Root was never a reactionary. His brief was for a moderate, ordered, and closely controlled progress. In the daily rub of minds with Roosevelt during the presidential years his conservatism became reasonably viable, and for one brief decade he unenthusiastically accepted the moral imperative of Roosevelt's thrust for social and economic justice.

The publicity over Payn and Root, coupled with increasing speculation about the Governor's political future, detracted from the legislative achievements of this second year. A law of 1899 opening corporation's books to agents of the supreme court was amended to open them to stockholders and creditors. An act granting a monopoly to a carriage company was supplanted by one designed to preserve competition in the automotive carriage industry. And a bill forbidding interest charges of more than 6 per cent a year was passed and signed.

The Governor did, however, lose or concede one important round to the machine. Pursuant to the recommendation of the tax commission appointed in the spring of 1899, a measure instituting a 1 per cent tax on all mortgages and banking capital was introduced in 1900. But at the request of J. P. Morgan and other finance capitalists, the Platt men amended it so as to exempt the New York Central Railroad and large corporations in general from its provisions. The state consequently lost six or seven million dollars in tax revenue. Although Roosevelt refused to support the Morgan-Platt amendments because of their discriminatory nature, he failed to fight them forcefully.

Several other important measures were enacted in 1900 with Roosevelt's active support. These improved the civil service laws, standardized the labels on linen cloth, and prohibited newspapers from soliciting funds from candidates for political office. They instituted safeguards on the letting of contracts for the New York City water supply, and they prevented the traction companies from laying four sets of car tracks on Bedford Avenue in Brooklyn. They projected a public park on the Palisades and reorganized and expanded the state forest, fish, and game program. They also limited the working hours of drug clerks and authorized bounties for the production of beet sugar. Roosevelt further vetoed or returned to the legislature some five hundred bills during his two-year term.

Among the approximately one thousand bills Roosevelt signed into law were two affecting the public school system. The first, which he spurred with an emergency message, banned race discrimination and repealed a previous authorization of separate schools for Negroes on a local-option basis.

Like most Americans of the period, the Governor did not regard Negroes in general as the equals of whites. But he did believe that many individual Negroes were superior to individual whites and he felt strongly that they should have full opportunity to prove their merit. "My children sit in the same school with colored children," he declared in defense of the bill.

The second school measure carried over from the fight for higher salaries for teachers. For three months during the fall of 1899 the Tammany-dominated Board of Estimate had refused to pay teachers' salaries in Brooklyn and Queens. Roosevelt responded by pushing through an emergency bill that directed city officials to transfer funds to meet their obligations to the teachers. He then approved a measure designed to prevent a recurrence. "The difference between the attitude of Tammany and the republicans," he angrily wrote, "is . . . that Tammany increased the salaries of all the useless offices but reduced the teachers almost to bankruptcy; whereas the republican party which is pre-eminently the party of the public schools has stood by these schools and teachers."

Roosevelt was keenly satisfied with his record as his term drew to a close. "I think I have been the best Governor within my time," he confided to his uncle, James Bulloch, "better either than Cleveland or Tilden."

The Governor's estimate of his worth was probably accurate. Within the shifting limits of such comparisons he had excelled both Tilden and Cleveland. All three were men of estimable integrity and ability; each had fought corruption, driven through important administrative reforms, and yet maintained a working relationship with elements of his party machine. But Tilden and Cleveland had been more passive than positive, and their administrations had suffered for it. Where they had refused to tread, Roosevelt had willingly broken new ground. They had been conservative of the power of the state; but Roosevelt, conscientiously seeking solutions to the problems created by the rampant industrial order, had broken sharply with the laissez-faire theory and existing concepts of state and local relations. They had been solicitous of the prerogatives of corporations; but Roosevelt, responding to the moderate progressive thought of the times, had begun to believe that public responsibilities, including tax payments, should attach to enormous wealth and power. And they had been oblivious to the plight of labor.

Besides all that, Roosevelt had taken major steps to preserve the wild life, forests, and natural beauty of his state. He had made a stab at the spreading curse of the tenements. And he had imbued many officials with a sense of the public trust and instilled in others the fear of dismissal. Even the *World,* which implied that it might have crossed party lines to support him had he run for re-election, conceded that "the controlling purpose and general course of his administration have been high and good."

It would be an exaggeration to say, as an upstate editor did say shortly before Roosevelt was nominated for Vice-President, that his "only qualification . . . for the office of Vice-President is fitness for the office of President." But it would not be extreme to suggest that he had several critical qualifications for the higher office. Of these, the most significant were his manifest capacity for growth and his signal ability to influence events by seizing the initiative at the strategic moment—the sure measures of a superior leader. In only one important province, and that the one he regarded himself as strongest in —foreign affairs—were Roosevelt's qualifications suspect. Time alone would reveal whether he also possessed the strength to conquer the *"Sturm und Drang"* impulses of his early manhood.

Chapter 8

The People's Choice

*"Tis Teddy alone that's runnin', and he ain't
r'runnin', he's gallopin'."*

—Mr. Dooley

ROOSEVELT HAD reached the fork in the road. From June,
1899, when Westerners hailed him as a presidential candidate
as he went out to the Rough Riders' reunion in Las Vegas,
until June of the following year, when the Republican convention met at Philadelphia, his political future evoked recurrent speculation. By the time the convention delegates detrained in the Quaker City discussion of whether he would
run for a second term as governor or would be forced up and
out to the vice-presidency overshadowed all other questions.

Roosevelt most wanted to return to Albany, although he
would have settled for the civil governorship of the Philippines. But he had no desire to accept the then empty honor of
the vice-presidency. "I am a comparatively young man . . .
and I like to work," he wrote Lodge in February, 1900. "I
do not like to be a figurehead." Nor did the prospect of presiding over the Senate hold any appeal. "I should be in a cold
shiver of rage at inability to answer hounds like Pettigrew
and the scarcely more admirable Mason and Hale," he continued. "I would be seeing continually things that I would like
to do, and very possibly would like to do differently from the
way in which they were being done." Nevertheless, a number
of factors militated in favor of the vice-presidential nomination. Some were within his control; most were beyond it.

On January 20, shortly after Roosevelt's refusal to reappoint Louis Payn had embarrassed the Platt machine anew,
the "Easy Boss" had urged the vice-presidential nomination
upon the Governor. "Platt is afraid," Roosevelt explained to
Lodge, that "unless I take it nobody will be made Vice-President from New York, and that this would be a pity."

The Colonel's naïveté was characteristic. He almost always

130

tended to believe well of his associates, and generally with good result. His confidence brought out the best in men and often inspired near-fanatical loyalty and devotion. But sometimes it backfired. When men's moral sensibilities were perverted or their material stakes were great, as with Tom Platt and later the managers of the United States Steel Corporation, Roosevelt could be deceived. Furthermore, TR never quite realized the overpowering impact of his own vibrant personality. Even such strong characters as Elihu Root and Cabot Lodge sometimes succumbed to it; and too often Roosevelt assumed that failure to challenge his enthusiastically expressed ideas implied agreement.

Roosevelt had left Platt without committing himself. Although Lodge counseled that the vice-presidency was the "better" and "safer" road to the presidency, he soon decided against it. "I was eager to have a regiment in the war and if there was another war I should try to have a brigade," Roosevelt wrote Benjamin Odell, "but nothing would hire me to continue as a colonel or brigadier general in time of peace." He added to Platt that since he had failed to amass a fortune, he felt honor bound to leave his children a record of achievement in politics or letters. "Now, as Governor, I can achieve something," he concluded, "but as Vice-President I should achieve nothing."

Both Platt and Odell were unimpressed; nor did they change their attitude when TR told them that he would "a great deal rather be anything, say professor of history, than Vice-President." Roosevelt's whole program—civil service reform, corporate publicity and taxation, and enforcement of the factory laws—had rocked the Republican machine's foundations. Platt was determined to avoid a second and possibly more sustained attack. Roosevelt gradually grasped Platt's real motives. "I have found out one reason why Senator Platt wants me nominated," he wrote Lodge:

. . . the big-monied men with whom he is in close touch and whose campaign contributions have certainly been no inconsiderable factor in his strength, have been pressing him very strongly to get me put in the Vice-Presidency, so as to get me out of the State. It was the big insurance companies, possessing enormous wealth, that gave Payn his formidable strength, and they to a man want me out. The great corporations affected by the franchise tax have also been at the Senator. In fact, all the big-monied interests that make campaign contributions of large size and feel that they should have favors in return, are extremely anxious to get me out of the State.

Roosevelt's resolve to serve a second term as governor was sharpened by his insight into Platt's design. He also desired to dissipate the suspicions of cowardice raised by his resignation from the police commissionership four years before. "I should feel like a coward if I went away from this work," he added, "because I ran the risk of incurring disaster and took a position where I could not fail, for the simple reason that I could not succeed." Throughout the spring of 1900, therefore, TR tried to suppress the developing boom for his nomination as McKinley's running mate. He told reporters in Chicago on April 26 that the governorship of New York was next to the presidency in importance and that he would return to private life before accepting the vice-presidential nomination; and in a formal address that night he refused to comment though his audience gave him a standing, fifteen-minute ovation and chanted, "We want you, Teddy, yes we do." Two weeks later he went to Washington to assure McKinley and Mark Hanna that he intended to stand for reelection in New York. When he repeated his opposition to the vice-presidency to Elihu Root, the Secretary of War smiled disarmingly and replied: "Of course not, Theodore, you're not fit for it."

Meanwhile Roosevelt wrote numerous negative letters to his Western friends. He thought for a while that he had contained the boom, but he was never quite sure. "If I were actually nominated; and if I were unable to stem the convention's desire to nominate me, it might be impossible to refuse," he confided to Joseph B. Bishop in April. "Still, maybe I could refuse anyhow. And I am almost sure I can prevent the nomination."

Tom Platt viewed the Governor's activities with tongue in cheek. Roosevelt's appeal to the rank and file in the West was irresistible, and Platt knew it. During the sixteen years since young Roosevelt had staked his claim in the hearts of Westerners they had followed his career as if he had been a native son. Long before they had volunteered to serve under him in Cuba they applauded his fight for civil service and his battles against crime and vice in New York. "Beneath Roosevelt's chivalry and the picturesque style which has aroused the enthusiasm of the Nation," the *Kansas City Star* said on the eve of the convention, "there is an intense sense of duty and a moral courage that is invincible."

The record of Roosevelt as a civil officer is a quite sufficient plea upon which to go before the people. It is of a character to make plain his enmity toward corruption and his devotion to public morality. . . .

Platt also knew that the Governor's popularity was not confined to the West. Eastern reformers had sometimes recoiled and party leaders had frequently squirmed, but TR had again and again captured the imagination of the middle classes. More than any young national leader of his era, Roosevelt exemplified the perennial personal virtues—honor, courage, and duty—and he quickened America's conscience because of it. Even the *New York Sun,* which was always suspicious of TR's economics, conceded as much just after the Republican Convention of 1900 ended:

People got to saying, "This man ROOSEVELT seems to do about what he thinks is right and doesn't care a rap for the consequences. He must be all right."

When, against that background, Roosevelt refused to say that he would not accept if chosen and insisted on going to Philadelphia on the grounds that it would be cowardly not to go, his nomination for the vice-presidency was virtually foreordained. As Platt supposedly said, "Roosevelt might as well stand under Niagara Falls and try to spit water back as to stop his nomination by this convention."

The night the convention opened in Philadelphia on June 19 Platt told Roosevelt that he would prevent his renomination for governor if he turned down the vice-presidential nomination. TR replied "that this was a threat, which simply rendered it impossible for me to accept, that if there was to be war there would be war, and that that was all there was to it." Thereupon, Roosevelt added, "I bowed and left the room." Platt's account differs, but it is clear that there had been a tense scene.

But even as Roosevelt resisted Platt, the waters were surging over. Roosevelt had earlier sparked a spontaneous demonstration by striding briskly to his seat in a black civilian version of the Rough Rider's slouch campaign hat—"an acceptance hat," so one delegate dubbed it. And for hours that night scores of Western delegates noisily paraded up and down the corridors outside Hanna's suite shouting "We want Teddy." Meanwhile Quay's Pennsylvania forces announced their endorsement of the New York Governor while Platt, Quay, and Foraker pressed his nomination on various convention leaders.

All through the next day the demands for Roosevelt's nomination continued to mount. The Colonel was told that his political future hung in the balance; he was warned that the West might go to Bryan if he rejected the nomination; and he was admonished that it was his duty to honor the wishes of his legions of admirers. He may also have been threatened with elimination from politics. Succumbing finally to these enormous pressures, he agreed to accept the nomination if the delegates willed it. Late that night Mark Hanna, who had earlier received a wire from McKinley stating that he did not intend to stand in Roosevelt's way if the convention wanted to nominate him, also submitted.

The next day, after McKinley was renominated, a portentous hush fell over the convention as LaFayette Young, head of the Iowa delegation, rose to his feet to withdraw the name of Jonathan Dolliver, Iowa's favorite son, and place Theodore Roosevelt's in nomination. The rank and file then broke loose. Hats flew into the air, state standards were raised from the floor, and pictures and banners appeared out of nowhere as the vast assemblage sprang spontaneously to its feet. The band struck up "There'll Be a Hot Time in the Old Town Tonight." And the delegations roared their congratulations as they marched exuberantly past the New York section where Roosevelt sat grimly in his seat, expressionless except for a tightening of lines around his mouth. In her box up above, Edith Roosevelt gasped momentarily, then flashed a smile.

The balloting followed, and when Lodge announced the near-unanimous result, the rank and file gave forth the mightiest and most sustained cheer of the entire convention. Roosevelt was nominated, reported an obscure country weekly, not because of the bosses, "but because the convention recognized Theodore Roosevelt as that which Henry C. Payne of

Wisconsin had called him—'not New York's son, but the nation's son.' "

Nevertheless, the Governor's emotions remained mixed. Roosevelt's "tail-feathers were all down," Nicholas Murray Butler, who saw him an hour after he had made his decision the night before, remembered. "The fight had gone out of him and he had changed his former tune to that of 'I cannot disappoint my Western friends if they insist. . . . I cannot seem to be bigger than the party.' "

Roosevelt's personal letters say much the same. They also reveal that he was reconciled to his lot: "It was simply impossible to resist so spontaneous a feeling." "I would be a fool not to appreciate and be deeply touched by the way I was nominated." "I believe it all for the best as regards my personal interests." ". . . had I been running for re-election as Governor I could not have helped feeling an uneasiness of mind as to my own fate." "Mrs. Roosevelt has begun to look at the matter our way now." And finally:

Every real friend of mine . . . will speak of me as exactly what I am—the man chosen because it is believed he will add strength to a cause which however is already infinitely stronger than any strength of his—a man absolutely and entirely in the second place whom it is grossly absurd and unjust to speak of in any other capacity.

The cause was Republicanism. It was the gold standard, the protective tariff, and the supremacy of the nation over state and region. It was the unrestricted development of big business and the casting aside of the old isolation. It was integrity, efficiency, and high-mindedness—the skulduggery of the bosses, the maladministration of the Army, and the McKinley administration's assault on the civil service notwithstanding. It was anti-Bryanism, anti-Populism, and anti almost everything else that threatened the party's success. It was, in a word, whatever the Republican orators chose to make it.

Roosevelt chose to make the coming campaign a moral crusade for good government and a referendum on the new foreign policy. He had virtually a free rein in so doing, for the President again confined himself to nebulous pronouncements from his front porch in Canton, Ohio.

Mindful of the dignity of his new situation, Roosevelt told Hanna at the outset that he emphatically opposed appearing "like a second-class Bryan." He tried to nip in the bud a plan to form Rough Riders' marching units all over the country. And he announced that he intended to campaign on his accomplishments as governor, not on his military record. But he also declared that he felt "strong as a bull moose."

That summer and fall Roosevelt canvassed the nation with a thoroughness no vice-presidential candidate had theretofore matched and only one presidential candidate, Bryan, had surpassed. Besides a trip to Oklahoma, where he fired his opening volley from the camp grounds of the Rough Riders' reunion, he made a quick excursion into the Middle West and an extended tour through the Rocky Mountain states where he experienced one long triumphal homecoming: "RANGE GREETS ROOSEVELT"; "WYOMING IS STIRRED UP"; "ROOSEVELT ROUSES BUTTE."

All told, Roosevelt covered 21,000 miles in twenty-four states, spent eight weeks on the road, and made several hundred speeches. Everywhere he preached his four-square gospel of duty, responsibility, Republicanism, and Americanism; and the curious, excited, and adulatory crowds that came out of the hinterland to swarm about the rear platform of his special train at every whistle stop could no more contain their enthusiasm than he could suppress his moralistic exhortations. "Tis Teddy alone that's runnin'," exclaimed the inimitable Mr. Dooley, "and he ain't r'runnin', he's gallopin'."

Roosevelt's nominal opponent was the Democratic vice-presidential candidate, Adlai E. Stevenson of Illinois; but his real adversary was William Jennings Bryan. Few pulses ever beat more quickly for the plain people everywhere than did that of the Great Commoner from Nebraska. For three decades the farmers and small townspeople of the South and the Middle West basked in his prairie-like simplicity and whole-souled sentimentality, and three times they bestowed upon him their highest accolade—the Democratic presidential nomination. Neither in eloquence nor in devotion did Bryan ever fail them. Nineteen years after they first gave him their charge he selflessly resigned as Secretary of State to serve better by his lights the cause of peace that he and they loved, and as he neared death a decade after that he fought unabashedly to uphold their fundamentalist faith against an evolutionary

doctrine that Roosevelt had mastered as an adolescent a half
century before. Again and again this great-hearted Christian
phrased with poetic insight and preached with evangelical
passion their swelling protest against the cruel maladjustments
wrought by the new industrial order; and for his broad
understanding of the economic nature of their problems, even
more than for his abiding compassion for all mankind, was he
truly distinguished.

As Henry Steele Commager, one of the few modern historians to see Bryan whole, asserts, he linked the agrarian
progressivism of the Populists with the sophisticated urban
progressivism of the later Roosevelt. And if he did not conceive, he did pioneer in the advocacy of "more important
legislation than any other politician of his generation." For
what Bryan lacked in profundity, he possessed to overflowing
in instinct. He had a firmer grasp of the public essentials, if
not of the technical details, of the money and tariff questions
than Hanna, McKinley, and their Wall Street compatriots.
And until Roosevelt came into his own in his second term,
Bryan's social thought was the more advanced. His one great
failing was his lack of the scientific spirit and his resultant inability to refine his arguments. He was to the end more de-
scriptive than analytical. A born generalizer, it was enough
for Bryan that he should conceive his mission as the liberation
of the government from the hands of the plutocrats. When
he first burst upon the national scene four years before, he
proclaimed of the cause he led:

On the one hand stand the corporate interests of the United
States, the moneyed interests, aggregated wealth and capital, imperious, arrogant, compassionless. . . . On the other side stand
an unnumbered throng, those who gave to the Democratic party a
name and for whom it has assumed to speak. Work-worn and dust-
begrimed, they made their mute appeal, and too often find their
cry for help beat in vain against the outer walls, while others, less
deserving, gain ready access to legislative halls.

That had been in 1896. The cause was now essentially the
same, though Bryan's early campaign speeches focused on the
imperialism issue. "Imperialism finds no warrant in the Bible,"
the Great Commoner thundered up and down the land. "The
command, 'Go ye into all the world and preach the gospel to
every creature,' has no gatling gun attachment," he declaimed.

"Love, not force, was the weapon of the Nazarene; sacrifice for others, not the exploitation of them, was His method of reaching the human heart"—so he exclaimed to the tens of thousands of Baptists, Methodists, and Presbyterians who made his campaign even more revivalist-like than Roosevelt's.

In effect, Bryan was asking the American people to deny the righteousness of a war they had heroically won and of a world prestige they had suddenly acquired. This was an underestimation of human passion. The emotions that had carried the nation exuberantly to war two years before were still potent; the zealous pride in the national achievement still swollen. The colonial empire was a *fait accompli* rather than a debatable political issue, and the United States was now a major power in a world of great powers, not of Nazarenes. The insurrection of the Filipino patriot, Aguinaldo, invoked the application of force rather than Christian charity; and even as Bryan's impassioned phrases poured forth, American troops were relentlessly applying that force. Not even the editorial spokesmen of American Protestantism succumbed to the Great Commoner's rolling periods. "God's hand," said the Methodist Episcopal *Zion's Herald,* was behind the circumstance "that those most beautiful islands of the Pacific, named for one of the worst monarchs that ever sat on the throne of Spain, should come into the possession of the most Protestant nation of the nineteenth century. . . . The present year of grace is 1900, and not 1800."

Roosevelt's reactions to Bryan's indictment embodied his cascading fervor for honor, duty, and the flag. They embraced his Social Darwinian conception of the evolutionary stages of the races. And they reflected his grasp of many of the hard facts of the international struggle for position. Thus he deprecated the suggestion that the Philippines be abandoned, invoking the same strategic, commercial, and chauvinistic rationale which had actuated him, Lodge, and Mahan to press for their acquisition in the first place. We would have "to pledge ourselves to perpetual war with them and for them," he argued. He declared that the American guardianship was a sacred trust deriving from "the most righteous foreign war that has been waged within the memory of the present generation." And he repeatedly drew a specious parallel between Jefferson's administration of the Louisiana Territory and the projected Republican administration of the Philippine Islands.

But Roosevelt's main theme was that the United States stood on the threshold of greatness. "It rests with us now to decide whether . . . we shall march forward to fresh triumphs or whether at the outset we shall cripple ourselves for the contest," he warned the Republican convention in his speech seconding McKinley's renomination. "We challenge the proud privilege of doing the work that Providence allots us, and we face the coming years high of heart and resolute of faith that to our people is given the right to win honor and renown as has never yet been vouchsafed to the nations of mankind."

Roosevelt's rhetoric, romanticism, and egocentric nationalism notwithstanding, his remarks at least touched the periphery of those momentous questions that have been a half century in the settling: Was the United States to play an assertive role commensurate with its emerging power in the affairs of the world? Was it to bury itself in an ostrich-like isolationism? Or was it to indulge in a nebulous internationalism unsupported by military force? Roosevelt and the imperialists incorrectly believed there was no real choice. They sensed that the revolution in communications had so altered traditional concepts of time and space that the old isolationism was as anachronistic by the turn of the century as the pony express. They recognized that the sheer fact of industrial might made America a *de facto* member of the community of powers. And they vehemently argued what the anti-imperialists, and especially Bryan, would not concede—to abandon the Philippines was to invite a scramble by England, Germany, Japan, and Russia, and possibly to precipitate world war.

Yet the Colonel's armor was penetrable. The Philippines were militarily indefensible; within the decade he himself would pronounce them an "Achilles' heel"—a tacit admission that the overextension of lines was not necessarily synonymous with the emergence from isolationism. Nor would the imperialists' loose expectations of a burgeoning Far Eastern trade be realized in Roosevelt's generation or even in the two that followed. But the most glaring flaw was moral. In the opinion of sensitive men then and since, the "honor and renown" Roosevelt read into the Philippine venture came with the enlightened administrative policies that culminated in Philippine independence in 1946, not with the brutal subjugation of Aguinaldo's partisans. It is a tribute to Bryan's right-mindedness, if not to his tactical wisdom, that he worked to that end from the beginning.

If Roosevelt's insight into foreign affairs was at once more romantic and more realistic than the Great Commoner's, his comprehension of domestic issues was in all but a few respects far shallower. Like William Allen White, whose vacuous, yet strangely stirring editorial, "What's the Matter with Kansas," had catapulted him to fame in the summer of 1896, TR was deluded by fear of free silver. Neither in 1896 nor in 1900 did Roosevelt understand that the Westerners' and Southerners' grievances derived from more than moral laxity, wool-hat demagoguery, or a bad turn in the weather. Neither in 1896 nor in 1900 did he concede that the underlying issue involved more than "decent government and the honest payment of debts." He wildly charged in 1896 that Bryan and the Democrats represented the "spirit of lawless mob violence"; and he repeated and embellished the indictment in 1900. As White long afterward said in words as applicable to Roosevelt as to himself: "How intellectually snobbish I was about 'sound economics.' . . . Being what I was, a child of the governing classes, I was blinded by my birthright. . . . It seemed to me that rude hands were trying to tear down the tabernacle of our national life, to taint our currency with fiat." And so, White concluded, "swallowing protection as a necessary evil and McKinley's candidacy as the price of national security, I went into the campaign with more zeal than intelligence, with more ardor than wisdom."

Roosevelt's delusion was made easier by the character of Bryan's impassioned hosts. One major element included the remnants of the Populist party. And though TR would later espouse that part of the Populist manifesto of 1892 which read, "We believe that the powers of government . . . should be expanded . . . to the end that oppression, injustice, and poverty shall eventually cease in the land," he gave little evidence of his future beliefs in 1900 and even less in 1896.

Another great division was spearheaded by John Peter Altgeld, who had compounded his "crime" in pardoning the surviving Haymarket anarchists by courageously attacking Cleveland's handling of the Pullman strike of 1894. Roosevelt seemed not to realize that Altgeld was actually a sensitive and responsible spokesman for the submerged urban masses; and in both campaigns he pummeled the Illinois Governor unmercifully and unjustifiably, expostulating at one point that Altgeld "would connive at wholesale murder and would justify it by elaborate and cunning sophistry for reasons known only to his own tortuous soul." So sweeping were TR's charges, in fact, that Hanna anxiously consulted him about them after an especially unbalanced speech in St. Paul in the fall of 1900.

Hanna failed, of course, to dampen Roosevelt's ardor; nor did anyone else. Neither age nor experience brought moderation, mellowing, or development; until the day of his death TR remained an extremist in speech when the battle was on.

For all Roosevelt's irresponsible assertions, including his failure to speak fairly to Bryan's proposals for an inheritance tax, graduated income tax, reduced tariff, and expanded money supply, TR did come out with one constructive proposal in 1900—the regulation of big business. Drawing on his experience as governor, he recommended publicity of capitalization and profits, taxation of corporations, and "the unsparing excision of all unhealthy, destructive and anti-social elements." This program was indefensibly vague. It failed to specify whether the states or the federal government should take the initiative. And it paled into insignificance beside Bryan's comprehensive, if also inadequate, proposals. Yet its call for the regulation rather than the dissolution of the great corporations dimly foreshadowed the future.

In spite of McKinley's front-porch vapidities and Bryan's impassioned oratory, the President's re-election was never in doubt. Election Day saw his popular vote soar several hundred thousand above his total in 1896 and his majority reach the highest level since Grant won a second term in 1872. Roosevelt's contribution to this impressive victory cannot be measured with accuracy; but by common agreement it was considerable. He had spoken, however egregiously, to the issues as no other Republican of prominence had done. And he had carried into the campaign the most responsive personal following ever rallied by a vice-presidential candidate. Even McKinley's sympathetic biographer concedes that Roosevelt's "forthright censure of the trusts did much to counterbalance the deference to business which paralyzed Republican leadership on economic questions, and to attract the enthusiastic support of younger and more progressive elements of the party."

The special session of Congress following the inaugural

ceremonies four months later lasted only four days, so Vice-President Roosevelt never had a chance to prove that he could have presided over the Senate with equanimity; and it is of no moment. He tarried in Washington less than a week after Congress adjourned, then returned to Sagamore Hill for the spring and early summer.

Unburdened by pressing duties for the first time since the winter of 1889, TR experienced perhaps the most pleasant vacation of his life. His seven children were still bound to the family bosom, though Alice, witty, contrary, and worldly beyond her seventeen years, was straining to break away. TR enjoyed her immensely, for she shared his lust for life. But she was already enamored by the superficially unconventional. Only with difficulty could he contain her. She eventually married a stand-pat Republican politician, Nicholas Longworth, who became Speaker of the House when the business civilization reached its apogee under Calvin Coolidge.

Ted was then just short of fourteen, in his first year at Groton, and already able to beat TR in tennis. The others, ranging down to chubby and effusive Quentin, who at three and one-half often got in on the fun, all had interests their father enjoyed. They rowed, hiked, waded, and swam together on fair days; romped, read, and recited poetry on rainy days. Inevitably, TR pushed the boys too hard—"I would rather one of them should die than have them grow up weaklings," he snapped at a woman who criticized their playing football. And he apparently drove Ted to a minor nervous breakdown at one point. Yet he had flashes of understanding for the limitations of the mind, if not of the will. He rarely demanded more than an individual could give, and as Wagenknecht observes, he resignedly accepted the fact that most men's best is not very good. "If Archie, through sheer inability, failed in mathematics," he wrote, "I should not in the least hold it against him; but where Ted gets on probation because he has been such an utter goose as pointlessly to cut his recitations I am not only much irritated but I also become apprehensive as to how Ted will do in after life."

The new Vice-President continued to make occasional speeches during the spring and summer of 1901. In April he spoke at the Newsboys' Lodging House, his father's favorite charity. In May he opened the Pan-American Exposition in Buffalo. And in June he addressed the Long Island Bible Society. A month later he held an informal seminar on the piazza at Sagamore for a group of Yale and Harvard undergraduates who stayed far into the evening listening to him urge upon them the need for men of character to enter politics. Then, on September 6, he spoke to the Fish and Game League on Isle la Motte in Lake Champlain.

The afternoon that the Vice-President spoke on Isle la Motte, President McKinley was mortally wounded by a mad man at the exposition Roosevelt had opened in Buffalo four months before. For five days McKinley hovered between life and death, but on the sixth day, Friday, September 13, he sank rapidly. Repeating the title of his favorite hymn, "Nearer, My God, to Thee," he murmured finally "It is God's way," then sank into semiconsciousness. At 2:15 in the morning of September 14 the President died.

William McKinley had been a well-intentioned man, unsure of the challenges of his times, but striving slowly and as conscientiously as he could to rise to them. His last public address, delivered the day before he was shot, had been his finest. He had declared that the old isolationism was dead and he had counseled the modification of the tariff system of which he himself was the symbol. A transitional President at best, his election in 1896 had marked the end of the old order; his passing in 1901 the ushering in of the new.

McKinley and Roosevelt had never been close; nor had either's opinion of the other ever been high. To the end, McKinley had been unnerved as well as amused by Roosevelt's shrill bellicosity and flagrant disrespect for the established forms. From the beginning, Roosevelt had been contemptuous of McKinley's caution, indecisiveness, and lack of conviction. Yet Roosevelt, like many strong-minded men whose lives touched McKinley's, was moved by the President's homely virtues—by his personal honesty, devotion to his invalid wife, unswerving loyalty to friends, and reluctance to hurt even those who, like Roosevelt, had themselves hurt him. He seemed genuinely saddened by his death. "He comes from the typical hard-working farmer stock of our country," Roosevelt wrote Lodge in a letter that unwittingly played on McKinley's tragic belief that it was a President's function to reflect rather than to lead. "In every instinct and feeling he is closely in touch with . . . the men who make up the immense bulk of our Nation. . . . His one great anxiety while President has been to keep in touch with this body of people and to give expression to their sentiments and desires."

Roosevelt had rushed by special train from Burlington, Vermont, to Buffalo, on being informed of the President's misfortune. There, so his most critical biographer concedes, he comported himself with dignity and restraint for three days. On September 10, the physician's reports being encouraging, he left to join his wife and the children in the Adirondacks in the belief that his withdrawal would reassure the country. He reached the Adirondacks, Mrs. Roosevelt wrote Bamie, "naturally much relieved at the rapid recovery of the President." On Friday morning, as the President's physician in Buffalo abandoned hope, Roosevelt and a party climbed Mount Marcy. They had descended as far as Lake Tear of the Cloud and were eating lunch beside a brook at two o'clock in the afternoon when a man came puffing up the trail bearing a message from Elihu Root: "The President appears to be dying, and members of the Cabinet in Buffalo think you should lose no time in coming."

Roosevelt reached his base at six that night. After sending a messenger six miles ahead to the nearest telephone, he retired at nine. He was awakened at eleven by the same messenger. The President was dying; a special train would pick up the Vice-President at North Creek, thirty-five miles distant. All that night Roosevelt sat on a buckboard as relays of horses and drivers rushed him over the gutted roads where a wrong turn meant a drop over a precipice. He arrived at North Creek at half-past five Saturday morning and at Buffalo at half-past one that afternoon.

The new President went at once to the house where the old President lay dead. After paying his respects to the bereaved widow, he was driven to the home of a friend, Ansley Wilcox, where all of the McKinley Cabinet except John Hay and Secretary of the Treasury Lyman J. Gage, solemnly awaited him. Root suggested that the oath be taken at once. Roosevelt thereupon bowed slightly and addressed the group: "I wish to say that it shall be my aim to continue, absolutely unbroken, the policy of President McKinley for the peace, the prosperity, and the honor of our beloved country." The oath followed, Roosevelt adding his own redundant touch: "And so I swear."

Roosevelt then took a brief walk with Root. They returned

just before Mark Hanna drove up to the Wilcox house. When the President saw Hanna appear, he bounded out to meet him. It was a tense moment. Hanna had loved McKinley like a brother; he also aspired to the office Roosevelt now held. Yet Hanna, like Roosevelt, had large habits of mind. When the President repeated the assurances he had given the Cabinet, Hanna replied that although he would not then commit himself to Roosevelt's nomination in 1904, he would do all in his power to make the administration a success during the next three years. "I trust," he concluded, "that you will command me if I can be of any service."

The date was September 14, 1901, six weeks before Roosevelt's forty-third birthday. He was the youngest President in the nation's history.

PART THREE

The Square Deal Begins

Chapter 9

The First Fell Blows

> *When I became President, the question as to the method by which the United States Government was to control the corporations was not yet important. The absolutely vital question was whether the government had power to control them at all.*
>
> —Theodore Roosevelt, *An Autobiography*

FOR FIVE months after the simple ceremony at Buffalo an uneasy calm hung over the American business community. The mighty masters of industry and finance understood that Roosevelt was no Eugene V. Debs, nor even a William Jennings Bryan. But they also knew that he lacked reverence for the "system" their constructive labor and political influence had created. They remembered that he had struck out at monopoly as a fledgling legislator two decades before. They recalled that as Civil Service Commissioner he had flouted the "system's" Grand Old Protector—the Republican party. And they could not forget, for they were still challenging the legislation in the courts, that he had imposed a tax on corporations while governor. Nevertheless, they hoped that he would prove himself in the image of McKinley—their "very supple and highly paid agent," as Henry Adams termed the late President. Until Roosevelt destroyed their forced optimism by striking out boldly on his own, their editorial spokesmen worked heroically to imbue him with his lamented predecessor's values.

President Roosevelt is "in perfect sympathy with the triumphant policies of Mr. McKinley," the *New York Tribune* said. It would be wrong to think, warned the *New York Times,* "that the temper of President Roosevelt's mind will incline him to seek for himself some more shining glory than that which has crowned the administration of his predecessor." The new President, the *New York Sun* added, "is a man on whom

149

the American people can rely as a prudent and a safe and sagacious successor to William McKinley."

He represents the same political party and spirit and policies which were represented by Mr. McKinley; his political future, his whole reputation, depends on his fidelity to the sentiment of his party. President Roosevelt's career has been as a strict party man, happily for the public. His policy as President can be assumed from the policy of his party. It will not depend on the possible vagaries of an individual judgment.

Wall Street half sensed that these statements would prove more wishful than realistic. It assumed, however, that the President would take it into his confidence if he decided to alter McKinley's policies. Great was its consternation, therefore, when Attorney-General Philander C. Knox announced on February 18, 1902, that the President had directed him to invoke the Sherman Antitrust Law against J. P. Morgan's latest paper creation, the Northern Securities Company. There had been no warning save the logic of Theodore Roosevelt's career.

The first memorable event of the Roosevelt era, the resurrection of the Sherman Law struck financial circles like a shaft of lightning. Even Pierpont Morgan was stunned. Roosevelt had not acted as a "gentleman," he grumbled to his dinner guests that night. Morgan's partner in the Northern Securities venture, the railroad magnate, James J. Hill, was less restrained. "It really seems hard," he wrote to a friend, "that we should be compelled to fight for our lives against the political adventurers who have never done anything but pose and draw a salary."

The lesser men of the financial world mirrored those two Goliaths' reactions. As the *Detroit Free Press* sardonically observed, "Wall Street is paralyzed at the thought that a President of the United States would sink so low as to try to enforce the law."

Roosevelt's bold decision to give life to the Sherman Law reflected in the broadest sense his concern for the state of the nation. Urban slums were multiplying, and crime and corruption were growing apace. Political machines based on the frustrations of the submerged lower classes or the greed of the high business order were tightening their grasp on the body politic. Nature's heritage was being ruthlessly squandered out of apathy, ignorance, or avarice. And worse even than that, there was rising such a concentration of business power as made a mockery of the democratic process and threatened the foundations of the republic itself.

In the face of these awesome trends, Theodore Roosevelt stood as the accidental head of a political party whose leadership blatantly opposed their arrestment. The most powerful deterrent to the new President's freedom to advance the public interest was the United States Senate. By the turn of the century that body had arrogated to itself much of the authority which Jefferson, Jackson, and Lincoln had vested in the executive office. Most of its members owed their seats to machine-dominated state legislatures, and most of them served special business interests. Only such a unique concatenation of events as marked the Roosevelt era would force them to compromise, and no power or event would compel many of them to submit.

The Republican leaders of the Senate were at once more ideological and more effective than their counterparts in New York. Many were men of personal wealth, the fruit of earlier careers in business or of continuing and rarely disinterested investment. They were often leaders of their state machines. And they frequently radiated charm and graciousness. With some exceptions, such as Matthew Quay of Pennsylvania, who narrowly escaped the penitentiary, their private morality was high. And even their public morality was estimable by prevailing standards. The powerful "Four," Nelson W. Aldrich of Rhode Island, John C. Spooner of Wisconsin, Orville H. Platt of Connecticut, and William B. Allison of Iowa, were cut of fine, if purely conventional cloth; and so were Mark Hanna and numbers of others. They were not to be compared with Quay or to Boies Penrose, the Pennsylvania aristocrat whose career was virtually an unrelieved stench.

Yet even the best of these men were unable to divorce themselves from their backgrounds. The modern concept of conflict of interest was foreign to their make-up, and they freely promoted their own business interests in the United States Senate. They disdained the most elementary considerations of social or economic justice. And they were supremely confident that the arrogant business society they so faithfully represented was an unexampled blessing to the American people. Intelligent, and in some instances even learned, they were unmarked by intellectual depth or consistency. They fixed upon those theories of John Stuart Mill and William Graham Sumner which subserved their purposes, and they contemptuously dismissed those that confuted them. They supported government subsidies for business both overtly and covertly; but they self-righteously invoked the authority of laissez faire against efforts to regulate and tax either corporate or individual wealth. Calvin Coolidge's dictum that "the business of the United States is business" well stated the G.O.P.'s dominant philosophy in the 1920's; but it applied even more pertinently to the Republican oligarchy Theodore Roosevelt inherited from William McKinley in 1901. As Roosevelt put it in his *Autobiography*: "These men still from force of habit applauded what Lincoln had done in the way of radical dealing with the abuses of his day; but they did not apply the spirit in which Lincoln worked to the abuses of their own day."

So it was that party leaders gasped and outside observers chuckled when the President unloosed his bolt at Morgan five months after he took office. Symbolically, he had crashed headlong into the "system" that made business, through its ideological partners or political hirelings in the House and the Senate, the *de facto* governing body of the nation.

From the start of his administration Roosevelt had seen the difficulties of his position. He also realized, and doubtless enjoyed, the irony of his sudden rise to eminence. But whether he at first realized the dormant power of his new office is debatable. Possibly he did, given his experience as Governor of New York. Yet he also knew that he would have to compromise in order to get legislation passed. Accordingly, he had at once entered into warm, seemingly deferential, relations with the men of power.

McKinley's assassination in September had been a devastating blow to the high priests of the market place. Stock prices had declined at news of the shooting, and they had fallen again when the President died. The volcanic Morgan was variously reported to have been enraged and stupefied, to have cursed wildly and to have muttered soulfully. And Charles M. Schwab of the United States Steel Corporation had even violated the unwritten code by predicting that business would surely suffer if McKinley failed to recover.

Business leaders meanwhile tried to master the situation. Their editorial spokesmen had yet to publish their wishful affirmations of Roosevelt's conservatism when they exerted personal pressure upon the new President through his brother-in-law, Douglas Robinson. He had been urged, Robinson wrote Roosevelt in a letter sent to Buffalo by special messenger, "to impress upon you the fact that you must . . . be as close-mouthed and conservative as you were before your nomination for Governor" and that you should "assure the country that you intend to carry out the administration policy."

I must frankly tell you that there is a feeling in financial circles here that in case you become President you may change matters so as to upset the confidence . . . of the business world, which would be an awful blow to everybody—the West as well as the East—as that means tight money.

The advice had been superfluous. Roosevelt had already announced his intention of continuing the McKinley policies in a statement that even Democratic and independent newspapers had heartily applauded. You have done "admirably, splendidly," and have not "made a single mistake," Lodge wrote from England soon afterward.

Nevertheless, an infectious change of pace soon marked the White House. "Every day or two . . . [Roosevelt] rattles the dry bones of precedent and causes sedate Senators and heads of departments to look over their spectacles in consternation," the *Detroit News* commented. "Mr. Roosevelt talks to every one alike," a British embassy official reported to his government, "and apparently in President McKinley's time Senators were accustomed to have their views received with a certain deference." The President was receiving scores of people such as had rarely crossed the White House threshold in the past and would rarely do so in the future—writers, reformers, scientists, professional social workers, and labor leaders. He was walking regularly to the little Grace Reformed Chapel on 15th and O Streets where he attended services almost every Sunday he was in Washington. And he was beginning to conduct diplomacy on horseback or while scrambling among the wilds of Rock Creek Park. Even crabbed Henry Adams admitted mild exhilaration. "Theodore helps us by his gaiety, and delights

Hay by his sense of fun," Adams wrote. " 'Cabot didn't mind having the newspapers say that he was head of the kitchen-cabinet,' said Theodore, 'but he was frantic with fury when they said he was learning to ride, so as to go out with me.' " In numerous other ways, including borrowing books from the Library of Congress, Roosevelt was giving his administration a uniquely personal distinction. "Roosevelt's first three months in the Presidency were interesting, even spectacular," Mark Sullivan wrote in *Our Times.*

His high spirits, his enormous capacity for work, his tirelessness, his forthrightness, his many striking qualities, gave a lift of the spirits to millions of average men, stimulated them to higher use of their own powers, gave them a new zest for life. "He brought in," said Harry Thurston Peck, "a stream of fresh, pure, bracing air from the mountains, to clear the fetid atmosphere of the national capital."

There was still no word, however, on the key question: Would Roosevelt continue McKinley's benevolent policy toward big business?

The first sign came with the release of Roosevelt's annual message on December 3, 1901. A verbose and lengthy document, it was designed to allay the fears of business while suggesting a program of moderate action. Paragraph balanced paragraph and sentence balanced sentence as Roosevelt made countless mental reservations. Finley Peter Dunne's Mr. Dooley summed up its apparent spirit:

"Th' trusts," says he, "are heejoous monsthers built up be th' inlightened intherprise iv th' men that have done so much to advance progress in our beloved counthry," he says. "On wan hand I wud stamp thim undher fut; on th' other hand not so fast."

Mr. Dooley and other contemporary observers did not know that the President had earlier rejected suggestions by the House of Morgan that he revise drastically his measured call for reform. While the message was being drafted, Morgan sent two associates, George W. Perkins and Robert Bacon, to Washington to persuade the President to stand pat. Roosevelt received them courteously though they argued, he told Douglas Robinson, "like attorneys for a bad case." They would not have done so were they not representatives "of a man so strong and dominant a character as Pierpont Morgan." The President added that they wanted him "to go back on my messages to the New York Legislature and on my letter of acceptance for the Vice-Presidency."

I intend to be most conservative, but in the interests of the big corporations themselves and above all in the interest of the country I intend to pursue, cautiously but steadily, the course to which I have been publicly committed again and again, and which I am certain is the right course.

The President also had trouble with Mark Hanna. "Go slow," McKinley's former confidant warned Roosevelt on October 12. Soon afterward Hanna took exception to the President's proposed criticism of overcapitalization. Not even labor wanted corporation control "made a political issue," he admonished Roosevelt. The President then agreed to delete the questionable passage. But in the message as sent to Congress Roosevelt stated that "one of the chief" of the "real and grave evils" threatening the nation was "overcapitalization."

Granting its indecisive tone, the section on corporations was still a reasoned statement of the President's views. Roosevelt never had taken anything but a Darwinian view of business growth; he therein reaffirmed it. The corporations' development "has not been due to the tariff nor to any other government action," he noted, "but to natural causes in the business world, operating in other countries as they operate in our own." Furthermore, "concerns which have the largest means at their disposal and are managed by the ablest men are naturally those who take the lead in the strife for commercial supremacy among the nations of the world." Foreign markets are "essential"; it would "be unwise to cramp or to fetter the youthful strength of our nation."

Roosevelt also realized the existence of grave and ominous abuses. These should be eradicated by federal regulation. "It is no limitation upon property rights or freedom of contract to require that when men receive from government the privilege of doing business under corporate form . . . they shall do so upon absolute truthful representations as to the value of the property in which the capital is to be invested," the President asserted. As a first remedial step he proposed compulsory publicity, his theory being that a specific program could not be devised until after the facts were known.

Conscious that his proposals for national regulation would affront the numerous and vociferous defenders of states' rights, the President attempted to outflank them with historical reasoning. "When the Constitution was adopted, at the end of the eighteenth century," he wrote in a passage that graphically revealed his evolutionary approach to constitutional law, "no human wisdom could foretell the sweeping changes, alike in industrial and political conditions, which were to take place at the beginning of the twentieth century."

At that time it was accepted as a matter of course that the several States were the proper authorities to regulate, so far as was then necessary, the comparatively insignificant and strictly localized corporate bodies of the day. The conditions are now wholly different and wholly different action is called for. I believe that a law can be framed which will enable the National Government to exercise control along the lines above indicated. . . . If, however, the judgment of the Congress is that it lacks the constitutional power to pass such an act, then a constitutional amendment should be submitted to confer the power.

The real portent of these recommendations went largely unrecognized. The *Hartford Courant* warned that federal control "is a few steps ahead of government ownership, and is in the same path"; and a few other newspapers commented in the same vein. But the reaction as a whole was broadly favorable. Many conservative newspapers expressed relief that the President's recommendations had been relatively restrained; some, including the *Wall Street Journal*, endorsed them openly; and others, viewing them with a cynicism born of realism, suggested that Congress could readily ignore them.

Why this mild reaction? One explanation is that big business and its defenders had feared the worst—an explosive, single-minded assault on the iniquities of "the criminal rich" and the "malefactors of great wealth." Another is that they were confident that the President's proposals would be buried by Congress. William McKinley was no longer in the White House, but God was in his heaven and Aldrich, Hanna, Spooner, and those who thought like them were still in control of the United States Senate. Did they not stand unalterably for the status quo, or for change in only the slightest degree?

If more assurance were needed, the conservative Cabinet that came down from McKinley gave it. The member most directly involved, Attorney-General Philander C. Knox, was able and public-spirited. But he was conservative in temperament and a corporation lawyer in background. He could also be expected to be dwarfed in influence by Elihu Root. Root's imposing talents, forceful personality, and intimate friendship with Roosevelt lent credence to reports that his hand would extend far beyond the War Department where he was already performing with brilliance. His attitude toward corporation control was no secret: he largely opposed it.

Had Pierpont Morgan, E. H. Harriman, and their minions been sharper students of human nature, they might have been more apprehensive. Roosevelt had at his command the means for independent executive action. Eleven years earlier a Republican Congress had enacted the Sherman Antitrust Law. Modern scholarship indicates that the measure had been passed in relatively good faith despite assertions that although no one knew what it would do to the trusts, almost everyone agreed that "something must be flung out to appease the restive masses." Nevertheless, a succession of presidential administrations had invoked it sparingly, when at all. Harrison instituted seven suits, Cleveland eight, and McKinley, under whom more trusts were formed than ever before, three. Indeed, the most notable prosecution had been against the benighted labor leader, Eugene V. Debs; and this in the face of Congress' conviction that labor unions were exempted from its provisions. Until 1902, moreover, not a single action against a business combine had been instituted on the initiative of Department of Justice headquarters in Washington; excepting only the four labor cases growing out of the Pullman strike of 1894, every one of the suits under Harrison, Cleveland, and McKinley had been originated by zealous district attorneys in the field. Indubitably, the utilization of the Sherman Law as a broad instrument of national policy awaited the application of a bold and imaginative intelligence.

Just five weeks after Theodore Roosevelt took the presidential oath the spawning of new trusts had come to a temporary climax as incorporation papers for the Northern Securities Company were filed in Trenton, New Jersey, at the instance of J. Pierpont Morgan.

"What a whale of a man!" was the way one of his contemporaries described the imperious Morgan. "There seemed to radiate something that forced the complex of inferiority . . . upon all around him, in spite of themselves," he continued. "The boldest man was likely to become timid under his piercing gaze. The most impudent or recalcitrant were ground to humility as he chewed truculently at his huge black cigar." In the parlance of the "Street," wrote James Ford Rhodes, he was known as "Jupiter." The appellation "was properly bestowed," Rhodes added, "for his word was 'I command.' "

This First Lord of American Finance was no more committed to the pure theory of capitalism, however, than the propagandists who fashioned its folklore. He too idealized the concept of an economy unfettered by governmental restraints. But on the critical abstraction—that of a genuinely open market—he was from the beginning a radical deviant. Like Aldrich and the other senators whose views reflected or paralleled his own, Morgan did not believe in free competition. Always, he yearned for the stability and security of an economy ordered by gentlemen bankers and corporation managers; always, he feared the instability of the hard and creative clash of undisciplined economic units.

Firm in the conviction that competition was wasteful, destructive of confidence, and erratic in impact, Morgan had been striving since 1885 to regularize the organization of the railroads in particular. By Roosevelt's accession he had already reorganized thousands of miles of Eastern lines with results that dramatically bore out the injurious, no less than the beneficial, effects of finance-capitalist control. He had also acquired a major interest in James J. Hill's Northern Pacific and Great Northern lines. Striking out in partnership with Hill, he had then masterfully extended his interests over the Burlington road into Chicago.

The acquisition of the Burlington line by the Morgan-Hill interests had been a bitter blow to the intrepid E. H. Harriman, long-time antagonist of Hill and dominant figure in the Union Pacific Railroad. Harriman believed that the conjunction of the Burlington and the Northern Pacific threatened his own "empire" to the south, and he boldly demanded permission to buy a one-third interest in the Burlington. Morgan and Hill peremptorily refused, whereupon Harriman started an all-out fight for control of Morgan and Hill's Northern Pacific road. For a few frenzied hours the battle of the titans caused Northern Pacific shares to soar to more than $1,000 a share; but finally Harriman failed of his objective by a narrow margin. He had provoked such a disturbance and made such heavy inroads in the Northern Pacific, however, that Morgan and Hill retreated. The order to combine rather than compete was given out, and the Northern Securities Company was organized to implement it. The new corporation brought together the stock of all three roads, the Northern Pacific, Union Pacific, and Burlington, under a board composed of the Morgan, Hill, and Harriman interests and the latter's bankers, Kuhn, Loeb & Company. One-third of the Northern Securities Company's stock was "water"; more important still, shippers through the entire upper West had no recourse but to pay such charges as the new combine fixed.

President Roosevelt had given no intimation of his feelings when the Northern Securities Company was formed in the fall of 1901; nor had he mentioned the company in his December message. Some time during the early winter of 1901, however, perhaps when he learned that Minnesota had instituted proceedings against it, he decided to investigate. Only to Attorney-General Knox, who was soon castigated as a "country lawyer" by irate Wall Street men, did Roosevelt give his confidence.

Pierpont Morgan's concern encompassed more than the President's violation of the "gentlemen's code." He feared that the action presaged a broadside attack on his other interests, several of which were closer to his leonine heart than the Western railroads; and soon after the suit was instituted he sped to Washington to impress Roosevelt with the gravity of his action and, particularly, to ascertain his future intentions.

"If we have done anything wrong," the lordly financier exclaimed to the President of the United States, "send your man [the Attorney-General] to my man [one of Morgan's lawyers] and they can fix it up." Roosevelt, who seems to have been somewhat awed by Morgan's commanding presence (though not enough so to alter his policy), replied simply, "That can't be done." Knox added that the administration wanted to stop such combinations rather than destroy them. Morgan then came to his main point. "Are you going to attack my other interests, the Steel Trust and the others?" he asked. "Certainly not," the President responded, "unless we find out that in any case they have done something we regard as wrong."

"That is a most illuminating illustration of the Wall Street point of view," Roosevelt remarked after Morgan left the White House. "Mr. Morgan could not help regarding me as a big rival operator, who either intended to ruin all his interests or else could be induced to come to an agreement to ruin none."

Morgan was not alone in resenting the President's failure to reveal his confidence. Elihu Root felt that he too should have been informed, and he visited his irritation on Knox in the erroneous belief that he caused the President's closemouthedness. Mark Hanna must also have been irritated, though he failed to show it. He had accompanied Morgan on one of his two visits to the White House, but had refused to urge Roosevelt to change his policy. "I warned Hill that McKinley might have to act against his company," the large-minded Ohioan said. "Mr. Roosevelt's done it."

The reasons for Roosevelt's cloak-and-dagger attitude are unclear. His only recorded comment suggests that he feared the stock market would have been upset had word got out. In all likelihood, however, he simply decided that an independent assertion of executive power would best serve his interests. More effectively than any words he might write or utter such action would demonstrate that he was President in fact as well as in name; that he had finally broken the McKinley nexus. It would also signify the weakening of that business-government partnership which Roosevelt was compelled by his own inner necessity to attack. And most important of all, for Roosevelt could suppress his moral compulsions temporarily, it would win the support of the middle classes while impressing Congress with the need to modify its opposition to his legislation program or suffer the consequences in the executive arena. As Mowry suggests, "With the path to effective regulation blocked by a stubborn, conservative Congress, the only way for Roosevelt to bring the arrogant capitalists to heel was through the judicious use of the anti-trust laws." Thus the President would have seriously weakened his position or subjected himself to agonizing intellectual turmoil had he consulted with Root, the Senate Four, or the Morgan group.

For nearly two years after suit was instituted in the winter of 1902 the Northern Securities case wended its way through the lower courts. The feeling was strong that the Supreme Court would reaffirm its opinion in the Knight Case of 1895—

to wit, a mere stock transaction was not in itself an act of commerce—and upon that reasoning the combine's able lawyers based the burden of their arguments. When the Court finally rendered its decision on March 14, 1904, however, it upheld the government's action by a five to four majority. John Marshall Harlan, one of the strongest minds to grace the High Tribunal in the late nineteenth century and the author of the dissenting opinion in 1895, this time spoke for the majority.

For the Court to accept the contention that the act violated state sovereignty, Harlan declared, would mean "nothing less than that Congress, in regulating interstate commerce, must act in subordination to the will of the states when exerting their power to create corporations." And such a view, the tough-minded jurist concluded, could not "be entertained for a moment." Thus was laid another section of the roadbed for a broad extension of federal regulatory power during the next half century.

President Roosevelt's pleasure in the Court's ruling was tempered by the fact that Oliver Wendell Holmes, the first and most eminent of his appointees to the Supreme Court, cast his vote with the minority. Harlan's was an interpretation of the law, said Holmes, that would "disintegrate society so far as it could into individual atoms." The tremendous size of the railroad combination was but "an inevitable incident" in their development and was hardly a legitimate reason for ordering their dissolution.

Roosevelt characteristically blamed Holmes's dissent on lack of courage. "I could carve out of a banana a judge with more backbone than that," he reportedly exploded. Always thereafter Holmes and Roosevelt's relationship was subtly hedged in. "Holmes should have been an ideal man on the bench," Roosevelt unforgivingly wrote Lodge two years later. "As a matter of fact he has been a bitter disappointment." The great jurist carried his resentment beyond Roosevelt's grave. Refusing to read a laudatory biography of the late President in 1921, he mused about the incident: "[The affair] . . . broke up our incipient friendship. . . . [Roosevelt] looked on my dissent to the *Northern Securities case* as a political departure (or, I suspect, more truly, couldn't forgive anyone who stood in his way). We talked freely later but it was never the same. . . ." Holmes added a characterization like the one he made of Franklin D. Roosevelt a decade hence. "[Theodore] . . . was very likeable, a big figure, a rather ordinary intellect, with extraordinary gifts, a shrewd and I think pretty unscrupulous politician. He played all his cards—if not more. *R.i.p.*"

The incident was regrettable, for the President's conception of the law roughly paralleled the evolutionary interpretation Holmes had written into his epochal *Common Law* more than twenty years earlier. (Holmes never acknowledged the coincidence, preferring the formulation of one of Roosevelt's senatorial contemporaries: "What the boys like about Roosevelt is that he doesn't care a damn for the law.") Indeed, the President had offered Holmes the seat in 1902 partly in the belief that he would bring breadth and balance to the corporation-oriented High Tribunal—Holmes's labor opinions in Massachusetts had especially impressed him. And though, as Holmes complained, Roosevelt's irritation over the Northern Securities dissent was personal and political, it was also ideological. Too perceptive a student of history to accept the fiction that legal decisions are made in a social and political vacuum, Roosevelt had sought a jurist whose philosophy was consonant with his own; who was, as he apparently told Holmes before he appointed him, a party man in the tradition of Marshall. "The ablest lawyers and greatest judges are men whose past has naturally brought them into close relationship with the wealthiest and most powerful clients," the President wrote shortly before he announced the appointment of Holmes, "and I am glad when I can find a judge who has been able to preserve his aloofness of mind so as to keep his broad humanity of feeling and his sympathy for the class from which he has not drawn his clients. I think it eminently desirable that our Supreme Court should show in unmistakable fashion their entire sympathy with all proper effort to secure the most favorable possible consideration for the men who most need that consideration. . . ."

The prosecution of the Northern Securities Company, which was followed by a successful suit against Swift & Company, heartened social critics everywhere—the more so because of Congress' hostility to comprehensive regulatory legislation. The Republican leaders in both the Senate and House had treated the President's moderate recommendations in December, 1901, with the indifference they habitually reserved for such "visionary" proposals; and during the summer of 1902

Roosevelt had taken the issue to the people, who gave warm approval to his fighting, yet balanced, speeches. When the new Congress convened in December, 1902, he pressed for legislation with considerably more vigor than he had done the year before.

"This country cannot afford to sit supine on the plea that under our peculiar system of government we are helpless in the presence of the new conditions," Roosevelt warned in his second annual message. "The power of the Congress to regulate interstate commerce is an absolute and unqualified grant, and without limitations other than those prescribed by the Constitution." Should the proposed laws transgress the authority granted to Congress, he asserted, "we should not shrink from amending the Constitution so as to secure beyond peradventure the power sought."

These were forceful generalizations. Finally, however, Roosevelt accepted a modest program embracing inspection and publicity of corporate earnings. He would have welcomed more, and he briefly supported a sweeping measure offered by Representative Charles E. Littlefield of Maine. But when Aldrich threatened to defect and Senator Hoar of Massachusetts blundered by appending an even more radical bill of Littlefield's to a measure to create a Department of Commerce and Labor, Roosevelt backed down. He had no alternative, given Aldrich's position. Nevertheless, the President characteristically deluded himself. It was "far more satisfactory to work" with Aldrich, Hanna, Spooner and the rest—"the most powerful factors in Congress"—than with "the radical 'reformers,' like Littlefield," he wrote William Howard Taft.

Roosevelt's pique was understandable. He had already threatened artfully to call a special session if Congress failed to give him a Bureau of Corporations (he ingeniously told the press that John D. Rockefeller was secretly influencing Congress against the measure). He had also made arrangements by then to enact the Elkins anti-rebate measure and to pass a law increasing the Attorney General's power to expedite antitrust proceedings.

Viewed as a whole, and including the epochal Supreme Court cases which Roosevelt initiated, the President's corporation program proved a profoundly creative undertaking. The new Department of Commerce and Labor possessed obvious merits. The Bureau of Corporation's provisions for inspection and partial publicity of corporative activities were a long stride forward. The Elkins Act's proposed elimination of long-standing abuses by powerful shippers was a major, if still in-adequate, reform. And the legislation strengthening the At-torney-General's authority to expedite cases under the Sherman Law was by any criterion salutary.

The trust problem was still far from resolved. Yet the way was prepared for an expansion of the executive power by Roosevelt and those of his successors who grasped the increas-ing complexity of the modern industrial and financial order. At a time when the American people's government was peri-lously close to becoming a mere satellite of big business, Theo-dore Roosevelt's masterful assertion of both his moral and political authority had reaffirmed the people's right to control their affairs through their elected representatives.

A devoted Democrat with little taste for the President's per-sonality most trenchantly stated this overriding fact. Recoiling from his own editor's constant "nagging" of Roosevelt, Joseph Pulitzer privately enjoined him to stop in the spring and sum-mer of 1907. "Support him on the main line—no hyper-criticism of his minor faults," the brilliant publisher ordered the *World's* leading editorial writer, Frank Cobb:

If Roosevelt had never done anything else, and if he had com-mitted a hundred times more mistakes, and if he were one hundred times more impulsive, changeable, unpresidential in dignity, loud and vociferating in manner and speech—. . . if he had done noth-ing else except to start the great machinery of the government and the most powerful force and majesty of the law in the direction of prosecuting these great offenders, he would be entitled to the greatest credit for the greatest service to the nation. This one initia-tive impulse and persevering instinct must be held as offsetting a hundred wrong impulses of a minor character. The greatest breeder of discontent and socialism is lack of confidence in the justice of the law, popular belief that the law is one thing for the rich and another for the poor.

Theodore Roosevelt, wrote the man whose newspaper had opposed his election as Governor in 1898, as Vice-President in 1900, and as President in 1904, "has subjugated Wall Street."

Chapter 10

A Historic Departure

> —*occasionally great national crises arise which call for immediate and vigorous executive action, and . . . in such cases it is the duty of the President to act upon the theory that he is the steward of the people, and . . . that he has the legal right to do whatever the needs of the people demand, unless the Constitution or the laws explicitly forbid him to do it.*
>
> —Theodore Roosevelt, *An Autobiography*

"[THE] TURBULENCE and violence you dread is just as apt to come from an attitude of arrogance on the part of the owners of property and of unwillingness to recognize their duty to the public as from any improper encouragement of labor unions," the President warned Robert Bacon in the fall of 1902 as a summer-long coal strike threatened to incite strife in the great urban centers of the East. "Do you think you are fully alive to the gross blindness of the operators?" Roosevelt asked his old friend Bishop of the *New York Evening Post*. "Do you realize that they are putting a heavy burden on us who stand against socialism; against anarchic disorder?"

What sophisticated Mark Hanna had averted in 1900 had come to pass in 1902. On May 12 virtually the entire anthracite industry in the gloomy, cavernous regions of eastern Pennsylvania had been struck. Two years earlier the operators had made a 10 per cent wage concession to the mine workers in response to Hanna's earnest entreaties. But that had been an election year, and almost no price had seemed too high for William Jennings Bryan's defeat.

With the Great Commoner safely consigned to the Chautauqua circuit in 1902, the operators felt free to follow their normal inclinations. Last-ditch resistance became again their battle order; and when President John Mitchell of the United Mine Workers invited them to discuss a new wage scale in February, they rebuffed him forthwith.

Mitchell desired above all to avoid a strike. He turned therefore to the National Civic Federation, an organization of labor, industrial, and political leaders dedicated to industrial peace. After considerable maneuvering, Mark Hanna, the Federation's chairman, arranged for the presidents of the major coal companies to meet with UMW officers and Federation representatives in New York City.

The ensuing conference proved barren of results, the operators refusing either to recognize the miners' union or to treat their grievances on an industry-wide basis. Their attitude seemed reasonable. The right-of-the-employer concept was deeply ingrained in the public mind, and there were few in America aside from labor leaders and a coterie of intellectuals who perceived how anachronistic the rise of large-scale industry had made it. Clinging to the historic, agrarian-molded conception of individual liberty, the middle classes refused to regard mass unionism as the logical counterweight to mass industrialism; and though they often conceded that workers should be free to join a union, they firmly believed that the employer should suffer no compulsion to recognize it. Not even in the darkest days of this bitter strike, therefore, did the miners' hope for recognition of their union receive broad sympathy.

Yet the average coal company's holdings were so varied and its financial resources so great—six railroad corporations owned upward of 70 per cent of the anthracite mines—that big unionism offered the only means of relief for the mine workers. That was the crux of the recognition issue, and the operators, who were far from novices in the field of labor relations, knew it. As Pulitzer's *World* argued editorially a few months later, "It is preposterous to put the coal trust in the position of a champion of free labor, or any sort of freedom except the freedom to mine coal or to stop mining as it pleases—to raise prices arbitrarily at will—to pay the wages it shall decide upon and exact any hours or conditions of work that it may decree without regard to the public, to its miners, or to the law."

The mine workers' decision to strike on May 12 had not been hastily made. Mitchell had persuaded them against an immediate strike call in April; and at the final meeting sponsored by the Civic Federation he offered to accept a 5 per cent wage increase though the rank and file were demanding 20. But the operators remained intransigent. Even Mark

Hanna, who had been burning the long-distance wires and cabling American business leaders in Europe in a desperate effort to effect a compromise, finally threw up his hands in disgust. "Well! they will not only strike," he angrily exploded, "but they will get ten per cent increase before they settle."

The wage issue at least was more complex than appeared. The anthracite industry was even then "sick," and the operators were probably correct in arguing that an increase in wages would necessitate a rise in prices. Indeed, they offered to open their books to Mitchell, who suggested that they raise prices if necessary. They replied that they would then be subjected to inroads by bituminous coal dealers, already a source of stiff competition. "Anthracite mining is a business, and not a religious, sentimental, or academic proposition," George F. Baer, President of the Philadelphia and Reading Coal and Iron Company and the industry's chief spokesman, remarked a week before the strike started. Baer would later take an even more theological view of management's right to direct the industry's affairs.

Contrariwise, the operators failed to appreciate the compulsions behind the miners' drive for an ever higher standard of living—the only tenable excuse for their beastlike sweat and toil. Roosevelt reflected on this a decade later: "The majority of the men . . . if they wished to progress at all, were compelled to progress not by ceasing to be wage-earners, but by improving the conditions under which all the wage-earners in all the industries of the country lived and worked, as well, of course, as improving their own individual efficiency." In the face of a dramatic increase in the cost of living that almost wiped out the miners' wage increases of two years before, however, the operators persisted in holding out.

Neither were the operators disposed to treat with the miners' other grievances. Hours were long and in some jobs extreme. Machinery for a fair evaluation of the individual miner's daily output was deficient, ton weight varying between 2,740 and 3,190 pounds. The men often spent many hours underground without compensation because of a shortage of cars. And they were subjected to a paternalism that belied the American dream. Even worse was the destruction of life, limb, and health. Irving Stone graphically describes it in his impassioned biography of Clarence Darrow: "Six men out of a thousand were killed every year; hundreds were maimed by explosions and cave-ins; few escaped the ravages of asthma, bronchitis, chronic rheumatism, consumption, heart trouble. By the age of fifty the miners were worn out and broken, good for little but the human slag heap."

When, against this background, the operators turned a deaf ear to Mitchell and Hanna's pleas for compromise—"[The miners] don't suffer," snarled George Baer, "why, they can't even speak English"—the coal workers had little recourse but to strike. Less than three weeks after they went out on May 12 a substantial number of engineers, firemen, and pumpmen joined them. It was the greatest work stoppage to that time.

In Washington that spring President Roosevelt followed the strike with increasing alarm. Violence was minimal at first; and the press generally sympathized with the miners. Until well into the summer, moreover, the stockpiles held up. Yet the strike was not two weeks old before the price of coal began to rise sharply. Meanwhile accounts of clashes between strikers and non-strikers began to appear beside reports that the independent operators were prevented from coming to terms by the six great railroads which controlled the means of distributing the coal. Nor were the operators disposed to tighten their own belts. "Official after official has had his salary increased," the *United Mine Workers' Journal* irately charged, and "President Truesdale, of the Lackawanna, got an increase of $10,000 per year."

Of all the charges and countercharges, the one which most interested the President was that the anthracite industry was a powerful, closely knit trust. Late in May the *Springfield Republican* pointed out that there was but one seller of coal to the dealer and consumer and that they must meet his terms or go without. "It would be difficult to conceive of a monopoly more perfectly established or operated than this monopoly which holds complete possession of a great store of nature most necessary to the life of the day," the *Republican* contended. "There is but one way to deal with [it] . . . public control or ownership."

By August the President was seriously considering antitrust proceedings against the coal companies. But after Attorney-General Knox advised him that suit would fail for want of evidence under the Sherman Law, he dropped the idea. "There is literally nothing, so far as I have yet been able to find out, which the national government has any power to do in the matter," he wrote Lodge, who was fretting over the strike's probable impact on the congressional elections in November. "Nor can I imagine any remedial measure of immediate benefit that could be taken in Congress," Roosevelt continued. "That it would be a good thing to have national control, or at least supervision, over these big coal corporations, I am sure; but that would simply have to come as an incident of the general movement to exercise control over such corporations."

The President's observations were to the point, given Congress' bedrock conservatism. Yet the public temper was rising daily and would continue to rise until the strike was settled. By early August panic buying and profiteering had pushed the price of pea coal from $2.40 a ton to $6 in New York; and by October some schools in New York and New England would be forced to shut down for lack of fuel. Available stocks, which were everywhere low, would then be commanding from $30 to $35 per ton. Meanwhile the anthracite operators impeded conversion to bituminous by tying up their coal cars.

To make matters worse, conservatives now launched a counteroffensive. Late in the summer Roosevelt's erstwhile mayoral opponent, Abram S. Hewitt, charged that mild-mannered John Mitchell was trying to make himself "the dictator of the coal business." Hewitt's charge pierced Mitchell's defenses, for the UMW leader burned for personal acceptance by management; within the decade he would destroy his career in quest of it. Almost abjectly, he replied through the *Independent* that recognition of the UMW "is not and never has been the paramount issue of the present strike."

Many moderate editorial voices echoed Mitchell's disavowal. Nevertheless, the deep prejudice against unions which had been tempered theretofore by the manifest arrogance of the operators began to assert itself. When reports of violence in the coal fields filled the news columns in September—on-the-spot observers charged they were grossly exaggerated by the metropolitan press—many middle-class conservatives accepted Hewitt's emotion-packed assertion as conclusive. The real issue, said the new president of Princeton University, Woodrow Wilson, was the union's drive "to win more power."

Whether the nation as a whole would also have turned against the miners is debatable. The UMW's resolve to prevent non-union men from returning to the pits, the violence that

must have ensued, and the costly discomfort to the public
from the shortage of coal all suggest that the middle classes
would have shifted their sympathies eventually; the unrelieved
arrogance of the operators together with the popular resentment of business malpractices in general suggest that support
of the mine workers would have continued. It is virtually
certain, however, that Roosevelt could have swung opinion
either way had he elected to take a one-sided stand.

The President's personal intervention came only after all
possibilities except federal seizure of the mines had been seemingly exhausted. During the summer effort after effort had
failed to bring the operators to terms. Even Hanna proved
powerless to move them though he and Mitchell persuaded
the bituminous miners from going out in sympathy. "It is one
of the proudest moments of my life that I can state . . . that
the men stood by their word," Hanna told a Chautauqua audience after the bituminous convention voted against a sympathy
strike on July 17.

Meanwhile Cabot Lodge showered importunities on Roosevelt. "By the first week in November if the strike does not
stop and coal begins to go down we shall have [a political]
. . . overturn," he warned. "Is there any form of pressure we
can put on the operators who are driving us to ruin? The
unions are just as obstinate but the rising public wrath makes
for them and they stand all the firmer."

Although Roosevelt saw Lodge's point, he felt helpless to
act. "I am genuinely independent of the big monied men in
all matters where I think the interests of the public are concerned," he replied, "and probably I am the first President
of recent times of whom this could be truthfully said. . . .
But where I do not grant any favors to these big monied men
which I do not think the country requires that they should
have, it is out of the question for me to expect them to grant
favors to me in return. . . . I am," he concluded, "at my wits'
end how to proceed."

The President continued, however, to grope for a practical
solution. After talking to Root, Knox, Quay, and Governor
Murray Crane of Massachusetts, he decided to invite the operators to confer with him. He contemplated telling them that
he would "advise action [presumably to Congress] along the
lines I have explained in my speeches but of a much more
radical type in reference to their business unless they wake

up." But the same day he made that decision Crane publicly called on him to meet with both the operators and miners. Roosevelt thereupon abandoned the idea of negotiating with the operators alone. On October 1 he requested the leaders of both groups to confer with him. Still under the delusion that anthracite could not be replaced by bituminous, he wrote his sister Bamie that there would have been no warrant in interfering in a strike of iron workers, for iron was not a necessity. But, he continued, "I could . . . [not] see misery and death come to the great masses of the people in our large cities and sit by idly."

The presidential summonses were duly honored, though not in good grace by the operators. A little before eleven on the morning of October 3, the leaders of the operators and the coal miners entered Blair House to await the President. They stood in knots at opposite ends of a long, second-floor room talking self-consciously. Shortly the President, who had been painfully injured in an automobile accident three weeks before, was wheeled in.

Roosevelt opened the meeting by disclaiming either the right or the duty to intervene. He presumed, instead, on the conferees' good will. "With all the earnestness there is in me," he solemnly declared, "I ask that there be an immediate resumption of operations in the coal mines in some such way as will without a day's unnecessary delay, meet the crying needs of the people. I appeal to your patriotism, to the spirit that sinks personal consideration and makes individual sacrifices for the general good."

John Mitchell then rose to speak. Never, wrote Mark Sullivan, did the swarthy, ex-breaker boy appear to greater advantage. "His natural distinction of person and manner was accentuated by his affecting the sober garb and the 'reversed' collar of the clergyman," and though the gathering was of the strongest men, "he stood out easily as the most intelligent force of all, save Roosevelt." Eschewing recrimination—for many weeks the operators had been abusing Mitchell vilely— he spoke simply and directly:

I am much pleased, Mr. President, with what you say. We are willing that you shall name a tribunal which shall determine the issues that have resulted in the strike; and if the gentlemen representing the operators will accept the award or decision of such a tribunal, the miners will willingly accept it, even if it be against our claims.

Mitchell's measured words outraged George Baer, the operators' spokesman. Two and one-half months earlier the Reading president had invoked the divine right of plutocracy against suggestions that he agree to mediation. "The rights and interests of the laboring man will be protected and cared for," he had then written, "not by the labor agitators, but by the Christian men to whom God in His infinite wisdom has given the control of the property interests of the country, and upon the successful Management of which so much depends." Now, though no longer blasphemous, he stood just as firmly on business' right to conduct its own affairs. His flintlike eyes flashed fire at the President no less than at Mitchell as he referred to the "crimes inaugurated by the United Mine Workers, over whom John Mitchell, whom you invited to meet you, is chief" and lectured Roosevelt that "the duty of the hour is not to waste time negotiating with the fomenters of this anarchy." There should be no governmental interference, he added, except through the Courts of Common Pleas in the mining districts (the established bulwarks of the status quo).

Throughout the long day, broken only by lunch, the operators continued to castigate Mitchell, the mineworkers, and the President. They dismissed the union members as anarchists and criminals; they told the President he was asking them to "deal with a set of outlaws"; and they openly accused him of making "a grandstand play." There was "only one man in that conference who behaved like a gentleman," Roosevelt reported, "and that man was not I."

Between expletives, the operators made three concrete proposals: (1) the government should send federal troops into the anthracite regions; (2) the United Mine Workers should be prosecuted under the terms of the Sherman Antitrust Law; and (3) the miners should be forced to return to work at once, their grievances to be adjudicated by the local courts. Mitchell stoically rejected all three proposals, and late in the afternoon the conference terminated.

Momentary depression gripped Roosevelt that night. "I have tried and failed," he wrote Mark Hanna. Mitchell's proposition was "entirely fair and reasonable," he continued. "I felt he did very well to keep his temper. Between times they insulted me for not preserving order." He did not know what his next move would be. "I feel most strongly that the attitude of the operators is one which accentuates the need of the Government having some power of supervision and regulation over such corporations. I would like to make a fairly radical experiment on the anthracite coal business to start with!"

To Roosevelt's credit, he resisted the action that would have resolved his political and economic, if not his ideological, dilemma. He could have broken the strike with a stroke of his pen by calling out federal troops as the operators requested and President Cleveland had done during the Pullman strike of 1894. Coal would then have been mined, prices would have dropped in time for the November elections, and he would have received the acclaim that is the man of action's desideratum. So acute was public distress and so exaggerated reports of union violence, that he might well have won overwhelming support from all but labor men had he pursued such a decisive course. Even newspapers which had been sympathetic to the United Mine Workers were demanding an end to conflict between strikers and non-strikers. The union men "can not expect, and we believe do not ask, for public support of a strike that threatens to degenerate into a murderous plot," the *Philadelphia North American* thundered. "It is not a coal strike, but an insurrection," the *New York Journal of Commerce* angrily charged.

In the face of this rising hysteria, the President maintained his balance. "Have you ever read Hay and Nicolay's *Lincoln?*" he wrote Robert Bacon. "Just as Lincoln got contradictory advice from the extremists of both sides at every phase of the struggle for unity and freedom, so I now have carefully to guard myself against the extremists of both sides. The men who wish me to proceed under the Sherman antitrust law against the miners' union are if possible one shade more foolish than the others who wish me to proceed under the same law against the coal operators as such." He added that the same was true of those who wanted him to call out the troops "on the present state of facts and without further investigation."

The President did not know it, but he had come almost to the crossroads. Shortly after the failure of the conference in Blair House, he sent Carroll Wright to Mitchell with a proposal that the strikers return to work pending an investigation by a presidential commission. He pledged himself to do all that he could to implement the commission's report. But as Mitchell explained in turning it down, the miners had already gone halfway and had no reason to believe the operators would "do us justice in the future."

There now occurred an event which served powerfully to make the operators more tractable. For some time the operators had held that great numbers of miners would go back to work if protected from reprisals by zealous union members. When, accordingly, Governor William A. Stone of Pennsylvania called out the entire state militia to maintain order, moderate observers sensed that the critical test had come. Let the operators now "put 100,000 men to work" under the protection of the militia, the *New York Times* asserted, or else "send for Mitchell and settle the strike on the best terms they can make."

The operators' worst fears were soon realized, for the great majority of strikers continued to stay out. Baer and his imperious associates were almost trapped. Just one alternative short of concessions to the miners remained. The government might still be persuaded to break the strike with federal troops. It was a thin reed, but the *New York Sun* waved it as if it had been a battle standard. "Pennsylvania is in a state of anarchy beyond the power of her entire Guard to control," the *Sun* proclaimed. The public demand for suppression of the Filipino guerrillas had been fulfilled. "Why is not the same far-seeing patriotism and resolute loyalty to the flag and to the preservation of the rights it guarantees to its citizens now guiding those concerned with the coal strike, officially or otherwise?"

While the editors of the *Sun* and other conservatives were censuring Roosevelt for bringing the operators and strike leaders together, another conservative was endorsing the President's conduct. "I am especially disturbed and vexed by the tone and substance of the operators' deliverances," Grover Cleveland wrote Roosevelt. Could not the operators and miners be persuaded to make a truce until the country's most pressing needs were fulfilled? Cleveland's proposal was even more impractical than the one Roosevelt had pressed upon Mitchell after the failure of the conference; yet it assured the President of Cleveland's good will.

Impressed by the failure of the strikers to return to work under the protection of the Pennsylvania troops and emboldened by the moral support of the nation's most eminent living conservative, Roosevelt now evolved a plan as drastic as any he ever formulated: he would send federal troops into the anthracite fields to seize the mines and run them as a receivership.

The President had not come lightly to this momentous decision. "You were no alarmist," he wrote Murray Crane shortly afterward, "and when you saw the coal famine impending, with untold misery as the result, with the certainty of riots which might develop into social war to follow, I did not feel like longer delaying."

The position of the operators, that the public had no rights in the case, was not tenable for a moment, and what most astounded me therein was their . . . ignorance of the fact that their violence and unreason and their inability or refusal to consider the terrible nature of the catastrophe impending over the poor were all combining to produce a most dangerous feeling in the country at large—a feeling which might have effect in great social disturbance. . . . Even without such a crisis the first long-continued spell of bitter weather meant misery and violence in acute form in our big cities.

Roosevelt called in Knox and Root soon after he made his decision. "I explained that I knew this action would form an evil precedent . . . and that they should both write letters of protest against it if they wished." Knox interposed legal objections, then submitted gracefully. ("Ah, Mr. President," he responded when Roosevelt later asked his counsel on another matter, "why have such a beautiful action marred by the taint of legality?") Root acquiesced reluctantly, purportedly because he was not sure the President would act. "Theodore was a bit of a bluffer occasionally," he recalled, "and at the same time he had nerve to go on—to take a chance his statements would have the deciding effect and, if not, to go on and trust the country would back him up."

For his part, Roosevelt professed to believe that he was simply giving the Constitution a broad construction. His plan, he explained in his *Autobiography*, illustrated what "I have called the Jackson-Lincoln theory of the presidency"; or, as he put it to Murray Crane, it was the opposite of "the Buchanan principle of striving to find some constitutional reason for inaction."

Representative James E. Watson's recollection of an exchange with Roosevelt at the time probably comes closest to re-creating the President's real attitude: " 'But,' I said to [him], '. . . what about the Constitution of the United States? What about seizing private property for public purposes without due process of law?' I recall very vividly. He stopped suddenly, took hold of my shoulder and turned me about facing him and looked squarely into my eyes as he fairly shouted, 'The Constitution was made for the people and not the people for the Constitution.' "

Meanwhile the President sought out a general who "possessed the necessary good sense, judgment, and nerve to act." He found him in Major General J. M. Schofield, "a most respectable looking old boy, with side-whiskers and a black skull-cap, without any of the outward aspect of the conventional military dictator." Roosevelt told Schofield that if forced to move it would be only because the crisis was almost as serious as the Civil War. He added that the general was to obey only his orders and that if served with a writ he was to send it to the President as had been done under Lincoln. He then gave his plan an aura of constitutionality by secretly arranging for Governor Stone of Pennsylvania to request federal troops on signal. He did not, however, take Stone into his confidence; nor did he delude himself that he was acting on a liberal interpretation of the Constitution.* (A half century later Roosevelt's "stewardship" theory was ringingly denounced in the federal courts when a government attorney invoked it in support of President Truman's seizure of the steel industry in 1952. "With all due deference and respect for that great President [Roosevelt] . . . ," declared Judge David A. Pine, "I am obliged to say that his statements do not comport with our recognized theory of government, but with a theory with which our government of laws and not of men is constantly at war.")

In a move that testified subtly to the extraordinary power Pierpont Morgan wielded over American life, Root meanwhile

* Art. IV, Sec. 4 specifies that federal troops may be called out "on application of the legislature, or of the executive (when the legislature cannot be convened) against domestic violence." At the time Roosevelt contemplated action there was no evidence that the state militia was unable to control violence.

visited the financier in New York. Root had asked for and
been granted permission to act as a private citizen. Morgan
had no especial sympathy for the miners or their grievances;
but he was incensed at the operators for botching their affairs
and was fearful that the strike would have serious social consequences. He must also have been agitated by Roosevelt's
plan for a government receivership. So when Root suggested
that the President appoint an independent arbitration commission, Morgan heartily endorsed the idea.

On Sunday, October 12, Morgan pressed Root's proposal
on George Baer who came up from Philadelphia. Two days
later, Morgan and Robert Bacon speeded to Washington to
present the operators' tentative approval to the President. "It
was a strange experience for Morgan," Frederick Lewis Allen
writes. "Only a few months before he had faced Roosevelt as
a man accused of the offense of setting up machinery to bring
peace among warring railroad companies; this time he faced
him as an ally in setting up machinery to bring peace between
railroad companies and organized labor."

There now unfolded a high drama, or as Roosevelt dubbed
it, "a ludicrous comedy." The agreement Morgan wrung from
the operators called for the commission to include "a man who
by active participation in mining and selling coal is familiar
with the physical and commercial features of the business,"
but it failed to provide for a labor representative. The mine
workers resented the omission; and though they agreed to the
general plan, they requested a fairer representation, specifically the addition of a union man and a Roman Catholic cleric.
The operators demurred; they also refused to accept former
President Cleveland, whom Roosevelt wanted to appoint in
place of the army engineer called for in the agreement. An
impasse again threatened.

Root resolved it temporarily by telegraphing Morgan, who
had returned to New York, to send down a member of his
firm for consultation. "That night Bob Bacon and Perkins
came on from Morgan, both of them nearly wild," Roosevelt
wrote a few days later. "The operators were balking. They
refused positively to accept the two extra men, and Morgan
said he could not get them to accept it. It appeared," the President continued, "that the men who were back of them, who
were in the narrow, bourgeois, commercial world, were still
in a condition of wooden-headed obstinacy and stupidity."

For two hours the President argued with Morgan's emissaries, who kept an open line to the financier and Baer in New York. The operators were anxious to settle—they had undoubtedly learned that drastic action was in the offing—and they were willing to accept a Catholic prelate, even a liberal one. But they would not agree to the appointment of a labor leader, for they continued to regard union recognition as the paramount issue.

Suddenly the President conceived a solution. He would appoint a union man to the sociologist's post, but would call him a sociologist. "I at last grasped the fact," Roosevelt explained to Lodge, "that the mighty brains of these captains of industry had formulated the theory that they would rather have anarchy than tweedledum, but if I would use the word tweedledee they would hail it as meaning peace."

With that brilliant stroke the President cut the Gordian knot. The operators saved face among themselves if no one else. The miners won a fair representation, Roosevelt naming E. E. Clark, Grand Chief of the Order of Railway Conductors, as the sociologist. And the President avoided an action that was clearly extraconstitutional and probably unconstitutional. The infant discipline of sociology was also given a new distinction. "Sociologist," wrote Roosevelt after Clark's name on the list handed the press, "means a man who has thought and studied deeply on social questions and has practically applied his knowledge."

The miners returned to the pits almost at once, and five months later the arbitration commission submitted a report moderately favorable to their demands. Wages were broadly increased by 10 per cent. Hours were generally reduced to nine and in a few jobs to eight per day. Many of management's more flagrant abuses were corrected, though the old method of weighing coal continued. And the Anthracite Board of Conciliation was created to settle future differences. The operators won their point on nonrecognition; but only formally, for representatives of the UMW were granted a seat on the new Board of Conciliation. The operators also received a 10 per cent increase in the price of coal. Peace had come to the anthracite fields.

The passing of a half century has failed to diminish the historical significance of the President's achievement. It is probably true, as his detractors contend, that he was animated more by fear of social upheaval than genuine sympathy for the mine workers' plight; that his plan to use federal troops reflected an authoritarian disregard of legal restraint; and that Lodge's hysterical pleas for action in the interest of everyday Republican politics hastened his decision to act. But it is also true, as the *Springfield Republican* declared at the time, that he had thwarted the operators' drive to crush the United Mine Workers:

This is the great distinguishing fact of what is to be the memorable coal strike of 1902; for while the operators still nominally refuse to recognize the mine workers' union, that union nevertheless is a party to the President's plan of arbitration and is so recognized by him. What the operators said they never would concede has been conceded, and hence, and hence only, does the strike draw rapidly to an end.

Perhaps labor could have got even more than it did. The impassioned agitator, Mary H. "Mother" Jones, thought that it could have; and she so informed John Mitchell. But Samuel Gompers believed otherwise; he congratulated Mitchell on the UMW's "splendid" achievement. Clarence Darrow, who served as counsel to the mine workers, also felt labor had won.

The personal significance of the President's action was not that he ended the strike, though he prided himself that he had. Nor was it in the great service he incidentally rendered the American labor movement, though he also took satisfaction in that. It was, rather, that in both his contemplated use of federal troops and in his actual success in winning an arbitration agreement he had by his own lights acted fairly. The precedents were overwhelmingly for government intervention in management's interest. By refusing to follow them, by making the government, as Mowry phrases it "a third force and partner in major labor disputes," Roosevelt gave meaning to what he was to call his "Square Deal." The anthracite intervention, coupled with his blows against the trusts, indelibly stamped him within a year of his accession as the first President of the modern era who was not indissolubly wedded to the business point of view.

Chapter 11

Affairs of State

> *"When I left the presidency, I finished seven and a half years of administration, during which not one shot had been fired against a foreign foe. We were at absolute peace, and there was no nation in the world . . . whom we had wronged, or from whom we had anything to fear."*
> —Theodore Roosevelt, *An Autobiography*

No FUNCTION of executive leadership more fascinated Roosevelt than the conduct of foreign affairs. He cheerfully accepted the responsibilities that were thrust upon him and went out of his way to shoulder others that were not. He gloried in the opportunities for national expression afforded by a world in flux. He viewed with impatience and at times forebodings his countrymen's slowness to face the realities of the world struggle for power. He acted with impetuosity and restraint, with bluster and sensitivity, with belligerence and accommodation. And he acted always to promote the American national interest as he conceived it. Neither the idealistic peace movement of the Bryans and the Carnegies nor the gathering internationalism of the era diverted him from that course, though he often used the internationalist vocabulary and eventually supported arbitration agreements of a sort.

During Theodore Roosevelt's presidency the United States established a proprietary interest in Latin America. It interjected itself self-consciously into European power politics. It took an assertive interest in the Pacific and parts of the Far East. It modernized its army and expanded its battle fleet. It helped negotiate peace between the Tsar-wearied Russians and the empire-minded Japanese. And it pursued a generally enlightened policy toward its newly acquired colonial dependencies.

Roosevelt was not the sole architect of these momentous policies. Some were inherited from the McKinley administration, some were conceived by the President's able subordinates, and many grew logically out of the stresses and strains of a world in turmoil. Still others reflected the influence of Admiral Mahan. Yet the controlling intelligence was Roosevelt's. Concluding that there could be no retreat from a power position that the Spanish-American War had dramatized but which the revolution in communications and the rise of industrialism had forged, he stamped his imprint upon American foreign policy with a force exceeded by only a few wartime Presidents and equaled, perhaps, by no peacetime President. From 1902 through early 1909 the unfolding drama of American foreign relations is essentially the story of the vigorous interplay of Roosevelt's personality and the surging mainstream of events.

Two weeks after he took office Roosevelt plunged into the administration of the colonial dependencies. His attitude of *noblesse oblige,* his belief that the United States should impose a better order on the ruins of the one it had destroyed, and his conviction that despotism was the high road to disaster, all impelled him to take an enlightened interest in the administration of the empire; and so did his urge to spread American culture in the manner of the great nations of the past:

Rome expanded and passed away, but all western Europe, both Americas, Australia and large parts of Asia and Africa to this day continue the history of Rome. . . . Spain expanded and fell, but a whole continent to this day speaks Spanish and is covered with commonwealths of the Spanish tongue and culture. . . . England expanded and England will fall. But think of what she will leave behind her . . .

Accepting literally Rudyard Kipling's charge to

"Take up the White Man's burden—
Send forth the best ye breed—"

Roosevelt announced in late September, 1901, that "absolutely no appointments in the insular possessions will be dictated or controlled by political considerations" lest the United States tread the path of Spain. To that dictum he adhered during the next seven years. At almost the same time he urged that the United States make the Filipinos "fit for self-government after the fashion of the really free nations." To this estimable goal he also adhered, acting always, however, within the limits set by his conception of America's vital interests.

The administration of the insular empire under Roosevelt was not without controversy. One of the earliest incidents involved the President's effort to resolve a long quarrel between the Filipinos and the Spanish Dominicans who had acquired tremendous holdings of choice farmlands under the Spanish.

Shortly before Roosevelt became President, William Howard Taft had proposed that the United States purchase title to the disputed lands and restore them to the Filipino farmers. In February, 1902, Roosevelt decided to send Taft to the Vatican to make the necessary arrangements. Three months later Taft was received with gracious circumspection by venerable Leo XIII. The Vatican consented to sell the friars' lands, but the negotiations broke down when it refused to withdraw the Dominicans as the Filipinos and the American hierarchy, which wanted to send over American priests, desired. Taft reopened the negotiations a year later. "The matter assumed all the aspects of a New England horse trade," Henry Pringle writes; not until November, 1903, when the United States agreed to pay approximately 50 per cent more than the appraised value of the lands and to accept the Spanish friars, was it finally settled.

Superficially, the Vatican had won its case. But in reality the Roosevelt administration had won a decisive victory. The Spanish friars failed to regain their power—only 200 stayed on in the Islands—and the former church lands became the basis of a native yeoman class. By 1912, 50,000 Filipinos worked small farms purchased on generous terms from the American government.

This enlightened diplomacy was bitterly criticized by some American Catholics who refused to credit the charges against the friars and bitterly resented the establishment of a secular school system on the islands. The President refused, however, to yield to their protests. He heartily endorsed Taft's effort to create an educational system on the American model and he warned several times that it should be completely nonsectarian. "The teachers must not only be careful to abstain from taking sides for or against Catholicism or any other creed," he wrote Taft in July, 1902, "but they must be careful to abstain from action which gives the impression that they are thus taking sides."

Meanwhile an articulate minority of American Catholics tried to enlist Roosevelt's support in crushing a group of Filipinos who had severed ties with Rome—the Aglipayans. Roosevelt bitterly resented their proposal, and on June 22, 1904, he wrote Bishop Frederick Z. Rooker of Jaro in the Philippines one of the angriest letters he ever penned to a member of the Roman Catholic hierarchy. He said in part:

Now, my dear Bishop Rooker, to be frank with you, your letter makes it evident that what you in your heart desire is to take the place of the friars, and have American troops take the place of the Spanish troops in upholding a clerical and political despotism in the islands, without regard to the wishes of the islanders. You say that you wish the civil government to come to an end, the power to be taken out of the hands of the natives, and a military government established under some general like my good friend Wood, with instructions instantly and without regard to law to give you and your colleagues possession of all the churches and other property which the Aglipayans claim. In other words, you desire us to establish a military despotism in the interests of the Catholic Church. I think you must be singularly ignorant of the temper of the American people if you believe such a proposition feasible.

The President meanwhile sought to endow the island dependencies in the Caribbean and the Pacific with modest economic advantages. As John Blum writes, "he defied the sugar lobby, the Democrats, and a considerable fraction of Republicans to obtain for Cuba a tariff advantage essential for the economic stability of the government he had helped to establish there"; and he would have done likewise for the Philippines had the Republican Old Guard permitted him. But it did not. If the President had not known it before, he knew thereafter that no consideration of rational economics, of general welfare, and certainly not of the "White Man's burden" could touch the Grand Old Party's most sacred of cows.

Fortunately, other channels of executive action remained open. Before and after Roosevelt's inauguration in 1905 the economic, political, and social uplifting of the new colonials advanced markedly. Railroads, sanitation facilities, and schools were built. Colonial administrators were urged to give the islanders greater participation in the conduct of their affairs.

"I shall endeavor," Roosevelt said more than once, "progressively to increase the share which the Filipinos themselves take in the government of the islands, letting the advance in this direction be rapid or slow precisely in accordance with the capacity which the Filipinos themselves develop for self-restraint, moderation, and ability to combine the enjoyment of liberty with the enforcement of order." He failed finally to provide enough self-government to satisfy the anti-imperialists, and he gave too much to please the unregenerate Old Guard. Yet he turned over to his successor the most progressively governed colonial empire in the world.

Roosevelt steadfastly refused, however, to make a categorical promise of independence. He feared for one thing that Japan or Germany would move in if the United States moved out; he believed for another that the Filipinos were then incapable of self-government. He emphasized the latter in a moving letter to the high-minded anti-imperialist, Senator Hoar of Massachusetts:

Now I do not want to make a promise which may not be kept. Above all things, I want for myself and for the nation that there shall be good faith. Senator Hoar, I honor you and revere you. I think you are animated by as lofty a spirit of patriotism and of devotion to and belief in mankind as any man I have ever met in public life. I hate to seem in your eyes to be falling short of my duty on a great question. I ask you to believe that after much painful thought, after much groping and some uncertainty as to where my duty lay, I am now doing it as light has been given me to see it.

The President's attitude might have been more favorably reviewed by historians had he always expressed himself on that high plane. But he had not. During the campaign of 1900 he had called Aguinaldo's beleaguered patriots "Talgal bandits," "Chinese halfbreeds," and worse; he had refused to concede the legitimacy (whatever the practicality) of the native independence movement; and he had defended the American troops' cruel repression of Aguinaldo.

The organization and administration of the new possessions and the Cuban protectorate had been a collective enterprise. But Roosevelt was responsible for the more strictly diplomatic accomplishments of his administrations. One of the earliest of these was the settlement of the long-standing Alaskan boundary dispute.

Thirty-seven years before Secretary of State William H. Seward arranged the purchase of Alaska, the British and Russian governments had ratified a treaty which loosely defined the line between British Columbia and the Alaskan Panhandle as running thirty miles inland from the head of tidewater. But after the discovery of gold in the Canadian Klondike in 1896, Canadians sought to redefine the boundary so as to give them access to the gold fields. National passions momentarily flared as Whitehall found itself caught between American enmity and Canadian resentment against imperial rule. In October, 1899, however, Secretary of State Hay arranged a *modus vivendi.*

Roosevelt never had believed that the Canadian claim was valid. "If we suddenly claimed a part of Nova Scotia you would not arbitrate," he wrote Sir Arthur Lee while he was still Vice-President. "This Canadian claim . . . is entirely modern. Twenty years ago the Canadian maps showed the lines just as ours did." For several months after he took the presidential oath, however, Roosevelt "let sleeping dogs lie." Not until March, 1902, when he learned that gold might be discovered in the disputed territory, did he act. Then, in a first display of "Big Stick" diplomacy, he brought the full force of his powerful personality to bear upon the British and Canadians. If gold is discovered, the President told a London *Times* correspondent in a White House interview, "I shall send up engineers to run our line as we assert it and I shall send troops to guard and hold it." A few weeks later he ordered Root to move "additional troops . . . as quietly and unostentatiously as possible to Southern Alaska, so as to be able promptly to prevent any possible disturbance."

Admitting that he wished "to save his face," Sir Wilfrid Laurier, the Canadian Prime Minister, finally suggested arbitration. Only after he realized that the presence of three Americans on the proposed six man commission portended no worse than a deadlock did Roosevelt consent; and then he let it out that he would instruct the American commissions "in no case to yield any of our claim."

Negotiations continued during the summer and fall of 1902, though the President diverted much of his energy to the settlement of the anthracite strike and the Panama Canal controversy with Colombia. Then, in January, 1903, Hay and Sir Michael Herbert, the British Ambassador, signed a treaty providing for an arbitration tribunal of six "impartial jurists of repute" who would "consider judicially the question submitted to them." Three were to be selected by the President of the United States; three by His Britannic Majesty.

The treaty received a rough reception in the Senate. At one point the President was forced to make its wording more palatable, and for a while it seemed doubtful that the Senate would ratify it under any circumstances. Finally, however, Roosevelt confided to Lodge that he would appoint Root, Senator George Turner of Washington, and Lodge himself if the Senate approved the treaty. Lodge thereupon whispered the President's intentions about the Senate chamber, and opposition vanished.

The formal announcement of the President's appointments provoked a resoundingly hostile reaction. "All my illusions are gone," Sir Michael Herbert exclaimed. Roosevelt "is obstinate and unreasonable." Laurier was similarly outraged; he even talked of breaking off further negotiations. Nor did the American press spare the President.

"President Roosevelt ought not to appoint . . . [Lodge] to the place," the *Springfield Republican* declared. "[Lodge] has been playing for years to the gallery where the England-haters sit," the *Hartford Courant* added, "and to the determination of this boundary question he does not bring the judicial mind."

Roosevelt saw no reason to regard his appointments as a breach of faith. He had consistently made clear his determination to secure a decision favorable to the United States, and he continued to press the American case on the British even after the commissioners were named. At the instance of Lodge, he also considered ending negotiations. But after discussions with Hay and Ambassador Choate, he dismissed the proposal. The Alaskan controversy is "altogether too important a matter to take a snap judgment or to forfeit a single chance of bringing it to a successful conclusion," he cabled the Senator in London. "There is not at present one single act which would justify so much as considering the breaking off of the negotiations."

Nevertheless, the President refused to relax his resolve to run the boundary line with American troops should a settlement fail. He was supported in this by Hay, Choate, and Root, all of whom were conservative in temperament and two of whom were Anglophiles. Indeed, it may well have been this threat to run the line on his own that moved Lord Alverstone to support the burden of the United States' demands. Thus Beale concludes: "The plan to use troops resulted not just from the desire of an impetuous President to bully or to have his own way; it grew in part at least out of a calm decision of cautious advisers, who feared growing frontier tension created by a lawless population might blow up into a dangerous international incident if uncontrolled."

The Alaskan boundary dispute was neither the first nor the last time Roosevelt "spoke softly" and waved a "big stick" to impress upon rival powers the righteousness or dominance of American claims. During the winter of 1902-03 he pressed Kaiser Wilhelm II's Imperial Germany hard; and in 1904 he told all Europe that the United States was assuming the duty of policing the more impecunious Latin American nations.

The origins of the Venezuelan crisis and the Roosevelt Corollary to the Monroe Doctrine were deep-rooted and tangled. Both grew out of the perennial instability of Latin American governments. Both underlined Roosevelt's concern for the United States' strategic interests in the Caribbean. And both reflected America's new power position vis-à-vis Europe. Of the two, the Venezuelan affair was the more immediately serious, the Roosevelt Corollary the more far-reaching. Out of one grew the other.

The Venezuelan crisis had come to a head in early December, 1902. Despairing of diplomatic efforts to collect debts due their nationals, Germany and Great Britain attempted to coerce Venezuela by blockading its coastline and seizing or sinking its gunboats. The American government had first learned of Germany's intentions in December, 1901. Hay seemingly acquiesced, warning only that the United States would tolerate no territorial aggrandizement; but on December 17 Roosevelt ordered Culebra, off Puerto Rico, to be transferred to the Navy Department in order that a base might be established "in case of sudden war." More precautionary measures followed. Arrangements were made to mobilize the fleet in the Caribbean at the end of the year. In the early Summer the Navy ordered "a careful reconnaissance of the terrain most likely to be occupied by German forces as well as a detailed examination of all localities where landing operations might be affected." And Admiral Dewey was put in command of the Caribbean fleet, an unprecedented assignment for a four-star admiral.

On December 8, 1902, the day Dewey raised his flag on the gunboat *Mayflower*, Germany and Great Britain severed relations with Venezuela. Within a fortnight they seized several Venezuelan naval vesels, bombarded two forts at Puerto Cabello, and established a formal blockade of the Venezuelan coast. Roosevelt thereupon moved the battle fleet to Trinidad, 500 miles closer to Venezuela. Apparently he also talked pointedly to the German Ambassador.

Results soon followed. Hay warned the German chargé d'affaires that Congress might call on the President to uphold the Monroe Doctrine. Meanwhile, Ambassador Theodor von Holleben sent two urgent warnings to Berlin. And on December 10 Speck von Sternburg, an old friend of the President's, was called to Berlin to give his impressions to high German officials. He stunned them, if the account he wrote Roosevelt is correct. "Nothing could have pleased me more," he confided to the President, "because it gave me a chance to tell them the truth. I've told them every bit of it and I have used rather plain talk. . . . Fear I've knocked them down rather roughly, but should consider myself a cowardly weakling if I had let things stand as they were." Against this background Germany agreed to arbitrate; it also decided to replace Ambassador von Holleben with von Sternburg, a change Roosevelt had long urged.

The Venezuelan affair proved a watershed in the President's thinking. At the start of the crisis he had believed that European intervention in Latin America was tolerable if it did not lead to territorial aggrandizement. By its end, however, he had begun to foresee the consequences of such a policy. Less than a month afterward he took the first tentative step toward formulation of the "Roosevelt Corollary" to the Monroe Doctrine. The catalytic agent was a talk with von Sternburg in mid-March. "Speck was in today," Roosevelt wrote Hay in confidence, "evidently inspired from Berlin, to propose for our consideration in the future the advisability of having the great Powers collectively stand back of some syndicate which should take possession of the finances of Venezuela."

The German proposal had an abstract appeal. There was no assurance that the Venezuelan dictator had reformed permanently. Nor was there a guarantee that similar crises would not occur in any of a dozen Latin American nations. Yet the plan implied compromise of the substance of the Monroe Doctrine, and Roosevelt was quick to sense it. His "first blush" judgment, he told the new German Ambassador, was that it "would pave the way for reducing Venezuela to a condition like that of Europe, and that the American people interpreted the Monroe Doctrine as meaning of course that no European power should gain *control* of any American republic." The whole debt-collection process, he observed to Hay, could prove a "subterfuge" for exercising control.

Conditions in debt-ridden and revolution-wracked Santo Domingo finally impelled Roosevelt to decisive action. The affairs of that island republic differed from those of a number of other Latin American nations only in their particulars; and in July, 1903, four months after the Venezuelan crisis had ended, the German, Italian, and Spanish governments forced the Dominican authorities to sign protocols for the payment of monthly installments on the debts owed their nationals. Thereafter matters grew steadily worse. In January, 1904, the harried Dominican Minister of Foreign Affairs made a special trip to Washington to prevail upon the American government, in Roosevelt's words, "to establish some kind of protectorate over the islands, and take charge of their finances."

The President would have preferred to avoid involvement completely—he had, he said, "about the same desire to annex it as a gorged boa constrictor might have to swallow a porcupine wrong-end-to"—but he agreed to send down an informal mission. Then, on February 1, insurrectionists fired on an American cruiser, the *Yankee*. A few days later new disturbances broke out. American plantation owners and investors now implored the government to act, and on February 5 Roosevelt cabled Rear Admiral Wise to take "immediate steps for protection of United States citizens and property." Two weeks later he directed Admiral Dewey to go to Santo Domingo and get "a full, impartial searching account of the situation as it now presents itself to your eyes." He was still reluctant, however, to undertake a major intervention. "I hope it will be a good while before I have to go further," he wrote Ted. "But sooner or later it seems to me inevitable that the United States should assume an attitude of protection and regulation in regard to all these little states in the neighborhood of the Caribbean."

Fearful of another ugly crisis like that over Venezuela and predisposed anyway to resolve the larger problem, Roosevelt took a decisive step: on May 20 the President set forth the principles of the Roosevelt Corollary to the Monroe Doctrine in a letter which Root read at a Cuban anniversary dinner in New York: "If a nation shows that it knows how to act with decency in industrial and political matters, if it keeps order and pays its obligations, then it need fear no interference from the United States," he wrote in part. "Brutal wrongdoing, or an impotence which results in a general loosening of the ties of civilizing society, may finally require intervention by some civilized nation; and in the Western Hemisphere the United States cannot ignore this duty."

A violent, and mixed, reaction ensued. Roosevelt professed to be "amused at the yell," but he was actually irritated at his critics' refusal to face the facts. It was "the simplest common sense, and only the fool or the coward can treat it as aught else," he angrily charged. "If we are willing to let Germany or England act as the policemen of the Caribbean, then we can afford not to interfere when gross wrong-doing occurs. But if we intend to say 'Hands off' to the powers of Europe, sooner or later we must keep order ourselves."

Roosevelt never backed down from that position. His annual message six months later emphasized that the United States entertained neither "land hunger" nor other ulterior ambitions toward the "other nations of the western hemisphere save such as are for their welfare." It also underlined his reluctance to undertake the policeman's role. "We have plenty of sins of our own to war against," the message said, "and under ordinary circumstances we can do more for the general uplifting of humanity by striving with heart and soul to put a stop to civic corruption, to brutal lawlessness, and violent race prejudices here at home than by passing resolutions about wrong-doing elsewhere."

Roosevelt soon found it necessary to act under the Corollary's terms. The situation in Santo Domingo had steadily deteriorated through the summer and autumn of 1904. The national debt soared to $32,000,000 and was still rising. One of the main customs houses fell under control of a New York corporation which claimed an unpaid debt of $4,500,000. The Italians, French, and Belgians were protesting that Santo Domingo was violating the protocols of 1903. And the

Morales administration was being attacked from within. It was Venezuela all over again, or so it seemed. Roosevelt and Hay determined to prevent a repetition of the final chapter. On December 30 the Secretary of State directed the American minister to Santo Domingo to ascertain "discreetly but earnestly" whether President Morales "would be disposed to request the United States to take charge of the collection of duties." Morales proved amenable, and on February 7, 1905, a protocol providing for American control of the republic's customs houses was arranged. One of the stormiest controversies of Roosevelt's presidential career followed.

From the start, many senators viewed the President's proceedings with grave misgivings. Roosevelt's standing enemies, Senators John Morgan of Alabama, Augustus O. Bacon of Georgia, and a handful of Republican anti-imperialists now charged that the protocol would lead to an American protectorate over the island republic; they refused to approve when the President submitted it for ratification on February 15. While Roosevelt fumed—"Bacon is a man of meticulous mind, a violent partisan, with no real public spirit"—and conditions in Santo Domingo daily grew more precarious, the Senate sat tight. Both the regular and special sessions expired without a favorable vote.

Meanwhile Santo Domingo's troubles worsened. On March 14 an Italian cruiser appeared off the coast; at almost the same time the French and Belgians renewed pressure for payment of their debts. The crisis Roosevelt sought to avert was thus upon him. Either the United States moved in or the three European nations took action on their own. Even Senator Morgan recognized that something had to be done. And to the President's disgust, he proposed that the great powers be encouraged to act in concert. This was precisely what Roosevelt's diplomacy, which was predicated on opposition to the spread of European influence in Latin America, was designed to forestall.

The President held off for a few more days. But on March 28 the American minister cabled that the Dominican government was in "domestic peril," that a *modus vivendi* was "absolutely necessary," and that the European powers awaited an American decision to appoint a collector of customs. Roosevelt at once called in Spooner, Foraker, Lodge, and Knox to discuss the situation with him and Taft, who had replaced

Root as Secretary of War. All "heartily" agreed that he should take over the Dominican customs as President Morales wanted, Minister Dawson recommended, and the European nations approved; and all submitted to Taft's genial chaffing for their surrender to "usurpation of the executive." The President then consulted with the Democratic minority leader, Senator Arthur Pue Gorman of Maryland, an old foe. Gorman also agreed that the President should appoint a customs collector in spite of the Senate's earlier failure to ratify the protocol. Thus fortified by the support of the leaders of both parties, Roosevelt made the necessary arrangements for the collectorship.

An American was appointed general receiver and collector of Santo Domingo's customs, and for some years thereafter the islanders enjoyed such financial stability as they had never before experienced. Roads were built, schools established, and a revenue service created. The foreign debt was drastically scaled down, and the Dominican share of customs collections rose beyond all previous totals. The threat of European intervention was also dissipated. On the other hand, the seeds of "Dollar Diplomacy" were sown when it was proposed in 1906 that the European-held debt be taken over by a private American bank.

The success of the experiment in Santo Domingo failed to cool the tempers of the anti-Roosevelt forces in the United States Senate. When the protocol again came to a vote in 1906 it failed once more to win the necessary two-thirds majority. Not until February, 1907, was the arrangement formalized; and then Root's conciliatory influence was responsible. The whole affair was unfortunate. The measured, reluctant, and extraconstitutional action of a responsible chief executive, it gave superficial credence to the charges that he aspired to powers that were not lawfully his. It enlarged the partial truth that his diplomacy had the sensitivity of a blunderbuss. And it deepened Latin American hostility toward the powerful neighbor to the north.

The Santo Dominican incident sharply points up both the strength and weakness of Roosevelt's Latin American diplomacy. The President's intervention broke the crisis, gave relief to the Santo Dominicans, and made the eighty-three-year-old Monroe Doctrine a viable instrument of national policy. But by using the crisis to enunciate the general principle of

American obligation to intervene in future crises—the so-called "Roosevelt Corollary"—Roosevelt incited resentment throughout Latin America and cost the United States the good will of European idealists. Furthermore, the public declaration was largely unnecessary. When President Monroe made his memorable pronouncement in 1823 the United States was a third-class power dependent on moral suasion and the British Royal Navy; when President Roosevelt set forth his corollary in 1904 the United States was a first-class power, one that had already brought Imperial Germany to bay. Had the President stood on his own maxim—"actions speak louder than words"—and confided his intentions to diplomats alone, he might have served his country's purposes more fully. But by speaking out publicly, he converted a triumph of action into a near tragedy of words.

Chapter 12

Noble Ends and Less Noble Means

> *By far the most important action I took in
> foreign affairs . . . related to the Panama Canal.
> Here again there was much accusation about my
> having acted in an "unconstitutional" manner
> — . . . and at different stages of the affair
> believers in a do-nothing policy denounced me
> as having "usurped authority"—which meant,
> that when nobody else could or would exercise
> efficient authority, I exercised it.*
> —Theodore Roosevelt, *An Autobiography*

FROM THE September day in 1513 when Vasco Núñez de
Balboa first gazed upon the placid blue waters that led to the
fabled East, men of imagination had dreamed of linking the
Atlantic and the Pacific oceans with a canal across the Central
American isthmus. But for four centuries their vision had been
thwarted by the formidable engineering obstacles that weighed
upon it. Not even the genius of Ferdinand De Lesseps had
been able to give it substance; and only after Theodore Roosevelt marshaled the political, financial, and scientific resources
of the United States behind it in a sustained assertion of
power was it finally realized.

A half century before Roosevelt became President the
United States and Great Britain had agreed through the Clayton-Bulwer Treaty of 1850 to facilitate construction of an
unfortified canal open to the commerce of all nations in times
of both war and peace. As the United States grew mighty in
the aftermath of the Civil War, however, the treaty was persistently denounced by American nationalists; and when the
battleship *Oregon* was forced to steam around South America
to reinforce the fleet off Cuba in 1898, demands for repudiation of the treaty and for construction of an American-owned
and fortified canal reached a crescendo. A new treaty was
consequently drawn up in 1900—the First Hay-Pauncefote
Treaty. By its terms the United States was authorized to con-

struct and administer the proposed canal, but not to fortify it or close it in time of war. This arrangement was poorly calculated to appease a body politic already pressing for unilateral action. And though it was received with moderate favor in conservative circles, it met a thunderous opposition by the jingo press, partisan Democrats, Irish-Americans and German-Americans, and professional twisters of the British lion's tail. It also incited the measured and articulate opposition of Theodore Roosevelt, then governor of New York. "I most earnestly hope that the pending treaty . . . will not be ratified unless amended so as to provide that the canal, when built, shall be wholly under the control of the United States, alike in peace and war," he declared in a public statement. "This seems to me vital, from the standpoint of our seapower, no less than from the standpoint of the Monroe Doctrine."

John Hay was hurt and irritated by Roosevelt's statement. "Cannot you leave a few things to the President and the Senate who are charged with them by the Constitution?" he angrily wrote the Governor. "Do you really think the Clayton-Bulwer Treaty preferable to the one now before the Senate? There is no third issue, except dishonor."

Roosevelt's reply was tender yet firm. "I hesitated long before I said anything about the treaty through sheer dread of two moments—that in which I should receive your note, and that in which I should receive Cabot's," he wrote. "You have been the greatest Secretary of State I have seen in my time, but at this moment I can not, try as I may, see that you are right." He added that a canal constructed under the treaty's terms would be a military liability since the fleet would be tied up in its defense. He also contended that it would vitiate the Monroe Doctrine:

If we invite foreign powers to a joint ownership, a joint guarantee, of what so vitally concerns us but a little way from our borders, how can we possibly object to similar joint action say in Southern Brazil, or Argentina, where our interests are so much less evident? If Germany has the same right we have in the canal across Central America, why not in the partition of any part of Southern America?

Meanwhile Lodge supported amendments that reserved the right of fortification to the United States and excised an article inviting interested powers to concur in the treaty. As thus altered the First Hay-Pauncefote Treaty was approved by the Senate on December 20, 1900. "Now the onus is on England," the Massachusetts Senator wrote in his personal journal. "If she accepts well. If she, out of infinite stupidity, refuses, then we can honorably go on, & abrogate the treaty and build the canal." Actually, Great Britain did reject the amended treaty; but she eventually ratified a second treaty virtually incorporating the Senate amendments.

When Roosevelt became President in September, 1901, the Second Hay-Pauncefote Treaty had not yet been laid before the Senate. He urged ratification in his first annual message on December 3, and thirteen days later the Senate so acted.

Before a route was selected, the Roosevelt administration became involved in such high and low comedy as the American people had seldom before witnessed. When the curtain crashed down at the end the pockets of a *mésalliance* of American, Colombian, and French adventurers were filled to overflowing. Ferdinand De Lesseps's vivid imagination and bold daring were vindicated. And the United States had a legacy of ill-will which the Good Neighbor policies of later Presidents have failed to this day to dissipate entirely. In addition, Roosevelt's desire for achievement was gratified, his engineering judgment affirmed, and the strategic interests of the United States well served.

After De Lesseps's grandiose project collapsed in 1889 with a boom that reverberated around the world, American interest shifted to Nicaragua where engineering difficulties seemed less imposing and the political climate more favorable. In 1899 a commission headed by Rear Admiral John G. Walker recommended in a preliminary report based largely on administrative considerations that the Nicaraguan route be used. This recommendation was well received in the Senate; but it failed to win support in the House, which demanded that a new commission be formed to explore all possible routes. Nor did the Walker Commission's report evoke favorable response in scientific circles. By the late 1890's much technical opinion favored completion of De Lesseps's project.

The Nicaraguan route might still have been selected had it not been for the sensational lobbying of the De Lesseps's company's receivers. Organized as the New Panama (Canal) Company, they conspired to influence a decision favorable to Panama and to unload their franchise on the American government for the princely sum of $109 million. To these ends an enterprising New York attorney, William N. Cromwell, was retained to press the company's case in high places. A $60,000 contribution was made to the Republican campaign fund in 1900. And a comic-opera revolution was instigated in the long restive state of Panama.

The manipulations of Cromwell and his unfriendly ally, a flamboyantly imaginative Frenchman named Philippe Jean Bunau-Varilla, defy total reconstruction. But it is clear that Cromwell was responsible in some part for the omission in the Republican platform of 1900 of a preferential statement for the Nicaraguan route; that he was responsible in large part for Mark Hanna's decision to carry the fight for a Panamanian route to the floor of the Senate; and that he probably reinforced Roosevelt's interest in the Panamanian route. It is similarly clear that the versatile Bunau-Varilla capitalized on every opportunity, the most fortuitous a gift from nature, to win his case. Thus when Mt. Momotombo in Nicaragua spewed forth a molten stream of lava just as debate on Senator Spooner's bill for the Panama route was coming to a head in June, 1902, Bunau-Varilla hastily purchased ninety Nicaraguan stamps portraying the majestic mountain and a great cloud of smoke at its summit. He then placed one on each Senator's desk with an appropriate inscription: "An official witness of the volcanic activity of Nicaragua." Three days after that byplay, the Panama faction won a key test by a 42-to-34 vote.

As a result of these bizarre events, a wrong inference about the decision to select the Panama route has often been drawn. Indubitably, Cromwell influenced Hanna, Hay, and the President. Again and again they reflected his point of view, and in the end they accepted a settlement consonant with his recommendations. But there is not a scrap of evidence to indicate they they were animated by ulterior considerations as Cromwell surely was. Even more in 1902 than in 1900 the burden of engineering opinion, including that of the Walker Commission, favored the Panama route; and the President was fully informed of and in agreement with that opinion.

Nevertheless, Roosevelt's negotiations with Colombia for permission to construct the canal through the isthmus constitute one of the ineradicable blots on his record. It is the measure of his arrogance toward underdeveloped countries, in fact, that he seems not to have considered treating Colombia as a truly sovereign power. As he wrote Hay in the summer of 1902 when he learned that matters were proceeding unsatisfactorily, "I think they [the Colombians] would change their constitution if we offered enough."

In Colombia, meanwhile, the harassed and high-minded dictator, José Manuel Marroquín, sat on another volcano—one compounded of greed, nationalism, and political intrigue. American policy now caused it to erupt.

Early in 1903 Secretary Hay wrung an agreement—the Hay-Herran Treaty—consonant to American interests from the Colombian minister, one Dr. Tomas Herrán. Three days after Herrán signed the treaty on January 22 Bogotá instructed him to withhold his signature. The arrangements were unsatisfactory to the Colombian government, the Colombian Senate, and the Colombian people. The treaty called for payment of $40 million to the New Panama Canal Company; $10 million and a $250,-000 annual subsidy to Colombia. It granted the United States perpetual control of a zone five kilometers wide across the isthmus. And it provided for a system of mixed courts that would have compromised Colombia's sovereignty further. So vehement was the reaction in Colombia that Marroquín, whose dictatorship was neither as total nor as stable as Washington assumed, refused even to identify himself with the treaty; he forwarded it to the Colombian Senate without signature or affirmative recommendation.

Roosevelt and Hay had been outraged by Colombia's rejection of their handiwork. Had not the Colombian government initiated talks in December, 1900, out of fear that the United States would choose the Nicaraguan route? Why should it now oppose terms which were absolutely necessary to American construction and operation of the canal—terms which Colombia's accredited envoy had approved?

The fault was partly Herrán's. He had made no effort to withdraw his signature upon receipt of his belated instructions; neither had he informed Hay of their import. American intelligence was also poor and misleading. The American minister to Colombia failed to report accurately the gathering opposition at Bogotá. And neither he nor his successor ever fully informed the administration of the importance high-principled Colombians attached to the sovereignty features of the treaty. Dismissing such protests as "unimportant and largely hypocritical," they gave Hay and Roosevelt the impression that the Colombian government placed gold above honor, as many Colombian officials did.

The dictates of military security removed all possibility that the United States would modify its demands for control over the projected canal zone. Even President Marroquín recognized this. "I find myself in a horrible perplexity," he wrote one of his generals. ". . . [In] order that the North Americans may complete the work by virtue of a convention with the Government of Colombia, it is necessary to make concessions of territory, of sovereignty and of jurisdiction, which the Executive Power has not the power of yielding; and if we do not yield them . . . we will lose more sovereignty than we should lose by making the concessions they seek." "History will say of me," the distraught dictator added, "that I ruined the Isthmus and all Colombia, by not permitting the opening of the Panama Canal, or that I permitted it to be done, scandalously injuring the rights of my country."

Other Colombian leaders also saw their government's dilemma; and in a desperate effort to salvage something, they tried to place a lien on the $40 million the United States was prepared to pay the New Panama Canal Company. Arguing that it would be immoral for the United States to allow the Colombian government to expropriate any of the $40 million slated for the New Panama Canal Company, Cromwell persuaded Hay to send the American minister in Bogotá a long memorandum that committed the United States "to the complete support of the New Company's financial interests." This was a staggering diplomatic blunder. Nothing short of an ultimatum to sign or submit to force could have had a more deleterious impact on the treaty's prospects; and if any single action constituted its death blow, it was that note, a copy of which was sent to the New Panama Canal Company's office in Paris.

In reality, no one action was responsible. President Marroquín had long known that his political opposition intended to prevent a settlement while he was in office regardless of the terms. And Hay's blunders—the note of April 28 was but one of several—served more to accentuate than to cause the Colombian's determination to reject the Hay-Herrán Treaty.

When, therefore, the Colombian Senate decisively rejected the treaty on August 12, 1903, Roosevelt vented his indignation. The "Dagos" had acted "exactly as if a road agent had tried to hold up a man," he wrote privately. "They are mad to get hold of the $40,000,000 of the Frenchmen." "I do not think that the Bogotá lot of jack rabbits should be allowed permanently to bar one of the future highways of civilization."

Unwisely influenced by Cromwell, misinformed by diplomatic dispatches from Bogotá, and victimized by Hay's obtuseness, Roosevelt's anger was understandable, if not excusable. He backtracked just a little in his *Autobiography:*

I am well aware that the Colombian people have many fine traits; that there is among them a circle of high-bred men and women which would reflect honor on the social life of any country; and that there has been an intellectual and literary development within this small circle which partially atones for the stagnation and illiteracy of the mass of the people; and I also know that even the illiterate mass possesses many sterling qualities. But unfortunately in international matters every nation must be judged by the action of its government. The good people in Colombia apparently made no effort, certainly no successful effort, to cause the government to act with reasonable good faith toward the United States; and Colombia had to take the consequences.

Meanwhile, Roosevelt pondered a course of action. The United States could seize Panama under the so-called right of "international domain" as a militant minority of newspapers were demanding. It could construct the canal under a tortured interpretation of an 1846 "right of transit" treaty as Professor John Bassett Moore of Columbia University was urging. It could support a revolution in Panama, which had revolted against Colombia (New Granada) many times in the past and where discontent was again rife. Or it could return to the Nicaraguan route as many Southern Democrats were suggesting.

By the time the President made his decision he had also emerged as his own Secretary of State. He never doubted that the canal would be constructed, and he doubted very little that it would be routed through Panama. As he wrote Hay, "the great bulk of the best engineers are agreed that that route is best . . . [and] what we do now will be of consequence, not merely decades, but centuries hence, and we must be sure we are taking the right step before we act."

The "right step" was hard to choose. Roosevelt's first inclination was to act on the basis of Professor Moore's sophistic report. "If under the treaty of 1846 we have a color of right to start in and build the canal," he wrote Hay after reading Moore's memorandum at Sagamore Hill, "my offhand judgment would favor such proceeding." By early autumn Roosevelt had prepared a rough draft of a message to Congress requesting authority to proceed independently on the grounds that it was "out of the question to submit to extortion." The interests of the United States and of world commerce demanded "that the canal should be begun with no needless delay," the proposed message stated. It added that the "testimony of the experts is very strong, not only that the Panama route is feasible, but that in the Nicaraguan route we may encounter some unpleasant surprises."

In the meantime the President rejected suggestions that the United States foment a revolt by the Panamanians or that he make a militant public statement. TR unburdened himself on October 10 to Albert Shaw who was on the point of coming out for a revolution in his *Review of Reviews:*

I cast aside the proposition made at this time to foment the secession of Panama. Whatever other governments can do, the United States cannot go into securing by such underhand means, the secession. Privately, I freely say to you that I should be delighted if Panama were an independent State, or if it made itself so at this moment; but for me to say so publicly would amount to an instigation of a revolt, and therefore I cannot say it.

Fortunately, the President neither had to "say it" nor to submit his proposed message to Congress. On November 5 a revolutionary junta declared Panama's independence of Colombia, and four days later the United States extended *de facto* recognition to the new republic.

Of all the episodes in the Panama story, the most extraordinary were those encompassing that revolution. They revealed Cromwell and Bunau-Varilla at the high tide of their resourcefulness and influence; they showed Roosevelt and Hay at their circumspect best; and they displayed the Colombian government at its confused and disorganized worst. They also saw the Panamanians fulfill aspirations a half century old. It was these aspirations, in fact, that formed the springboard for Cromwell and Bunau-Varilla's activities and which allowed Roosevelt to acquiesce silently, yet in reasonably good conscience, to what he could not advocate publicly.

Panama had long lacked both the capital and political climate essential to material and cultural progress. Separated from Bogotá by a near impenetrable tropical jungle and a lofty mountain range, she was fifteen days' traveling time from the capital city, where the ruling gentry regarded her alternately with disdainful indifference or avaricious curiosity. Panamanians had repeatedly demonstrated by armed rebellion their dissatisfaction with absentee rule. Six times during the fifty-three years prior to the climactic revolution of 1903 American sailors or marines had gone ashore to restore the order necessary to the open transit across the isthmus guaranteed by the Treaty of 1846; and four times—in 1861, 1862, 1885, and 1900—the impotent Colombian government had itself requested American military intervention. As Roosevelt contended in his *Autobiography*, Colombia's "connection with the Isthmus would have been sundered long before it was" had it not been for American intervention.

Against such a background, those masters of intrigue and persuasion, Cromwell and Bunau-Varilla, had little trouble in finding Panamanians whose revolutionary fervor burned fiercely at the prospect of an independent Republic of Panama endowed with the $10 million the United States had been prepared to pay Colombia. During the summer of 1903 Cromwell and Bunau-Varilla sustained the hopes of a small band of Panamanian conspirators. And in the early autumn of 1903, when the conspirators were on the point of abandoning the project for lack of funds and encouragement, Bunau-Varilla gave them both. The result was revolution.

Roosevelt and Hay knew from reports of special observers and from conversations with Cromwell and Bunau-Varilla that a revolution was in the making. Indeed, Cromwell later boasted that he had planned the revolution in his New York law office. The President could readily have suppressed it; but Hay advised him that the United States should act "to keep the transit clear" and warned that American intervention "should not be haphazard nor, this time should it be to the profit, as heretofore of Bogota." Hay also confided to Bunau-Varilla on October 16 that American naval forces had been ordered "to sail towards the Pacific." Coming after an earlier interview with Roosevelt which he construed as favorable, Bunau-Varilla hardly needed to know more.

On November 2 the captains of United States warships already dispatched to isthmian waters were ordered to "maintain free and uninterrupted transit" and to "prevent landing of any armed force, either government or insurgent at any point within fifty miles of Panama." This meant that Colombia would be unable to reinforce its tiny garrison in Panama. Then, at 5:49 A.M. on November 3, forty-nine minutes after the Panama City fire brigade started to distribute weapons to crowds in the streets, the revolution against Colombia was accomplished. Except for a brief shelling by a Colombian gunboat which killed an innocent bystander and mortally wounded an ass, there was no violence. The Colombian governor of Panama, José Domingo de Obaldía, participated in the conspiracy, and the Colombian army detachment in Panama City sold its services to the revolutionary cause as financed by the New Panama Canal Company.

The next day the Panamanians celebrated their independence with a formal ceremony. The Colombian general was presented with $30,000, most of his officers with $10,000 each, and every soldier in the ranks with fifty gold dollars. The American consul joined in a gala parade, and the President-to-be, Dr. Manuel Amador Guerrero, delivered an oration:

> The world is astounded at our heroism! Yesterday we were but the slaves of Colombia; today we are free. . . . President Roosevelt has made good. . . . Free sons of Panama, I salute you! Long live the Republic of Panama! Long live President Roosevelt! Long live the American Government!

Dr. Amador was almost premature. The same day he was proclaiming long life to the new republic and its North American friends, the commander of the 500 Colombian regulars in Colón was threatening to kill every Yankee in the city unless his force received rail passage to Panama City. But before he summoned the necessary nerve, a detachment of United States marines landed under orders to prevent the Colombians from using the railroad. The success of the revolution was thus assured.

Washington received the news the morning after this last threat was dissipated. Within an hour and a half Secretary Hay, acting on instructions from Roosevelt, directed the American consul at Panama City to recognize Dr. Amador's *de facto* government. Five days later the President received the ubiquitous Bunau-Varilla as Minister Plenipotentiary of the Republic of Panama.

Less than a week after that Bunau-Varilla signed for the Republic of Panama a treaty which enabled the Panama Canal to be constructed on terms favorable to Panama, the United States, the New Panama Canal Company, and probably civilization as a whole. Written partly by Bunau-Varilla and partly by Hay, who consulted with Roosevelt, Root, Knox, and Albert Shaw, it made Panama a virtual protectorate of the United States. The treaty granted the United States perpetual "use, occupation, and control" of a strip across the Isthmus ten miles wide, and it authorized the United States to fortify the canal and safeguard the independence of Panama. Panama was awarded $10,000,000, and a $250,000 annual payment to begin nine years later. The New Panama Canal Company received $40 million, Colombia nothing.

For Roosevelt the sword of righteousness had again thrust through the shield of iniquity. Just as the American colonies "had revolted from England because England declined to treat them as free men with equal rights," so had "Panama revolted from Colombia because Colombia, for corrupt and evil purposes or else from complete governmental incompetency, declined to permit the building of the great work which meant everything to Panama." Nor need the Colombians, who offered to ratify the Hay-Herrán Treaty by executive decree, now expect the United States to respond to their change of front. "In their silly efforts to damage us they cut their own throats," the President charged. "They tried to hold us up; and too late they have discovered their criminal error." Their belated offer proves beyond cavil that when the same government said earlier it had no power to take that step "it was guilty of deliberate bad faith." Consequently, the President concluded, "nothing could be more wicked than to ask us to surrender the Panama people, who are our friends, to the Colombian people, who have shown themselves our foes."

Roosevelt held in the main to that analysis over the years. True, he allowed his boundless pride in the achievement to overrule his discretion by declaring in an address at the University of California in 1911 that "I took the canal zone and let Congress debate, and while the debate goes on the canal does also." And in his *Autobiography* he asserted that "From the beginning to the end our course was straight-forward and in absolute accord with the highest standard of international morality." But other statements in his *Autobiography* were more representative:

> I did not lift my finger to incite the revolutionists. . . . I simply ceased to stamp out the different revolutionary fuses that were already burning. . . . I deeply regretted, and now deeply regret, the fact that the Colombian Government rendered it imperative for me to take the action I took; but I had no alternative, consistent with the full performance of my duty to my own people, and to the nations of mankind.

It is doubtful that the case for and against Roosevelt's conduct will ever die. The story is too dramatic, the characters too romantic, the maneuverings too intricate. This much, however, is certain: Roosevelt's primary motive was his conviction that the Panama route would best serve American interests. Had he been less quick to react against Colombia's rejection of the Hay-Herrán Treaty and had he been more accurately informed, he might have realized his objective without creating a heritage of ill-will. He might even have resolved the conflict by paying the Colombians a sum equal to that granted Cromwell's shadowy clients. But because he persisted in regarding the Colombians as blackmailers, and because delay was foreign to his nature and possibly subversive of his presidential ambitions in 1904, he pursued a blameworthy course.

Chapter 13

In His Own Right

*In politics we have to do a great many things
we ought not to do.*

—Theodore Roosevelt

MARCH 4, 1905, dawned clear and brisk. The wind was moderate, the sky pale blue. In the East, where the oversized dome of the Capitol broke the horizon, a tuft of storm clouds hovered; but by noon they had disappeared. This was Theodore Roosevelt's day of glory.

A few minutes after noon Roosevelt stepped forward on the east portico of the Capitol to face Chief Justice Melville E. Fuller. In the background stood high government officials, foreign diplomats and their ladies, personal friends, the ubiquitous Roosevelt family, and an honor guard of Rough Riders. Slowly and deliberately, his eyes fastened on the Chief Justice, Roosevelt placed his left hand on an open Bible, raised his right hand, and repeated the measured phrases of the presidential oath.

The President was heavier and more sharply lined, especially about the eyes, than he had been four years before. His face was wider, his shoulders broader, his neck thicker. He was much larger through the midriff, and he seemed stronger than he had as a young man when his square face alone conveyed the impression of physical strength. Even his voice, always imperfect and too high in pitch, had the timbre of a man proved, proved in battle in another era and proved in office in the years just gone by. Theodore Roosevelt was now in command. As he repeated the last words of the presidential oath the throng that milled about the plaza between the Capitol and the Library of Congress gave forth a mighty roar—the first display of an enthusiasm that eclipsed all previous inaugurations save Andrew Jackson's first.

The "Giver of Good," said the President in his inaugural address, had richly endowed the American people. "We are the

206

heirs of the ages, and yet we have had to pay few of the penalties which in old countries are exacted by the dead hand of a bygone civilization." Still, we had faced perils which "called for the vigor and effort without which the manlier and hardier virtues wither away." We now faced new ones. "The conditions which have told for our marvelous material wellbeing, which have developed to a very high degree our energy, self-reliance, and individual initiative, have also brought the care and anxiety inseparable from the accumulation of great wealth in industrial centers." Upon their resolution, exclaimed this first major statesman of the new order, depended the welfare of the American people and perhaps of mankind itself. "If we fail, the cause of free self-government throughout the world will rock to its foundations." But we need not fail. The qualities now needed were no different than ever. They were those "of practical intelligence, of courage, of hardihood, and endurance, and above all the power of devotion to a lofty ideal." They had made great the men who founded the Republic under Washington, and they had made great the men who preserved it under Lincoln. They could also make great the present generation.

Through the remainder of that March afternoon, Roosevelt was zestful, ebullient, and even prideful. On the reviewing stand an hour or two later he alternately sat and stood, grinned and laughed, waved and applauded. He stamped his feet and bent his knees to the rhythm of "There'll Be a Hot Time in the Old Town Tonight." He glowed when a troop of Rough Riders, fortified by three days of liquid preparation for the indignity of riding artillery rather than cavalry mounts, rode uproariously by. And he chatted freely, almost constantly, with members of the presidential party.

The President was also mindful of the charges that he had usurped congressional power and exploited colonial peoples. "I really shuddered today as I swore to obey the Constitution," the President supposedly joked at the outset of the parade. As the Puerto Rican contingent passed in review, he turned to Senator Bacon, the anti-imperialist from Georgia, and remarked with a chuckle: "They look pretty well for an oppressed people, eh, Senator?" Roosevelt again fixed his gaze on the discomfited Georgian when a finely drilled body of Filipino Scouts swung past the reviewing stand to the buoyant strains of "Gary Owen." "The wretched serfs disguised their feelings admirably," he shouted as Bacon turned his face from the scene.

The President's high spirits were warranted. He knew that his effectiveness had been circumscribed by the accidental nature of his rise to power; that Congress had tolerated him and at times angrily compromised with him, but had supported him only when his recommendations coincided with its own views. But now he was President by popular mandate rather than by assassin's hand. He had swept scores of Republicans into office with him. And he had already shown by messages, speeches, and informal maneuvers that he would no longer pay lip service to the dead hand of McKinley or again be so deferential to the will of the Senate oligarchy. "Tomorrow I shall come into my office in my own right," he is said to have exclaimed on the eve of his inauguration. "Then watch out for me."

If the President's inaugural address exemplified those high and statesman-like ideals to which Roosevelt so urgently aspired, the events preceding the election had revealed that ruthlessness and low cunning that made him the master politician of his own age and one of the masters of all ages. During the three years the President was serving the nation and incidentally enhancing his prestige by battling the trusts, intervening in the coal strike, and acquiring the Panama Canal Zone, he had also been waging a fiercely single-minded campaign for his nomination and election in 1904. He manipulated the patronage with cold disingenuousness. He signed a controversial pension bill. And in the third of those years he slowed the momentum of his antitrust campaign and temporarily reaffirmed the historic alliance between the Republican party and big business that his earlier policies had begun to weaken.

Roosevelt's triumphal election in November, 1904, had actually been an anticlimax. The real contest had been for the nomination, and it had been won more than a full year before —won against Mark Hanna, the man who symbolized the McKinley policies Roosevelt had so spontaneously promised to continue upon assuming office.

Marcus Alonzo Hanna was no Joseph G. Cannon committed to the preservation of the status quo at any cost but the political; neither was he a Nelson W. Aldrich dedicated to its maintenance at all costs including the political. Rather, the portly, convivial Ohioan was a genuinely sophisticated conservative. A successful businessman on his own, he had tried most of the standard means of repressing labor during his early career only to conclude that an open-handed policy was more profitable than recurrent strife. Although he had coined the slogan "Stand pat" for the campaign of 1900, Hanna understood that the predatory ways of capital would have to be changed, the rights of labor more broadly affirmed, if social upheaval were to be averted. He had little sympathy, consequently, with his Republican colleagues in the Senate who wished to convert the slogan of 1900 into a political philosophy. Why, then, did Roosevelt move against him?

The reason was power. Hanna had it and Roosevelt wanted it. The President wanted it, assuredly, to gratify his ego. Like all great leaders, he took almost primitive satisfaction in the exercise of power. Yet, just as Abraham Lincoln was distinguished from Stephen A. Douglas by the depths of his idealism rather than of his ambition, so Theodore Roosevelt was set off from most of his contemporaries by his dedication to the public interest. Had Roosevelt's moral sensibilities been less acute he might have been likened to Hanna himself, a good and well-intentioned man, but hardly a great man; and had they been genuinely dull he might have been compared to Platt, or Quay, or Penrose, men to whom power was the consuming end of life. Roosevelt might even have emerged as a violent demagogue, for he had not a few of the attributes, including the ability to oversimplify, smear, and stir the masses.

If Roosevelt wanted Hanna's power to gratify his baser urges, he also wanted it to assure the success of those high public purposes to which his vaulting ambition and lust for power had long been directed. Hanna was hardly prepared to rally the Grand Old Party behind those parts of the President's program which were too advanced for his own tastes. The question of whether Roosevelt's maturing progressivism, a progressivism that was even then dimly pointing toward basic changes in American society, or Hanna's program of piecemeal concessions that failed to modify the capitalists' control of the body politic, would win out was far from idle. And since Hanna wanted at the least to continue the role of Warwick and at the most to become President himself, Roosevelt believed he had either to crush him or suffer the constriction of most of the policies he himself represented.

Whatever the baseness or loftiness of Roosevelt's motives, however groundless his rationalizations and praiseworthy his justifications, his drive to unseat the man who had made McKinley was at once subtle, open, and pitiless. The President allied himself with and was even obsequious to the unsavory bosses Quay and Penrose and the archconservative Foraker of Ohio. He appointed a great host of Quay, Penrose, and Foraker's friends, not a few of them the "low morality" types whom Civil Service Commissioner Roosevelt had so despised, to the government service. And finally, after Foraker had boxed in Hanna by calling on the Ohio Republican Convention to endorse the President in the spring of 1903, Roosevelt forced Hanna's hand by publishing a private telegram from the Senator. This low blow left Hanna little alternative but to allow the Convention to endorse the President. From the Ohio Convention, Roosevelt was the head of the Republican party outside Congress. "It simplified things all around," he exulted to Lodge. "Hanna was my only formidable opponent so far as the nomination . . . [was] concerned."

Nine months later Mark Hanna lay dead of typhoid fever. To the end he had maintained cordial relations with the President. Roosevelt had visited him during his final illness, and fittingly so. More than any man in the United States, Hanna could have ruined Roosevelt in the formative years, 1901–02. But in spite of his own ambition, his contempt of Roosevelt's flamboyance, and distrust of many of his policies, Hanna had chosen to place public and party interests above his own fortunes. Roosevelt said as much in a moving letter to Elihu Root the day after his Olympian adversary died:

I think that not merely I myself, but the whole party and the whole country have reason to be grateful to him for the way in which, after I came into office, under circumstances which were very hard for him, he resolutely declined to be drawn into the position which a smaller man of meaner cast would inevitably have taken; that is, the position of antagonizing public policies if I was identified with them.

Hardly less than his obsession with power, Roosevelt's dexterous use of the patronage in his campaign against Hanna has been disillusioning to the President's defenders. Actually, Roosevelt was incomparably more restrained than Lincoln, who appointed a string of inferior men to high office in order to secure the success and promote the great objects of his administration. But because Roosevelt was so emphatically on the record, and especially because he was so boorishly self-righteous, his compromises have subjected him to harsh censure.

The most flagrant violation of principle was the appointment of James S. Clarkson of Iowa, the archspoilsman who had led the Republican hosts in their assault on the fourth-class postmasterships under Wanamaker, to a non-policy-making plum in New York in 1902. Clarkson, explained the President to the numerous and vociferous critics of his appointment, was "in no way to be criticized" for his "occasional" removals of Democratic postmasters in years gone by. Indeed, he was "an honorable and capable man." To some, however, Roosevelt was more candid. "In politics," he confessed, "we have to do a great many things we ought not do."

Although the President thus lowered the bars on minor offices, he usually stood firm on major appointments. His attitude toward the Isthmian Canal Commission was a case in point. The construction of the Panama Canal by the first great government corporation in American history was a worthy tribute to the President's pragmatic, trial-and-error administrative techniques. He took more pride in it than any other of his concrete achievements. And it was his personal decision to support Dr. William C. Gorgas, who insisted on pursuing Walter Reed's theories on yellow fever, that made the undertaking possible. When, accordingly, Senator Quay asked Roosevelt to appoint one of his constituents to the Isthmian Commission in 1904, the President forthrightly refused. "I hate to be in any way unreciprocative," he wrote the powerful Pennsylvanian. "But it does seem to me that in handling this Commission I should do nothing on the ground of locality."

I have had to refuse to appoint an admirable young fellow in whom Lodge was intensely interested, though I was able to place him on the Philippine Commission. In any ordinary appointments I am only too glad to consider political recommendations and the recommendations of my friends. . . . But when we come to a position like this I feel as I do when I am choosing a judge for the Supreme Court.

The year before Roosevelt came up for election he brought indictments against an imposing array of Republicans for defrauding the Post Office Department and pushed an investigation of land corruptionists in Oregon, among them a Republican congressman. He instituted a rigid civil service system in the Philippines, backed a measure sponsored by Lodge and Root for the improvement of the consular service, and gave forceful and informed support to Root's reorganization of the Army. He also added 50,000 positions to the classified civil service lists during his seven and one-half years in office. In spite of minor concessions to the bosses and paternal solicitude for unemployed ex-Rough Riders, the general level of his appointments was the highest since the halcyon days before Jackson. Never, said Lord Bryce, had he seen a more eager, high-minded, and efficient set of public servants, men more useful and more creditable to their country, than the men he placed in positions of heavy responsibility. "Theodore Roosevelt," wrote the great administrative historian, Leonard D. White, stood "head and shoulders above his predecessors since the days of James K. Polk."

Roosevelt went beyond the customary geographical considerations in selecting men of character and ability for government office. Before he appointed Oscar Straus, the first Jew to serve in a Cabinet post, Secretary of Commerce and Labor in 1906, he sought the advice of the pillar of New York's civic-minded German-Jewish community, Jacob Schiff. At a banquet of prominent Jews in honor of Straus some weeks later, Roosevelt exclaimed that he had not even thought about Straus's religion when contemplating his appointment. But Schiff, whose hearing was failing, bungled the cue. "Dot's right, Mr. President," he exclaimed. "You came to me and said, 'Chake, who is der best Jew I can appoint Segretary of Commerce.' "

In similar vein, Roosevelt sometimes appointed a Roman Catholic, a labor union man, a white Southern Democrat or a Negro Southern Republican as he strove to make his administration reflect the rich ethnic diversity of American society. Invariably, he did so with an eye for the immediate political advantage. He consorted with Booker T. Washington, the first American Negro invited to break bread in the White House, because Washington was supporting him in his fight to wrest control of the party machinery from Mark Hanna; and he gave high place to other qualified Negroes for the same reason. But he also recognized Negroes and members of other suppressed groups in ways that clearly transcended his political interests.

Roosevelt was too sophisticated a Reform Darwinist to believe blatantly in racial supremacy, though a mild undercurrent of racism seems to have lingered in his unconsciousness. His thought coincided roughly with the moderate, informed opinion of the times; and it was in fact more advanced than that of reformer-economists like John R. Commons and politician-intellectuals like Cabot Lodge and Woodrow Wilson. Yet Roosevelt was never enthusiastic about the mass immigration of Irish, Slavs, and Southern Europeans—of Jews and Greeks and Roman Catholics. He believed their numbers were too great, their conditions of life too impoverished, and their cultural backgrounds too different for easy assimilation. And he erroneously concluded that they were easy prey to political radicalism as well as to social and moral degradation. Unable to slow their influx—he unsuccessfully recommended immigration restriction and then appointed a commission of experts which submitted a racist report—he characteristically reacted by promoting their assimilation. To this end he fulminated against discrimination and worked actively to open the channels of opportunity. "I grow extremely indignant at the attitude of coarse hostility to the immigrant," Roosevelt wrote the Rev. Lyman Abbott, publisher of the influential, Protestant-oriented *Outlook:*

I have tried to . . . appeal to their self-respect and make it easy for them to become enthusiastically loyal Americans as well as good citizens. I have one Catholic in my Cabinet and have had another, and I now have a Jew in the Cabinet; and part of my object in each appointment was to implant in the minds of our fellow-Americans of Catholic or of Jewish faith, or of foreign ancestry or birth, the knowledge that they have in this country just the same rights and opportunities as every one else . . . just the same ideals as a standard toward which to strive. I want the Jewish young man who is born in this country to feel that Straus stands for his ideal of the successful man.

Roosevelt's attitude toward the declining birth rate offers additional insight into his implicit repudiation of racial, as distinct from national or cultural, superiority. "The American stock is being cursed with the curse of sterility, and it is earning the curse, because the sterility is wilful," he wrote in 1911.

"If it were confined to Americans of old stock . . . we could at least feel that the traditions and principles and purposes of the founders of the Republic would find their believers and exponents among their descendants by adoption." And in that case, "I, for one, would heartily throw in my fate with the men of alien stock who were true to the old American principles rather than with the men of the old American stock who were traitors to the old American principles." But unfortunately, he lamented, "the children of the immigrants show the same wilful sterility that is shown by the people of the old stock."

Roosevelt's intense preoccupation with an Americanism that embraced personal morality as well as national loyalty and unity pervaded his views on religion. Throughout his life he was a regular churchgoer, and by the testimony of some of his intimates, a devoutly religious man as well. "When a man believes a thing, is it not his duty to say so?" he said to the pastor of the St. Nicholas Dutch Reformed Church in New York at the age of seventeen. "If I joined the church, wouldn't that be the best way for me to say to the world that I believed in God?"

Roosevelt never wavered in his formal commitment to the church. Bill Sewall remembered that he took the Bible into the North Woods as a Harvard undergraduate and that he would slip away to peruse it by himself. "Some folks read the Bible to find an easier way into Heaven," Sewall once said. But "Theodore reads it to find the right way and how to pursue it." Nevertheless, Roosevelt's innermost convictions are unclear even to this day. As Hagedorn writes, "He trumpeted his moral convictions from the housetops and up and down the land, until even his friends begged for mercy. But his relation to the unseen was something else." Only three or four times in his maturity is he reported to have spoken freely of his faith; and in most of those instances the report is suspect or deficient.

Curiously, Roosevelt had been even more dependent on religion than most young men during his adolescence and early manhood—a reflection, perhaps, of what Morison calls "his capacity for total investment." At Harvard he taught an Episcopal Sunday school class until forced to resign because of his refusal to give up his Dutch Reformed affiliation; and he prayed regularly each morning during his college years. It was to religion, moreover, that he turned for solace in the traumatic aftermath of his father's death. "It is lovely to think of our meeting in heaven. . . ." "Lord, I believe; help thou mine unbelief." "Nothing but my faith in the Lord Jesus Christ could have carried me through this, my terrible time of trouble and sorrow." Those were his diary entries at the time. During Roosevelt's twenty-first year, however, the evidences of deep religious feeling began to abate; nor do they seem to have resurged in the double tragedy of his mother's and first wife's death when he was twenty-five.

It is true that Roosevelt continued to pay formal obeisance to the Judeo-Christian God and occasionally to the Trinity as well. But nowhere in the published addresses and writings of his later years is there anything resembling a movingly spiritual confession of faith. Nor was he ever disturbed by the Darwinian findings which were rocking the substance of traditional theology as he came into manhood. "I know not how philosophers may ultimately define religion," he wrote, "but from Micah to James it has been defined as service to one's fellowmen rendered by following the great rule of justice and mercy, of wisdom and righteousness." For Theodore Roosevelt, who lacked even Lincoln's mysticism, that was enough. As Gamaliel Bradford concludes in a dozen lines that atomize the volume and more of essays designed to prove Roosevelt's spirituality: "I cannot find God insistent or palpable anywhere in the writings or the life of Theodore Roosevelt. He had no need of him and no longing, because he really had no need of anything but his own immensely sufficient self. And the abundant, crowding, magnificent presence of this world left no room for another. Bishop's *Life of Roosevelt* ends with a quotation [from Roosevelt] which seems to sum up the whole story: 'It is idle to complain or to rail at the inevitable; serene and high of heart we must face our fate and go down into the darkness.' I do not see God here anywhere at all."

If Roosevelt's rejection of both dogma and spirituality made for a broad tolerance of religious diversity, his commitment to religion as a social and ethical force nevertheless imposed limits on that tolerance. His ultimate test was whether a religion transgressed the moral code that comprised the warp of the Judeo-Christian heritage. He was chary, accordingly, of the Church of the Latter-day Saints. Yet, with uncharacteristic restraint, he opposed a proposed constitutional amendment against polygamy partly on the grounds "that there is less polygamy among the Mormons . . . than there have been bigamous marriages among an equal number of Christians." Roosevelt knew, it is perhaps no exaggeration to conclude, that the history of mankind is writ large with foolish and futile religious persecutions.

Roosevelt's regard for the moral law and his insight into the pressure of environmental forces made him more sympathetic to Catholicism than most middle-class Americans of his times. He had little patience with the doctrine of papal infallibility and he especially resented the Roman Church's authoritarian structure. His frequent endorsements of the separation of church and state, his emphatic support of the free public school system, and his implied criticisms of parochial education even suggest a latent anti-Catholicism. But in the final analysis he was most impressed by Rome's beneficial influences—with its potential ability to infuse immigrants with those Judeo-Christian ethical values that were the fount of his own inspiration and out of which Protestantism itself had sprung.

Nor was Roosevelt daunted by the prospect of a Catholic residing in the White House at some future date. Indeed, he welcomed it, for it implied a complete assimilation. Too pragmatic to be bound by doctrinaire principles himself, he was confident that other men of responsibility and patriotism would prove similarly chainless. He accordingly took pleasure in striking out at Protestant bigots and asserting that he would happily support a Roman Catholic for the presidency if he happened to be the best qualified man. Predicting in September 1904 (a most politic timing, it is true), that there would be many Catholic Presidents in the years to come, he expressed the hope that if any one of them know "anything of me or my conduct, he will feel that I have acted along just the lines that he can afford to act." Over the years Roosevelt could and did consort in good conscience with Catholic and Episcopal bishops, with Jewish rabbis and Methodist ministers, and with laymen of all denominations, including the Unitarian Taft.

When viewed against this background, Roosevelt's ceaseless cultivation of political support by minority groups becomes more morally defensible. Had he been a religious bigot or an Anglo-Saxon supremacist dedicated to purity of the so-called race, his comportment might have stamped him as a sheer opportunist. But his commitment was to the preservation of

American institutions, not to defense of a particular in-group, and it was more intellectual than political in origin. To discriminate against an American citizen because of his own or his father's birthplace was to the mature Roosevelt "a base infamy—utterly un-American and profoundly unpatriotic."

Had Roosevelt never faced an electorate he would have been as concerned about Americanization of the newer immigrants as he was as an active politician. But since he had to face the electorate and since he believed "in being thoroughly practical in politics," he spared no effort to win every last vote in every last minority group or organization that he had served during his twenty-year political career. During the campaign of 1904 the word went out in a dozen different tongues from the ward heelers and precinct leaders that the President had appointed Jews and Catholics to high office, that he had defended immigrant working men against exploitation by the great coal barons, and that he had represented the little man against the privileged few in his strike against the trusts.

The whole man in 1904 was not only one of ideals, courage, and forthrightness, he was a man of surprising fear and no little expediency. Just as the appointment of Clarkson in 1902 had been designed to promote Roosevelt's cause at the nominating convention of 1904, so was a decision to broaden the pension base for Union veterans in the late winter of 1904 by executive decree calculated to advance his fortunes in the election that followed that convention. The President's unilateral action, roared W. Bourke Cochran, grandiloquent orator, Tammany chieftain, and spoilsman of the first order, was a clear-cut case of usurpation of Congress' authority. The *New York Times* emphatically agreed. Rarely, said an angry editorial, had the American people witnessed such an "impudent" exercise of executive power. Pulitzer's *World* professed to see a more fundamental issue. "There is an impression that we are to elect a President next November," it loftily declared. "It is a mistake. Unless Mr. Roosevelt be totally at sea regarding the nature of his office, we are to elect a czar."

The Republicans in Congress discreetly held their tongues; they had paid higher prices than "executive usurpation" for the veteran vote in the past. Their President was meanwhile embarrassed, but far from chastened, by the outcry. "I came to the conclusion," Roosevelt said in a labored explanation, that if we waited on Congress "we would either have no legislation or else improper legislation."

Yet the President was also convinced that he was morally right, that the pensions were deserved. Their recipients were not ex-contractors who had waxed rich at the government trough during the war; nor were they tariff-protected manufacturers seeking one more favor. They were, as Roosevelt who had honored them long before he became a politician, ringingly declared, "the men who fought for union and liberty" and "not only saved this Nation from ruin, but rendered an inestimable service to all mankind."

Roosevelt well knew that during the four years the "plain people" had been at war Elihu Root took his degree at Hamilton College and Robert Lincoln finished his studies at Harvard. J. P. Morgan, a widower without children at twenty-four, procured a substitute to serve in the Army and began the career that was to make him the most powerful man in the nation by the time Roosevelt became President. John D. Rockefeller also hired a substitute, then bent over his books in the produce commission business in Cleveland, invested in oil, and watched his annual income rise to $17,000 by 1865. Philip D. Armour made his first great "killing" by selling pork "short" as Grant marched through the Wilderness to Richmond. And Jay Gould, Jay Cooke, Andrew Carnegie, Colis P. Huntington, Jim Fisk, and dozens of others who preferred the emoluments of the market place to the miseries (or glories) of the battlefield either launched their careers or embellished their already sizable fortunes while the muskets rattled and the cannon roared. When silence fell on Appomattox their futures were as secure as money could make them.

It was for "the plain people" who survived the holocaust that Roosevelt's pension order was designed. Whatever the political nuances of his decision to sign it (he self-righteously refused to admit any) his justification was plausible. Admitting that there was an "unreasoning or demagogic demand for excessive and improper amounts" and claiming that he had prevented Congress from submitting to it, he reminded Jacob Riis that "there are very many excellent people who have lived softly, and who have no idea of what it is all one's life to earn one's living by toil, and then, without having been able to save, to face failing strength at the end of one's days." The age of sixty-two had been selected, he added in a passage that pre-

saged the later, more socially conscious Roosevelt, "not at
random, but after careful inquiry which satisfied us that in
most great manufacturing and railroad establishments new
men of the age of 62 who might apply for work were peremptorily refused. . . . There are exceptions, of course, but the
average toiler, the average wageworker, whose work is physical, has at 62 lost half his capacity to do his work. In New
Zealand, at 65 such a man, even if a civilian, is given an old-
age pension, larger in amount by over one-half than the
amount we thus allow." The Civil War veteran shall have such
a pension, TR emphatically concluded, "because the presump-
tion is that he needs it."

In a world just beginning to face the need to take care of
the aged, the President's ruling was socially meaningful, however inadequate, discriminatory, and political its application.
Thirty-one years were to go by and five Presidents were to
pass in and out of the White House before Roosevelt's reasoning would be applied to civilians as well as veterans; and then
it would be in the first administration of his distant cousin and
sometime disciple.

Just as Roosevelt sought the support of the minority groups
and Union veterans for his campaign in 1904, he welcomed
the backing of big business in general and of Wall Street in
particular. In a maneuver that further blurred the distinctions
between the parties, the Cleveland Democrats had beaten back
drives to include free silver and income tax planks in the party
platform in 1904 and then named Judge Alton B. Parker of
New York to carry the once progressive Democratic standard.
A confirmed Gold Democrat and a colorless campaigner,
Parker was a moderate states' rightist and a strong anti-
imperialist. He was the antithesis of Bryan in personality and
he differed radically from the Great Commoner in social
philosophy. He also offered a striking contrast to Roosevelt,
"The Republican Bryan," as embittered Old Guardsmen were
by then calling the President.

Although Democratic newspapers had received Parker's
nomination with mixed reactions, they had quickly closed
ranks. From one end of the country to the other they announced that the campaign would be waged on the issue
of personalities. Theodore Roosevelt, declared Colonel Henry
Watterson's *Louisville Courier-Journal,* embodies "absolutism"
and the "Gospel of Force"; Alton B. Parker, said Pulitzer's

editors on the *World,* stands for "conservative and constitutional Democracy."

Wall Street leaders sulked. There was enough truth in these assertions to challenge the wisdom of their supporting Roosevelt against the conservative Parker. Until the day of Hanna's death the Harriman, Rockefeller and similar interests had hoped that the Ohio Senator would somehow wrest the nomination from the Rough Rider in the White House. As a meeting of railroad executives had urged Hanna in January, 1904, "Stop making presidents and become one yourself." But with the passing of that monumental symbol of "McKinleyism" in February, they had resigned themselves to the inevitable. Six weeks before Roosevelt's power-packed steamroller forced his unanimous nomination at Chicago before mechanically cheering delegates (the galleries were wildly enthusiastic), even the *New York Sun* had leaped atop the boiler:

RESOLVED: That we emphatically endorse and affirm Theodore Roosevelt. Whatever Theodore Roosevelt thinks, says, does, or wants is right. Roosevelt and Stir 'Em Up. Now and Forever; One and Inseparable!

The rest of the Old Guard had gone along, or were soon to do so. Henry Adams had thought that they would not. "Roosevelt has no friends," he wrote in January with characteristic effort at effect. "I doubt whether he has in all Washington, including his own Cabinet, a single devoted follower; for even Cabot can hardly be called a devoted follower of anyone, except as a kitten follows its own tail . . . every man in the organization will dread his re-election. Half of them, and all the money, will sell him out."

That summer, however, money flowed into Republican headquarters like a great tidal wave. J. P. Morgan contributed $150,000; H. H. Rodgers and John D. Archbold of the Standard Oil Company, $100,000; C. S. Mellon, $50,000; E. H. Harriman, $50,000; and William Nelson Cromwell, $5,000. All told, $2,195,000 swelled the Republican war chest, 72½ per cent the gift of corporations.

Historians still differ over the meaning of Wall Street's munificent support of Roosevelt's campaign in 1904. Some contend that it proved the issue was parties rather than men—that a Democratic Congress was a more potent threat than a

Republican Congress even with Roosevelt in the White House. The editors of the *New York Sun* so believed: "We prefer the impulsive candidate of the party of conservatism to the conservative candidate of the party which the business interests regard as permanently and dangerously impulsive." Others argue that the lords of the market place and the heads of the counting houses were too astute to fear Roosevelt; that they were persuaded by Elihu Root's logic: "You say Roosevelt is an unsafe man. I tell you he is a great conservator of property and rights." And many, of course, interpret it both ways.

Roosevelt himself badly wanted Wall Street's support. But he wanted to believe that he wanted it only on his own terms. Although he had been consistently more temperate in his criticisms of businessmen throughout 1904, he now righteously directed the Republican National Committee to return the contributions of officials of the Standard Oil Company, which was then under investigation. He further warned that there should be no intimation to business that he would become conservative in return for financial aid. "I should hate to be beaten in this contest," he wrote, "but I should not merely hate, I should not be able to bear being beaten under circumstances which implied ignominy."

The force of the President's renouncement of Standard Oil money is unfortunately weakened by his failure to attempt to stay the main stream of contributions by other corporations. It is further weakened by his request that Root spread through the financial community the word that he was really protecting business from revolution. Root's text bears reading:

There is a better way to protect property, to protect capital, to protect . . . enterprises, than by buying legislatures. There is a better way to deal with labor, and to keep it from rising into the tumult of the unregulated and resistless mob than by starving it or by corrupting its leaders. . . . That way is, that capital shall be fair . . . fair to the consumer, fair to the laborer, fair to the investor; that it shall concede that the laws shall be executed. . . . Never forget that the men who labor cast the votes, set up and pull down governments, and that . . . the continued opportunity for enterprise, for the enjoyment of wealth, for individual liberty, is possible, only so long as the men who labor with their hands believe in American liberty and American laws.

Those remarks laid bare the essence of Roosevelt's policies.

No competent scholar has challenged them as a statement of what Roosevelt was actually doing. But many historians have used Roosevelt's endorsement of them as the point of departure for a cynical appraisal of his motives. It proves, they imply or declare, that he was more a sophisticated conservative than a genuine progressive, that he hated the "malefactors of great wealth" because he feared their excesses would provoke revolutionary violence, not because they were fundamentally unjust.

There is surely a large measure of truth in that analysis. One need but recall Roosevelt's harangues against the Haymarket anarchists, against Altgeld, Bryan, and the Silver Democrats, to realize how obsessive was his fear of upheaval from below. "We shall have to do this in order to prevent that," is the suggestive comment of Richard Hofstadter. Obviously, many of the sophisticated conservatives with whom Roosevelt associated—Lodge, Hanna, Root—were drawn to him because of this phase of his political character.

Nevertheless, significant differences separated the President and his conservative friends. Roosevelt was temperamentally disposed to act; they tended to stand pat until the external pressures became overwhelming. Roosevelt became morally indignant when confronted with injustice; they remained largely indifferent. Roosevelt would become intellectually involved in the reform itself—in its social and economic merit—and would make it part of his body of affirmative beliefs; they would view it as a necessary evil. Above all else, it was this positive accent that distinguished Roosevelt from his sophisticated conservative consorts, the real proponents of strategic retreat. The President's goal was a better, a more just and less privileged America; theirs, a more ordered America. This had been evidenced by Roosevelt's actions during his years in the legislature, by the economic reforms of his governorship, and by the recommendations of his first term. It would be further evidenced by the policies of his second term.

Regrettably, there had been no need for Roosevelt to compromise himself in the campaign of 1904. His election was a foregone conclusion, so firm was his hold on the American people's affections. That hold had already been demonstrated by countless incidents, none more moving that his reception on a whistle-stop tour of the West in the spring of 1903. "Wherever I stopped at a small city or country town," he wrote John Hay, "I was greeted by the usual shy, self-conscious, awkward body of local committeemen, and spoke to the usual audience of thoroughly good American citizens— a term I can use in a private letter to you without being thought demagogic!"

For all the superficial differences between us, down at bottom these men and I think a good deal alike, or at least have the same ideals, and I am always sure of reaching them in speeches which many of my Harvard friends would think not only homely, but commonplace. . . . The veterans felt that I had fought too, and they claimed a certain right of comradeship with me which really touched me deeply; and to them I could invariably appeal with the certainty of meeting an instant response. Whatever their faults and shortcomings, and however much in practise they had failed to come up to their ideal, yet they had this ideal, and they had fought for it in their youth of long ago. . . .

The President had also been amused—by the gifts of two bears, a lizard, a horned toad, and a horse, and by the undiluted democracy of the mayor of Butte, Montana:

As soon as we got in the banquet hall and sat at the head of the table the mayor hammered lustily with the handle of his knife and announced, "Waiter, bring on the feed." Then in a spirit of pure kindliness he added, "Waiter, pull up the curtains and let the people see the President eat!"—but to this I objected. . . . Of the hundred men who were my hosts I suppose at least half had killed their man in private war. . . . As they drank great goblets of wine the sweat glistened on their hard, strong, crafty faces.

On November 8, 1904, the people whose ideals Theodore Roosevelt exemplified had turned out by the millions to give him the greatest popular majority to that time. Judge Parker's campaign had fallen flat, as it had been foredoomed to do, and not even the revelation of the President's support by Wall Street did more than create a mild flurry of excitement. Roosevelt's adroit and self-righteous handling of the issue—the President dismissed the exaggerated implications of Parker's charges as "unqualifiedly and atrociously false," but ignored the objective portions—may even have redounded to his advantage.

At any rate, the returns gave the President an unprecedented popular majority of more than 2,500,000 and an electoral majority of 196. Roosevelt carried every state in the North, including Missouri, and he swept scores of Republican congressmen in with him. His election, conceded the *New York Sun*, was "one of the most illustrious personal triumphs in all political history."

Yet the President's personal popularity failed to offset completely the widening disenchantment with his party on the state level; five of the states he carried elected Democratic governors. Even in that, however, there were elements of vindication; also of irony. As the British Ambassador reported to Whitehall, the President's oft-repeated attacks on "political machines and party government by 'bosses' has encouraged . . . the principle of independent judgment."

Roosevelt was both astonished and elated by the magnitude of his victory. On election night, in accordance with a decision he had made some time before, he renounced further ambition. "I am deeply sensible of the honor done me by the American people . . . ," he said. "I appreciate to the full the solemn responsibilities this confidence imposes upon me, and I shall do all that in my power lies not to forfeit it."

On the fourth of March next I shall have served three and a half years, and this three and a half years constitutes my first term. The wise custom which limits the President to two terms regards the substance and not the form. Under no circumstances will I be a candidate for or accept another nomination.

A sincere and high purposed affirmation of the national tradition, that statement was also the worst political blunder of Theodore Roosevelt's career.

PART FOUR

The Square Deal Matures

Chapter 14

Another Measured Advance

*Three of the most cherished powers of pri-
vate business had been the right to set its own
prices for services, the right to maintain its
books and records in secrecy, and the right to
negotiate with labor without interference by a
third party. The President's 1905 message
challenged . . . all these rights. . . .*
                                    —George E. Mowry
                       The Era of Theodore Roosevelt

ROOSEVELT'S MAJESTIC triumph at the polls in November,
1904, had not changed the Old Guard's sentiments toward
him. To the leaders of his own party this greatest popular
hero since Andrew Jackson was still a maverick who must
be contained and even repressed; and as they detrained in
Washington early in December for the lame-duck session of
the Fifty-eighth Congress, the Republicans had breathed defiance. "Congress," growled Joseph G. Cannon, the grizzled,
tobacco-chewing Speaker of the House, "will pass the appropriation bills and mark time."

Cannon's forecast proved accurate. By Roosevelt's inauguration on March 4 Congress had pigeonholed most of the recommendations—railroad regulation, employers' liability legislation, tariff relief for the Philippines, and a child labor law
for the District of Columbia—the President made in his annual message of December 6. It had also failed to act on a
special message urging ratification of the critical Santo
Domingo treaty. Decidedly, there had been an aura of resentment, of studied insolence, about the final session of the
Fifty-eighth Congress.

Roosevelt had not really expected more. "Congress does
from a third to a half of what I think is the minimum that
it ought to do, and I am profoundly grateful that I get as
much," he explained to Leonard Wood. True, he was exasperated by the Senate's cavalier treatment of the Santo Domingo

treaty. "The Senate adjourns. I am then left to shoulder all the responsibility due to their failure . . . and have to spend an industrious summer engaged in the pleasant task of making diplomatic bricks without straw." But he was delighted that the lame-duck session had voted funds for the construction of two more battleships: "This navy puts us a good second to France and about on a par with Germany. . . . For some years now we can afford to rest and merely replace the ships that are worn out or become obsolete, while we bring up the personnel." And he was quietly confident that he had won the first skirmish in the looming battle for railroad rate regulation.

Roosevelt had originally hailed the Elkins Anti-rebate Act of 1903 as a signal accomplishment. Within a year of its enactment, however, he had concluded that more comprehensive regulation was needed. But he had waited until the people gave him their mandate in November, 1904, before pressing. Then, in his most unequivocal annual message to that time, he had forcefully delineated the lines of advance.

The President's paramount objective was to win authority for the Interstate Commerce Commission to set "maximum" railroad rates. This was necessary, he told Congress, because "as the law now stands the commission simply possess the bare power to denounce a particular rate as unreasonable." The Commission's ruling should take effect immediately after it had been made (instead of after prolonged litigation), and it should remain in effect unless reversed by the courts. Otherwise the great highways of commerce could not be kept "open to all on equal terms." Nor should Congress be deterred by philosophical objections to big government. The question was empirical. National supervision, Roosevelt asserted, was the only means by which "an increase of the present evils . . . or a still more radical policy" could be prevented.

The President struck at the opportune moment. Many powerful shippers were defying or circumventing the Elkins Act's provisions. Other discriminatory practices, including freight differentials that wrought hardship on whole sections of the country, were rampant, and the consolidation of lines was threatening great numbers of farmers and small manufacturers with the loss or drastic reduction of service. It was also widely and inaccurately believed that rates in general were excessive.

The result was such a broadly based demand for reform as the nation had not theretofore witnessed.

Militant farmers and their organizations were bitterly prescribing the old Populist remedy, government ownership of the roads. Southern and Western state legislatures were memorializing Congress for relief from the "iniquities" of the railroad operators or were threatening to act on their own as they had done during the Granger era. And more important still, for the farmers had tried and failed with William Jennings Bryan, the small-town middle classes were swelling the chorus. Business and professional men who had cast Democratic ballots only when Blaine had run against Cleveland, men who had equated Bryanism with social revolution and financial madness—these and many, many more were furiously decrying the abuses of the railroads. Even conservative churchmen were viewing the rate issue as a moral problem.

The Old Guard was visibly shaken. Repeatedly in the past it had dismissed or deflected mass pressures for reform; there were some who argued that it could do so again. There were others, however, who painfully concluded that it could no longer hold the weakening line. These realists knew that the corporations' spokesmen in the Senate could still turn a deaf ear to the outcries of the agrarians and ignore with impunity the feeble demands of labor. But they were not so confident that they could resist the combined pressure of the agrarians and the urban middle classes and yet remain indefinitely in power. From Joseph G. Cannon and Nelson W. Aldrich on down, therefore, the leaders of the Old Guard reluctantly decided to give the President and the reformers the shadow of their program. They or their predecessors had done this before—with the original Interstate Commerce Act of 1887, the Sherman Antitrust Act of 1890, and even the Elkins Act of 1903. They would now do it again, this time by endowing the courts with such broad powers of review that the Commission's decisions would become virtually impossible to implement. Yet even this devious strategy was formulated under duress, for at heart many preferred inaction. Had it not been for the sustained and commanding influence of Theodore Roosevelt, they might well have done nothing, the political consequences notwithstanding.

The struggle that marked the Old Guard's decision to hoist

the white flag proved bitter and dramatic. It saw the President abandon hope of tariff reform, submit to artful insult by Aldrich and his lieutenants, and back down from an advanced position. But it also saw him drive the Old Guard from its bastions, hold together a political party that a wrong move might have split asunder, and give the American people meaningful railroad legislation for the first time in history.

The first skirmish was handily won by the President. Flushed by his stunning victory in November, Roosevelt had considered urging tariff revision as well as railroad reform when he drafted his annual message. Had not the Republicans beaten "the Democrats on the issue that protection was robbery, and that when necessary we would amend or revise the tariff ourselves"? Discreetly, he revealed his feelings to the party faithful. He might call a special session of Congress in September to revise the tariff, he wrote Nicholas Murray Butler. It was possible that he would send in a special tariff message early in the new year, he confided to Cannon. Indeed, he had composed a draft of his proposed remarks; perhaps the Speaker would care to read them!

The President neither sent in a special message nor called an extra session. Hardly had he made those first gestures toward revision than he began to draw back. The obstacles were too imposing. A minority of Republicans, mainly Midwesterners, favored revision. They could be counted on for informed, vociferous support; but their numbers were inconsequential. In opposition stood a phalanx of stand-patters. They were headed by Cannon in the House and Orville H. Platt in the Senate, and they included virtually the entire Republican leadership. Committed by interest and conviction to the protectionist principle, they unalterably opposed a major reduction in schedules. For reasons of political expediency, they also opposed minor adjustments. "We know from long experience," Cannon candidly explained years later, "that no matter how great an improvement the new tariff may be, it almost always results in the party in power losing the following election."

Nevertheless, Roosevelt made measured soundings throughout November, 1904. They were not encouraging. "I am having great difficulty," he reported to Butler in early December. "The trouble is that there are large parts of the country which want no tariff revision. . . . They say, with entire truth, that neither in the platform nor in any communication of mine is there any promise whatever that there shall be tariff revision. . . . My argument in response is that I am meeting not a material need but a mental attitude. . . . What I am concerned about is to meet the expectation of people that we shall consider the tariff question, and the need of showing that the Republican party is not powerless to take up the subject."

Nine days later the President despaired of the chances of tariff revision, at least by the lame-duck Congress. There was, he informed Butler, "a strong majority against it—a majority due partly to self-interest, partly to inertia, partly to timidity, partly to genuine conviction. . . ." Nor was there anyone among the small minority of revisionists who possessed the "remarkable ability" needed to frame the law and steer its passage through Congress. A month later he privately conceded defeat. "On the interstate commerce business, which I regard as a matter of principle, I shall fight," he wrote Lyman Abbott. "On the tariff, which I regard as a matter of expediency, I shall endeavor to get the best results I can, but I shall not break with my party."

The President's statements were partly rationalizations. He recognized the need for tariff revision and he would have liked to effect it; his letters leave no doubt of that. Yet his decision to subordinate, and possibly to abandon, the issue did little real violence to his principles. Roosevelt's tariff views had paralleled the change in his attitude toward government regulation of industry and his repudiation of laissez-faire in general. By the mid-1890's and possibly before, he had come to believe that protectionism was a necessary instrument of national policy, one consonant with the obligation of the state to regulate in the interests of the whole. The mature Roosevelt could no more have weakened American industry's competitive advantage over foreign manufacturers by promoting free trade than he could have jeopardized America's world power position by jettisoning the battle fleet. The issue was urgent, not open to compromise, and only incidentally Republican. Not even the bitter protests of his Western followers would move Roosevelt from his protectionist commitment when he emerged as the knight-errant of the progressive movement in 1912.

Still, Roosevelt knew that there were abuses, that the schedules on some products were so high that they made the term "competitive concept" a mere play on words. Except in their impact upon colonial policy, however, he hardly regarded them as critical. As he explained to Butler, "I think there are certain schedules that should be reduced, but I do not think it at all a vital matter to reduce them, so far as the welfare of the people is concerned." Hence his willingness to exchange tariff reform for rate regulation. This was regrettable, for Roosevelt's inability to alter the tariff was one of the major failures of his presidency. But it had to be, so numerous and powerful were the high priests of protectionism within his party. Had he made a genuine effort to revise the tariff at any time during his seven and one-half years in office, he would have destroyed his effectiveness. Even as he virtually threw in the sponge, however, he decided to use the threat of action on the tariff to soften the Old Guard. As Blum shrewdly points out, he raised the dreaded specter at the outset of the fight for rate regulation and revived it at strategic moments thereafter until his offensive was fairly organized.

Of all the agitations then current, that for tariff reform was the most baleful to "Uncle Joe" Cannon. Although railroad reform stood to alienate some important Republicans, it bid to appease many more, notably farmers and other shippers. But tariff reform threatened to antagonize tens of thousands of party stalwarts—the small manufacturers who comprised the very sinews of the Republican party. In spite of his plan to have the lame-duck session "mark time," therefore, Cannon came quickly to terms in the winter of 1904–05. In return for inaction on the tariff, he allowed the President's railroad program as embodied in the Esch-Townshend bill to roll through the House by a staggering majority of 356 to 17. The Senate then refused to consider the measure; but it did provide for committee hearings following the adjournment of Congress. Hence the President's quiet confidence following his inauguration in March.

Meanwhile Roosevelt prepared to take the issue to the people—and to the enemy. He went to the enemy first, addressing the Union League Club of Philadelphia late in January, 1905. He had drawn his ground well. Philadelphia was long notorious for its craven politics, its corrupt business leaders, its complacent "nice people"; it was the financial capital of the state that regularly sent Quay and Penrose to the United States Senate; and it was one of the great railroad centers of the nation. Like the Old Guard it indifferently commissioned to represent it, the City of Brotherly Love stood immovably for the status quo.

The President said little in Philadelphia or anyplace else that he had not said before. But he did speak more emphatically, more effectively, and more authoritatively. His listeners could not but perceive what the leaders of the Senate were still unwilling to concede—that Roosevelt was President in his own right. He reminded the Union Leaguers, as he was shortly to remind the nation in his inaugural address, that "the great development of industrialism means that there must be an increase in the supervision exercised by the Government over business-enterprise." He observed, as he had done in his first message to Congress three years before, that the framers of the Constitution could not possibly have foreseen that present-day developments made state regulation impractical and national regulation mandatory. And he called again for amendment of the Constitution if necessary. His peroration nailed down his conservative-progressive Square Deal:

. . . there must be lodged in some tribunal the power over rates, and especially over rebates . . . which will protect alike the railroad and the shipper on an equal footing. . . . We do not intend that this Republic shall ever fail as those republics of olden times failed, in which there finally came to be a government by classes, which resulted either in the poor plundering the rich or in the rich . . . exploiting the poor.

From then until the rate issue was settled eighteen months later, Roosevelt maintained his fire. After the lame-duck session ended without Senate action on the day of his inauguration, he again feinted with the tariff. In April and May he campaigned through the Middle West and Southwest while en route to the annual Rough Riders' reunion at San Antonio. And during the summer of 1905 he warned the Old Guard that he might still call for tariff reform. Early in the fall he even went into the South where he repeatedly praised the Confederate military leaders, commented pridefully on his own Southern blood, and declaimed on the need for railroad legislation. It was as though he "himself fired the last two shots from the *Alabama* instead of his uncle," the incredulous correspondent for the *Washington Star* reported. "Wherever the President's visit is discussed you will hear men who believed in and fought for the Confederate cause speak of him with the affection of a comrade."

It was well that Roosevelt thus mobilized his forces, for the railroads, reinforced by the National Association of Manufacturers, had already organized theirs. While the President was warning that his program was the only alternative to socialism, an imposing battery of railroad lawyers was arguing before the Senate Committee on Interstate Commerce that it constituted a one way track to the destruction of private property. Nor did the railroads confine their fire to the Senate committee room. The distinguished scholar, William Z. Ripley, described their activities:

Bogus conventions, packed for the purpose . . . passed resolutions unanimously, to be scattered broadcast by free telegraphic dispatches all over the country. "Associations for the Maintenance of Property" held conventions; the fact being duly advertised. Palpably garbled news items from Washington were distributed without cost. . . . An elaborate card catalogue of small newspapers through the United States was made; in which was noted all the hobbies, prejudices, and even the personal weakness of the editors. . . . Dakota farmers got suggestions as to the danger of the proposed legislation affecting their rates. Kentucky planters were warned of the probable effect upon tobacco prices.

This powerful propaganda barrage failed of its target, mainly because the public recognized it for what it was even as it was born. The deep-seated grievances of the farmers and small shippers, the rising indignation of professional men, the shocking revelations of the muckrakers, and the relentless pounding of the President of the United States—all these made the movement for regulation politically irresistible. Observer after observer recognized this at the time. As the *Chicago Tribune* reported, "Many Senators are willing to serve the railroads and big shippers, but they have no desire to arouse a popular sentiment which might deprive them of their seats." By December, 1905, when the Fifty-ninth Congress finally convened, the reform wave had swept such stalwart Old Guardsmen as William B. Allison of Iowa and John Spooner of Wisconsin onto its crest. One question, and one question alone, remained: what shape would the impending legislation take?

The answer to that question affords as much insight into

Roosevelt as any event in his presidential career. It reveals especially his extraordinary skill and balance. The President insisted from the start that the attack be organized and disciplined, that it encompass the enemy's defeat, but not its annihilation. His order of battle, written into his annual message to Congress in December, 1905, was a model of calculated restraint. The President observed that the railroads, for all their faults, "had done well and not ill" to American society. He warned that rate regulation was "a complicated and delicate problem." And he declared that because of the "extraordinary development of industrialism along new lines . . . which the lawmakers of old could not foresee and therefore could not provide against," well-meaning corporations had been driven into malpractices by the struggle for survival.

Having recognized the railroads' material services, Roosevelt then revealed the idealism that caused him always to reject the business civilization's ultimate values. "There can be no delusion more fatal to the nation," he warned, "than the delusion that the standard of profits, of business prosperity, is sufficient in judging any business or political question—from rate legislation to municipal government." He would, accordingly, set up a moral and legal standard that would free "the corporation that wishes to do well from being driven into doing ill, in order to compete with its rival, which prefers to do ill." The rebate evil should be eliminated completely, the Interstate Commerce Commission should be empowered to fix maximum rates after appeal and investigation, and delays in implementing the Commission's findings should be drastically reduced. Those were his objectives. He would go a little beyond them; he would not stop short of them.

As incorporated in the Hepburn bill, Roosevelt's rate recommendations passed the House early in 1906 by a majority even more imposing than that mounted on the Esch-Townshend bill the previous year. The Hepburn bill then went to the Senate, where progressives sought vainly to overcome its inadequacies and the Old Guard tried urgently to compound them.

One problem was that the Hepburn bill failed to provide means to determine rates realistically. Roosevelt had called for uniform accounting procedures and for government inspection similar to that exercised over the national banks. This was a first, and important, step toward a full solution; but it was inconclusive. Without authority for the Interstate Commerce Commission to evaluate the worth of the railroads, it was impossible to fix a fair rate. This was widely recognized at the time. But it was Senator La Follette who most forcibly impressed it upon the President.

Robert Marion La Follette had stormed out of Wisconsin, which he had given a gubernatorial administration that serves to this day as a prototype of enlightenment, to be sworn in at the opening session of the Fifty-ninth Congress in March, 1905. A radical in the traditional sense—he was a root thinker to the point of single-mindedness—he would brook neither intellectual nor political compromise. Again and again during the twenty years he sat in the United States Senate this humorless, fiercely intense tribune of the upper Mississippi Valley championed unpopular causes, often with grave risk to his influence and not inconsiderable ambition, but almost always with honor to his convictions. Historians who shared his isolationist sympathies, and many who did not, would eventually set him down as the greatest twentieth-century senator of the progressive persuasion, excepting only, perhaps, George W. Norris of Nebraska.

La Follette had come to Washington in the high hope that the second Roosevelt administration would herald the full flowering of the national progressive movement. And though he brought reservations about the President—there was, he suspected, too much of the trimmer in his make-up—he also knew that Roosevelt had an intelligent regard for the opinion of experts and was reputedly open to advice.

The redoubtable Wisconsin freshman's hopes had begun to sink when Roosevelt failed to come out for evaluation of railroad properties in his annual message. They sank further when he realized that the Hepburn bill would go to a final vote in the Senate without that important provision. Rebelling inwardly against the tradition that kept freshmen senators out of debate, La Follette maintained his silence for week after week. Nor did he discuss his views with the President. In accordance with his policy of working with those in whom the real power was vested, Roosevelt was not confiding in La Follette and others of his stamp. In February, 1906, however, the Wisconsin Senator's hopes were momentarily revived when Lincoln Steffens arranged for him to meet with the President.

For two hours late one Sunday night these two embattled leaders of the American social-justice movement discussed the rate problem in the privacy of the White House. Conceding the logic of La Follette's economic analysis, Roosevelt rejected its politics. "But you can't get any such bill as that through this Congress," he exclaimed as the Wisconsin Senator finished. "I want to get something through."

La Follette characteristically replied that Roosevelt should capitalize on the popular sentiment for rate reform by sending a special message to Congress. If that failed, he should take the issue to the next Congress. And if that also failed, he would have at least familiarized the public with the only effective course of action; and that, concluded the unyielding Senator, would be a monumental achievement.

Both men were proved right. Roosevelt went on to win his immediate, limited objective, then took the more advanced issue to the people in succeeding years. La Follette meanwhile contributed to the general enlightenment, or, so Roosevelt complained, confusion, by raising the basic question. "I became utterly out of patience with his attitude. . . ." he wrote of La Follette a year later, "for . . . had it been effective, [it] would have meant the loss of the bill with absolutely no compensating gain." Still, the President added, he "often serves a very useful purpose in making the Senators go on record, and his fearlessness is the prime cause of his being able to render this service."

The futility of the course La Follette wanted Roosevelt to pursue was decisively demonstrated in April, 1906, when the Wisconsin freshman resolutely broke with tradition and took the floor of the Senate chamber, a 148-page manuscript clutched in his hand. As he started to speak senator after senator stalked off the floor; but before he completed his presentation two days later most had returned—some out of idle curiosity, some to engage him in open debate, and some, like Jonathan Dolliver of Iowa, the President's floor leader of the moment, to become converts to his point of view. For to those whose minds were open, La Follette's logic was irrefutable. As Roosevelt knew, however, the majority of the Old Guardsmen's minds were closed. Their design was to mitigate the popular pressure, not to solve the railroad problem. When La Follette's proposal for physical evaluation was put to the roll-call test, only six Republicans voted for it.

While La Follette was striving for the impossible, Roosevelt was earnestly mustering votes for the possible and a little that was not. The formidable character of his task had again been driven home when Cabot Lodge declared on February 12 that freight rates were not generally excessive. "I have the gravest doubts," the haughty Senator exclaimed, "as to the wisdom of government rate-making even in the most limited form." Lodge's opposition must have hurt the President. But so highly did he value his friend's affection that it failed to affect their relationship. "I say deliberately," Roosevelt wrote Lyman Abbott soon afterward, "that during the twenty years [Lodge] has been in Washington he has been on the whole the best and most useful servant of the public to be found in either house of Congress. . . . Lodge is a man of very strong convictions." And this means, he added in a flash of self-revelation, "that when his convictions differ from mine I am apt to substitute the words 'narrow' and 'obstinate' for 'strong'; and he has a certain aloofness and coldness of manner that irritate people who don't live in New England. But he is an eminently fit successor of Webster and Sumner." Roosevelt never changed that judgment of his closest friend.

Even as Lodge flailed the heart of the President's program, the Old Guard leadership concluded that Roosevelt had the votes to win the right to fix maximum rates. It decided, therefore, to attack the flank by amending the Hepburn bill with such broad provisions for judicial review that the I.C.C.'s rate-making power would be dissipated. The architect of this strategy was Nelson W. Aldrich of Rhode Island.

A natural aristocrat of modest birth, Aldrich was by some estimates the ablest senatorial conservative of his times. He had been educated in the common schools of the mill town, East Killingly, Connecticut, gone into the wholesale grocery business in Providence as a youth, and been mobilized into the federal military service in 1862 at the age of twenty. Stricken by typhoid fever after six months of war, he had returned to Providence to move up the business and social ladder. By his middle twenties he had been made junior partner in the grocery firm, and by his middle thirties he had become president of the First National Bank and of the Providence Board of Trade. He had meanwhile married well.

A boyhood interest in debate and a mature concern with civic affairs soon caused Aldrich to gravitate to politics. He became head of the City Council in Providence, served one term in Congress in the late 1870's, and was made a United States senator by the Republican organization in the early 1880's. In Washington, where the irreverent dubbed him "Morgan's floor broker in the Senate," Aldrich's impressive talents soon won him recognition as one of the most persuasive young spokesmen of the burgeoning industrial and financial order. Witty, urbane, and gracious to his peers, a connoisseur and patron of painting, Aldrich was intellectually facile if not profound. He was imperious by nature, and he was both more arrogant and less flexible than Elihu Root. Aldrich had always been distantly contemptuous of his inferiors, and as he grew older he became increasingly aloof, disdaining the intimacy of most other senators, yet wielding greater influence perhaps than anyone else in the Senate.

Aldrich's failing was the common one of the self-made man: he was insensitive to the inequities in the economic system that had yielded undue preferment to his own superior abilities. The welfare of labor, the farmers, and the consumers fell not within his compass except incidentally, and in the classic manner of his type he believed that government should subsidize and otherwise foster the ends of business while desisting from regulatory action. A millionaire several times over, the father-in-law of John D. Rockefeller, Jr., the holder of vast oil and railroad securities, Aldrich nevertheless failed to fit the formula of David Graham Phillips's muckraking *Treason of the Senate.* His conservatism, like that of his colleague and staunch supporter, Orville Platt of Connecticut, who had no millions and owned little stock, was ideological, and in the field of finance, narrowly constructive. By temperament, by experience, and by conviction, Nelson W. Aldrich was a Hamiltonian.

It was probably inevitable that the distinguished Rhode Islander should emerge as the leader of Roosevelt's opposition. By 1906 Mark Hanna was two years in his grave. Spooner and Allison were acting as Roosevelt's lieutenants on the rate bill for reasons of expediency. And Platt, "not as brilliant, but . . . of fine ability, of entire fearlessness, and of a transparently upright and honorable nature" in the President's apt description, had died the summer before. Of the genuine conservatives, only Philander C. Knox, who had resigned as Attorney-General to become junior senator from Pennsylvania, approached Aldrich in character. And he led no faction.

A number of factors strengthened Aldrich's plan to vitiate Roosevelt's railroad program by amendment. The most fortuitous was the Hepburn bill's failure to specify the scope of the courts' review. Roosevelt believed that limited review of the I.C.C.'s findings was both necessary and proper; and after being advised that omission of a provision for same would result in a ruling of unconstitutionality, he had his lieutenants attack the problem when the bill reached the Senate. His object, as Blum writes, was to devise an amendment that would "perpetuate explicitly the ambiguities implicit in the House's version." But in thus tampering with the House bill, Roosevelt opened the door for the Old Guardsmen to cloak their prorailroad arguments in the hallowed language of constitutionalism.

To a few, such as Knox, the constitutional question was substantive. In a memorable speech on March 28 the former Attorney-General declared that judicial review was "a right painfully won from tyrannies of the past" and that it "would be as a reproach to those of us who are lawyers . . . should we urge the bill or . . . supinely permit it to become law." But to most conservative Republicans the real issue was how best to circumvent regulation of maximum rates. Little or nothing in the backgrounds of Elkins of West Virginia, Penrose of Pennsylvania, Depew of New York, Foraker of Ohio, and numerous other Old Guardsmen suggests they were remotely animated by concern for a great legal tradition.

If the Old Guard's shift from rate-making to judicial review illuminated the art of political sophistry, Aldrich's floor leadership revealed the politics of desperation. Unable to muster a majority for such a broad review clause as would have thwarted the President's purposes, his fertile mind devised still another stratagem. He would turn over floor leadership of the Hepburn bill, then under Dolliver's control, to a Democrat. Not a respectable Democrat with whom the President could cooperate, but a beak-nosed, one-eyed master of personal invective whom Roosevelt had once compared to Robespierre and Marat and had not spoken to for four years— Benjamin R. "Pitchfork Ben" Tillman of South Carolina.

The South Carolina Senator exemplified both the worst and the best in the Southern "popocrat" tradition. A vicious Negro-baiter, an early anti-imperialist, and an inveterate friend of the federal pork barrel, Tillman was as devoted a servant of his white, back-country constituents as most Northern Republicans were of the railroad managers and manufacturers. Like many Southerners of demagogic bent, his compassion was considerable if erratic, and had he not been perverted by the race problem he might have emerged as a respected progressive. "Pitchfork Ben" believed with the President that the real need was railroad legislation in the public interest, and he proposed to get it by spelling out the narrowest possible judicial review. He even sought to prohibit temporary injunctions, the device by which the railroads indefinitely avoided the I.C.C.'s rulings.

Roosevelt was exasperated by the Rhode Island Senator's blow. "Aldrich," he fumed privately, had "completely lost both his head and his temper." Indeed, the President feared he might lose everything by identifying himself with the Tillman-La Follette radicals. Not only might the amendment restraining the use of temporary injunctions be ruled unconstitutional, there was no assurance that Roosevelt could realign his forces should the alliance with Tillman and La Follette break down. Roosevelt soon decided to take the gamble, however, and in truth it was not too great. "The more I think over this railroad rate matter and the antics of the men who are, under all kinds of colors, trying to prevent any kind of effective legislation," he wrote Allison, "the more I think through their own action the so-called 'conservative' or so-called 'railroad senators' have put us in a position where we should not hesitate to try to put a proper bill through in combination with the Democrats." The Republicans, he indignantly complained to another correspondent, "have tried to betray me."

Roosevelt accordingly entered into negotiations with the despised South Carolinian through a mutual friend. The President hoped that they could agree on a bill that would be acceptable to the Spooner-Allison Republicans in the center; but when this failed because Tillman's provisions were too radical for Spooner and Allison, Roosevelt agreed to go all the way with Tillman and La Follette if they could muster a majority. Tillman failed by two votes, however, to marshal the support he needed.

The President thereupon returned to his original position— that of an explicit perpetuation of "the ambiguities implicit in the House's version." Under Allison's persuasive cloakroom leadership the Republicans then closed ranks behind Roosevelt's program. The Democrats also went along; and on May 18, 1906, the Hepburn bill passed the Senate with only three negative votes. The President had won his primary objective.

Charges and countercharges followed: cries of betrayal from the Tillman-La Follette left; claims of victory by the Aldrich-Knox right. Despite his failure to form the majority that would have carried his amendments, Tillman felt that the President had let him down. With injured countenance and ostentatious restraint, "Pitchfork Ben" had arisen from his seat just a few days before the final vote to read an "inside history of recent events" from a carefully prepared manuscript. He "confessed" that he had entered into a "conspiracy" with the President; he charged that the administration had surrendered to Aldrich; and he flatly asserted that Roosevelt had spoken derogatorily of prominent Republicans, namely, Knox, Spooner, and Foraker.

If Tillman's first two charges were routine, the third was sensational. Roosevelt had already strained relations with the Old Guard to the breaking point; the revelation that he had criticized members of his own party to the leader of the opposition could sever the last thin cord. It was with cold discomfort, therefore, that Lodge listened to the colorful South Carolinian's accusations. As soon as Tillman concluded, he rushed to a telephone to read to the President a stenographic report of the South Carolinian's remarks. Lodge returned to the Senate chamber a few minutes later with what the exigencies demanded—an official denial. Tillman's assertion, said the President in the statement that Lodge read into the record, was "a deliberate and unqualified falsehood."

And so Benjamin R. Tillman of South Carolina was initiated into Roosevelt's "Ananias Club." His membership was not earned. Roosevelt rarely spoke with moderation in the heat of controversy. And though he repeated his denial a few days later in what his daughter Alice dubbed a "posterity letter," he significantly added: "I cannot remember the details of the conversation."

The claims of victory by the Aldrich forces had no foundation. When Roosevelt scuttled the Tillman-La Follette program he withdrew only to his original position. Blum proves beyond cavil that the bill that finally went through embodied the ambiguous phraseology that Roosevelt had first insisted upon. Thus it was Aldrich, his power compromised by Roosevelt's leadership and Allison's defection to the President's side, who had actually submitted. "[Aldrich] . . . has come nearer being unhorsed and thrown in the ditch in this struggle," Tillman observed, "than ever before since I have been here." Only by climbing on the bandwagon at the end had he saved his face and a measure of his prestige.

Overlooked at the time, moreover, was a clause that put all interstate pipelines under the I.C.C.'s control. On May 4, two weeks before the final roll call in the Senate, Roosevelt had sent in a report describing the Standard Oil Company's near monopoly of pipelines. He accompanied it with a forceful special message accusing Standard of overcharging New England consumers three to four hundred thousand dollars a year, mainly "by unfair or unlawful methods." Cabot Lodge, who almost invariably responded to pressures from his Massachusetts constituents, had then framed the amendment classifying all pipelines as common carriers.

Roosevelt had earned the right to exult and even to exaggerate. The Hepburn bill "contains practically exactly what I have both originally and always since asked for," he wrote. "Pitchfork Ben" Tillman knew that it did not contain what the President had "always" supported. But the vituperative South Carolinian also knew what Aldrich tried in the end to ignore: passage of the Hepburn bill was a testament to Roosevelt's superb powers of leadership. In a speech made after his relations with the President had returned to their customarily low level, the unpredictable Tillman acknowledged that fact. Had it not been "for the work of Theodore Roosevelt, in bringing this matter to the attention of the country," he graciously said, ". . . we would not have had any bill at all," and "whatever success may come from it will be largely due to him." Of course, he added, the idea was proclaimed in three successive Democratic platforms. Other senators echoed Tillman's words. "I do not believe a bill of this character would have passed the Senate," Henry M. Teller of Colorado declared, "if the President had not given life to this enterprise." Without Roosevelt, intoned Joseph A. Bailey of Texas, "even this imperfect and insufficient bill could have never become a law."

Roosevelt never had any illusions that the Hepburn Act was perfect. He underestimated its inadequacies, notably its failure to strike at freight differentials. And he overestimated its immediate impact. But even as he had fought for its broad principles, he had regarded it as experimental; always he planned to amend it on the basis of practical experience.

To dwell on the measure's limitations is to obscure the magnitude of the President's achievement. Once again he had demonstrated his mastery of the political process; once again his bold and imaginative leadership had forged the Grand Old Party into a crude instrument of reform. By feinting and threatening, by advancing and retreating, by inciting the people and cooperating with the opposition, he had wrenched from its leaders legislation that many of them bitterly opposed. Even more important, he had created another counterforce to the overweening power of monopoly. To the conservative elements of the nation, government by commission was "creeping socialism"; to the extreme left, it was perversion of the socialist dogma. But to the pragmatic center it was simply a rational response to the need to curb the railroads' antisocial power and yet preserve the advantages of large-scale organization. The appraisal of Professor Ripley, who had been disappointed when Roosevelt failed to support amendments he had urged at the time, is still persuasive. Passage of the Hepburn bill, wrote Ripley, "was an historic event—the most important, perhaps, in Theodore Roosevelt's public career—and a not insignificant one in our national history."

Chapter 15

Trials, Triumph, and Tragedy

> *But for all that, this contemner of "reforms"*
> *made reform respectable in the United States,*
> *and this rebuker of "muckrakers" has been the*
> *chief agent in making the history of "muck-*
> *raking" in the United States a national one,*
> *conceded to be useful.*
> —Robert M. La Follette, *Autobiography*

THE LONG fight for the Hepburn bill illuminated only a few of Roosevelt's many facets and was but one of several episodes which made 1905 and 1906 the most constructive years of his presidency. During these first two years "in his own right" Roosevelt took America into the world, stamped his imprint upon a score and more of domestic matters, and engaged in ceaseless controversy. He jousted good-naturedly with Bryan, who accused him of stealing his program. He alienated many idealistic magazine writers by damning them as "muck-rakers." He quarreled publicly with his ambassador to Austria-Hungary, a pleasant gentleman whose career was ruined by the foibles of his ambitious wife. He made a serio-comic effort to convert the nation to simplified spelling. And he pushed through Congress public health measures of momentous importance.

Many of the President's controversies hardly merit review. His quarrel with Ambassador and Mrs. Bellamy Storer proves only that Roosevelt was mildly indiscreet in his enthusiasm for the promotion of Archbishop Ireland. Thus Pringle, after dismissing Storer's charge that Roosevelt had authorized him to inform Pope Pius X of the President's desire, speculates: "It is not difficult to imagine Roosevelt pacing up and down in front of his guests at Oyster Bay and insisting explosively that 'Ireland is just the man for Cardinal . . . the Pope should appoint him . . . I fully sympathize.' "

If the Ireland affair was soon forgotten, the President's vain effort to impose simplified spelling upon an anguished people lives on in the minds of literary purists. Roosevelt took naturally to the recommendations of the Spelling Reform Association, a learned organization headed by his friend, Professor Brander Mathews of Columbia University. And when the Association proposed three hundred changes in spelling in 1906, he directed the Government Printing Office to comply. Although 90 per cent of the new spellings were already in the standard dictionaries under optional or alternative listings— they mainly embraced such changes as "honour" to "honor," "dropped" to "dropt," "fulfill" to "fulfil"—the ensuing reaction was as heated as the one provoked by another Roosevelt's effort to change the date of Thanksgiving Day some three decades later.

The *New York Times* weightily predicted that all newspapers "will take the kindly view that the President's heterographical freaks are misprints and will correct them into English." An irate contributor to the *Rochester Post-Express* charged that the whole scheme is backed "by certain large publishing interests and designed to carry out an immense project for jobbery in reprinting dictionaries and schoolbooks." And Henry Watterson declared in his *Louisville Courier-Journal* that the President's name should be written "Rucefelt," "the first silabel riming with goose." But the most indignant outcry was raised three thousand miles away. The "President's American," it was freely said on the isle that had spawned the language, is usurping the "King's English." The Supreme Court of the United States also issued an opinion. Any citation of a previous decision which invoked the new spelling "was not a literal quotation," the Chief Justice sternly informed the Solicitor-General.

Roosevelt knew when a cause was lost. "I could not by fighting have kept the new spelling in," he explained to Mathews after the House angrily directed that all government publications, including executive department documents, observe the standard practice, "and it was evidently worse than useless to go into an undignified contest when I was beaten." They had made a tactical error. "Do you know that the one word as to which I thought the new spelling was wrong—thru —was more responsible than anything else for our discomfiture?" The President would not, however, concede complete defeat. "In my own correspondence I shall continue using the new spelling," he added. He did.

Meanwhile, more substantial matters were absorbing the President's energy. For fifteen years reformers inspired by the Department of Agriculture's chief chemist, Dr. Harvey Wiley, "a very mountain among men, a lion among fighters," as one admirer described him, had been agitating for a federal law to require accurate labeling of preserved foods, beverages, and drugs. They had mobilized an articulate opinion in support of their proposals, and they had twice won approval for their bills in the House. But they had failed to make headway in the Senate, the Republican spokesman for the food and drug industries combining with the Southern Democratic proponents of states' rights to keep their bills in committee.

The President's commitment to their cause was belated—a reflection, perhaps, of that accommodation to conservatives which marked much of his conduct in the election year 1904. Not until the summer of 1905 after talks with his personal physician, Dr. Wiley, and others, did Roosevelt agree to support their proposals; and then he did so with misgivings. As he remarked in November, "it will take more than my recommendation to get the law passed, for I understand that there is some very stubborn opposition." And as he did not say, he was prepared to sacrifice almost everything for railroad regulation. Nevertheless, he recommended federal regulation of "interstate commerce in misbranded and adulterated foods, drinks, and drugs" in his annual message on December 5.

Roosevelt's brief recommendation incited a short, but bitter, fight in the Senate. Refusing to allow a bill sponsored by Weldon Heyburn of Idaho to emerge from committee, Aldrich sneered openly at the "chemists of the Agricultural Department" and speciously asserted that "the liberty of all the people of the United States" was at stake. Nor did the imperious Rhode Islander recant when Porter J. McCumber of North Dakota rejoined that the real issue was a man's right to receive what he asks and pays for, "not some poisonous substance in lieu thereof."

For a month and one-half after Aldrich's onslaught the Heyburn bill lay buried in committee. On February 15, 1906, however, Aldrich told Beveridge that he would permit it to be brought out for consideration; six days later the measure rolled through the Senate. Four states'-rights Democrats voted against it, and Aldrich, in a not unusual gesture of contempt, abstained. Aldrich offered no explanation for his startling reversal, and his adulatory biographer fails to explore his reasoning. But the circumstantial evidence is overwhelming. Samuel Hopkins Adams' exposures of the patent medicine industry in *Collier's* had set off a new round of protest. The American Medical Association was threatening to take the issue into partisan politics. And Roosevelt himself had entered a personal appeal. In addition, and perhaps as important, Aldrich wanted to clear the decks for the final debate on the railroad bill.

Nevertheless, the Pure Food bill might still have died in the House. Cannon was indifferent and Roosevelt was too engrossed in the fight for railroad legislation to give it much attention. But the publication in late February of Upton Sinclair's gruesome indictment of the meat-packing industry, *The Jungle,* added a dramatic new dimension. Roosevelt was so revolted by Sinclair's findings, in fact, that he at once directed Secretary of Agriculture James "Tama Jim" Wilson to investigate the novelist's charges:

I wish you would carefully read through this letter yourself [he had enclosed a personal appeal from Sinclair]. . . . The experiences that Moody has had in dealing with these beef trust people convinces me that there is very little that they will stop at. You know the wholesale newspaper bribery which they have undoubtedly indulged in. Now, I do not think that an ordinary investigation will reach anything. I would like a first-class man to be appointed to meet Sinclair. . . . We cannot afford to have anything perfunctory done in this matter.

The President meanwhile engaged in a brisk and revealing exchange with Sinclair. "I agree with you that energetic, and, as I believe, in the long run radical, action must be taken to do away with the effects of arrogant and selfish greed on the part of the capitalist," Roosevelt wrote the young and sensitive novelist. However, he continued, he deplored the "pathetic belief" of the characters who "preach socialism" in the last chapter of *The Jungle*. There were communities where "self-raising is very hard for the time being," the President added, but "there are many, many men who lack any intelligence or character and who therefore cannot thus raise themselves." He would help those crippled by accident (as the employers' liability bill he was then urging Congress to pass was designed to do) and he would regulate big business; but he was not then ready to go further. "A quarter of a century's hard work over what I may call politico-sociological problems has made me distrust men of hysterical temperament," he pointedly added. Yet, he resolutely concluded, "all this has nothing to do with the fact that the specific evils you point out shall, if their existence be proved, and if I have power, be eradicated."

During the next several weeks the meat-packing investigation weighed increasingly heavily on the President. He appointed two special investigators, Commissioner of Labor Charles P. Neill and the veteran social worker, James B. Reynolds, to verify Sinclair's findings. And he took his old friend, Albert J. Beveridge of Indiana, into his confidence. Beveridge was never a member of the Senate's inner circle, his self-assurance, independence, and progressive viewpoint offending the Old Guard. Like Roosevelt, however, he had continued to grow intellectually. He had already voted consistently for railroad regulation and before the year was out he would become a passionate partisan of the graduated income tax and child labor legislation.

Beveridge had been aware of the nauseous conditions in the stockyards and packing houses for some time. With the President's hearty assent, but without a promise of active support, he now framed a meat inspection measure which passed the Senate on May 25 as an amendment to the Agricultural Appropriations bill. The House committee on agriculture sat on it, however, and it appeared that the impassioned outpourings of Sinclair, Mark Sullivan, and the others would come to naught. For in the committee chairman, James W. Wadsworth, a stand-pat, walrus-mustached, gentleman farmer from Geneseo, New York, the packers had a man almost as solicitous of their interests as the paid lobbyists who milled about the Capitol's corridors.

Meanwhile the long struggle for the Hepburn bill ended. Roosevelt was now free to throw the power of his office behind the pure food and meat inspection legislation; with characteristic zest and no little finesse, he did so.

The facts uncovered by Neill and Reynolds are "hideous," the President wrote Wadsworth on May 26. "I was at first so indignant that I resolved to send in the full report to Congress." But after reflection, he continued, he decided to withhold it if Wadsworth would push through the Beveridge amendment. "I should not make the report public with the idea of damaging the packers," he ominously added. "I should do it only if it were necessary in order to secure the remedy."

But Wadsworth and the packers' friends were too anxious to prevent effective inspection to act rationally; they soon came up with crippling amendments. Roosevelt thereupon sent the House a special message urging passage of the Beveridge amendment. The first part of the Neill-Reynolds report, carefully designated as "preliminary," was appended. The inference was clear: the President would publish the full and more damning report should the House fail to swing into line.

As Roosevelt anticipated, the confirmation of Sinclair's charges had a devastating impact upon the packing industry's sales, especially in Western Europe. One packinghouse executive described the decline as "disastrous"; another reported that his company's sales had "been more than cut in two."

The packers therefore decided to support a federal meat-inspection measure in the cynical expectation that it would restore confidence in their products. Almost overnight the same lobbyists who had castigated the Beveridge amendment as "unconstitutional" and "socialistic" reversed themselves. What they and their powerful employers now wanted, and what Wadsworth was prepared to give them, was "an inspection law . . . strong enough to still public clamor, while not so drastic as to inconvenience them too greatly." But what the President wanted, and what he was prepared within limits to fight for, was "a thorough and rigid, and not a sham, inspection."

The result was conflict, and in the Roosevelt pattern, compromise. After a bitter exchange of letters in which the President wrote Wadsworth that his substitute amendment was "very, very bad," and the Congressman replied that Roosevelt was "wrong, 'very, very wrong,' " they came together. The President agreed that the government should bear the cost of inspection. He also yielded to the packers' objections to Beveridge's proposal that the date of inspection be stamped on the cans. But Roosevelt won clear-cut victories on two other points: inspectors were to be appointed under the civil service laws; the government was authorized to stop inspections in plants that failed to comply with its recommendations. This meant that the packers would have either to conform or lose the now coveted government stamp of approval.

The President also won a substantive victory on the most important issue of all—court review. Wadsworth had urged a clause that would have enabled the packers to evade the law by endless litigation. Roosevelt was outraged by this proposal. "I wish to repeat that if deliberately designed to prevent the remedying of the evils complained of," he wrote Wadsworth on June 15, "this is the exact provision which the friends of the packers and the packers themselves would have provided. . . . Why have you not put such a provision in the post-office law as it affects fraud orders; in the law as it affects fraudulent entries of homesteads, and so forth?"

Roosevelt then published his "very, very bad" letter. Wadsworth was crushed, or nearly so. Reluctantly, he submitted to a compromise clause which restricted the packers' right to appeal the inspectors' rulings in the courts. Meanwhile the way was cleared for passage of the original pure food bill. Four months later Wadsworth lost the seat he had held almost continuously since 1881. An embittered and discredited man, he could only growl that the "bloody hero of Kettle Hill" was "unreliable, a faker, and a humbug."

Once again the President basked in the glow of achievement. "The railroad rate bill, meat inspection bill & pure food bill . . . mark a noteworthy advance in the policy of securing Federal supervision and control over corporations," he told Lyman Abbott. "I send you herewith the pen with which I signed the agricultural bill, containing the meat inspection clauses," he wrote Beveridge. "You were the man who first called my attention to the abuses in the packing houses. You were the legislator who drafted the bill which in its substance now appears in the amendment to the agricultural bill. . . ."

But to Upton Sinclair, Dr. Wiley, and all the other reformers who had recruited the armies Roosevelt had so brilliantly maneuvered, the President sent nothing. Nor did he mention them in his *Autobiography*. It was not that Roosevelt was ungenerous or wholly impatient with men of theory. He himself was the most eminent intellectual to sit in the White House since John Quincy Adams, and his administration reflected it. Never had a President shown such a considered respect for the opinion of welfare workers and social critics, of natural scientists and experts in general; never had there been such a triumph of applied theory as marked the conversation movement under Theodore Roosevelt.* And never, either, had a President been so acutely sensitive to the compromises forced upon him by political necessity and so rankly partisan in their defense. Incident after incident attests to this.

Roosevelt never publicly acknowledged his debt to Tillman and his Democratic colleagues on the Hepburn bill. Nor, until late in his second administration, did he begin to have reservations about supporting the Republican Old Guardsmen whose opposition to his own advanced theories had repeatedly compelled their compromise and at times their emasculation. During the congressional elections of 1906 he called for a united Republican front; and when Samuel Gompers dared to challenge it with a scorching indictment of "Uncle Joe" Cannon's labor record, he boiled over with resentment. "This administration has had no stouter friend than the Speaker of the House," Roosevelt wrote in obvious self-delusion. "I need not say . . . that it is a simple absurdity to portray him as an enemy of labor. . . . He is a patriotic American. He is for every man, rich or poor, capitalist or labor man, so long as he is a decent American; and he is entitled to our support because he is a patriotic man."

The President continued meanwhile to give William Jennings Bryan short shrift. The closest Roosevelt ever came to admitting a similarity of view with the Great Commoner was at a Gridiron Club dinner in January, 1905. Bryan disarmingly accused the President of abstracting plank after plank from the Democratic platform and Roosevelt disingenuously confessed the crime. The trouble, he explained with mock regret, was that he had to expropriate the good things in the Democratic platform because Mr. Bryan would never be in a position to apply them.

But as Pringle has cogently written, Roosevelt was in the main "curiously intolerant toward the Commoner." Even in late 1905 and early 1906 when Bryan was threatening to read out of the Democratic party members who opposed the President's effort to regulate railroads, Roosevelt was fulminating against him in private: "He is neither a big nor a strong man . . . he is shallow, but he is kindly and well-meaning, and singularly free from rancor." "Bryan, LaFollette, and others like them, so far as I know, have always refused to attack labor people or to denounce their wrongdoing, no matter how flagrant—for

* See Chapter 19.

corporations, though their indirect influence may be powerful, have practically no votes, while the labor vote is very strong indeed." "As for Bryan . . . what a shallow demagogue he is. I do not believe he is a bit worse than Thomas Jefferson, and I do not think that if elected President he will be a worse President. The country would survive."

There was more than partisan Republicanism, more than Roosevelt's concealed discomfort at his own compromises, in those strictures. For even as the President picked up the pieces of the Populist-Democratic platform and began dimly to see that in himself, if not in his party, Hamiltonianism and Jeffersonianism were merging, he feared where the advanced reformers might take him. More than ever before he was now the hero of the moderate left; but no more than before did he believe that the nation's problems could be resolved by supplanting business control of American society with that of the agrarians and labor.

The lust for power and prestige, the self-interest approach to public issues, the potential for political corruption—all these qualities were possessed alike by the right and the left, the exploiters and the exploited, the favored and the unfavored. They buttressed Roosevelt's fears of unregulated competition; they provoked his consuming aversion to government in the interests of a particular class; and they served as the intellectual springboard for the great centralizing tendencies of his administrations. They also explain his obsession with personal character, for upon the integrity of the office holder and the disinterested intelligence of the administrator did the success of the classless, centralized state depend. Even Lincoln Steffens, after observing in 1904 that Roosevelt "has been sneered at for going about the country preaching . . . good conduct in the individual, simple honesty, courage, and efficiency," concluded that "the literal adoption of Mr. Roosevelt's reform scheme would result in a revolution, more radical and terrible to existing institutions, from the Congress to the Church, from the bank to the ward organization, than socialism or even anarchy. Why, that would change all of us —not alone our neighbors, not alone the grafters, but you and me."

It was not to be. Roosevelt's critics on the right even deny the moral and intellectual base of his mighty thrust toward the welfare state, arguing as they must that the President's real goal was the personal aggrandizement of power. Contrariwise, his detractors on the left, including the latter-day Steffens, scorn both his rationale and his results. No basic change in the power structure was wrought by Roosevelt's deeds and even less was wrought by his words, they contend to this day. In their analysis, his projection of a classless government was chimerical. And perhaps it was. But the biographical point remains: Roosevelt regarded himself as the steward of all the people's interests and as the active and effective leader of a classless government.

Like the Founding Fathers, Roosevelt believed that man's lust for power had to be contained. But he went far beyond that monumental testament to their conviction—the separation of powers and the creation of an artificial system of checks and balances—in bringing his views to pass. His expansion of the executive branch and his continuing effort to convert the Supreme Court to a public interest philosophy, coupled with his later demand for the recall of judicial decisions on the state level, constituted a direct assault on their creation. And it had to be, given Roosevelt's realization that business domination of the judiciary as well as of the legislature had made separation of powers more theoretical than actual. Yet he remained consistent with the Founding Fathers in one regard: he insisted always that the left be kept in balance. Hence his exaggerated fear of Bryan and La Follette, his refusal until 1912 to align himself with any of the great movements of protest, and his irrepressible impulse to strike verbal blows at the left even as he advanced its interests.

Whatever the enduring value of Roosevelt's theory of balance through government regulation, it had practical limitations at the time. For one thing, it presupposed that government control of the corporations would induce more fundamental changes than it actually did. Long after Roosevelt left office big business continued to have a disproportionate voice in Congress, to dominate the regulatory agencies he had devised to control it, and to send its political spokesmen to the White House, though never again with quite the same freedom to trample on the public interest as in the pre-Roosevelt era. For another, it profoundly overestimated the power of the left at that point in history. Neither the agrarians nor labor, and certainly not the reformers, were then in a position to assume effective control of American society. Bryan's elec-

tion in 1896, 1900, or 1908 might have spawned a spate
of reform legislation, but it would hardly have sired the revolution Roosevelt feared. By the President's own analysis, the
power of business was inextricably intertwined with the
social and political fabric of the nation, especially the courts.
But Roosevelt, his mind's eye partly on the future and partly
on the past (he never fully weaned himself from the Whig
historians upon whom he had been nurtured), could not
quite see this during the middle years of his presidency. Nor
could he realize that the rise of labor, the agrarians, and even
the intellectuals to a rough equality with business must perforce be accompanied by excesses and probably by violence,
given business' persistent and entrenched opposition to that
rise. More than anything else, in fact, his failure to accept
the inevitability of such convolutions explains his flaming
intolerance of the militant left.

No incident of Roosevelt's presidential career more graphically illustrates this intolerance than his blistering attack on
the "muck-rakers." Leveled first in the semiprivacy of a Gridiron Club dinner in late January, 1906, the attack was repeated publicly in the middle of April. "In *Pilgrim's Progress,*"
the President said, "the Man with the Muck-rake is set forth
as the example of him whose vision is fixed on carnal instead
of on spiritual things . . . the man who never does anything
else, who never thinks or speaks or writes, save of his feats
with the muck-rake, speedily becomes, not a help to society,
not an incitement to good, but one of the most potent forces
for evil."

Roosevelt's blazing indictment had apparently been sparked
by the publication of David Graham Phillips's sensational series, "The Treason of the Senate," in William Randolph
Hearst's *Cosmopolitan.* Many of Phillips' insights pierced the
veneer of disinterestedness that the most confirmed railroad
senators presented to the public. And a hard stratum of truth
underlay the great body of his work. But his misstatements,
innuendoes, and exaggerations offended many readers and
his character assassinations obscured the fact that a political
philosophy, rather than personal corruption, was on trial.
Roosevelt, who knew "poor old Chauncey Depew," Aldrich,
Spooner and the rest for what they were—unreconstructed
Hamiltonians—was understandably exercised.

The President may also have feared that the coincidence

of Phillips's indictment and the administration's renewed attack on the trusts—three major railroads were indicted in December and suit was filed against the Standard Oil Company in March—would stiffen the Old Guard's resistance to the Hepburn bill, the fight for which was then coming to a climax. There is evidence, too, that the real object of Roosevelt's assault was Hearst himself:

> Hearst has edited a large number of the very worst type of sensational, scandal-mongering newspapers . . . being a fearless man, and shrewd and farsighted, Hearst has often been of real use in attacking abuses which benefited great corporations, and in attacking individuals of great wealth who have done what was wrong. . . . He will never attack any abuse, any wickedness, any corruption, not even if it takes the most horrible form, unless he is satisfied that no votes are to be lost by doing it. He preaches the gospel of envy, hatred and unrest. . . . He cares nothing for the nation, nor for any citizens in it.

Roosevelt seems to have been motivated most, however, by fear that the reform movement was becoming extreme. "The dull, purblind folly of the very rich men; their greed and arrogance, and the way in which they have unduly prospered by the help of the ablest lawyers, and too often through the weakness or short-sightedness of the judges or by their unfortunate possession of meticulous minds"—all this, he wrote, was inducing an enormous increase in socialist propaganda. The outpourings of *Cosmopolitan, McClure's,* and *Collier's* contained "a little good, a little truth" mixed in with a "great amount of evil," Roosevelt told Secretary of War William Howard Taft. But to others, especially the scholarly journalist, Ray Stannard Baker, whose exposure of railroad malpractices in *McClure's* had done much to marshal support for the President's program, Roosevelt insisted that he was not trying to thwart reform.

Baker had been shocked when he learned in the spring of 1906 that Roosevelt had assailed the magazine writers in January: "It was difficult for me to understand this attack, considering all that had recently happened, all that the President owed to the investigations and reports of at least some of the magazine writers." He had then tried to dissuade Roosevelt from repeating the "muck-rake" speech in April. "Now, the letting in of light and air in the matter of current business conditions, toward which you yourself have contributed more than any other man, and for which your administration will, I sincerely believe, be chiefly remembered," he wrote the President on April 7, "is neither pleasant nor profitable for the rascals upon whom the light is turned." Conceding that some of the exposures had been extreme, Baker asked whether they "have not, as a whole, been honest and useful? and would not a speech, backed by all of your great authority, attacking the magazines, tend to give aid and comfort to these very rascals, besides making it more difficult in the future not only to get the truth told but to have it listened to?"

Roosevelt promised only that he would make clear the objects of his attack. "One reason I want to make that address," he replied, "is because people so persistently misunderstand what I said, that I want to have it reported in full."

Actually, Roosevelt's remarks in the public version of the "muck-rake" speech in April were carefully qualified. He hailed "as a benefactor" every writer who attacks evil, provided he is honest and refrains from "indiscriminate assault upon character." He warned against misinterpreting his words in one phrase, and predicted in the next that such would be their fate. "Some persons are sincerely incapable of understanding that to denounce mud-slinging does not mean the endorsement of whitewashing," he ruefully observed:

At the risk of repetition let me say again that my plea is, not for the immunity to but for the most unsparing exposure of the politician who betrays his trust, of the big business man who makes or spends his fortune in illegitimate or corrupt ways.

The President's request for a fair hearing was not universally honored. Within twenty-four hours the magazine writers were all lumped together by the newspapers—the sensitive, searching ones like Baker and Lincoln Steffens, the perfervid emotionalists like Phillips and Thomas Lawson, the author of *Frenzied Finance*. Triumphantly, the conservative press, long starved for utterances by Roosevelt it could endorse without strain, trumpeted the glad tidings across the land. "It was a great day while it lasted, but it came too hot," the *New York Sun* gloated. "Muck-rakers worked merrily for a time in their own bright sunshine, and an unthinking populace applauded their performance. Now there are few to do them reverence." The people, said the *Philadelphia Press,* "are sick of the muck-rake" and "a healthy reaction has begun." But had it?

The President's speech failed to stay the engulfing wave of reform. Many moderate newspapers rallied to the defense of the responsible "muck-rakers." The term itself became one of approbation, and for several years thereafter the muckrakers flourished.

Many of the muckrakers were embittered even so. "I met the President many times afterward," Baker recalled, "and there were numerous exchanges of letters, but while I could wonder at his remarkable versatility of mind, and admire his many robust human qualities, I could never again give him my full confidence, nor follow his leadership." Lincoln Steffens, to whom Roosevelt had given carte blanche to investigate the executive branch of the government just two and one-half weeks before the Gridiron Club speech, professed to be unperturbed. The President, he wrote, "said that he did not mean me."

The indictment of the muckrakers was a minor tragedy. Historians have found it as hard as Baker to understand why Roosevelt struck such a devastating blow at the men and women whose writings had so abetted his own program. By uncritically accepting the muckrakers' reminiscences, by viewing the letter to Taft as a closed statement of Roosevelt's philosophy, and by misconstruing the broad tenor of the speech itself, they have even concluded that the President was a pseudo-progressive at heart. In so doing they have underplayed Roosevelt's plaintive warning against misinterpretation and his explicit exoneration of those "who with stern sobriety and truth assail the many evils of our time." More important still, they have discounted or ignored the fact that he concluded the public version of the "muck-rake" address with two proposals hardly calculated to make men of wealth and their spokesmen in the Senate rest easy—federal supervision of *all* corporations engaged in interstate commerce and a progressive inheritance tax on swollen fortunes.

Significantly, those recommendations did not go unheralded by contemporary commentators. Many moderates who would have (and had) dismissed the inheritance tax proposal disdainfully had it come from Bryan announced their support. The radical Democrats feigned displeasure that "that Republican" in the White House had stolen another plank from the Democratic platform. And numerous conservative newspapers lashed both proposals mercilessly. The *New York Evening Post* was vitriolic:

It will be a mortification to his friends, and a real public misfortune, that his mouthing has made Bryan appear a reactionary, Hearst a conservative, and has elevated Debs and Powderly to the level of Presidential statesmanship.

In reality, the President's insight into fiscal policy was less acute than Bryan's. Except for his firm grasp of the inevitability of centralization in industry and the need to devise effective methods of federal control, his knowledge of economics was rudimentary. He construed the inheritance tax as a moral rather than an economic instrument; and not until later, when he belatedly took up the graduated income tax, was he animated so much by a considered appraisal of revenue needs (though the enactment of his own welfare program would have made the creation of new sources of tax revenue mandatory) or a desire to level as by a moralistic urge to strike at the malefactors of great wealth.

There should be, the President argued in the "muck-rake" speech, a sharp distinction between fortunes "gained as an incident to performing great services to the community . . . and those gained in evil fashion by keeping just within the limits of mere law-honesty." He added that "no amount of charity in spending [ill-won] fortunes in any way compensates for misconduct in making them." He realized, of course, that it was impossible to make the distinction; and because of his reluctance to penalize those whose incomes were by his unspecified criteria earned, he was slow to espouse the income tax. So great was his contempt for the idle rich and their offspring, however, that he came easily to the conclusion that regardless of how huge fortunes were amassed, they should not be passed down in full. "They rarely do good and they often do harm to those who inherit them," he sermonized in his last annual message to Congress. From the attack on the muckrakers on, accordingly, Roosevelt repeatedly urged Congress to enact a steeply graduated inheritance tax.

Chapter 16

The Peacemaker I

*Forty years before Americans were willing
to listen . . . [Roosevelt] urged active participation in world decisions for which he felt we
shared responsibility and whose consequences
he felt we could not escape.*
—Howard K. Beale, *Theodore Roosevelt*

EVEN BEFORE the President's domestic program reached its
finest flower in 1906, Roosevelt had sounded the death knell
over the old isolationism and won recognition for his country
as a world power of the first magnitude. He had further committed the United States to internationalism of a form. Never
thereafter would the American people live in relative isolation
from the affairs of Europe or the Eastern Hemisphere, though
they would often imagine that they were. Never again would
the leaders of the Old World act without regard to American
interests, though they would sometimes tragically miscalculate
America's response to their actions.

The Roosevelt who sheathed the sword of ultranationalism
to plunge into the struggle for world peace in 1905 and 1906
was a wiser and more reflective man than the Roosevelt who
had exulted over war in 1898, urged repudiation of a half-
century-old treaty with the British in 1900, and rode rough-
shod over Latin American sensibilities in 1902. He thought
as much as always in terms of power—"I never take a step in
foreign policy unless I am assured that I shall be able eventually to carry out my will by force," he asserted in 1905 and
numerous times before and after. And he continued to urge
that the battle fleet be strengthened. But he now possessed a
clearer perception of the ramifications of power.

No longer did Roosevelt gauge events solely in terms of
their impact upon the immediate interests of the United States,
as he had frequently done in the past. No longer did he believe
that a display of force was invariably more effective than
patient negotiation or that America had only to flex its muscles

and go it alone. When, just six months before he brought peace to Russia and Japan in 1905, he declared in his inaugural address that America's attitude toward all nations "must be one of cordial and sincere friendship" and that it must be shown "not only in our words, but in our deeds," he indubitably meant it. Had it not been for the fetters imposed by his own views on colonialism, he might well have fulfilled that high aspiration.

These changes were nowhere more marked than in the President's Far Eastern policy. He still clung to many of the old imperialistic precepts, and he believed until near the end that China was fraught with opportunity for American economic penetration. "Before I came to the Pacific Slope I was an expansionist," he exclaimed in San Francisco in May, 1903, "and after having been here I fail to understand how any man . . . can be anything but an expansionist." Thus he continued to give vigorous support to John Hay's "Open Door" and to reflect the ideas of Captain Mahan and, more critically, of Brooks Adams. Yet—and this is the real measure of his intellectual growth—Roosevelt saw the world in more and more complex terms.

"He commenced to realize," writes Beale, "that the struggle for supremacy in Eastern Asia was closely related, sometimes in a complicated and baffling fashion, to a struggle for dominance in Europe, and that both of these component struggles were parts of a world struggle that encompassed much besides either Europe or the Far East. . . . [He] came to comprehend the discouraging but basic fact that, if America was to become a world power among imperial rivals as he wished her to do, she must enter a game in which . . . each nation was trying to increase its own power but was determined that no other power or group of powers should attain sufficient strength to threaten it and its friends."

One result was a *volte-face* toward Russia. Roosevelt had originally viewed that giant's remorseless advance into Turkestan and the wild reaches of Siberia during the late nineteenth century with the fascination he had written into his *Winning of the West*. True, he had vague forebodings that Russia might some day "take possession of Northern China and drill the Northern Chinese to serve as her army." But as late as the eve of his elevation to the presidency he professed to be undisturbed. "Undoubtedly the future is hers unless she mars it from within," he wrote in July, 1901. "But it is the future and not the present." Meanwhile Russia's advance into China would exert a stabilizing influence on that backward, amorphous, and warlord-ridden nation; indeed, it would prove a blessing to "civilization."

Under the heavy responsibility of the presidential office, however, Roosevelt's views began to change. America's dynamic thrust toward world power, the tragic dream of economic penetration of China—these and the growing *rapprochement* with Great Britain shed an ominous new light on the Russian question. Where once Roosevelt had been enamored of the Eurasian giant's latent power and had even speculated that Russia might be "the hope of a world that is growing effete," he now began to ponder the implications of that power. A note of apprehension and distrust of Russian ambitions crept into his correspondence. When the Russians massacred thousands of Jews at Kishinev in 1903 he was revolted; the tsarist government's failure to withdraw its troops from Manchuria pursuant to an agreement with China and resultant flouting of the Open Door angered him further. "I wish, in Manchuria, to go the very limit I think our people will stand," he wrote Hay in the summer of 1903. The Russians have comported themselves with "well-nigh incredible mendacity," the President complained to Albert Shaw about the same time. "I believe in the future of the Slavs if they can only take the right turn," he later confided to Spring-Rice, who had been trying to impress him with the Russian menace for almost a decade. "But I do not believe in the future of any race *while it is under a crushing despotism. . . .*"

Roosevelt's once harsh attitude toward Japan meanwhile softened perceptibly. There was much in the Japanese national character that he had always admired—military competency, industrial efficiency, and sacrificial quality. And though he believed that the Japanese had much to learn from the West, particularly about the treatment of women, he felt that Americans could profit from contact with the Japanese. He was notably impressed by their success in eliminating "the misery" that cursed America's great cities. But the President was not wont to interject consciously his personal likes and dislikes into his appraisal of the American national interest. Even after he turned against the Tsar's government he continued to feel warm toward the Russian people; and he always did respect

Germans heartily, the anti-German tenor of much of his diplomacy notwithstanding.

Roosevelt's growing cordiality toward Japan was animated by the belief that Japan had resigned itself to American possession of Hawaii and the Philippines and by the conviction that Japan constituted the natural counterweight to Russia in the Far East. Hence his approval of the Anglo-Japanese Alliance of 1902. Yet the President never dropped his guard completely. "It is always possible that Russia and Japan will agree to make up their differences and assume an attitude of common hostility toward America," he warned his Ambassador to Russia in December, 1904; or, as he bluntly phrased it to the Japanese Ambassador during a luncheon conversation six months before, "Japan might get the 'big head' and enter into a general career of insolence and aggression." But he did not think this likely as long as the United States treated Japan with respect and recognized its "paramount interest in what surrounds the Yellow Sea."

Convinced that the interests of America and the civilized world called for stability in the Far East, the President held himself ready to promote it. Nor did he feel any compunction about acting on this, his personal estimate of the situation. Indeed, in an action that heavily underlined the irreconcilables faced by numerous architects of twentieth century foreign policy, he strained the executive authority to its uttermost limit in the summer of 1905 to achieve his objective.

Shortly before the President opened the memorable Russo-Japanese peace conference his special representatives in London and Tokyo, Senator Lodge and Secretary of War Taft, pledged the United States to silent partnership in the Anglo-Japanese Alliance. Of necessity, the commitment was unofficial. Roosevelt would have welcomed a formal treaty with His Majesty's government, for he regarded British and American interests as identical in their larger compass. But he was too shrewd a political leader to cut himself off from the people by proposing such a radical break with tradition. So he settled on the personal arrangements made by Lodge and Taft. They were not binding, except in a gentlemanly sense. Yet their import was clear: on the word of its President and without the knowledge of its people, the United States government had agreed to act in concert with Great Britain and Japan should a Far Eastern crisis develop. As Taft had confidentially explained to Count Taro Katsura, the Japanese Prime Minister, Tokyo could count upon his government "quite as confidently as if the United States were under treaty obligations."

Two decades were to pass before the American people learned of this signal circumvention of the treaty-making power. A rumor that the United States had unofficially joined the Anglo-Japanese Alliance was published in Japan a few months after the fact, but it was denied by Washington. Only when the historian Tyler Dennett uncovered the evidence while doing research for his *Roosevelt and the Russo-Japanese War,* published in 1925, did the secret come out.

Thus Roosevelt had once again exceeded the limits of his authority as he comported himself in the grand manner of the strong Presidents. And once again he had acted out of deep-felt concern for his country's well-being—but only after mature reflection and consultation with responsible advisers. Confident in the wisdom of his course and serene in the belief that he was serving as the peoples' steward, he felt no need for other justification. Nor did he feel obligated to inform the people at the time.

The most far-reaching aspect of the new Anglo-American-Japanese accord was recognition of Japan's suzerainty in Korea by the so-called Taft-Katsura Agreement. Korea had been wrenched from its tie to the Confucian polity by Japan's victory in the Sino-Japanese War of 1894–95. And though the Japanese and Russians had then guaranteed Korea nominal independence, the Tsar's government had persistently tightened its hold on her during the next decade. At the same time, the Russians had continued to occupy Manchuria.

Desperate to dissipate the Russian threat, Japan finally offered Russia a free hand in Manchuria in exchange for one in Korea. But the Russians, as Sir Bernard Pares writes, were aiming "at nothing less than establishing a Russian hegemony over Asia . . . including . . . the expulsion of the British from India." Repeatedly Tsar Nicholas II refused to respond to Japanese entreaties that he evacuate Manchuria or soften his Korean policy. Finally, on February 5, 1904, Tokyo "gave a last and earnest warning," then withdrew its minister from St. Petersburg. Three days later, in a maneuver they had used against China in 1894 and would develop to perfection thirty-seven years later, the Japanese launched a surprise attack on the Russian fleet at Chemulpo. They made no formal declaration of this, the start of the Russo-Japanese War.

Spectacularly successful both on land and sea, the Japanese stood as masters of all Korea and part of Manchuria by the spring of 1905. They thus made British recognition of their authority in Korea a prime factor in renewal of the Anglo-Japanese Treaty of 1902; and they in effect demanded a similar recognition from the United States.

Roosevelt had followed the course of the war with absorbed interest. He was informed that the Japanese occupation forces were subjecting the Koreans to indignities that made American imperialism seem salutary. And he knew that the Japanese were making a concerted effort to restrict American business activity in Korea. He must also have known, though he could not admit it, that American refusal to recognize Japan's aggrandizement of Korea might have restored the moral leadership which the subjugation of the Filipino guerrillas had so badly compromised; that it might even have evoked words of praise from his severest domestic critics, the "goo-goos." But he further understood that such action would have spiked his project for a Far Eastern balance of power built on the friendship and mutual recognition of the interests of his own country and Japan. Adapting himself to conditions as he found them, therefore, he warmly agreed with Taft that the United States approved Japan's "suzerainty over" Korea while Tokyo disavowed designs on the Philippines. "Your conversation with Count Katsura absolutely correct in every respect," the President cabled Taft on July 31, 1905. "Wish you would state to Katsura that I confirm every word you have said."

Roosevelt never publicly explained his Korean policy, and understandably, given the continued delicacy of Japanese-American relations. Nevertheless, his intimates knew why he had acted as he did. Events had boxed him into a situation analogous to that encountered by Franklin D. Roosevelt at Yalta with the Communists in *de facto* control of Poland. As Elihu Root, irked by charges that his beloved friend had "sold out" the Koreans, insisted twenty-five years later, the President had no alternative course aside from complete withdrawal. "Many people are still angry because we did not keep Japan from taking Korea," Root reflected. "There was nothing we could do except fight Japan; Congress wouldn't have declared war and the people would have turned out the Congress that had. All we might have done was to make threats which we could not carry out."

By the time the Taft-Katsura memorandum formalized the Anglo-American-Japanese comity, the President stood on the threshold of his most magnificent, and in a sense most frustrating, diplomatic achievement—mediation of the Russo-Japanese War. The background was long and complex.

Roosevelt had not quite assumed full direction of Far Eastern affairs when the war broke out in February, 1904. His initial reaction followed lines Secretary Hay had earlier laid down. Both Russia and Japan were urged to observe "the neutrality of China" and interested neutral powers were urged to cooperate to the same end. That, apparently, was all. Afterward the President wrote Spring-Rice that he "notified Germany and France in the most polite and discreet fashion that in the event of a combination against Japan" the United States would "promptly side with Japan and proceed to whatever length was necessary on her behalf." But neither the editors of Roosevelt's *Letters* nor Beale have found evidence that he delivered such a warning. Possibly Roosevelt confused what he actually said with what was in his mind at the time or with what he later believed he should have said. And possibly Ambassador Jusserand and Speck von Sternburg failed to report what they may have regarded as informal remarks meant for them rather than their governments.

Meanwhile Roosevelt's enthusiasm for the Japanese continued to rise. By the technological, militaristic, and administrative criteria that loomed so large in his thinking, they were proving themselves civilized. "What nonsense it is to speak of the Chinese and the Japanese as of the same race," the President said to Hay. "I should hang my head in shame if I were capable of discriminating against a Japanese general or admiral, statesman, philanthropist or artist, because he and I have different shades of skin," he wrote on the eve of the peace conference. The white Russians, not the yellow Japanese, were the inferior people. "They are utterly insincere and treacherous; they have no conception of the truth . . . and no regard for others . . . no knowledge of their own strength and weakness." Was not the Tsar "a preposterous little creature."

Nevertheless, the President thought basically in terms of an

American interest related to that of civilization as a whole. To be sure, he sometimes conjectured that it might be best for Russia and Japan to bleed themselves to enfeeblement; and he occasionally contemplated an ultimate war between the United States and Japan. But he never gave serious consideration to either possibility. Maturely and morally, he concluded that the war should be ended rather than prolonged. A friendly America would give Japan no provocation for hostile action; and in any event, Russia was more dangerous. "If Russia wins she will organize northern China against us," Roosevelt predicted to Hay when the war was but five months old. "Therefore, on the score of mere national self-interest, we would not be justified in balancing the certainty of immediate damage [from Russia] against the possibility of future damage [from Japan]."

The President consequently strove to promote a peace that would end the war and yet reflect Japan's military victories. To Chentung Liang-Cheng and Baron Takahira, the cordial Chinese and Japanese ambassadors to Washington, to Count Arturo Cassini, the despised representative of the Tsar, and to those old stand-bys, Speck von Sternburg and Jean Jules Jusserand, Roosevelt repeatedly proposed mediation. But for more than a year he was cast about on the shoals of European rivalries. No nation could afford to antagonize the Russians. France was already allied with them; Germany was striving soulfully to woo them; and Great Britain was in the throes of a fateful indecision. Nor would the Russians themselves listen to peace proposals. "Cassini throws a pink fit at any reference to peace," Hay remarked as late as November, 1904.

Lacking the financial resources to fight indefinitely, or even for many more months, Japan now perceived the wisdom of negotiating while the fortunes of war were still with her. Rumors that she would entertain mediation cropped out in February, 1905, and in March Ambassador Takahira and Baron Kaneko, a Harvard classmate of Roosevelt's, began secret conferences with the President. Their government demanded victor's terms, including an indemnity.

The Tsar resisted. An obtuse autocrat at worst and a reckless gambler at best, he preferred to stake the future on one more showdown with the Japanese fleet; and this over against the colossal defeats of his forces, the near bankruptcy of his government, and the massive unrest of his people. The showdown came in the Battle of the Sea of Japan on May 27 and 28. In one of the most impressive naval victories yet to be won, Admiral Togo virtually destroyed Admiral Rozhdestvensky's thirty-two-ship fleet which had steamed around the world from Europe for the engagement. And so, wrote Pares, there was fulfilled a fate that had been sure to overtake it "from the day it set sail on its desperate errand under the ill-starred flag of the Romanoffs." Three days later the Japanese, having ascertained that Roosevelt agreed with their principal demands, asked the President to initiate mediation.

Even imperious Wilhelm II now importuned his stubborn cousin, "Nicky," to agree to mediation. Under this and other pressure, the Tsar began to weaken, though hardly to break; and there ensued a difficult preliminary negotiation which has been brilliantly pieced together by Beale. Through it all Roosevelt showed himself wisely sensitive to the childlike whims of the Tsar and discreetly firm with the Japanese, who were beginning to stand hard on their new-won dignity. Privately the President raged. "The more I see of the Czar, the Kaiser, and the Mikado the better I am content with democracy, even if we have to include the American newspaper as one of its assets," he complained to Lodge. But in his relations with the principles he acted with "consummate tact."

During the early summer Roosevelt ironed out most of the surface conflict in separate meetings with the delegates: Count Sergei Witte and Baron Roman R. Rosen for the Russians; Ambassador Takahira and Baron Jutaro Komura for the Japanese. Then, on August 5, he surpassed himself with a memorable display of social urbanity and diplomatic finesse aboard the presidential yacht *Mayflower*, anchored in the harbor of Oyster Bay. The occasion was a luncheon for the envoys and the issue was precedence. Who would be seated to the President's right? Which nation would be toasted first? Who would precede whom into the dining room? Upon such trivialities hung the fate of tens of thousands of common soldiers and sailors.

Witte, who admitted being "morbidly sensitive" to criticism of his shaken country, was beset by fear that the President, "a typical American, inexperienced in and careless of formalities, would make a mess of the whole business" and that the Japanese might "be given some advantage" over the Russian envoys. "I will not suffer a toast to our Emperor offered after one to the Mikado," he warned Baron Rosen on the eve of the conference. Nor were Takahira and Komura, who stood half a foot under Roosevelt and a full foot under the tall and powerful Witte, disposed to waive the proprieties. Their country's resounding defeat of the Russians symbolized nothing if not the yellow man's rise to equality or more with the white man, and their resultant arrogance had already made its mark on American public opinion.

Happily, Roosevelt devised an ingenious solution. After introducing the Russians to the Japanese when they came aboard the presidential yacht, he engaged in general conversation in French; then, his butchered phrases still pouring out, he simultaneously guided the chief of each delegation across the threshold and into the dining salon where their plates were filled from a round buffet table. After everyone was served, he exclaimed: "Gentlemen, I propose a toast to which there will be no answer and which I ask you to drink in silence, standing." He then drank "to the welfare and prosperity of the sovereigns and peoples of the two great nations, whose representatives have met one another on this ship." It was, he said, "my most earnest hope and prayer, in the interest . . . of all mankind that a just and lasting peace may speedily be concluded among them."

The President had carried it off. The subsequent conversation was even more relaxed than circumstances warranted, and when Takahira and Rosen departed, they shook hands warmly. Roosevelt was tremendously relieved; he was also pleased with himself. "I looked forward to this affair with a good deal of anxiety," he confided that night to Joseph B. Bishop, "knowing that a single slip on my part which could be construed as favoring one set of envoys over the others would be fatal. . . . I think we are off to a good start."

The luncheon on the *Mayflower* was but a prelude to the larger drama. From any perspective, Roosevelt had embarked on a perilous course. The stakes were fabulously high. Success promised peace—the end of pointless bloodletting, the extinction of the threat of worldwide conflict. It meant that Roosevelt would be acclaimed by men of good will the world over; that he would be showered with laurels such as no American had ever before received. Failure meant that the war would continue or that the powers of Europe would carve out a peace representative of their own special interests. It also portended personal humiliation for the President and loss of prestige for his country. Nor was that all. Success in the primary objective —peace—threatened failure in the secondary objective: advancement of the United States' interests. What would be the fate of the President's good neighbor policy toward Japan if the terms of the peace he had promoted failed to satisfy the Mikado's government?

It is the measure of Roosevelt's character that knowing all this he undertook the mission. There are, of course, the stock psychological explanations—his unfailing compulsion to act, his perpetual gravitation toward the center of the stage, his conviction that glory was the supreme end of life. But in all probability, higher motives than those were controlling. Indeed, Beale concludes that the President's purpose was purely and simply to end the carnage and stabilize the balance of power in the Far East. "I thought it my plain duty to make the effort," the President wearily, yet happily, remarked to Bishop the night of the *Mayflower* luncheon. "I should be sorry to see Russia driven completely off the Pacific coast," he had confided to Lodge two months before, ". . . and yet something like this will surely happen if she refused to make peace."

The final terms proved more advantageous to Russia than Roosevelt thought necessary. The Tsar had remained adamant, disdaining to the end the Japanese demand for an indemnity; he also opposed transfer of Sakhalin Island to Japan. Fortunately for his obdurate Majesty, Sergei Witte had managed by good luck and high skill to swing the mercurial American temperament from support of Japan to sympathy for Russia. He had also faithfully reflected his sovereign's obduracy at the council table. The result was prolonged deadlock. Concluding that the negotiations would terminate in failure with all that implied, Roosevelt had made an indirect personal appeal to the Mikado near the end. And well that he had, for the Russian envoys were under orders from the Tsar to "finish the negotiations and come home at once." To Witte's astonishment and Komura's despair, Tokyo had submitted. On August 30 the Japanese agreed to waive the indemnity and accept the southern half of Sakhalin Island, rather than the whole, as they had been demanding.

Peace of a sort had finally come to the Far East. As Roosevelt freely acknowledged, France and Germany had contributed to the final achievement. Nevertheless, it was a uniquely personal triumph for the President, one that earned for him and his government the acclaim of the nations. The Tsar, the Mikado, the Kaiser, the King of England (whose government had been inactive), and hundreds of prominent men the world over now poured forth their congratulations. Some were perfunctory; but many were heartfelt.

"This is the happiest news of my life," exclaimed the aging Pope Pius X, who would live just long enough to protest the start of a much greater war. "Thank God for President Roosevelt's courage." "You have probably saved the lives of a quarter of a million men," the American Ambassador to Russia reported. "Whatever the actual influences which induced the Government at Tokyo to accept the terms," the editors of the *Literary Digest* concluded, "the whole world is agreed that President Roosevelt is the man who marshaled them in such a way as to bring about the desired result."

As in all creative acts, however, the cost was high. Even as many Americans basked in their President's glory, even as they conceded that Roosevelt had done for humanity what no one else could have done, they lamented the price of greatness. They spoke critically of "entangling alliances"; they remarked nostalgically of the old isolationism; they read knowingly of the wave of anti-Americanism that rose in Japan in the wake of the settlement. And some, Mark Twain among them, even protested that peace had preserved the tottering regime of the autocratic and irresponsible Nicholas II. Better that the Russians should be liberated from their "age-long chains," said that master satirist of royalty and its works.

And perhaps it would have been better—as it would also have been better if the United States had not become identified with Japan's failure to realize the full fruits of her victories. More than one historian has added the heavy burden of hindsight to those ponderous judgments. But to what real enlightenment? To accept the premises of those who argue that Roosevelt should have foreborne the peacemaker's role that fate had thrust before him is to accept premises which lead logically, albeit extremely, to preventive war. Not yet has moral Western man succumbed to that ultimate degradation of the human spirit. So the wheel perforce turns full circle— back to the night of the luncheon aboard the *Mayflower* and the President's unaffected statement to his friend Bishop that he had felt it "my plain duty to make the effort."

John Hay had not lived to see his country become the focal point of world interest at Portsmouth. Never a robust man, he had been steadily declining since the summer of 1900. Partly out of loyalty to party and friend, largely out of sheer inertia, he had hung on until after the inauguration in March—long enough for the Senate to emasculate a series of arbitration treaties he had laboriously negotiated and then insult him personally by declining to pass a resolution authorizing him to accept the Grand Cross of the Legion of Honor from the French. Early in the morning of July 1, 1905, two weeks after he returned to his summer home in New Hampshire from a fruitless trip to Europe in quest of health, he died.

Private secretary to Abraham Lincoln, friend of Roosevelt's revered father, and one of the main architects of Anglo-American amity, Hay had been for the President a link with the past. "I dearly loved him; there is no one who with any of us can quite fill the place he held," Roosevelt wrote Hay's widow the day of his death. "He was not only my wise and patient advisor in affairs of state; he was the most devoted and . . . charming of friends." The sentiments were genuine, if not inclusive.

The death of the man who had articulated the Open Door policy inspired a spate of uncritical newspaper appraisals. Hay was ranked with the greatest Secretaries of State; he was credited with achievements that were more Roosevelt's than his; and he was given responsibility for the administration's "signal success." Although Roosevelt publicly pronounced Hay's death a "national bereavement," he revealed his pique to Lodge, Taft, Beveridge and others. But not until the publication of three volumes of Hay's letters in 1909 did he give full vent to his feelings.

Curiously, the burden of Hay's comments proved favorable to Roosevelt. "He has plenty of brains, and as you know, a heart of gold," he wrote. Hay did play down the President's role in the Panama and Alaskan boundary episodes, however, and he otherwise showed less deference than the President desired. "[Roosevelt] . . . began talking at the oysters, and the pousse-café found him still at it," Hay had confided to Adams near the end of Roosevelt's first year in office. "When he was one of us, we could sit on him—but who, except you, can sit on a Kaiser?"

To Lodge on January 28, 1909, in a nine-page letter as

revealing of its author's values as of its subject's character and achievements, Roosevelt reduced Hay to a stature somewhat below that which historians have given him:

> I think he was the most delightful man to talk to I ever met, for . . . he continually made out of hand those delightful epigrammatic remarks which we would all like to make, . . . But he was not a great Secretary of State. . . . He had a very ease-loving nature and a moral timidity which made him shrink from all that was rough in life. . . . His close intimacy with Henry James and Henry Adams —charming men, but exceedingly undesirable companions for any man not of strong nature—and the tone of satirical cynicism which they admired . . . marked that phase of his character which so impaired his usefulness as a public man. [Hay] . . . never initiated a policy or was of real assistance in carrying thru a policy; but he sometimes phrased what I desired said in a way that was of real service; and the general respect for him was such that his presence in the Cabinet was a strength to the administration. He was always afraid of Senators and Congressmen who possest any power or robustness. . . .

Roosevelt then reproduced documents to prove that he, not Hay, had been principally responsible for settling the Alaskan dispute. He wrote that he himself had done the "vital work" on Panama. He charged that Hay would not act when a crisis occurred in China. And he asserted that Hay "could not be trusted where England was concerned."

Neither Roosevelt's letter to Lodge nor the comments by Hay which provoked it comprise a pleasant chapter. Lincoln, the man both men most admired, could not have written them. But Roosevelt had to. His extraordinary concern for his place in history would not permit him to leave unchallenged statements that he regarded as misleading or derogatory to himself.

If the President's reflections on Hay expose his own hypersensitivity, his selection of Elihu Root as the new Secretary of State reveals his larger strength. His natural rapport with men of strong character virtually foreordained that he would turn to Root, though he thought fleetingly of Taft, who had replaced Root as Secretary of War eighteen months before. "I wished Root . . . partly because I am extremely fond of him and prize his companionship as well as his advice, but primarily because I think that in all the country he is the best man for the position," Roosevelt explained to Beveridge. "He will be a tower of strength to us all," he wrote Lodge. "I not only hope but believe that he will get on well with the Senate, and he will at once take a great burden off my mind in connection with various subjects, such as Santo Domingo and Venezuela."

Root was to fulfill the President's hope, though his works as Secretary of State proved less notable than as Secretary of War. Then he had been a host unto himself—efficient, constructive, and within the limits of his cautious outlook, bold. But Elihu Root had been already engaged in his constructive labors when Roosevelt became President in September, 1901. And he had continued to be a real power until he had resigned on February 1, 1904, with Roosevelt's praises ringing in his ears—"I shall never have, and can never have, a more loyal friend, a more faithful and wiser adviser." When Root returned to Washington in July, 1905, however, it was to the service of a man who had been resoundingly endorsed by the American people, was more dominant than ever, and had been making the basic decisions on his own for many months. The old order had passed and it could not be recreated.

Yet Root hardly proved ineffectual. As Roosevelt later said, "He fought me every inch of the way. And, together, we got somewhere." The President wisely gave Root almost complete freedom to formulate and carry out policy in the Western Hemisphere. Root won the Senate's approval of a new treaty with Santo Domingo in February, 1907; he promoted cordial relations with Canada; and he became one of the early architects of the modern "Good Neighbor" policy. He also assumed virtually sole responsibility for the administration's Manchurian policy.

Chapter 17

The Peacemaker II

> *"In [Roosevelt's] . . . consciousness of the possibility of world war and of America's involvement in it, and hence of America's concern to help avoid it, he was unusual in an America that was for the most part innocent of the danger of war and certain that a war in Europe or Asia would not concern us if it did come."*
>
> —Howard K. Beale, *Theodore Roosevelt*

THE MUFFLED outcry of the isolationists over the President's mediation of the Russo-Japanese War became an angry roar when Roosevelt interjected America into a smoldering crisis in French Morocco at virtually the same time. In this action as in the Far Eastern one the President sought to promote peace through an uneasy balance of conflicting interests. And in this crisis as in that one Roosevelt dutifully shouldered responsibilities that a lesser man might have declined. Once again he emerged as the only statesman with the prestige, power, and presumed disinterest to be acceptable to all concerned. And once again he acted in the realization that fulfillment of his larger objective might compromise the lesser interests of his own country, though he worked adroitly to avoid it.

The immediate issue was the Open Door in Morocco. By agreements completed in April, 1904, the British recognized French control over Morocco in return for French recognition of British pre-eminence in Egypt. These arrangements antagonized the Germans, who had come to the imperialist stage too late to play a role commensurate with their newly consolidated might, and their seething ambitions consequently spilled over. On March 31, 1905, Emperor Wilhelm II disembarked from a German warship off Tangier, rattled his saber, and defiantly announced that the Sultan of Morocco was an independent sovereign within whose domain all foreign powers were entitled to equal rights. The war clouds that had hovered over

Europe since the end of the Franco-Prussian War thus threatened to deluge the continent once more.

Roosevelt was again caught in a dilemma. France's case
was so weak, her breach of a trust established in 1880 so
flagrant, that world opinion might normally have forced her
to abandon her Moroccan venture. But the Moroccan situation
could not be isolated from the matrix of power in Europe nor
from Britain's interest in Egypt. To stand against France in
Morocco was to oppose Great Britain in Egypt.

Roosevelt's feelings toward the British were partly emotional; but they were not blindly so, as Hay's sometimes were.
The President often railed at the supercilious qualities of eminent and not so eminent Englishmen. And like Lodge and
many other militant ultranationalists, he felt unconsciously
inferior to the British. But his strident patriotism would not
allow him to admit the mother country's cultural superiority;
even in his historical writings he only begrudgingly acknowledged the great heritage she had bequeathed her mighty offspring. Nevertheless, Roosevelt had slowly and painfully convinced himself that American and British interests complemented each other. By the fall of 1905 the British Ambassador
was reporting to Whitehall that although Roosevelt's "prejudices are all the other way," he had at times "seemed really
friendly." Two years later when the President received James
Bryce, author of *The American Commonwealth*, as the new
ambassador, he cast aside his prepared remarks "and made a
long impromptu speech full of expressions of friendliness to
the King and to Great Britain and conveying the earnest desire
for best relations and reciprocal understanding between the
two countries."

Roosevelt's feelings toward the Germans were at once less
censorious and more guarded than those toward the British.
The compulsion for order and efficiency he admired in the
Japanese was accentuated in the case of the Germans, and his
own approach to administration was in some part Germanic.
He was also less sensitive than many Americans to the nationalism, militarism, and assertiveness of so many Germans. He
could, it is true, laugh surreptitiously at the Kaiser's pompos-
ity; and he smiled knowingly at the sycophancy of the men who
surrounded him. Yet he did have a kind of admiration for
Wilhelm which he impressed on German diplomats when it
suited his purposes. (He once complimented him supremely

by saying that he would have carried his ward in a democratic election.) Always, however, the President regarded Imperial Germany as a dangerous rival; and never was he the subordinate partner in the calculated friendship he and Wilhelm long maintained.

Although Berlin sensed Roosevelt's predisposition toward the British and French, it hoped even so that he would serve as Germany's *amicus curiae* in the Moroccan affair. From early 1905 on, influential Germans subjected him to unremitting pressure to do so. They pointed out that France and Spain's primacy in Morocco could lead to the exclusion of other commercial nations. They protested that Germany had no ambitions in Morocco beyond maintenance of the Open Door. And they argued that the British would privately welcome action. Would not the United States join Germany in encouraging the Sultan to request an international conference? Would not Roosevelt cooperate by releasing a protest of his own simultaneously with one by Germany?

The President responded circumspectly. He told Speck von Sternburg that an active Moroccan policy would expose him "to the bitterest attacks" in Congress and that "our interests in Morocco are not sufficiently great to make me feel justified in entangling our Government." He also said the same to others. Meanwhile, however, Wilhelm became beset by fear that England would support France in a showdown; through his ambassador he virtually importuned Roosevelt to urge the British against such a fateful course. But the President, who was on a bear hunt in Colorado, shrewdly refrained. As he explained to Taft, he did not want to make the English "think we are acting as decoy ducks for Germany." He added, however, that he was "sincerely anxious to bring about a better state of feeling between England and Germany"; he also suggested that the Secretary of War conduct a cautious inquiry into the British attitude, but only if he found the Ambassador, Sir Mortimer Durand, "in any rational mood and you think the nice but somewhat fat-witted British intellect will stand it."

During May and early June tension continued to rise, especially after the Sultan issued an invitation for a conference of the powers. The dramatic dismissal on June 6 of Foreign Minister Théophile Delcassé, the resolute architect of France's Moroccan policy, reduced it temporarily; but the dismissal also emboldened the Kaiser. As rumors of an impending showdown spread through the great chancelleries of the Western World, the Imperial government grew increasingly belligerent. Fearing finally that war might ensue, the French reluctantly began to relax their opposition to an international conference. Roosevelt thereupon concluded that the time had come to intervene.

The President's friendship with amiable Jean Jules Jusserand, with whom he had often played tennis and scrambled over the boulders of Rock Creek Park, now proved fruitful. Taking the Ambassador into his confidence almost completely, he impressed upon him the gravity of the crisis and convinced him of his own disinterested purposes (the President's problem was to avoid creating the impression that he was pro-German). A measure of Roosevelt's success is the sympathetic report Jusserand later made to this government:

Examining . . . the means by which he might help us in avoiding war, the very idea of which struck him with horror, the President has concluded that the only chance to do what might be useful, would be perhaps to flatter this excessive vanity of William II, to which he attributes, in large measure, the present difficulties.

Roosevelt's intercession, combined with the force of events, swung over the French. But a new impasse soon threatened. France demanded a preliminary understanding before meeting at the council table; Germany insisted that the issues be decided at the formal conference. The fate of the conference, and perhaps of world peace, hung precariously in the balance.

The President reacted with characteristic ingenuity. Using Speck von Sternburg as a sounding board, he played such a song of praise as would inevitably beguile a man of Wilhelm's vanity. He said the Kaiser "stands as the leader among the sovereigns of to-day who have their faces set toward the future." He argued that the French decision to accept a conference was "a genuine triumph for the Emperor's diplomacy." And he suggested that the Emperor's "high and honorable fame might be clouded" should "questions about minor details" produce "the dreadful calamity of war."

For the second time, Roosevelt's resourcefulness apparently tipped the scales. Wilhelm agreed to an advance agenda; he also promised that if there should be differences at the conference he would in every case support whatever decision Roosevelt regarded as "the most fair and the most practical."

The President then conveyed this promise to the French with the resultant resolution of their doubts.

The President would have preferred no further part. Congressional resentment was strong and vociferous; and in January, 1906, Senator Bacon introduced a resolution designed to remind Roosevelt of the Founding Fathers' allegedly isolationist faith. Even Elihu Root questioned the wisdom of his participation. But Lodge rose to the President's defense with a high-blown assertion that it was in the American tradition to use "moral influence . . . to prevent war." And when the conference, which opened in Algeciras, Spain, in mid-January, deadlocked, Roosevelt unhesitatingly interceded again.

With talk of war emanating from all sides, the President offered a four-point compromise program on February 19. His recommendations reflected his basic sympathies as well as his estimate of the total situation. They provided for the Open Door in principle; but they proposed in effect to turn over control of the Moroccan police to France and Spain. The Kaiser understandably demurred, and it seemed for a while that the conference would actually fail. Finally, on the basis of representations from the Russians, Roosevelt decided to make a direct appeal to His Imperial Majesty on March 7. Again playing on Wilhelm's vanity, and also his honor, he quoted Speck von Sternburg's earlier promise that the Emperor would defer to his decision in the event of an insoluble difference between the German government and France. Wilhelm could do little but submit; after failing to convert Roosevelt to a compromise plan of his own, he did so.

The President's imaginative diplomacy had saved the conference and probably the peace as well. He had strengthened the bonds with his country's natural allies, France and Great Britain, and had managed at least to preserve them with Germany. He had also taken America another long stride into the world. The episode, concludes Mowry, "was eloquent testimony to Roosevelt's growing appreciation that the frontiers of twentieth-century American security often lay along the Yangtze and the Rhine, at Algeciras and Rome and Paris, and in a host of other places, some of them unknown or obscure even to members of Congress."

Roosevelt again proved magnanimous in victory. To Jusserand he wrote that he had been able to give him his confidence only because he knew that "you would treat all that was said and done between us two as a gentleman of the highest honor treats what is said and done in the intimate personal relations of life." And of Speck von Sternburg, whose contribution may have been even greater than Jusserand's, he said: "Loyal though Speck was to his Government, down in his heart the honest, brave little gentleman did not believe Germany was acting as she should act." But to His Majesty, Wilhelm II, the President was less than candid. He sent him his "sincerest felicitations on this epochmaking political success at Algeciras" and assured him that his policy had been "masterly from beginning to end."

As for his own role, the President remained discreetly silent. Only to Whitelaw Reid, in a long, heavily documented letter which he warned must "be considered as of the most strictly confidential character," did he set forth the record of events. The letter was designed for a posterity which until recently rejected it.

President Roosevelt's mediation of the Russo-Japanese War and his intervention in the Moroccan dispute deservedly earned him the Nobel Peace Prize for 1906. At long last the responsibilities of his office had made him a mature man. This was exemplified by his reproof of "those who would lightly undergo the chance of war in a spirit of mere frivolity, or of mere truculence" and was confirmed by his effort to secure general peace through an international agreement to limit naval power and arbitrate minor disputes.

Roosevelt had first issued a call for an international conference in October, 1904. Following the outbreak of the Russo-Japanese War, he withdrew it. Then, when the Tsar indicated a year later that he would like to call the conference himself, the President readily deferred. The Tsar's sponsorship would give the United States a freer hand; it would also spare Roosevelt, who still scorned the "peace-at-any-price" people on the grounds that they failed to realize that "justice is greater than peace," the odium, as he phrased it, of "posing too much as a professional peacemaker."

During the long interval between the original call and the actual convening of The Second Hague Peace Conference on June 15, 1907, Roosevelt gave considerable thought to the meeting's agenda. He warned that the Conference should not be regarded as a panacea. "Just at present the United States Navy is an infinitely more potent factor for peace than all the peace societies of every kind and sort," he wrote President Eliot of Harvard. "At The Hague I think we can make some real progress, but only on condition of our not trying to go too far." Meanwhile he flirted with suggestions to limit the size of armies, then drew back after concluding that the world armaments manufacturers' lobby was too puissant and that the Kaiser would under no conditions agree. He continued, however, to press for naval limitations and "obligatory arbitration as broad in scope as now appears to be practicable."

The Conference proved a bitter disappointment, adjourning on October 18, 1907, without material accomplishment. As the American delegate, Joseph H. Choate, reported, "There is very great reluctance on the part of these fighting nations to bind themselves to anything." Roosevelt himself failed to press vigorously for arbitration because of the attitude of the United States Senate. "[It] does not represent any real advance for me or anyone else," he explained to the British Foreign Secretary, Sir Edward Grey, "to sign a general arbitration treaty which itself merely expresses a 'pious opinion' that there ought hereafter to be arbitration treaties whenever both parties think they are advisable—and this was precisely the opinion that most of my own good friends in the Senate took as regards the last batch of arbitration treaties which I sent them." Nevertheless, he added, "I will do my best to get this Government to agree to any feasible scheme which will tend to minimize the chances for war occurring without previous efforts to secure mediation or arbitration." Before he had a chance to act, eight European nations led by Germany scuttled even that moderate proposal.

The President's cautious internationalism and his newly developed abhorrence of war continued, of course, to be delimited by his unwavering devotion to the national interest and by his contempt for the backward nations. He never agreed to endorse arbitration of disputes involving the national honor or interest. Nor did he ever abandon his belief that the "civilized" nations should discipline the "barbarous" ones. To be sure, he conceded that the problem was relative, that it was difficult to "state exactly which power ceases to be free and civilized and which comes near the line of barbarism or despotism." But in practice he allowed his own conception of the national interest to rule.

The President's China policy was a case in point. Roosevelt had the intellectual equipment to have evolved a China policy that would have served American interests and kept ill-will at a minimum. He had a keen conception of the Russian menace, an almost prophetic vision of China's future importance, and unparalleled daring and imagination. But because he held firm to his technological criteria of civilization, because he insisted on upholding false values of prestige, and particularly because he overestimated his country's economic stake in China, he failed.

Admittedly, Roosevelt inherited his China policy from McKinley and left its conduct largely in Hay's hands until 1904. Yet Hay kept him informed. He agreed in the main with Hay's policies. And he himself made several critical decisions during Hay's tenure. As Beale shows, it was the President who insulted the Chinese by insisting that the mixed foreign court at Shanghai rather than the Chinese government should be authorized to sentence a group of Chinese citizens found guilty of "violent incitements to insurrection" against the Chinese government. It was the President who tried to compel the Chinese to support a nominally American railroad company which had laid but twenty-eight miles of track out of a projected thousand miles in five years of financial chicanery and general mismanagement. (Lodge and Roosevelt agreed that the maintenance of American prestige was at stake.) And it was the President who directed policy throughout the Chinese boycott of American goods in 1905. Of these incidents, the latter was the most significant. The attitudes and actions which provoked it were deeply enmeshed in the Western social fabric, and they cut to the core of the imperialistic philosophy, even in its then softened version.

The precipitating issue was the Chinese Exclusion Treaty of 1883 which came up for renewal in 1904. Roosevelt had long favored the exclusion of Chinese laborers on economic and social grounds. "There is no danger of having too many immigrants of the right kind," he said in his annual message of 1905 and in numerous private letters. Nor does it make any "difference from what country they come." However, he argued, "we should not admit masses of men whose standards of living and whose personal customs and habits are such that they tend to lower the level of the American wage-worker."

The issue was actually more complex than that. Immigration officials often visited indignities on those Chinese who were admitted, among them high government officials and distinguished scholars. The United States refused naturalization to *all* Chinese ("Congress has done its work so well that even Confucius could not become an American," Hay remarked). And West Coast politicians were so sensitive to the prejudices of their constituents that they demanded unilateral exclusion legislation in the spring of 1904 regardless of the outcome of pending treaty negotiations.

Whatever the limitations of the President's own views, they were far in advance of his countrymen's at large. He personally favored admission of qualified Chinese to citizenship. He wanted to extend America's cultural hold on China. And he was reluctant to make commercial intercourse with China more difficult than it already was. But in the spring of 1904, fearing more the wrath of the West Coast voters than the indignation of the impotent Chinese, he sacrificed statesmanship to politics. On April 5 of that election year he informed his Cabinet that he would approve a separate exclusion bill. Then, in one of the weakest actions of his presidential career, he signed a measure so providing.

Meanwhile anti-American sentiment in China rose feverishly. Its source was not the reactionary Boxers, but the men of China's future—the progressive-minded intellectuals, students, and businessmen who foresaw for China the industrialized development that Roosevelt himself foresaw in his more reflective moments. Led by Sun Yat-Sen among others, they resolved to assert China's independence; and they proposed to boycott American goods as a first step.

The President's response was both enlightened and authoritarian. He was so angered by the "barbarous methods" which inspired the boycott that he ordered reform even before the textile and other interested American business groups beseeched him for relief. "We are a civilized nation," Roosevelt wrote the secretary of the Immigration Bureau on June 12, and "we are trying to teach the Chinese to be civilized. . . . We ought not to treat a Chinese representative in a way which we would not for a moment tolerate if applied by the Chinese to some of our representatives." He then issued an executive order prescribing humane treatment of visiting Chinese by American immigration officials and directing "immediate dismissal" of any official who failed to conform.

Chinese grievances were too long standing and the new nationalists' desire to assert their independence too intense for a change in the form of American policy to divert the nationalists; on July 20, 1905, the boycott was instituted. It spread rapidly from Shanghai through South China and thence to Hawaii, the Philippines, and the Japanese ports of Nagasaki and Yokahama. It varied widely in effectiveness and was nowhere total; yet it was severe enough to evoke frantic pleas for diplomatic action. As one consul reported, our businessmen in China have "gone mad" and are acting like "regular wild Indians."

The President's contempt for the "inferior" Chinese now began slowly to surge to the surface. He continued to fulminate against the obtuseness that had incited the crisis. "I have the right," he testily wrote Senator George C. Perkins of California, "to expect that the Pacific coast representatives will aid me in undoing the injustice in our treaties . . . which has probably been the whole, and certainly the main, cause of the present boycott." But he was unable to hold to that rational viewpoint entirely. To the veteran China hand, William Rockhill, he laid bare his fatal flaw. The Chinese, wrote Roosevelt, "despise weakness even more than they prize justice, and we must make it evident both that we intend to do what is right and that we do not intend for a moment to suffer what is wrong."

Nevertheless, the President resisted his rising impulse to resort to force until well into November, 1905. Gratified when the Chinese government formally condemned the boycott on August 31, he attempted to marshal public opinion behind a revision of the exclusion laws. The United States had failed to do its "duty toward the people of China," he bluntly told an export-conscious audience in the cotton belt on October 20. At the same time, however, he warned that America must maintain its "rights."

Meanwhile anti-American sentiment in China intensified in spite of the near extinction of the boycott. The President's daughter, Alice, was insulted by the Cantonese and forced to cancel a visit to their city. Riots broke out in several places, including Shanghai, where the Chinese nationalists sought greater jurisdiction over the privileged foreign settlement. And an American admiral who had accidentally shot a Chinese woman was mobbed.

The President decided, accordingly, to pursue the firmest possible course; on November 15 he ordered the Secretary of the Navy to concentrate "as strong a naval force as possible" off the China coast. Preparations to form an expeditionary force of 15,000 troops followed, and by mid-February the battleship *Oregon* was hovering off Hong Kong and Canton while the gunboat *El Cano* was cruising on the Yangtze River. Then, on February 26, Roosevelt submitted a series of humiliating demands to the Imperial government. Eight days later the Emperor issued an Imperial edict condemning expressions of antiforeign sentiment by his subjects.

Roosevelt's gunboat diplomacy had restored tranquillity, maintained the Open Door, and refurbished the national ego. But it had also embittered China's men of the future. It would be absurd to blame the whole subsequent China tangle on the President's coercive policies; many and graver blunders were to be made in the years to come. It is also difficult to see how Roosevelt could have avoided a firm policy (except for the unnecessary display of force), given the violence of Chinese activity, the frenetic pressures of American business and labor leaders, and the Western milieu of which the United States, however less imperiously, was yet a part. Within this frame of reference, Roosevelt had done almost all that was possible. He had upbraided American officials for their execrable discourtesy; he had urged Congress to modify the exclusion policy (though after he himself had submitted to it); and he had taken the question to the people. How then had he failed?

The President failed because he, his advisers, and all but a handful of American commentators persisted in regarding China as a colonial with all that the term implied. Ideally, the United States should have courted, rather than condemned, the new nationalists. It should have encouraged, rather than discouraged, Chinese efforts to whittle down the extraterritorial privileges of Occidentals. And it should have opened its doors to cultivated Chinese as Roosevelt himself wanted to do. But the domestic political maelstrom, coupled with the President's inability to break totally with his imperialistic, might-is-right heritage, prevented it from so doing.

The President meanwhile became involved in a somewhat similar crisis with Japan. For several years that compound of economic insecurity, racial prejudice, and political demagoguery which lay behind the Chinese exclusion law had also been swelling the West Coast's resentment of the Japanese. Finally, in the fall of 1906, the San Francisco Board of Education ordered all ninety-three Japanese, Chinese, and Korean students in the San Francisco system to attend a segregated school.

From across the Pacific there now surged a great wave of protest. Raging and storming over "the idiots in the California legislature," Roosevelt sought desperately to roll it back. "Let me repeat that everything in my power will be done," he said in response to a cable from Baron Kaneko. "The action of these people in San Francisco no more represents American sentiment as a whole than the action of the Japanese seal pirates last summer represented Japanese sentiment." Meanwhile the President tried to shame the Californians. He called the Board's action "a wicked absurdity" and "a crime against a friendly nation" in his annual message; he also threatened to use "all the forces, civil and military" at his command to rectify it. The next month he sent in a special message requesting the people of San Francisco to resolve the issue "as a matter of comity." Finally he invited the Board to confer with him.

Early in February the President received an eight-man delegation at the White House. After several conferences at which Elihu Root sat at Roosevelt's left, prepared to tap the table when the President became too vehement, a compromise was worked out: aliens of any nationality would be admitted to nonsegregated schools if they knew English and fell into the proper age group; Roosevelt would recommend that the immigration law be amended to exclude coolies.

The resultant reduction of tension proved temporary. The California Assembly passed a bill limiting ownership of land by Japanese and Chinese. In May a mob attacked a Japanese restaurant in San Francisco. And in June the Board of Police Commissioners refused licenses to six Japanese employment bureaus. Meanwhile reports of possible conflict between the United States and Japan filtered into Washington through diplomatic channels.

At this juncture Roosevelt decided to send Taft to Tokyo. The amiable Secretary of War arrived in the Japanese capital in October, 1907. After being "feted all over the place," as he phrased it, he completed negotiations already in process for the so-called "Gentlemen's Agreement." Under its terms both

Japan and the United States agreed to limit emigration of their nationals to types acceptable to each other. This meant that the trickle of coolies into California would virtually dry up.

At about the same time, the President completed arrangements for a gesture on the grand scale—the dispatch of the American battle fleet around the world. His main reasons for this bold decision were his desire to stimulate domestic support for his naval construction program and to dramatize to the impressionable Japanese the magnitude of American power. This suggests that he had not taken the war talk of the summer of 1907 seriously, for the Philippines and Hawaii would be left unguarded while the fleet was in European waters. Actually, he had taken it seriously; but he contemplated a future rather than an immediate war, Japan's naval strength being at least a third less than the United States' at the time. He accordingly viewed the fleet's visit to Japan as a deterrent. "My own judgment is that the only thing which will prevent war is the Japanese feeling that we shall not be beaten," he confided to Root at the height of the tension. Nevertheless, the commander of the Great White Fleet which steamed out of Hampton Roads on December 16 carried firm orders to be prepared for and to resist attack.

No enemy fired a gun except in salute, and on the return of the fleet fourteen months later its primary missions had seemingly been fulfilled. The Japanese had received the officers and men with a spectacular demonstration of hospitality and blandness, and Congress had authorized the construction of two more battleships (the President had spurred action with dark hints of war). There had also been controversy. The chairman of the Naval Affairs Committee was so angered by Roosevelt's decision to dispatch the fleet without Congress' approval that he had threatened to withhold funds for its supply. The President had replied that he had enough money to get the fleet to the Pacific, that it would definitely go to the Pacific, and that it could then stay in the Pacific. "There was no further difficulty about money," Roosevelt recalled in his *Autobiography*.

Roosevelt also asserted in his *Autobiography* that the world cruise was "the most important service that I rendered to peace." Historians are not so sure. Beale suggests that it strengthened the Japanese naval party and anti-American elements which were already in conflict with pro-American groups in Japan. And Braisted points out that "a powerful American fleet defending the Philippines in 1909 was potentially no less threatening to Japan than had seemed Japan's intervention in Hawaii to the United States only twelve years before." It is also probable that the spectacle of American naval power quickened Kaiser Wilhelm II's burning resolve to build up the Imperial German Navy.

By the end of Theodore Roosevelt's presidency the Asiatic balance he had striven so laboriously to create was working against American commercial interests. In silent defiance of the Open Door, Russia and Japan had agreed to divide north China, Mongolia, and Korea between them; and by an exchange of notes between Secretary Root and Baron Takahira on November 30, 1908, the United States had implicitly recognized Japan's economic ascendancy in Manchuria. Roosevelt's acceptance of this shift of power further confirmed his maturity, for the alternative to Root's measured attempt to persuade Japan to be moderate was war or a firm threat of war. If the world cruise of the fleet was a blunder, what would the mustering of sufficient force to disrupt the new Russo-Japanese comity or to drive the Japanese out of Korea and Manchuria have been?

Roosevelt's realization that America's Far Eastern position was untenable sharpened during his retirement. Perceiving the implications of President Taft's "dollar diplomacy," he urged him in December, 1910, to abandon commercial ambitions in Manchuria and China in return for Japanese concessions on immigration. "Japan is not rich, her main interests are on the Continent of Asia. . . ," he wrote Taft on December 8. Two weeks later he warned that to wage "a successful war about Manchuria would require a fleet as good as that of England, plus an army as good as that of Germany." He added that although the " 'open-door' policy in China was an excellent thing . . . , it completely disappears as soon as a powerful nation determines to disregard it, and is willing to run the risk of war rather than forego its intention."

Neither Taft nor most of his successors heeded Roosevelt's advice, and on December 7, 1941, the tragedy played out. The responsibility of President Theodore Roosevelt was comparatively light; but that of Theodore Roosevelt as warmonger in

1898 was correspondingly heavy. If he and his imperialistic friends had not been so anxious to penetrate China commercially in the 1890's and early 1900's, the Open Door might never have become an article of faith second only to the Monroe Doctrine. Two generations of American policy-makers would not then have been constrained to uphold it.

Chapter 18

More Troubles and Greater Tribulations

If a man has a very decided character, has a strongly accentuated career, it is normally the case of course that he makes ardent friends and bitter enemies. . . .
—Theodore Roosevelt to G. O. Trevelyan

THE PRESIDENT continued, meanwhile, to be a storm center of controversy on the domestic front. He created it, he fell into it, and he searched it out. When he was not rebuking his trusted friends, he was taunting his long-sworn enemies. And if he was fleetingly at peace with both, as occasionally he was, it was rarely the peace that passeth understanding. Nor could one predict what the swirling winds that bore his wrath would next envelop. During the same two years the President made his mark in European affairs, pacified the Japanese, and flaunted the power of the American navy, he crossed swords with a people he had sought sincerely to uplift—the Negroes. He unloosed his fury on a private citizen whose sole offense was an imagination that transcended the observed facts of nature. And he himself fell victim to the financial and industrial barons whose motives he had so long suspected.

The President's clash with the Negroes grew out of an incident at Brownsville, Texas. On August 14, 1906, a group of Negro soldiers from nearby Fort Brown allegedly killed a white bartender and wounded a policeman in a wild midnight raid on the town. No one of the alleged participants was ever positively identified; nor did any one of them ever admit responsibility. They were never tried before a court of law, military or civil, and to this day their guilt remains unproved. Yet Roosevelt, in a flagrant breach of the Anglo-American code of justice, punished three companies of Negro troops with extraordinary severity. He was influenced to this action by the report of the soldiers' commanding officer, who reluctantly concluded that his troops were blameworthy, and by the

290

findings of two separate investigations, one by a Major August B. Blockson, the other by the Inspector General of the Army.

Major Blockson's report charged that the raid had been "pre-concerted" and that many members of the three Negro companies stationed at Fort Brown had entered into a "conspiracy of silence" to protect the men who had actually done the shooting; he recommended that they "be made to suffer with others more guilty." After an intensive effort to break the "conspiracy" failed, possibly because there was none, the President ordered almost the entire complement of the three companies in question "discharged without honor . . . and forever barred from re-enlistment." Of the 160 or more soldiers thus summarily dismissed, several were near retirement and six had won the coveted Medal of Honor in campaigns against the Indians, the Spaniards, or the Filipino insurrectionists.

Although the order was signed on November 5, Roosevelt withheld its release until after the congressional elections of November 6, presumably to mitigate its political impact. The *New York Herald* held that a shift in the Negro vote would have reduced the Republican majority in the House of Representatives from 59 to 14, and the *Washington Post* pointed out that a switch of one half the Negro votes in Cincinnati could have defeated the President's son-in-law, Representative Nicholas Longworth.

Roosevelt's imperious action provoked a country-wide reaction. Many Southern newspapers applauded his course, but the Northern press sharply criticized it and the Negro editors and civic leaders vehemently condemned it. The *New York Age* called the discharge order an "outrage upon the rights of citizens who are entitled in civil life to trial by jury and in military life to trial by court-martial." And the pastor of the Abyssinian Baptist Church of New York exclaimed that although Roosevelt was "once enshrined in our love as our Moses," he is now "enshrouded in our scorn as our Judas." Only in Tuskegee, Alabama, was there silence; and it was brutally painful. The President had "blundered," Booker T. Washington privately wrote, and ". . . the enemy will, as usual, try to blame me for all of this. They can talk; I cannot, without being disloyal to our friend, who [*sic*] I mean to stand by throughout his administration."

Roosevelt rode out the storm, but at no enhancement of his reputation for justice. For in Joseph B. Foraker, who emerged as the beleaguered Negro soldiers' *amicus curiae,* he encountered a bold and resourceful adversary. The veteran Ohio senator aspired to the presidency in 1908, and he needed an issue to capture the public's imagination. Although Foraker believed at first that the soldiers were guilty, he made an intensive private investigation in the hope that he might turn up something; and by early December, when Congress convened, he had convinced himself that the affair was in truth an "American Dreyfus Case." From then on the Ohioan carried the torch of justice almost alone. But not until March 2, 1909, two days before Roosevelt left office in triumph and Foraker left it in disgrace, a victim of the President's wrath and the revelation of his unseemly relations with the Standard Oil Company, was it lighted; and then but dimly. On that date Roosevelt signed a compromise measure authorizing appointment of a high military court to review the individual cases of all the discharged soldiers.

The two-year controversy between the imperious President and the audacious Senator was brisk with acrimony. The most regrettable incident occurred at the Gridiron Club dinner in January, 1907. Failing to accept the newspapermen's barbs in good grace, Roosevelt delivered a long, humorless defense of his policies. He then flung the gauntlet at Foraker, who sat less than twenty feet away, his face ashen. With the temerity that had always set him off from the herd, Foraker retrieved it. For twenty minutes he tongue-lashed the President of the United States, charging finally that Roosevelt's handling of the Brownsville case had been illegal, unconstitutional, and unjustifiable.

Furious, Roosevelt sprung to his feet demanding time for a reply. He got it—after waves of applause for Foraker slowly abated. Speaking through clenched teeth, his eyes squinting and his face flushing, the President denied the Senate's right to interfere and dogmatically asserted that he alone had the power to mete out justice to the discharged soldiers. "The only reason I didn't have them hung was because I couldn't find out which ones . . . did the shooting," he added. Some were "bloody butchers." He then stormed out of the hall, leaving, so Foraker recalled, "no good taste in anybody's mouth and no good feeling in anybody's heart."

Less than twenty-four hours later the President recovered his balance. "Foraker ought not to have been called upon to speak," he wrote Beveridge, "but, as he was called upon, I do not blame him much for the speech he did make."

The saddest part of the Brownsville affair, sadder even than the President's comportment at the Gridiron Club dinner, was the impression it gave of Roosevelt's attitude toward Negroes. Possibly his indictment would have been less sweeping and his punishment less severe had white troops been involved. Yet his published correspondence fails to suggest it. Two days after the order he wrote:

When the discipline and honor of the American Army are at stake I shall never under any circumstances consider the political bearing of upholding that discipline. . . . To show you how little the question of color enters into the matter, I need only point out that when a white officer was alleged to be guilty in speaking of the incident of commenting unfavorably on the black troops generally, I directed an immediate investigation into his words and suitable proceedings against him should he prove to have been correctly quoted.

Roosevelt never deviated from that position. To underscore it he let it out while the conflict was at its peak that he planned to appoint a prominent Negro to a high federal post in Cincinnati (Foraker, who was caught unaware, testily told newspapermen to consult "the third Senator from Ohio—Booker Washington"). The President further tried to redress the balance during these last, troubled years by directing the Army to consider the organization of a Negro battalion of heavy artillery. And in 1908 he threatened the Nashville, Chattanooga & St. Louis Railway Company with legal action unless it provided Negro passengers with facilities. Roosevelt also coupled a ringing denunciation of lynching with a rational appeal for improved Negro education in his annual message of 1906:

It is out of the question for our people as a whole permanently to rise by treading down any of their own number. The free public school, the chance for each boy or girl to get a good elementary education, lies at the foundation of our whole political situation. . . . It is as true for the Negro as for the white man.

The President's effort to redeem his reputation for fairmindedness met only moderate success. His strictures against lynching failed to mollify the Negro press because he sapped their strength by estimating that one-third of the lynchings in the South were actually incited by rape. (He had earlier complained to Owen Wister about Charleston aristocrats who "shriek in public about miscegenation, but . . . leer as they talk to me privately of the colored mistresses and colored children of white men whom they know.") To the end Brownsville remained an open wound, one that historians would open still wider. But some, even then, placed the affair in perspective. Among them was Booker T. Washington. "The bulk of the Negro people are more and more inclined to reach the decision that even though the President did go against their wishes in dismissing the soldiers at Brownsville," Washington wrote in June, 1908, "he has favored them in nine cases out of ten and the intelligent portion of the race does not believe that it is fair or wise to condemn such good friends as President Roosevelt and Secretary Taft because they might have done what they considered right." The patient educator added that it "is not the part of common sense to cherish ill will against one who has helped us in so many ways as the President has."

Meanwhile other of Roosevelt's friends were defending his strictures against nature-fakers. Of all the controversies of the presidential years, this was the most needless. No weighty public matter stood in the offing; no election hung in the balance. All that the President could gain was the satisfaction of speaking his mind, and he could gain that only by compromising the dignity of his office.

Like so many of Roosevelt's seemingly impulsive acts, the assault had been long in building up. The first round was fired in the *Atlantic Monthly* several years before when John Burroughs flailed the Rev. William J. Long, a pseudo nature writer who attributed human characteristics and other absurdities to wild animals. During the next several years other prominent naturalists also criticized Long. Roosevelt meanwhile repressed his own irritation. Finally, in the spring of 1907, he lost control, giving out an interview under the title "Roosevelt on the Nature Fakirs." "You will be pleased to know," he wrote Burroughs, "that I finally proved unable to contain myself, and . . . sailed into Long and Jack London and one or two others of the more preposterous writers of 'unnatural' history." "I know that as President I ought not to do this," he added, "but

I was having an awful time toward the end of the session and I felt I simply had to permit myself some diversion."

The Reverend Long replied in kind. "I find after carefully reading two of his big books," he said in a public letter, "that every time Mr. Roosevelt gets near the heart of a wild thing he invariably puts a bullet through it. From his own records I have reckoned a full thousand hearts which he has thus known intimately. In one chapter alone I find that he violently gained knowledge of 11 noble elk hearts in a few days."

Rarely had the President given his hungry critics such an opportunity. Many concluded that Long's false nature writing was less offensive than Roosevelt's wanton killing; and many more contended that the President's attack on a private citizen was ungentlemanly and cruel.

Yet neither Roosevelt nor his friends were willing to drop the matter. The director of the New York Zoological Park, the curator of Mammalogy and Ornithology at the American Museum of Natural History, and a number of other naturalists defended the President in the September, 1906, issue of *Everybody's* on their own initiative. And in the same issue Roosevelt expounded on the commitment to science which had been his ruling motive:

We abhor deliberate or reckless untruth in this study of natural history as much as in any other, and therefore we feel that a grave wrong is committed by all who, holding a position that entitles them to respect, yet condone and encourage such untruth.

Resentment against the President's undignified conduct was still seething when he became involved in a far more significant imbroglio. This time his role was confidential.

Rumors of an impending break in the stock market had started in December, 1906, when Roosevelt submitted a radical annual message to Congress. An expansion of the constructive parts of his muck-rake speech and of a hard-hitting address delivered at Harrisburg, Pennsylvania, it declared that all big business was really engaged in interstate commerce and should therefore be brought under federal control. It called for compulsory publicity of corporations' accounts, government inspection of their books, and physical valuation of railroad properties, and it contended that the "authority" for these measures was inherent in the Constitution.

Tough-mindedness pervaded the message. The President dutifully denounced monopoly; but he proposed no inclusive assault on the trusts. "Our effort should be not so much to prevent consolidation . . . ," he wrote, "but so to supervise and control it as to see that it results in no harm to the people." Only through "such adequate control and regulation . . . as will do away with the evils which give rise to the agitation against them" could government ownership of the railroads be averted. The belief that "such control would do away with the freedom of individual initiative and dwarf individual effort" was absurd. The stock market had dipped, then steadied. Nevertheless, rumors persisted that the President would make an unsettling move, perhaps against the great Harriman empire, which was then under investigation by the Interstate Commerce Commission. And when the market suddenly broke sharply on March 14—Harriman's Union Pacific dropped twenty-five points—railroad officials openly cried "persecution." "I would hate to tell you to whom I think you ought to go for an explanation of all this," Harriman bitterly exclaimed to reporters.

The President was now in a quandary. Should he try to stave off panic by directing the Interstate Commerce Commission to let up? (The Fifty-ninth Congress had expired without taking action on the proposals made in his annual message.) Or should he encourage the reform movement on the theory "that we have got to make up our minds that the railroads must not in the future do things which cannot bear the light?" He apparently decided to hold to reform but to soften its impact by conciliatory words. On March 15 he directed the Commission to investigate the railroad industry with particular reference to physical evaluation, legitimacy of stock issues, and vertical and horizontal integration. "I desire from you," he wrote the Commission, "recommendations definite and precise in character to secure a far more thoro-going supervision and control than we now have over the great agencies of interstate transportation." Two and one-half months later, however, with talk of panic still current, he declared at Indianapolis that he did not believe the railroads were overcapitalized.

The situation worsened during the summer of 1907. The President was subjected to heavy pressure from businessmen to let up, especially after Judge Kenesaw Mountain Landis, whom Roosevelt characterized as having "the face of a fanatic

—honest, fearless, well-meaning, but tense to a degree that makes me apprehensive," rocked the corporate world by imposing a fine of more than $29 million against the Standard Oil Company for violating the Elkins Act on some fourteen hundred separate counts.

Yet the President refused to give substantial ground. "I have tried my best not to take up any old offenses," he wrote a Boston banker on August 12, "but I cannot grant an illegal immunity. If we have to proceed against anyone it is because he has sinned against the light." Eight days later Roosevelt dropped a bomb of his own at Provincetown. He charged that "certain malefactors of great wealth" were actually forcing a panic in the hope that it would effect a "reversal" of his regulatory policies "so that they may enjoy unmolested the fruits of their own evil-doing," then urged the criminal prosecution of businessmen law-breakers. Unfortunately, he asserted, "the average juryman wishes to see trusts broken up . . . but is very reluctant to find the facts . . . when it comes to sending to jail a reputable member of the business community for doing what the business community has unhappily grown to recognize as well-nigh normal in business."

Nothing untoward followed the President's forceful reaffirmation of his policies, for the financial disturbances were caused by an international overextension of credit rather than by Roosevelt's pronouncements. Not until mid-October when reports of a group of swashbuckling banker-speculators' attempt to corner the copper market with funds drawn from their own unstable trust companies and the larger and sounder Knickerbocker Trust Company of New York were blazoned in the press did a major crisis occur. Long lines of frantic depositors formed overnight, and by the end of the week runs had forced the affected institutions to close. Throughout the nation, but especially in New York, credit lines became taut. The Westinghouse Company went into receivership; the Stock Exchange in Pittsburgh suspended operations; Western banks demanded more and more money from their New York depositories. And the great Trust Company of America faced imminent collapse.

At this juncture J. Pierpont Morgan brought his commanding abilities to bear. On Wednesday morning, October 23, as Roosevelt rushed back from a hunt in the Louisiana canebrakes and Secretary of the Treasury George B. Cortelyou arranged to deposit $25 million of government funds in New York's national banks, Morgan bolstered the Trust Company of America with a heavy private deposit. The next morning government deposits were added to Morgan's central fund. Together with a new pooling of Wall Street's resources, these kept both the Trust Company and the Stock Exchange open until the regular closing on Friday.

The President was greatly relieved. On Friday he sent Cortelyou a public letter designed to help restore general confidence. "I congratulate you upon the admirable way in which you have handled the present crisis," Roosevelt said in part.

I congratulate also those conservative and substantial businessmen who in this crisis have acted with such wisdom and public spirit. By their action they did invaluable service in checking the panic which, beginning as a matter of speculation, was threatening to destroy the confidence and credit necessary to the conduct of legitimate business.

Within limits, the President was right. Whatever their past errors, the "conservative" bankers of New York had acted wisely and speedily. Morgan had been a central bank unto himself. "At a time when the almost universal instinct was to pull one's own chestnuts out of the fire, to escape new commitments, to dodge responsibility," wrote Frederick Lewis Allen, "he risked everything, again and again, on the success of his campaign." He had, in addition, wielded power greater than that of the President of the United States.

If Morgan had more courage and a higher conception of the commonweal than most of his fellow financiers, he was nonetheless willing to turn a profit. The money shortage had carried on into the next week, and by the week-end the prominent brokerage firm of Moore & Schley, which held a great block of the Tennessee Coal and Iron Company's stock, was in danger of failing. Morgan again acted decisively.

On Saturday, November 2, an emissary of Moore & Schley suggested that the United States Steel Corporation buy out the small, but competing, Tennessee Coal and Iron Company. Its bonds could then be substituted for the Tennessee Company's, saving Moore & Schley and averting a general crisis among brokerage firms. Morgan pondered over the proposal. He might have bailed out Moore & Schley by other means. Grant B. Schley later admitted that all the firm really needed was five or six million dollars in "real money" and Judge Elbert H. Gary, the Steel Corporation's president, conceded that a loan would have sufficed. At the time, however, Moore & Schley rejected Morgan's offer of a five million dollar loan as insufficient. Spurred by his partner, George W. Perkins, Morgan then decided to pursue the merger on the theory that the T. C. & I.'s coal and iron deposits alone were worth the price. After prolonged argument with Henry Clay Frick, he prevailed on the Steel Corporation's Finance Committee to buy T. C. & I. at par with United States Steel bonds.

Judge Gary was at once more cautious and more subtle than the bull-like Morgan; at his insistence the deal was made contingent on President Roosevelt's agreement. Twice before Gary had made arrangements with the President or his representatives—for the Steel Corporation in the fall of 1905 and for the International Harvester Company in the winter of 1907. In each of these "gentlemen's agreements" Gary had agreed to open all the company's books and records to the Bureau of Corporations with the understanding that they would be used "by the President alone for his guidance in making such suggestions to Congress concerning legislation as might be proper, expedient, and for the actual benefit of the general public." In each case the administration had agreed that the President, rather than the Attorney-General, would decide what matters should be kept confidential. Neither agreement exempted the corporations from prosecution for irregularities, but the Morgan-Gary men assumed that Roosevelt would withhold action until they had been granted time to conform to the law. The President did not so promise. But as his failure to institute suit suggests and his repeated recommendations to Congress for regulatory legislation confirm, Wall Street's assumption that he was more interested in sustained regulation than haphazard dissolution was correct. Indeed, the major difference in outlook was that the financiers conceived themselves as equal partners in the business-government relationship (a marked decline from their status as senior partners when Roosevelt succeeded McKinley), and the President regarded them as junior partners.

In these circumstances, Morgan readily agreed that a conference with Roosevelt was desirable. Late that Sunday night Gary and Frick departed for Washington. They met with the President (whom they found at breakfast) and Root early the next morning. Blandly, Gary explained that the United States Steel Corporation had an opportunity to purchase the Tennessee Coal and Iron Company at a "price somewhat in excess of its true value." If the President would approve the purchase before the Stock Exchange opened at ten that morning it "would be of great benefit to financial conditions, and would probably save further failure of important business concerns." Gary and Frick then professed purity of motive. "Judge Gary and Mr. Frick inform me that as a mere business transaction they do not care to purchase the stock," Roosevelt afterward wrote Attorney-General Bonaparte. They say that "but little benefit will come to the Steel Corporation from the purchase; that they are aware that the purchase will be used as a handle for attack upon them on the ground that they are striving to secure a monopoly of the business and prevent competition. . . . But they feel that it is immensely to their interest, as to the interest of every responsible businessman, to try to prevent a panic and general industrial smashup at this time. . . . I answered that while of course I could not advise them to take the action proposed, I felt it no public duty of mine to interpose any objection."

The episode haunted Roosevelt. It was torn out of context by the Democrats in the campaign of 1908; it was raised during the investigation of the United States Steel Corporation in 1911 with grave political consequences; and it was revived sporadically during the rest of Roosevelt's life. Pringle has woven it into a kind of "babe in the woods" account of Roosevelt's relations with "The Wicked Speculators." And some historians continue to regard it as prima-facie evidence of Roosevelt's two-facedness.

Indubitably, Roosevelt had been imposed upon: the United States Steel Corporation's acquisition of the Tennessee Coal and Iron Company strengthened its already favored position within the industry and measurably increased its assets. But what else could the President have done? He was advised that rejection of the proposal would induce a new panic and possibly a real depression. He was told that the decision had to be made before the Stock Exchange opened that morning. And he was assured that Morgan and the others were acting in good conscience. He did, accordingly, what circumstances dictated: he accepted the word of Gary and Frick as that of gentlemen.

The President's tacit consent to the merger should also be viewed in the context of his maturing trust philosophy. By then he entertained little brief for the Sherman Law except as a political or moral weapon; during the year and one half following the Panic of 1907 he would invoke it only in the most extreme cases. Thus he was broadly predisposed to approve the merger. And though he hedged in his letter to Bonaparte by emphasizing that the Steel Corporation's holdings would still comprise less than 60 per cent of those of the industry at large, the transaction as he understood it was consistent with his own philosophy.

But as the long term results of the merger suggest, Roosevelt's inability to define the indirect no less than the direct limits of tolerance was critical. The contention that control of less than 60 per cent of the industry failed to constitute a monopoly had a superficial appeal; and in 1920 the Supreme Court itself succumbed to it, refusing to order the Steel Corporation's dissolution after a long and exhausting suit. But the real effect of the merger was the partial subversion of the interests of a section of the nation. Controlled thereafter from Pittsburgh and New York, T. C. & I. was forced to pursue policies consonant with the interest of U.S. Steel rather than the economy of the Southeast. It was subjected to "basing point" prices that by some accounts prevented it from capitalizing fully on its ability to produce more cheaply than the parent corporation's northern subsidiaries; its natural propensity to expand and diversify its production was seriously curbed; and the steel-consuming industries in the region it served grew less rapidly than they would have had T. C. & I. been free to meet their demands.

Probably neither Morgan nor Gary, and surely not Frick, foresaw all this at the time. Whatever their misrepresentations to Roosevelt in the White House conference, the conspiratorial element is lacking in their talks in New York at the height of the Panic.

Otherwise, the Panic of 1907 proved salutary. By dramatizing the faults of the banking and currency system it sparked meliorative legislation in 1908 and thoroughgoing reform under Woodrow Wilson. After Roosevelt again called for corrective legislation in December, 1907, Senator Aldrich introduced a bill authorizing national banks to issue additional notes up to $500 million in times of emergency. The notes were to be based on municipal, state, and railroad bonds, and they were to be taxed in order to expedite their retirement once the money market loosened. This was somewhat less than the President had recommended.

A bill that anticipated the Federal Reserve Act of 1913 was meanwhile introduced in the House. But politics, insecurity, and a lack of economic imagination combined to force its rejection. Cannon and Aldrich found it too unorthodox. Roosevelt considered it inflationary; also "very puzzling." Furthermore, he leaned too heavily on Aldrich. As he facilely wrote a few weeks later:

I would like to see a thoroly good system of banking and currency . . . and yet this is the only measure that has been proposed that we can seriously consider. The trouble is that the minute I try to get action all the financiers and businessmen differ so that nobody can advise me, nobody can give me any aid; and only Senator Aldrich has prepared a bill.

A substitute administration offering, the Vreeland bill, now passed the House. As merged with Aldrich's bill and enacted into law, it broadened the base for note issues in the South and the West. But it still gave heavy advantage to the East and Southern Democrats and Republican progressives pummeled it unmercifully. Carter Glass of Virginia charged that the three-man committee of bankers empowered to handle the reserve fund would reflect the interests of the great financial institutions and could readily strangle small country banks. He added that it "perpetuates and accentuates the rigidity of a bond-secured currency system," and he finally dismissed it as "50 per cent House infamy and 50 per cent Senate infamy." John Sharp Williams of Mississippi said that it ought "to be entitled the 'Cannon-Aldrich political emergency bill.'" And La Follette said considerably more.

The criticisms were partisan and overdrawn. The Aldrich-Vreeland bill was a temporary expedient rather than an inclusive reform, and its provision for a study commission was of momentous importance. Nevertheless, many of the opposition's points were well taken, and the Federal Reserve Act would incorporate them. As Roosevelt's critics fairly contend, his failure to fashion substantial banking and currency reform stands as one of the signal defeats of his presidency.

Like Roosevelt's other failures, however, it fades into insignificance beside his towering contribution to the conservation movement.

Chapter 19

For the Generations Yet Unborn

When the historian . . . shall speak of Theodore Roosevelt, he is likely to say that he did many notable things, but that his greatest work was inspiring and actually beginning a world movement for staying territorial waste and saving for the human race the things on which alone a peaceful, progressive, and happy life can be founded.
—Robert M. La Follette, *Autobiography*

OF ALL Roosevelt's constructive endeavors, the movement for conservation was most marked by sustained intellectual and administrative force. In none other did the President blend science and morality quite so effectively; in only one other, foreign policy, did he submerge partisan politics nearly so decisively. For more than seven years, often against the avowed opposition of the most powerful leaders of his own party and at the bitter end against the combined opposition of both parties, he pressed Congress and the states to place the future public interest above the current private interest. And though he was repeatedly criticized, rebuffed, and insulted, he refused even to compromise significantly.

Roosevelt freely confessed that his program was built upon the labors and visions of scientists who had given, or were to give, the flower of their lives to its advancement. "They actualiy did the job that I and the others talked about," he said at Harvard two years after he left the White House. "I know what they did because it was something in which I intensely believed, and yet it was something about which I did not have enough practical knowledge to work except through them. . . ." Nevertheless, the President's was the ultimate responsibility.

Roosevelt would have thrown himself into the conservation movement whatever the circumstances of his presidency. But he would hardly have promoted it with such extraordinary boldness and imagination had it not been for his inspiring relationship with Gifford Pinchot, Chief Forester of the United States and one of American history's most constructive secondary leaders.

The scion of an old Huguenot family of moderate wealth and high public spirit (the Pinchots in 1900 made the grant that started the Yale Forestry School), Gifford was thirty-six years old when Roosevelt became President. A tall, sinewy man with piercing eyes, a thin straight nose, and a long sharp chin that a drooping mustache barely softened, he wore an air of compelling urgency. He was constantly converting, or trying to convert, and only his natural graciousness and the high fortune of his friendship with the President early spared him the fate of many another zealot. For more, even, than most men with a mission, Pinchot was fanatically confident of the righteousness of his cause. Upon its altar he would eventually sacrifice his governmental career.

Not until Roosevelt became governor of New York did the two men become close. During the winter of 1899 Pinchot stopped in Albany for an overnight visit, arriving "just as the Executive Mansion was under ferocious attack from a band of invisible Indians, and the Governor of the Empire State was helping a houseful of children to escape by lowering them out of the second-story window on a rope." After the children had been "saved," the forester had proved his mettle by knocking Roosevelt "off his very solid pins" in a boxing match. He and his host had then discussed forestry.

While one of the nation's most singularly productive friendships was thus being sealed, the conservation cause was going badly in Washington. By Roosevelt's accession more than twenty-six million acres of public lands had been withdrawn from private entry. But the figures were deceptive, for the prevailing leasing system permitted private exploitation of minerals, timber, and water-power sites even in the so-called reserves. Although Cleveland had halted the process by executive order ten days before his second term expired, McKinley had soon signed a compromise measure which opened the reserves to indiscriminate mining and prospecting. Between 1898 and 1905, when this "vicious piece of legislation," as the Public Land Commission termed it, was repealed, three million acres of government timber land passed permanently into private hands.

Roosevelt had barely moved into the White House after

McKinley's death in September, 1901 before he unloaded his baggage in the conservationists' camp. On his return from his predecessor's funeral, Pinchot and Frederick H. Newell, the father of the Reclamation Service, spelled out the far-reaching forestry and reclamation plans they and their able associates had long hoped to institute. "The new President knew what we were talking about," Pinchot recalled. "We left, two very happy men, authorized to draft for the Message what we thought it ought to say on our twin subjects. It was a Heaven-sent chance."

The message President Roosevelt sent into the Congress two months later gave forceful expression to Pinchot and Newell's advanced scientific views; and in the manner of his partly ghost-written statements, to his own as well. "The fundamental idea of forestry is the perpetuation of forests by use," Roosevelt declared. He then recommended that the reserves be kept open to "selective cutting." They should also be utilized as natural reservoirs, supplemented where necessary by great storage dams "too vast for private effort" to finance. This could not be accomplished by the states alone. "It is as right for the National Government to make the streams and rivers of the arid region useful by engineering works for water storage," he said in a passage that foreshadowed his later, more strident centralism, "as to make useful the rivers and harbors of the humid region by engineering works of another kind." Too often, he testily added, the states had allowed streams to pass into private ownership. "Whoever controls a stream practically controls the land it renders productive," he reminded the Congress, and ". . . the doctrine of private ownership of water apart from land cannot prevail without causing enduring wrong."

Roosevelt had then plunged headlong into the seven years' struggle to put his proposals into effect. On December 19, 1901, he urged Congress to create a national forest reserve in the Appalachians. Meanwhile he threw his as yet untested power behind a Democratic-sponsored irrigation and reclamation measure, the Newlands bill, which McKinley had failed to support and which Joseph G. Cannon, then chairman of the Appropriations Committee, was opposing. Cannon's opposition was animated by an unreasoned commitment to economy, by fear that the reclaimed areas would offer competition to Midwestern agriculture, and by a coarse anti-intellectualism. As he later snapped in another context, he stood "not one cent for scenery" and he never did have much use for the "college professors, students, wise men and so on through the length and breadth of the country, who investigate. . . ." Nor was "Uncle Joe" moved by a presidential appeal. "I do not believe that I have ever before written to an individual legislator in favor of an individual bill," Roosevelt wrote, "but I break through my rule to ask you as earnestly as I can not to oppose the Irrigation measure. Believe me this is something of which I have made a careful study, and great and real though my deference is for your knowledge of legislation, and for your attitude in stopping expense, I yet feel from my acquaintance with the far West that it would be a genuine and rankling injustice for the Republican party to kill this measure. I believe in it with all my heart from every standpoint."

I am just about to sign the River and Harbor bill. . . . Now this is a measure for the material benefit of your State and mine and of the other states with harbors and navigable rivers. Surely it is but simple justice for us to give to the arid regions a measure of relief, the financial burden of which will be but trifling, while the benefit to the country involved is far greater than under the River and Harbor bill. I cannot too strongly express my feeling upon this matter.

Cannon refused to clarify his position, and the Newlands bill rolled through the House without his support. On June 17, 1902, Roosevelt enthusiastically signed it into law. The first important enactment of his presidency, it authorized the creation of a reclamation service, assigned revenues from land sales to the construction of reservoirs and irrigation works, and established a creative, heavily subsidized program for the arid lands. By its authority thirty irrigation projects, including the Roosevelt Dam in Arizona, were in progress or already completed when Roosevelt left office in March, 1909.

During the remainder of his first term Roosevelt continued to see much of Pinchot. At the forester's suggestion he set aside the Dismal River and Niobrara Forest Reserves for a controlled experiment in tree planting in Nebraska where an earlier and more limited experiment had shown that marketable trees could grow on sand hills regarded as worthless. This second experiment proved similarly successful, serving in Pinchot's words as the forerunner of the "great Shelter Belt Plan begun under President Franklin D. Roosevelt, and so brilliantly suggested and successfully directed by Raphael Zon."

But not until after he was elected in his own right did Roosevelt's flaming conviction really scorch the anti-conservationists. Reinforced by his popular mandate, the President launched a full-scale campaign to stay the exploitative processes of a century and a quarter. From the winter of 1905 on scarcely a detail eluded his creative attention as he vigorously promoted the cause in public speeches, messages to Congress, and executive actions. There followed such an era of enlightenment as the nation had never before experienced and would not again see until Franklin Roosevelt, himself nurtured on Theodore's conservation theories, came to power.

The first harvest came in on February 1, 1905. On that date Roosevelt signed a measure transferring the Forest Reserves from the jurisdiction of the inefficient Land Office in the Department of the Interior to the Bureau of Forestry, renamed the Forest Service, in the Department of Agriculture. The measure also conferred upon Pinchot such power as was to make him the Galahad of the conservationists and the bête noire of their opponents. Two months later the Forest Service was authorized to make arrests for the violation of its regulations.

The forestry movement was now coming of age. The most powerful interests in the West, including the National Wholesale Lumber Dealers' Association, had finally concluded that the selective cutting and other techniques urged upon them by Pinchot and his dedicated colleagues were feasible. It was no accident that the transfer bill was passed just after they endorsed it at the American Forest Congress in January, 1905.

The Forest Service soon became more independent of Congress than anticipated. By a little-noticed cause given an inclusive interpretation by the Attorney-General, the Agriculture Appropriations Act of 1905 authorized the Service to use the revenues from the sale of the lands or products of the reserves for administration of existing reserves and the creation of new ones. A small revolution ensued. "While we could still say nothing but 'Please' to private forest owners," Pinchot recalled, "on the national Forest Reserves we could say, and we did say, 'Do this,' and 'Don't do that.' We had the power, as we had the duty, to protect the Reserves for the use of the people, and that meant stepping on the toes of the biggest interests in the West. From that time on it was fight, fight, fight."

Under Roosevelt's driving leadership the Forest Lieu Land Act of 1897 was repealed. (This measure, writes Roy Robbins, was believed by many Westerners to have "done more to aid the speculators and corporations than to aid the actual settler.") Hard on its demise a leasing system for use of the grass lands within the forest reserves was established. Under and in violation of prevailing regulations, pastures had been ruthlessly overgrazed, government lands had been fenced in by private operators, cattlemen had fought bloody battles against sheepmen, and both had made life miserable for the homesteaders. The new order was buttressed by Roosevelt's resolve to enforce the laws against fencing. "I cannot consent to a clause continuing for a year, or for any length of time, the present illegal fencing," he explained to Senator Francis E. Warren of Wyoming, whose solicitude for the sheep industry later earned him the sobriquet, "the greatest shepherd since Abraham." The President continued:

The opposition we have . . . now comes primarily from the big men who graze wandering flocks of sheep, and who do not promote the real settlement of the country. These are the men whose interests are diametrically hostile to those of the homemakers, who wish to eat out and destroy the country where he desires permanently to live, and who, when they have thus ruined the land of the homesteader and small stockman, move elsewhere to repeat the process of devastation.

Actually, Roosevelt's understanding was deeper than his strictures against illegal fencing implied. He knew that many homesteaders and small cattlemen had also resorted to illegal fencing, if only in self-defense. He shared the cattlemen's animus toward the sheepmen. And he realized that the fenced-in lands were generally less overgrazed than the open range. As he conceded in a special message the next year, fencing the public domain "would be thoroughly desirable if it were legal."

The President also knew that the 160-acre limit on homesteads was grossly inadequate for the semi-arid country. He persistently labored to correct this, and shortly before he left office Congress raised the allotment to 320 acres. As he argued, however, the only rational solution was to base the allotment on the particular needs of the area. Otherwise, he pointed out as early as December, 1905, "needless suffering and failure on the part of a very considerable proportion of the bona-fide settlers who give faith to the implied assurance of the government that such an area is sufficient" would result.

Meanwhile the President focused his sights on the fast-growing electric power industry. For some years, writes Pinchot, utility companies had been securing the best water-power sites "through every workable use or misuse of the public-land laws and the laws relating to navigable rivers. . . . The Government's problem, as we saw it, was to ensure the fullest possible development of water power and its sale to the consumer at the cheapest possible price. That meant the prevention of monopoly where we could, and effective regulation of it where we couldn't." For these reasons Roosevelt had vetoed a bill in 1903 that would have turned Muscle Shoals, which later became the heart of the TVA, over to piecemeal private development.

From 1906 on, when a number of sites were leased to the Edison Electrical Company of California, a policy of controlled, fifty-year leases obtained. To assure orderly development, Pinchot withdrew 2,565 sites from entry during the next two years, often on the pretext that he planned to establish ranger stations on them. In these actions, as in most others, he leaned heavily on the President's broad shoulders. "Without T.R.'s support," he wrote, "all reasonable regulation of the development of water power on the National Forests would have broken down."

Several times during his last two years in office Roosevelt vetoed bills which failed to conform to his regulatory program; and on January 15, 1909, in one of the most memorable of such actions, he sweepingly rebuked both Congress and the puissant electric power lobby. "I esteem it my duty," he said in rejecting a measure authorizing construction of an unleased and unregulated dam in Missouri, "to use every endeavor to prevent this growing monopoly, the most threatening which has ever appeared, from being fastened upon the people of the Nation." This bill "does not contain the conditions essential to protect the public interest."

Shortly after Roosevelt and Pinchot began to apply the principle that "the public rights come first and private interest second" to the electric power industry, the President imposed it upon the mining industry. Valuable coal lands had long been passing into private hands at prices disgracefully disproportionate to their true value. Now, by direction of the President on June 29, 1906, the process was finally slowed. More than fifty million acres believed to contain coal and other minerals were temporarily withdrawn from public entry in order that they might be classified, and before Roosevelt left office eighteen million additional acres were withdrawn in Alaska. To be sure, the President's frequent requests that Congress establish a royalty fee system under government price and transportation controls fell on deaf ears. But as Samuel P. Hays observes, the Geological Survey at least "valued the coal lands according to the quality of the deposits and their accessibility, and established prices which would aid development, while preventing speculation."

By 1907 Congress, the timber, grazing, and mining interests of the West, and the overwhelming majority of conservatives in the East were surfeited with Theodore Roosevelt. From 1907 on the President faced a manifestly hostile Congress, one that resisted him on almost all major issues and repudiated him on some. Had Roosevelt been a less resourceful man, he might have served out his final years in fretful impotence. But because he held it the executive's duty to lead, he managed to maintain the authority of his office. By his discriminating use of the veto power he held the main line against his opponents' embittered assaults; and by continuing his audacious use of other powers he even advanced in some areas. His conservation program reached full maturity, in fact, at the very time it fell under the sharpest attack.

The first of a succession of showdowns between President and Congress came during the short session of 1907. Resentment of Roosevelt and Pinchot's policies had increased in direct proportion to their effectiveness. When the Agricultural Appropriations bill was sent in from the House, Senator C. W. Fulton, an Oregon Republican who bowed not to "Uncle Joe" Cannon in the vigor of his anti-intellectualism, castigated the Chief Forester and his colleagues as impractical "dreamers and theorists" ensconced within "marble halls"; he also opposed a provision to increase Pinchot's salary.

Less than a month later Fulton offered an amendment to the Agricultural Appropriations bill specifying that no forest reserve should thereafter be created within the states of Oregon, Washington, Idaho, Montana, Colorado, or Wyoming (extremist Westerners actually wanted the reserves returned to the states, under whose benign authority private interests had already ravaged great blocks of land). The anti-Roosevelt feeling in the Senate was so concerted that Fulton's amendment was adopted without a roll-call vote, and shortly before the session ended the amended Agricultural Appropriations bill reached the President's desk. Fulton and his friends waited, serene in the belief that Roosevelt would sign it. (The Department of Agriculture and all its subordinate agencies, including the forest reserves, depended on its authorization for funds during the coming fiscal year.) They were completely unprepared for the explosion that followed.

Responding instinctively to this sullen attack on the public interest, Pinchot formulated an ingenious counterattack: Roosevelt should proclaim National Forests in all suitable remaining public lands during the ten days he had to sign or reject the bill. "We knew precisely what we wanted," Pinchot recalled. "Our field force had already gathered practically all the facts. Speedily it supplied the rest. Our office force worked straight through, some of them for thirty-six and even forty-eight hours on end, to finish the job." As the proclamations were completed, Pinchot took them to the White House for Roosevelt's signature. They were then sent to the State Department for safekeeping until twenty-one new forest reserves embracing sixteen million acres in the six states affected by Fulton's amendment were provided for. The President formally proclaimed them on March 2 just before he signed the Agricultural Appropriations bill into law.

Six years later Roosevelt described with transparent glee how "the friends of the special interests in the Senate" had been outwitted. "The opponents of the forest service turned handsprings in their wrath, and dire were their threats against the Executive; but the threats could not be carried out, and were really only a tribute to the efficiency of our action." But a memorandum dictated at the time suggests that he was concerned lest historians interpret his action as arbitrary:

If I did not act . . . and if Congress differs from me in this position, it will have full opportunity in the future to take such position as it may desire. . . .
Failure on my part to sign these proclamations would mean that

immense tracts of valuable timber would fall into the hands of the lumber syndicates.

The President's "midnight" proclamations rang down the curtain for many Westerners. Forgotten in their bitterness were the ties that had made them regard the young reformer-ranchman as their own; that had impelled them to pour out of the mountains and off the great plains to serve under his command in 1898; and that had turned "Boss" Platt's cynical maneuvering into an uncontrollable stampede at the Republican Convention of 1900. Not only to the lumber syndicates, the mining corporations, and the great sheep and cattle barons, but to many of the "plain people" Roosevelt professed so to love, the President by 1907 was a deadly enemy of their region. The spurious charge the governor of Washington now leveled against Pinchot—he "has done more to retard the growth and development of the Northwest than any other man"—could only have had Roosevelt as its real object.

Not all the opposition to the Roosevelt-Pinchot policies was unfounded; nor did it all emanate from the servants of "special privilege." The problems were so diverse and the interests involved so irreconcilable that there remain to this day areas of unresolved conflict. The complaint of the states that the national reserves reduced their tax base is reasonable, if not in the broad view consequential. Understandable, also, are the protests of those operators, small even more than large, who had come by custom to regard the nation's resources as theirs to exploit. Man once unfettered does not submit gracefully to bureaucracy no matter how great its flexibility or laudable its social and scientific purposes. The leasing fees, the proscriptions of fencing, the prohibition of excessive grazing—these and other regulations irked free-wheeling Westerners on the make.

Small entrepreneurs complained that the great lumber companies benefited unfairly from the creation of reserves because they had already engrossed the lands that gave ingress. They also charged that the selective-cutting techniques prescribed by the Forest Service were easier for the large interests to finance. The gigantic Weyerhaeuser Timber Company could conform to the principles of a long-term investment, but few small companies had the financial resources to take the long view. Inevitably, they resented having it imposed upon them.

Roosevelt's reaction was ambivalent at best and disingenuous at worst. He continued to emphasize the anti-monopolistic tenor of his policies; and with some justification. A million and one-half acres were opened to settlement by small farmers under his administration and his water-power program was clearly designed to bring natural monopolies under public control. Yet he also complained privately that the "people refuse to face squarely the proposition that much of these lands ought to be leased and fenced as pastures, and that they cannot possibly be taken up with profit as small homesteads." But the point is not worth belaboring. His commitment to scientific forestry was so firm and his insight into the advantages of corporate organization in a technological age so deep that he could not have altered his course. Regulation was the only socially desirable solution.

Pinchot's personnel policies compounded the paradox. The old Forestry Division had been plagued by an inferior staff, especially in the field, where ward politicians, ex-bartenders, and other misfits comprised an embarrassingly large part of the ranger force. At Pinchot's instance Roosevelt had placed foresters under the civil service laws in December, 1904. The reform proved so salutary that in 1908 a New York consulting firm compared the administration of the Forest Service "most favorably" with private industry and reported that its investigators had "rarely, if ever, met a body of men where the average of intelligence was so high or the loyalty to the organization and to the work so great."

But from Cannon on down professional politicians resented the loss of patronage. More ironic still, Westerners who had earlier protested the low quality of the Forestry Division now fulminated against the high quality of the reconstituted Forest Service. No longer could they evade regulations on the grounds that the men who devised and enforced them lacked competence. Like the meat packers, the railroad officials, and other businessmen who had felt Roosevelt's controlling hand, their philosophy proved under fire to encompass little more than their own self-interest.

Meanwhile the President's love of nature carried him into skirmishes for the preservation of the country's magnificent natural monuments—Niagara Falls and Arizona's Grand Canyon, Oregon's Crater Lake and New Mexico's Petrified Forest, the undulating Blue Ridge Mountains and dozens upon dozens of others. In private letters, speeches, and messages to Congress he expressed his heartfelt conviction that nature's wonders were the American people's own rightful heritage. "I cannot too often repeat that the essential feature in the present management of the Yellowstone Park, as in all similar places, is its essential democracy," he said as he laid the cornerstone of Yellowstone's gateway on April 24, 1903.

And so there were created under Roosevelt five National Parks—Crater Lake in Oregon, Platt National Park in Oklahoma, Wind Cave in South Dakota, Sully Hill in North Dakota, and Mesa Verde in Colorado. These doubled the number established by all his predecessors. There was passed under Roosevelt's spur the National Monuments Act of June, 1906, by authority of which he proclaimed sixteen National Monuments, including Wyoming's Devil Tower, California's Muir Woods, and Washington's Mount Olympus. There were established by executive orders issued between March 14, 1903, when Roosevelt first realized he had the power, and March 4, 1909, when he turned over the power, fifty-one wildlife refuges. ("Is there any law that will prevent me from declaring Pelican Island a Federal Bird Reservation?" he had asked. Informed there was none, he had replied: "Very well, then I so declare it.") And there was launched from the base built by Wiliam T. Hornaday, George Bird Grinnell, Frank M. Chapman, and the National Audubon Society a nature-appreciation movement that offers one of the few hopes that the march of the billboards, the gas stations, and the bulldozers may somehow be stayed and that such commercial barbarisms as Wisconsin's Dells may yet be redeemed.

As the time for Roosevelt to give up his stewardship drew near, he came increasingly to realize that the conservation movement's future lay pre-eminently with the states. They must abandon their particularism in order that regional, multipurpose river developments might be undertaken; they must be imbued with a sense of responsibility that the despoliation of their own public lands might be halted. To these ends Roosevelt appointed a path-finding body, the Inland Waterways Commission, on March 14, 1907. Six months later he announced that he would call a conference of governors to meet in Washington that winter. The long-range effects proved momentous.

The President's charge to the Inland Waterways Commission spelled out the need of a comprehensive plan for the improvement and control of the nation's rivers:

Works designed to control our waterways have . . . been undertaken for a single purpose, such as the improvement of navigation, development of power, the irrigation of arid lands, the protection of lowlands from floods, or to supply water for domestic and manufacturing purposes. . . . the time has come for merging local projects and uses of the inland waters in a comprehensive plan designed for the benefit of the whole country.

Within the year the Inland Waterways Commission confirmed and amplified the President's original charge. Presumably because he feared Congress might miss the point, Roosevelt appended to it a sharp attack on the electric power industry. "Among these monopolies . . . ," he wrote, "there is no other which threatens, or has ever threatened, such intolerable interference with the daily life of the people as the consolidation of companies controlling water power."

. . . I call your special attention to the attempt of the power corporations, through bills introduced at the present session, to escape from the possibility of Government regulation in the interests of the people. These bills are intended to enable the corporations to take possession in perpetuity of national forest lands for the purposes of their business, where and as they please, wholly without compensation to the public.

Neither the report of the Inland Waterways Commission nor the angry assertions of the President turned Congress from its pork-barrel ways. Resentful of Roosevelt's popularity, contemptuous of his interest in social planning, and solicitous of special interests, the Republican majority yearned openly for the day when its leader would no longer lead—when it would have again a President in the mold of McKinley. Sullenly, it sat on its hands. It got off them only to prohibit the President from appointing new commissions without congressional consent following his message of December 8, 1908. The historic handling of the inland waterways has been "short-sighted, vacillating, and futile," the President charged in that last annual message. The Army engineers responsible for the program (the chief of the corps had actually said that flood control, hydroelectric power, and irrigation should be subordinated to navigation) were "unsuited by their training and traditions to take the broad view" and they had failed above all "to grasp the great underlying fact that every stream is a unit from its source to its mouth, and that all its uses are interdependent." Congress should provide funds, the President fruitlessly concluded, "to frame and supervise the execution of a comprehensive plan."

It was those last two principles—"that every stream is a unit from its source to its mouth, and that all its uses are interdependent"—which comprised the springboard for the TVA, that monument to George W. Norris's persistence and the New Deal's acceptance of its legacy from the Square Deal.

Had Theodore Roosevelt's service to conservation ended with the proclamation of the sixteen million acres of Forest Reserves in 1907 or with his vigorous exposition of the findings of the Inland Waterways Commission, his conservation record would still have been distinguished beyond that of all of his predecessors. But it did not. The Governors' Conference of 1908 added one more star to his already glittering constellation.

Attired in the formal clothes he deemed appropriate to the occasion, Roosevelt mounted a temporary podium in the East Room of the White House on the morning of May 13, 1908. For fifty minutes, in the modulated, cultured tones as characteristic of his speech as the shrill falsetto ascribed to him by caricaturists, he spoke—to the members of his Cabinet; to the Associate Justices and the Chief Justice of the Supreme Court of the United States; to the Governors of thirty-eight states and territories, many of whom spared no love for either him or conservation; to the loyal leader of the opposition, William Jennings Bryan, who would make his third and last bid for the presidency that autumn; to Andrew Carnegie, dedicated for some years past to peace, philanthropy, and public welfare; to James J. Hill, the most enlightened of the great railroad magnates; and to a host of scientists, publicists, and representatives of the nation's learned societies. Grover Cleveland would also have been present had he not then been in his final illness.

The President's address was a testament of faith and a statement of hope. He started by declaring that conservation was "the chief material question that confronts us, second only —and second always—to the great fundamental question of morality." He emphasized the urgent need for a "coherent plan" of development. He reaffirmed that his object was not to lock up natural resources, but to use them in a way that would increase their yield for the next generation. "No wise use of a farm exhausts its fertility," he said. "So with the forests." He showered encomiums upon Gifford Pinchot, "to whom we owe so much of the progress we have already made." And he concluded by asserting that the rights of the public transcended private interests:

In the past we have admitted the right of the individual to injure the future of the Republic for his own present profit. The time has come for a change. As a people we have the right and the duty, second to none other but the right and duty of obeying the moral law, of requiring and doing justice, to protect ourselves and our children against the wasteful development of our natural resources.

No event of Roosevelt's turbulent career evoked a more favorable reaction than the conference he had thus opened. Even the *New York Evening Post* conceded that "this is distinctly a case where Mr. Roosevelt's love of the spectacular and skill in advertising have proved of public advantage." The *New York Sun*, noted the editors of the *Literary Digest*, "is the only paper we yet have seen which holds absolutely aloof from the enthusiasm of the occasion."

The epochal importance of the Governors' Conference can only be suggested. Not all the governors were sympathetic to the Roosevelt-Pinchot program, and before the sessions closed several of the Westerners militantly defended states' rights, that "darling of the great special interests" as Pinchot caustically termed them. Yet even they gave their names to the notable Declaration of the Governors, a landmark in the history of the conservation movement and the changing conception of federal-state relationships:

We agree that the sources of national wealth exist for the benefit of the People, and that monopoly thereof should not be tolerated.

We declare the conviction that in the use of the natural resources our independent States are interdependent and bound together by ties of mutual benefits, responsibilities, and duties.

We agree that further action is advisable to ascertain the present condition of our natural resources and to promote the conservation of the same; and to that end we recommend the appointment by each State of a Commission on the Conservation of Natural Resources, to co-operate with each other and with any similar commission of the Federal Government.

Less than a month later Roosevelt appointed the Federal Commission on the Conservation of Natural Resources under the chairmanship of the indefatigable Pinchot. Organized in four divisions—water, forest, land, and mineral resources— the Commission was charged to cooperate with the states in the interests of "the permanent welfare of the people" and to submit a preliminary report by January, 1909. The end product, writes Robbins, comprises "the most exhaustive inventory of our natural resources that has ever been made." Its value to scholars, government officials, and civic-minded citizens has been inestimable.

Most of the state executives kept the faith during the first great outburst of enthusiasm that followed the conference. Within a year or so of the final session forty-one state conservation commissions had been formed; and until their recommendations began actually to be applied, everyone, or almost everyone, was for conservation. Only "when it began to interfere with the profits of powerful men and great special interests," complained Pinchot, did the honeymoon come to an end.

Yet that is less than the whole. If, a half century later, many state governments stand paralyzed before the special interests that Roosevelt fought; if, thirty years after Roosevelt's death, private power companies continue to build dams without regard for the multi-purposes he urged; if, only rarely, a governor emerges with the courage and vision to rise above the short-sighted economy that Roosevelt deplored; if all this in our times is true, it is also true that the very substantial achievements of the past fifty years reflect the animating spirit of Theodore Roosevelt.

There was much difference of opinion about Roosevelt the politician, Dr. Charles Van Hise, conservationist, geologist, and president of the University of Wisconsin from 1903 to 1918, wrote two years after Roosevelt left the presidency:

He has been severely criticized by many, warmly commended by others, but his aggressive action for the conservation of our resources has been commended by all parties alike . . . what he did to forward this movement . . . will place him not only as one of the greatest statesmen of this nation but one of the greatest statesmen of any nation of any time.

Chapter 20

Toward the Welfare State

> *There has been a curious revival of the doc-*
> *trine of State rights . . . by the people who*
> *know that the States cannot with justice to both*
> *sides practically control the corporation and*
> *who therefore advocate such control because*
> *they do not venture to express their real wish,*
> *which is that there shall be no control at all. . . .*
> —Theodore Roosevelt in a
> speech at Harvard, 1907

ALTHOUGH THE Panic of 1907 had compelled the President to resume relations with the congressional conservatives, his unyielding fight for conservation proves that the *rapprochement* was not of the spirit. True, Roosevelt maintained the working alliance with the Old Guard on some issues until near the end, though it daily grew more precarious. And in the manner of his entire career, he continued to compromise, holding out for some measures, sacrificing others, and accepting the form in lieu of the substance on still others.

Roosevelt would have been gratified, for example, had Congress passed a national child labor bill. But on that issue as on numerous others, his party's massive conservatism thwarted him. So powerful was the manufacturers' hold on the Republican leadership that no executive pressure, no marshaling of sociological data, no high-minded appeals from disinterested reformers could break it. The President had little alternative, therefore, but to dismiss as impractical the impassioned pleas of Beveridge, who had taken the child labor movement to his heart, and to support instead a bill sponsored by Lodge which applied only to the District of Columbia, an area where child labor was virtually nonexistent. The President rationalized this near-mockery of justice by contending that it would warn the states that they must either pass similar legislation or suffer federal action in the future.

To dwell on Roosevelt's forced compromises with the Sixtieth Congress is to obscure the larger significance of his final years as President. On front after front he was moving out in advance of his party—moving so far and so rapidly that by 1908, a year before Herbert Croly published his *The Promise of American Life*, Roosevelt had skirted all, and occupied most, of the ground he was to deploy his armies over in 1912. Nor is it surprising that the President's ideas continued to develop, for if the challenges were not more imposing, they were more sharply delineated; and in great measure because of Roosevelt's own actions. It was partly the momentum of his earlier attacks on special privilege that now impelled Roosevelt to set forth piecemeal the positivist-regulationist program that the theoretician Croly would later formalize.

The essence of this program was a broad extension of federal authority. And one of the most widely accepted interpretations of it is that it constituted a signal reflection of Roosevelt's lust for personal power. Only a man who believed in power could have countenanced such a concentration of authority as Roosevelt repeatedly urged; only a man unafraid of power could have unloosed the broadsides that Roosevelt again and again rained upon the states'-righters. So the analysis runs.

There is, to repeat, a measure of truth in those assertions. The reader familiar with Blum's perceptive writings must be impressed by the influence that abstract and concrete concerts of power exerted upon the President's policies. Nor can he disregard Blum's suggestion that Roosevelt resented being inhibited by the law; that he, especially, "may have benefited from the limits on Presidential power which men who understood the problem in 1787 created." The Brownsville affair and numerous other incidents attest weightily to that. So does one of Roosevelt's candid revelations: "I don't think that any harm comes from the concentration of power in one man's hands, provided the holder does not keep it for more than a certain, definite time, and then returns to the people from whom he sprang."

Nevertheless, a fuller truth emerges: a great exertion of federal authority was the only feasible means of meeting the challenge of the times. That challenge was dramatized by the overweening arrogance of the Morgans, the Harrimans, the meat packers, and their like. But its primal force was the impersonal corporate power of the burgeoning industrial age and the shattering revolution in communications which made California closer to New York in Roosevelt's day than Virginia had been to Georgia when the Constitution was framed. To ignore this, to attribute the growth of centralized power under Roosevelt to his apparent compulsion for power, is to do enormous violence to history and to the President himself. For if Roosevelt's glands decreed that he must forever act, his high sense of justice and his empirical approach to problems determined the direction of his acts.

Theodore Roosevelt had never been alone in urging the positivist-regulationist state upon a reluctant Congress. He may have seemed a Caesar by comparison to the negative-minded Cleveland or the judicial-minded Parker. But there was little to choose between Roosevelt's policies and those of the affirmative-minded Bryan. The Great Commoner also understood that the upheavals induced by the Industrial Revolution made national action mandatory; and on many specific issues he generously cheered Roosevelt on. So persistent were the problems and so obvious the means to resolve them, indeed, that the national welfare state continued to develop under such an avowed constitutionalist as William Howard Taft.

Curiously, even Roosevelt's most psychoanalytically oriented critics have failed to challenge the high-minded motivation behind his conservation policies, though they embodied the broadest of all his augmentations of federal power. It is fruitful, therefore, to re-examine his evolving antitrust and labor policies and especially his attitude toward the judiciary.

The President's move against the Northern Securities Company in 1902 had been followed by a spate of antitrust proceedings—forty-three all told. The burden of these had been instituted hard on the election of 1904 and they had served in part to justify Roosevelt's faith in himself, to prove that he was a free moral agent in spite of the hostage the corporation's contributions to his campaign purportedly represented. They had failed, however, to resolve the trust problem. Anti-social practices continued in the face of the dissolution orders, and the vast majority of corporations were in no wise affected anyway.

Accordingly, the President was beset by misgivings even as he encouraged a succession of attorneys-general to prosecute the most flagrant violators. It should be remarked again that the constructive in him had always rebelled against the muckraking mentality's total indictment of big business. Roosevelt rarely, if ever, attacked from a purely anticorporation bias. To assert the supremacy of the federal government, to court (unconsciously perhaps) the favor of the "plain people," to suppress the most flagrant cases of "wrongdoing," or to strike down the most patent monopolies—these and the need to force Congress to support his program, as with the Hepburn bill, were his motives. But now, slowly yet ineluctably, the regulationist philosophy which had all along dominated his policy toward the railroads came to reign over most other areas as well. Without abandoning trust-busting completely, for he continued to believe that some trusts deserved destruction, Roosevelt gave regulation greater and greater emphasis.

By March, 1907, seven months before he tacitly agreed to the merger of the United States Steel Corporation and the Tennessee Coal and Iron Company, the President was writing the Interstate Commerce Commission that he did "not believe in the sweeping and indiscriminate prohibition of all combination which has been so marked and as I think so mischievous a feature of our anti-trust legislation." Could not the Commission explore further the possibility of authorizing "combinations by consent?" Then, with greater emphasis than ever before, he urged Congress in December, 1907, to place all interstate business under federal supervision. "This is not advocating centralization," he declared. "It is merely looking facts in the face and realizing that centralization in business has already come and cannot be avoided or undone, and that the public at large can only protect itself from certain evil effects of this business centralization by providing better methods for the exercise of control. . . ."

The pure-food law was opposed so violently that its passage was delayed for a decade; yet it has worked unmixed and immediate good. The meat-inspection law was even more violently assailed; and the same men who now denounce the attitude of the National Government in seeking to oversee and control the workings of interstate common carriers and business concerns, then asserted that we were "discrediting and ruining a great American industry."

The President's assertions drew strong support from a small coterie of sophisticated Wall Street men, among them George W. Perkins. That very winter the House of Morgan supported proposals which would have regularized the "gentlemen's agreements" by authorizing the Bureau of Corporations to pass on business projects in advance. By then, however, the great majority of corporate leaders outside the Morgan-Gary-Perkins axis were so exercised by Roosevelt's penetrating criticisms of businessmen that they blinded themselves to their own interests. Nor did small business take kindly to measures that would have accelerated the rise of giant corporations by sanctioning "reasonable" restraints on trade. As a result, neither the regular session of the Sixtieth Congress nor the short session a year later gave serious consideration to the proposals. The trouble, Roosevelt wrote in exasperation, was that the corporations preferred that the existing laws be "administered crookedly" rather than be revised in their own and the public interest. "Of course," he added, "as far as I am concerned such expectation is in vain."*

The President's charge may have been oversimplified, but it was not ill-considered. He had long accepted Brooks Adams' contention that the law is "the expression of the will of the strongest for the time being" and that as wealth increases "the representatives of the monied class acquire that absolute power once wielded by the Roman proconsul, and now exercised by the modern magistrate." He recoiled, however, from Adams' pessimistic conclusion that a legal system serving poor and rich alike was an illusory ideal. His goal was a legal system that knew neither class nor favor; he had sought often in the past, and he would seek more often in the future, to attain it.

For years Roosevelt had been angered by the system's tendency to impose heavy prison terms on petty criminals and to allow businessmen to violate both the civil and criminal statutes with relative impunity. He had been uncertain, however, as to a course of action. He believed that it would be unfair to prosecute for offenses which the government had condoned, in effect, by default. And he had consequently over-

* For an illuminating analysis of Roosevelt's effort to amend the Sherman Law in 1908, see Arthur M. Johnson, "Antitrust Policy in Transition," *Mississippi Valley Historical Review*, XLVIII (1961). Business broadly agreed that revision was desirable; but when Roosevelt threatened to veto any bill which failed to provide for effective regulation by government administrative bodies most business groups withdrew their support. The NAM, in particular, opposed the President's insistence on meaningful supervision. As Johnson concludes, "Whatever his shortcomings, Roosevelt's view of the national interest and the need to keep a balance between the ideal and the reality was broader than that of the groups attempting to influence the pending legislation."

looked many businessmen's earlier transgressions. But now, as he stepped up his campaign to make corporations obey the law, he concluded that businessmen who flouted the law should be treated with neither more nor less consideration than other criminals. So he repeated the strictures against juries which fail "to jail a member of the business community" that he had uttered at Provincetown the previous summer. "The two great evils in the execution of our criminal laws today are sentimentality and technicality," he reminded Congress. Both should be remedied; the former by "the gradual growth of a sound public opinion," the latter by strengthening and more clearly defining the law.

Nor did the President then cover his guns. Over the protests of his lieutenants, he fired at Congress one of the most bitter and radical special messages on record on January 31, 1908. He charged that "the representatives of predatory wealth—of the wealth accumulated on a giant scale by all forms of iniquity, ranging from the oppression of wage workers to unfair and unwholesome methods of crushing out competition, and to defrauding the public by stock jobbing and the manipulation of securities," were thwarting his program. He excoriated those "apologists of successful dishonesty" who declaim against all measures to strike down corruption "on the grounds that any such effort will 'unsettle business.' " He called again for stringent regulation of securities, adding that there "is no moral difference between gambling at cards . . . and gambling in the stock market." He upbraided "decent citizens" for permitting "those rich men whose lives are evil and corrupt" to control the nation's destiny. And he contemptuously dismissed that great body of editors, lawyers, and politicians "purchased" by the corporations as "but puppets who move as the strings are pulled."

The President then vented his rage on the judiciary. There has been, he caustically declared, a growing tendency for judges to "abuse" the injunction process in labor cases. The injunction was a necessary device for the prevention of violence and should under no circumstances be eliminated. Nevertheless, the "grave and occasionally irreparable wrong" sometimes inflicted upon those enjoined must be prevented. It was a travesty on justice for the law to acknowledge labor's right to engage in peaceable, organized action and for the courts to override that right "under the guise of protecting property rights."

The blazing indictment continued. The "high office of judge" should be regarded with the "utmost respect" as should those "brave and upright men" who mainly constitute the judiciary. But the judge who "truckles to the mob" and "shrinks from sternly repressing violence and disorder," or who makes the wage worker bitter "by misuse of the process of injunction or by his attitude toward all measures for the betterment of the conditions of labor," or by failing "to stop the abuses of the criminal rich," could not expect to escape public censure. This, the President concluded, "is but right, for except in extreme cases this is the only way he can be reached at all."

The message evoked an extraordinary reaction. In Congress, where the Bryan Democrats punctuated its reading with round after round of spontaneous applause, the great body of Republicans sat glumly, applauding perfunctorily, and then but infrequently. On the outside, conservative Easterners like Nicholas Murray Butler lost all sense of proportion and the *New York Times* actually said editorially that the President's "delusions of persecution . . . would ordinarily be commended to the attention of a psychiatrist."

But the national response was favorable. The agents of special privilege who wore the Republican label in Congress had never been broadly representative of the "plain people" who comprised the bulk of the Grand Old Party's membership. Independent Republican editorial voices joined Democratic newspapers in hailing the message of January 31 "as a classic," as one of "the really memorable state papers in the history of the nation," and as "a clarion call to duty." Once again, moreover, that faithful tribune of the people, William Jennings Bryan, rose to his great rival's support. Roosevelt's message, exclaimed Bryan, was a "brave" and timely "call to arms"; he urged Democrats "to accept promptly the issues that have been presented by the President."

Meanwhile the President continued his efforts to meliorate the lot of working men and women. He still refused to accept the closed shop and his fear of labor violence and dislike for "professional labor agitators" remained as acute as ever. Less than two months before the message of January 31 he had ordered federal troops into Nevada to suppress reported violence in a strike. But when he learned that the reports were exaggerated and that the state's pro-corporation governor designed to use the troops to break the workers' union he had withdrawn them forthwith.

Roosevelt did not, of course, subscribe to the near total environmentalism that is the warp and woof of so much twentieth century liberalism. He believed to the end in the individual's ability to control and rise above his environment and he was unfailingly disdainful of theoretical socialism. As he wrote Lincoln Steffens in June, 1908: ". . . under government ownership corruption can flourish just as rankly as under private ownership." Privilege must be eliminated; but privilege was not all. "I know from actual experience—from experience of the most intimate kind in the little village of Oyster Bay and out in the West at Medora, where there was not a special privilege of any kind in either place—that what is needed is the *fundamental fight for morality.*" Yet, as he wrote another friend, the tenets of many people who call themselves socialists "are not only worthy of respect but represent real advances." Among such "advances," presumably, were major features of Roosevelt's own conservation program.

Even as Roosevelt clung to the vestiges of the "survival of the fittest" theory, even as he continued to hold that much of man's weakness and evil was inherent, he drastically modified his working philosophy. By 1908 he perceived more clearly than ever before that the environment exerted tremendous, if not quite overpowering, influence, especially on the weak and the straitened. And in the newer mode of Reform Darwinism and the older tradition of *noblesse oblige,* he strove to mitigate the harsher conditions of labor through government action. Warmly and persistently he supported proposals for the eight-hour day and for workmen's compensation measures. "I spoke of the hard case of P. B. Banton, who was crippled for life while doing his duty on the Panama Canal and is now helpless with a wife and three children," he wrote a congressman in February, 1908. "Will it not be possible to have a general bill passed to remedy the injustice . . . ? No more righteous act could be passed by Congress." Or, as he wrote in his message of January 31:

The special pleaders for business dishonesty, in denouncing the present Administration for enforcing the law against the huge and corrupt corporations which have defied the law, also denounce it for endeavoring to secure sadly needed labor legislation, such as a far-reaching law making employers liable for injuries to their employees. . . . It is hypocritical baseness to speak of a girl who works in a factory where the dangerous machinery is unprotected as having the "right" freely to contract to expose herself to dangers to life and limb. She has no alternative but to suffer want or else to expose herself to such dangers . . . It is a moral wrong that the whole burden of the risk necessarily incidental to the business should be placed with crushing weight upon her weak shoulders. . . . This is what opponents of a just employers' liability law advocate. . . .

More significant than Roosevelt's widening acceptance of Reform Darwinism was his growing conviction of the need for big unionism. He continued to condemn the closed shop; but he came more and more to believe that big unionism was as necessary as big business was inevitable. Within the limits imposed by his ultimate faith in individualism, he warmly encouraged the labor movement. The principle of unionism was "beneficial," he repeatedly asserted; it was the "abuses" of power that must be guarded against.

The first President to keep an open door to union officials, Roosevelt conferred many times with Gompers, Mitchell, and other labor leaders. And though he never again played as dramatic a role as in the Anthracite Strike of 1902, he continued to make a modest contribution to labor's uplifting. When, for example, several railroads contemplated wage reductions in 1908 in order to recoup losses caused by the administration's regulatory program—or so the Louisville and Nashville angrily charged—Roosevelt ordered the Interstate Commerce Commission to investigate. "These reductions in wages may be warranted, or they may not," the President wrote. But in any event, the Commission should be prepared to mediate. It finally arranged a settlement that held the line on wages and created in the process a precedent for handling future controversies in the railroad industry.

Had Roosevelt had his way the principle of government mediation would have been made broadly inclusive. In his annual message of 1906 and again in that of 1907 he had urged "compulsory investigation of such industrial controversies as are of sufficient magnitude and of sufficient concern to the people of the country as a whole"—clear evidence that in the President's mind labor had come of age. When his attitude is contrasted to that of the National Association of Manufacturers, which was then girding its loins for an anti-union campaign that persists to this day ("better to fight than be assassinated in the interests of a coalition of politics and labor," the Association's journal warned in May, 1908), Roosevelt's progressivism is put in proper perspective.

Although organized labor was gratified by the advances in the President's thought, it still refused to take him to its bosom. Roosevelt's deep distrust of union officials as a class remained ill-concealed. And his reluctance to place labor violence in its social context continued. Roosevelt might have agreed with that part of the publisher E. W. Scripps's defense of the bomb-setting McNamara brothers which read: "We, the employers . . . have the jobs to give or withhold; the capital to spend, or not spend, for production, for wages, for ourselves; we have the press to state our case and suppress theirs; we have the Bar and the Bench, the legislature, the governor, the police and the militia." But he could only have spewed epithets over Scripps's conclusion that "violence and mob force" were labor's sole weapons and that "Working-men should have the same belligerent rights in labor controversies that nations have in warfare."

The President's failure to write his advanced recommendations into law gave labor a far more direct cause for disenchantment. The trouble, complained Samuel Gompers, was that Roosevelt "desired to maintain party leadership and that led to compromise with the reactionaries in the Republican party."

Gompers' analysis contained much truth; and the President's devious handling of the injunction issue in the 1908 campaign would understore it. Nevertheless, the AF of L chief's evaluation begs the critical political question. Could Roosevelt have broken with the Old Guard and yet fulfilled as many of his objectives as he did?

Chapter 21

The Campaign of 1908

> *I believe in a strong executive; I believe in power; but I believe that responsibility should go with power and that it is not well that the strong executive should be a perpetual executive.*
>
> —Theodore Roosevelt

THE SANDS were running out, and with them the President's waning influence over Congress and party. Within five months of the memorable special message of January 31 Roosevelt's successor would be nominated, and within ten months he would be elected. For the four months following Roosevelt would be in name what he already was in fact—a "lame duck" President. Then, on March 4, 1909, the middle-aged man who had committed himself to the "governing class" as a youth would return to the people.

A difficult matter for normal men, the loss of power was an excruciating prospect for this man of such extraordinary drive and talent—one which all his surging emotions rebelled against, one which his character alone supported, and then only after a supreme and sustained exertion of strength. Rarely has history witnessed a more painful and high-minded action than Roosevelt's voluntary relinquishment of a power that he had proudly proclaimed was greater than that of any crowned head in Europe. And rarely has it seen a great man come nearer to nobility than Theodore Roosevelt did when he resolutely refused over many months to submit to the enormous pressures that he violate his election-eve promise of 1904 and accept another term.

"It is a very unhealthy thing that any man should be considered necessary to the people as a whole, save in the way of meeting some given crisis," he wrote his fellow historian, Sir George Otto Trevelyan. "I regard the memories of Washington and Lincoln as priceless heritages for our people, just because they are the memories of strong men, of men who

cannot be accused of weakness or timidity . . . who, nevertheless, led careers marked by disinterestedness just as much as
by strength. . . ."

I may be mistaken, but it is my belief that the bulk of my countrymen, the men whom Abraham Lincoln called "the plain people"—
the farmers, mechanics, small tradesmen, hard-working professional
people—feel that I am in a peculiar sense their President, that I
represent the democracy in somewhat the fashion that Lincoln did,
that is, not in any demagogic way but with the sincere effort to
stand for a government by the people and for the people. Now the
chief service I can render these plain people who believe in me is,
not to destroy their ideal of me.

Roosevelt then related an incident that had moved him
greatly. "A few months ago three old back-country farmers
turned up in Washington and after a while managed to get
in to see me," he said. "They were rugged old fellows, as
hairy as Boers and a good deal of the Boer type. They hadn't
a black coat among them, and two of them wore no cravats;
that is they just had on their working clothes, but all cleaned
and brushed. When they finally got to see me they explained
that they hadn't anything whatever to ask, but that they
believed in me, believed that I stood for what they regarded
as the American ideal, and as one rugged old fellow put it,
'We want to shake that honest hand.' "

If Roosevelt's decision to step down was an act of high
statesmanship, the manner and choice of his successor was
considerably less. It was marked by poor judgment, was influenced by extraneous considerations of personality, and was
accomplished in typical power-political fashion.

The President's first choice was Elihu Root. Down through
the tumultuous years of the second administration Root had
continued to give Roosevelt wise counsel. He remained unmoved, however, by the compassion that had already pushed
Beveridge and would soon drive George W. Perkins in new
directions. Never did Root urge Roosevelt on; never did he
display the passion for social and economic justice that made
the Square Deal an end in itself. After he lost close contact
with Roosevelt and entered the United States Senate in 1909,
moreover, he lost even the veneer of ideological sophistication. As Richard W. Leopold observes, from then until his
retirement in 1915, he was "astonished, puzzled, irritated and

eventually overborne" by the progressive challenge to the values of his early manhood.

That Roosevelt could have believed Root capable of carrying on the Square Deal is a measure of his credulity. But it is also a measure of his deep concern with foreign policy, for in that province Root was superbly qualified. Roosevelt once called him "without question the greatest living statesman"; and he also remarked that "I would walk on my hands and knees from the White House to the Capitol to see Root made President." He was shrewd enough to realize, however, that Root's corporate background and conservative associations made him politically unpalatable. So he never seriously considered him. "What the people do not understand . . . ," he ruefully concluded, "is that if he were President they would be his clients."

The logical candidate was Charles Evans Hughes of New York. A stern, unbending Baptist, Hughes's heavy beard and pale blue eyes masked a will of steel. He had been catapulted to prominence in 1905 on the force of his brilliant investigation of the corrupt and mismanaged life insurance industry. Backed handsomely by the President the next year, he had narrowly defeated William Randolph Hearst in a gubernatorial contest that Roosevelt exuberantly pronounced "a victory for civilization." As governor, Hughes had fused the old political reformism with the new economic progressivism much in the manner of Roosevelt himself; and he became consequently the presidential choice of many progressive Westerners as well as of Eastern reformers of the *Evening Post* variety. Unfortunately, however, Hughes's most striking personal characteristic—his fierce independence—proved his Achilles' heel.

In the spring of 1907 after Roosevelt removed a minor federal officeholder in Rochester who opposed both Hughes and himself, the Governor self-righteously announced that he had been neither consulted nor informed. This studied rebuff to the President had then been blown up into a major declaration of independence by a feature writer for the *Evening Post*. Hughes was thus forced into the camp of the enemy—not of the left or the right, but of the impracticable, Roosevelt-baiting "goo-goos." The President never forgot the incident. Hughes is "a thoroly selfish and cold-blooded creature," he warned Taft more than a year later. "I strove to help him and he started the entire mugwump press cackling with glee about the way in which he had repudiated my help and did not care for it, and relied purely upon the people." The affair sealed Hughes's fate, if it had not already been sealed by Roosevelt's affection for William Howard Taft.

Taft's selection was not quite as incongruous as events later suggested. By performance and apparent conviction, he sympathized with Roosevelt's program. As he wrote with some irritation in 1907, "Mr. Roosevelt's views were mine long before I knew Mr. Roosevelt at all." From the President's strictures against the abuse of injunctions through his espousal of the inheritance tax, Taft had conscientiously, if reservedly, supported him. And he had been on the tariff issue more forthright than Roosevelt himself. He had proved in the Philippines that he could be moved by enlightened compassion. And if he believed with the President and others of the inner circle that reform was necessary to preserve the capitalistic structure, he also believed with Roosevelt, though not with all the others, that some reforms were ends in themselves.

Behind Taft's affable countenance, walrus mustache, and three hundred and more pounds of undulating flesh, however, was a man of marked limitations. They were not great; and they would not have disqualified Taft from the presidency in normal times. But the times were not normal. By the sheer force of his political genius, Roosevelt had made his party moderately responsive to the challenges that everywhere confronted it. But not even he had radically changed the Grand Old Party's basic character. The election of a La Follette, the conversion of a Beveridge, the surging progressivism of the rank and file—notwithstanding all that, the party's congressional leadership and corporate supporters remained militantly conservative and in many cases reactionary. Never during the Progressive Era, not even at the height of insurgency in 1910, would more than a quarter of the Republican delegation in either the Senate or the House raise the progressive battle flag. Taft lacked the wherewithal to bear it for the other three-fourths.

Taft was neither bold nor dynamic nor in the political sense resourceful. He was extraordinarily lazy, and he was given to petulance rather than, like Roosevelt, to wrath. His mental processes were painfully conventional, and he had little of Roosevelt's synthesizing intelligence and even less of his urge to create. For all his humanism and unexpected moral courage, he was a conservative in all his instincts. No more than Elihu Root and others of legalistic frame of mind could he approve Roosevelt's tactics, even though he thought he believed in his objectives. Had the battle been won, Taft might have been competent to hold the line. But the lines were still advancing and the intermediate objectives changing. The President's great battle order of January 31, which Taft had professed to approve, had called for an offensive that Roosevelt himself would have been hard-pressed to push to victory. Was Taft, whose experience had been that of a loyal lieutenant and top-drawer liaison officer, the man for the command?

Taft's ambitious wife and his father-like half-brother were confident that he was; but only because they were enamored of the presidency itself. They seemed not to understand, or at least to accept, the formidable obstacles that would confront any successor to Theodore Roosevelt. Indeed Mrs. Taft, who became the instrument of her husband's tragedy by putting her own desire to be First Lady above his more reasonable aspiration to a post on the Supreme Court, was impervious to the tidal wave of reform then engulfing the country. Recoiling from the President's special message of January 31, she advised her husband as early as February, 1908, not to "make any more speeches on the Roosevelt policies."

But there was another Taft who knew that William Howard was not the man for the command. "Roosevelt is a good fighter and enjoys it, but the malice of politics would make you miserable," Taft's aged mother warned her son shortly before she died. "They do not want you as their leader, but cannot find anyone more available."

By then Roosevelt had made his decision. As early as 1905 he decided that the Secretary of War was his most likely successor; thereafter he gave him every encouragement short of absolute commitment. True, he appeared to waver in 1906 when he again offered Taft a seat on the Supreme Court. There was a compelling need for distinguished men to sit on "the greatest court in Christendom" and pass judgment on the questions "which seem likely vitally and fundamentally to affect the social, industrial and political structure of our commonwealth," Roosevelt wrote. However, he also explained, he thought that Taft really wanted to become a member of the Court. "What you say in your letter and what your dear wife says [Mrs. Taft had impressed her views on the President in an urgent, half-hour interview arranged at her instigation] alter the case."

Following that fateful exchange the President's resolve to make Taft his successor deepened, though he did not act decisively until March, 1907. During the interim the generous-minded Secretary of War several times told Root, his wife, and the President himself that Roosevelt should run again. Although Roosevelt gave the suggestion short shrift, he did write William Allen White, who was cool to Taft, that he was "not going to take a hand in his nomination for it is none of my business." Then, in October, 1906, he strained his relations with the aggressive Mrs. Taft, if not with her husband, by warning that if Hughes's popularity continued to soar and Taft remained aloof he might have to back the New Yorker. In March, 1907, however, before Roosevelt's vendetta with Hughes completely soured him, the President virtually made the final commitment by directing that "a peculiar regard" for Taft's "judgment" be shown in all executive appointments in Ohio.

The preconvention campaign that the President now waged for his "beloved Will" proved as ruthless as the one he had fought against Mark Hanna for his own nomination in 1904. And the justification was less, for Hughes was closer to Roosevelt ideologically than Hanna had been. Once again the President played the patronage game to the hilt; and once again he artfully denied that he had: "I appointed no man *for the purpose* of creating Taft sentiment; but . . . I have appointed men in *recognition* of the Taft sentiment already in existence." But Roosevelt needed even more than that to win, or so he thought. Late in January, in a characteristically brilliant political maneuver, he stole Hughes's audience in the Governor's very hour of self-revelation.

Sentiment for Hughes's nomination for president had been steadily rising. Finally, under heavy pressure from his backers, he agreed to state his views on national issues in a widely advertised address to the Republican Club of New York on January 31, 1908. It was expected that the Governor's statement (it turned out to be friendly to Roosevelt and his progressive policies) would dominate the front pages the next morning. But the headlines on February 1 heralded a startlingly different event: "Roosevelt's onslaught . . ."; "Big Men

Roasted"; "Message Dazes"; "Hottest Message Ever Sent to Congress."

On the afternoon of January 31, too late for publication in the evening newspapers, the President had released the most sensational of all his messages to Congress. "If Hughes is going to play the game," he blandly told reporters, "he must learn the tricks."

And so Roosevelt the king-maker. In his biography of Thomas Hart Benton years before he had bitterly criticized Andrew Jackson for acting the same way.

Mrs. Taft's gnawing suspicions thus proved needless. So effective was the President's support of her husband that Taft's nomination was a foregone conclusion months before the Republican Convention opened at Chicago on June 19. Only a stampede for the President could have altered the outcome; and Roosevelt had commissioned Lodge to stave it off. "If you think it was pleasant to be the one to close the door & do what we both thought right you are in error," Lodge reported. "The hardest thing I ever had to do in public life was to use all the great tho' temporary powers of my place at Chicago to shut you out of the White House & put some one else (much as I love & admire that some one else) in."

But Lodge had succeeded in the face of a record forty-nine-minute demonstration for Roosevelt that interrupted his keynote address just before the end. "The President . . . retires by his own determination," declared this devoted friend who more than any one else except Edith Roosevelt appreciated the nobility of Roosevelt's self-abnegation. "His refusal of renomination . . . is final and irrevocable. Any man who attempts to use his name as a candidate for the presidency impugns both his sincerity and his good faith. . . . That man is no friend to Theodore Roosevelt."

Throughout the campaign that summer and fall the President directed a steady stream of thinly veiled instructions at the uncomfortable Taft. Many were exhortatory—"Hit them hard, old man!"—and some were shrewdly practical. Roosevelt warned Taft not to affront Speaker Cannon, no matter how insufferable that aging tyrant's support. He suggested that Taft curtail his golf playing, or at least refuse to be photographed "in costume" (he had always been careful about his own tennis, he explained). And he warned him not to appear on the same platform with the loathsome Foraker, whose unsavory relationship with the Standard Oil Company had recently been aired by Hearst. Roosevelt also urged Taft to be cautious on the tariff. (Taft had embarrassed the President and party by coming out for downward tariff revision in 1906.)

The warrior-politician found it hard, even so, to avoid the smoke of battle. He held to an early decision to make no speeches. He also tried to prevent his own booming personality from overpowering Taft's. "I think that the number of times my name is used should be cut down," he wrote after reading the draft of Taft's acceptance message. "You are now the leader, and there must be nothing that looks like self-depreciation or undue subordination of yourself." But in the end Roosevelt reached the front through a series of public letters; and in so doing he again scarred his reputation.

Much in the Democratic platform of 1908 warranted attack from Roosevelt's point of view. The foreign policy planks displayed little understanding of the realities of world power; they also threatened to undermine Roosevelt's delicately negotiated masterpiece, the "Gentlemen's Agreement" with Japan. As the President caustically said, the Democrats "desire to insult Japan by excluding all Japanese immigration, and at the same time recommend cutting down the navy so it could only be used for coast defense." The platform further called for immediate Philippine independence, a proposal Roosevelt regarded as fatefully premature.

The President also challenged the domestic planks. He regarded the statements on the trusts, which promised a limitation on the size of corporations rather than regulation of their activities, as impractical. He opposed the promise of over-all reductions in the tariff. And he took specious exception to a proposal for a guaranteed bank deposit scheme which presaged the Federal Deposit Insurance Corporation of the New Deal. Professing to approve it in principle, he urged Taft to attack it on the grounds that the banking structure must be radically changed before it could be implemented. But it was the injunction issue that inspired Roosevelt to show his political colors and suffer his heaviest wound.

True to the faith of his message of January 31 and four previous recommendations to Congress, the President had sent Lodge to the Republican Convention at Chicago under firm instructions to frame an injunction plank with teeth in it. But the Massachusetts Senator failed, partly because he was unsympathetic and largely because of the National Association of Manufacturers' decisive authority in Republican councils. As rewritten by the Association's president, James W. Van Cleave, Aldrich, and other conservative Republican leaders, the plank pledged the party to "uphold at all times the authority and integrity of the courts." Nor did it propose to limit the use of injunctions. That plank "will legalize what we have been trying to abolish," Samuel Gompers cried out in anguish. He then charged that labor had been "thrown down, repudiated and relegated to the discard by the Republican party."

At Gompers' instance, the Democrats had adopted a sweeping plank that could be interpreted as outlawing the use of the injunction in labor disputes. Roosevelt seized upon this plank as extreme, and he was partly honest in so doing. Nothing he ever said or wrote favored the outright abolition of injunctions. Always his brief was against their "abuse" by procorporation or antilabor judges. But in a not unusual act of self-delusion, he now contended that the Republican plank was truly "moderate" and that the G.O.P. had steered a middle course between the demands of labor and the manufacturers.

The issue simmered through the summer of 1908, then flamed up on October 13 when newspapers carried an open letter from Gompers repeating the charge that the Republicans had sold out labor. Gompers' letter also boldly urged workingmen to vote for Bryan. Furious, Roosevelt released a long and indignant letter to Senator Philander Knox calling on Bryan to say whether he agreed with Gompers' broad construction of the Democratic plank. He also criticized Gompers for charging in words that were actually less vehement than his own that the judiciary was subservient to corporations. And he struck particularly at Gompers' proposal to strengthen the secondary boycott. "No court could possibly exercise any more brutal, unfeeling, or despotic power than Mr. Gompers claims for himself and his followers in this legislation," he said. Roosevelt failed, however, to reply effectively to the basic political challenge; to wit, the Republican party was so submissive to the National Association of Manufacturers that not even the President of the United States had been able to write his reasonable views into the party's platform. For that letter, for past compromises, and for future blasts, tens of thousands of workingmen would in 1912 rally behind Eugene V. Debs or Woodrow Wilson.

Meanwhile Gompers replied in kind. "The mere fact that Mr. Roosevelt denounces a proposition as wicked does not so constitute it," he said in a second public letter. He noted that Roosevelt himself had called the reversal of the $29 million fine Judge Landis had imposed on the Standard Oil Company "a gross miscarriage of justice." He quoted the President's statement of January 31 that "It is futile to concede . . . the right and the necessity of organized effort on the part of wage earners and yet by injunctive process to forbid peaceable action to accomplish the lawful objects for which they are organized." He twitted Roosevelt for permitting "Genial Uncle Joe" Cannon and other Old Guardsmen to "slap" him in the face by nominating archconservative James "Sunny Jim" Sherman for Vice-President. And he asserted that Roosevelt, after failing to get the Republican platform committee to accept his own liberal platform, "not only swallows the whole pot pourri, but . . . directly and indirectly attack[s] me in the fight which my fellow workers and I are making in defense of equality before the law of the men of labor with all other citizens." He added an ironic footnote: In January, 1908, Roosevelt had called Gompers' attention to a chapter in George A. Alger's *Moral Overstrain* that sharply criticized the courts for guaranteeing the workingman "an academic and theoretic liberty which he does not want" and "denying him industrial rights to which he thinks he is ethically entitled." Then, four days before the Special Message of January 31, Roosevelt had written Gompers that he would "be amused to know" that he had sent copies of Alger's book to the anti-labor Supreme Court Justices, Day and McKenna.

The injunction controversy was unpleasant, but it had been waged openly. Indeed, Taft's frank defense of his issuance of injunction orders while a Federal judge in Cincinnati almost a decade before was refreshing. But there was another issue on which frankness seemed politically inexpedient—religion. A Unitarian of considered conviction, William Howard Taft did not believe in the divinity of Jesus Christ. He stood in distinguished company—with Benjamin Franklin, Thomas Jefferson, John Adams, and John Quincy Adams probably; with Abraham Lincoln and Theodore Roosevelt possibly; and with numbers of other eminent Americans whose services to their country had been not less noteworthy for their failure to conform to the reigning theology. But Taft was running against

William Jennings Bryan. The consequence was a painful experience for Taft and a frustrating one for Roosevelt.

All through the summer of 1908 the President fumed privately at the undercover campaign. Bryan was playing "strong in Chautauqua circles and elsewhere for the church vote," he wrote Taft. Meanwhile others raised the issue—"the bigoted, narrow-minded, honest, evangelical . . . Methodists, Lutherans, Baptists, and some Presbyterians," as Roosevelt, who received hundreds of protest letters, referred to them. "Think of the United States with a *President* who does not believe that Jesus Christ was the Son of God," wrote the editor of one religious journal, "but looks upon our immaculate Savior as a common bastard and low, cunning impostor!" From Chautauqua came the report that the Methodist ministers attending an Epworth League Convention had "gone wild" for Bryan. "They assert that no good Methodist can vote for a man who openly declares he does not believe in the divinity of Christ," the secretary of the Assembly said. On the other hand, the *Literary Digest* reported that the majority of religious publications viewed Taft's religion with equanimity and that one Catholic paper had argued that the issue was irrelevant since the "dominant Protestantism of the day is unconfest [*sic*] Unitarianism."

To compound Taft's troubles, many Protestants also asserted that he had been pro-Catholic in the Philippines. The charge was patently unfair. The Vatican had driven a hard bargain when it sold the friars' lands; but militant Catholics had bitterly disapproved the secular emphasis of the public school system established during Taft's commissionership.

Confused, surprised, and hurt, Taft proposed to issue a public statement. Under advice from Root and Roosevelt, however, he decided against it. Meanwhile the President kept silent with difficulty. He continued to inveigh against bigotry in his private letters, alluding repeatedly to Lincoln's unorthodox religious beliefs. And he once attended Unitarian services with Taft in the hope, as he phrased it, "that it would attract the attention of sincere but rather ignorant Protestants who support me." But in deference to Taft's interests he waited until the campaign was over before speaking out. Then, in words that reflected his Jeffersonian strain, he poured forth his convictions in a public letter to a correspondent from Ohio:

"You ask that Mr. Taft shall 'let the world know what his religious belief is.' "

This is purely his own private concern; it is a matter between him and his Maker, a matter for his own conscience; and to require it to be made public under penalty of political discrimination is to negative the first principle of our Government, which guarantees complete religious liberty, and the right to each man to act in religious affairs as his own conscience dictates. . . .

Discrimination against the holder of one faith means retaliatory discrimination against men of other faiths. The inevitable result of entering upon such a practice would be an abandonment of our real freedom of conscience and a reversion to the dreadful conditions of religious dissension which in so many lands have proved fatal to true liberty, to true religion, and to all advance in civilization.

Except for his anger over the intrusion of the religious issue, the President was jubilant as the returns came in. "We have them beaten to a frazzle, we have them beaten to a frazzle," he exclaimed again and again on election night. A few days later he penned Taft a warm, congratulatory letter. "You have won a great personal victory as well as a great victory for the party," he wrote his friend, "and all those who love you, who admire and believe in you and are proud of your great and fine qualities, must feel a thrill of exaltation over the way in which the American people have shown their insight into character, their adherence to high principle."

It *was* "a great personal victory"; but as much for Roosevelt as for Taft. The President-elect's majority dropped to one half of Roosevelt's record majority of 1904. Four states, including Ohio, elected Democratic governors while returning majorities for Taft. And the Republicans lost a great bloc of seats in Congress though they retained control of both houses. The import was clear: the country wanted more, not less, reform.

Taft's personal reaction was also ominous. He showed no zest at his triumph and he displayed no enthusiasm for the future. At three o'clock the morning after the election he wearily told a crowd outside his half-brother's house in Cincinnati that he hoped his administration would prove "a worthy successor of that of Theodore Roosevelt." He then went to bed.

A few weeks later he confided his anxieties to a friend. "If

I were now presiding in the Supreme Court of the United States as chief justice, I should feel entirely at home," wrote the man whose mother had warned him he was not qualified for the presidency, "but with the troubles of selecting a Cabinet, and the difficulties in respect to the revision of the tariff, I feel just a bit like a fish out of water." He concluded by saying that "my wife is the politician and she will be able to meet all these issues." He could not have been more wrong.

Chapter 22

The Changing of the Guard

*I have had the best time of any man of my
age in all the world. . . . I have enjoyed myself in the White House more than I have ever
known any other President to enjoy himself,
and . . . I am going to enjoy myself thoroly
when I leave the White House.*

—Theodore Roosevelt

THE MOST striking feature of the postelection interim was that
attention continued to center on Roosevelt. The four months
between Taft's election and his inauguration saw no abatement
of the controversy that had enveloped the President from 1902
on, no relaxation of his resolve to spread on the record his
blueprint for a new America. Until the end of the regime
Roosevelt remained a raging lion—spurred by pricks at his
rear, wounded by attacks on his flanks, frustrated by barriers
at his front, but roaring all the while.

And the roar was as lordly as it was angry. The foraging in
other seasons had been good; and the Congress that convened
in December, 1908, to bid all speed to this dynamic force
knew it. The achievements of the past seven years—the Hepburn, Employer's Liability, and Pure Food and Drug acts, the
antitrust measures, the conservation program, the progress on
the Panama Canal, the expansion of the fleet, and the intervention in world affairs—could not be written off. The pressures Roosevelt had generated for even greater reforms could
not be dismissed.

The President's last annual message ran to form. Roosevelt
"looks forward and not back," the *Washington Post* observed.
The message was actually a compelling statement of the President's still advancing progressivism, one that boldly proposed
action on every important issue except the tariff, and one that
categorically declared that the workingman should be guaranteed "a larger share of the wealth" he produced. It provoked
the *New York Commercial and Financial Chronicle* to com-

plain that if a fraction of Roosevelt's recommendations were put into law "they would commit the country to a course of new experiments and make over the face of social creation." And it inspired in the *New York Sun* a ray of hope—hope that within a few weeks "the seven-year flood of words" would at last dry up!

But the most suggestive comments on the President's call for centralization came from independent Democratic newspapers. Roosevelt had asserted that the telegraph and telephone companies should be placed under the jurisdiction of the Interstate Commerce Commission. And he had again charged that corporate wealth was using the "appeal to the old doctrine of States' rights" as a "cover" in its fight against "adequate control and supervision." The charge was neither new nor inaccurate. Roosevelt had leveled it many times before, often with fateful precision. But the significant point, as the *Literary Digest* reported, was that "a number of Southern and other Democratic papers are willing to give it a tolerant, and even a sympathetic hearing, while some of the most strenuous protests come from Republican sources."

The historic reversal in philosophy which has been the signal feature of twentieth century party politics was thus in the process of delineation. Repulsed by Roosevelt's neo-Jeffersonian ends, the Republicans were openly abandoning Hamiltonian means in order to thwart fulfillment of those ends; attracted by those same ends, the Democrats were abandoning Jeffersonian means so that they might be realized. The trend was by no means universal. The Republicans would waver until 1912, and on some issues, long after; the Democrats would not even be certain where they stood under Woodrow Wilson. But by the middle of the century the reversal would be relatively complete: the majority of Democrats in Congress would be wedded to the centralized welfare state; all but a small minority of Republicans would be opposed or unsympathetic to it. Theodore Roosevelt, grown increasingly frustrated by the tenets of his own party during his last two years in office, served mightily to hasten this momentous development.

Unfortunately, Roosevelt distorted the larger sense of his message by an acrimonious attack upon Congress itself. During the previous session an amendment limiting the activities of the Secret Service to the protection of the President and the investigation of counterfeiting had been adopted. Partly because he felt the Secret Service should combat anarchists and mainly because he wanted it to investigate corporation executives, Roosevelt had opposed the amendment. But the House had insisted on passing it. Some congressmen were still angered by the President's earlier prosecutions of congressmen for postal, land, and timber frauds. Others were reluctant to expedite the indictment of businessmen whose interests they had long served. And still others opposed the expansion of the Secret Service on high civil libertarian grounds.

Unable longer to hold back what he believed was the truth, the President baldly charged that the chief argument for the amendment had been "that the congressmen did not themselves wish to be investigated." Never did Roosevelt's relations with the legislature sink to a lower level than they did under the weight of that accusation. Unanimously, an outraged House approved the formation of a committee to investigate. Angrily, Senator Aldrich drafted a resolution of inquiry that even Cabot Lodge supported.

In the White House, meanwhile, the President fumed. On January 4 he sent in a special message softening his charges against Congress but repeating his assertion that weakening the Secret Service would prove a boon to "the criminal class." The members of the House were not edified; and in an action that went back to Jackson for a precedent, they voted by 211 to 36 to lay on the table the whole of the special message and that part of the annual message which referred to the Secret Service. They further resolved that the special message should be considered an invasion of the privileges of the House. Not even that ponderous rebuke chastened the President, however, and for weeks people feared to mention Roosevelt's name at many dinner tables.

To make matters worse, the President was by then embarked on a course more misguided even than his handling of the Brownsville affair. Infuriated by charges in the *Indianapolis News* and the *New York World* that the $40 million paid the New Panama Canal Company had gone to American businessmen, including his brother-in-law, Douglas Robinson, Roosevelt had directed the attorney-general's office to institute a libel action. His provocation was understandable, the *World* having finally charged him with deliberate misstatement of fact. Grand juries thereupon returned indictments against the publishers of both newspapers and Bryce wrote Sir Edward Grey that "The moral effect of convictions in cases of this kind would be excellent." But in the end federal district judges dismissed the cases. And well that they did. As the editors of Roosevelt's *Letters* suggest, a government victory "would . . . in the opinion of many men at the time and since, have placed the freedom of the press in jeopardy."

The charges and countercharges continued until the end of the reign. Roosevelt repeatedly lost his powers of discretion, but only rarely his sense of humor. "Taft told me with a chuckle," he wrote his son Kermit the second week in January, ". . . that one of his friends in New York has said to him that he supposed that between the election and his inauguration there would be a period of stagnation in Washington. I have felt like wiring him that the period of stagnation continues to rage with uninterrupted violence." Congress, however, lost both its discretion and its humor. Critical of the man, resentful of his conception of his office, and unsympathetic to his broad social purposes, it struck wildly, even irresponsibly at the President.

In early January Congress approved the bill authorizing a private power project in Missouri under conditions that mocked Roosevelt's plan for a carefully controlled development of such sites. The irate veto message discussed in Chapter 19 followed. On January 12 the Senate directed the Secretary of the Treasury to report all disbursements from the President's emergency fund. (No irregularities were found.) Shortly later a bill to create 4,000 positions in the Census Bureau without competitive examination was passed. Roosevelt responded with another angry veto message. Then, when the President transmitted to Congress on February 8 the Report of the Country Life Commission, the House refused to appropriate funds to publish it.

Nor were those the only examples of Congress' consuming passion to insult, defy, and expose the President in those last turbulent months. The supreme act of spite was the amendment to the Sundry Appropriation Bill* forbidding the President to appoint commissions of inquiry without specific authority from Congress. If evidence is lacking that Congress understood, feared, and resented the great expansion of executive power under Roosevelt, that action should fill the void. Yet even it failed to beard the mighty lion. "I replied to Con-

* See Chapter 19.

gress," Roosevelt recalled, "that if I did not believe the Amendment to be unconstitutional, I would veto the Sundry Civil Bill which contained it, and that if I remained in office I would refuse to obey it."

On October 27, 1908, Theodore Roosevelt had turned fifty years of age. Although he had no conscious intention of running again for the presidency, he was sure nonetheless that he would do something "to help onward certain movements for the betterment of the people." As he wrote Ted, who had gratified him by entering business "instead of leading a perfectly silly and vacuous life around the clubs or in sporting fields," he was equally certain that he would enjoy himself. "Every now and then solemn jacks come to me to tell me that our country must face the problem of 'what it will do with its ex-Presidents,' " he told his oldest son.

I always answer them that there will be one ex-President about whom they need not give themselves the slightest concern . . . and I add that they need waste no sympathy on me—that I have had the best time of any man of my age in all the world, that I have enjoyed myself in the White House more than I have ever known any other President to enjoy himself, and that I am going to enjoy myself thoroly when I leave the White House, and what is more, continue just as long as I possibly can to do some kind of work that will count.

The President had already made his immediate plans. He would first go into the dark depths of Africa to hunt big game and collect data and specimens for the Smithsonian Museum. ("I feel," he explained to an English friend, "that this is my last chance for something in the nature of a 'great adventure.' ") He would next visit Oxford to deliver the Romanes Lectures. (Gladstone, Huxley, Morley, and Bryce were among his predecessors, he wrote Lodge with both pride and awe.) Then, avoiding a "kind of mock triumphal procession" through Europe, he would return to the United States in the spring of 1910 to become a contributing editor to Lyman Abbott's *Outlook* at a salary of $12,000 per year. (He had rejected vastly more remunerative offers.)

While the President was formulating his plans and his enemies were wishing luck to the lions—"Only Four Weeks More of Roosevelt," the *Sun* proclaimed on February 4—a quieter drama was playing out at 1600 Pennsylvania Avenue.

During the campaign of 1908 Taft had welcomed, or at least accepted graciously, Roosevelt's counsel. After the election Roosevelt had continued as chief-of-staff long enough to advise the President-elect that a move to prevent Cannon's re-election as Speaker would probably prove abortive and that it would be foolish in any event "to have him in the position of the sullen and hostile floor leader bound to bring your administration to grief." This was sound advice; but it was also ominous advice. Sooner even than Roosevelt feared, Taft would be forced to side with either the insurgent or Old Guard wings of his party.

With an exertion of self-discipline more remarkable for his earlier dominance over his easygoing friend, Roosevelt had then stopped advising the President-elect. Difficult moments followed, especially when Taft showed himself insensitive to the conservation crusade and at the same time made plans to drop several members of Roosevelt's Cabinet. But as Pringle, who sometimes captures Roosevelt in fuller perspective in his sober biography of Taft than in his lively biography of Roosevelt, concludes, the President "loyally suppressed, save on one or two occasions, any temptation to give expression to the first seeds of doubt regarding the man he had pushed into glory." Indeed, Roosevelt told Archie Butt, his military aide, that "Taft is going about this thing just as I would do, and while I retained McKinley's Cabinet the conditions were quite different." He added that he could not "find any fault in Taft's attitude to me."

Only in a few cases did the President press his friends upon his successor. He arranged indirectly for his private secretary, William Loeb, to become Collector of the Port of New York. And on December 10 he sent Taft a memorandum listing the names of eleven men and a woman who had "been staunch adherents of Mr. Taft under stress of adverse assault in positions not of the first rank." Taft took care of most of the people on the list, which included a few former Rough Riders, though he dropped Roosevelt's old Twenty-first District Club friend, Deputy Commissioner of Immigration Joe Murray, and one other. Only for his Maine hunting guide and companion, Bill Sewall, did Roosevelt make a direct plea. On December 18 he was able to write "Friend William" that Taft had agreed to keep him on as Collector of Customs for the Eastern District of Maine. After thanking Sewall and his wife for their Christmas gift of heavy woolen socks, he warned Sewall to show his letter of recommendation to no one except Taft. Otherwise, he explained, "I should be deluged with requests for letters."

Additional touches of loyalty, affection, and appreciation marked the end of the regime. To Gifford Pinchot, Roosevelt confided his distress at Taft's failure to reappoint James Garfield Secretary of the Interior. "There had been a peculiar intimacy between you and Jim and me, because all three of us have worked for the same causes, have dreamed the same dreams, have felt a substantial identity of purpose," the President wrote. "Jim has made a sacrifice in entering public life that you and I have not made. . . . I think that he has been the best Secretary we have ever had in the Interior Department." Now, Roosevelt concluded, Garfield's "law practise has gone to the winds."

But it was on his relations with Pinchot himself that the retiring President poured out his heart in a letter that cast a long shadow over the future. "As long as I live I shall feel for you a mixture of respect and admiration and of affectionate regard," he wrote the forester two days before he left office. "I am a better man for having known you . . . *and I cannot think of a man in the country whose loss would be a more real misfortune to the Nation than yours would be* [the author's italics]. For seven and a half years," he continued, "we have worked together, and now and then played together—and have been altogether better able to work because we have played; and I owe to you a peculiar debt of obligation for a very large part of the achievement of this administration."

The President wrote one other important letter in those final days. Conscious of the partial failure of his Far Eastern policy, fearful of Germany's growing lust for naval power, and faithful as always to the views of Mahan, he addressed himself to the President-elect the day before the inauguration: "Dear Will, one closing legacy. Under no circumstances divide the battle fleet."

There remained only the personal farewells and the inaugural ceremony. On March 1 the President gave a dinner to his "Tennis Cabinet" and out-of-town associates. He seated Ambassador Jean Jules Jusserand on his right, Captain Seth

Bullock, United States Marshal of Oklahoma at his left, and twenty-nine other guests, including Bill Sewall, a professional wolf hunter named Jack Abernathy, and Elihu Root at the rest of the table ("there will never be such a smashing precedence again as to rank," wrote Archie Butt). The guests gave the President a bronze cougar by Proctor, Henry L. Stimson making the presentation when Seth Bullock choked with emotion. Later the President went to the home of the Garfields, where eleven members of the "Tennis Cabinet" presented him with a silver bowl. This time Jusserand, who was to have presided, broke down. The next afternoon many in the line at a reception for the diplomatic corps, including the Japanese Ambassador's wife, Baroness Takahara, wept openly. Meanwhile the President himself lost his composure when he found his wife and their daughter Ethel crying over the gift of a diamond necklace by a group of Washington society women. "He has the humour to carry these little scenes off well," Butt wrote, "and says he feels heartily ashamed of such apparent weakness." However, Butt reflected, "the love which does manifest itself on all sides, coming just now after the bitter attacks from the political world, has gone to their hearts."

One final civility followed. With characteristic generosity, Roosevelt invited the Tafts to spend the night of March 3 at the White House. Taft accepted in a letter signed "With love and affection, my dear Theodore." Their ladies also tried to be friendly, but Mrs. Taft lacked the grace. Even before she moved into the White House she made arrangements for many of the Roosevelts' favorite servants to be replaced the instant the change became official. Although the President and his wife were hurt, they failed to show it. Taft later described the dinner that night as a "funeral"; but Archie Butt reported that the dinner went better than expected, the President "talking as naturally and entertainingly as he does usually at his luncheons" and the salad course being reached before it was realized. When it came time to retire, Mrs. Roosevelt gently took Mrs. Taft's hand and said that she hoped her sleep would be sweet. "Thoughtful and gentle to the last," wrote Butt, ". . . she has stood, the embodiment of womanly dignity and social culture, before the entire nation, never unbending in the matter of official etiquette, yet always the gentle, high-bred hostess; smiling often at what went on about her, yet never critical of the ignorant and tolerant always of the little insincerities of political life."

The inaugural ceremony the next day was held indoors because of a blustery storm that Cabot Lodge, with more prescience than he knew, pronounced a "calamity." Solemnly, President Taft promised in his undistinguished address to uphold his predecessor's reforms; enthusiastically, former President Roosevelt rushed forward to congratulate him. "God bless you, old man," he exclaimed. "It is a great state document." Then, by an arrangement suggested by Roosevelt and warmly seconded by Mrs. Taft, the parties divided. Instead of riding down Pennsylvania Avenue with the new President, Roosevelt was escorted by the New York delegation to the railroad station where he and his wife were given a rousing sendoff. To the disgust of the Congressional committee, Mrs. Taft took the former President's place at her husband's side. The seven and one-half years of Theodore Roosevelt's presidency thus ended; the era of Theodore Roosevelt had just begun to reach a climax.

PART FIVE

The High Tide of Progressivism

Chapter 23

The New Nationalism

> *The whole tendency of [Roosevelt's] pro-*
> *gramme is to give a democratic meaning and*
> *purpose to the Humiltonian tradition and*
> *method. He proposes to use the power and*
> *resources of the Federal government for the*
> *purpose of making his country-men a more*
> *complete democracy in organization and prac-*
> *tise. . . .*
>
> —Herbert Croly, *The Promise of American Life*

WITHIN THREE weeks of Taft's inauguration Theodore Roose-velt, his twenty-year-old son Kermit, and a party of professional naturalists had embarked for Africa from the grimy port city of Hoboken, New Jersey. The new President had not seen the old President off. But he had sent gifts—a gold ruler, an autographed photograph of himself and a pathetically revealing letter. "When I am addressed as 'Mr. President,'" Taft wrote, "I turn to see whether you are not at my elbow." He predicted that Roosevelt would find him under suspicion by their Western friends when he returned. He guilelessly reported that Cannon and Aldrich had promised to stand by the platform and follow his lead. And he confessed that he lacked Roosevelt's facility for educating the public and arousing popular support. "I can never forget that the power that I now exercise was a voluntary transfer from you to me," he concluded, "and that I am under obligation to you to see that your judgment . . . shall be vindicated. . . ."

Edith Roosevelt had also remained at home. She had not wanted Theodore to go; but she had known that he must. His mother "was perfectly calm and self-possessed," Kermit said aboard ship that morning, but "her heart was almost broken."

Others had also been moved. "In all the striking incidents of your career," wrote Cabot Lodge, "I never saw one which impressed me more. It was not merely the crowd but the feeling which was manifested which was so striking. I can see you

355

now, as the ship moved slowly down the river, waving your hand to us from the bridge. . . . The newspapers have been filled daily with minute accounts of your progress. . . . The American people . . . follow it all with the absorbed interest of a boy who reads 'Robinson Crusoe' for the first time."

The field part of the expedition proved a spectacular success. "Bwana Makuba" (Great Master), as the Africans called the Colonel, took seriously the Smithsonian Institution's sponsorship—he had repeatedly protested that he was "going primarily as a naturalist"—and he soon shipped the National Museum a collection of flora, fauna, and mammals that raised its East African collection to among the world's greatest. He impressed his companions with the breadth of his knowledge. "[Roosevelt] . . . had at his command the entire published literature concerning the game mammals and birds of the world, a feat of memory that few naturalists possess," Edmund Heller, with whom he later wrote a two-volume scientific work, reported. "I constantly felt while with him that I was in the presence of the foremost field naturalist of our time, as indeed I was. . . ." During the long nights in camp, the Colonel even came into his "inheritance in Shakespeare." Roosevelt poetically re-created his mood in the foreword to *African Game Trails*:

"I speak of Africa and golden joys"; the joy of wandering through lonely lands; the joy of hunting the mighty and terrible lords of the wilderness, the cunning, the wary, and the grim. . . .

But there are no words that can tell the hidden spirit of the wilderness, that can reveal its mystery, its melancholy, and its charm . . . the strong attraction of the silent places, of the large tropic moons, and the splendor of the new stars; where the wanderer sees the awful glory of sunrise and sunset in the wide waste spaces of the earth, unworn of man, and changed only by the slow change of the ages through time everlasting.

The ten months' adventure had been free of conflict except for bouts with the wild beasts of the jungle. But almost the instant the Colonel emerged at Khartoum in mid-March the old order returned. In speeches that he himself reported "caused an outburst of anger and criticism among the Egyptian Nationalists, the anti-English and fanatically Moslem party," he applauded British rule in the Sudan as "really the rule of civilization" and declared that it was "incumbent on every decent citizen of the Sudan to uphold the present order of things."

Two weeks after those impolitic remarks the Colonel, Mrs. Roosevelt and Ethel, who had met him at Khartoum, were received by the King and Queen of Italy. Roosevelt found them, as he was to find most of the royalty he met during the next two months, "delightful people" of ordinary endowment. And so, perhaps, he might also have found the Pope, Pius X. But when the Papal Secretary, Merry del Val, informed him that as the condition of an audience with His Holiness, he must agree not to see a group of offensive American Methodist Missionaries in Rome (one had referred to Pius X as "the whore of Babylon"), Roosevelt refused. The Pope, he said, was a "worthy, narrowly limited parish priest; completely under the control of . . . Merry del Val." He then refused to see the Methodists who issued a "scurrilous" address of exultation when they learned he had rebuffed the Pope. "The only satisfaction I had out of the affair," the Colonel wrote Lodge, ". . . was that on the one hand I administered a needed lesson to the Vatican, and on the other hand I made it understood that I feared the most powerful Protestant Church just as little as I feared the Roman Catholics." He added that it was a good thing he had no further interest in public office, for the incident would have compromised his usefulness.

The grand tour continued. Roosevelt captivated the French with a homely exhortation at the Sorbonne on the "Duties of Citizenship." And in Christiania, where he accepted the Nobel Peace Prize at Andrew Carnegie's instance, he sparked the simmering peace movement with a call for limitation of naval armaments, expansion of the work of The Hague Tribunal, and formation of a League of Peace backed by force if necessary. He did not, however, spell out the details. Following a brief visit to Stockholm, the Colonel and Wilhelm II reviewed German army maneuvers. Afterward the Kaiser sent Roosevelt two photographs of them watching the troops. On one was the inscription: "When we shake hands we shake the world." Even before he left Berlin the Foreign Office urgently requested Roosevelt to return the photographs; but the Colonel refused. "His Majesty, the Kaiser, gave the photographs to me," he said, "and I propose to keep them." On the other hand, Roosevelt made no effort to impress upon Wilhelm his disapproval of his naval expansion program, perhaps because he was swept up by His Majesty's enthusiasm, more probably because he considered it hopeless. Furthermore, he had thrown down the gauntlet at Christiania. "The ruler or statesman," Roosevelt had said after coming out for a League of Peace, "who should bring about such a combination would have earned his place in history for all time and his title to the gratitude of mankind."

In London a week later Roosevelt served as the American representative at the funeral of Edward VII. The formal dinner given by King George V, he later told Taft, was the most "hilarious banquet" he ever attended. "Everyone went to the table with his face wreathed and distorted into grief." But before the first course was over, "we had all forgotten the real cause of our presence in London." The next day the former President of the United States rode with the French Minister of Foreign Affairs and a Persian Prince behind eight visiting monarchs.

A week and a half after Edward's funeral Roosevelt lectured the British on their administration of Egypt: "Now, either you have the right to be in Egypt or you have not; either it is or it is not your duty to establish and to keep order." He then advised them to get out if they were not prepared to rise to their responsibilities. But he added the earnest hope that in the interest of civilization and "fealty to your own great traditions," they would do their duty.

Seven days later Roosevelt delivered the Romanes lecture, "Biological Analogies in History." It was not an intellectual success. "In the way of grading which we have at Oxford," the Archbishop of York said, "we agreed to mark the lecture 'Beta Minus,' but the lecturer 'Alpha Plus.' While we felt that the lecture was not a very great contribution to science, we were sure that the lecturer was a very great man."

On June 18, 1910, the "very great man" disembarked at New York. During the fourteen months he had been conquering the jungle, slighting the Pope, enlightening the British, and sounding a hopeful note at Christiania, his chosen successor had been proving a political failure. Even as the Colonel waved, grinned, thumped, and expostulated amidst the most tumultuous of receptions, the shifting coalitions he had so skillfully maneuvered were crystallizing into uncompromising conservative and progressive factions.

The new President's misfortunes were only partly of his own making. Almost any man would have suffered by comparison to Roosevelt, one of the half dozen greatest natural leaders in American history. Nor could Taft be blamed for the temper of the times or the character of his party. At the very moment the national progressive movement was building up to its first roaring climax, the long-champing Republican majority in Congress was angrily reaffirming the marriage to the lords of the market place that Roosevelt had fought so hard to sunder. Only Roosevelt could have saved the situation; and not even he could have saved it without taking sides.

Human frailty also contributed to the polarization. Taft's lack of zest for conflict proved a heavy burden. He tended to submit rather than fight, or, because of laziness, to follow the course of least resistance. He delegated too much authority; and for want of information or willingness to explore a problem, he sometimes made offhand or impulsive decisions. He had a poor sense of timing. And he lacked the ability to inspire. Nor did he read so productively as Roosevelt nor welcome to the White House such a churning stream of people with ideas.

Taft's affinity for legalists also hurt. His Cabinet supplemented rather than complemented his own views, and his lament that "Roosevelt has no one to advise him of the conservative type, like Root or Moody or Knox or myself, as he did when in office," is as revealing of him as of TR; it also gives point to Senator Jonathan Dolliver's remark that the President was a "ponderous and amiable man completely surrounded by men who know exactly what they want." Taft's brother Henry, his half-brother Charles, and the President's wife, who was ill throughout most of his term, added to his difficulties. They wielded a heavy and conservative influence, inaccurately advising him on the temper of the country and fanning the flames of his growing suspicions of the absent Roosevelt.

But it was Taft's stubborn courage which first disrupted the party. True at first to his personal ideals and campaign promises, Taft called a special session to revise the tariff shortly after his inauguration. The House responded in reasonably good faith. When the bill reached the Senate, however, Aldrich and his friends blandly amended it 847 times, mostly upward. They also eliminated an inheritance tax clause, though they reluctantly replaced it with a modest tax on corporations. The President was irritated; but after he secured some modifications he lost the will to fight or even to veto the measure. He then rationalized his submission with the statement that the bill represented "a sincere effort on the part of the Republican party to make a downward revision." Nor did he then drop the matter. That autumn he went into the Middle West, where the Payne-Aldrich tariff was considered a barefaced perversion of the Republican platform of 1908, and exclaimed in Winona, Minnesota, that "I think the Payne bill is the best bill that the Republican party ever passed."

Roosevelt was already on safari in Africa when the controversy reached its peak. Such comment as he did make, however, was hardly to his credit. Responding to a smug letter from Lodge, he wrote that "what we have to meet is not an actual need, but a mental condition among our people, who believe there ought to be a change. . . ."

Triumphantly, Lodge had shown TR's letter to Aldrich. "He put the whole situation in those few lines," the Rhode Islander enthusiastically responded. "He is the greatest politician we have had. We are dealing with a mental condition and that is the exact trouble with the situation."

If the Colonel's views were clouded on this first of the issues that set his successor on the road to political disaster, they were clear and consistent on the second—conservation. Taft came into the presidency without conscious intention of undoing Roosevelt's great work though he certainly intended to modify it. From the start Gifford Pinchot (whom he regarded as "a good deal of a radical and a good deal of a crank") was suspicious, and with cause. "There is one difficulty about the conservation of natural resources," President-elect Taft had declared to the second Joint Conservation Conference of Governors on December 8, 1908. "It is that the imagination of those who are pressing it may outrun the practical facts." It was Taft's failure to make a fighting speech on that occasion, coupled with the dropping of Garfield, that sparked Roosevelt's last-minute withdrawals of potential water-power sites on the theory "that the incoming Executive would have to act affirmatively to give them away."

Worse still, Taft had selected a dubious conservationist, Richard Achilles Ballinger, to replace Garfield as Secretary of the Interior. Ballinger was a strict constructionist; or, as

Pinchot put it, a friend of the special interests. While Commissioner of the Land Office under Roosevelt he had opposed the President's mineral-lease program, preferring outright sale to rental. And on that and other accounts he had resigned his position after exactly a year in office. Returning to the government service in a higher position than Pinchot's, it was probably inevitable that he should clash with the zealous Chief Forester.

Taft's legalism increased the tension. Whatever the President's views on conservation, he had no stomach for the Roosevelt-Garfield-Pinchot methods. "After T.R. came Taft," Pinchot later wrote in high irritation. "It was as though a sharp sword had been succeeded by a roll of paper, legal size." Neither did Taft approve of the Hamilton-Marshall conception of implied powers—a doctrine Roosevelt would have had to invent had it not already been in the public realm—or of Roosevelt and Pinchot's reliance on scientific, as distinct from congressional, advice. As he admonished the California conservationist, William Kent, three months after his inauguration, "We have a government of limited power under the Constitution, and we have got to work out our problems on the basis of law."

Now, if that is reactionary, then I am a reactionary. . . . Pinchot is not a lawyer and I am afraid he is quite willing to camp outside the law to accomplish his beneficent purposes. I have told him so to his face. . . . I do not undervalue the great benefit that he has worked out, but I do find it necessary to look into the legality of his plans.

Pinchot and the new administration first clashed over the water-power sites. "I do not hesitate to say," Taft wrote Kent late in the spring of 1909, that the presidential power to withdraw public lands "was exercised far beyond legal limitation under Secretary Garfield—and, more than that, unnecessarily so." Resolutely, Taft authorized Secretary Ballinger to restore them to public entry pending a report by the Geological Survey. This cast the die, for by rejecting the view that the spirit of the law could best be served by temporary withdrawals while time-consuming permanent surveys were completed, Taft had repudiated one of Roosevelt's basic policies. Clashes between Pinchot and Ballinger followed with clock-like regularity. Ballinger so harassed the Reclamation Service that a number of engineers contemplated resigning in a body. He made establishment of legitimate ranger stations difficult. He played into the hands of the corrupt "Indian Ring" by canceling an arrangement whereby the Forest Service managed forests in the Indian Reservations to the Indians' advantage. And he allowed Postmaster-General Hitchcock to have an outsized hand in appointments.

Ballinger justified his actions on strict constructionist grounds; and perhaps he did act in good faith. But if so, his tendency toward loose construction when private interests were at stake has never been adequately explained. The most generous interpretation is that he mirrored the Western milieu out of which he came: he was intelligent enough to approve conservation in principle, and less broadly in practice. But when the issue was drawn his commitment proved almost invariably to be to the private entrepreneur; and hence, in the Roosevelt-Garfield-Pinchot view, to the ruthless exploitation or inefficient development of the nation's natural resources.

Ballinger's most controversial action involved the Morgan-Guggenheim Syndicate's acquisition of the Cunningham coal lands claims in Alaska. The details of this *cause célèbre* need not concern us here. But it should be said that it proved that more than legalism, or even states' rights, differentiated Ballinger's policies from Garfield's. When the evidence was finally in, Ballinger was revealed to have played fast and loose with the law in a way that made Pinchot and Garfield's elastic interpretations seem rigid by comparison; and he had done so in the private, rather than the public, interest. Sadder still, President Taft was revealed to have signed a spuriously dated document designed to bolster the administration's case against Pinchot's charges that Ballinger was promoting a "give-away" of the disputed Cunningham claims. And most portentous of all, Pinchot had been forced to resign.

By every criterion except the public interest, the fault was Pinchot's. With characteristic single-mindedness, he had decided within six months of Taft's inauguration to force the larger issue. During the summer and autumn of 1909 he had delivered one conservationist speech after another as the newspapers buzzed with rumors of his differences with Ballinger. And in late September, after it became clear that Taft intended to support Ballinger's handling of the fraudulent Cunningham claims, Pinchot told Taft he would stick to his guns even if the President had to fire him. Three months later Pinchot defied a presidential order by sending Senator Dolliver a letter defending two subordinates who had released information about Ballinger and the Cunningham claims. By prearrangement, the Iowan read it on the floor of the Senate chamber. "It is clear not only that they acted from a high and unselfish sense of public duty," Pinchot's defense ran, "but that they deliberately chose to risk their official positions rather than permit what they believed to be the wrongful loss of public property."

By his own admission, Pinchot had been insubordinate. "There is only one thing for you to do now," Elihu Root told the President as the issue was joined on January 3; four days later Taft dismissed the Chief Forester. "I would not have removed Pinchot if I could have helped it," he plaintively remarked a few days later. Although Taft replaced Pinchot with an outstanding conservationist, he retained Ballinger, thus stamping his administration as anticonservationist and anti-Roosevelt.

With thirty newspapers calling for Pinchot's nomination for President in 1912 and the periodical press rising almost as one in criticism of Taft, the pressure was now on the administration to produce. On June 25 Congress partially restored the President's authority to withdraw public lands from entry— the same power it had angrily wrested from TR three years before. And from then on Taft moved so relentlessly that his record of withdrawals compared favorably to Roosevelt's by the time he left office. But he failed, even so, to grasp Roosevelt's conception of controlled development. During his last two years in office he signed several bills granting perpetual and unrestricted franchises for the construction of dams, among them the James River project that TR had indignantly vetoed two months before Taft's inauguration.

The removal of Pinchot destroyed such confidence in Taft as Roosevelt may still have possessed. To be sure, he tried to withhold judgment until his return to the United States; but the burden proved unbearable. On each side there were ties of loyalty and affection. But on Pinchot's side there was also a great cause—one of the greatest of Roosevelt's presidency. It was inconceivable that Taft should have dealt it such a blow. "We have just heard by special runner that you have been removed," TR wrote Pinchot from the Lado Enclave in Africa on January 17, 1910. "I cannot believe it. I do not know any man in public life who has rendered quite the service you have rendered. . . . Do write. . . ."

Pinchot had already written. On December 31, 1909, a week before he was forced out, he sent the Colonel a sixteen-point bill of particulars against Taft. The gist was that "the tendency of the Administration thus far, taken as a whole, has been directly away from the Roosevelt policies." Then, on April 11, Pinchot met his former chief at Porto Maurizio in Italy.

There is no record of what Roosevelt and Pinchot said at that momentous meeting. "One of the best and most satisfactory talks with TR I ever had," Pinchot tersely wrote in his diary. "Lasted nearly all day, and till about 10:30 P.M." But Pinchot had already said enough in his letter of December 31 to make his position clear. And if he had not, he bore letters from Beveridge, Jonathan Dolliver, and William Allen White charging that the Payne-Aldrich Tariff was "just plain dishonest" and that Taft had taken "the certificate of character which Mr. Roosevelt had given him and turned it over to the Senator [Aldrich] from Rhode Island."

Roosevelt never felt the same toward Taft after that. On the day he saw Pinchot he wrote Lodge that Taft had virtually failed. "The qualities shown by a thoroughly able and trustworthy lieutenant are totally different, or at least may be totally different, from those needed by the leader, the commander," he remarked. Admitting that "a man with strong convictions is always apt to feel overintensely the difference between himself and others with slighter convictions," he then renounced ambitions of his own:

I have played my part, and I have the very strongest objection to having to play any further part. . . . I most emphatically desire that I shall not be put in the position of having to run for the Presidency, staggering under a load which I cannot carry, and which has been put on my shoulders through no fault of my own.

Nor did Roosevelt intend to help the Republican regulars. The Colonel had had almost a year to reflect on the character of his party. And in a passage that the Democrats would have given their party treasury to have made public, he testily rejected Lodge's suggestion that he campaign for the G.O.P. in

1910. "Twice I have asked the American people to elèct a Republican Congress," he reminded his friend, "in one case in spite of an indifferent record and in the other in spite of a poor record. . . . In each case the leaders of Congress have promptly gone back on their promises and have put me in the position of having promised what there was no intention of performing."

Three weeks later the former President passed another revealing judgment: "Our own party leaders did not rcalize that I was able to hold the Republican party in power only because I insisted on a steady advance, and dragged them along with me. Now the advance has been stopped."

Meanwhile Roosevelt's wife reported that people were urging her to keep her husband out of the country for a year and a half longer ("Why not for life?" wondered Henry Adams). Finally, on May 30, Elihu Root, who had compromised his own integrity in the Ballinger affair, met TR at the Dorchester House in London. Root defended Taft for an hour, after which, so he contended, the Colonel promised to stay out of politics for sixty days following his return home.

At about the same time the troubled President, whom Adams described as "feebly wabbling all over the place, and tumbling about the curbs," penned a long, poignant letter to his predecessor. Taft remarked on the heavy burden of Mrs. Taft's illness. She "is not an easy patient and an attempt to control her only increased the nervous strain." He dismissed the criticisms of the Payne-Aldrich Tariff measure, terming it "a good bill and a real downward revision." And he recounted with pride the constructive measures already cnacted or about to be enacted—railroad legislation, a postal savings system, statehood for New Mexico and Arizona, protection for railroad employees, and restoration of the President's authority to withdraw land from the public domain. He concluded by incorrectly asserting that the insurgents, rather than the Old Guard, had failed to abide by the party platform. Roosevelt dictated a generous but pointed reply. We are, he wrote, aware that the "sickness of the one whom you love most has added immeasurably to your burden . . . and feel very genuine pleasure at learning how much better she is." He then told Taft of his talk with Root, adding that he did not know the situation at home. "I am, of course, much concerned about some of the things I see and am told." "I have felt it best to do . . . absolutely nothing—and indeed to keep my mind as open as I kept my mouth shut!"

The Colonel should have known himself better. For a few weeks after his return a fortnight later he avoided affronting Taft publicly, though he ungraciously rejected the President's invitation to visit him in Washington. And in the face of pleas by the insurgents—Pinchot, Garfield, Beveridge, La Follette, and almost everyone else of importance who made the *hegira* to Sagamore Hill that summer—he refused to cast his lot openly with Taft's opposition. In fact, he worked conscientiously to promote party unity of a sort. But he finally gave in to his urge to express himself. Before the summer ended he had ringingly affirmed the advanced progressivism of the last two years of his presidency and a little more besides.

The first break came in August when Roosevelt challenged the Barnes machine for the temporary chairmanship of the New York State Republican Convention. If Taft had been capable of reading the signs, he would have viewed the Colonel's action as providential. A firm declaration of support for Roosevelt would have placed TR under personal obligation. It would also have narrowed their ideological gulf, for Barnes was an incorrigible conservative. But with characteristic maladroitness Taft made it appear that he favored the Barnes forces; nor did he suppress his perverse satisfaction when news that the New York County organization refused to endorse Roosevelt reached him in Washington. Thus was the Colonel's opinion of his successor's ineptitude confirmed. "Taft is utterly helpless as a leader," he confided to Ted.

I fear that he has just enough strength to keep with him the people of natural inertia, the good conservative unimaginative people who never do appreciate the need of going forward, and who fail to realize that unless there is some progressive leadership, the great mass of the progressives for lack of this legitimate leadership will follow every variety of demagogue and wild-eyed visionary.

Less than two weeks later TR set out on a three weeks' speaking tour of the West that carried him into sixteen states and saw him deliver at Osawatomie, Kansas the most radical speech of his career. More, even, than on his previous forays into the West, he was wildly acclaimed by plainly dressed crowds which stood long hours in the baking prairie sun awaiting his whistle-stop appearances; and more, perhaps, than ever before, they saw in Roosevelt the Moses who would lead them to the promised land.

The Colonel scaled the status quo's outer defenses at Denver on August 29 with an attack on the Supreme Court's decisions in the *Knight* case of 1895 and the *Lochner* case of 1905. Both decisions, he declared, struck "against popular rights, against the Democratic principle of government by the people, under the forms of law." The result was creation of a "neutral ground . . . which can serve as a place of refuge for the lawless man, and especially for the lawless man of great wealth, who can hire the best legal talent to advise him how to keep his abiding place equally distant from the uncertain frontiers of both state and national power."

Two days later Roosevelt stormed conservatism's inner bastion at Osawatomie. "The essence of any struggle for liberty has always been, and must always be to take from some one man or class of men the right to enjoy power, or wealth, or position or immunity, which has not been earned by service to his or their fellows," he said in words that could have been uttered by Marx.

Anticipating the furor they would set off, TR had preceded them with a quotation:

Labor is prior to, and independent of, capital. Capital is only the fruit of labor, and could never have existed if labor had not first existed. Labor is the superior of capital, and deserves much the higher consideration.

With characteristic directness, he had then rammed the point home: "If that remark was original with me, I should be even more strongly denounced as a Communist agitator than I shall be anyhow. It is Lincoln's. I am only quoting it."

Roosevelt's dream was actually the ancient one of equality of opportunity within a propertied framework. In the tradition of the Jacksonians far more than of Lincoln, he sought to purge business of its corrosive influence upon men, morals, and politics, but not to destroy it. Even at Osawatomie Roosevelt preached no proletarian uprising and envisioned no broad destruction of private property. Nor, significantly, did he call for the upbuilding of labor as a countervailing force. The "essence of the struggle is to destroy privilege, and give to the life and citizenship of every individual the highest possible value both to himself and to the commonwealth," he exclaimed in a passage that marked the full flowering of his views and gave title to his speech and the progressive movement's philosophy. The "New Nationalism puts the national need before sectional or personal advantage."

It is impatient of the utter confusion that results from local legislatures attempting to treat national issues as local issues. It is still more impatient of the impotence which springs from over division of governmental powers, the impotence which makes it possible for local selfishness or for legal cunning, hired by wealthy special interests, to bring national activities to a deadlock. This New Nationalism regards the executive power as the steward of the public welfare. It demands of the judiciary that it shall be interested primarily in human welfare rather than in property, just as it demands that the representative body shall represent all the people rather than any one class or section of the people.

TR then spelled out the reforms needed to achieve equality of opportunity: elimination of corporate expenditures for political purposes; physical valuation of railroad properties; regulation of industrial combinations; establishment of an expert tariff commission; a graduated income tax and, especially, a steeply graduated inheritance tax; reorganization of the nation's financial system; conservation of natural resources; workmen's compensation laws; state and national legislation to regulate the labor of women and children; and complete publicity of campaign expenditures.

Westerners applauded what they heard at Denver and Osawatomie. "The West loves and understands Roosevelt," the *Denver Republican* asserted. This region "takes it for granted that Theodore Roosevelt will be the next Republican candidate for President," the *World's* correspondent wired from Cheyenne, "so what is the use of getting excited about it." The *New York Tribune* urbanely agreed. Criticisms of Colonel Roosevelt "afford great comfort to a select class of persons," it observed, "for not to approve, or to give only a qualified approval to, the Colonel is a mark of distinction. It sets you apart from the common herd, with its love of moral platitudes and its incapacity for distinguishing between them and deep and original thought."

Other Eastern criticisms were not so lighthearted. Elihu Root patronizingly remarked that "the only real objection" was that Roosevelt had called the New Nationalism "new!" But he was disturbed nonetheless. "I shall be curious to know whether he really meant that he would deprive the courts of their power to pass on constitutional questions," he wrote Taft. Cabot Lodge also put on a bold public front by claiming that Western papers had quoted Roosevelt out of context; but down deep he was worried, and he so informed the Colonel. Meanwhile, in a fair sample of the unsophisticated Eastern reaction, the *New York Commercial* called Roosevelt a "peripatetic revolutionist" and his tour "a firebrand's triumphal march."

It was President Taft, however, who was hurt and angered the most. He complained that Roosevelt had gone far beyond the advocations of his White House days (which was not substantially true). He commented on Roosevelt's "ego," "swelled-headedness," and "wild ideas." And he argued that the Colonel's proposals were "impracticable" since they could be brought about only through "revolution or revision of the Constitution." But above all he was enraged that the Colonel had aligned himself with the enemy. "In most of his speeches he has utterly ignored me," he lamented to his brother Horace. "His attitude toward me is one that I find difficult to understand and explain. . . . He is at the head of the insurgents, and for the time being the insurgents are at the top of the way."

In spite of his fear that the G.O.P. was destined for defeat, Roosevelt proved incapable of staying out of the congressional campaign. His own ambitions were as yet unformed—he may have been thinking vaguely of 1916—but he still believed that only the Republicans had the capacity to govern. He foresaw with fateful accuracy, moreover, that complete division meant long-term disaster. So he decided to veer again toward the middle and even to endorse the Payne-Aldrich tariff; but to little constructive result, so turbulent was the backwash from Osawatomie.

In New York the Old Guardsmen simply would not forgive the Colonel—either for the "crime" at Osawatomie or for the "sins" of his presidency and governorship. To make matters worse, Roosevelt's reluctant decision to resume relations of a sort with Taft backfired. The two men had first met at Taft's summer residence in Beverly, Massachusetts, on June 30. Taft had made a heartfelt effort to break through the Colonel's defenses. "See here now," he told him, "drop the 'Mr. President.' " But for all his effervescent good will, his "bullies" and exclamations of "de-e-light," TR refused to resume the old relationship.

They met again on September 19 at New Haven. TR stole the early headlines by streaking out from Oyster Bay in a motorboat, putting in at Stamford because of rough weather, and proceeding on to New Haven by motor. He and the President had then conferred alone for an hour. The Colonel "told stories and the President wreathed his face with a purely physical smile and laughed aloud," Archie Butt reported, "but it was all strained."

Nevertheless, Taft agreed to support Roosevelt in his bid for the temporary chairmanship of the New York State Convention. Unfortunately, however, a member of Taft's entourage told newspapermen that the conference had been arranged at Roosevelt's request and that he had asked the President to help him out of his difficulties in New York. That did it.

Roosevelt issued a denial the next day, then poured out his feelings to Lodge. He had agreed to meet Taft on the representations of a third party, he said. "I did not ask Taft's aid or support in any shape or way, and it would never have entered my head to do so; although of his own accord he volunteered the statement that Barnes and Company were crooks, and that he hoped we would beat them." Taft meanwhile wrote his wife that "It was perfectly characteristic that after having sought the interview, as . . . [Roosevelt] undoubtedly did, . . . he should at once advertise that it was not at his instance." He added that Roosevelt had asked for his support. To Butt, however, Taft explained that he had offered his support unsolicited because he knew that the Colonel intended to ask for it.

Taft's later support of Roosevelt failed to mend the breach, partly because Roosevelt prevented the State Convention from endorsing the President for re-election. Then, when Root in "a jollying letter" written at Taft's request asked TR to speak for the President in Ohio, he categorically refused. "As for what you say about the President having helped here in New York," he replied, "I can only say that I went into the fight at all simply at the earnest request of the Taft men." The Colonel added that he had "been cordially helping the election of a

Republican Congress, having split definitely with the Insurgents, including good Gifford Pinchot, on this point."

I have never had a more unpleasant summer. The sordid baseness of most of the so-called Regulars, who now regard themselves as especially the Taft men, and the wild irresponsible folly of the ultra-Insurgents, make a situation which is very unpleasant. . . . I do not see how I could as a decent citizen have avoided taking the stand I have taken this year, and striving to reunite the party and to help the Republicans retain control of Congress and of the State of New York, while at the same time endeavoring to see that this control within the party was in the hands of sensible and honorable men who were progressives and not of a bourbon reactionary type.

Chapter 24

The Travails of Indecision

*Even so clear-headed a man as Root thinks
that Theodore has not the Presidency in his
mind, but that he aims at a leadership far in
the future, as a sort of Moses and Messiah for
a vast progressive tide of a rising humanity.*

—Henry Adams

HAD THEODORE ROOSEVELT been not quite so ambitious, or
even a shade less self-righteous, the history of twentieth century American politics must surely have been different. The
Taft forces were humiliatingly defeated in the congressional
elections of 1910, first by the insurgents in the Republican
primaries, then by the Democrats in the regular contests. For
the first time since Grover Cleveland the Democrats had won
control of the House, and for the first time in the Roosevelt
era the American people had broadly affirmed their progressivism by electing a string of progressive governors, most of
them Democrats. They had also returned almost all the incumbent progressive Republican senators and had added three
new ones to their ranks. Obviously, Taft and the Old Guard
were headed for defeat in 1912 and Theodore Roosevelt was
destined to have his party's nomination thrust upon him four
years after that.

Assuming that the Colonel's thoughts were on 1916, and
he was too young and ambitious for them not to have been,
his tactics and strategy were sharply limned. He must avoid
irreparable insult to the Old Guard, which was bowed but far
from crushed, and he must continue to cultivate relations
with the party's growing band of progressives. Following Taft's
defeat in 1912 he would resume leadership of the party. Resignedly, the Old Guard would accept him in the realization
that he was the party's strongest candidate; enthusiastically,
the progressives would embrace him in the belief that he reflected their views.

This course, if it was a course, was not without obstacles. On the one side stood the Roosevelt-haters. Conservatives by and large, they also included politicians of no apparent ideology— men to whom politics was purely a play for power, men who might even support another progressive, so eager were they to be done with TR's disruptive force. Could the Colonel compromise with such types indefinitely? He had done so for seven and one-half years as President, and with generally constructive results. Without office, however, he would have nothing constructive to show; nothing but party regularity and intellectual inconsistency.

On the other side stood the militant progressives—the men and women of creative vision and evangelical good will whose doctrinaire politics Roosevelt had so often deplored and whose fertile ideas he had so regularly expounded. Could the Colonel indefinitely please these—the Jane Addamses, Gifford Pinchots, and other idealists whose lives and heritage have so enriched the Republic—and yet maintain his precarious relationship with the conservatives, including his beloved friends Root and Lodge? Already, by 1910, this was a meaningful question. The reform sentiment that Roosevelt had so spectacularly affirmed at Osawatomie would have to be consolidated on more than party regularity and nurtured on more than intellectual equivocation. Should TR pull his punches too much, should he imply by his relations with the conservatives that he had not really meant what he said, then, surely, the reformers would gravitate to the relentlessly uncompromising La Follette as many were already doing or threatening to do. Probably Roosevelt could have won them back; but it was not the Colonel's nature to view his political future with optimism.

In the center stood Roosevelt himself—Roosevelt the progressive conservative and Roosevelt the conservative progressive; Roosevelt, the man of surprising subtlety and predictable bluntness; Roosevelt, the ruthless politician and the idealistic preacher; Roosevelt, the contemner of reformers and the purveyor of reforms; Roosevelt, the most consummate man of action the American public has ever known. Could he avoid stumbling over himself? Could he for five years do and say the contradictory things necessary to the preservation of his hold on both the right and the left? Could he accept the inevitable even after he had convinced himself that Taft's nomination in 1912 was in fact inevitable?

For well on to a year the Colonel pursued this, the course

of wisdom and expediency, if not of valor. The Colonel resumed friendly relations with Taft even as he cultivated them with La Follette. He was less than consistent on some issues and he reversed himself ignobly on at least one, tariff reciprocity. He both defended and criticized Taft in private, and he did the same with La Follette, Pinchot, and other militant progressives. He also backslid a bit from Osawatomie. But in the end he proved emotionally unable to walk the tightrope that both he and circumstances had strung.

The *rapprochement* with Taft was short-lived; nor did it ever recapture the easy informality of earlier years. Roosevelt could rekindle the flames of friendship as readily as he could stamp them out, but he could not re-create the old respect for Taft's competency. Never, not even in his beloved brother Elliott, who had died of alcoholism eighteen years before, could Theodore Roosevelt condone weakness; never could he tolerate ineptitude in men of public responsibility. And for all those flashes of courage that made his downfall a minor tragedy, Taft had been both weak and inept. "I do not believe he has been a bad President, and I am sure he has been a thoroughly well-meaning and upright President," TR wrote in September, 1910. "I think he is a better President than McKinley and probably than Harrison, but the times are totally different, and he has not the qualities that are needed at the moment." After Taft's obtuseness and Roosevelt's bustling vanity had brought about a situation beyond repair, the Colonel altered even that measured judgment of his chosen successor.

Meanwhile TR wrote Taft that he was "a trump" to invite him again to the White House. He commended his annual message of December, 1910. And he rendered friendly advice on foreign policy. Taft responded in kind. Reporting the progress of the Panama Canal, he observed that it would be completed around July, 1913, "a date at which both you and I will be private citizens and . . . can then visit the canal together." Then in March, 1911, when Roosevelt requested permission to raise a cavalry division if the seething Mexican situation boiled over, the President cordially acquiesced.

Three months later they met in Baltimore at a celebration honoring Cardinal Gibbons. There, so Mowry writes, they "shook hands heartily, whispered together, and at times broke into unrestrained laughter." A few days afterward Roosevelt sent the Tafts a silver wedding anniversary gift. Taft's thank-you note, dated June 18, 1911, was the last personal communication exchanged by the two men in years. By the third week in August Roosevelt was writing that the President "is a flubdub with a streak of the second-rate and the common in him, and he has not the slightest idea of what is necessary if this country is to make social and industrial progress." Taft's real trouble, he explained to Hiram Johnson in October, 1911, was his values. Like those of McKinley, Hanna, and most of America's business leaders, they were essentially materialistic.

What caused this final estrangement? TR's whole career was marred by a seemingly congenital inability to view his competitors with normal dispassion, and Mowry's speculation that he "could not have thoroughly approved of the leadership of any successor, much less that of a personal friend," is powerfully compelling. It is not unlikely, in fact, that from that one great flaw of character flowed much of the rest—the intolerance, the hypercriticism, the indignation at the reversal of "my policies." Yet even at their unalloyed worst, personality factors were no more than partial determinatives. They fixed the direction of Roosevelt's broad bias and they governed the magnitude of the final eruption; but they would have been historically inconsequential had they not been compounded by ideological issues. During the eight or ten months of his *rapprochement* with Taft, for example, the Colonel proved quite capable of mastering his most egregious compulsions. It is reasonable to conclude that he would have continued to hold them in check had not a new series of disruptive issues come to the fore in the spring of 1911. One of the most important of these was foreign policy.

In spite of his realistic work for peace, Roosevelt had never regarded America's vital interests as justiciable. To the end of his life he remained a *Realpolitiker,* his moral principles partly suppressed by his strident nationalism or merged in that *Zeitgeist* which identified America's national interests with the ultimate welfare of humanity. When, therefore, Taft backed a series of comprehensive arbitration treaties in the spring of 1911, Roosevelt was hard pressed to maintain the façade of approval that circumstances demanded. Indeed, he soon commenced to destroy it brick by brick.

Privately, the Colonel warned Lodge, who needed no reminder, against sanctioning such "maudlin folly" as the negotiation of "honor and independence." He also said much the same publicly, first in a signed article in the March issue of the *Outlook*, later in a seven-page letter published in the *New York Times*. Hurt and embittered, Taft refused to reply publicly though he privately attributed Roosevelt's opposition to his primitive drives and animosity toward himself. "The truth is he believes in war and wishes to be a Napoleon and to die on the battlefield," he wrote. "I shall continue . . . to discuss the treaties, and shall not notice the personal turn of his remarks. . . . It is curious how unfitted he is for courteous debate. I don't wonder he prefers the battle-ax."

Actually, the controversy transcended both personalities and politics. The two men's raging disrespect for each other doubtless contributed subconsciously to the fanning of the flames; but neither it nor Roosevelt's as yet unformed ambition for 1912 was casual. More even than conservation, this was an ideological conflict.

Like Bryan, Carnegie, and Woodrow Wilson, William Howard Taft envisioned the substitution of international law for sheer force. He believed devoutly that all disputes, including those involving national honor and interest, were justiciable; and in a series of extraordinarily frank and sensitive speeches defending the arbitration treaties before the Senate in the fall of 1911, he persuasively expounded these views. "We had the war of 1812, in which our neighbor, England, asserted rights that she would not now think of pressing," Taft said at Marquette on September 11. "I think that war might have been settled without a fight and ought to have been. So with the Mexican War. So, I think, with the Spanish war." The climax came at the University of Idaho on October 7. "I don't think," the President exclaimed to the students and faculty, "that it indicates that a man lacks personal courage if he does not want to fight, but prefers to submit questions of national honor to a board of arbitration."

To a Theodore Roosevelt, a Cabot Lodge, an Admiral Mahan, and even an Oliver Wendell Holmes, Taft's subordination of the national ego was the rankest heresy. How could patriotism be fostered? How could the manly virtues, without which the nation would follow Rome and all the other civilizations grown flaccid from effeteness and ultramaterialism, be maintained if national wrong were admitted and the will to assert renounced?

Nor was that the whole of Roosevelt's brief. If the Colonel

bore the national honor as a truculent youngster carried a chip on his shoulder, he understood power politics as well as the most cynical of his European contemporaries. He entertained no objection to a treaty with England, for he now regarded America and Britain's larger interests as identical or complementary. But he took vigorous exception to Taft's plan to sign similar treaties with all the other powers. As he wrote Lodge late in the spring of 1911:

> Of course as regards England . . . there is not any question that we could not arbitrate. . . . But with either Germany or Japan it is perfectly conceivable that questions might arise which could not submit to arbitration. If either one of them asked us to arbitrate the question of fortifying the Isthmus; or asked us to arbitrate the Monroe Doctrine, or the fortification or retention of Hawaii; or Germany's right to purchase the Danish islands in the West Indies; or Japan's right to insist upon unlimited Japanese immigration—why! we would not and could not arbitrate.

There was and is no easy answer. Taft was pushing hard on the only course that offers hope for the preservation of world civilization; Roosevelt was arguing that national survival had first priority. Actually, neither statesman was quite as extreme as his words of the moment suggested. The President was wholeheartedly committed to the fortification of the Panama Canal and the defense of the Monroe Doctrine. The Colonel was willing to push for arbitration as an eventual goal. But like Root and the many other thoughtful senators who helped emasculate the treaties, he felt that Taft was moving too rapidly and hence irresponsibly.

Other issues further widened the ideological gulf. One was conservation; another, Roosevelt's continuing criticism of the courts. As Taft's administration progressed he had become increasingly responsive to the needs of the conservation movement. He failed, though, to give it the moral support that had made it a crusade under Roosevelt and Pinchot. Had he spoken for conservation with the same zeal he defended the Payne-Aldrich Tariff or the arbitration treaties, he might have spared himself a heavy burden of pain. Nevertheless, by April, 1911, after he finally accepted Secretary of the Interior Ballinger's resignation "with great reluctance" and appointed an able and dedicated conservationist in his place, Roosevelt was writing that if only "Poor Taft" had done some of the same things two years earlier, his lot might have been different. But even this faint glimmer of approval was soon obscured by the black cloud that fell over Taft's Alaskan policy.

Distressed by Taft's appointment of "a thoroughly untrustworthy man" as governor of Alaska in 1909 and disgusted by Ballinger's handling of the Guggenheim claims, Roosevelt needed but the slightest breeze to fan his white hot coals. It came in the spring of 1911 when Taft restored to public sale forest lands on Controller Bay that Roosevelt had withdrawn from public entry. The Colonel construed this as playing into the hands of the Guggenheim monopolists. And on July 22, a month after he had conversed so amiably with Taft at the reception for Cardinal Gibbons, he published a slashing attack on Taft's conservation policies in general and his Alaskan policy in particular. The President's action, he wrote, made it possible for the Guggenheim interests to acquire control of the only remaining outlet to the Bering coal fields. Four days later Taft sharply defended his own course and criticized Roosevelt's by inference in a special message to Congress. "I fear," the President confided to poor Archie Butt, who was still striving manfully to be loyal to Taft without being disloyal to Roosevelt, that the Colonel "will regard this portion of my message as a direct slap at himself and will answer it as such."

Events justified the President's fears. Encouraged by the single-minded Pinchot, who no longer even conceded that Taft was "upright," Roosevelt struck back on August 5 and again on August 12 through editorials in the *Outlook*. One was signed, the other unsigned, and neither spared the nettled President's feelings. Yet even as the controversy thus degenerated, new advances punctuated Roosevelt's thought. Eschewing a simple recommendation for lease of the Alaskan coal lands, he came out for government construction and operation of the port facilities and the railroad line into the coal fields. This, he emphatically believed and openly declared, was the only alternative to private monopoly.

If Taft's foreign and conservation policies were central to Roosevelt's ideological estrangement from the President, the Colonel's attitude toward the law continued to be the most critical factor in Taft's separation from Roosevelt. A few months were still to pass before TR would carry his biting criticisms of the judiciary to their logical conclusion—the substitution of the people's will for the courts' judgment under limited conditions. But as conservatives long feared, Roosevelt was moving rapidly along that fateful path in the spring of 1911; and Taft realized it.

Curiously, the legal issue was intertwined with the trust question. Taft had always entertained reservations about the wisdom, and in some cases the legality, of many of Roosevelt's policies. As Secretary of War, he had demurred only mildly; and he had even acquiesced in the President's handling of the Brownsville affair. He had also submitted to Roosevelt's views on the trusts, which he seems not to have grasped fully. "What we believe in, if I understand it," he wrote TR shortly after his own nomination, "is the regulation of the business of the trusts as distinguished from its destruction." Once Taft assumed Roosevelt's sceptre, however, his compulsion to uphold the letter of the law—a compulsion that sometimes caused him to pursue policies more redolent of form than substance—became again his *leitmotif*. The result was the most unrelenting destruction of the trusts to that time and the most shattering of all blows to the two men's relations.

The signs were already posted when the Supreme Court laid down the so-called "rule of reason" doctrine in ordering the dissolution of the Standard Oil and American Tobacco companies in the spring of 1911. In so far as that doctrine read flexibility into the Sherman Antitrust Law, it confirmed Roosevelt's long-held view; he can perhaps be forgiven the smugness that crept into his comments. "I think it is a good thing to have had those two decisions," he wrote a friend, "but they do not reach the root of the matter." There was needed, he wrote in the *Outlook* on June 3, an independent commission with powers similar to those of the Interstate Commerce Commission. Regulation of corporations could then be "accomplished by continuous administrative action, and not by necessarily intermittent lawsuits." He added that the commission should be empowered to fix prices indirectly.

Roosevelt's recommendations failed to impress Taft. Conscious that he was enforcing the Sherman Law as it had not been enforced, even by Roosevelt himself, he gave his energetic Attorney-General, George W. Wickersham, his rein. The consequence was that while Standard Oil and American Tobacco Company executives were privately snickering at the government (the orders seemed not to affect their real power positions within the steel and tobacco industries; and, as Pringle writes, who among them "was indicted, fined or punished?"), the administration was taking its most fateful step of all. In the full flower of the political innocence that was both his charm and his undoing, Taft allowed a special assistant to the Attorney-General to file suit against the United States Steel Corporation on October 26, 1911. He did not even read the government's bill of particulars. There followed the most disastrous explosion in the Republican party's history.

The government's petition of October 26 made the startling inference that President Roosevelt had been hoodwinked by Messrs. Frick and Gary when they assured him that purchase of the Tennessee Coal and Iron Company by the United States Steel Corporation was essential to stoppage of the panic of 1907 and that no advantage would accrue to U.S. Steel. Despite the hard truth of this inference, the Colonel was too vain, or to put it more charitably, too human, to do other than deny it. He did so at once—vitriolically in his private letters and vehemently in an *Outlook* article of November 18. He complained to friends that Taft had been "enthusiastic" and "emphatic in his commendation of the merger" when Secretary of War. "It ill becomes him either by himself or through another afterwards to act as he is now acting." And he charged in the article in the *Outlook* that Taft's insistence on meeting the trust problem "by a succession of lawsuits" was about as practical as "a return to the flintlocks of Washington's Continentals."

The wheel had turned full circle. Roosevelt now appeared at one with Justice Holmes who had raised similar objections to the dissolution of the Northern Securities Company in 1904. Yet the wheel had also moved forward; and in so doing it left the great jurist, who held no brief for regulation either, to muse alone over the raw Social Darwinian theories of Herbert Spencer and William Graham Summer. "I don't disguise my belief," Holmes had written just the year before, "that the Sherman Act is a humbug based on economic ignorance and incompetence, and my disbelief that the Interstate Commerce Commission is a fit body to be entrusted with rate-making."

The Colonel's solution was the one he had been pointing toward as early as 1902 when "Mr. Dooley" chided him for his fuzzy categorization of "good" and "bad" combinations. TR called not only for continuous and comprehensive government regulation as he had done so often during the last years of his presidency, but he faced for the first time in a public statement the ultimate question—government control of wages, hours, and prices. In extreme cases, he said, the government should be empowered to exercise "control over monopoly prices, as rates on railways are now controlled."

Historians have widely interpreted the *Outlook* article as a direct bid for Wall Street's support. And so it was, in timing at least. Wiebe's studies show that the Morgan-Gary-Perkins forces were disaffected by the Taft administration's relentless enforcement of the Sherman Law and that they had earlier sought to avoid suit by reviving the "gentlemen's agreements" of the Roosevelt years and offering to correct such practices as the Department of Justice found offensive. But Wickersham, whose devotion to the letter of the law was as sustained as Taft's, had flatly refused. Furthermore, they had already proved themselves sympathetic to Roosevelt's broad regulatory proposals, including government price-fixing. As Judge Gary told the congressional committee that investigated the Steel Corporation that June, price-fixing would diminish cut-throat competition; and as he did not tell the committee, it would also have assured tremendous profits for his organization since the prices would have to be set high enough to cover the costs of the small, and less efficient, companies. Gary also argued that it was "a great mistake to suppose that we can dominate the market price, a great mistake." Under cross-examination, however, he conceded that the Steel Corporation's vertical organization, coupled with the benefits derived from comparative bookkeeping in its numerous plants, did give it a considerable advantage.

As suggested in Chapter 18, Roosevelt seems never to have shown any real insight into the purely economic effects of the subordination of the interests of a subsidiary company to those of a parent company. He was concerned with the more obvious abuses of power—railroad rebates, for example—rather than with the subtle and intangible, yet surely substantive, economic consequences of monopoly or oligopoly. Believing that the manufacturing industries were impelled by the same natural forces as the utilities to become monopolistic or oligopolistic, he readily concluded that what was right for one was right for the other—that the Steel Corporation should be regulated in the manner of the railroads rather than dissolved.

There were refinements and exceptions of course; also inconsistencies. As a moralist, TR concerned himself pre-eminently with processes. Since the Standard Oil and American Tobacco trusts, unlike the Steel Corporation, had been created by willfully dishonest, antisocial means, they were "bad" trusts and deserved to be atomized. This was right; this was retributive justice, so essential in his value system to the good and ordered society. Yet—and here was the inconsistency—he did not believe their effective dissolution was possible even though he had made the original decision to prosecute them as President. Hence his assertion that the Tobacco Trust had been dissolved in theory but not in fact.

The Colonel was not alone in this view. Many informed observers believed at the time and for long thereafter that the decrees against the Standard Oil and American Tobacco companies failed to alter their real power positions within their industries. Most economic historians now hold, however, that the disruption of the oil and tobacco trusts had a constructive impact on the industries concerned. They further contend that both the application and the threatened application of the Sherman and Clayton acts by the Roosevelt, Taft, and Wilson administrations reduced the incidence of business malpractices and retarded the growth of monopoly. As Eugene V. Rostow puts it, "The example of these basic decisions served as a powerful negative factor in business affairs. Certain lines of development were denied to ambitious men."

In these circumstances, TR's distinction between "good" and "bad" trusts belongs more to the limbo of morals than economics. Conversely, Taft's wholesale prosecution of the trusts gives his administration a luster often denied it. (His majority opinion in the *Addyston Pipe & Steel Co.* case, rendered when he was a Federal judge in 1898, is one of the classic statements of antitrust literature.) Nevertheless, there is widespread agreement that more than mere trust-busting was needed; that an incorporation statute such as Roosevelt had proposed and Taft had failed to push, or an agency like the Federal Trade Commission, which TR had also envisioned and Wilson later created, was also necessary. This being so, it is fair to conclude that Roosevelt's perception of the complexity of aspects of the trust problem and his sustained call for the rule of reason were as economically hard-headed as his belief that the Steel Corporation was a "good" trust was economically naïve.

Roosevelt had anticipated that his article would provoke

charges of collusion between himself and Wall Street, and he had acted to dispel them with a statement at once forthright and disingenuous:

Sincere zealots who believed that all combinations could be destroyed and the old-time conditions of unregulated competition restored, insincere politicians who knew better but made believe that they thought whatever their constituents wished them to think, crafty reactionaries who wished to see on the statute-books laws which they believed unenforceable, and the almost solid "Wall Street crowd" or representatives of "big business" who at that time opposed with equal violence both wise and necessary and unwise and improper regulation of business—all fought against the adoption of a sane, effective, and far-reaching policy.

The Colonel's main point was accurate. The business community and its representatives in Congress had in fact prevented the enactment of his regulatory program in 1908. What TR failed to observe, however, was that the Morgan-Gary-Perkins part of the "Wall Street crowd" he had so sweepingly arraigned had actually cooperated in the preparation of much of that program.

On the other hand, only a few big businessmen accepted in good faith Roosevelt's most critical hypothesis—big business should be subordinate to, rather than a partner of, the government. Among them were men of high civic purpose and personal disinterest, like the canny, freethinking Scot, Andrew Carnegie; also some younger men like the sophisticated, yet increasingly humanistic, George Perkins. Competition, exclaimed Perkins in the spring of 1911 in a speech that blended Gary's concern for business stability with Roosevelt's desire for social justice, had largely induced "the past horrors of the factory system"—low wages, restricted production, child labor, and "inadequate care for the safety of life and limb." Within a month of TR's outburst Carnegie wrote Perkins, who forwarded his letter to Taft, that Roosevelt's proposal for government price-fixing was the only effective solution to the trust problem. And by the end of the year Perkins would place at the Colonel's disposal his own bulging pocketbook, the product of the service to the Morgan and other interests he was then giving up.

However all that may be, the steel suit and Roosevelt's enunciation of a trust program so advanced that it remains unrealized to this day catapulted him into the presidential arena. As the *Charleston Post* correctly surmised, " 'Theodore' and 'Will' have parted political company sharply at last, and . . . there is going to be a struggle between them as representing conflicting schools of thought within the Republican party."

The Colonel was at once amused, pleased, and confused. He was amused at the interest in what "was really merely a repetition of what I had been saying for nine years at least." He was pleased that it "seemed to be the one really practical platform put forth by any leader, the one platform that represented sincerity of belief as to the need of reform and practical good sense in advocating what could be really achieved." And he was confused, or so he protested, by the demands that he issue a categorical declaration of his political intentions:

Most men seem to live in a space of two dimensions; and so they wish either for me to declare myself a candidate, or to declare that I will not accept the nomination under any circumstances. I cannot, as a matter of duty, take either position. I am not a candidate, I shall not become one, I do not think it will be necessary to accept the nomination; but if the matter of my candidacy should appear in the guise of a public duty, then however I might feel about it personally, I would not feel that I ought to shirk it. But I see no signs of it so appearing.

Indubitably, TR was honest even to himself. Whatever his subconscious desires, his rational self opposed a bid for the nomination. His place in history was already high and secure, and he quite agreed with Nick Longworth and other conservative intimates that it would be "a veritable calamity" to run again. He would even have moments of regret after the die had been cast. "I've got no glory to get out of being President again," he told Felix Frankfurter that winter. "I have no particular religious beliefs" and no sense of assurance that there is a hereafter. "The one thing I want to leave my children . . . is an honorable name. They have that now."

Furthermore, the Colonel's near superhuman energy was beginning to flag. This was not perceptible to the public. At fifty-three TR's stamina was still incredible. The arduous speaking tour in the spring of 1911; the scramble walks, long hikes, rowing trips, and hunts; the whirling talks with visitors at Sagamore or in the *Outlook* office on Fourth Avenue; the ceaseless outpouring of articles—all are suggestive of that.

Roosevelt would not measurably weaken until after he had been stricken with malarial fever while exploring the River of Doubt in South America in 1914. And even in the five years of life after that setback the fighting instinct which compelled him again and again to rise to challenges would drive him to remarkable feats of energy. Nevertheless, Roosevelt in 1911 was admitting to himself and close friends that he felt tired.

Finally, the political realities had not changed significantly. The Taft forces firmly controlled the party machinery, and only a minor revolution could unseat them. Such an upheaval would not be easy to accomplish given La Follette's growing resolve to strike boldly on his own. The Wisconsin Senator's personal following was large, though not large enough to gain him the nomination, as Roosevelt coldly concluded. And much of it, including Roosevelt partisans like Gifford Pinchot, who had announced for La Follette only after concluding that TR would not run, would move unhesitatingly into Roosevelt's camp if the Colonel gave the sign. But not all of it would. Inevitably, La Follette's hard-core supporters would be resentful and possibly recriminatory. Nor could La Follette himself be expected to submit gracefully. In vanity, in creative drive, in moral fervor, and in lust for power—in virtually everything but personal charm and the breadth of view which was TR's greatest distinction, the Midwestern regionalist was Roosevelt's peer. And in uncompromising quality—or stubbornness—he was his superior. Should TR decide to fight Taft for the presidential prize, he must first give battle to the rock-hewn senator from Wisconsin.

But other, more compelling, reasons weakened Roosevelt's resolve to remain aloof during the long summer and fall of 1911. The most powerful was the mounting evidence that he, and he alone, was the popular choice. TR still thrived on personal popularity. He loved to be engulfed by surging crowds, to preach to great assemblages, to bask in their roaring shouts of approval and demonstrations of faith. When, therefore, the cry for his nomination went up all over the country following his statements on the trusts, it was almost foreordained that he should reconsider his position.

Nor could the prospect of another term have been as unappealing in late 1911 as it had been in 1908. The rankling congressional resentment which had so comprised the dignity and effectiveness of his last year in office would hardly have abated substantially had he been re-elected in 1908. But by 1911 the old order had changed markedly. The archconservative, Aldrich, had retired. Allison was dead. Foraker had been forced out. And Joe Cannon's power had been circumscribed by a coalition of Democrats and insurgent Republicans led by an emerging progressive star, George W. Norris of Nebraska.

More important still, the progressive movement was surging forward. In spite of Roosevelt's belief in 1908 that the country was surfeited with reform, or at least with him, notwithstanding Taft's post-election contentions that he had been elected to consolidate rather than to advance, the demand almost everywhere was for more reform. This was evidenced by the early reaction against Taft's conservation policies, by the signal defeat of the conservative Republicans in the 1910 congressional elections, and by the meteor-like rise of La Follette; it was further attested by the emergence of men like Woodrow Wilson in the ranks of the Democrats and by the increasing strength of the progressive Republicans in and out of Congress; and it was confirmed by the popular approval accorded Roosevelt's views on the relations of capital and labor and kindred problems.

Admittedly, there was no assurance that the conservative Republicans in Congress would go along with Roosevelt much more than they had before. Yet TR stood to carry many progressive Republicans into office with him. He could also count on considerable support from the Democrats. So there it was— power, prestige, and a political matrix that promised greater opportunity for fulfillment than ever before. The times cried for action. Could TR turn his back on them? Could he again contain, as he had so nobly done in 1908, the vaulting ambition which had been the springboard for so many long plunges in the past? Could he live indefinitely at Sagamore surrounded by the mementos of a past glory?—a glory which, however great, was less than that which now beckoned.

Chapter 25

The People Shall Rule

The life of the law has not been logic; it has been experience. The felt necessities of the time, the prevalent moral and political theories, intuitions of public policy, avowed or unconscious, even the prejudices which judges share with their fellow-men, have had a good deal more to do than the syllogism in determining the rules by which men should be governed.
— Oliver Wendell Holmes, *The Common Law*

SEVEN MONTHS were still to pass before Colonel Roosevelt would stand at Armageddon. But by December, 1911 the forces that would drive him there were proving harder and harder to resist. From all sides and from all sections of the country letters imploring TR to run were pouring in. They came from Republican regulars who coldly calculated that Roosevelt's was the bandwagon to ride. They came from nationalists who viewed La Follette as a regionalist and from moderates who regarded him as an extremist. They came from radical Westerners who concluded that only the Colonel could win. They came from men with little or no place in politics— from TR's favored "plain people"; from friends of long standing affection; from personal supporters of no acquaintance whatsoever. And they came from social reformers like Colorado's great children's judge, Ben Lindsey. Inevitably, under this heartening demonstration of confidence, the Colonel began to weaken.

By the middle of December Roosevelt was casting an appraising eye at the trial balloons his friends had sent up. And by the end of the month he was clearly implying that he would accept the nomination if it came as the result of "an overwhelming public sentiment." But even then he would not admit that he wanted it. "I should regard it as utterly unfortunate"; it "would be a veritable calamity." Besides, he might lose. "If I were nominated, very possibly I should be beaten," he confided to the president of the University of California, "and if I were elected, such impossibilities would be expected of me that I do not see how I could avoid causing bitter disappointment to sincere and good people."

TR had lost little of those fears which lingered always near the surface and sometimes surged above it. Nor was this fiercest campaigner of the era yet prepared to command a lost cause; to lead his still inadequate armies against all those hoary bastions of privilege and complacency he had so often verbally harassed. Until July, 1912, Colonel Theodore Roosevelt led no Pickett's charges and ordered no Rapido crossings. Only when he became convinced that victory was possible, if not absolutely certain; only when he persuaded himself that he had heard the clarion call of duty, then, and then only, did he unfurl his battle flag and plunge his sword. In December, 1911 the chances of success were still slight, the call of duty still muted, though they were daily growing greater and louder.

Yet Roosevelt had already made a major, preparatory step. His moving renunciation of 1904, he now said, applied only to three consecutive terms. The real danger "would come from a man who had been in office eight years and may be thought to have solidified his power by patronage, contracts and the like, using that power to perpetuate himself," he explained to a friend, Herbert Parsons. "Oh! good Herbert," he added parenthetically, "I cannot help grinning as I dictate these words at your solemnity over the possible danger to free institutions from the Contributing Editor of The Outlook who has just come to Town hanging onto a strap in a crowded car."

TR's complaints that he felt tired and old had also stopped. He never admitted it, but the pleasures of Sagamore and the challenges of his editorial work were not enough. Frankfurter understood his drives better than most: "[When] a fellow was gifted like TR was gifted for public life, he had to do that, just as Gutzon [Borglum] had to sculpt, work with his hands. You could see that [after the Colonel had exclaimed, 'Oh, if only Taft knew the joys of leadership!'] he just sort of jumped out and was going to lead the armies for regeneration. All this about, 'We stand at Armageddon,' wasn't just flapdoodle. That's the way he felt."

Roosevelt understood, moreover, that the prestige and power he was then enjoying would wane after November, 1912. The steady stream of visitors, the tidal wave of mail, the headlines that heralded his every word—all this, he knew, stemmed from the muddled situation created by the hapless man in the White House. Had Taft's administration been popular and his control of the party commanding, then, surely, the politicians and the idealists, the disaffected and the men of good hope, would not have made the *hegira* to Sagamore Hill.

The future also looked less promising than it had a year earlier. La Follette's bid for the nomination was earnest and powerful, if not powerful enough. Should the Colonel decline the authority that was being urged upon him, leadership of the party's progressive hosts would devolve on the Wisconsin Senator following Taft's defeat in the national campaign. Could TR wrest it back between 1912 and 1916? Probably he could have; yet the question remains.

If some of the above is speculative, Roosevelt's conclusion that it was his plain duty to run is not. Again and again it was impressed upon him that he alone could hold the Republican party together. He was told that Taft's defeat for re-election would split the G.O.P. beyond repair; that La Follette's drive for the nomination was destined to end in bitter frustration. He was told that only he could advance the progressive principles he had so persuasively expressed at Osawatomie; that he, not La Follette, represented a progressivism at once sane and constructive. And most important of all, probably, for his thirst for power was never quenched, it was borne upon him that he had a chance to win.

All through December and on into January, however, Roosevelt held back. He protested repeatedly that he was not a candidate and did not want to become one; he also refused to encourage his friends. Yet he refrained from closing the door with a Sherman-like declaration. And as the appeals grew steadily more urgent his replies changed perceptibly in emphasis. By early January he obviously wanted to run—but only on his own terms.

The crux of the Colonel's terms was that the voters should demand his nomination. "My usefulness . . . would depend not merely upon the people wishing me to be President, but upon their having good reason to believe that I was President because of their wishes, because of their desire that I should do a given job, which they felt I could do better than anyone else, and not because of any personal ambition on my part." Therefore, he wrote the publisher, Frank Munsey, on January 16,

"I must not put myself in a position which would look as if I were seeking the office."

From then on events moved swiftly. Responding to a plea from Michigan's Governor Chase Osborn, TR virtually threw his hat into the ring two days later. "I am inclined to come to the conclusion that it is impossible for me much longer to remain silent," he wrote. "In this morning's mail came two letters from Governor Glasscock of West Virginia and Governor Hadley of Missouri, written to the same general effect as yours." He would agree, he continued, to reply openly to a joint letter signed by these and other governors stating that the people of their states "desire to have me run for the Presidency, and [want] to know whether in such a case I would refuse the nomination."

I want to make it very clear that I am honestly desirous of considering the matter solely from the standpoint of the public interest, and not in the least from my own standpoint; that I am not seeking and shall not seek the nomination, but that of course if it is the sincere judgment of men having the right to know and express the wishes of the plain people that the people as a whole desire me, not for my sake, but for their sake, to undertake the job, I would feel in honor bound to do so.

This "spontaneous appeal" of the governors was a disingenuous device. Yet it was neither dishonest nor truly deceptive. Roosevelt had merely manufactured a political vehicle for expression of an already puissant sentiment.

The issue soon came to a climax. The secret leaked early in February when a copy of TR's letter to Munsey was published. The next week the governors' prearranged request that TR "soon declare whether, if the nomination for the Presidency come to you unsolicited and unsought, you will accept it" was released. Then, as the Colonel arrived in Columbus on February 21 to address the Ohio Constitutional Convention, he casually told a reporter that "My hat is in the ring." Three days later he replied formally to the petition from the governors. "I will accept the nomination for President if it is tendered to me," he wrote, "and I will adhere to this decision until the convention has expressed its preference." He could no longer turn back.

The Colonel was in Boston for a meeting of the Harvard Board of Overseers the day his reply was released. His host,

Robert Grant, reported his impressions to James Ford Rhodes a month later. "Before I give you in detail his reasons and comments," Grant wrote, "let me say that I never saw him in better physical shape."

He is fairly stout, but his color is good, and he appeared vigorous. I saw no signs of unusual excitement. He halts in his sentences occasionally; but from a layman's point of view there was nothing to suggest mental impairment, unless the combination of egotism, faith in his own doctrines, fondness for power and present hostility to Taft . . . can be termed symptomatic . . . I have never spent a more absorbing twenty-four hours. He was a most delightful guest. He had his usual laugh at the people who said he drank,—and this story has been revived with the new one that he is crazy. He drank nothing but the wines we had at dinner and he took tea in the afternoon. As you well know, his habits are simply normal. . . .

"But you will agree that Taft has made a good President this last year?" He acquiesced without enthusiasm. . . . He protested that he owed nothing to Mr. Taft, but that the President owed everything to him; that Mr. Taft had in all States immediately after becoming President affiliated himself with the factions hostile to his (Roosevelt's) friends. . . . Indeed, he asserted that he was interested in carrying out his ideas, and that the plea of disloyalty did not weigh with him. . . .

"But will any of the party leaders support you?" I inquired.

"No," he said. "None of them; not even Lodge, I think. I don't see how he can. . . . I like power; but I care nothing to be President as President. I am interested in these ideas of mine and I want to carry them through." He said that he believed the most important questions today were the humanitarian and economic problems, and intimated that the will of the people had been thwarted in these ways, especially by the courts on constitutional grounds, and that reforms were urgent. . . .

That Theodore is in earnest and sincere, there is no room for doubt in my mind. People who hate him,—and their number is legion in our walk of life—credit him neither with sincerity nor honesty. . . . At the same time it is to be remembered that he has the reputation of being the most farsighted politician in the Country, and he unquestionably believes that we are on the eve of an economic revolution, and that it is better for the Country that the Republican party should point the way rather than the Socialists should control the situation and leadership. . . .

. . . I am so in sympathy with his desire to right humanitarian wrongs, and such a true admirer of his . . . though I disapprove of what he has done, and feel a little as if a baby had been left on my doorsteps. . . . On the other hand, I was on very pleasant terms with Mr. Taft, who I hear on the best authority is *much* wounded and very sad over Theodore's defection. . . .

Roosevelt's declaration was indeed a heavy blow to the distraught man in the White House. "I told you so four years ago and you would not believe me," Mrs. Taft exclaimed. "I know you did, my dear, and I think you are perfectly happy now," the President replied. "You would have preferred the Colonel to come out against me than to have been wrong yourself." In point of fact, the waters ran deeper.

No less than Theodore Roosevelt, William Howard Taft believed that his cause was righteous and high; and he at once announced his resolve to keep the campaign for the nomination on the highest possible plane. "I believe the arguments pro and con will force themselves upon the electorate without the use of denunciation and personal attack," he warned his supporters. And unlike Roosevelt, in whom the vein of sentiment had hardened into ice, the President still brooded over the destruction of their friendship. He hoped, so a mutual friend told TR after visiting Taft, that "when all this turmoil of politics has passed, you and he would get together again and be as of old."

With La Follette, however, it was different. No memories of happier years, no gratitude for past favors or respect for peerless abilities bound the iron-willed Senator to the dynamic ex-President. They had sometimes waged common cause in the past, it is true; and they seemed during 1911 to be doing it again. But the alliance had been cautious and always informal. Roosevelt's belief that statesmanship was the art of the possible and La Follette's conviction that it was the leadership of a crusade come victory or defeat made mutual trust impossible. Thus the Colonel had commended the National Progressive Republican League, formed in January, 1911 to advance progressive principles and to promote La Follette's candidacy; but he had refused to join it. And though he had been cordial to the Wisconsin Senator's candidacy, he had always backed off from a categorical commitment. As for La Follette, he never considered anyone except himself an acceptable candidate in 1912.

The indomitable Senator's ego was so swollen, in fact, that he seems actually to have believed that the Colonel had pledged himself to his candidacy. When, therefore, the enthusiasm of many of his own supporters began to wane in late November while that for Roosevelt commenced to rise, he feared conspiracy. And when it became apparent early in the new year that Gifford Pinchot, Frank Munsey, and Medill McCormick, publisher of the *Chicago Tribune*, would scuttle La Follette's already battered ship on a signal from the former President, his fears were confirmed. The showdown came not at the memorable Periodical Publishers' dinner in Philadelphia on February 2, where the overworked Senator broke down, but on January 29 in La Follette's Washington headquarters.

The outlook had been so bleak from November on that in the second week of December La Follette contemplated withdrawing in favor of Roosevelt. On December 11 he authorized the California conservationist, William Kent, and the two Pinchot brothers, Gifford and Amos, to draw up a letter to that effect; but he changed his mind the next morning. As the Roosevelt boom became steadily more powerful thereafter, La Follette became correspondingly less tractable. He agreed to have lunch with Roosevelt at Amos Pinchot's apartment in New York on December 17, then backed out. The Colonel, who kept the engagement, proved still noncommittal about his own plans, declaring only that although Taft should be beaten, he doubted that he could be. Meanwhile, the evidence that La Follette had no following of consequence in the East continued to mount.

Finally, without consulting the Senator, La Follette's lieutenants called the meeting of January 29 in Washington. There now began, wrote Amos Pinchot in his *History of the Progressive Party*, "another painful and long drawn out series of conferences with La Follette. . . . Most of his supporters were by this time convinced that his strength, always confined to the rural districts of the West and Middle West, had sunk to a point where it was to La Follette's own interest to get out of the campaign as quickly as possible." But the Senator could not, or would not, agree, so intense was his hatred of Roosevelt and so confirmed his belief in his own cause. Indignantly, he rejected the suggestion that he withdraw. "I told them," he wrote in a 1913 edition of his autobiography, "that I had never played that kind of politics and never would; that I did not recognize Roosevelt as standing for Progressive principles; that I had resisted from the time of its proposal every effort on the part of Pinchot and others to make me serve as a stalking horse for Roosevelt's candidacy."

And so another chapter of the tumultuous progressive movement was written. In truth, La Follette had been used as a stalking horse, but by Roosevelt's supporters rather than by the Colonel himself. And though many of them had really preferred La Follette, for they believed his progressivism more sincere than Roosevelt's, they had known all along what the Wisconsin leader's unconquerable spirit would not openly admit: he never had a chance. The sensational publicity given La Follette's temporary breakdown at the publishers' dinner four days later was but the *coup de grâce.*

Meanwhile, Roosevelt was assuming the roles of strategist, politician, and ideologist—or, as he would have preferred it, practical idealist. They proved not always complementary; and within the month his commitment to progressive principles carried him into a situation from which his consummate political skill never succeeded in extricating him.

Spurred by Herbert Croly and the Pinchot brothers, TR severed the faint reed of hope that conservatives might support him out of fear that Taft could not be re-elected with a militant address in Columbus on February 21.

The Colonel started by evoking the heritage of Lincoln and repeating phrases become familiar, if not respectable, with the passing of time: "We Progressives believe that . . . human rights are supreme . . . that wealth should be the servant, not the master, of the people." As Lincoln said, this nation "belongs to the people." "So do the natural resources which make it rich." Our charge is to "stop the waste of human life in industry and prevent the waste of human welfare which flows from the unfair use of concentrated power and wealth in the hands of men whose eagerness for profit blinds them to the cost of what they do." "The only prosperity worth having is that which affects the mass of the people. We are bound to strive for the fair distribution of prosperity." We must "exercise over big business a control and supervision" based on the realization that bigness is not necessarily bad. Nor should we shrink "from bringing governmental regulation to the point of control of monopoly prices if it should ever become necessary to do so." Unquestionably, "our fundamental purpose must be to secure genuine equality of opportunity."

More followed in similar vein. Then, about one-third of the

way through, Roosevelt plunged into the political question of the era—popular representation. "I believe in . . . direct preferential primaries." "I believe in the initiative and the referendum, which should be used not to destroy representative government, but to correct it whenever it becomes misrepresentative." "I do not believe that there is any great necessity for [the recall] as regards short-term elective officers. . . . I believe it should be generally provided, but with . . . restrictions."

All that was uncomfortable, if not quite fatal. Most conservatives recoiled from one or all of those proposals; but they regarded them as only mildly revolutionary. Had the Colonel stopped there, the situation might yet have been salvaged. Instead, he deliberately crashed headlong into conservatism's strongest and most hallowed bastion—the judiciary. In phrases that even Pringle calls "fine and courageous," he demanded the recall of judicial decisions involving constitutional interpretation on the state level. "In New York, in Illinois, in Connecticut, lamentable injustice had been perpetuated," Roosevelt asserted. There have been "foolish and iniquitous decisions" and they "have almost always been rendered at the expense of the weak," of the "wage-workers," of the men who "toil on the farm and on the railway, or in the factory." The judges who wrought these injustices were "well-meaning men," but their "prime concern was with the empty ceremonial of perfunctory legalism, and not with the living spirit of justice." He would not vote for the recall of judges themselves, TR added, even "for as flagrant a decision" as that which declared unconstitutional New York State's Workmen's Compensation law. "But most emphatically I do wish that the people should have the right to recall the decision itself." The prevailing system was "a monstrous perversion of the Constitution into an instrument for the perpetuation of social and industrial wrong and for the oppression of the weak and helpless."

Roosevelt realized that his proposals pitted the rule of men against that of law; or, so he insisted, the rule of the majority of men against the law as construed by a minority of men. He knew, too, that the latter position had powerful advocates— men who "believe, and sometimes assert, that the American people are not fitted for popular government, and that it is necessary to keep the judiciary 'independent of the majority of all the people.' " But he cared not.

I take absolute issue with all those who hold such a position. I regard it as a complete negation of our whole system of government; and if it became the dominant position in this country, it would mean the absolute upsetting of both the rights and the rule of the people.

If the American people . . . should of right be the servants and not the masters of the men whom they themselves put in office, then Lincoln's work was wasted and the whole system of government upon which this great democratic Republic rests is a failure.

Whatever the merit of his proposals, TR's purity of purpose is beyond cavil. The Roosevelt who spoke at Columbus on February 21, 1912 was not the politician who supported Blaine in 1884. Nor was he the master statesman who had so deftly guided the Hepburn bill to passage, constructively co-operated with Cannon, Aldrich, and other Old Guardsmen, and made his party moderately responsive to reform. He was, rather, the compulsive idealist: the charismatic leader who for all his temporizing and equivocating, for all his bold pronouncements and weak follow-throughs, had studded his record with more acts of courage, more audacious maneuvers, and more frontal assaults on privilege than any of his major contemporaries except La Follette or Bryan.

Politically, there had been no need for Roosevelt to say the things he said at Columbus. Except for the most intransigent supporters of La Follette—and their number was never great —the Colonel held the insurgent West in the palm of his hand. It was the East, not the West, that had to be won; and he knew it.

The Colonel also knew that the recall of judicial decisions would stir up a whirlwind all over the country. Henry L. Stimson, tough-minded Learned Hand, and men of similar quality had warned him against his earlier flirtations with the recall; and so had numbers of lesser men. But to no effect. TR's passion for moral justice was so acute, his conviction that the courts were serving privilege so deep-rooted, that he had to act. In the failure of his long struggle to convert the judiciary from a static to an organic conception of the law, the recall of judicial decisions was the last resort.

The reaction proved more severe than any Roosevelt had theretofore provoked. The *New York World* suggested that it might better have been called "the charter of demagogy." The *New York Times* observed that it would be "alarming" and "appalling," a threat "to our institutions" were it not certain that Roosevelt "had gone far beyond" public opinion. And the *New York Sun* labeled it "the craziest proposal that ever emanated from himself or from any other statesman." But the Colonel must have expected as much.

Nor could TR have been surprised at Cabot Lodge's heartfelt lament. "I have had my share of mishaps in politics but I never thought that any situation could arise which would have made me so miserably unhappy as I have been during the past week," the Senator wrote on February 28. "I knew of course that you and I differed on some of these points but I had not realized that the difference was so wide." Lodge added that he would remain silent rather than oppose Roosevelt openly in convention. TR generously replied:

> My dear fellow, you could not do anything that would make me lose my warm personal affection for you. For a couple of years I have felt that you and I were heading opposite ways as regards internal politics. I shan't try to justify my viewpoint because it would seem as if I were attacking yours.

But TR could hardly have anticipated the disapproval that swept through progressive ranks. From Washington came the report that "even the more radical of the Progressives in Congress acknowledge that the Colonel's utterances are distasteful to the lawyers among the Republican insurgents," and Roosevelt's own files reveal that many, many others were deeply disturbed. As that quondam progressive and sometime lion, Senator William E. Borah of Idaho, growled, the recall of judicial decisions was "bosh."

Wounded though he was, the Colonel stayed on the firing line. On the advice of Learned Hand and other realistic progressives, he emphasized that he did not favor the recall of judges in all states; that his proposals had absolutely no relation to "ordinary suits, civil or criminal, as between individuals"; and that they did not apply to the Supreme Court. But he held to his belief that social and economic reform hinged on political reform; and in speech after speech he drove deeper and deeper the wedge that was breaking the Grand Old Party asunder.

"I have scant patience with this talk of the tyranny of the majority," TR expostulated before a roaring crowd at Carnegie

Hall on March 20. "The only tyrannies from which men, women, and children are suffering in real life are the tyrannies of minorities." He then named them—the coal trust, the water-power trust, the meat-packing trust. "I am not thinking of . . . bribery and crime," he added. "I am thinking as much of their respectable allies and figureheads, who have ruled and legislated and decided as if in some way the vested rights of privilege had a first mortgage on the whole United States, while the rights of all the people were merely an unsecured debt." Either they would be stripped of their power or the Republic would fail. "I stand on the Columbus speech."

If on this new continent we merely build another country of great but unjustly divided material prosperity, we shall have done nothing. . . . We stand against all tyranny, by the few or by the many. We not merely admit, but insist, that there must be self-control on the part of the people . . . but we also insist that the people can do nothing unless they not merely have, but exercise to the full, their own rights.

Eight days later TR was in St. Louis pleading the cause "of the crippled brakeman on a railroad, of the overworked girl in a factory, of the stunted child toiling at inhuman labor, of all who work excessively or in unhealthy surroundings, of the family dwelling in the squalor of a noisome tenement, of the worn-out farmer in regions where the farms are worn out also."

Less than a fortnight later Roosevelt spoke in Philadelphia where he had bludgeoned the defenders of the status quo more than once in the past. Now, in a bold and forthright address entitled "The Recall of Judicial Decisions," he did so again. Noting that a group of eminent New York lawyers had formed an association to combat the referendum and recall, TR charged that their real purpose was "to uphold privilege and sustain the special interests against the cause of justice and against the interest of the people as a whole." In similar manner, he added, a group of distinguished New Yorkers had defended the Dred Scott decision sixty-five years before.

"This is a strong statement," Roosevelt conceded, "and I would not make it of ordinary men who are misled by reading those New York papers owned or controlled by Wall Street." But Joseph Choate and his associates were not ordinary men. "These men are not to be excused on the plea of ignorance."

As Choate knows, the proposal "is precisely and exactly in line with Lincoln's attitude toward the Supreme Court in the Dred Scott case, and with the doctrines he laid down for the rule of the people in his first inaugural as President." Its purpose was not to make the legislature supreme, Roosevelt argued, but to "make legislature and court alike responsible to the sober and deliberate judgment of the people, who are masters of both legislature and courts."

> In the long run this country will not be a good place for any of us to live in . . . if we permit our government to be turned aside from its original purpose and to become a government . . . by corporation attorneys on the bench . . . serving the cause of special privilege and not the cause of the people.

Such, then, were the intellectual highlights of Theodore Roosevelt's preconvention campaign for the Republican presidential nomination in 1912. Men will always differ over their merits. Roosevelt had no more faced the long-range question of the tyranny of the majority than his opponents had come to grips with the immediate question of the tyranny of the minority. ("An ignorant judge may be informed, a corrupt judge may be detected and exposed, but a judge cowed into impotence or tempted to excess by dependence upon the constant favor of the appointing power or the continued smile of public approval is of all men most pitiable and most dangerous," warned Congressman John W. Davis of West Virginia.) But that Roosevelt had dramatized existing perversions of the law, that he had offered a concrete, if ill-considered, plan for their resolution, and that he had kept his own and the progressive faith while comporting himself with high and resolute courage, no man can deny.

TR's strictures did not lack constructive result. Nicholas Longworth and the bulk of conservative Republicans in Congress remained supinely inactive. But that very spring John W. Davis framed, and a majority of Democrats and a few handfuls of progressive Republicans supported, a measure, later written into the Clayton Antitrust Act, to eliminate the abuse of the labor injunction. In spite of the American Bar Association's condemnation of the recall of judicial decisions a few months later, moreover, many thoughtful lawyers were moved to reflect on the problems the former President had raised.

"I was one of those who favored the resolution," Felix Frankfurter wrote the next winter. "But as I left the meeting, I had a conviction that the . . . American Bar Association fell short of its responsibility in not going beyond negative criticism and inquiring into the cause of the ferment. . . . The fallacy of a specific remedy may be crushingly exposed," Holmes's eminent disciple continued, "but we cannot whistle down the wind of a widespread, insistent, and ill-vouched feeling of dissatisfaction." When the conditions of life are changing, Frankfurter added in a comment that marked the coincidence of his own, Holmes's, and Roosevelt's perception, the law cannot remain static.

Eleven years later when La Follette revived the issue in his presidential campaign against Coolidge and Davis, Frankfurter pronounced the historical verdict on TR's attack on judicial excesses in 1912. "No student of American constitutional law can have the slightest doubt that Mr. Roosevelt's vigorous challenge of judicial abuses was mainly responsible for a temporary period of liberalism which followed in the interpretation of the due process clause," he wrote, "however abhorrent the remedy of judicial recall appeared to both bar and bench."

The public opinion which the Progressive campaign aroused subtly penetrated the judicial atmosphere. . . . Roosevelt shrewdly observed: "I may not know much about law, but I do know one can put the fear of God into judges." The "fear of God" was needed to make itself felt on the bench in 1912.

Chapter 26

Thou Shalt Not Steal

> *The cause of our opponents has now become
> naked—the cause of the political bosses and
> of special privilege in the business world.*
>
> —Theodore Roosevelt

THE COLONEL had been too long in the jungle to permit the
enemy to do the stalking. Even as he commandeered the high
ground with his principled public addresses, his scouts were
scouring the underbrush for the convention delegates that
alone would sustain his cause. And when in the process they
flushed the President of the United States, TR rushed pell
mell from the heights to engage in the hand-to-hand combat
which was not in his blood to resist. What might have been
a reasoned debate between high-minded public servants of
divergent outlook degenerated into a ferocious personal brawl.

Ironically, the judicial-minded Taft made the first lunge.
On Lincoln's birthday, 1912, he also invoked the heritage of
the Great Emancipator. He contended, however, that Lincoln
would have dismissed those "political emotionalists or neu-
rotics" who would "reconstruct our whole society on some
new principle, not definitely formulated, and with no intelligent or intelligible forecast of the exact constitutional or
statutory results to be attained." No one who heard Taft
could have misinterpreted the implication.

Meanwhile Taft's managers forced almost the entire con-
glomeration of Southern officeholders into line as Congressional Republicans revived the old charge, never really
proved or disproved, that TR had compromised with E. H.
Harriman in 1904. Then, after Lodge's son-in-law charged
in late April that Roosevelt had personally protected the
International Harvester Company from prosecution under
the Sherman Law in 1907, the President engaged in an
acrimonious exchange with his once beloved friend.

Neither singly nor in combination, however, could these
incidents have caused the stream of venom that soon issued

from Roosevelt. Elihu Root, whose flashes of insight are illuminating in spite of his inability to understand TR's philosophic base, had known it would come. "I have an immense admiration for him," he wrote in March.

I think that, rightly directed, his tremendous personality would be a great national asset. All these things combined fill me with regret over what he is now doing. He is essentially a fighter and when he gets into a fight he is completely dominated by the desire to destroy his adversary. He instinctively lays hold of every weapon which can be used for that end. Accordingly he is saying a lot of things and taking a lot of positions which are inspired by the desire to win. I have no doubt he thinks he believes what he says, but he doesn't. He has merely picked up certain popular ideas which were at hand as one might pick up a poker or chair with which to strike.

Taft had yet to feel the full force of Roosevelt's attack when those lines were written. But the first blows were already raining. TR's strategy was to contest in states which had primaries and to try to institute primaries in states that did not. Failing in the latter, he would appeal directly to convention delegates. His tactics were less clear, though a pattern emerged after he began his campaign. He argued that he was the only progressive who had a chance to win the nomination and carry the election. He labeled Taft a conservative, and as the campaign became more intense, a reactionary. And he identified the President with both bossism and corruption at the polls.

Nevertheless the Colonel's campaign went badly through March and on into April. The Wisconsin delegation was La Follette's to the man. North Dakota went almost two to one for the insurgent Senator (TR blandly instructed his manager to announce that the North Dakota delegation would support him after "a complimentary vote for La Follette"). New York, Indiana, Michigan, and Kentucky selected Taft delegations. And the South made ready to affirm its loyalty to the organization.

Roosevelt became increasingly bitter under the impact of these defeats. He charged the Taft people with "bare-faced fraud" in New York and in a host of other states. He denounced as "deliberate faking" rumors that he would bolt the Grand Old Party if Taft were nominated. He shamelessly linked Taft with the notorious Senator Lorimer of Illinois, though the President had earlier confided to TR his hope that the Senate would unseat him. And throughout the West he unabashedly denounced Taft's Canadian Reciprocity tariff agreement.

Not until the tide suddenly changed and Roosevelt began to roll off primary victories in late April did Taft again claw back. En route to Boston on April 25, the President told whistle stop crowds that he had come "to reply to an old and true friend of mine, Theodore Roosevelt, who has made many charges against me. I deny those charges. I deny all of them. I do not want to fight Theodore Roosevelt, but sometimes a man in a corner fights. I am going to fight." And fight he did. He asserted that during the course of "his long and useful and honorable life" Roosevelt had not learned "to be a good loser." He ridiculed the Colonel's trust policy. He predicted that Roosevelt's nomination would cause a depression. And he expressed grave concern that the anti-third term tradition should be broken:

One who so lightly regards constitutional principles, and especially the independence of the judiciary, one who is so naturally impatient of legal restraints, and of due legal procedure, and who has so misunderstood what liberty regulated by law is, could not safely be intrusted with successive presidential terms.

The strain proved unbearable. That night Taft returned to his train weary, depressed, and shaken. The thick flesh on his unlined face sagged almost lifelessly and his step, usually light and graceful, was heavy, even ponderous. He sat down alone on one of the lounges. There, writes Pringle, Siebold of the *World* found him "slumped over, with his head between his hands." The President looked up as the newspaperman entered. "Roosevelt was my closest friend," he blurted out. He then broke down and wept.

Still, Taft kept going. He argued that he had put through progressive measures which Roosevelt himself had failed to get through Congress. But he did not admit that they constituted a tiny creek compared to progressivism's mighty mainstream—a mainstream whose channel Roosevelt had done so much to carve. Nor did he point out that most of them had been pushed through by a majority of Democrats and a minority of Republican progressives, or that dynamic executive leadership could have produced far more important legislation.

Yet the President could not regard himself as other than he was—a man of pacific temperament constrained to fight desperately for the semblance of self-respect. "Condemn me if you will," Taft exclaimed at Lowell, Massachusetts, on April 30, "but condemn me by other witnesses than Theodore Roosevelt. I was a man of straw, but I have been a man of straw long enough. Every man who has blood in his body, and who has been misrepresented as I have been is forced to fight." A week later he made an even more humiliating remark in Hyattsville, Maryland. "I am a man of peace, and I don't want to fight. But when I do fight I want to hit hard. Even a rat in a corner will fight."

On the other extreme where the redoubtable La Follette was waging a futile battle against fate, there was no sorrow, no yielding, no heart-rending appeal. The political tenor of "Fighting Bob's" campaign was captured on a postcard sent out by his Nebraska campaign manager: "I WANT THE NAMES OF ALL WHO ARE READY TO FIGHT FOR LA FOLLETTE TO THE END." And its ideological tone was embodied in the Senator's harsh charges that Roosevelt was a trimmer. To the end he remained an heroically stubborn figure, as one newspaperman described him:

Supposedly coming from a sickbed, . . . [he] looks anything but a sick man. He is tense, vigorous and full of fighting ire. Picture this "little giant" with the bushy head of hair, tramping up and down the platform, face, hands and figure in nervous action as he drives home his points. Picture him leading carefully up to his arraignment of the popular idol of the day [Roosevelt] and . . . "getting away with it."

Meanwhile the ferocious struggle between Roosevelt and Taft raged to its tumultuous conclusion. Early in April the Colonel took most of the Pennsylvania delegation from the President and the corrupt Penrose machine. (TR was backed by the less notorious, but hardly less corrupt, Flinn machine.) And from then until early June victory followed victory. California, Minnesota, Nebraska, Maryland, and South Dakota went into Roosevelt's column. The Colonel swept New Jersey. And he carried thirty-seven out of forty-eight delegates in Taft's own state, Ohio.

TR's resounding triumph in the President's home grounds was the most exhilarating and portentous of all his victories. The campaign itself had been degrading. Exhausted and frayed by thousands of miles of travel and hundreds of speeches, both men had lowered the bars more than ever before. The beleaguered President had called Roosevelt a "dangerous egotist," a "demagogue," and a "flatterer of the people"; the high-riding Colonel had labeled Taft a "puzzle-wit," a "fathead," and worse. Yet they had also spoken on the philosophical questions that divided the party.

The outcome in Ohio had raised the lid and the smashing triumph in New Jersey had blown it sky high. Roosevelt could now claim that he had won enough delegates to be nominated. "The result in Ohio has settled the contest," he exclaimed. "I will have a great deal to say, and I won't stand it for a moment" if "the discredited bosses and politicians . . . decide against me."

Actually, the Colonel fell about seventy delegates short of the majority needed for nomination. So boldly had his managers pressed his case, however, that 254 seats were open to contest. About 100 were legitimate challenges. The remainder were manufactured—the product of TR and his followers' frenetic charges of fraud. But that Roosevelt could win even the legitimate challenges was doubtful, for they were to be reviewed by the Taft-controlled Credentials Committee.

By the time the Credentials Committee began hearings on June 7, eleven days before the Convention convened, TR was caught ineluctably in his own momentum. He had either to carry the Convention with him or crash through and out on his own. There was no honorable alternative. Whether he knew this is not clear; nor is it of any moment given the powerful compulsions and the mighty external forces that were propelling him.

Of the compulsions, that for victory was the most gripping. TR's mental state was such that he must take over the active leadership of the Republican majority or bequeath it his ghost. Compromise, the great constructive tactic of the past, was out, for to swing the nomination to a moderate progressive like Charles Evans Hughes or Governor Herbert S. Hadley of Missouri would be to relegate himself to political oblivion. "I'll name the compromise candidate," Roosevelt had expostulated just after his triumph in Ohio. "He'll be me. I'll name the compromise platform. It will be our platform."

Neither this consuming need to fulfill himself nor his searing desire to destroy Taft completely explains TR's resolve to fight to a finish. The fact is Roosevelt and his friends sincerely believed that he was being robbed; that the National Committee, which found in favor of Taft with callous regularity from June 7 on, was dishonest. "Under the direction, and with the encouragement, of Mr. Taft," read a statement the Colonel released on June 22, "the majority of the National Committee, by the so-called 'steamroller' methods, and with scandalous disregard of every principle of elementary honesty and decency stole eighty or ninety delegates."

Roosevelt's vast support by the man in the street—he polled 1,157,397 votes in the primaries to Taft's 761,716—also made TR's cause at least as righteous as it was self-righteous. "I have felt that we are fighting for a very high ideal," he wrote privately three days before the National Committee commenced its hearings. "The cause of our opponents has now become naked—the cause of the political bosses and of special privilege in the business world. It is the cause of corruption and of bad government. . . ."; or, as he phrased it in his statement of June 22, his opponents placed "on the temporary roll call a sufficient number of fraudulent delegates to defeat the legally expressed will of the people, and to substitute a dishonest for an honest majority."

The story of the Convention itself bears little retelling. There was the Colonel, his countenance wrought with indignation and determination, arriving in Chicago three days early on the urgent entreaties of his angry, explosive lieutenants. "The issue is both simpler and larger than that involved in the personality of any man," he exclaimed to an overflow crowd of screaming supporters in the Chicago Auditorium the night before the Convention opened. "Tonight we come together to protest against a crime which strikes straight at the heart of every principle of political decency and honesty, a crime which represents treason to the people, and the usurpation of the sovereignty of the people by irresponsible political bosses, inspired by the sinister influences of moneyed privilege. . . . We fight in honest fashion for the good of mankind; . . . we stand at Armageddon, and we battle for the Lord."

There was the felt presence of Robert Marion La Follette, more dogmatic and neither less self-righteous nor egocentric than Theodore Roosevelt, spouting orders into the long-distance telephone at Washington. So consuming was his hatred of his progressive adversary that he was willing to let Taft and the Old Guard win rather than throw his support to TR; and in a decision that probably cost Roosevelt the nomination, he refused to combine forces in support of a temporary chairman. Then, when some of his subordinates defied his wishes, he forthwith repudiated them. "This nomination is not with Senator La Follette's consent," a lieutenant dutifully announced. "We make no deals with Roosevelt. We make no trades with Taft." And thus, La Follette's biographers conclude, the Roosevelt forces were "robbed . . . of the psychological band-wagon advantage they had hoped to gain by uniting. . . . The convention knew that delegates instructed for La Follette would not go to Roosevelt on the ballot for President."

There was Elihu Root in morning coat and gray striped trousers, wielding the chairman's gavel and vainly calling for order following the defeat of TR's candidate for temporary chairman by 558 to 502 votes. As he had once served Roosevelt and the nation, and before and between them the great corporations, this eminent lawyer, whose principles were at once so high and so narrow, was now serving Taft and the Old Guard; or, so the Colonel phrased it, "the representatives of reaction." With heavy heart, for he had accepted the chairmanship only as "a difficult and embarrassing duty," Root fatefully ruled that delegates whose seats were in contest could vote on all cases except their own. The ruling conformed to traditional procedure; it also assured Taft's victory.

There was the spectacle on and around the convention floor: the fist fights and near fist fights; the vitriolic cries of "liar," "swindler," "robber," and "thief"; the chants of "We Want Teddy" that swept down from the galleries and set off a roaring forty-five minute demonstration in the aisles; the imitation steamroller toots and whistles that rent the air whenever the Taft forces offered a motion. There were the flowery words and empty sentences of that pathetic pleaser of crowds, Warren Gamaliel Harding of Ohio, whom Taft had selected to place his name in nomination; and there was, finally, the grim determination of the 344 Roosevelt delegates who refrained from voting on the Colonel's order and then marched out of the hall as it was announced that the President had been renominated on the first ballot with 561 votes.

There were also the scenes in the Colonel's suite in the Congress Hotel where TR and his advisers gathered in council of war. "We are frittering away our time," Hiram Johnson of California, whose state had returned a 77,000 majority for Roosevelt only to have Root rule in favor of the Taft slate, grimly asserted. "We are frittering away our opportunity. And, what is worse, we are frittering away Theodore Roosevelt." There was the Colonel himself silently walking up and down the floor. Could he bolt from the party he had led as President for seven and one-half years; could he form a new party without financial support except from the grass roots? Of a sudden, the decision was made for him. The millionaires Frank Munsey and George Perkins, who had been bent over in earnest conversation in a corner of the room, straightened up. "And with a decisive gesture from Munsey, who seemed the more agitated of the two," wrote Amos Pinchot, "both men . . . moved over to Roosevelt, meeting him in the middle of the room. Each placed a hand on one of his shoulders and one, or both of them, said, 'Colonel, we will see you through.' At that precise moment the Progressive Party was born. . . ."

Finally, there was the climactic scene in Orchestra Hall on Saturday night, June 22, where a near hysterical throng of Roosevelt men—the 344 delegates who had stormed out of the convention, the scores upon scores of delegates who had been refused their seats, and thousands of alternates and spectators—met in rump convention. Shouting, stamping, and singing, they interrupted the Colonel again and again as he started the most historic of all his speeches by hissing "Thou Shalt Not Steal" and ended it by declaring that he would make the third-party fight "even if only one State should support me."

What is the historical verdict? Historians agree that Roosevelt had been "robbed"; not of the seventy to a hundred delegates he loosely claimed, but of about twenty-five. These would have been enough to create a deadlock. Probably the nomination would have then gone to Roosevelt. Each day of the convention one or more Taft delegates went over to the

Colonel; and had the voting gone beyond one ballot, many others must surely have done the same. Nor could Taft have held indefinitely his sixty Negro delegates. The product of the most insidious politics—they had sold out the interests of their own people—they were being subjected to heavy pressure by sophisticated Chicago Negro leaders to abandon the President who had largely reversed Roosevelt's moderately uplifting policies toward members of their race. They were also being offered cash bribes by some of the Roosevelt forces. It is doubtful, moreover, that La Follette's forty-one delegates would have suffered the fetters he imposed upon them had there been a deadlock, for they were not all as uncompromising and vindictive as their extraordinary leader.

If the twenty-five "stolen" delegates would have enabled TR to win the nomination, he might also have won it for a progressive other than himself or La Follette without them. In fact, some Taft leaders did offer to support Governor Hadley of Missouri as a compromise candidate. But Roosevelt angrily rejected their proposal. Had the Colonel remained at Oyster Bay he might have consented, though it is unlikely that his vanity would have allowed it. On the scene at Chicago, in any event, he was caught up in the swirling adulation of his outraged followers and blinded by the wrathful fervor of his own burning indignation. To have vested authority over this holy cause in a more ordinary man or to have compromised with the satanic forces which had defied the Eighth Commandment would have been to mock the tragic drama unfolding before TR's eyes. He was right when he ringingly affirmed to the rump convention on Saturday night that the cause was far nobler than any one man; he was also right when he implied that he alone could lead it.

Chapter 27

Armageddon

> *He had the hold of the hero. By his words and deeds he gave a defining and supporting frame for the aspirations of those insufficiently clear or strong to support their aspirations by their own endeavor. Men, in the hope of finding their better selves, attached themselves to him.*
>
> —Elting E. Morison, *Turmoil and Tradition*

As ROOSEVELT knew it must, the Progressive party convention that met seven weeks later in the same auditorium where the Republican steamroller had flattened the Eighth Commandment, was destined to prove a failure of politics and a triumph of ideals. The practical politicians upon whom success depended were notable for their absence. A few came, including Flinn of Pennsylvania and Walter Brown of Ohio, neither of whom had any other place to go. A handful of insurgent Republicans led by Beveridge of Indiana, handsome, well groomed, and confident as always of his intellectual prowess, also came. Beveridge had opposed the formation of the new party and had refused to participate in the rump convention in June for reasons of expediency. But out of devotion to principle, not a small measure of vanity, and fealty to the Colonel and their mutual friend Perkins, he now prepared to deliver the keynote address and serve as chairman.

Otherwise the signs were ominous. Of the seven governors who had signed the round-robin call for TR to wage war against Taft seven months before, only two were courageous enough to join the Progressive party: Chase Osborn and highstrung Hiram Johnson, who agreed to become Roosevelt's running mate. Hadley of Missouri refused to come over, arguing that progressive control of his state could be achieved only through the Republican party; and so with most of the other governors. William E. Borah took the same position

410

as did the majority of progressive Republican senators and representatives.

Roosevelt was bitter. "What a miserable showing some of the so-called Progressive leaders have made," he grumbled. "They represent nothing but sound and fury . . . they have not the heart for a fight, and the minute they were up against deeds instead of words, they quit forthwith."

Yet the Colonel also had moments of understanding for some. "Nothing has touched me more than the willingness of men in whom I earnestly believe to leave their official positions and come out in this fight," he wrote a Department of Justice agent. "But . . . I feel that the sacrifice ought not to be made unless the good that will be done outweighs the damage. . . . I do not feel that our cause is sufficiently bright to warrant me to have men like you and those . . . named come out for me. . . . Events shaped themselves so that I had no alternative except to lead, but I am under no illusion about it. It is a forlorn hope." Nevertheless, he was determined to sustain it. Do not "let it get beyond the men I have mentioned," he warned, "for even in a forlorn hope it does not do to let your soldiers think that their commander won't lead them to victory—although there are occasions when it is his highest duty to fight no matter how great the risk of defeat."

If the Colonel's army lacked regulars, it suffered nothing for volunteers. Rarely, and perhaps never, has a political convention contained such a concentration of substantial and dedicated citizens, of men and women so fervently devoted to cause and leader alike, as now closed ranks at Chicago. "Here were the successful middle-class country-town citizens," wrote William Allen White, "the farmer whose barn was painted, the well-paid railroad engineer, and the country editor."

It was a well dressed crowd. We were, of course, for woman suffrage, and we invited women delegates and had plenty of them. They were our own kind, too—women doctors, women lawyers, women teachers, college professors, middle-aged leaders of civic movements, or rich young girls who had gone in for settlement work. Looking over the crowd, judging the delegates by their clothes, I figured that there was not a man or woman on the floor who was making less than two thousand a year, and not one, on the other hand, who was topping ten thousand. Proletarian and plutocrat were absent—except George Perkins. . . .

. . . On the speaker's stand, we had notables from all over the land: college presidents, heads of scientific foundations. Our prize exhibit was Jane Addams. . . . When she came down the aisle back of the speaker's stand where the other notables wearing Bull Moose badges were arrayed in proud and serried ranks, the delegates and the scattered spectators in the galleries rose and cheered. Not even the Colonel got much more rousing cheers than Jane Addams, when she rose to second his nomination.

Why had they come? Some, obviously, to tie their kites to Roosevelt—the cynical, flint-faced underlings of Flinn and his like; men of vast materialistic design and little if any moral purpose. Their numbers were not great, but they were, large enough to be embarrassing. The true fanatics were also there, come to this convention as to the great protest assemblages of the past to indulge in an orgy of political emotionalism. Later Roosevelt would ungraciously designate them "the lunatic fringe."

But what of the convention's real leaders, the middle-class respectables White so graphically describes? Richard Hofstadter suggests that they were animated by personal resentment over their loss of general status to the new elite—the coarse, crude, compassionless men of business and finance who surged to the top on the mighty convulsions of the Industrial Revolution; the crass materialists whom Roosevelt and the Adams brothers so feared and deplored; the vulgar new leaders whose ostentatious mansions had become the focal points of the new high society in the great urban centers and summer resorts of the nation; the amoral men of power whose puissant wealth, so Roosevelt charged, had bought off the editors, the lawyers, and the college professors; the nouveaux riches whose bulldozing tactics were reducing to an ant heap the once mountainous influence of the people of long-established, but by the new standards, relatively modest means.

What was more natural than that the younger members of these submerged genteel families should emerge as the secondary leaders of the Progressive movement? They had the time, the money, and the political habit in a dilettante way. Their grandfathers and their fathers had been abolitionists, mugwumps, and civil service reformers. They themselves were active in civic affairs, their relative decline in power notwithstanding. And they now realized, if only because of the rise in prices attributed to the trusts, that they stood in the lengthening shadow of the power and wealth concentrated in the hands of the new barbarians.

Unquestionably, as Hofstadter emphasizes, resentment born of declining status contributed to the reform impulses of some Progressives. Undeniably, vanity, ambition, and other worldly considerations figured large in their acceptance of Roosevelt's commissions. Cut off from service in the Democratic party by crude immigrant bosses, frustrated within the Republican party by the spokesmen of the men of new wealth, they inevitably gravitated to Roosevelt. With him they could bask in the prominence and assert the authority they deemed their rightful inheritance; with him they could curb the plutocrats' power and recapture in part their own lost status.

At best, however, the concept of status revolution offers little more than a partial insight into a limited number of Progressives. As Norman Wilensky shows, the men who marched with Theodore Roosevelt came almost universally from the same social and economic class as those who manned the bastions for William Howard Taft in 1912. They differed only in age, the Roosevelt men averaging ten to fifteen years younger than the Taft men. This meant that the Bull Moosers had been impressionable college students or rising young men of affairs when the great intellectual revolt against laissez-faire and natural law broke in the last quarter of the nineteenth century. Now, in 1912, they had the energy, maturity, and prestige to fight for ideas that had been growing on them during two decades of civic and political apprenticeship.

Assuredly, the striking feature of the platform they met at Chicago to adopt was its scientific, moral, and humanitarian tone. Their platform contained a full measure of angry indictments, sweeping generalizations, and partisan distortions. But it also embodied a constructive distillation of the current social wisdom—a wisdom that derived from the decade and more of analysis of American society by the muckrakers, by economists and historians, by the new psychologists and sociologists, and by all those investigatory commissions that Roosevelt as President had appointed. For all that platform's naïvetés, including the colossal one of the recall of judicial decisions, it comprised a blueprint for a more humane, enlightened, and constructive America. It is hardly an accident that virtually all of its planks have since been written into law.

Nor is it less remarkable that the Progressive party should have attracted the people it did, given man's capacity for compassion, his compulsion for order, and his urge both to conserve and create. Roosevelt expected to receive, and he did broadly receive, the support of college professors and presidents the nation over because he promised to implement programs their minds had long nurtured and cultivated. And so with Pinchot's scientific management conservationists, those scientists and gentlemen who had been at once a cause and an effect of the Progressive movement. It would have been strange indeed had they not followed their unfailing patron into a party which offered them complete freedom to write its conservation plank. Nor was it much different with Jane Addams and all those other well-born women social workers who had become reformers out of resentment against man's inhumanity to man. Aggrieved though they were by the Colonel's militant preparedness views, they saw in the planks calling for minimum wages for women and the national abolition of child labor the fruition of much of their life's labors. The same may be said for the clergymen who joined the crusade in spite of Woodrow Wilson's powerful pull. Theodore Roosevelt, the greatest preacher and the most strident moralist of all, was offering nothing less than an opportunity to write the Social Gospel into law. "I doubt," wrote New York City's distinguished councilman, Stanley M. Isaacs, four decades later, "if anyone today can realize the personal inspiration that came from direct contact with TR or can appreciate the fervor that animated those of us who shared in the early Progressive Party years."

TR gave us new goals, a broad new purpose—faith in our country's ideals and willingness to press forward along lines we knew to be right, never willing to compromise where a vital moral issue was at stake, and confidence in the ultimate success of justice and sound ideas, provided they were pressed with courage and a disregard of personal consequences.

If great numbers of Progressive leaders were thus men of creative moral vision and social respectability, they were nonetheless emotional for it. At Chicago, where TR arrived the night before the convention opened on August 5 exuberantly exclaiming that he felt "as strong as a bull moose," their impassioned outcries soared to the rafters and thence across the land. At the slightest provocation, and sometimes at no provocation at all, ten thousand and more voices poured out the soul-stirring cadences of those great martial hymns, "Onward Christian Soldiers" and "The Battle Hymn of the Republic." Again and again thousands of delegates, alternates, and alternates' alternates who had come at their own expense cheered, waved, and stamped as a succession of speakers affirmed the exaltation of their cause.

"We stand for a nobler America," thundered the emotion-wrought Beveridge (listening to him rehearse the keynote address in his room the night before, George Perkins broke into a sob and left the room with tears coursing down his cheeks). We know "the price we must pay, the sacrifice we must make, the burdens we must carry . . . yet we enlist and we enlist for the war. For we know the justice of our cause, and we know, too, its certain triumph."

The climax came on the second day when Roosevelt appeared before the convention. He came, he afterward wrote, to say the things that were "deepest" in his heart, and he had entitled his address his "Confession of Faith." Mowry describes the scene:

As he stood on the platform in the old familiar attitude, his body swaying with delight, his left hand in his pocket and his right vigorously waving a reply, fifteen thousand people roared their welcome. For fifty-two minutes, wildly waving red bandannas, they cheered him as they had never cheered anyone else. Here were no claques, no artificial demonstration sustained by artificial devices. . . . Men and women simply stood on their feet for an hour to welcome a man because they liked him and believed in him. When Roosevelt himself finally sought to stop the demonstration, the crowd once more broke into song:

> Thou wilt not cower in the dust,
> Roosevelt, O Roosevelt!
> Thy gleaming sword shall never rust,
> Roosevelt, O Roosevelt.

At long last the singing stopped and Roosevelt prepared to speak. A newspaperman observed that he seemed bewildered, unable to understand the temper of his audience. "They were crusaders; he was not," the reporter wrote. Yet Roosevelt the politician knew what the amateurs who filled the Coliseum did not know or could not admit if they did know—the failure of progressive Republican politicians to join the Progressive party on the state level had foredoomed him and the party to disaster. And because of that knowledge, Roosevelt at that moment and for the three months that followed was more truly a crusader than he had ever been. "Now friends," he exclaimed at the end of a speech that the Wilson scholar, Arthur S. Link, terms a classic synthesis of the most advanced progressive thought of the times, "this is my confession of faith." ". . . I hope we shall win. . . . But win, or lose, we shall not falter. . . . Our cause is based on the eternal principle of righteousness; and even though we who now lead may for the time fail, in the end the cause itself shall triumph. . . . We stand at Armageddon, and we battle for the Lord."

Yet the ways of the Lord are sometimes mysterious. Even before this most religious-like convention in American political history was ended, Roosevelt's handling of the trust question had sown seeds of doubt in the minds of a great body of the faithful.

Reflecting their agrarian frame of reference, Midwestern Progressives and a sprinkling of Easterners insisted that the party platform call for strengthening the Sherman Law. The day after Roosevelt's address the Committee on Resolutions framed a plank to that effect. The platform was then sent up to Roosevelt's rooms where George Perkins, who served as TR's chief aide throughout the convention and campaign, persuaded the Colonel to delete it.

The next day Perkins sat confidently in the Coliseum as Dean William Draper Lewis of the University of Pennsylvania Law School read the platform to the convention. Suddenly Perkins started. Lewis was reading the antitrust plank as originally approved by the Committee on Resolutions. "That does not belong in the platform," Perkins shouted to Amos Pinchot. "We cut it out last night." He then rushed out of the auditorium.

Perkins later prevailed on Roosevelt to delete the plank; and as printed and distributed the Progressive party platform neither endorsed nor called for strengthening the Sherman Antitrust Act. The radicals' distrust of Perkins, whom they believed only to be protecting his vast holdings in the United States Steel Corporation and the International Harvester Company, was thus confirmed. "Perkins . . . smiling and simpering in triumph like a sinister specter—in his gray alpaca suit to match the slightly sprinkled gray of his brown hair and gray mustache, and . . . steel-gray heart . . . was not one of us," William Allen White wrote. He "misunderstood" Roosevelt. White's characterization, accepted by virtually all Midwestern Progressive leaders and written thence into the history books, is a palpable injustice to Perkins. It is also a misreading of Roosevelt himself, one that blithely ignores the long evolution of TR's views on the trusts as well as his denunciation of the Sherman Act's philosophy in his address accepting the Bull Moose charge.

"Half of . . . [the Progressives] are really representative of a kind of rural toryism, which wishes to attempt the impossible task of returning to the economic conditions that obtained sixty years ago," Roosevelt had written just the summer before. "The other half wishes to go forward along the proper lines, that is, to recognize the inevitableness and the necessity of combinations in business, and meet it by a corresponding increase in governmental power over big business; but at the same time these real progressives are hampered by being obliged continually to pay lip loyalty to their colleagues, who, at bottom, are not progressive at all, but retrogressive."

Many Progressives also disapproved of Roosevelt's handling of the party's relations with Southern Negroes. Partly to win the Northern Negro vote and partly because of humanitarianism, Progressive leaders had encouraged Northern Negroes to come into the Progressive hold. When the convention convened at Chicago the delegates' ranks were studded with Negroes—mute testimony to their faith in Roosevelt, Brownsville notwithstanding. Large numbers of Negroes had also joined the party in the South, and three Southern states sent contesting delegations, mixed and all white, to Chicago. Their leaders appealed in advance to Roosevelt, who on August 1 announced his decision in a moving letter to Julian L. Harris, son of the author of *Uncle Remus*.

Roosevelt first pointed out that the Republican party in the South "exists only to serve the purposes of a small group of politicians, for the most part white, but including some colored men, who have not the slightest interest in elections." He then predicted that a similar fate would befall the Progressive party should it appeal "to the Negroes or to the men who in the past have derived their sole standing from leading and manipulating the Negroes."

I earnestly believe that by appealing to the best white men in the South, the men of justice and of vision as well as of strength and of leadership, and by frankly putting the movement in their hands from the outset we shall create a situation by which the colored men of the South will ultimately get justice as it is not possible for them to get justice if we are to continue and perpetuate the present conditions.

That decision plagued TR for the duration of the campaign. The majority of Northern Negro delegates swallowed hard and stayed on; but a small number walked angrily out of the party —a few into the arms of Woodrow Wilson, who was to treat them worse, and most into those of Taft, who already had done so. The Colonel was hurt, especially when Booker T. Washington came out for Taft; nevertheless, he adhered resolutely to the policy.

Meanwhile, TR girded himself for battle with his principal adversary, Governor Woodrow Wilson of New Jersey. Roosevelt and his followers had hoped that bibulous Champ Clark of Missouri would be the Democratic nominee, and their depression ran deep when Wilson won a grueling contest on the forty-sixth ballot at Baltimore the week after they had stormed out of the Republican convention in Chicago.

Wilson and Roosevelt had once been cordial, if not intimate, friends. "Woodrow Wilson is a perfect trump," TR wrote in 1902 when Wilson was named president of Princeton University. But their friendship gradually weakened, for Wilson strongly disapproved Roosevelt's strident nationalism. He also became disenchanted with TR's personality.

I have not seen much of Mr. Roosevelt since he became President, but I am told that he no sooner thinks than he talks, which is a miracle not wholly in accord with the educational theory of forming an opinion.

As Governor of New Jersey in 1911 Wilson had won national recognition by his masterful imposition of a formidable body of progressive legislation upon a divided legislature. The day after he was nominated, Governor Osborn of Michigan spread consternation through the Colonel's ranks by publicly declaring that there was now "no necessity for a new party." He also urged Roosevelt not to run. Praising Wilson as "a christian, [*sic*] a scholar and a fearless citizen," he added that Wilson was "not owned by anybody" and would "lead the people against the financial overlords in orderly but earnest fashion."

In spite of TR's realization that he could not win and that the party he was founding could not survive—"I would have had a sporting chance if the Democrats had put up a reactionary candidate," he said on the eve of the Bull Moose convention—he held fast. His prejudices against the Democrats were too deep, his desire to destroy Taft too consuming, and his urge for leadership too irresistible. He replied to Osborn, who had meanwhile written that "Woodrow Wilson represents . . . what you represent," that Wilson's election would result in a resurgence of the Democratic bosses and that two-thirds of his own supporters would go to Taft if he withdrew. Until Wilson was fifty years old, Roosevelt wrote another friend, "he advocated with skill, intelligence and good breeding the outworn doctrines which are responsible for four-fifths of the political troubles of the United States." Then, as governor, he "turned an absolute somersault so far as at least half of these doctrines was concerned."

The most significant feature of the campaign that summer and fall was the modification Roosevelt induced in the "other half" of Wilson's doctrines; also the partial retreat which the New Jersey Governor forced the Colonel to make. Writing off Taft as undeserving of serious debate, TR charged Wilson with "rural toryism"; he argued that his proposal to break up the giant corporations was anachronistic; and he contended that Wilson's low-tariff views, which he interpreted as embracing free trade, would harm American workingmen. But he hammered most forcefully at Wilson's reluctance to countenance big government. "Mr. Wilson is fond of asserting his platonic devotion to the purposes of the Progressive party," TR declared at San Francisco on September 14. But Wilson also holds that " 'The history of liberty is a history of the limitation of governmental power, not the increase of it.' " How, he asked, could he square that view with the Progressives' proposals for workmen's compensation, regulation of conditions in factories, control of railroads and the trusts, and all the rest? "We propose to use the whole power of the government to protect all those who, under Mr. Wilson's laissez-faire system, are trodden down in the ferocious, scrambling rush of an unregulated and purely individualistic industrialism," Roosevelt concluded.

Actually, as John Wells Davidson shows, TR had inadvertently quoted Wilson out of context. The "history of liberty" remark had been preceded by a qualifying paragraph which the newspapers failed to reproduce. Nevertheless, a tremendous gulf still separated the two men. Wilson sought to bridge it, for he was wounded by Roosevelt's hammering. "I realize that while we are followers of Jefferson," Wilson asserted in early October, "there is one principle of Jefferson's which no longer can obtain in the practical politics of America."

You know that it was Jefferson who said that the best government is that which does as little governing as possible. . . . That was said in a day when the opportunities of America were so obvious . . . that all that was necessary was that the government should withhold its hand and see to it that every man got an opportunity to act if he would. But that time is past. America is not now, and cannot in the future be, a place for unrestricted individual enterprise.

Wilson also focused increasingly on social justice as the campaign progressed. He refused to endorse the Progressives' demand for a minimum wage law for women, arguing that it would drive the general wage level down to the minimum. Nor did he come out for a national child labor law as Roosevelt and his party advocated. By the end of the campaign, however, he had several times endorsed the Progressive party's broad social objectives. "I want to say here, as I have said on so many other occasions," the Democratic candidate declared in Minneapolis, "that there is a great deal in the program of the new third party which attracts all public-spirited and hopeful men, that there is a great program of human uplift included in the platform of that party."

Meanwhile Wilson maintained a relentless fire on Roosevelt's proposal to place trust regulation under a commission of experts without specifying in law the abuses to be regulated. Under Wilson's harassment and the concurrent complaints of the radical Progressives, the Colonel finally submitted. In mid-October he released a statement endorsing in part the antitrust plank Perkins had struck out of the platform in Chicago.

If, for instance, a corporation should be found crushing out competition by refusing to sell when the patron bought off competitors, or by underselling in districts, or in the dozen of other ways that Congress should learn were being practised and should say were illegal, I would have the statute say point blank, with no loophole for escape, that the corporation was guilty.

Roosevelt's statement had been issued from a hospital bed in Chicago where he lay recuperating from a bullet wound. On October 14, as he stepped into his car in Milwaukee, he had been shot by a fanatic. The bullet went through the former President's overcoat, spectacles case, and folded manuscript, fracturing his fourth rib and lodging a little short of his right lung. Stunned, TR fell backward momentarily, coughed, and then stood up again. "Stand back. Don't hurt the man," he shouted at the crowd. Then, over the protests of attending physicians, he insisted that he be driven to the auditorium to deliver an address.

"Friends," he exclaimed to the crowd that sat rigid before him five minutes later, "I shall ask you to be as quiet as possible. I don't know whether you fully understand that I have just been shot; but it takes more than that to kill a Bull Moose. . . . I had my manuscript—and there is a bullet—there is where the bullet went through . . . and it probably saved me from it going into my heart. The bullet is in me now. . . . And now, friends . . . I want you to understand that I am ahead of the game, anyway. No man has had a happier life than I have led. . . . I cannot understand a man fit to be a colonel who can pay any heed to his personal safety. . . . Friends, I am thinking of the movement. . . . He shot to kill. He shot—the shot, the bullet went in here—I will show you. . . . Now, friends, I am not speaking for myself at all. I give you my word, I do not care a rap about being shot; not a rap. . . . Now, friends—[speaking to someone on the stage], I am not sick at all. I am all right. . . . Now friends, what we Progressives are trying to do is to enroll rich or poor . . . to stand together for the most elementary rights of good citizenship. . . . My friends are a little more nervous than I am. Don't you waste any sympathy on me. I have had an A-1 time in life and I am having it now."

Of a sudden TR seemed to forget his wound. "At one time I promoted five men for gallantry . . . two of them were Protestants, two Catholics, and one a Jew. . . . If all five of them had been Jews I would have promoted them." He continued, moving now into the theme of his prepared address. "I make the same appeal in our citizenship. . . . It is essential that there should be organizations of labor. This is an era of organization. Capital organizes and therefore labor must organize." Roosevelt then called for capital to treat labor fairly and for labor to repudiate crime and violence. "I know these doctors, when they get hold of me, will never let me go back, and there are just a few things more that I want to say to you," TR declared. "Mr. Wilson has distinctly committed . . . [himself] to the old flintlock, muzzle-loaded doctrine of States' rights. . . . We are for the people's rights. If they can be obtained best through the National Government, then we are for national rights. . . . Mr. Wilson has distinctly declared that you shall not have a national law to prohibit the labor of children. . . . I ask you to look at our declaration and hear and read our platform about social and industrial justice and then, friends, vote for the Progressive ticket without regard to me. . . ."

The Colonel had spoken for almost an hour. Yet, as Pringle writes, "Men did not judge . . . [his performance] histrionic or childish." Such was Theodore Roosevelt's uniqueness.

The election returns a few weeks later confirmed Roosevelt's fears. Wilson won in a landslide with 435 electoral votes. He failed, however, to win a popular majority, receiving 6,286,124 votes to Roosevelt's 4,126,020 and Taft's 3,483,922. Eugene V. Debs also polled close to a million votes in a remarkable demonstration of the left wing's distrust of the three major candidates, their parties, and their programs. On the other hand, the Democrats captured both houses of Congress and numerous governorships while the Progressives won but a scattering of congressional seats and elected only one governor.

Roosevelt ran best in the urban areas—he swept Pennsylvania, Michigan, California, and three smaller states—and he fared poorer than expected in the West, his ringing defenses of conservation antagonizing anticonservationist Westerners. He also failed to win over Democratic and independent progres-

sives; party loyalty, Wilson's eloquence, and the lingering belief that the Colonel was a trimmer all worked against him. As
the reformer, Anna Howard Shaw, wrote Jane Addams shortly
after the Progressive convention, "I wish I could believe . . .
[TR] intended to do a single honest thing, or that he would
carry out a single plank in the platform if he were elected
. . . I cannot." That statement mirrored the views of thousands
of nonpolitical reformers who never understood the constructive compromises of Roosevelt's presidency.

Yet the crusade had not been in vain. Roosevelt's vigorous
and explicit statement of the case for social justice had sharpened the mounting offensive against privilege and exploitation.
It had further forced Wilson and many of the leaders of his
party to face the paradox inherent in their commitment to both
national reform and the philosophy of states' rights.

Theodore Roosevelt's personal services to the great movement that was the signal feature of the era that bears his name
virtually ended with the Bull Moose campaign. Within the following four years the Democratic party under Woodrow Wilson would write the burden of the Bull Moose party's planks
into law and Roosevelt himself would go into temporary
eclipse. He would come out of it near the end of Wilson's first
administration to perform one last memorable service and
some disservice to the country he loved.

PART SIX

One Last Great Cause

Chapter 28

The Variety of Him

> *... the vitality of him, the charm, the humor, the intellectual avidity, the love of people, the flaming devotion to his country.*
>
> —Hermann Hagedorn

ALTHOUGH ITS leader would return at the head of another great command, the Progressive party itself was doomed to die. Its fate had been sealed in the summer of its birth by the failure of Republican officeholders to support it; and with all his personal magnetism, Theodore Roosevelt had not the power to sustain it indefinitely. The only questions were how long the death rattle would last and whether the Great Bull Moose would make one last ferocious lunge before it rolled over and died. The answers lay in Roosevelt's personality, the metamorphosis of Woodrow Wilson and the Democratic party, and the coming of World War I.

The Colonel's first impulse was to turn away. He considered himself finished, and early in 1913 he plunged into the writing of his autobiography. Yet he was under heavy obligations to the four million Americans who had affirmed their faith at the polls and especially to the thousands of semiprofessionals who had cut loose from the Grand Old Party to serve under his banner. Great hosts of these still believed that the party could supplant the G.O.P.; sizable numbers were determined to see that it did. Their leader felt duty bound to go along with them, at least until the Congressional elections of 1914 exposed the party's fatal weakness.

The first order of business was to stop a drive by Gifford Pinchot and Western radicals to deprive George Perkins of his influence in party councils. Ascribing the movement to "baseless prejudice," Roosevelt indignantly refused to "throw to the wolves one of the staunchest allies and supporters we have had." The radicals thereupon submitted, though they won the right to include a strong antitrust plank in the platform they adopted at a convention in Chicago the month after the elec-

427

tion. The Colonel himself attended the Chicago meeting; and from then until the 1914 elections he repeatedly affirmed the party's permanence. "We believe that there are literally millions of progressives now associated with the Democratic and Republican parties who agree with our principles," he wrote a group of leading Minnesota Progressives in January, 1913. "There shall be no retreat from the position we have taken. High of heart and strong of hand, we front the future; and the future is surely ours."

Yet Roosevelt hardly believed his own words as he uttered them. "I regret to add that I agree with your forecast," he replied to a pessimistic letter from Hiram Johnson in January, 1913. "Our chance depends upon there being a break in the Democratic party . . . [Wilson] showed his adroitness during the campaign, and he may well be able to show similar adroitness during the next four years in the Presidency, and with the same result."

Well, my dear Governor, if these views are correct, the chances of immediate victory or at least of victory obtained under my leadership, are not great. . . . In any event I do believe that great good has come from the fight we have made, and that the principles for which we stand have made and will make real progress.

But it was not in the Colonel's nature to withdraw permanently from the surging stream of events. When floods inundated the lower Mississippi Valley in the winter of 1913, he seized the opportunity to reiterate his demand for multipurpose development of the entire watershed. It was "criminally wasteful" for the "richest nation on earth" to "hesitate or haggle" over adoption of such a program, he wrote. There must be a "national effort to turn floods into power, arid regions into gardens, and marshes into farms" through a single enabling act of Congress, "establishing a policy and providing continuing funds, exactly as was done in the case of the Panama Canal."

Meanwhile Roosevelt delivered the presidential address for 1913 to the American Historical Association. "I am to deliver a beastly lecture—'History as Literature'—" he confided to Lodge. He added that none of the Association's members "believe that history is literature" but that he had spent "much care" on the address even so. He did not spare the disbelievers, whom he had once characterized to Trevelyan as the "small men who do most of the teaching," when he confronted them.

Roosevelt's poetic strain was too strong and his potential as a stylist too great for him to approve the dryness of the new historical writing—itself a reflection, ironically, of the scientific spirit which infused his own thought. Inevitably, he overstated the case for literary excellence, though with such lyric force as almost to win it. He understood the importance of monographs. "I pay high honor to the patient and truthful investigator," he said. "He does an indispensable work." But he wanted more, far more than most men could give. What was needed was "the great master who can use the materials gathered, who has the gift of vision, the quality of the seer, the power himself to see what has happened and to make what he has seen clear to the vision of others." His protest, Roosevelt explained, was against those "who believe that the extension of the activities of the most competent mason and most energetic contractor will supply the lack of great architects." The master historian must have vision and imagination, the power to grasp the essentials and reject the nonessentials, the "power to embody ghosts, to put flesh and blood on dry bones, to make dead men living before our eyes." He must, the author of *The Winning of the West* declaimed, "have the power to take the science of history and turn it into literature."

In passages as revealing of his ultimate affirmation of human kind as any he ever wrote, Roosevelt then called for deeper understanding and firmer moral judgment. "Side by side with the need for the perfection of the individual in the technic of his special calling goes the need of broad human sympathy, and the need of lofty and generous emotion in the individual." The great historian must also be a great moralist. "It is no proof of impartiality to treat wickedness and goodness as on the same level." To be sure, it was wrong to let abstract principles intrude on facts as Carlyle had done in his *Frederick the Great*. Nevertheless, when great events lack a great historian the poet will fix them in the minds of men. Shakespeare had so fixed the character of Richard III; and it is the lines of Keats, who had even forgotten Balboa's correct name, "which leap to our minds when we think of the 'wild surmise' felt by the indomitable explorer-conquerer from Spain when the vast new sea burst on his vision."

Warning his fellow historians that the revolt against the spectacular and the exceptional, against war, oratory, and politics, had gone too far, Roosevelt declared that "there are hours so fraught with weighty achievement, with triumph or defeat, with joy or sorrow, that each such hour may determine all . . . that are to come thereafter." Then, in a Churchillian peroration that rings down through the years, he challenged his listeners to re-create the epochal movements of the past. "Some day," he concluded, "the historians . . . will portray the conquest of the continent. . . . They will show how the land which the pioneers won slowly and with incredible hardship was filled in two generations by the overflow from the countries of western and central Europe. The portentous growth of the cities will be shown, and the change from a nation of farmers to a nation of business men and artisans. . . . The formation of a new ethnic type in this melting pot of nations will be told. The hard materialism of our age will appear, and also the strange capacity for lofty idealism which must be reckoned with by all who would understand the American character."

In February, 1913, Roosevelt's autobiography began to appear in the *Outlook* in serial form. Like all autobiographies it justified its subject's career, and like most autobiographies it was flawed by grievous omissions. Its literary quality was uneven, though some sections were superbly written, and its point of view was that of the Progressive rather than the Republican Roosevelt. But for all of that, it was and is the most illuminating autobiography ever written by a former President and probably by any major American political leader.

At odd hours in the late spring of 1913 TR also wrote his part of *Life Histories of African Game Animals,* a two-volume collaboration with the naturalist, Edmund Heller. Published under Roosevelt and Heller's name (TR had offered to list the naturalist's name first), it was commended by the *Bulletin of the American Geographic Society* as "a very valuable contribution both to geography and zoology" and by C. Hart Merriam as "far and away the best book ever written on the big-game animals of any part of the world."

Meanwhile Ethel married Richard Derby in the little Episcopal church in Oyster Bay where the family worshiped. The guest list reflected the shattering upheaval of the previous year; also Roosevelt's conviction that he had been cheated out of the Republican nomination. Cabot Lodge attended, but he lacked congenial company. "We did not send invitations to Root or Taft or Nicholas Murray Butler," TR explained to Winthrop

Chanler, "because they would have been just as unwelcome guests as Barnes or Penrose or Guggenheim." "Root took part in as downright a bit of theft and swindling as ever was perpetrated by any Tammany ballot box stuffer, and I shall never forgive the men who were the leaders in that swindling."

In May the Colonel pressed a libel suit against an obscure Michigan editor who had written that "Roosevelt lies and curses in a most disgusting way; he gets drunk too, and that not infrequently, and all of his intimates know about it." Determined, as he phrased it, "to expose the infamy of these slanders," the Colonel easily won the suit. The editor failed to produce a single witness to confirm his assertions, though TR did swear mildly when excited, and Roosevelt produced a host of depositions to disprove them. At TR's request, damages were set at six cents.

That same spring Roosevelt made a memorable sally into art criticism. He had never been as sensitive to the fine arts as to literature and history. Yet his curiosity was so avid and his belief in the ennobling force of aesthetics so firm that he was unfailingly responsive. He considered the Gothic cathedrals of Western Europe "the most magnificent architecture that our race has ever been able to produce," and he admired Raphael, Michelangelo, and Rembrandt among the painters. His favorite contemporary sculptor was Saint-Gaudens. As President, Roosevelt had directed the United States Mint to employ Saint-Gaudens to design coins. Then, when the sculptor decided for artistic reasons to omit the phrase "In God We Trust" from the new coins, Roosevelt supported him in the face of a popular outcry. Roosevelt had also appointed a Fine Arts Council of distinguished architects, painters, and sculptors to advise the government on the design and placement of public buildings. ("I am going to do what these men want, Gifford; it is a move for civilization; it is the right thing to do. It is a great deal better than appointing third-class postmasters.") Before the council disbanded under Taft at the behest of pork-barrel congressmen and commercial interests, an enlightened plan for the preservation and development of the Mall was adopted. The result, a former member of the Council wrote in the *American Architect* the year after TR's death, was "an epoch" in our history. Theodore Roosevelt's administrations marked the first real case "of Executive appreciation of Fine Arts" since John Quincy Adams.

On March 27, 1913, Roosevelt described his impressions of the historic international exhibition of modern art at the Sixty-ninth Regiment Armory for the *Outlook* under the title, "A Layman's View of an Art Exhibition." Unabashedly, he compared the Cubists and the Futurists or Near-Impressionists to the "lunatic fringe" of the progressive movement in one passage and to the "later work of the paleolithic artists of the French and Spanish caves" in the next. And he took particular exception to a Duchamp which "for some reason is called 'A Naked Man Going Down Stairs,' [*sic*]," but could just as fittingly have been named " 'A Well-Dressed Man Going Up a Ladder.' " Yet he perceived, even as he failed wholly to understand; his reaction to the exhibition's raging creativity was far more sophisticated than that of most professional critics. "It is vitally necessary to move forward and to shake off the dead hand, often the fossilized dead hand, of the reactionaries," Roosevelt wrote. The necessary penalty of creativity "is a liability to extravagance."

There was one note entirely absent . . . and that was the note of the commonplace. There was not a touch of simpering, self-satisfied conventionality anywhere in the exhibition. Any sculptor or painter who had in him something to express and the power of expressing it found the field open to him. . . . There was no stunting or dwarfing, no requirement that a man whose gift lay in new directions should measure up or down to stereotyped and fossilized standards.

And so with TR's understanding of literature. It is true that the moral and political conventions of the times delimited his appreciation—that he failed to come into rapport with the naturalistic novelists whose rise roughly paralleled his own because they described the "unspeakable" or because he rebelled against their determinism. As he explained to the minor novelists Owen Wister and Winston Churchill, Mrs. Roosevelt could evaluate literary works purely on their aesthetic quality, but he could not. "I am old-fashioned, or sentimental, or something, about books!" he admitted. "Whenever I read one I want, in the first place, to enjoy myself, and, in the next place, to feel that I am a little better and not a little worse for having read it." TR believed with Bernard Shaw that comedy is more realistic than tragedy, and he more than once advised Wister and other novelist friends to "Let in some sunlight, somehow . . . life, after all, does—go—on."

The result was a string of social, moral, and political pronouncements that have sadly compromised Roosevelt's reputation in academic circles. Henry James was "a miserable little snob" for abandoning his native land and writing of the drawing room. The characters of Zola were "hideous human swine." To find the merits of Rabelais and Boccaccio was to examine "a gold chain encrusted in the filth of a pigpen." Kipling's *Stalky & Co.* was unhealthy, "for there is hardly a single form of meanness which it does not extol." Even *Peck's Bad Boy* was unfortunate. "I want every boy to be manly and able to fight for his own rights and those of his country," TR wrote a youngster who expressed fondness for the book, "but I want him to be gentle and upright also."

Roosevelt's harsh strictures against Tolstoy have exposed him to the sharpest criticism. TR conceded that the Russian pacifist was "a great writer, a great novelist," and that "even as a professional moralist and philosophical adviser of mankind in religious matters he has some excellent theories and on some points develops a noble and elevating teaching." He feared, however, that Tolstoy's preachments "would have an influence for bad." The *Kreutzer Sonata*, TR wrote in the *Outlook* in 1909, was marked by a "moral perversion" that could only have come "from a man who, however high he may stand in certain respects, has in him certain dreadful qualities of the moral pervert." Yet when the former President lectured the militaristic Germans in Berlin the next year, he chose to say that "it would also be a bad thing not to have Tolstoy, not to profit by the lofty side of his teachings."

Criticism of Roosevelt's views on literature may be overdrawn. TR was invariably interested; and for all his forced optimism, for all his strident moralizing, his letters and essays are filled with perceptions that transcend the conventions that controlled his conclusions. If it is true that insights rather than generalizations survive, Roosevelt's criticisms cannot be cavalierly dismissed.

Nor is TR's love of reading unimportant. Here was a statesman whose interests were more catholic than all but a handful of his country's men of letters and probably most of its college professors. He may have lacked, and by his own disarming confession he did, the critical capacity (more likely the introspective turn of mind) to assess *Hamlet* and *Macbeth* in depth. But as Wagenknecht, one of the few scholars to cut through the clichés that are the life-blood of judgments on TR, convincingly shows, Roosevelt's breadth was incredible. He knew, often in the original, Villon, Ronsard, Mistral, Körner, Topelius, Goethe, Dante, Dumas, and hundreds of others. He was versed in the minor Scandinavian sagas, the Arabian tales, the core of Rumanian literature. And he even earned his honorary presidency of the Gaelic Literature Association by anticipating the revival of interest in Celtic literature.

Here also was a statesman who had read the bulk of his own country's literature and knew personally perhaps a majority of the nation's best writers. A rare quality in any man of action, this was a unique quality in a President. There had been Presidents before who were intellectuals—notably Jefferson and the Adamses; and there was one after him—Woodrow Wilson. There were a few others who were receptive to intellectuals. But there was no modern President save TR who had such deep bonds with and unaffected interest in the nation's writers. Just as Roosevelt's attacks on the courts worked a subtle change on the judicial mind, just as his responsiveness to social and natural scientists quickened the acceptance of their ideas, so did his patronage of writers influence the national mood. One has only to contrast the cultural void created by a McKinley's or Eisenhower's apotheosis of the businessman to the virile intellectualism generated by Roosevelt to understand this.

Admittedly, TR's boyish exuberance made him a natural foil for aesthetes like brooding, cynical Henry Adams. Roosevelt, wrote Adams in one of those searing aphorisms that live more for the prejudices they confirm than the truths they reveal, was "pure act." And there was hardly a first-rate literary mind in the country that was not contemptuous of TR's heavy-handed imposition of social conventions upon aesthetic standards. Yet the central fact remains: Roosevelt stimulated, and even inspired, dozens of young authors over the years. And if he did not discover, he nevertheless brought into the open the genius of Edwin Arlington Robinson, whom he appointed to a minor government post with the admonition "to think poetry first and Treasury second."

Indeed, Roosevelt's patronage of his friend Robinson was the first thing Robert Frost remembered about TR. "As I think of him," Frost said, "I remember him as the only President I ever met, as the only President who ever took that much interest in a poet . . . [TR] was our kind. He quoted poetry to me. He knew poetry. Poetry was in his mind; that means a great deal to me."

Stephen Vincent Benét felt much as Frost did. "I do not mean to say in the least that his [TR's] judgment of books was infallible—no man's is," Benét wrote. However, he added, Roosevelt had "a love for the thing itself." The testimony is endless. Hamlin Garland recalled the Colonel exclaiming at lunch one day during World War I: " 'Do you know that the rhythms of archaic French are much finer and manlier than the rhythms of modern French?' Whereupon, he quoted with immense gusto and dramatic force a page or two from the Song of Roland and followed it up by the quotation of a poem from a modern French writer." Van Wyck Brooks remembered a similar performance—"the most remarkable exhibition of presence of mind and phenomenal memory I had ever heard of," he wrote. "If ever there was obviously a man of genius," said Brooks in a judgment that TR himself never accepted, "it was Theodore Roosevelt."

The interim between the Bull Moose campaign and the outbreak of World War I also saw the most harrowing physical experience of Roosevelt's life. Early in the summer of 1913 he decided to combine a lecture trip to South America with an ascent of the Paraguay River. "It won't be anything like the African trip," TR wrote Kermit, who postponed marriage to join his father. "There will be no hunting and no adventure."

When the Colonel reached Rio de Janeiro on October 21, however, he heard of an unmapped river, the River of Doubt, which flowed north toward the Amazon from the Brazilian plateau. "We will go down that unknown river!" he at once announced. The Brazilian government thereupon agreed to organize a major expedition, "the Expedicão Scientifica Roosevelt-Rondon."

On February 27, 1914, the Colonel, Kermit, and a party of twenty began the hazardous exploration of the River of Doubt. They were soon beset with troubles. Insects proved almost unbearable, eating through their clothes and biting painfully into their flesh. Two boats were lost when the river rose unexpectedly one night. Hostile Indians killed one of their dogs. A boat capsized and one of the boatmen was lost. Kermit escaped death only by grasping an overhanging limb after being swept over a falls. Food ran dangerously low. Another boat was lost. Equipment was discarded. One of the men went insane, killed a member of the party, and fled into the wilderness. Finally, the Colonel, who had been weakened by intermittent attacks of fever, slipped and gashed his leg in a heroic effort to prevent two capsized boats from being ground against the rocks.

The Colonel's wound became infected; his malarial fever grew worse and his temperature rose to 105 degrees. The naturalist, George K. Cherrie, expected to find him dead each morning, and once Roosevelt told Kermit and Cherrie to go on without him. "I feel I am only a burden to the party," he said. TR also contemplated suicide, but decided against it for fear that Kermit would insist on bringing his body out. "The fever was high and father was out of his head," Kermit later wrote.

The scene is vivid before me. Father first began with poetry; over and over again he repeated, "In Xanadu did Kubla Khan a stately pleasure dome decree," then he started talking at random, but gradually he centered down to the question of supplies, . . . and he would then ask me if I thought Cherrie had had enough to eat to keep going. Then he would forget my presence, and keep saying to himself: "I can't work now, so I don't need much food, but he and Cherrie have worked all day with the canoes, they must have part of mine."

On April 30, two months after they had started the descent, the Colonel and his party ended their journey at Manaos. They had completed a major exploration, made significant collections for the American Museum of Natural History, and traveled 1,500 miles. TR had lost fifty-seven pounds, satisfied his last great urge for non-military adventure, and suffered illnesses that would cause his gradual physical deterioration. He had also written the major portion of a minor adventure classic, *Through the Brazilian Wilderness*, and had his name formally given by the Brazilian government to the River of Doubt. "My dear Sir," the fever-wracked former President of the United States telegraphed the Brazilian Minister of Foreign Affairs on reaching Manaos, "I thank you from my heart for the chance to take part in this great work of exploration."

Even while Roosevelt had been fighting for his life in the jungle, his name had been embroiled in controversy at home. On April 6, 1914, the new Secretary of State, William Jennings Bryan, guilelessly signed a treaty with Colombia which virtually admitted that the United States had dealt that nation less than substantial justice in acquiring the Panama Canal Zone. The treaty, as approved by President Wilson, expressed "sincere regret that anything" should have marred relations between the two nations and called for payment of a $25 million indemnity to Colombia.

The Colonel first learned of the treaty with Colombia after his descent of the River of Doubt; and from that moment until his death he suffered paroxysms of rage at its mention. "I regard the proposed Treaty as a crime against the United States, an attack upon the honor of the United States, . . . and a serious menace to the future well-being of our people," he wrote the Democratic leader, Senator William J. Stone, in July, 1914. "Either there is warrant for paying this enormous sum and for making the apology, or there is not." And he believed emphatically that there was not. "Every action we took was in accordance with the highest principles of public and private morality," the Colonel concluded in a statement that both the facts and his own earlier assertions belied.

The United States Senate eventually rejected the Colombian treaty. But in 1921, after Roosevelt's death, the Harding administration renegotiated it in order to win oil concessions for American corporations. Although the apology was then omitted, the $25 million settlement which TR had called "blackmail" was still included. But in one of the most casuistic speeches in his long career Cabot Lodge argued in the Senate that his deceased friend would have approved.

On August 1, 1914, four days after Austria-Hungary declared war on Serbia, TR unburdened himself to Arthur Lee. "As I am writing, the whole question of peace and war trembles in the balance; and at the very moment . . . our own special prize idiot, Mr. Bryan, and his ridiculous and insincere chief, Mr. Wilson, are prattling pleasantly about the steps they are taking to procure universal peace by little arbitration treaties which promise impossibilities, and which would not be worth the paper on which they are written in any serious crisis," the Colonel wrote. "It is not a good thing for a country to have a professional yodeler, a human trombone like Mr. Bryan as Secretary of State, nor a college president with an astute and shifty mind, a hypocritical ability to deceive plain people, unscrupulousness in handling machine leaders, and no real knowledge or wisdom concerning internal and international affairs as head of the nation."

Three days later Kaiser Wilhelm's superbly conditioned armies goose-stepped across the Belgian border.

Chapter 29

The Bugle That Woke America

*There were some of them did shake at what was
told,
And they shook best who knew that he was
right.*

—Edwin Arlington Robinson

WITHIN THREE months of the Imperial German Government's
invasion of Belgium Theodore Roosevelt had thrown himself
into the mightiest struggle of his career—the campaign to persuade the American people to enter World War I and to prosecute it with vigor after they had entered it. In the four and
one-half years of life that remained Roosevelt was to deal his
great adversary, Woodrow Wilson, even heavier blows than he
had earlier dealt Taft. He was to suppress his progressivism
for the first two of those years and he was to liquidate the Bull
Moose party in one of the angriest conventions in American
history. He was to see his influence sink to its lowest point
since 1900, then surge to new heights. And he was to set for
his countrymen an unparalleled example of intolerance and
hatred, of duty and devotion, and of high and resolute courage.

Roosevelt's early reactions to the coming of the war to
Europe elude facile generalization, partly because he said one
thing in private and another thing in public; he also seems to
have reversed himself on some issues as the significance of the
war emerged in sharper relief. Nevertheless, his views on two
or three of the main issues are clear. He sympathized wholeheartedly with Belgium. He believed emphatically that England
had to prevent Germany from stamping its iron heel on all
Europe. And he feared the long-range effect of Germany's defeat.

Charles Booth, the English reformer and shipping executive,
Herbert Croly, Felix Frankfurter, and two or three other
young Americans were visiting Roosevelt on August 4, 1914,
the day Great Britain entered the war. They all agreed that the
destruction of Germany would be a calamity; but they also

439

agreed that the Kaiser's armies had to be beaten. "You've got to go in! You've got to go in!" TR passionately exclaimed to Booth in the library at Sagamore. "I say all this," he went on, "though probably in a few years Germany will be an ally of ours in our fight against Japan."

A few days later an emissary from the German Embassy sought out Roosevelt at Progressive party headquarters in New York. The German bowed stiffly on being ushered in, then said that his Imperial Majesty wished Roosevelt to know that he had always remembered the great pleasure it had given him to receive and entertain the Colonel at the palace in Potsdam. He added that the Kaiser felt certain that he could count on Roosevelt's sympathetic understanding. TR returned the bow, looked the emissary straight in the eye, and icily replied: "Pray thank his Imperial Majesty for me for his very courteous message and assure him that I am deeply conscious of the honor done me in Germany and that I shall never forget the way in which His Majesty the Emperor received me in Berlin, *nor the way in which His Majesty King Albert of Belgium received me in Brussels.*"

On August 22, however, Roosevelt put himself on the record in a way he later rued. He would not then pass judgment on the violation of the treaties guaranteeing Belgium's neutrality, he wrote in the *Outlook*. "When giants are engaged in a death wrestle, as they reel to and fro they are certain to trample on whoever gets in the way of either of the huge straining combatants." He amplified his views the next month in a curiously contradictory article. "We can maintain our neutrality only by refusal to do anything to aid unoffending weak powers which are dragged into the gulf of bloodshed and misery through no fault of their own."

Of course it would be folly to jump into the gulf ourselves to no good purpose; and very probably nothing that we could have done would have helped Belgium. We have not the slightest responsibility for what has befallen her, and I am sure the sympathy of this country for . . . Belgium is very real. Nevertheless, this sympathy is compatible with full knowledge of the unwisdom of uttering a single word of official protest unless we are prepared to make that protest effective; and only the clearest and most urgent National duty would ever justify us in deviating from our rule of neutrality and noninterference.

Early in 1915 TR published this and other essays under the title *America and the World War*. The equivocal passage of August 22 was replaced with a sweeping indictment of Wilson's call for "a neutrality so strict as to forbid our even whispering a protest against wrong-doing, lest such whispers might cause disturbance to our ease and well-being."

We pay the penalty of this action—or, rather, supine inaction—on behalf of peace for ourselves, by forfeiting our right to do anything on behalf of peace for the Belgians in the present. . . . It is a grim comment on the professional pacifist theories as hitherto developed that, according to their view, our duty to preserve peace for ourselves necessarily means the abandonment of all effective effort to secure peace for other unoffending nations which through no fault of their own are trampled down by war.

The Colonel's critics were quick to pounce upon him for his apparent change of front. "I was pretty lonely, and almost everybody attacked me for not 'standing by the President,'" he lated said. "For the first sixty days, I . . . supported President Wilson . . . on the assumption that he was speaking the truth, had examined the facts, and was correct in his statement that we had no responsibility for what had been done in Belgium." Then, he continued, "I went over the Hague Conventions myself" and found that "they did demand action on our part." Indeed, he concluded, "if I made any error whatever, it was standing by . . . [Wilson] just sixty days too long. I have never committed the error since. . . ."

TR's explanation of his dramatic reversal is both enlightening and confusing. It ignores the fatalistic acceptance of brute power implicit in his assertion that "giants . . . engaged in a death wrestle . . . are certain to trample on whoever gets in the way." It fails to mention his own qualifications. We should make no official protest, Roosevelt had written in the original version, "unless we are prepared to make that protest effective." And it even omits reference to the statement that only by refusing "to do anything to aid unoffending weak powers which are dragged into the gulf of bloodshed and misery through no fault of their own" can the United States maintain its neutrality.

The Colonel's explanation further ignores his private conclusion that the President should have protested the invasion of Belgium. As he wrote Arthur Lee on August 22, the day his ambiguous *Outlook* article appeared, "I do not know whether I would be acting right if I were President or not, but it seems to me that if I were President I should register a very emphatic protest, a protest that would mean something, against the levy of the huge war contributions on Belgium. . . . The Germans, to suit their own purposes, trampled on their solemn obligations to Belgium and on Belgium's rights . . . any power which now or hereafter may be put at the mercy of Germany will suffer in similar shape."

The Colonel appended a postscript which suggests that he was holding in because of a high-minded desire to avoid embarrassing Wilson. "Of course this letter is only for you and Ruth," he wrote. "I am an ex-President; and my public attitude must be one of entire impartiality—and above all no verbal or paper 'on to Berlin' business." Meanwhile, he informed a newspaperman who attempted to draw him out that "what we have to do is not to put obstacles in the way of the Administration."

Roosevelt's indignation at Belgium's fate and Wilson's refusal to protest it had increased as the summer waned. On September 5, E. A. Van Valkenberg and Dean Lewis met him on a train bound for New Orleans to deliver a Labor Day speech for Progressive congressional candidates. "Germany is absolutely wrong," TR expostulated as the two Progressive leaders entered his compartment. "Her own White Book places her squarely in the wrong . . . [nothing] she can possibly do in the future will extricate her."

About two weeks later the newspaperman, O. K. Davis, asked TR directly what he would have done had he been President at the outbreak of war. The Colonel replied that Sir Edward Grey had needed only a few more days to force a conference on Germany. "We certainly could have supplied those few days, if Washington had cared to do so, or had known how . . . I should have felt myself a criminal, if I had been President, and had not done so." TR added that "The Kaiser's haste in declaring war shows that he recognized the fact that, if he did not begin hostilities at once, he would be prevented from doing so."

Still, the Colonel had doubts. "Of course," he reflected, "it might not have prevented it permanently, for the Kaiser and Germany were bent on attacking France, and possibly England also. . . . If Germany—that is, the Kaiser and von Moltke and the army war-lords—really believe that they can dominate the whole world, then nothing would permanently keep them from making the effort."

Two weeks later the Colonel repeated those views to Spring-Rice. "I would not have made such a statement," he added, "unless I was willing to back it up. . . . Only a limited number of people could or ought to be expected to make up their minds for themselves in a crisis like this; and they tend, and ought to tend, to support the President." Adding that it would be "mere clamor and nothing else" for him to talk about "what ought to be done or ought to have been done," TR warned that his views should be kept confidential. Then, almost as an afterthought, he sapped the strength of his contention that Wilson could have delayed the outbreak of war:

Of course, I only acted in the Japanese-Russian affair when I had received explicit assurances, verbally from the Russians and in writing from the Japanese, that my action would be welcome; and three or four months of talk and negotiation had preceded this action on my part.

The Colonel might have attacked Wilson's policies openly long before November, for he was daily growing more resentful of the President's adjuration to be neutral in thought as well as in deed, had it not been for his obligations to his Progressive supporters. His lieutenants insisted that he again lead an advance—Beveridge, Bainbridge Colby, Garfield, Johnson, Gifford Pinchot, and Victor Murdock were all running on state tickets—and TR had dutifully and wearily undertaken the assignment.

On the stump that fall TR, "always cheerful in public, always with his head high, and with his old appearance of confidence and unshaken determination," said most of the same old things in the same old manner. But they lacked the same old meaning. Wilson and the Democratic party were outflanking Roosevelt and the Bull Moose legions; and even if the Colonel had not been exacerbated by the President's diplomacy, he had sooner or later to face the fact that Democratic legislative successes were destroying the Progressive party's *raison d'être*.

The first fruits of Roosevelt's ideological victory over Wilson in 1912 was the Federal Trade Commission Law of September

26, 1914. Envisaging, in the words of Arthur S. Link, "such a positive regulation of business as Roosevelt had advocated and Wilson had condemned," it outlawed unfair business practices in a sweeping general statement that delegated the responsibility for interpretation to the members of the Commission. Three weeks later Wilson signed the Clayton Antitrust Bill into law. Under that measure's famous labor section, which Samuel Gompers enthusiastically and prematurely labeled "labor's Magna Carta," use of the injunction against labor unions was theoretically modified. This was what Roosevelt had called for in the great messages of his last two years in office, what he had tried unsuccessfully to write into the Republican platform of 1908, and what he had campaigned so eloquently for in 1912.

However grimly satisfying the Colonel's vindication by Wilson and the Democrats, it made the campaign of 1914 more difficult. To complicate matters further—and probably to explain the disparity between his private and public statements from September on—Roosevelt also felt constrained to soften his projected attack on Wilson's foreign policies. As Midwestern Progressive leaders sharply warned him early in the fall, many voters felt that the United States would be at war with Mexico and involved in Europe were he President. The result was the most fruitless canvass Roosevelt had undertaken since 1884.

Tired and disheartened, TR sat talking with O. K. Davis on a train going from Philadelphia to New York near the end. The Colonel remarked on the futility of it all, on the crowds' enthusiasm for himself and their lack of interest in the Progressive candidates he urged them to support. Suddenly, however, his mood changed dramatically. "Well, O.K.," he exclaimed, leaning over and whacking the newspaperman on the knee in a gesture of triumphant liberation, "I've got only a few hours more of this campaign, and then I shall be through. . . . Hereafter no man can claim anything from me in politics. Not a single obligation is left. I have done everything, this fall, that everybody has wanted. This election makes me an absolutely free man. Thereafter I am going to say and do just what I damned please."

The wraps were now off. Five days after the election TR publicly lashed Wilson's failure to protest Germany's invasion of Belgium. Early in December he arraigned the President for tolerating violence in Mexico. And from then until the night before his death four years later he maintained an unremitting fire on the President. Roosevelt's strictures were unvaryingly colored with partisanship. But they were almost always constructive—if one believes that defense of American rights in Mexico and preparation for war with Germany were actually constructive goals—and they were never remotely obstructionist. TR's consuming purpose was the advancement of his country's interests as he conceived them, and neither his volcanic hatred of Wilson nor his emerging ambition to return to the White House more than fanned flames that were already raging.

The controversy over Belgium was a skirmish as compared to the battle that soon raged over preparedness policy. The lines were first drawn early in the fall of 1914. In spite of the soft-pedaling of his views on Belgium and Mexico, TR had come out forthrightly for defense increases during the congressional campaign. His statements had evoked little support and no small measure of derision; and though they had probably sparked a handful of like-minded men to speak out, notably Lodge's son-in-law, A. P. Gardner, they had particularly incited the President's ire. "We shall not alter our attitude . . . because some amongst us are nervous or excited," Wilson coldly remarked in his annual message on December 8, 1914. A change of policy "would mean merely that we had lost our self-possession, that we had been thrown off our balance by a war with which we had nothing to do, whose causes cannot touch us, whose very existence affords us opportunities of friendship and disinterested service which should make us ashamed of any thought of hostility or fearful preparation for trouble."

Thus the President had chosen to stake everything on the hope that the United States could end the war by mediation. It was a noble dream, one that Roosevelt had pursued at Portsmouth and was even then criticizing Wilson for not having tried at the outbreak of hostilities. Men must always honor the President for it. Yet mediation and preparedness were not mutually exclusive. As Roosevelt had consistently and realistically held, strength could portend greater force for peace than weakness in the world as it then was.

"Upon my word," TR wrote Lodge when Wilson first ridiculed the preparedness agitation in October, "Wilson and

Bryan are the very worst men we have ever had in their positions." "If Germany smashes England I should regard it as certain that this country either had to fight or to admit that it was an occidental China," he confided to another friend. "In any event I feel that an alliance between Germany and Japan, from which we would suffer, is entirely a possibility, if Germany comes out even a little ahead in the present war."

The Colonel's growing concern over the implications of an Allied defeat was widely shared. If the submarine controversy had not interjected a major diversionary factor in the spring of 1915, the preparedness crusade might well have been fought out on that broader issue. As it was, Roosevelt and Lodge missed no opportunity to advance the Allies' cause. They supported the President's refusal to institute an embargo on munitions on the grounds that it would hurt Britain and France. They opposed Wilson's plan to purchase foreign-owned ships confined to American ports for fear it would lead to conflict with the British. And they even attacked Wilson's measured protest against Great Britain's unnecessarily inclusive contraband policy. The President "has remained silent in regard to the violation of Belgium's neutrality by Germany," Lodge complained to TR in January, 1915, ". . . and then he suddenly finds his voice in a protest to England, one of the Allies, about interference with our trade."

As it became apparent that winter that the war might become one of attrition, Roosevelt advised the British to reconsider their contraband policy. "Our trade . . . is of vastly more service to you and France than to Germany," he wrote Edward Grey. Should German submarines "now begin to destroy ships carrying foodstuffs to Great Britain," he continued, "the effect might be not merely serious but appalling."

[The] trade in contraband is overwhelmingly to the advantage of England, France and Russia, because of your command of the seas. You assume that this command gives you the right to make the advantage still more overwhelming.

TR added that the majority of administration leaders "see that political advantage will unquestionably lie with those who try to placate the German-American vote and the professional pacificist [sic] vote."

The German-Americans wish to put a stop to all exportation of contraband because such action would result to the benefit of Germany. The pacificists are inclined to fall in with the suggestion, because they feebly believe it would be in the interest of 'Peace'—just as they are inclined heartily to favor any peace proposal, even though it should leave Belgium in Germany's hands and pave the way for certain renewal of the war.

The Colonel also suggested that the British and French governments capitalize upon reports of German war atrocities and objectives by publishing official versions of such stories. He warned, however, that he "should most heartily reprobate putting out any fact which was not absolutely established." With the deepening of his emotional involvement, he was to disregard that warning.

By the winter of 1915, indeed, TR had convinced himself that the United States should enter the war. Early in the year J. Medill Patterson, publisher of the *Chicago Tribune*, raised the question. "You even seem to want to get us into war on the Allied side," Patterson said. "Is it just Belgium, or do you feel that America itself is menaced?" TR replied that although Germany would probably not attack the United States at once, she would soon challenge American interests in the Caribbean. "In this way," he continued, "we would be thrown into hostilities with Germany sooner or later and with far less chance of success *than if we joined with the powers which are now fighting her.*"

TR was too astute to destroy his effectiveness by calling for war at a moment when Congress was enthusiastically endorsing the President against the proponents of preparedness. So he continued to hammer on preparedness, the embargo, and Mexico.

He chafed under his self-imposed fetters. "Lord, how I would like to be President in view of . . . the huge German-Irish element and the possible sinking of the *Lusitania*," he wrote the famed reporter, Cal O'Laughlin, on May 6, 1915. Less than twenty-four hours later the giant, unarmed British liner was torpedoed without warning off the coast of Ireland. More than eleven hundred men, women, and children, one hundred and twenty-eight of them American citizens, went down with the ship.

Roosevelt first heard of the *Lusitania* tragedy in a crowded courtroom at Syracuse where he was standing trial for libel against the notorious New York Republican boss, William Barnes, Jr. He made no comment. But that night he was called from his bed by a telephone call from an editor in New York City. "That's murder!" the Colonel exclaimed as the immensity of the disaster was borne upon him. "Will I make a statement? Yes, yes, I'll make it now. Just take this":

This represents not merely piracy, but piracy on a vaster scale of murder than old-time pirates ever practiced. . . . It is warfare against innocent men, women, and children, traveling on the ocean, and our own fellow countrymen and countrywomen, who are among the sufferers. It seems inconceivable that we can refrain from taking action in this matter, for we owe it not only to humanity but to our own national self-respect.

The next morning TR warned his lawyers that his statement had probably alienated the two German-Americans on the jury. "I cannot help it," he added. "There is a principle at stake here which is more vital to the American people than my personal welfare is to me." His fears proved groundless; the jury returned a verdict in his favor.

Meanwhile the President began the drawn-out process of note-writing which eventuated in Bryan's resignation as Secretary of State and Germany's temporary submission to his demands. The *Lusitania* disaster distressed Wilson more than Roosevelt, for his sensitivity to the value of life was far greater. The President believed, however, that the solution lay in a negotiated peace. He had no intention of asking Congress for a war resolution; and even if he had contemplated such action, he was warned by powerful Democratic leaders that the people would not support it. As a Kansas Progressive reported to TR, the Midwest's sense of outrage "died down as suddenly as it had risen." Even Cabot Lodge confined his public remarks to a general affirmation of the right of Americans to travel on belligerent ships, though he asserted privately that Wilson should sever relations and seize German vessels in American ports if the Imperial Government failed to make amends.

TR's contention that Wilson could have taken the nation into war at the time is thus open to challenge. In fact, Roosevelt was virtually alone in denouncing the President's noble declaration at the height of the crisis that "There is such a thing as a man being too proud to fight." America could not act on Wilson's theory, TR responded, "if it desires to retain or regain the position won for it by the men who fought under Washington and by the men who, in the days of Lincoln, wore the blue under Grant and the gray under Lee."

Roosevelt's personal letters were even more direct. "There is a chance of our going to war; but I don't think it is very much of a chance," he wrote his son Archie on May 19. "Wilson and Bryan . . . are both of them abject creatures and they won't go to war unless they are kicked into it. . . ." Had he been President, TR wrote Arthur Lee, "I would . . . have taken a stand which would have made the Germans either absolutely alter all their conduct or else put them into war with us." He added that "If the United States had taken this stand, in my judgment we would now have been fighting beside you."

The destruction of the *Lusitania* obscured the real issue—war in the national interest. From that fateful day on, TR concentrated almost solely on neutral rights. And though he never lost his conviction that the national interest demanded that the United States should fight on the Allies' side, the preservation of American rights now became an end in itself. On that issue Roosevelt based his renewed demands for preparedness; and upon it he eventually based his call for war. He sensed, at times, that he sounded extreme; that, as he phrased it to Arthur Lee, he was "making people think that I am a truculent and bloodthirsty person, endeavoring futilely to thwart able, dignified, humane Mr. Wilson in his noble plan to bring peace everywhere by excellently written letters." But he believed himself morally obligated to give the country the leadership the President had in his view defaulted. "I put the case as strongly as I can," he explained. "I speak as often as I think will do good."

During the next twenty-one months Roosevelt did more than any other citizen including the President of the United States to condition the American people to the coming of war. He became the avowed enemy of the rabid German- and Irish-Americans, of the agrarian isolationists and the urban pacifists, and of those men and women of good hope led by Hamilton Holt and William Howard Taft who anticipated Woodrow Wilson's great vision of an international order by forming the

League to Enforce Peace. He emerged, conversely, as the leader and spokesman of many of those same Republican conservatives who had rejected him in 1912.

The Colonel found boundless opportunities to fire verbal blasts at the despised professor in the White House during these twenty-one months. He tried to be fair. When Bryan resigned in protest against the second *Lusitania* note, he issued a statement pledging his "heartiest support" to Wilson in any steps he might take "to uphold the honor and the interests of this great Republic, which are bound up with the maintenance of democratic liberty and of a wise spirit of humanity among all the nations of mankind." But he was so completely out of sympathy that he could not appreciate the effectiveness of the President's note-writing. Nor would Roosevelt concede the political obstacles under which Wilson labored. For all TR's charges of cowardice and lack of leadership, Wilson courageously pursued policies that influential congressional blocs representing the Democratic and Republican agrarians, the urban Irish-Americans, and the Middle Western German-Americans bitterly opposed.

In these circumstances, the unrelieved stream of expletives that poured forth from Roosevelt's lips is defensible, if at all, only in the context of his larger aim—war in the national interest, and, as the generation that has witnessed Hitler's ultimate defilement of Bismarck's creation of "blood and iron" is now coming to believe, in the interest of the civilized world.

Tragically, however, the Colonel was also animated by that rampant nationalism and inflated conception of the national honor which forever prevented him from scaling the spiritual heights. The evidence is almost conclusive that he would have been just as extreme had the issue been merely the upholding of America's technical rights in Mexico, where the impoverished masses were then in rebellion against their aristocratic, clerical, and foreign overlords. Thus even as TR termed the President that "infernal skunk in the White House" and irritably dismissed one of his protests to Germany as "No. 11,765, series B," he excoriated the "feebleness, timidity, and vacillation" of Wilson's Mexican policy.

However unreasonable the Colonel's scorn for the President's diplomacy, his broadsides against Wilson's preparedness policy were justifiable, given the President's own assumptions. Wilson's decision to hold Germany to "strict accountability" destroyed the premises on which his original opposition to preparedness rested, i.e., the United States was not in danger of becoming involved in the war. From that moment on Wilson was obligated to prepare for the war that must come if Germany refused to back down. But in the face of all the warnings raised by Roosevelt and the other advocates of preparedness, the President moved with the speed of a glacier. The *Lusitania* was five months in the depths of the Atlantic before he made his first public call for defense increases, and his "strict accountability" policy was twelve months old before he took the issue forcefully to the people. And then it was largely to restate propositions that Roosevelt had been arguing for the seventeen preceding months.

Ironically, when the President finally did act on Roosevelt's logic, Lodge suggested that he was inspired by purely political considerations. "Wilson evidently has come to the conclusion that there is a rising popular feeling for preparedness and, seeing votes in it, is prepared to take it up," he wrote TR in the summer of 1915 as the President made his first tentative overtures toward preparedness. "Last winter he did everything he could to stop any improvement in the Army and Navy, sneered at Gardner and held him up as merely trying to make political capital because he was urging then, as he is now, the necessity of doing something."

There was probably more "political capital" in playing preparedness down than up, so intense was the antiwar sentiment throughout the country. But whatever the President's motives, his dramatic *volte-face* in the fall of 1915 confirmed Roosevelt's judgment on preparedness. From the fall of 1915 on, as Bryan lamented, Wilson spoke partially in Rooseveltian terms. The President failed, however, to act with Rooseveltian dispatch or to propose an army program commensurate with Roosevelt's conception of the nation's needs.

The Colonel quickly seized the opportunity afforded by Wilson's belated conversion to press a proposal he had never deemed possible of enactment in the past—universal military service. As the preparedness debate came to a head in the winter of 1915-16, he made a herculean effort to persuade the public and the administration to support it. "I would have the son of the multimillionaire and the son of the immigrant who came in steerage, sleep under the same dog-tent and eat the same grub," TR announced. "It would help mightily to a mutual comprehension of life." In the end, however, the fight for universal service failed. The "plain people" in the West and the South and organized labor throughout the country wanted no part of it; nor could Wilson, who was having to coerce and cajole Congress into passing a modest army program, have got it through.

Meanwhile, the administration's program was taking shape. Instead of calling a special session of Congress when he first convinced himself of the need for preparedness, the President waited for the regular session to convene in December, 1915. Then, on the recommendation of Secretary of War Lindley M. Garrison, he came out for creation of a volunteer force of 400,000 semireservists—the so-called Continental Army. Roosevelt at once charged that the proposal was inadequate; and when Lodge, the National Security League, and a number of prominent Republicans endorsed it in the realization that they could not expect more, he became furious. "I am so out of sympathy with what seems to be the prevailing currents of American opinion that I keep my judgment suspended . . . ," he wrote Lodge.

Apparently the Republicans are expecting to beat Wilson by keeping as neutral as he is as regards international duty, by supporting him in his sham-preparedness program and letting him pose before the country as the author of that program and as the champion of preparedness, and by then trusting that on the tariff and by some more or less secret understanding with the German vote they may be able to replace him by some one to whom the Germans won't object. . . .

Nevertheless, Lodge decided to compromise. "I have repeatedly said that this Administration has wasted one year in providing for the defense of the country and I want to prevent them if I can from wholly wasting another year," he explained to TR. "We may not be able to get much but every little counts."

As it turned out, he got very little; and he was fortunate to get that. Led by Claude Kitchin of North Carolina, Southern agrarians flatly refused to back the Continental Army scheme on the grounds that it was both militaristic and unnecessary. They insisted instead on expanding the inefficient National Guard. In this they were supported by the Republicans, most of whom lacked the courage to resist the Guard's powerful lobby. Wilson was thus forced to compromise or suffer the complete defeat of his program. He chose the first course, and when he did so Secretary of War Garrison resigned in protest. Garrison became in consequence a minor martyr to many preparationists, but not to TR.

A measure increasing the Regular Army's strength to about 220,000 officers and men finally went through after a protracted battle which saw Wilson bring all the force of his personality and power of his office to bear on the resentful agrarian-progressives in the House. Provision was also made to place the National Guard under federal supervision and to increase substantially its strength.

Roosevelt was too disgusted by the unconscionable delay— the National Defense Act of 1916 followed the outbreak of war by two years and the enunciation of the "strict accountability" policy by eighteen months—to appreciate the leadership the President had at long last exerted. Nor did he regard the measure as a victory for his own point of view. It was, he said, "as foolish and unpatriotic a bit of flintlock legislation as was ever put on the statute book. It is folly, and worse than folly, to pretend that the National Guard is an efficient second line of defense." He also felt that Congress' failure to provide for a capable reserve force repudiated implicitly the thesis that the United States should prepare for participation in the war then raging.

The naval bill was different. Wilson's request in December, 1915, for a vast construction program incited only moderate opposition; and after he gave a spectacular series of addresses climaxed in St. Louis, where German-American resentment of British naval power was strong, by an oratorical call for "incomparably the greatest navy in the world," the majority of Democrats and Republicans in Congress swung behind his recommendations. The result was the largest and most comprehensive naval program to that time. It was based on two propositions Roosevelt had been arguing since the start of the war: the United States should be prepared to negotiate from strength, and it should be capable of defending its far-flung strategic interests.

On one important issue only had TR failed the preparedness crusade. Agrarian-progressives and their allies in labor and reform circles had contended from the outset that the movement was inspired by big business in general and the munitions makers in particular. After Wilson went over to preparedness in 1915, they laid plans to impose the cost of the program upon those groups. Republicans "will vote for the biggest preparedness appropriation and then fight all methods to finance it . . . ," Kitchin resentfully wrote Bryan. "I am persuaded to think that when the income tax will have to pay for the increase in the army and navy, they will not be one-half so frightened over the future invasion by Germany."

Kitchin's analysis was overdrawn, but not excessively. When he pushed a bill in the summer of 1916 to raise the income tax in the upper brackets, institute a steeply graduated inheritance tax, and assess the profits of munitions makers as well, the overwhelming majority of Republicans in both houses of Congress, including Roosevelt's son-in-law, Nicholas Longworth, fought it bitterly.

That Lodge and other conservatives opposed a more equitable tax structure was natural. But that Roosevelt, in whom the Progressive leadership was vested until July, 1916, failed to sound a clarion call for a great democratization of effort (as he was to do after the United States entered the war) is one of the minor tragedies of his career. A generation was to pass before the naïve belief that the munitions makers and the House of Morgan had inspired the preparedness movement and American entry into the war would begin to down. TR could have struck it a blow at its birth.

How much the preparedness program of 1916 owed to Roosevelt's driving leadership can only be conjectured. His bitter strictures against Wilson, the pacifists, and the so-called hyphenated Americans provoked an adverse reaction among many moderates. His extremism also alienated many who agreed with his position. Yet he just as certainly roused the fears and inspired the courage of many, many others. There was not a preparedness society in the country that did not look to TR for leadership, not a major newspaper that was not moved to discuss editorially the issues he had raised; nor, probably, was there a politician in Washington who was not influenced one way or the other by his searing pronouncements. By 1916 "preparedness" and "Roosevelt" were virtually synonymous; and if the Colonel was not literally "The Bugle That Woke America," he was surely the leader of the corps that did.

Chapter 30

The Campaign for American Rights

The delegates [Progressives] who go to Chicago will have it in their power to determine the character of the administration which is to do or leave undone the mighty tasks of the next four years.

—Theodore Roosevelt

WHILE THE preparedness fight was coming to a head in the spring of 1916, Roosevelt was girding for yet another battle—one that would concentrate all his surging idealism and flaming patriotism, all his political artistry and personal venom, into a mighty drive to supplant Wilson with a President whose devotion to preparedness and American rights matched his own.

With each twist and turn in President Wilson's diplomacy during 1915 and early 1916 Roosevelt's urge to remove him from power had become more compelling. Months before the election of 1916 the Colonel had fastened upon a strategy that made suppression of his progressivism mandatory and led logically to his ultimate insult to the crusaders of 1912—the suggestion that they give Henry Cabot Lodge the Bull Moose presidential nomination. It was to win the Republican nomination for himself, and, failing in that, to force the Republicans to select a candidate who was "right" on the great issues of the times. He would use the Progressive party's potential strength at the polls as the bludgeon wherewith to achieve one or the other of these ends, and he would then take the party triumphantly back into the organization that had given it birth. The broad outlines of this strategy were disclosed as early as January, 1916, when TR compelled the Progressive National Committee to issue a statement calling on its members to return to the Republican fold in a supreme effort to turn out the Democrats.

If the Colonel was willing to draw the veil on the progressive movement in the vain hope that he could compel the

455

Republican party to rise to responsibilities that the Democrats had eschewed, he was nonetheless determined that his own nomination, if it came, would come in full recognition of his views on preparedness and Americanism. He fervently wanted the nomination. "Don't imagine that I wouldn't like to be at the White House this minute," he exploded that winter. "This was my year—1916 was my high twelve," he wrote with heavy heart after Wilson had been re-elected. "In four years I will be out of it. . . . I did not want to run in 1912. Circumstances compelled me to run then. This year it was different."

But except for the deference to the Old Guard's economic prejudices implicit in his failure to endorse the agrarian-progressives' tax program, Roosevelt cast politics to the winds in the spring of 1916. In March he in effect invited the American people to elect him President and then go to war. "I . . . say that it would be a mistake to nominate me unless the country has in its mood something of the heroic—unless it feels not only devotion to ideals but the purpose measurably to realize those ideals in action," he declared in a public statement. And in May he took his militant message to the Middle West, the seedbed of the nation's three great isolationist strains—ruralism, pacifism, and German-Americanism.

Roosevelt went first to Detroit, where Henry Ford's pacifist views had received a long, full hearing. There he gave a rousing speech for universal military service interrupted by a slender woman who stood up in the balcony, American flag in hand, and cried out to thunderous applause: "I have two sons. I offer them." Gravely, the Colonel replied: "Madam, if every mother in the country would make the same offer, there would be no need for any mother to send her sons to war."

After being engulfed by a roaring crowd of fifty thousand at Kansas City, TR then turned east to St. Louis. More furiously than ever before, he lashed the German-Americans. "It is our purpose this fall," he declared in that German-American center on the Mississippi, "to elect an American president and not a viceroy of the German emperor." One week later the Republican convention, its ranks heavily laden with German-Americans and its managers prepared to defer to German-American sensibilities at any cost, convened at Chicago.

The Colonel's performance had destroyed his last slim hope for the presidency, and he knew that it had. "If there had been a chance of winning the Republicans' support," he remarked after his return to Oyster Bay, "I killed it by my tour of the West."

In reality, there had been little chance. A small group of Easterners were willing to let bygones be bygones. And a great host of rank and filers wanted the Colonel. Just two spontaneous outbursts would punctuate the Republican convention the following week, one when a speaker inadvertently mentioned Roosevelt's name, the other when it was placed in nomination. But the Midwestern professionals had no intention of letting Roosevelt capture the heights. Long before TR dropped his hat on the edge of the ring, they had decided to nominate a man tinged with enough progressivism to be acceptable to the Bull Moosers, orthodox enough on the tariff to keep contributions from manufacturers rolling in, and mild enough on the war to appease the German-Americans. They went to the Supreme Court of the United States to find him.

"I wish I knew something about [Charles Evans] Hughes," Representative Gardner had written his daughter in January, 1916, as the movement for the jurist's nomination had first begun to gather momentum. "All I know is that he wears a beard and stopped horseracing in New York. . . . The machine is getting ready to nominate . . . [him]." Roosevelt added in May that the movement for Hughes "is primarily a politicians' movement made for the very reason that no one knows where he stands, and therefore represents the ideal, dear to the soul of the politician, of the candidate against whom no one can say anything." Gardner and Roosevelt were not far wrong. The Republican party would have to wait until it met in convention on June 7 to find out what its leading candidate stood for, and even then it would not quite be certain. Nor would it know much more after he had campaigned for four months.

Meanwhile, some Republican leaders tried to pave the way for Roosevelt's endorsement of the Republican candidate by framing a platform consonant with the Colonel's views. Before they entrained for Chicago, Lodge and Borah drew up an aggressive document which they submitted for approval to George Perkins, who served as TR's liaison man. When they reached Chicago, however, they found the majority too intent on appeasing the German-Americans and rural isolationists to accept their draft. Resignedly, they rewrote it.

The first plank to go was one for universal military service. "They all admitted, readily enough, that we must come to universal military training, but they did not think the people were ripe for it, and were afraid to risk it," Lodge explained to TR. "I did what I could with the aid of Jimmy Wadsworth." Calls for an army of 250,000 and a navy second to none were also deleted. As finally adopted, the planks on foreign policy paid lip-service to the Colonel's philosophy; but they ignored most of his charges against Wilson's diplomacy. They also called for "a straight and honest neutrality between the belligerents," the antithesis of what Roosevelt, Lodge, and the Eastern interventionists desired. Not without perception did a Progressive national committeeman write TR that the Republican platform measured "up to your demands to about the same degree the Kaiser's answers did to Wilson's notes."

While the Republicans were meeting in the Coliseum, the Bull Moosers were staging a remarkable demonstration of fealty to TR in the Chicago Auditorium. Large numbers of Progressives—probably the overwhelming majority of the convention—opposed war, whether against Germany or Mexico. But their affection for the Colonel was so great and their realization that they could not survive without him so acute, that they prepared to swallow the bitter with the sweet. Protesting only in undertones, they endorsed a platform that evaded the critical taxation issue, that only perfunctorily endorsed the memorable reform planks of 1912, and that called for universal military service, a regular army of 250,000, and the second largest navy in the world (TR continued to believe that Great Britain should have the largest). Angrily, the *New Republic* summed it up:

The platform of an ostensibly progressive party fails to utter one single conviction which need cause any uneasiness to the established order. It does not tamper with the foundations of political and economic power. . . . Militant progressivism is converted into a nebulous nationalism which can be made to mean all things to all men.

The blackest hour was yet to come. The Republican professionals in the Coliseum could neither forget 1912 nor ignore the seething hatred the German-Americans now felt for the Colonel. In the face of a minor boom for Roosevelt on the lower echelons, they resolutely held to their plan to nominate Hughes, who remained substantially uncommitted on the great questions of the times. TR was outraged. "I guess there is no need to tell you," he said to Medill McCormick over a private line connecting Sagamore Hill with George Perkins' rooms in the Blackstone Hotel, "that I think Hughes a good deal of a skunk in the attitude he has taken." He would "breathe a sigh of relief" if he were not nominated himself, he added when Lodge came on the wire, ". . . but in international matters and in the present situation I know I am worth two of Hughes."

The Colonel's contempt for Hughes proved less than consuming. To be sure, he vehemently reiterated his opposition to the jurist in telephone conversations with Perkins and other Progressive and Republican leaders. And he even offered the notorious Boies Penrose, who was "right" on preparedness and Americanism if little else, the majority leadership of the Senate in return for his support in the Republican convention. He refused, however, to force the G.O.P.'s hand by saying that he would again run on the Progressive ticket if Hughes received the Republican nomination. Gifford Pinchot implored him to do so. "We have been playing poker with them," he heatedly asserted, ". . . without chips in that direction." But Roosevelt brusquely dismissed the proposal. "I wish to say this," he said to his forester friend when he again raised the issue, ". . . there is a very wide difference between making a young Colonel and a retired Major General lead a forlorn hope." He added later that he would refuse to support Hughes until "he repudiated the German-American alliance," but that he was "not going to dictate to that Convention as if I were a Tammany Chieftain."

In point of fact, the Colonel was already dictating to the Progressive convention. The Bull Moosers wanted Roosevelt and no one else, and they were straining powerfully to nominate him and have done with it. But against the urgent entreaties of Pinchot, William Allen White, and others, TR insisted that Perkins prevent the Progressives from balloting until after the Republicans had made their nomination. Perkins, who was later to be charged by the western radicals with destroying the Progressive party, dutifully followed his leader's instructions. By Friday night, June 9, however, it was apparent that he could not control the delegates much longer. The Bull Moosers were going to nominate Roosevelt the next morning regardless of his or Perkins' protests; and the Republicans were just as surely going to bestow their accolade on Hughes.

In desperation, Perkins put Nicholas Murray Butler on the

phone with the Colonel at 3 A.M. Saturday to discuss alternative candidates. "How do you do, President of Columbia College," TR remarked when the pompous educator came on the wire. He then dismissed Butler's three suggestions—Elihu Root, Philander C. Knox, and former Vice-President Charles W. Fairbanks—and countered with Leonard Wood. "Of course he would understand very speedily that the tariff and such matters were entirely outside his realm and would get on the Army and Navy question and Americanism at once," Roosevelt added. "He wouldn't have to do as Brother Hughes will have to do—improvise." Although White had said earlier that Wood's selection would "suit me beautifully," Perkins blanched. "I think it was a very grave mistake to suggest Wood," he admonished the Colonel a little later. "He is not acceptable to anybody. He is a military man. It puts you in a bad light." Roosevelt saw Perkins' point. "It has been rejected and I will not follow it up at all," he answered.

Meanwhile Roosevelt suggested Cabot Lodge as his alternative candidate. Perkins again demurred, proposing instead that the Progressive convention adopt a resolution of opposition to Hughes and then nominate Roosevelt as Pinchot and White had earlier urged. Vehemently, the Colonel rejected the idea. "That is one of the most extraordinary things I have ever heard," he exclaimed. "I want to say right here, although you may not agree with me, that I am sure I was right in speaking of Wood and Lodge."

Perkins thereupon backed down, conceding that Lodge was "the only man familiar with the international situation" who might be acceptable to both conventions. "I know Lodge's record like a book," TR replied. "There has never been anything against it at any time, except, of course, George, that he does not have as advanced views as you and I."

Perkins remained unenthusiastic even so. Early that morning he and other Progressive leaders made a last effort to dissuade TR from submitting Lodge's name to the Progressive convention. Roosevelt proved implacable. "I do not ask our people to accept one of the burglars," he testily told former Governor Robert Bass of New Hampshire. "I do not ask them to accept any man who isn't of the highest character and who does not stand absolutely square on the issues of the day." That ended it.

Late that morning the faithful Perkins went sorrowfully be-

fore the Bull Moose convention and read a statement from
Roosevelt warmly commending Lodge as one of the "staunchest fighters for different measures of economic reform in the
direction of justice." As he finished, a great gasp of incredulity
went up from the floor. The delegates felt that Roosevelt "had
done something not merely fantastic but grossly insulting,"
Amos Pinchot recalled. "They had been kept in the dark,
treated like children—pawns in a game into the nature of
which they had had no inkling. I saw men and women sitting
as if stunned, like unjustly punished children, with tears
streaming down their cheeks." With catcalls and boos filling
the air, they shouted down a new appeal from Perkins that
they nominate Hughes. They were done with deals, or so they
thought. Deliberately, and with a touch of irony in his voice,
Bainbridge Colby thereupon placed Roosevelt's name in nomination. Hiram Johnson seconded it in a speech calling on TR
to rise to his responsibilities. Then, three minutes after the
Hughes movement reached floodtide in the Republican convention, the Progressives angrily and overwhelmingly gave
their unqualified nomination to Theodore Roosevelt. Roosevelt's response came by telegraph that afternoon, Saturday,
June 10.

"I cannot accept it at this time," the message read. "I do not
know the attitude of the candidate of the Republican party
toward the vital questions of the day. Therefore, if you desire
an immediate decision, I must decline the nomination." Roosevelt suggested, however, that his conditional refusal to run be
submitted to the national committee. "If Mr. Hughes's statements, when he makes them, shall satisfy the committee . . .
they can . . . treat my refusal as definitely accepted."

The Colonel had partially carried his objective, but at the
cost of wounds that would never heal. His artfulness had been
bared as rarely before. And his commendation of Lodge as
"one of the staunchest fighters . . . for economic reform . . ."
lives on as the hollow mockery of a once glorious crusade.
Cabot Lodge was no black reactionary, nor even an unyielding
defender of the status quo. But if his heart ever throbbed with
the passion for social justice and economic reform that inspired the Bull Moose legions and their leader, its beat has
never been recorded. That very summer he failed to support
the child labor bill that Wilson drove through Congress.

Yet, as Amos Pinchot, whom TR soon consigned to the

Progressive party's "lunatic fringe," later conceded, the circumstances were unique. No man can gainsay that in Roosevelt's mind the cause that now enveloped him was not noble; that preparedness for war did not transcend all other issues. The Colonel may have suppressed his progressivism more than was necessary; and he undoubtedly allowed his contempt for Wilson to becloud his judgment of the President. But he was absolutely faithful to his own conception of the main issues. More than any other major political figure of the era, Henry Cabot Lodge stood as one with him on those issues. That Roosevelt should have turned to Lodge in the hour of crisis is as understandable from his point of view as it was unforgivable from that of the Progressives. As Amos Pinchot wrote in the reflective mood of a later year, "There are generally extenuating circumstances for every political act in which the element of betrayal seems present." The Colonel's treatment of the Bull Moosers "was bad; at the time . . . unforgivable."

And yet, in the light cast on these events by Roosevelt's own peculiar philosophy, there was a certain justification. . . . He believed that the most important thing in the world was for America to enter the war on the side of the Allies. Comparatively speaking, domestic issues did not exist for him. He was wrapped up in the war. . . . In 1916 Wilson was a pacifist.

. . . Roosevelt felt—and how much his personal animosity toward Wilson warped his judgment cannot be told—that the essential thing was to get rid of Wilson. For him to run as a Progressive would have meant to re-elect Wilson. . . .

There was also a degree of logic in TR's eventual acceptance of Hughes, whom he had earlier passed off as "another Wilson with whiskers." The Colonel was bitter that Hughes had been nominated without showing his colors. "A more sordid set of creatures than the Republicans who nominated Hughes could not be imagined," he angrily wrote. "They are a trifle better than the corrupt and lunatic wild asses of the desert who seem most influential in democratic councils, under the lead of that astute, unprincipled and physically cowardly demagogue Wilson; but they are a sorry lot." As always, however, Roosevelt looked to the future. He took hope in reports that Hughes would appoint Elihu Root Secretary of State. He held that Hughes's understanding of the progressive philosophy was at least "far ahead of all the other leading Republicans." And he persuaded himself that Hughes was "an able, upright man" capable of learning with "comparative quickness" and possessed of the temperament to "rise to a very big height" in time of crisis.

The Colonel had also had a gratifying luncheon conversation with Hughes on June 28, two days after the Progressive National Committee reluctantly agreed to support the Republican nominee. "I believe as you do that he will make a straight-out fight for preparedness and national defense," he confided to Lodge soon afterward. "He told me he personally believed in universal service, but was doubtful as to the expediency of coming out for it at this time." Furthermore, Roosevelt was outraged by the Democrats' comportment at St. Louis, where ex-Governor Martin Glynn of New York had electrified the convention and given the party its campaign theme with a rolling reiteration of the thesis that "We didn't go to war" every time an American right had been violated in the past.

TR's hard-forced enthusiasm for the Republican candidate was destined to be short-lived, for the unwritten terms of Hughes's candidacy made a forthright campaign impossible. "To satisfy Mr. Roosevelt, Hughes must quarrel with the Old Guard," Pulitzer's *St. Louis Post Dispatch* pointed out:

To satisfy the pro-Germans he must quarrel with the pro-British, who demand war with Germany. To satisfy Wall Street, he must quarrel with the Western radicals. To satisfy the jingoes and the Munitions Trust, he must quarrel with most of the country. To satisfy privilege and plutocracy, he must quarrel with the people. Even as a candidate Mr. Hughes dare not have a policy, because to have a policy is to antagonize one element or another of his followers.

In spite of a recurring throat condition that made speech excruciatingly painful, Roosevelt agreed to campaign for Hughes. It proved a difficult chore. As TR confessed midway through the campaign, "it has been no light task for me in my speeches to avoid seeming to clash with Hughes and, at the same time, not to go back on any of the things for which I stand." On the whole, however, the Colonel gave full and free expression to his views on the hyphenates, universal military training, and European and Mexican policy. Requested to confine his remarks to the tariff at one point, he exploded: "I did not come here to talk tariff, the crowd did not come here to hear me talk tariff, and I'll be hanged if I do talk tariff. I'll talk what is in me."

Only on intervention was Roosevelt inconsistent. Sometimes he argued that a firm policy would have prevented the *Lusitania's* destruction. But more often he implied that the United States should have gone to war when the British liner was torpedoed. In Battle Creek, Michigan, he charged that "men who now with timid hearts and quavering voices praise Mr. Wilson for having kept us out of war are the spiritual heirs of the Tories of 1776, and the Copperheads of 1864." And in Denver he declared that he would have gone to war in a minute had he been President when the *Lusitania* was torpedoed. Elsewhere TR asserted that when he was President other nations knew he was not "too proud to fight." He also blasted the professional hyphenated Americans to the distress of harried Republican managers.

Roosevelt reached his nadir at Cooper Union on November 3. Unable longer to control himself, he cast aside his manuscript near the end of his speech and remarked that the President was then visiting his summer home, Shadow Lawn. He added in a voice nearly breaking with emotion:

> There should be shadows now at Shadow Lawn; the shadows of the men, women and children who have risen from the ooze of the ocean bottom and from graves in foreign lands; the shadows of the helpless whom Mr. Wilson did not dare protect lest he might have to face danger; the shadows of babies gasping pitifully as they sank under the waves; the shadows of women outraged and slain by bandits. . . . Those are the shadows proper for Shadow Lawn; the shadows of deeds that were never done; the shadows of lofty words that were followed by no action; the shadows of the tortured dead.

There was neither cant nor hypocrisy nor even conscious partisanship in those cruel words. In the minds of Theodore Roosevelt and thousands of super patriots the country over, Woodrow Wilson had failed to uphold the national honor as it was then construed.

The Colonel had given more of himself than he had planned. Yet he had not given quite enough. Unlike Wilson, who understandably believed that he had kept the country out of war, or Hughes, who mistakenly believed that a firmer policy would continue to prevent war, Roosevelt stood for war. But the war he was asking for was more for the maintenance of American rights than the preservation of the Anglo-Franco-American balance of power or even of international law. Not once during the campaign did TR state his rational conviction: the United States should have been fighting on the Allies side regardless of the submarine issue.

It is easy now to say that Roosevelt and his friends should have stated their objectives fully. And it is probably true that their failure to treat the war in a larger context than American rights contributed to the disillusionment of the postwar generation. But that only underscores the realities of 1916. The American people were wracked with dissension over the submarine issue; Roosevelt, almost alone, had spoken frankly to that question. Had it not been for his scorching strictures, the nation might never have been roused to a war pitch. He had led the country just as far as it was willing to be led, or dragged. He could not have done more and maintained a position of leadership. As he exclaimed again and again, "A nation is not wholly admirable unless in time of stress it will go to war for a great ideal wholly unconnected with its immediate national interest."

The Colonel's postelection comments illuminate the convictions that had inspired him. "I was grimly accepting, at great personal cost, a man whose election would have been hailed as a great personal triumph over me by the stand-patters," he wrote William Allen White, "because I felt that Wilson's reelection would be a damage to the moral fibre of the American people." Roosevelt agreed that Hughes's failure to talk progressivism had cost him the election; that the West "fixed its eyes on Hughes' pussy-footing and lack of vision, and on the machine and reactionary support of him." And he heartily approved the movement to "progressivize" the Republican party launched by White, Gifford Pinchot, James Garfield, Harold Ickes and other Progressive leaders. But he was distraught over the nation's failure to respond to the American rights issue and the character of the Democrats' campaign. "Hiram Johnson wrote me that in California one large factor in the vote for Wilson was the 'he kept us out of war cry,' especially affecting the women," TR explained to White. "This is yellow, my friend! plain yellow!"

During the interim between the election and Woodrow Wilson's classic call for war on April 2, 1917, TR's impatience with the President's failure to read a great moral issue into the Allied cause grew greater daily. When accounts of the deportation of tens of thousands of Belgian workers to Germany were published in the United States in late December, Roosevelt joined Root, Bacon, Stimson and others in urging Wilson to act. And when the President presciently warned the world on January 22 that there must be "a peace without victory," that a victor's peace would rest "only as upon quicksand," he stormed furiously. "Any peace, which does not mean victory over those responsible for these outrages, will set back the march of civilization," he wrote.

Any announcement by the United States, that Belgium and Germany are fighting for the same thing, is a falsehood, and by inference an approval of wickedness. Any announcement that the United States desires peace to come without a victory which will restore Belgium to her people, puts the United States in an attitude of aiding and abetting international immorality, and ranks this people against the cause of international righteousness.

Wilson's indecisiveness after the severance of relations with Germany on February 4 further infuriated the Colonel. "I don't think he is capable of understanding the emotion of patriotism, or the emotion of real pride in one's country," he wrote Hiram Johnson on February 17. "Whether we will really go to war or not, Heaven only knows, and certainly Mr. Wilson doesn't."

The Zimmerman Note was the final blow. Informed by newspapermen of Germany's proposal that Mexico recapture its "lost territory in New Mexico, Texas, and Arizona" in return for an alliance if the United States entered the war, TR turned a stream of expletives on the President. "Boys," he said, after recovering and flashing his irresistible grin, "I'm sorry, but you have now heard some of the more or less—mostly less—justly famed Roosevelt profanity. . . . I don't apologize for it—this man is enough to make the saints and the angels, yes, and the apostles, swear, and I would not blame them. My God, why doesn't he do something? It's beyond me."

Roosevelt refrained from attacking the President publicly for a few more weeks. As he explained to Lodge on February 28, "I have applied for leave to raise a division, [and] I doubt the propriety of doing so." He added that he wished "Root would speak up unequivocally, as he thinks." "I am as yet holding in," he wrote Lodge two weeks later, "but if he does not go to war with Germany I shall skin him alive." Fearful that the President would hold indefinitely to armed neutrality or resort only to limited naval warfare, Roosevelt finally decided to speak out. "I shall write a brief and courteous, but unequivocal statement of our present condition in the face of Germany," he confided to the Massachusetts Senator on March 18. "I have kept silent for seven weeks. Whatever the effect on myself, I think that the situation now calls for some statement by me."

Two days later TR went to the Union League Club where he had been flailed as a revolutionist in another era. He failed now to refer directly to the President or to the events of the preceding two and one-half years. But he argued persuasively and eloquently that the United States was hiding behind Great Britain's shield. "Let us dare to look the truth in the face," he declared. "Let us dare to use our own strength in our own defense and strike hard for our national interest and honor. There is no question about 'going to war.' Germany is already at war with us. The only question for us to decide is whether we shall make war nobly or ignobly."

Meanwhile the tragedy was playing out at 1600 Pennsylvania Avenue. On March 20, the day Roosevelt issued his war call before the Union League Club, President Wilson listened to his Cabinet argue that war existed in fact and advise him to call Congress into session on April 2 to declare it. Wilson was hesitant. "Every reform we have won will be lost if we go into this war," predicted the man whose administration had implemented so much of Roosevelt's platform of 1912. "War means autocracy. The people we have unhorsed will inevitably come into the control of the country for we shall be dependent upon the steel, oil, and financial magnates. They will run the nation."

The tortured President continued to search his soul through the last days of March. Finally, after reluctantly concluding that "the right is more precious than peace," he wrote his war message and sent for Frank Cobb of the *New York World.* Cobb reached the White House in the early hours of the morning of April 2. And there, in a scene that will live forever in the minds of sensitive men, Wilson poured out his feelings.

" 'Once lead this people into war,' the President said, the

manuscript of his war message on his desk, 'and they'll forget there was ever such a thing as tolerance. To fight you must be brutal and ruthless, and the spirit of ruthless brutality will enter into the very fibre of our national life, infecting Congress, the courts, the policeman on the beat, the man in the street.' Conformity would be the only virtue, said the President, and every man who refused to conform would have to pay the penalty.

"He thought the Constitution would not survive it; that free speech and the right of assembly would go. He said a nation couldn't put its strength into war and keep its head level; it had never been done.

" 'If there is any alternative, for God's sake let's take it,' he exclaimed."

That night, April 2, 1917, the President asked a joint session of Congress to declare a war "for democracy, for the right of those who submit to have a voice in their own Governments, for the rights and liberties of small nations, for a universal dominion of right by such a concert of free peoples as shall bring peace and safety to all nations and make the world itself at last free."

Four days later the United States entered the war upon the outcome of which Theodore Roosevelt also believed and had longer, though more chauvinistically, maintained, the survival of freedom depended.

Chapter 31

The Last Battle

*I have no message for France; I have already
given her the best I had.*

—Theodore Roosevelt

WOODROW WILSON's anguished decision to take the American
people into war was Theodore Roosevelt's ultimate vindication. As his countrymen waged war on the Imperial German
Government during the next eighteen months, the Colonel
gave heroically of his time, his energy, and his health in support of their efforts. He emerged as the recognized leader of
the administration's constructive, and until the coming of
peace, loyal opposition. And for one fleeting moment at the
start he even stood as one with the Democratic President.

"The President's great message of April 2 was literally un-
answerable," the Colonel wrote in the *Metropolitan*. "All good
Americans will back . . . [him] with single-minded loyalty in
every movement he makes to uphold American honor, defend
American rights, and strike hard and effectively in return for
the brutal wrong-doings of the German Government."

But the wounds had cut too deep for the unity long to endure. Wilson's message was "a terrible indictment of everything he has done and said, and everything he has left undone
and unsaid, during the past two years and eight months,"
Roosevelt soon wrote James Bryce. "I will forgive him everything if he will see that America fights not only with swords
but with hatchets also."

If Roosevelt demanded total submission before he would
forgive, Woodrow Wilson demanded that and more. The President was neither so cold and arrogant nor so inflexible and
domineering as his critics have often portrayed him. The British
Foreign Secretary, Arthur Balfour, found him "firm, modest,
restrained, eloquent, well-informed, and convincing." And
others found him similarly appealing. It is even said that his
sense of his own dignity was less than TR's. Wilson "did not
seem to value it, while Roosevelt sometimes overvalued his,"

wrote one who knew them both. Yet the failings that mark those who value ideas above men were surely there. The passing of a generation and the waging of a Second World War were to see the triumphant resurgence of the President's noble ideals, but they would not see the vindication of his remorseless Calvinism. The long chain of broken friendships that he left behind—the awe, loyalty, and even reverence often lived on—contrasts starkly with the web of affection that even the "lying thieves" of 1912 spun over the grave of the Colonel. Roosevelt never suffered from Wilson's inability to thrive on the give and take of strong men; nor was TR, for all his ruthlessness in the heat of conflict, unable to forgive and forget once the lines had shifted.

The first clash between Roosevelt and Wilson after the nation's entrance into the war was personal, though it had powerful public overtones. For more than a year TR had been drawing up plans for a volunteer division. It was to be officered on the higher levels by regulars and on the lower echelons by business and professional men. ("The broncho-buster type will be very much lacking," the Colonel asserted.) After six weeks it was to be sent to France for combat training in order, TR explained, "that it could be sent to the front in the shortest possible time."

As war impended in the winter of 1917, Roosevelt had bombarded Secretary of War Newton D. Baker with letters and telegrams requesting authorization to act. He offered to finance the division privately until Congress took action. And he called Baker's attention to his record in the Spanish-American War— "I served in the first fight as commander first of the right wing and then of the left wing of the regiment; in the next, the big fight, as Colonel of the Regiment; and I ended the campaign in command of the brigade." "I wish respectfully to point out that I am a retired Commander in Chief of the United States Army, and eligible to any position of command over American troops to which I may be appointed." But to little avail. "This is one of the most extraordinary documents I have ever read!" Wilson commented after examining one of TR's more urgent communications. "Thank you for letting me undergo the discipline of temper involved in reading it in silence!"

Finally, on April 10, Wilson granted the former President an hour-long interview. Both men exuded cordiality, the President's secretary, Joseph P. Tumulty, reported. They exchanged anecdotes and "seemed to enjoy what the Colonel was accustomed to call a 'bully' time." They also sparred. TR told Wilson his war message would rank "with the great state papers of Washington and Lincoln" *if he made it good.* The President explained that his desk was piled high with applications from assorted Indian fighters, Texas Rangers, and Southern "colonels" though none, of course, of Roosevelt's eminence. He outlined his plans for a selective service law (which TR agreed to support and did support). And he remarked that the war in France was no "Charge of the Light Brigade."

The Colonel left in high spirits, thumping Tumulty on the back and promising him a place in the division (but not, he explained to a confidant, near headquarters where Tumulty could report his observations to the White House). "I had a plain talk with the President, and if it were anyone but Mr. Wilson, I'd say that it is all fixed up," TR exclaimed on his return to Sagamore Hill. "Yes," the President said after Roosevelt breezed out of his office, "he is a great big boy. I was . . . charmed by his personality. There is a sweetness about him that is very compelling. You can't resist the man."

Roosevelt had also talked with the Secretary of War while in Washington. At the instance of Franklin D. Roosevelt, whose preparedness views had been closer to TR's than to Wilson's, Baker called on the Colonel shortly after TR saw the President. He found him surrounded by senators and friends discussing plans to have the selective service bill provide for volunteer divisions. "[TR] came out when I arrived and greeted me cordially, put his hand through my arm and took me upstairs to one of the bedrooms," Baker recalled. Roosevelt then repeated the reasons for granting his request. The Secretary made no promises although Roosevelt felt that he "could twist him about my finger could I have him about for a while." The trouble with Baker, TR later wrote, is that he has a blind faith in the General Staff and graduates of the Military Academy. "He does not realize that a muttonhead, after an education at West Point—or Harvard—is a muttonhead still. . . . The Secretary has changed his position so rapidly he reminds me of the flywheel of an engine. But," he added of the courageous ex-reform mayor of Cleveland, "the dear little fellow isn't to blame."

Inevitably, the "Roosevelt Division" became a *cause célèbre.* Applications for service poured in by the tens of thousands as a swelling volume of opinion called on Wilson to give the old warrior his rein. "The appearance of an ex-President of the United States leading American soldiers to the battle front," wrote "Marse" Henry Watterson in his *Louisville Courier-Journal,* would "electrify the world." The battered hero of the Marne, Marshal Joffre, who headed a French mission to the United States that spring, agreed that it would; and when he said as much at a formal dinner in his honor, the State Department censored newspaper accounts of his remarks. Meanwhile passage of the selective service bill was delayed for two weeks while Lodge and other Roosevelt men in the Senate amended it to authorize volunteer divisions of troops above and below the draft ages. "It is a pity," General Pershing commented privately, "that . . . [Roosevelt] has not been able to take a broader view . . . but I presume a man's ambition eventually will warp his view of things."

The amended selective service measure became law on May 18, 1917, and TR at once telegraphed the President for authority "to raise two divisions for immediate service at the front." Wilson replied, as Hagedorn writes, in words chosen "to reduce the patriot to the romantic adventurer." The President said that though he would like to pay Roosevelt the compliment, "this is not the time for compliment or for any action not calculated to contribute to the immediate success of the war." He added that the "business now in hand is undramatic, practical, and of scientific definiteness and precision." And so in a sense it was.

Yet, as the man soon to emerge as the "Tiger of France" understood all too well, "scientific definiteness and precision" were no substitute for courage, inspiration, and hope. In a graphic open letter to Wilson published in his Paris newspaper *L'Homme Enchaîné,* Georges Clemenceau summed up the case for TR:

> . . . in all candor, that at the present moment there is in France one name which sums up the beauty of American intervention. It is the name of Roosevelt, your predecessor, even your rival but with whom there can now be no other rivalry than heartening success . . . [Roosevelt] is an idealist, imbued with simple vital idealism. Hence his influence on the crowd, his prestige, to use the right expression. . . . The cause of humanity, which is also your cause, will owe to . . . [the soldiers of France] something approaching a miracle. . . . believe me—send them Roosevelt.

Most of the announced reasons for refusing Roosevelt's request appear untenable today. Selective service was a rational application of democratic doctrine, but its effectiveness hardly hinged on the rejection of all volunteer forces. The only other living ex-President of the United States, William Howard Taft, was prepared to serve in a nonmilitary capacity (and also to wish Theodore "no worse luck than to be sick in bed while Woodrow runs his war"). Neither was TR so inflexible that he would not have agreed to staff his divisions with other than the regular officers he had chosen—the finest in the army. Even the argument that Roosevelt lacked military experience breaks down before the facts, which TR heatedly urged upon Baker, that the regulars would have to undergo almost as much training in the new warfare as the draftees and that he was prepared to accept a subordinate command. On the evidence then available, many a general officer was tragically less qualified for command than Roosevelt, one of the most brilliant administrators ever to occupy the White House. There was plausibility, moreover, in a painful statement TR made Ambassador Jusserand shortly before the issue was settled. "I am too old. . . . I should crack. But," Roosevelt continued,

I could arouse the belief that America was coming. I could show the Allies what was on the way and then, if I did crack, the President could use me to come back and rouse more enthusiasm here and take some more men over. That is what I am good for now, and what difference would it make if I cracked or not?

One factor was not irrelevant—the Colonel's irrepressibility. As the President remarked to a luncheon guest the day he rejected Roosevelt's final appeal, "it would be dangerous to send over someone likely to try to show Europe how it should manage its affairs." TR himself adverted to it indirectly by assuring Jusserand that "The President need not fear me politically." But could the Colonel have kept that faith? Would he have accepted Wilson's decision not to drive on to Berlin in November, 1918, as Pershing and Foch wanted to do? Could he have been silent or discreet about a dozen other political-military matters? Could he have comported himself as an Eisenhower rather than as a MacArthur? General Hugh L. Scott, then Chief of Staff, thought not. "Consider what a ridiculous figure you would cut," he warned Secretary Baker, "attempting to punish Mr. Roosevelt by court-martial!"

The episode was as unfortunate as it was inevitable. It exposed the President's cold self-possession. ("I really think the best way to treat Mr. Roosevelt is to take no notice of him," he told Tumulty. "That breaks his heart and is the best punishment that can be administered.") It accentuated TR's hatred of Wilson. And it sharpened the impression that the Colonel was basically a military adventurer.

The impression was not inaccurate. The romance and glory of the battlefield still burned bright in TR, and even before the United States entered the war he had written William Allen White that "I think I could do this country most good by dying in a reasonably honorable fashion, at the head of my division in the European War." Now, in the bitterness and frustration of Wilson's denial of his heart's desire, he projected himself into the military careers of his four sons. "I am immensely delighted, . . . for I had no idea that you could make a *regular* regiment in a line position," he wrote Ted, who had been given command of the 1st battalion of the 26th regiment of the First Division. "I think it was most wise of . . . [Kermit] to get transferred to the armored car service," he told his second son's wife. "Kermit is a natural officer of the fighting line." "One of your Generals gave . . . [Archie] the Croix de Guerre," he wrote Clemenceau in March, 1918, "and I am prouder of his having received it than of my having been President."

Just as the warrior sent forth his sons to battle to prove their courage and share with him the greatest satisfaction he ever knew, so did the statesman send them forth to perform their national duty. "We must dare to be great; and we must realize that greatness is the fruit of toil and sacrifice and high courage," wrote the man whose career had come as close, probably, as any political leader's could to exemplifying those values. The ultimate measure of national character, he wrote in a typically romantic-realistic vein, was war: "No qualities called out by a purely peaceful life stand on a level with those stern and virile virtues which move the men of stout heart and strong hand who uphold the honor of their flag in battle." What anguish would have been his had he not had four sons to give when the offer of his own life was declined!

Meanwhile the Colonel threw himself into the battle of the

home front with a zeal unsurpassed in all his career. He briefly considered offering his services to Wilson in any capacity. But partly because he feared "the President would treat me as an importunate and self-seeking beggar," he decided not to. He also decided not to ask General Pershing for command of a brigade of regulars. "I am not certain that to give it to me would mean a service to any one except myself," he explained, "whereas if allowed to raise four divisions of volunteers I would be doing a service of prime importance both to this country and to the Allies." Instead, he cast himself in the roles of preacher-at-large to the American people and critic-in-general of the Wilson administration.

Roosevelt characteristically chose the *Kansas City Star*, which served the heartland of isolationism, as his main outlet. Between September, 1917, and January, 1919, he wrote more than one hundred syndicated articles for its pages. He also made repeated appearances on the public platform, often while wracked with pain from the malignant malarial fever he had suffered in Brazil and from abscesses of his thigh and ear. In the fall of 1917 and again the spring and fall of 1918 he made major tours of the Middle West, and on each trip close observers perceived that his iron determination, and little more, was holding him together. TR himself thought the end had come in February, 1918, when a friend found him lying in agony on a bed in the Hotel Langdon in New York. "I don't mind having to die," he slowly remarked as he roused himself. "I've had my good time . . . and I don't mind having to pay for it. But," he concluded with a sudden display of fire, "to think that those swine will say that I'm out of the game."

Throughout the war the Colonel's unvarying theme was a "one hundred per cent, undivided loyalty" that tolerated neither dissent from nor obstruction to the war effort. He expounded it with incredible vigor and awesome virulence, and he scored his record in so doing (as Wilson also did his) with scars so ugly that the passing of forty years has failed to erase them.

Roosevelt could neither sympathize with the antiwar attitudes nor comprehend the moral courage of the conscientious objectors, whom he regarded as "slackers, pure and simple." He flailed them unmercifully and he relegated them finally to the camp of the enemy. He endorsed loyalty oaths for teachers and urged the dismissal of those who refused to take them. He advocated the abolition of the teaching of German in the public schools. He suggested that German-language newspapers be compelled gradually to publish in English on the theory that "moral treason in English is at least open, whereas in a foreign language it is hidden." He approved the prosecution of two Columbia University students who had advised their fellow students not to register for the draft; and he similarly endorsed the indictment of the Milwaukee Socialist and pro-German, Victor Berger. He regretted that the German apologists George S. Viereck and Bernard Herman Ridder were not given the same treatment. Yet—and the point is relevant in view of reports that he would face the electorate as the Republican presidential candidate in 1920—he was unfailingly forthright. Repeatedly his bitterest excoriations of German-American "disloyalty" were made in the German-American centers of the Middle West.

Even as TR fanned the already raging flames, he strove to keep the fire within bounds. In the summer of 1917 he denounced the series of race riots that swept eastward from East St. Louis. In the spring of 1918 he condemned the lynching of a German alien in Collinsville, Illinois. And from the beginning to the end of the war he warned against blanket indictments of the hyphenates. "It is," he asserted again and again, "an outrage to discriminate against a good American in civil life because he is of German blood." But his words fell as water on burning kerosene; the conflagration he himself had set off evaporated them.

TR was also quick to read "Bolshevist" and "German Socialist" into labor strife. By the end of the war he was preaching that campaign of intolerance which catapulted Attorney-General A. Mitchell Palmer to passing fame and enduring notoriety in 1919. "Any foreign-born man who parades with or backs up a red flag or black flag organization ought to be instantly deported to the country from which he came," Roosevelt wrote in the *Star* on November 14, 1918. "Appropriate punishment should be devised for the even more guilty native-born."

Again and again during the war the Colonel spoke out for a press free to print the truth; but it was a truth that collated only with his own one hundred per cent Americanism. He approved the administration's suppression of the famed Socialist periodical *Masses;* he decried its failure to take the same action against the mass-circulation Hearst papers for their incitement of "the hatred of our people against allies who are faithfully fighting beside us." He also castigated Wilson and his administration for censoring publications for partisan political purposes. But on the main line—the right to impose cloture on those who opposed the war effort—he held firm. Thus his celebrated attack on the Sedition Bill of 1918 was directed at a clause prohibiting "contemptuous or slurring language about the President," not at its strictures against disloyalty. "If it is passed," TR wrote in the *Star*, "I shall certainly give the Government the opportunity to test its constitutionality."

The Colonel's concern for the right to criticize was real and personal. By the late autumn of 1917 he had emerged as Wilson's most powerful and effective critic—so embarrassingly effective that it was rumored that Burleson planned to impose the iron glove of censorship on the *Metropolitan* and *Kansas City Star*. And by the end of hostilities Roosevelt's scathing pen had exposed all of the administration's major failings (and attributed to it a number of others that were not its fault). He seems only to have feared that the President would silence him by appointing him to an official position. As he remarked to a friend who found him hurrying through a mass of proofs, "It's a collection of my war articles and speeches. I'm afraid Wilson is going to appoint me to something, and I want to get the book out before he shuts me up."

Roosevelt had begun his articles in the *Star* with a powerful blast at America's failure to have "a single man on the fighting line" after eight months of war. He followed it with an indignant protest against the War Department's failure to equip the draftees with rifles—"Broomstick Preparedness," he called it. Thereafter he hammered furiously at the administration's indecisiveness and lack of a sense of urgency—its failure to decide quickly on a specific rifle for infantrymen; its seeming indifference to the task of transporting a great army to France; its leisurely approach to the shipping crisis; and its failure to produce aircraft and artillery. The titles of TR's editorials reveal his bent: "Broomstick Apologists," "A Square Deal for the Training Camps," "Fighting Work for the Man of Fighting Age," "Mobilize Our Manpower," "Tell the Truth and Speed Up the War," "The Cost of Unpreparedness," "Let George Speed Up the War," "Gird Up Our Loins."

It was hardly in TR to speak well of Wilson; and though he

sometimes did, notably when the President called for complete victory in his annual message to Congress in December, 1917, such occasions were rare. Yet Roosevelt's partisanship should not be overexaggerated. It blinded him to the President's many estimable qualities, and it infused his otherwise constructive criticisms with personal venom and rancor. But it bears repeating that Roosevelt's wartime record was marred by little, if any, obstructionism. Always, his brief was for greater effort.

That record also fails to reveal TR as the reactionary that his harsh injunctions against the pacifist-progressives and his renewed communion with the Republican Old Guard suggest. To be sure, he privately classified La Follette and other antiwar progressives with "that unhung traitor, Hearst." He first urged that La Follette be expelled from the Senate, then settled on censure as the more expedient course (he feared La Follette would be martyrized). And he still refused to recognize, much less endorse, the memorable progressive enactments of Wilson's first administration. Yet the embers of his own progressivism continued to smolder and in 1918 again to flame. At war's end it was Woodrow Wilson, preoccupied with the great questions of the peace as Theodore Roosevelt had been preoccupied with those of preparedness from 1914 to 1917, whose progressivism had burned down. The Colonel's attitude toward tax policy and kindred questions are revealing of this.

TR's understanding of finance was still hazy. ("I have not made any speech *only* on the Liberty Loan, because while I may not share any other quality with Abraham Lincoln, I do share his lack of intimate acquaintance with finance," he wrote Herbert Hoover in the fall of 1917.) Nevertheless, he maintained an active interest in the social and moral aspects of such problems. He regarded the administration's bill for a 60 per cent ceiling on excess profits taxes as inadequate. And against the counsel of Lodge, he backed Hiram Johnson, Norris, La Follette, and Borah in their demand for an even higher tax. With the blessing of George Perkins, he asserted on the platform and in his published writings that it would be "mischievous not to put a stop to the making of unearned and improper fortunes out of the war" and that America must have "a heavily—a very heavily—graduated tax on the excess profits . . . a tax as heavy as Great Britain has now imposed."

The Colonel was similarly concerned with the inequities,

actual and proposed, in the draft system. He chided the YMCA for including men of military age on its staff. "It is an ignoble thing for an able-bodied man to be in . . . a position of bodily safety." He excoriated President Wilson for allegedly holding up Edsel Ford's induction into service until he could be legally deferred. "These other young Americans face death and endure unspeakable hardships and misery and fatigue . . . and have surrendered all hope of money-getting, of comfort and of safety," he indignantly wrote. "But young Mr. Ford, in ease and safety, is in the employ of his wealthy father." And he bitterly attacked the program, devised late in the war, to send new draftees to college preparatory to commissioning them without service in the ranks. The program, he said, was unfair to those already serving overseas. It was also undemocratic:

The average working-man or small farmer has not had money enough to educate his son so that the boy can now enter college without further training. . . . Such a working-man or farmer ought to wish, and does wish, that his son be tested on his merits by actual service in the ranks. . . . [There should be no] privilege given to money. . . .

By 1918 Roosevelt's booming exhortations had made him the loyal opposition's uncrowned leader and the Republican party's foremost candidate for the presidency in 1920. "I suspect," Raymond Robbins remarked in July to William Barnes, the Old Guardsman who had sued Roosevelt for libel three years before, "we are going to nominate TR in 1920 by acclamation."

"Acclamation, hell!" Barnes replied. "We're going to nominate him by assault."

The Colonel was pleased, even sanguine, until personal tragedy dulled his edge. "Yes, I will run," he said, "if the people want me, but only if they really want me. I will not lift a finger for the nomination." He had, he continued, discussed the matter with a number of Republican senators and representatives who "appeared to be sincerely desirous of accepting the fact that we were about to face a changed world and that mere negation and obstruction and attempts to revive the dead past spelled ruin." He told them that "I am not in the least concerned with *your* supporting *me* either now or at any future time; all I am concerned with is that you should so act that *I* can support *you*."

Roosevelt meant what he had always meant: the Republican party should become "the Party of sane, constructive radicalism, just as it was under Lincoln." Otherwise, he firmly added, "I have no place in it."

It was an idle dream. Had TR been elected President in 1920 the shape of events would surely have been different. But could they have been much different than in the last years of his presidency? Roosevelt's party had shown its colors during his own turbulent administration and under Taft's as well. It had shown them in its opposition to the progressive legislation of the first Wilson administration; and it would show them again in the administrations of Harding, Coolidge, and Hoover and thence through the long, bitter years of obstruction to the New and Fair Deals. It is hard to believe that Roosevelt, for all his creative fervor, could have done in the 1920's what he had failed so dramatically to do from 1901 to 1912—change the Republican party's social and economic bias. A handful of Republicans—La Follette, Johnson, Norris, and their like—would burn the progressive candle down through the twenties; but they were the very senators whom TR most despised because of their opposition to the war. Nevertheless, the Colonel, satisfied finally that the preparedness fight was won and the Bull Moose party buried, could not but dream of a progressive Republican future.

On March 28, 1918, at Portland, Maine, Roosevelt urgently warned party and nation that they must tread the moderate progressive path during the postwar years. He reaffirmed his belief in a tightly and federally regulated capitalism. He called for the encouragement of private enterprise, but not at the expense of labor's "full right to cooperate and combine and full right to collective bargaining and collective action." And he again adumbrated the New Deal by advocating aid to farmers, multipurpose river valley developments, public housing projects, reductions in the hours of labor, and sundry social security measures including old age, sickness, and unemployment insurance.

The Portland address was Theodore Roosevelt's progressive legacy. Though it would soon repudiate it, the speech was grist for the Old Guard's propaganda mill in the spring of 1918; the more so because it also featured a broadside attack on the

Democrats' conduct of the war. The Republican National Committee had it printed and distributed by the tens of thousands during the congressional campaign that summer and fall.

The Colonel was delighted with the fire he had lit. "I think I do not overstate the matter," he wrote William Allen White in high spirits, "when I say that the Maine Progressives felt that my speech and its reception amounted to the acceptance, by the Republicans of Maine, of the Progressive platform of 1912 developed and brought up to date." He did not, however, really deceive himself. Even as he railed against the Bolsheviks to the end of his life, he continued to fear that the Grand Old Party would allow "the Romanovs of our social and industrial world" to return to power.

Meanwhile the pall of death enveloped Sagamore Hill. The old warrior never expected all of his sons to return; he and Mrs. Roosevelt, he later said, were "quite prepared that none of them should come back." Had he not always been captivated by children, one might read into the affection he now lavished on his grandsons and daughters an urgency born of the war. "I came back here Monday evening," he wrote Ted's wife in October, 1917, "and day before yesterday your three darling children arrived."

I can't say how I have enjoyed them. Gracie is the most winning little thing I have ever known. . . . The first evening I read her Peter Rabbit and Benjamin Bunny, while Mother as an interlude read her Little Black Mingo—Gracie felt that to have us read alternately prevented monotony. Ted's memory was much clearer about the pigs than about me; he greeted me affably, but then inquired of a delighted bystander . . . "What is that man's name?" . . . This afternoon I took the three down to that haven of delight, the pig pen; . . . Little Edie by the way is sometimes laid on the sofa in my room for me to take care of while I am dressing.

But it was on twenty-year-old Quentin, the most promising of his own boys, that the Colonel's thoughts settled in the summer of 1918. TR had earlier tried to get the "idiotic ruling" that prevented Quentin's fiancée, Flora Payne Whitney, from going to France to marry him suspended. For, he explained to Ted, "It is well to have had happiness, to have achieved the great ends of life, when one must walk boldly and warily close to death." It was not to be.

The second week in July, just as TR was preparing to serve

as a pallbearer for former Mayor John Purroy Mitchel who had been killed in a training accident in Louisiana, he learned that Quentin had destroyed a German plane in combat near Château-Thierry. "Whatever now befalls Quentin," the Colonel wrote Ethel, "he has now had his crowded hour, and his day of honor and triumph. Mitchell [sic] had neither; he died before he was able to get to the front and to render service and to feel the thrill generous souls *ought* to feel when they have won the honorable renown of doing their duty with exceptional courage and efficiency."

Five days later a newspaperman informed Roosevelt at Sagamore Hill that Quentin had gone down behind the German lines. He received the news in silence, striding up and down the veranda. Finally, after wondering aloud how he would break the news to Mrs. Roosevelt, he summoned his courage and entered the house. A half hour later he reappeared with a written statement: "Quentin's mother and I are glad that he got to the front and had a chance to render some service to his country, and show the stuff that was in him before his fate befell him." The date was July 17, 1918.

Three suspenseful days followed. On July 18 Roosevelt delivered the keynote address to the Republican State Convention at Saratoga Springs, resolutely asserting that "It is more than ever my duty to be there." He received at Saratoga the most heartfelt personal ovation of his career; also a flicker of hope. A cablegram from Ted's wife reported that Quentin's death was "absolutely unconfirmed." The Colonel returned to Sagamore Hill the next day to find similar reports from his son-in-law, Richard Derby, and from General Pershing. But on the afternoon of July 20, just twenty minutes *before* TR received and addressed a delegation from the Japanese Red Cross, a warm and sympathetic telegram from President Wilson confirmed the original report. Quentin was dead! He had been buried "with military honors by German airmen at Cambrai at the spot where he fell."

It was then, wrote the Colonel's young friend, Hermann Hagedorn, that the boy in TR died.

For five and a half more months the man in TR lived on. Never was the mature Roosevelt's conception of duty and honor put to a harder test. For a while Quentin's last letters continued to arrive; and once Ethel's young son Richard, Quentin's favorite nephew, heard an airplane overhead and exclaimed, "perhaps that's Uncle Quentin." Finally, in late July, the Roosevelts fled their beloved Sagamore for the first time since their marriage to spend two weeks in Dark Harbor, Maine, with Ethel and Quentin's bereaved fiancée. "It is no use pretending that Quentin's death is not very terrible," TR wrote Kermit's wife. ". . . There is nothing to comfort Flora at the moment; but she is young; I most earnestly hope that time will be very merciful to her, and that in a few years she will keep Quentin only as a loving memory of her golden youth, as the lover of her golden dawn, and that she will find happiness with another good and fine man. But of course it would be all wrong for me to tell her this *now*. As for Mother, her heart will ache for Quentin until she dies."

And so it was also with the father. The public never heard him express his grief. But his valet observed him sitting on a chair, an open book before him, gazing out at the horizon, murmuring, "Poor Quinikins!" There were also fleeting moments of doubt. "To feel that one has inspired a boy to conduct that has resulted in his death, has a pretty serious side for a father," TR wrote a stranger. Nevertheless, he added, "I would not have cared for my boys and they would not have cared for me if our relations had not been just along that line." To the novelist Edith Wharton he said that there was no use in his writing about Quentin, for "I should break down if I tried." And to General Pershing, whose wife and three daughters had perished in a fire three years before, he wrote that "I should be ashamed of myself if I did not try in a lesser way to emulate . . . [your] courage." But it was to Arthur Lee that he expressed his philosophy most cogently: "It is very dreadful that [Quentin] should have been killed; it would have been worse if he had not gone."

The father's informal memorial, an editorial in the *Kansas City Star* entitled "The Great Adventure," fittingly made no mention of his son's name.

Only those are fit to live who do not fear to die; and none are fit to die who have shrunk from the joy of life and the duty of life. Both life and death are parts of the same Great Adventure. Never yet was worthy adventure worthily carried through by the man who put his personal safety first. Never yet was a country worth living in unless its sons and daughters were of that stern stuff which bade them die for it at need; and never yet was a country worth dying for unless its sons and daughters thought of life not as something concerned only with the selfish evanescence of the individual, but as a link in the great chain of creation and causation. . . .

But honor, highest honor, to those who fearlessly face death for a good cause; no life is so honorable or so fruitful as such a death. Unless men are willing to fight and die for great ideals, including love of country, ideals will vanish, and the world will become one huge sty of materialism. And unless the women of ideals bring forth the men who are ready thus to live and die, the world of the future will be filled by the spawn of the unfit. . . .

For Roosevelt there now remained one last struggle—the winning of the peace. He did not survive to its end; and the tactics he would have pursued can only be conjectured. But he said and wrote enough during its early stages to make his ultimate objective clear. He stood for a peace that would redress Belgium for the wounds she had suffered, reduce Germany to military impotence, and perpetuate the grand alliance that had won the war.

Roosevelt had never forgiven Woodrow Wilson for his call for a "peace without victory" in January, 1917, for his assertion that all the belligerents were fighting for the same general ends. Upon America's entrance into the war TR's conviction that the vital interests of the United States and the Allies were virtually identical had gained wide acceptance; and what he had so often said privately during the long ordeal of neutrality he thereafter said publicly. He upbraided the President for insisting that the United States was an associate, rather than a partner, of the Allies. He vehemently demanded that America declare war on Turkey and Bulgaria. And he briefly advocated that American combat troops be placed under British and French command to expedite the prosecution of the war.

Nor did TR delude himself that the United States alone was winning or had won the war. Five weeks after Quentin was shot from the skies he reminded the American people of their debt to Great Britain. "If she had not controlled the seas," he wrote in the *Kansas City Star* on August 18, "not an American battalion could have been sent to the aid of France as she struggled to save the soul of the world, and no help could have been given gallant Italy or any others of these Allied nations to whose stern fighting efficiency we owe it that this earth is still a place on which free men can live."

Several weeks after the armistice Roosevelt publicly evaluated the factors responsible for victory: (1) the French army;

(2) the British navy; (3) the British army; (4) the Italian army. "Our own gallant army and navy did exceedingly well," he added, "but came in so late that the part they played, taking the four and a half years as a whole, does not entitle them to rank with the instrumentalities given above."

It was this appreciation of the decisive role of Allied power, coupled with fear that Germany would come back with a vengeance, that underlay TR's call for the unconditional surrender of Germany. He was, no doubt, influenced by a thirst for revenge. And his passion was surely heightened by his contempt for Wilson. "Let us dictate peace by the hammering guns and not chat about peace to the accompaniment of the clicking of typewriters," he expostulated. Yet at root he was rational, however unwise. "A premature and inconclusive peace now," he wrote in May, 1918, "would spell ruin for the world, just as in 1864 a premature and inconclusive peace would have spelled ruin to the United States. . . . Twenty years hence by mere mass and growth Germany would dominate the Western European powers." "Germany must accept whatever terms the United States and its allies think necessary in order to right the dreadful wrongs that have been committed and to safeguard the world for at least a generation to come from another attempt by Germany to secure world dominion," he declared on the eve of the armistice. "The surest way to secure a peace as lasting as that which followed the downfall of Napoleon is to overthrow the Prussianized Germany of the Hohenzollerns as Napoleon was overthrown."

More, even, than Roosevelt's anger over Wilson's call for a Democratic Congress in 1918, those views governed Roosevelt's attitude toward the President's peace program. Arguing that Wilson's Fourteen Points portended "not the unconditional surrender of Germany but the conditional surrender of the United States," he openly ridiculed them as "Fourteen Scraps of Paper." The proposals for freedom of the seas and general disarmament particularly incensed him. Freedom of the seas "would have meant Germany's victory and the subjugation of not only Germany's foes, but of all neutrals like ourselves," he realistically contended. Indeed, Wilson's failure to appreciate the importance of British naval power to America's well-being so enraged him that he now left the ranks of the loyal opposition. The Republican party, he wrote Sir Arthur Balfour, Lloyd George, and Clemenceau, does "not believe in what we understand to be Mr. Wilson's interpretation of 'the Freedom of the Seas.' " He declared that "in any free country, except the United States," the Democratic defeat in the Congressional elections on November 5 "would have meant Mr. Wilson's retirement from office and return to private life." And he added that his party did not support the President's startling proposal to force Britain's hand by threatening a naval race. (Of all men in the United States, Roosevelt, the onetime master diplomatist, should have allowed Wilson to bluff.) "We feel that the British Navy . . . should be the most powerful in the world, and we have no intention of rivaling it, any more than we have any intention of rivaling the French military preparedness, because we recognize that France must prepare her army in a way not necessary for the United States," he told the British and French leaders. He repeated in the *Star* that the "worse thing we could do would be to build a spite navy, a navy built not to meet our own needs, but to spite some one else."

Elements of realism as well as a fateful shortsightedness marked Roosevelt's attitude toward the League of Nations. Here, too, he was doubtless influenced by his hatred of Wilson. But to imply that his spleen was controlling is to defile one of the purest and noblest, if also most egocentric, patriots the nation has yet produced. It is also to ignore the consistency of the Colonel's career.

Although Roosevelt had never totally dismissed the ancient dream of a parliament of the nations, his commitment had always been cautious and measured. He did not believe the nations of the world were yet ready to subordinate their national drives to the collective will; nor, in his own country's case, did he think it desirable to do so. He was too nationalistic —perhaps realistic—to scuttle the Monroe Doctrine. "All the coasts and islands which in any way approach the Panama Canal must be dealt with by this Nation, and by this Nation alone," he wrote as the League issue was coming to a head. And notwithstanding the great blow he himself had rendered the old isolationism, the tragic limitations of his nationalism prevented him from perceiving that America's future lay in cooperative action. "If the League of Nations means that we will have to go to war every time a Jugoslav wishes to slap a Czecho-slav in the face," he said to his personal physician, "then I won't follow them." He added that "we don't want any more scraps of paper." He also wrote in the *Star* that "the affairs of hither Asia, the Balkan Peninsula, and of North Africa are of prime concern to the powers of Europe, and the United States should be under no covenant to go to war about matters in which its people have no concern and probably no intelligent interest."

Even so, the Colonel's attitude toward the League was cautiously affirmative. Partly because Taft and Root, with both of whom he had resumed cordial relations, favored the League, and partly perhaps, because of his Nobel Peace Prize address in 1910, he prepared in the summer of 1918 to support it with reservations. "I think I have found a *modus vivendi!*" he wrote Taft on August 15. "I will back it as an *addition to,* but not as a *substitute for,* our preparing our own strength in our own defense."

From then until his death Roosevelt gave a carefully measured endorsement to the League, arguing always that it should be built around the concert of powers that had won the war. He publicly recommended that the United States and Great Britain sign a *universal* arbitration treaty, though not, he hastened to advise Kipling privately, "on the hands-across-the-sea or Anglo-Saxon brotherhood theory." As a matter of fact, he added, "I doubt if there is such a thing as an Anglo-Saxon, but at any rate I am not one. . . . I am just plain straight American."

Otherwise, TR disapproved of President Wilson's decision to go to Paris, approved the appointment of Henry White to the peace commission, and supported a proposed congressional resolution to separate the peace treaty from the League of Nations Covenant. He also demanded that the Covenant recognize the Monroe Doctrine and that its members be authorized to regulate their own internal affairs, including tariff and immigration policy. Then, in an editorial dictated three days before his death, he endorsed Taft's proposed reservations, which were substantially the ones he had been advocating himself.

Whether, as Henry Pringle flatly asserts, the Colonel "would have joined the battalion of death that killed the League of Nations" had he lived, is impossible to say. Shortly before Christmas, 1918, Lodge spent two mornings at TR's bedside reportedly drawing up the broad reservations upon which he later stood. Possibly he did; his basic reservations, as distinct from his petty ones, differed little from Taft's and Roosevelt's.

But that TR would have indulged Lodge in all his obstructionist maneuvering, particularly his pandering to the Irish-Americans, is conjectural. TR was probably too deeply committed to
Anglo-Franco-American comity, to the moderate views of
William Howard Taft, and perhaps to his own words over the
years for that. Still, he would have opposed the treaty as Wilson brought it home. And whether as President in 1921 he
would then have compelled the Republican party to abide by
the campaign promises of a great phalanx of its leaders—Taft,
Root, and Hughes included—to join a modified league remains
an open question. His public statements, coupled with Britain's
disposition to accept America's nationalistic reservations, suggest that he might have; his belief that an alliance with Great
Britain would prove more substantive than membership in any
peace organization, and especially his aversion to all that
Woodrow Wilson represnted, indicate that he would not have.

On October 27, 1918, Roosevelt turned sixty. "I am glad
. . . ," he wrote Kermit, "for it somehow gives me the right to
be titularly as old as I feel. I only hope that when you are sixty
you'll have as much happiness to look back upon as I have
had, and be as proud of your sons and daughters as I am of
mine; and somehow I believe you'll then still be as much in
love with Belle as I am with your Mother, and will feel that
you owe her as much as I owe your Mother."

The next day, in the last major address of his thirty-six-year
political career, the Colonel answered Wilson's appeal for a
Democratic Congress before a furiously Republican crowd in
Carnegie Hall. For two tense hours, his jaw thrust forward, his
teeth clicking, and his manuscript waving as of old, he blasted
the President's record, motives, and proposals. He seemingly
forgot that just twenty years earlier a Republican President
had requested that there be no "divided councils" as the nation
prepared to make peace; or that the Republican candidate for
governor of New York had called for a Republican Congress
on the grounds that the world would interpret a Republican
defeat "as a refusal to sustain the efforts of our peace commission to secure the fruit of war." Yet the circumstances were
not quite identical. For if Woodrow Wilson's appeal was justified, as in a sense it was, Theodore Roosevelt's thunderous
attack on that appeal was at least defensible in terms of his
party's war record. ". . . [The President] asks for the defeat of
pro-war Republicans," TR roared. "He does not ask for the

defeat of anti-war Democrats. On the contrary, he supports such men if, although anti-war, they are pro-Administration."

Six days after the Republicans swept the Congressional elections the Colonel entered Roosevelt Hospital with inflammatory rheumatism. Told that he might be confined to a wheel chair for the rest of his life, he mused a moment, then replied: "All right! I can work that way, too." Old friends dropped in to see him, among them William Howard Taft. Hamlin Garland came with a proposal that a garden be planted around Quentin's grave, but Mrs. Roosevelt vetoed it. Someone else talked of the reports, by then a foregone conclusion, that TR would be nominated by the Republicans in 1920. The Colonel professed indifference. "Since Quentin's death the world seems to have shut down on me," he said. "But if I do consent," he added with a flash of the old fire, "it will be because as President I could accomplish some things that I should like to see accomplished before I die." Then, recalling the G.O.P.'s long hostility toward so many of his views, TR raised himself up in bed and snapped: "And, by George, if they take me, they'll take me without a single modification of the things I have always stood for!"

Uncured and still wracked with pain, Roosevelt returned to Sagamore Hill on Christmas Day. There, chatting with neighbors, browsing among his books, and eying fondly the mementos of his tumultuous career, he lived on for almost two weeks. He wrote the editorial endorsing Taft's reservations to the League which appeared in the *Star* after his death. He composed a scorching and intolerant message on Americanism for a meeting of the American Defense Society. And he dictated a final memorandum that suggests that he was prepared again to hold his party together, his progressive declarations notwithstanding: "Hays—see him; he must go to Washington for 10 days; see Senate & House; prevent split on domestic policies."

On the eleventh day, Sunday, January 5, the Colonel stayed in his bedroom overlooking Long Island Sound. He read aloud with his wife, dictated a letter to Kermit, and worked over the proofs of an article for the *Metropolitan*. Late in the afternoon as Mrs. Roosevelt, who had been playing solitaire, rose to leave, TR looked up from his book and said, "I wonder if you will ever know how I love Sagamore Hill."

A little earlier than usual that night the Colonel asked his Negro valet if he thought "I might go to bed now." The valet,

James Amos, had almost to lift him into bed. Mrs. Roosevelt then came in and kissed him good night as she had done to Quentin the night he slept at Sagamore Hill for the last time. Between eleven and twelve o'clock he said, "James, please put out the light." He never spoke again. Sometime after four the next morning, January 6, 1919, Theodore Roosevelt died in his sleep.

He was buried without eulogy, music, or military honors in a plain oak casket on a hillside plot near Sagamore Hill that he and Mrs. Roosevelt had earlier selected. About four hundred personal friends, fifty children from the public school in Oyster Bay where he had sometimes played Santa Claus, and one hundred dignitaries attended the simple ceremony. Among them was the man he had hurt the worst and who had loved him the most—William Howard Taft. Some time after the assemblage dispersed, Taft was seen standing alone meditating over the grave.

For weeks the tributes poured forth. "ONE WORD is repeated a thousand times . . . ," the *Literary Digest* reported. "It is the simple but eloquent word 'American.'" America's contribution to the Great War, said the *Philadelphia North American* in a statement echoed throughout the nation, was "the product of the will, the passionate conviction, and the devoted services of Theodore Roosevelt, private citizen, more than any other force." In England Rudyard Kipling wrote a memorial, "Great-heart." And in the chamber of the Senate a grief-stricken Cabot Lodge closed his eloquent eulogy with the quotation: "So Valiant-for-Truth passed over and all the trumpets sounded for him on the other side." Even the man who had served as the buffer between the Colonel and President Wilson was affected. "You will, no doubt, be greatly distressed at the news," gentlemanly Newton D. Baker wrote General Pershing the morning Roosevelt died. "About many things my disagreements with him were fundamental, but like all Americans I had a sympathy for his irresistible energy and courage. . . . In practically every field of human endeavor he has made his mark. . . ."

As Irvin S. Cobb put it, "You had to hate the Colonel a whole lot to keep from loving him."

Like most men of heroic proportions, Theodore Roosevelt had made major blunders and miscalculations. He had suffered an acute and far-ranging vision to be blurred by a too sweeping commitment to force or the threat of force. He had blinded himself, except in the memorable year of his Bull Moose heresy, to the moral limitations imposed on his party by its hostage to the men and values of the market place. He had repelled men who should have taken him seriously by his boyish enthusiasms and matchless lust for life. And he had often conveyed the impression of opportunism by the ease with which he had shifted causes and allegiances in the harsh conviction that politics is the art of the possible.

Yet, as in all generalizations about this extraordinary man, the need to qualify and elaborate remains. If Roosevelt the conservative retained to the end a Burkean fear of revolution, Roosevelt the progressive had proclaimed from the beginning a democratic functionalism grounded in almost fuller faith in man—in his free moral capacity, his educability, and his power to act finally with disinterest—than Jefferson's. No great American statesman has ever been more committed to an open society based on talent; no American President has ever flirted more seriously with majority rule. Nor, paradoxically, has any major American political leader ever reposed greater confidence in government by experts; nor, still more paradoxically, expounded so emphatically a philosophy of moral absolutes.

If, in the summing up, Roosevelt indulged too indiscriminately in platitudes, as surely he did, and if he extolled character at the sacrifice of depth and breadth of mind, as conservatives have immemorially done, his preachments are nonetheless viable. It is true that they rested on nothing more substantial than his own intuition and intelligence—as he once exclaimed when asked how he knew that justice had been done, "Because I did it." And it is also true that although this was well enough for him, the intuition being deep and the intelligence penetrating, it was not enough for all the men who subsequently held the office he had himself so distinguished. Men of estimable character with one exception and men of narrow intellectual horizons with some exceptions, only a few of them understood, as the mature Roosevelt finally did, that a moralism unsupported by social and economic reality is the most meaningless of platitudes.

But for all of that, for all, even, of the relativism of the modern mind, the feeling persists that men of character, if blessed also with depth and breadth of view, will always come to a working consensus as to the nature of justice in a given situation. And if such is in truth the case, the ideal of the morally responsible and duty-conscious citizen that Roosevelt so imbued in the minds of his own generation must live on in those that follow.

Whatever the Colonel's ultimate place in the hearts of his countrymen—and it yearly grows larger and warmer—there is no discounting those incisive perceptions and momentous deeds that made him such a dynamic historical force from his civil service years to the day of his death. In an age when the excesses of the profit system were undermining the moral foundations of American society, when one great body of reformers was invoking the antiquated ways of the agrarian order and another was uncritically accepting a mechanistic interpretation of man himself, when two of the nation's most ripened historical minds, Brooks and Henry Adams, were evolving theories that closed the ring on all hope, Roosevelt the practical idealist was molding the new determinism and the old individualism into the only synthesis compatible with the American political temperament; the only program that offers hope that industrialism will ultimately serve American society for good rather than ill. Eschewing laissez-faire capitalism no less than doctrinaire socialism, he saw with the pragmatist's genius that "Ruin faces us if we . . . permit ourselves to be misled by any empirical or academic consideration into refusing to exert the common power of the community where only collective action can do what individualism has left undone, or can remedy the wrongs done by an unrestricted and ill-regulated individualism." More, perhaps, than anything else, it was the coincidence of that insight and Roosevelt's disposition to act that explains his dramatic and exhilarating impact on his times.

Long after the rationalizations, the compromises, the in-fights, the intolerance and all the rest have been forgotten, Theodore Roosevelt will be remembered as the first great President-reformer of the modern industrial era—the first to concern himself with the judiciary's massive property bias, with the maldistribution of wealth, and with the subversion of the democratic process by businessmen and their spokesmen in Congress, the pulpits, and the editorial offices; the first to comprehend the conservation problem in its multiple facets, the first to evolve a broad regulatory program for capital, and the first to encourage, however cautiously, the growth of countervailing labor unions; the first President, in fine, to understand and react constructively to the challenge to existing institutions raised by the technological revolution. And if for the affront his militarism and chauvinism gave the human spirit, he will never be truly revered, he will yet for his unique personal qualities and remarkably constructive achievements, among them the realistic pursuit of peace in a world that he understood better than most, be greatly loved and profoundly respected.

Notes

Notes

General

As my references within the text indicate, I have written this book mainly from published works. There are, of course, significant exceptions. I have done supplementary research in the Roosevelt Papers at the Library of Congress, in Roosevelt's several diaries at the Library of Congress and the Houghton Library of Harvard University, and the voluminous scrapbooks kept by Roosevelt's family and friends and now on deposit in the Widener Library at Harvard. I have also used many of the relevant public documents—legislative journals, Civil Service Commission and Police Commission reports, *Congressional Record,* and Roosevelt's published messages as governor and President. In connection with another work, moreover, I have done systematic, basic research for most of Part VI—the World War years. But in general I have relied on two invaluable sets of Roosevelt's writings: Elting E. Morison and John M. Blum (eds.), *The Letters of Theodore Roosevelt* (8 vols., Cambridge, 1951–54); and Hermann Hagedorn (ed.), *The Works of Theodore Roosevelt* (20 vols., National Edition, New York, 1926). I doubt that I could have written this biography without either of them. They will be cited hereafter as *The Letters* and *The Works* respectively. Albert Bushnell Hart and Herbert Ronald Ferleger (eds.), *Theodore Roosevelt Cyclopedia* (New York, 1941), has been useful as a reference guide.

Since the following chapter notes include only the works I have actually used, as distinct from the hundreds and perhaps thousand or more books I have consulted over the years, the serious student's attention is directed to a number of bibliographies. The most exhaustive such work on Roosevelt himself, one that merits separate publication, is in Edward Wagenknecht, *The Seven Worlds of Theodore Roosevelt* (New York, 1958). The best general bibliography for the presidential and immediate postpresidential years is in George E. Mowry, *The Era of Theodore Roosevelt* (The New American Nation Series, New York, 1958); the best for the years 1912–16 in Arthur S. Link, *Woodrow Wilson and the Progressive Era* (The New American Nation Series, New York, 1954). Oscar Handlin *et al.* (eds.), *Harvard Guide to American History* (Cambridge, 1954), is indispensable for the whole of Roosevelt's life and times. But see especially the critical analysis of the secondary literature in Dewey W. Grantham, Jr., "Theodore Roosevelt in American Historical Writing, 1945–1960," *Mid-America,* XLIII (1961).

Part I / The Making of a Man

Chapter 1. The First Battle

Although I disagree strongly with many of his inferences and conclusions, Henry F. Pringle's scintillating *Theodore Roosevelt: A Biography* (New York, 1931) has contributed immeasurably to the conception of this chapter and to many that follow. In revision I have profited from Carleton Putnam, *Theodore Roosevelt: The Formative Years* (New York, 1958), the superb first volume of a projected multi-volume biography. Besides *The Letters* and the scrapbooks in the Widener Library, I have drawn liberally on TR's unpublished diaries (the diaries covering the legislative period have been published in part as Appendix I, *The Letters*, Vol. II.) Other primary sources include Theodore Roosevelt, *An Autobiography*, first published in 1913 and later reissued as Vol. XX of *The Works; Proceedings of the Theodore Roosevelt Memorial Meeting of the State Charities Aid Association* (privately printed, New York, 1878); and New York State Assembly, *Journal of the Assembly, 1882* (6 vols., Albany, 1882–84). The recollections of Isaac Hunt and others, quoted herein, are in the "Harvard Club Transcripts," a transcript of the proceedings at a Harvard Club dinner in New York in 1920, at the Theodore Roosevelt Memorial Association Library in the Roosevelt House, New York; also the recollections of Joe Murray as told to Hermann Hagedorn. Roosevelt's *The Naval War of 1812* is in Vol. VI of *The Works.*

Of the secondary materials, Howard Lawrence Hurwitz, *Theodore Roosevelt and Labor in New York State, 1880–1900* (New York, 1943), has proved informative and suggestive. It is, I think, unnecessarily harsh, and it should be read against the broader and more understanding treatment in Putnam's *The Formative Years*. In addition, I have drawn on or quoted from the following works: Howard K. Beale, "TR's Ancestry, A Study in Heredity," *New York Genealogical and Biographical Record*, LXXXV (1954); Hermann Hagedorn, *The Boy's Life of Theodore Roosevelt* (New York, 1918); Corinne Roosevelt Robinson, *My Brother, Theodore Roosevelt* (New York, 1923); Paul Russell Cutright, *Theodore Roosevelt the Naturalist* (New York, 1956), a good appreciation by a professional zoologist; Frances Theodora Parsons, *Perchance Some Day* (privately printed, New York, 1951), cited by Putnam; William Roscoe Thayer, *Theodore Roosevelt, an Intimate Biography* (New York, 1919); Charles G. Washburn, *Theodore Roosevelt, the Logic of His Career* (New York, 1916); Owen Wister, *Roosevelt: The Story of a Friendship* (New York, 1930); William Wingate Sewall, *Bill Sewall's Story of T.R.* (New York, 1919); Donald Wilhelm, *Theodore Roosevelt as an Undergraduate* (Boston, 1910); Curtis Guild, Jr., "TR at Harvard," *Harvard Graduate Magazine*, X (1938); and J. Laurence Laughlin, "Roosevelt at

Harvard," *Review of Reviews*, LXX (1924). Also, Poultney Bigelow, *Seventy Summers* (2 vols., New York, 1925).

Chapter 2. A LEADER EMERGES

Besides the obvious sources—*The Letters, Autobiography, Journal of the Assembly* for the relevant years, and *Scrapbooks*—I have again used Pringle, *Theodore Roosevelt*, and Hurwitz, *Theodore Roosevelt and Labor*, extensively. Again, too, I have made several revisions on the basis of Putnam's *The Formative Years*. My characterization of Cleveland reflects Allan Nevins' highly moralistic *Grover Cleveland: A Study in Courage* (New York, 1932). Among the many other works used are: Samuel Gompers, *Seventy Years of Life and Labor* (2 vols., New York, 1925); Jacob Riis, *Theodore Roosevelt the Citizen* (New York, 1904); Chauncey Depew, *My Memories of Eighty Years* (New York, 1922); Henry Cabot Lodge (ed.), *Selections from the Correspondence of Theodore Roosevelt and Henry Cabot Lodge, 1884–1918* (2 vols., New York, 1925); and the *Proceedings of the Eighth Republican Convention* (Chicago, 1884). I have evolved my account of the Republican Convention of 1884 from the varying interpretations given in Pringle's and Putnam's biographies; in John A. Garraty, *Henry Cabot Lodge* (New York, 1953); James C. Malin, "Roosevelt and the Elections of 1884 and 1888," *Mississippi Valley Historical Review*, XIV (1927); DeAlva Stanwood Alexander, *A Political History of the State of New York* (4 vols., New York, 1906–23), and by the same author, *Four Famous New Yorkers* (New York, 1923); contemporary newspaper accounts as found in the *Scrapbooks;* and numerous general works. A few of Roosevelt's campaign speeches are in *Campaigns and Controversies*, Vol. XIV, *The Works;* excerpts from others may be found in the *Scrapbooks*. John Blum's essay, "Theodore Roosevelt: Years of Decision," published as Appendix IV, *The Letters*, Vol. II, has been a continuing source of stimulation. For reasons implicit in my treatment throughout, however, I incline to be more tolerant of the "eclectic intellectual home," so incisively described therein, that Roosevelt created to accommodate the divergent pulls of pure theory and pure politics. One of the more surprising recent reassessments of TR's early years is Richard Hofstadter, "Idealists, Professors, Sore-Heads," *Columbia University Forum*, V (1962). In appreciative vein, Hofstadter writes: "Roosevelt paved the way for Progressivism and helped restore the prestige of educated patricians . . . by demonstrating the compatibility of their type with masculine virtues."

Chapter 3. THE WESTERNER: RANCHER, HUNTER, AND HISTORIAN

The best account of the death and funeral of Roosevelt's wife and mother is in Putnam, *The Formative Years*. Pringle's treatment is also moving. I have supplemented these accounts with clippings from the *Scrapbooks,* excerpts from *The Letters,* and quotations from Theodore Roosevelt, *In Memory of My Darling Wife* (privately printed), and Arthur H. Cutler's typewritten statement as cited by Putnam. Hermann Hagedorn's pioneering narrative, *Roosevelt in the Bad Lands* (Boston, 1921), forms the base for my brief treatment of TR's western experience. In revision I drew on the seemingly definitive story in Putnam, *The Formative Years.* Otherwise I used *The Letters; Scrapbooks;* Lincoln Lang, *Ranching with Roosevelt* (Philadelphia, 1926); Cutright, *Theodore Roosevelt the Naturalist;* and Ray H. Mattison, "Roosevelt and the Stockmen's Association," *North Dakota History,* XVII (1950). I have also read Roosevelt's three books, *Hunting Trips of a Ranchman, Ranch Life and the Hunting Trail,* and *The Wilderness Hunter.* They comprise Vol. I and part of Vol. II of *The Works.*

The expositions of Roosevelt's *Thomas Hart Benton* and *Gouverneur Morris,* published as Vol. VII of *The Works,* are my own. Briefer analyses may be found in the biographies by Putnam and Pringle. I have chosen to quote liberally from Frederick Jackson Turner's review of the fourth volume of Roosevelt's *The Winning of the West,* which appeared in *The American Historical Review,* II (1896), in order to emphasize how seriously professional historians regarded the work at the time. I do not agree with all of Turner's judgments. Further evidence of Roosevelt's high repute among contemporary professional historians may be found in the analysis of the reviews of Vols. I and II offered by George B. Utley, "Theodore Roosevelt's *The Winning of the West:* Some Unpublished Letters," *The Mississippi Valley Historical Review,* XXX (1944). A brief, favorable assessment may also be found in Wagenknecht's uniquely interesting *The Seven Worlds.* Two severely critical appraisals of TR as an historian are the essays by H. J. Thornton and Raymond C. Miller published respectively in William T. Hutchison (ed.), *The Marcus W. Jernegan Essays* in *American Historiography* (Chicago, 1937); and James Lea Cate and Eugene N. Anderson (eds.), *Medieval and Historiographical Essays in Honor of James Westfall Thompson* (Chicago, 1938). Harvey Wish, *The American Historian* (New York, 1960), also gives a brief evaluation. The most perceptive and balanced treatments are Robert W. Sellen, "Theodore Roosevelt: Historian With a Moral," *Mid-America,* XLI (1959), and Elwyn B. Robinson, "Theodore Roosevelt: Amateur Historian," *North Dakota Historian,* XXV (1958).

PART II / The Road to the White House

Chapter 4. FOR THE GOOD OF THE NATION

The classic account of the Haymarket tragedy is Henry David, *The History of the Haymarket Affair* (New York, 1936). I have used it along with *The Letters* and Ray Ginger, *Altgeld's America* (New York, 1958). Putnam's treatment of TR's attitude is more sympathetic than mine. The account of the mayoral campaign of 1886 is drawn from *The Letters; Scrapbooks;* Hurwitz, *Theodore Roosevelt and Labor;* Allan Nevins, *Abram S. Hewitt, With Some Account of Peter Cooper* (New York, 1935); Louis F. Post and Fred C. Leubuscher, *An Account of the George-Hewitt Campaign in the New York Municipal Election of 1886* (New York, 1886); Albert Jay Nock, *Henry George* (New York, 1939); and Jacob Riis, *Theodore Roosevelt.* I have also found the chapter on George in Daniel Aaron, *Men of Good Hope* (New York, 1951) illuminating. The treatment in Charles A. Barker, *Henry George* (New York, 1955), is definitive on George.

The estimate of Edith Carow Roosevelt is based on two confidential sources; on Hermann Hagedorn, *The Roosevelt Family of Sagamore Hill* (New York, 1954); and on scattered references in *The Letters* and in memoirs too numerous to cite. Putnam is partial to TR's first wife. My evaluation of Lodge, in so far as it is moderate, reflects Garraty's multi-dimensional study, *Henry Cabot Lodge.* Roosevelt's relations with Lodge may also be traced in Lodge (ed.), *Selections.* Because of the unspecified changes made by Lodge in the original letters, they should be used with caution.

For the description of TR's activities as Civil Service Commissioner, I have relied heavily on *The Letters* and *Scrapbooks* and particularly on the *Annual Reports* for the relevant years. I have also quoted from the *Letters of Theodore Roosevelt: Civil Service Commissioner, 1889–1895,* a pamphlet issued in 1958 under the direction of then Commissioner Harrison Ellsworth. It contains several theretofore unpublished letters. In addition, I have drawn on Theodore Roosevelt, "Six Years of Civil Service Reform," *Scribner's Magazine,* XVIII (1895); Eric F. Goldman, *Charles J. Bonaparte, Patrician Reformer* (Baltimore, 1943); Dorothy Canfield Fowler, *The Cabinet Politician: The Postmasters General, 1829–1909* (New York, 1943); Carl Schurz, *Speeches, Correspondence and Political Papers* (Frederic Bancroft, ed., 6 vols., New York, 1913); Herbert A. Gibbons, *John Wanamaker* (2 vols., New York, 1926); and William Dudley Foulke, *Roosevelt and the Spoilsmen* (New York, 1925). In revision I have modified my treatment slightly on the basis of Leonard D. White, with the assistance of Jean Schneider, *The Republican Era, 1869–1901* (New York, 1958). White is more sympathetic to (and probably more understanding of) the problems faced by Wanamaker and others who crossed TR than I am. He is especially appreciative of Wanamaker's organizational and executive ability. But also see the comments on Roosevelt in Ari Hoogenboom, "The Pendleton Act and the Civil Service," *American Historical Review,* LXIV (1959).

Chapter 5. THE FIGHT FOR THE RIGHT

There is no adequate secondary account of Roosevelt's tenure as Police Commissioner although the late Howard K. Beale's unpublished first volume of TR's life is said to contain an exhaustive treatment. The chapter in Pringle, *Theodore Roosevelt,* is palpably unfair; that in Lincoln Steffens, *The Autobiography of Lincoln Steffens* (2 vols., New York, 1931), perceptive, but cynical and not wholly reliable. Riis, *Theodore Roosevelt,* is informative, but uncritical. My reconstruction of the commissionership is based mainly on *The Letters, Scrapbooks, Reports* of the New York City Police Department, and especially on the scrapbooks kept by TR's fellow commissioner, Avery D. Andrews. These are now in the collection at Harvard. I have also found Andrews's unpublished manuscript, "Theodore Roosevelt as Police Commissioner," of considerable value. A copy is in the Theodore Roosevelt Memorial Association Library. In addition, I have consulted and occasionally quoted from Roosevelt's *An Autobiography;* Gustavus Myers, *The History of Tammany Hall* (New York, 1901); Joseph Bucklin Bishop, *Theodore Roosevelt and His Time* (2 vols., New York, 1920); Wister, *Roosevelt;* Lodge (ed.), *Selections;* and Charles F. Parkhurst, *My Forty Years in New York* (New York, 1923). I have further used *Campaigns and Controversies,* Vol. XIV, *The Works.*

Chapter 6. THE GREAT ADVENTURE

Besides such standard sources as *The Letters, Scrapbooks,* and *An Autobiography,* I have relied on Bishop's and Pringle's biographies of TR and Garraty's of Lodge. I have also quoted from William Allen White, *Masks in a Pageant* (New York, 1930); William L. Langer, *The Diplomacy of Imperialism, 1890–1902* (2 vols., New York, 1935); Hermann Hagedorn, *Leonard Wood: A Biography* (2 vols., New York, 1931); Philip C. Jessup, *Elihu Root* (2 vols., New York, 1938); and Catherine Drinker Bowen, *Yankee from Olympus: Justice Holmes and the Supreme Court* (Boston, 1944). The excerpts from Long's diary are taken from Stefan Lorant, *The Life and Times of Theodore Roosevelt* (New York, 1959); the statement by Will James from the excellent chapter, "Racism and Imperialism," in Richard Hofstadter, *Social Darwinism in American Thought,* rev. ed. (Boston, 1955). Among the numerous other works I have used are James Ford Rhodes, *The McKinley and Roosevelt Administrations* (New York, 1922); Julius W. Pratt, *Expansionists of 1898* (Baltimore, 1936); Samuel Flagg Bemis, *A Diplomatic History of the United States* (rev. ed., New York, 1950); Richard Hofstadter, *The American Political Tradition and the Men Who Made It* (New York, 1948); and

Matthew Josephson, *The Politicos* (New York, 1938), and *The President Makers* (New York, 1940).

I have found the analysis of Roosevelt's views on Darwinism and imperialism in Blum's essay, "Theodore Roosevelt: The Years of Decision," especially discerning. Margaret Leech, *In The Days of McKinley* (New York, 1959) supersedes George S. Olcott, *The Life of William McKinley* (Boston, 1916). I used it in revision. Although I continue to believe that McKinley could have and should have averted war, *In The Days of McKinley* offers the best account yet published of the enormous pressures to which he was subjected. A fine brief history of the war is Frank Freidel, *The Splendid Little War* (Boston, 1958). Roosevelt's own view is given in Theodore Roosevelt, *The Rough Riders,* Vol. XI, *The Works.* The interested student might also consult his reviews of Alfred T. Mahan's *The Influence of Sea Power Upon History* and of Brooks Adams' *The Law of Civilization and Decay,* reprinted in Vols. XII and XIII of *The Works.* Charles A. Beard's appreciative comments on TR's review of Adams' work are in his introduction to the Vintage Edition of Brooks Adams, *The Law of Civilization and Decay* (New York, 1955). Also see Albert K. Weinberg, *Manifest Destiny: A Study of Nationalist Expansionism in American History* (Baltimore, 1935); Richard Hofstadter, "Manifest Destiny and the Philippines," in *America in Crisis,* Daniel Aaron, ed. (New York, 1952); and John P. Mallan, "The Warrior Critique of a Business Civilization," *American Quarterly,* VIII (1956). I have also quoted from William Reynolds Braisted, *The United States Navy in the Pacific, 1897–1909* (Austin, Texas, 1958).

The most recent study of the coming of war, Ernest R. May, *Imperial Democracy* (New York, 1961), tends to confirm the classic accounts of McKinley's weakness. As May writes, "In all probability, McKinley had no thought of evading the manifest will of Congress and the people."

Chapter 7. THE FINAL PREPARATION

TR's governorship has been covered exhaustively in a doctoral dissertation, regrettably unpublished, G. Wallace Chessman, "Theodore Roosevelt, Governor," (Harvard University, 1950). I have used it in revision. There is no published work of consequence. Pringle's chapter is superficial. Alexander's *A Political History* is limited. Hurwitz *Theodore Roosevelt and Labor* is informative, but unappreciative of the multiple demands made on TR. It is nonetheless useful. A number of other works have also contributed to various phases of my treatment. They include: Harold F. Gosnell, *Boss Platt and His New York Machine* (Chicago, 1924); Thomas Collier Platt, *The Autobiography of Thomas Collier Platt,* edited by Louis J. Long (New York, 1910); Roosevelt, *An*

Autobiography; Richard Hovey, *John Jay Chapman, an American Mind* (New York, 1959); Henry Herman Kohlsaat, *From McKinley to Harding* (New York, 1923); Jessup, *Root;* Chauncey M. Depew, *My Memories of Eighty Years* (New York, 1922); and Joseph I. C. Clarke, *My Life and Memories* (New York, 1925).

The substance of my exposition is drawn from *The Letters,* Vol. II, and a number of illuminating notes therein, including O'Neil's report to Van Duzer; the *Scrapbooks; Public Papers of Theodore Roosevelt, Governor* (2 vols., Albany, 1899–1900); *Journal of the Assembly of the State of New York* (7 vols., Albany, 1899–1900); and the *Journal of the Senate of the State of New York* (4 vols., Albany, 1899–1900). My characterization of Root, originally quite harsh, now reflects in part the brief estimate in Elting E. Morison, *Turmoil and Tradition: A Study of the Life and Times of Henry L. Stimson* (Boston, 1960). The "Note on Roosevelt's Nomination for the Governorship" (no author named), in Appendix II, *The Letters,* Vol. II, offers the most plausible explanation I have read of the controversy between TR, Chapman, *et al.* over the issue of a separate, Independent ticket nomination.

Richard M. Abrams, "A Paradox of Progressivism: Massachusetts on the Eve of Insurgency," *Political Science Quarterly,* LXXV (1960), gives the progressive movement a new dimension. Abrams points out among other things that Massachusetts had the most advanced corporation and labor legislation in the nation on the eve of the progressive movement. I find this particularly provocative, given the massive Midwestern bias of progressive historiography in general. When considered in conjunction with TR's record in New York, it suggests that progressivism was not as uniquely Midwestern as is commonly believed.

Chapter 8. THE PEOPLE'S CHOICE

The most inclusive account of the events leading to TR's nomination is G. Wallace Chessman, "Theodore Roosevelt's Campaign Against the Vice Presidency," *The Historian,* XIV (1952). Margaret Leech, *In The Days of McKinley,* offers new insights into McKinley's attitude toward TR. I have been unable to weave them into my copy, however. Basically, I have depended on Chessman's article and *The Letters, Scrapbooks,* and numerous memoirs, including Nicholas Murray Butler, *Across the Busy Years: Recollections and Reflections* (2 vols., New York, 1939–40); Kohlsaat, *From McKinley to Harding;* Herbert Croly, *Marcus Alonzo Hanna, His Life and Works* (New York, 1912); Platt's *Autobiography;* and White's *Autobiography.*

The story of the campaign has been reconstructed in part from most of the above mentioned works and largely from newspaper clippings in *The Scrapbooks.* My appraisal of Altgeld reflects two constructive appraisals, Harry Barnard, *Eagle Forgotten: The Life of John Peter Altgeld* (Indianapolis, 1938), and Ginger, *Altgeld's America*. My understanding of the populist movement derives from John D. Hicks, *The Populist Revolt* (New York, 1931); from chapters in C. Vann Woodward, *Origins of the New South* (Baton Rouge, La., 1951); Francis B. Simkins, *Pitchfork Ben Tillman, South Carolinian* (Baton Rouge, La., 1944); Theodore Saloutos and John D. Hicks, *Agricultural Discontent in the Middle West* (Madison, Wisc., 1951); and articles, monographs, and doctoral dissertations too numerous to cite here. I agree with the assertion in Samuel P. Hays, *The Response to Industrialism: 1885–1914* (Chicago, 1957), that the economic analysis in works such as Carl C. Taylor, *The Farmer's Movement, 1620–1920* (New York, 1953), and Allan G. Bogue, *Money at Interest: The Farm Mortgage in the Middle Border* (Ithaca, 1955), proves that the farmers' suffering was caused less by money lenders, whether Eastern or Southern and Western, and tariff-protected industrialists than by marketing problems that we have yet to resolve. But I see little in these newer works that refutes the validity of the Populist-Bryan program (as distinct from its analysis of the reasons for the farmers' plight) in so far as it embraced lower tariffs, government-supported regional credit devices, graduated income tax, and a general expansion of the money supply. I find, accordingly, that the older works continue to be illuminating. The racist and other egregious impulses attributed to the Populists and their agrarian successors in Richard Hofstadter, *The Age of Reform; From Bryan to F. D. R.* (New York, 1955), are put in proper historical context by Norman Pollack in "Hofstadter on Populism: A Critique of 'The Age of Reform,' " *Journal of Southern History,* XXVI (1960).

Bryan awaits a good biography. Richard Hofstadter, *The American Political Tradition* (New York, 1948), presents a devastating portrait. The picture in Eric Goldman's graphic *Rendezvous with Destiny* (New York, 1952) is similarly penetrating and not more flattering. I lean toward the affirmative assessment in Henry S. Commager, *The American Mind* (New Haven, 1952). Bryan's major speeches for the two campaigns are in William Jennings Bryan, *The First Battle* (Chicago, 1896) and *The Second Battle* (Chicago, 1900). Since the above was written, an extended essay, Paul W. Glad, *The Trumpet Soundeth: William Jennings Bryan and His Democracy, 1896–1912* (University of Nebraska Press, 1960), has been published. Glad makes Bryan intelligible to the urban mind and broadly succeeds, I think, in giving him his due. Conversely, Leech, *In the Days of McKinley,* seems to me to give McKinley far more than his due. Yet it has many excellences. It contributes particularly to an understanding of the decision to take the Philippines. But also see the relevant chapters in Bemis, *A Diplomatic History,* and Thomas A. Bailey, *A Diplomatic History of the American People* (3rd ed., New York, 1946).

It occurs to me as this goes to press that the reader may infer from my treatment of the campaign of 1900 that the election actually turned on the imperialism issue. Historians familiar with Thomas A. Bailey, "Was the Presidential Election of 1900 a Mandate on Imperialism?" *Mississippi Valley Historical Review,* XXIV (1937), and the numerous works that touch on the question know that the available evidence indicates that it did not. They are similarly aware, as most of the standard diplomatic histories point out, that Bryan's response to the charge that other powers would take the Philippines should the United States move out was a nebulous proposal for a protectorate.

A General Note on the Presidential Years

George E. Mowry, *The Era of Theodore Roosevelt: 1900–1912* (New York, 1958), is the best work on the presidential years. It supersedes the chapters in Pringle, *Theodore Roosevelt,* and in Rhodes, *The McKinley and Roosevelt Administrations.* Mowry's book appeared too late to influence my conception. I have, however, made some revisions and included some new materials on the basis of it. Mowry takes Roosevelt seriously, as Pringle and most of the historians who drew on him did not always do; he succeeds admirably in relating him to his times. In lighter vein, there is much colorful material on the Roosevelt years in Vols. II and III of Mark Sullivan, *Our Times* (New York, 1927, 1930).

For general background I have consulted, but not used, a number of political-intellectual histories, the most important of which are: Henry Steele Commager, *The American Mind;* Goldman, *Rendezvous With Destiny;* Arthur Ekirch, Jr., *The Decline of American Liberalism* (New York, 1956); and Richard Hofstadter's *Age of Reform.*

I have also found Harold U. Faulkner's *The Quest for Social Justice: 1898–1914* (New York, 1931), and the same author's *The Decline of Laissez-Faire: 1897–1914* (New York, 1951) informative. Hays, *The Response to Industrialism,* revises many of the older judgments found in Faulkner and others.

It is needless to add that I have based much of the following chapters on *The Letters,* Vols. III-VI, and on the Homeward Bound Edition of Roosevelt's *Presidential Addresses* (8 vols., Review of Reviews Co., 1910). *The Works,* Vol. XV, contains a comparatively small number of TR's messages to Congress. I have continued to use the *Scrapbooks* and have supplemented them with *The Literary Digest* for the years under review. I have also used the *Congressional Record* liberally, though not systematically, a detailed and exhaustive study of the legislative process being beyond the scope of this volume.

PART III / The Square Deal Begins

Chapter 9. THE FIRST FELL BLOWS

The broad outlines of the sparkling account of TR's first blows against the trusts given in Pringle, *Theodore Roosevelt*, have not changed. Mark Sullivan, *Our Times: America Finding Herself* (Vol. II of *Our Times*) is also rich in human interest. I have extracted the Pulitzer correspondence from it. I have also used Talthasar Meyer, *A History of the Northern Securities Case* (University of Wisconsin Bulletin, No. 142, Madison, 1906); the court record, *Northern Securities Co., et al. v. United States*, 193 U.S. 360, 1904; and several treatises on the trust problem. Of the latter, Hans B. Thorelli, *Federal Anti-Trust Policy: Organization of an American Tradition* (Baltimore, 1955), offers a thorough, up-to-date, and generally favorable appraisal of TR's early antitrust program. A keen insight into the business mind is found in Edward C. Kirkland, *Dream and Thought in the Business Community, 1860–1900* (Ithaca, N.Y., 1956).

Biographies of the central figures include Frederick Lewis Allen, *The Great Pierpont Morgan* (New York, 1949); James G. Pyle, *The Life of James J. Hill* (New York, 1917); and George Kennan, *E. H. Harriman* (2 vols., Boston, 1922). All should be used with caution. In addition, see Elmer Ellis, *Mr. Dooley's America: A Life of Finley Peter Dunne* (New York, 1941).

The background of Roosevelt's decision to appoint Holmes is given in John Garraty, "Holmes' Appointment to the Supreme Court," *The New England Quarterly*, XXII (1949). Garraty's treatment is fuller than mine and properly emphasizes TR's interest in Holmes's attitude toward the Insular Cases. Also see Mark A. DeWolfe Howe, *The Correspondence of Mr. Justice Holmes and Sir Frederick Pollock* (2 vols., Cambridge, 1941); Felix Frankfurter, *Mr. Justice Holmes and the Supreme Court* (Cambridge, 1938); and Worthington C. Ford (ed.), *The Letters of Henry Adams: 1892–1918* (2 vols., Boston, 1932).

An informative note on Littlefield's activities is in *The Letters*, Vol. III. Arthur M. Johnson, "Theodore Roosevelt and the Bureau of Corporations," *Mississippi Valley Historical Review*, XLV (1959), is illuminating.

Chapter 10. AN HISTORIC DEPARTURE

The dramatic account in Sullivan, *America Finding Herself*, has not been altered substantially by recent scholarship. I have supplemented it from my usual primary sources, *The Letters*, *Scrapbooks*, *The Literary Digest*, and in this case the *Report* of the

Anthracite Coal Commission, U.S. Department of Labor Bulletin No. 46 (Washington, 1903). I have also used Marguerite Green, *The National Civic Federation and the American Labor Movement, 1900–1925* (Washington, 1956); a number of standard labor histories, including Foster Rhea Dulles, *Labor in America: A History* (New York, 1949); and especially Robert J. Cornell, *The Anthracite Coal Strike of 1902* (Washington, 1957). Eliot Jones, *The Anthracite Coal Combination in the United States* (Cambridge, 1914), has been useful, and so has Edward Berman, *Labor Disputes and the President of the United States* (New York, 1924).

Among the other works I have drawn upon or quoted from are: Lodge (ed.), *Selections;* Jessup, *Root;* Elsie Gluck, *John Mitchell, Miner* (New York, 1929); Irving Stone, *Clarence Darrow for the Defense* (New York, 1941); Mother [M. H.] Jones, *Autobiography,* M. F. Parton (ed.), (Chicago, 1925); Gompers, *Life and Labor;* Mowry, *The Era of Theodore Roosevelt;* and Roosevelt, *An Autobiography.* Judge Pine's statement is in the *New York Times,* April 30, 1952.

For this edition I have revised a couple of points on the basis of some of the materials in Robert H. Wiebe, "The Anthracite Strike of 1902: A Record of Confusion," *Mississippi Valley Historical Review,* XLVIII (1961).

Chapter 11. AFFAIRS OF STATE

The secondary literature on foreign affairs during Roosevelt's presidency is enormous. No effort will be made to survey it. As I hope my text makes clear, however, I have been strongly influenced by Howard K. Beale, *Theodore Roosevelt and the Rise of America to World Power* (Baltimore, 1956). Except for a set of neo-isolationist conclusions that seem curiously distended from the body of the work, Beale's book is the most exhaustive and balanced treatment extant of selected phases of Roosevelt's conduct of diplomacy. I have, of course, profited from many other works also. Of these, special mention should be made of Julius W. Pratt, *America's Colonial Experiment* (New York, 1950); Dexter Perkins, *The United States and the Caribbean* (Cambridge, 1947); the same author's classic *The Monroe Doctrine, 1867–1907* (Baltimore, 1937); Samuel F. Bemis, *The Latin American Policy of the United States* (New York, 1943); Garel A. Grunder and William E. Livezey, *The Philippines and the United States* (Norman, Okla., 1951); M. M. Knight, *The Americans in Santo Domingo* (New York, 1928); Russell H. Fitzgibbon, *Cuba and the United States, 1900–1935* (Menasha, Wis., 1935); and many other specialized studies.

I have also used S. W. Livermore, "Theodore Roosevelt, The American Navy and the Venezuelan Crisis," *American Historical*

Review, LI (1946); Thomas A. Bailey, "Theodore Roosevelt and the Alaskan Boundary Settlement," *Canadian Historical Review,* XVIII (1937); H. C. Hill, *Roosevelt and the Caribbean* (Chicago, 1927); and Charles C. Tansill, *Canadian-American Relations, 1875–1911* (New Haven, 1943). Of the biographies, Henry F. Pringle, *The Life and Times of William Howard Taft* (2 vols., New York, 1939); Garraty, *Henry Cabot Lodge;* Jessup, *Root;* and Tyler Dennett, *John Hay, From Poetry to Politics* (New York, 1933), have been most helpful.

Additional sources include: Nelson Manfred Blake, "Ambassadors at the Court of Theodore Roosevelt," *Mississippi Valley Historical Review,* XLII (1955); *The Literary Digest* for the relevant years; *Special Report of William H. Taft on the Philippines,* Sixtieth Congress, First Session, Sen. Doc., VII, No. 200; Frederick James Zwierlein, *Theodore Roosevelt and Catholics* (St. Louis, 1956); and a microfilm reel of reports to Whitehall by British ambassadors, now in the library of the Theodore Roosevelt Memorial Association at the Theodore Roosevelt House. I have also used Roosevelt's *An Autobiography* and *The Letters,* Vols. III and IV.

For this edition I have tempered slightly my treatment of Lodge's appointment to the arbitration commission on the basis of Charles S. Campbell, *Anglo-American Understanding, 1898–1903* (Baltimore, 1957), and the comments of James Hewes in a letter to the author, June 3, 1961.

Chapter 12. NOBLE ENDS AND LESS NOBLE MEANS

To most of the works cited for the previous chapter should be added the fine study by Dwight C. Miner, *The Fight for the Panama Route* (New York, 1940). I have followed it closely. Also see Philippe Bunau-Varilla, *Panama; the Creation, Destruction and Resurrection* (London, 1913); the note in Vol. III of *The Letters;* and Gerstle Mack, *The Land Divided* (New York, 1944), a superb book. I have found the version in Chapter 26 of Julius W. Pratt's *A History of United States Foreign Policy* (New York, 1955) the best of the brief accounts. Pratt is understanding of the force of the engineering opinion in favor of Panama, critical of TR's refusal to try further negotiations with Colombia. Pringle's treatment is overdrawn and suffers from his failure to consider the impact on TR of the engineering aspects of the situation. Nevertheless, his insight into certain of Roosevelt's drives cannot be dismissed. Arthur H. Dean, *William Nelson Cromwell* (New York, 1957), views Cromwell's comportment as exemplary, or as he puts it, "unselfish and patriotic."

Chapter 13. IN HIS OWN RIGHT

The account of the inaugural is reconstructed from contemporary newspaper reports in the *Scrapbooks* and *The Literary Digest*. For the Hanna incident and TR's manipulation of the patronage in general see Croly, *Hanna;* Thomas Beer, *Hanna* (New York, 1929); A. Bower Sageser, *The First Two Decades of the Pendleton Act* (Lincoln, Nebraska, 1935); *The Letters* and relevant notes; Mowry, *The Era of Theodore Roosevelt;* and, in particular, Blum, *Republican Roosevelt*. For the appointment of Straus, also see Oscar S. Straus, *Under Four Administrations: From Cleveland to Taft* (Boston, 1922). Straus quotes TR in January, 1906, when he first asked him to enter the Cabinet: "There is still a further reason: I want to show Russia and some other countries what we think of the Jews in this country."

Alfred D. Chandler, Jr.'s essay, "Theodore Roosevelt and the Panama Canal: A Study in Administration," is in *The Letters*, Vol. VI, Appendix 1. An analysis of the report of the Immigration Commission is in Oscar Handlin, *Race and Nationality in American Life* (Boston, 1957). John Higham, *Strangers in the Land* (New Brunswick, N.J., 1955) has also contributed to my understanding of the immigration problem. Roosevelt's religion is discussed in Hermann Hagedorn, "The Unknown Theodore Roosevelt," an unpublished essay; in Christian F. Reisner, *Roosevelt's Religion* (New York, 1922), a compilation of conventional observations by contemporaries; and in Gamaliel Bradford, *The Quick and the Dead* (Boston, 1931). I have also used TR's diaries. The best biographies of Booker T. Washington are Basil Mathews, *Booker T. Washington, Educator and Interracial Interpreter* (Cambridge, 1948); and Samuel R. Spencer, Jr., *Booker T. Washington and the Negro's Place in American Life* (Boston, 1955). I have also found the relevant chapters in John Hope Franklin, *From Slavery to Freedom* (New York, 1947), stimulating. Professor Franklin is more critical of TR and Booker T. Washington than my conviction that economic uplift was precedent to civil rights at that time permits me to be. Pringle, Mowry, and Blum all write perceptively of the campaign of 1904 as does Josephson in his *The President Makers*. I have filled out their various accounts with stories from contemporary newspapers and material from Jessup's biography of Root. I have also quoted from Ford (ed.), *The Letters of Henry Adams*. Parker has no biographer. The reader still rankled by TR's opportunism in the Clarkson appointment might take succor in his statesmanship and sure purpose as appraised by William Seal Carpenter, *The Unfinished Business of Civil Service Reform* (Princeton, 1952), to wit, "Before he left the presidency, Theodore Roosevelt had brought many thousands of positions within the classified service until 63.9 per cent of the whole executive civil service was included."

The statement by Leonard D. White is from his "The Public Life of 'T.R.' " *Public Administration Review*, XIV (1954). For an account of more campaign demagoguery by Roosevelt and Hay, see Pringle's *Roosevelt* or Barbara W. Tuchman, " 'Perdicaris Alive or Raisuli Dead,' " *American Heritage*, X (1959).

Part IV / The Square Deal Matures

Chapter 14. Another Measured Advance

This chapter is largely based on two brilliant essays by John Blum, "Theodore Roosevelt and the Legislative Process; Tariff Revision and Railroad Regulation, 1904–1906," and "Theodore Roosevelt and the Hepburn Act: Toward an Orderly System of Control," published as appendices I and II of *The Letters*, Vols. IV and VI. I have added to them and revised somewhat with materials from the *Scrapbooks* and the *Congressional Record*. I have also drawn from the following biographies or memoirs: Nathaniel Stephenson, *Nelson W. Aldrich* (New York, 1930); Simkins, *Pitchfork Ben Tillman;* S. H. Acheson, *Joe Bailey: The Last Democrat* (1932); Blair Bolles, *Tyrant from Illinois: Uncle Joe Cannon's Experiment with Personal Power* (New York, 1951); Robert M. La Follette, *Autobiography* (Madison, 1913); Belle Case La Follette and Fola La Follette, *Robert M. La Follette* (2 vols., New York, 1953); Leland L. Sage, *William Boyd Allison: A Study in Practical Politics* (Iowa City, 1956); Ray Stannard Baker, *An American Chronicle* (New York, 1945); and Garraty, *Lodge*.

I have quoted at length from William Z. Ripley, *Railroads: Rates and Regulation* (New York, 1912), and have also used Russel B. Nye, *Midwestern Progressive Politics* (East Lansing, Mich., 1951). The best account of the pipeline amendment controversy is in Arthur Menzies Johnson, *The Development of American Petroleum Pipelines: A Study in Private Enterprise and Public Policy, 1862–1906* (Ithaca, N.Y., 1956), although my account is based on the *Congressional Record*. Johnson points out that the amendment had little economic impact on the oil industry, but that it was nonetheless a landmark in the expansion of federal regulatory power. An illuminating note on the grievances of Nebraskans against the railroads is Richard Lowitt, "George W. Norris, James J. Hill, and the Railroad Rate Bill," *Nebraska History*, XL (1959).

Chapter 15. Trials, Triumphs, and Tragedy

I have added little to Pringle's sprightly account of the controversy over simplified spelling—a few contemporary editorial comments, but no more. My description of the fight for the Pure Food Act and the Meat Inspection Amendment to the Agricultural bill comes partly from *The Letters, The Literary Digest,* and the *Scrapbooks,* partly from the exciting story in Mark Sullivan, *Our Times,* vol. II, and partly from the following memoirs, biographies, and monographs: Dr. Harvey Wiley, *An Autobiography*

(Indianapolis, 1930); Oscar E. Anderson, Jr., *The Health of A Nation: Harvey W. Wiley and the Fight for Pure Food* (Chicago, 1958), an able study that describes TR's subsequent falling out with Wiley; Louis Filler's thoughtful and interesting *Crusaders for Liberalism* (Yellow Springs, Ohio, 1950); and Claude G. Bowers' full dress *Beveridge and the Progressive Era* (New York, 1932). I have also used Faulkner, *The Quest for Social Justice.*

The quotation by Steffens is from his introduction to his *The Shame of the Cities* (New York, 1904). The muckraking incident is drawn from Filler, *Crusaders for Liberalism;* C. C. Regier, *The Era of the Muckrakers* (Chapel Hill, N.C., 1932); Baker, *American Chronicle;* Steffens, *Autobiography;* and Arthur Wallace Dunn, *Gridiron Nights* (New York, 1915), and the usual contemporary sources. My appraisal has also been influenced by the reflective comments of Walter Lippmann, "The Themes of Muckraking," in his *Drift and Mastery* (New York, 1914), and by the evaluation in Hofstadter, *The Age of Reform.* TR's speech is in *The Works,* Vol. XVI. The suggestion that the "muck-rake" speech may have been animated by TR's desire to soften the Senate in preparation for the fight over the Hepburn bill is Richard Lowitt's.

Chapter 16. THE PEACEMAKER I

This chapter closely follows Beale, *Theodore Roosevelt and the Rise of America to World Power.* I have supplemented his work with excerpts from *The Letters, Scrapbooks,* and *The Literary Digest.* I have also taken advantage of such standard works as Alfred W. Griswold, *The Far Eastern Policy of the United States* (New York, 1938); Tyler Dennett, *Roosevelt and the Russo-Japanese War* (New York, 1925); Thomas A. Bailey, *Theodore Roosevelt and the Japanese-American Crises* (Stanford, 1934); and a number of scholarly articles.

I have further used John Hay, *Letters and Extracts from the Diary,* edited by Henry Adams (3 vols., Washington, D.C., 1908). Jessup's *Root* contains much good material on Root's tenure as Secretary of State, while Richard W. Leopold, *Elihu Root and the Conservative Tradition* (Boston, 1954), offers a thoughtful evaluation. William Appleman Williams, *The Tragedy of American Diplomacy* (Cleveland, 1959), and George F. Kennan, *American Diplomacy, 1900–1950* (Chicago, 1951), have proved stimulating in different ways; so, too, Williams' *American-Russian Relations, 1781–1947* (New York, 1952), though I disagree with many of his underlying assumptions.

Chapter 17. THE PEACEMAKER II

Besides the works of Beale and the other authors cited under the preceding heading, I have drawn on: E. C. Sandmeyer, *The Anti-Chinese Movement in California* (Urbana, Ill., 1939);

Eleanor Tupper and George E. McReynolds, *Japan in American Public Opinion* (New York, 1937); Pringle, *Taft;* Thomas A. Bailey, "The Root-Takahira Agreement of 1908," *Pacific Historical Review*, IX (1940); Eugene N. Anderson, *The First Moroccan Crisis, 1904–1906* (Chicago, 1930); Outten J. Clinard, *Japan's Influence on American Naval Power, 1897–1917* (Berkeley, Calif., 1947); Braisted, *The United States Navy in the Pacific, 1897–1909;* Gordon Carpenter O'Gara, *Theodore Roosevelt and the Rise of the Modern Navy* (Princeton, 1943); William Clinton Olson, "Theodore Roosevelt's Conception of an International League," *World Affairs Quarterly*, XXIX (1959); and Raymond A. Esthus, "The Changing Concept of the Open Door, 1899–1910," *The Mississippi Valley Historical Review*, XLVI (1959), an important essay. Also three other important works: Fred H. Harrington, *God, Mammon, and the Japanese* (Madison, Wis., 1944); Charles Vevier, *The United States and China, 1906–1913* (New Brunswick, N.J., 1955); and Robert E. Osgood, *Ideals and Self-Interest in America's Foreign Relations* (Chicago, 1953), which covers these and all the other chapters on foreign policy. The citations of the reports of the British ambassadors are taken from the microfilm reel of same in the Roosevelt Memorial Association Library.

Chapter 18. MORE TROUBLES AND GREATER TRIBULATIONS

Pringle's treatment of the Brownsville episode has not been surpassed. I have filled it out and modified it slightly on the basis of my reading of *The Letters*. I have further drawn from Emma Lou Thornbrough, "The Brownsville Episode and the Negro Vote," *The Mississippi Valley Historical Review*, XLIV (1957); James A. Tinsley, "Roosevelt, Foraker, and the Brownsville Affair," *Journal of Negro History*, XLI (1956); and Everett Walters, *Joseph Benson Foraker: An Uncompromising Republican* (Columbus, Ohio, 1948). Morison, *Turmoil and Tradition*, describes Stimson's support of Roosevelt. It is less critical of TR than my account and those cited above. It is significant, I think, that Roosevelt did not mention the episode in his *An Autobiography*.

Cutright's exposition in depth of the nature-fakers affair in his *Theodore Roosevelt: The Naturalist* supersedes the account in Pringle, *Theodore Roosevelt*. I have drawn on his sources. My treatment of the Panic of 1907 was originally based on the conventional sources, notably, Pringle, *Theodore Roosevelt;* Allen, *Pierpont Morgan;* William C. Schluter, *The Pre-War Business Cycle, 1907–1914* (New York, 1923); Alfred D. Noyes, *Forty Years of American Finance, 1865–1907* (New York, 1909); and several extended notes in *The Letters*, Vol. V. I have tempered my evaluation of Morgan, however, on the basis of the account set forth in John A. Garraty, *Right-Hand Man: The Life of George W. Perkins* (New York, 1960). As the text indicates, I have also drawn on two important essays by Robert H. Wiebe, "Business Disunity and the Progressive Movement, 1901–1914," *Mississippi Valley Historical Review*, XLIV (1958), and "House of Morgan and the Executive, 1905–1913," *American Historical Review*, LXV (1959). Wiebe's statement that "a respectable number of country bankers . . . applauded" the Aldrich-Vreeland Act modifies the assertions by Glass, Williams, and La Follette which I have taken from the *Congressional Record*, Sixtieth Congress, First Session. For the trust problem I have used Henry R. Seager and Charles A. Gulick, Jr., *Trust and Corporation Problems* (New York, 1929), and with particular profit, George W. Stocking, *Basing Point Pricing and Regional Development: A Case Study of the Iron and Steel Industry* (Chapel Hill, N.C., 1954). On the other hand, Ward S. Bowman, Jr. argues in a review article in *The University of Chicago Law Review*, XXII (1954) that Stocking's evidence fails to support the thesis that relative retardation in the South was caused by acquisition or basing point prices. He does not, however, disagree with the proposition that the merging of U.S. Steel and T. C. & I. or the use of a basing point system had no anticompetitive effects on production in the South as elsewhere. Rather, Bowman's point is that the relative retardation of the South is not established by Stocking's analysis. He holds, as do many other economists, that the South's plight was attributable to numerous other factors. The standard treatment of taxation is Sidney Ratner, *American Taxation* (New York, 1942).

Chapter 19. FOR THE GENERATIONS YET UNBORN

In addition to *The Letters* and their several informative notes, I have relied heavily on Gifford Pinchot, *Breaking New Ground* (New York, 1947). Pinchot's book is partisan and fails to do justice to some of the proconservation men with whom he disagreed. Nevertheless, for its anecdotes, for its insights into the best sides of Roosevelt's character, and for its revelation of Pinchot's missionary zeal, without which in my view the conservation movement might never have matured, it is a work of surpassing importance. I have, of course, modified its conclusions in the light of such standard works as E. Louise Peffer, *The Closing of the Public Domain: Disposal and Reservation, 1900–1950* (Stanford, 1951); Roy M. Robbins, *Our Landed Heritage: The Public Domain, 1776–1936* (Princeton, 1942); John Ise, *The United States Forest Policy* (New Haven, 1920); Jerome Kerwin, *Federal Water-Power Legislation* (New York, 1926); Benjamin Horace Hibbard, *A History of the Public Land Policies* (New York, 1939); Samuel Trask Dana, *Forest and Range Policy:*

Its Development in the United States (New York, 1956); and Peggy Heim, "Financing the Federal Reclamation Program, 1902 to 1919: The Development of Repayment Policy" (unpublished Ph.D. dissertation, Columbia University, 1953). I have also drawn on William T. Hornaday, *Thirty Years War for Wildlife* (New York, 1931), and Arthur B. Darling (ed.), *The Public Papers of Francis G. Newlands* (2 vols., New York, 1932), and J. A. O'Callaghan, "Senator Mitchell and the Oregon Land Frauds, 1905," *Pacific Historical Review*, XXI (1952). Pringle, *Theodore Roosevelt*, reviews TR's conservation record (favorably) in two paragraphs. Roosevelt, *An Autobiography*, has a good chapter, perhaps the best in the book. Arthur De Witt Frank, *The Development of the Federal Program of Flood Control on the Mississippi River* (New York, 1930), confirms, in so far as it expresses any judgments, the validity of Roosevelt's and Pinchot's strictures against the Army engineers. Erich W. Zimmermann, *Conservation in the Production of Petroleum* (New Haven, 1957), is an informed and scholarly study. I think, however, that Zimmermann reads too much of the preservationist, as distinguished from conservationist, into Roosevelt and Pinchot. Cutright, *Theodore Roosevelt, The Naturalist*, has much fascinating and relevant material. Whitney R. Cross, "Ideas in Politics: The Conservation Policies of the Two Roosevelts," *Journal of the History of Ideas*, XIV (1953), is suggestive and I think meritorious. Indubitably, the ideals and example of TR influenced FDR. The statement by Dr. Van Hise is from his *The Conservation of Natural Resources in the United States* (New York, 1911).

As my text suggests, I have also revised a number of judgments on the basis of Samuel P. Hays, *Conservation and the Gospel of Efficiency: The Progressive Conservation Movement, 1890–1920* (Cambridge, 1959), the most exhaustive and in many respects, penetrating, study of the movement yet published. Hays plays down too much the antimonopolistic tenor of the Roosevelt-Pinchot waterpower policies, but he puts their forest and range policies in sharp perspective. He is especially informative in his analysis of the roles of McGee and Leighton, in his appreciation of the movement's scientific base, and in his analysis of the differences between the conservationists and preservationists (a subject I have been forced to ignore for reasons of space). On the other hand, I find little in Hays or anything else I have read to negate the contention in J. Leonard Bates, "Fulfilling American Democracy: The Conservation Movement, 1907 to 1921," *Mississippi Valley Historical Review*, XLIV (June, 1957), that "The organized conservationists were concerned more with economic justice and democracy in the handling of resources than with mere prevention of waste." Pinchot's values are ably explored by M. Nelson McGeary in *Gifford Pinchot: Forester-Politician* (Princeton, 1960). McGeary clearly perceives both the scientific and democratic aspects of Pinchot's thought and actions.

Chapter 20. TOWARD THE WELFARE STATE

This chapter has been written mainly from *The Letters, The Works, Scrapbooks,* and *The Literary Digest.* I have not treated Herbert Croly at length, either here or in later chapters, mainly because I am convinced that Roosevelt's actions and speeches had as much impact on Croly, probably, as Croly's writings had on Roosevelt. I am also of the opinion that Roosevelt would have taken almost the same positions he did had Croly never lived. This view is documented in Charles Forcey, *The Crossroads of Liberalism* (New York, 1961). On the other hand, Croly undeniably had a sharp impact on the intellectuals of his times and thus on the climate of opinion in which TR functioned. See, for example, Goldman's *Rendezvous With Destiny.* David W. Noble, *The Paradox of Progressive Thought* (Minneapolis, 1958), ably dissects Croly's ideas. The statements attributed to Scripps are taken from Stone, *Clarence Darrow;* that by Gompers from his *Autobiography.* I have also quoted from Brooks Adams, *The Law of Civilization and Decay* (Vintage Edition, New York, 1955). Berman, *Labor Disputes and the President,* offers a measured evaluation of TR's decision to send troops into Nevada. Berman concludes: "The incident again shows the necessity for investigation by some impartial agent before the President orders troops sent to the scene of a strike. The alarming tone of Governor Sparks' first telegram to the President probably caused the latter to fear the evil consequences of delay, but, as he himself said to the officer in charge of troops . . . 'Better twenty-four hours of riot, damage, and disorder than illegal use of troops.' Though his action in sending soldiers so hastily is deserving of criticism, his insistence that they be strictly impartial and his pressure on the Governor to have the legislature convened and to make provision for doing its own policing, when he realized that he had been placed in a false position, are worthy of praise."

Chapter 21. THE CAMPAIGN OF 1908

Besides the obvious sources—*The Letters, Scrapbooks, The Literary Digest,* and *The Works*—I have drawn on Leopold, *Root;* Lodge (ed.), *Selections;* and numerous other secondary works. Pringle's fine biography of Taft, earlier cited, has been especially useful. Merlo J. Pusey's *Charles Evans Hughes* (2 vols., New York, 1951), unfailingly informative, though not always critically so, has also been helpful. The comments by Archie Butt in this and the following chapter are taken from Lawrence F. Abbott (ed.), *The Letters of Archie Butt* (New York, 1924). The correspondence on the Roosevelt-Gompers controversy is in *Injunc-*

tions: Hearings before the Committee on the Judiciary, House of Representatives. Sixty-Second Congress, Second Session (Washington, D.C., 1912). Yet another irony in the Roosevelt-Gompers relationship is that by 1908 Roosevelt perceived the greater equity in workmen's compensation, as distinguished from employers' liability, laws. He persuasively argued for same in his message of January 31 and in a second special message two months later. Congress responded by establishing a limited compensation system for government employees. Gompers failed, however, to support the President. Not until after Roosevelt left the presidency did the A.F. of L. leader finally comprehend the superiority of the compensation principle.

Chapter 22. THE CHANGING OF THE GUARD

I have supplemented *The Letters, The Works, Scrapbooks,* and *The Literary Digest* with liberal extractions from Pringle's two biographies, *Theodore Roosevelt* and *William Howard Taft;* also from Butt, *Intimate Letters.* The italics in Roosevelt's farewell letter to Pinchot are mine. The quote from Lord Bryce is taken from the microfilm reel previously cited. Morison, *Turmoil and Tradition,* offers a more charitable interpretation than I of Roosevelt's decision to press the libel suits. But see the note in *The Letters,* Vol. VI. Hays, *Conservation and the Gospel of Efficiency,* confirms Roosevelt's and Pinchot's realization before the inauguration that Taft was unfriendly toward their conservation policies. The best analysis of the report of the Country Life Commission, which Congress refused to publish, is Clayton S. Ellsworth, "Theodore Roosevelt's Country Life Commission," *Agricultural History,* XXXIV (1960). Ellsworth reveals Taft's indifference to the Commission's recommendations. He also shows that the Wilson administration put many of the Commission's recommendations, some indirect and others direct, into law. Farm organizations were exempted from the Clayton Antitrust Act; extension education was provided by the Smith-Lever Act of 1914; vocational education was promoted by the Smith-Hughes Act; federal aid to roads was given by an act of 1916; more adequate credit facilities were established through the Federal Reserve Act of 1913, the Federal Warehouse Act of 1916, and the Federal Land Bank Act of the same year; also, the Underwood-Simmons Tariff of 1914 reduced the rates on industrial products purchased by farmers.

PART V / The High Tide of Progressivism

GENERAL

The ground here has been clearly staked out by George E. Mowry, *Theodore Roosevelt and the Progressive Movement*

(Madison, 1946). I have followed his guide lines, though wandering here and there and modifying certain of his conclusions. I have also benefited enormously from Pringle's *Taft*, and from Arthur S. Link's *Wilson: The Road to the White House* (Princeton, 1947), and Link's *Woodrow Wilson and the Progressive Era: 1910–1917* (New York, 1954). My greatest debt continues to be to the editors of *The Letters*, Vol. VII of which covers the period under review. I have also, of course, drawn liberally on Roosevelt's *The Works*. I have been especially impressed in revision by Andrew M. Scott, "The Progressive Era in Perspective," *The Journal of Politics*, XXI (1959).

Chapter 23. THE NEW NATIONALISM

This chapter is based on the works mentioned above, on press commentaries in *The Literary Digest*, and on numerous books cited earlier. The most valuable of the latter include, Goldman, *Rendezvous;* Cutright, *Theodore Roosevelt the Naturalist;* Lodge (ed.), *Selections;* Butt, *Intimate Letters;* Pinchot, *Breaking New Ground;* Jessup, *Root;* White, *Autobiography;* and Roosevelt's *The Works*. I have also used Kenneth W. Hechler, *Insurgency: Personalities and Politics of the Taft Era* (New York, 1940); Ford (ed.), *The Letters of Henry Adams;* and F. W. Taussig, *The Tariff History of the United States* (New York, 1914). Conflicting interpretations of the Ballinger-Pinchot affair are Pringle, *Taft,* and Mowry, *Progressive Movement;* also, Alpheus T. Mason, *Bureaucracy Convicts Itself: The Ballinger-Pinchot Controversy of 1910* (New York, 1941). Hays, *Conservation and the Gospel of Efficiency,* also treats it. Archibald W. Butt, *Taft and Roosevelt: the Intimate Letters of Archie Butt* (2 vols., Garden City, N.Y., 1930), is the source of the remarks by Archie Butt in this and the three following chapters. David H. Burton, "Theodore Roosevelt and Egyptian Nationalism," *Mid-America,* XLI (1959), fairly indicts TR's obtuseness towards Egypt. Warren F. Kuehl, *Hamilton Holt* (Gainsville, Florida, 1960), illuminates aspects of the background of TR's Nobel Prize Address.

As this book goes to press, Elmo R. Richardson's monograph, *Politics of Conservation* (Berkeley, California, 1961), has come to my attention. Based on Ballinger's private papers and many other previously unused manuscript sources, this work sharply upgrades Ballinger's reputation—he emerges as an able conservative of integrity and public spirit. Richardson also makes past actions more understandable, illuminates the administrative complexities of conservative policy, and proves that more westerners supported conservation than is commonly believed. At the same time, he confirms the great contributions of Roosevelt and Pinchot.

Chapter 24. THE TRAVAILS OF INDECISION

The Letters, The Works, Scrapbooks, The Literary Digest, and The Outlook together with Pringle's Taft and Mowry's Progressive Movement are the main sources for this chapter. I have also drawn from Mowry's Theodore Roosevelt and the Progressive Era, wherein he is much more sympathetic to and understanding of Roosevelt's approach to the trust problem than in the earlier Progressive Movement. Wiebe's articles have again proved enlightening, while Garraty's Right-Hand Man has confirmed my own conclusion that Perkins was sincere and conscientious. I have further drawn on Amos R. E. Pinchot, History of the Progressive Party, 1912–1916, edited by Helene Maxwell Hooker (New York, 1958), and Felix Frankfurter, Felix Frankfurter Reminisces: Recorded in Talks with Dr. Harlan B. Phillips (New York, 1960). Among the numerous other works I have used are Pinchot, Breaking New Ground; Hechler, Insurgency; Hays, Conservation and the Gospel of Efficiency; and L. E. Ellis, Reciprocity, 1911 (New Haven, 1939). Of further interest is the statement by John J. Leary, Jr. that TR told him in 1916 that Taft's failure to reappoint the Country Life Commission was "the last straw." It is in Talks with T.R. From the Diaries of John J. Leary Jr. (Boston, 1930). Judge Gary's statements are extracted from Special Committee on Investigation of the U.S. Steel Corporation. Hearings. House of Representatives (Washington, 1911).

For a favorable and reflective appraisal of Chief Justice White's "rule of reason" doctrine, see Eugene V. Rostow, Planning for Freedom, The Public Law of American Capitalism (New Haven, 1959). The most exhaustive and judicious synthesis of antitrust policy I have read is Simon N. Whitney, Antitrust Policies, American Experience in Twenty Industries (2 vols., New York, 1958). Whitney concludes, as does Rostow, that the broad deterrent effect of the antitrust laws has been greater than the visible effects of special prosecutions would suggest. I am particularly impressed by Whitney's implicit confirmation of the broad outlines of Roosevelt's attitude toward big business. His closing statements read in part: "Few if any responsible writers would push such a program [for pure competition] to the extreme, lest the benefits of large-scale operation and the profit motive be lost. . . ." "The pure competition of small firms . . . would not be dynamic or progressive." "Not competition alone, but the combined force supplied by competition and by ambitions of a noncompetitive nature, will make a progressive economy."

Chapter 25. THE PEOPLE SHALL RULE

I have here drawn on almost all the works cited under the three previous headings. Of the new materials, Robert Grant's letter to James Ford Rhodes is in The Letters, Vol. VIII, Appendix II;

Felix Frankfurter's retrospective comments on the recall of judicial decisions in Archibald MacLeish and E. F. Prichard, Jr., (eds.), *Law and Politics: Occasional Papers of Felix Frankfurter, 1913–1918* (New York, 1939). The quotation by John W. Davis is from one of his speeches in 1912 in support of his bill to eradicate the abuse of the injunctive power. My general statements on Davis are based on an examination of his papers which are temporarily in my possession.

The reader dissatisfied with my analysis of Roosevelt's motivation in seeking again the presidency might profitably consult Morison's *Turmoil and Tradition*. Morison puts the case for TR's personal ambition more compellingly and more succinctly than any historian I have read. An interview with Judge Learned Hand on January 25, 1958, is the basis for my statement that he advised TR not to come out for the recall of judicial decisions and to clarify his position after he had come out for it.

Chapter 26. THOU SHALT NOT STEAL

Here again the sources are essentially the same as those listed under *General,* Chapter XXIII, and Chapter XXIV. I should say, however, that in addition to *The Letters* and *The Literary Digest,* I have drawn particularly heavily on Pringle's *Taft.* Belle Case La Follette and Fola La Follette, *Robert M. La Follette,* has also contributed new material; and so, also, Jessup's *Root.* My account of the convention is reconstructed partly from contemporary newspaper accounts, partly from memoirs and autobiographies earlier cited, and largely from Mowry's *Progressive Movement.*

Chapter 27. ARMAGEDDON

To all my standard sources should be added Hofstadter's *Age of Reform;* George E. Mowry, *The California Progressives* (Berkeley, 1951); Bowers, *Beveridge;* and Link, *Woodrow Wilson and the Progressive Era.* Also, Woodrow Wilson, *A Crossroads of Freedom,* edited by John Wells Davidson (New Haven, 1956); Ira Kipnis, *The American Socialist Movement: 1897–1912* (New York, 1952); David Shannon, *The Socialist Party of America* (New York, 1955); Ray Ginger, *The Bending Cross: A Biography of Eugene Victor Debs* (New Brunswick, N.J., 1949); and Nye, *Midwestern Progressive Politics.* Additional sources include Henry May, *Protestant Churches and Industrial America* (New York, 1949); White, *Autobiography;* Robert M. Warner, "Chase S. Osborn and the Presidential Campaign of 1912," *Mississippi Valley Historical Review,* XLVI (1959); and Alfred D. Chandler, Jr., "The Origins of Progressive Leadership," *The Letters,* Vol. VIII, Appendix III. The most recent and most inclusive treatment of the controversy over the antitrust plank is in Garraty, *Right-Hand Man.* Garraty points out that the records have been lost and that, in any event, the changes were matters of detail rather than of principle. He confirms, however, that regardless of the wording of the platform, the real issue was trust-busting *versus* government regulation. Roosevelt's speech at Milwaukee is in *The Works,* Vol. XVII. Also see Robert Donovan, *The Assassins* (New York, 1955). For insight into why one group of conservationists—the pure nature lovers or preservationists—who were at odds with Pinchot because of his insistence that the forests be opened to controlled commercial use, supported Taft rather than TR, see Linnie Marsh Wolfe, *Son of the Wilderness: The Life of John Muir* (New York, 1945).

The statement by Stanley M. Isaacs is from a letter to the author, June 5, 1961. I have taken the liberty of running a couple of sentences together. The generalization on the Progressives' social and economic backgrounds is from Norman Wilensky, "The Republican Old Guard during Insurgency: 1908–1912," (Ph.D. dissertation, Yale University, 1961). Wilensky surveyed the backgrounds of nine hundred Old Guardsmen from every state.

PART VI / One Last Great Cause

Chapter 28. THE VARIETY OF HIM

See Garraty, *Right-Hand Man,* for evidence that Perkins was far more dedicated to preserving the Progressive Party than Harold Ickes, W. A. White, and other Westerners believed. The most discerning short treatment of Wilson's domestic program is in Link, *Woodrow Wilson and the Progressive Era.* A vastly more detailed account of the first phase is in the same author's *Wilson: The New Freedom* (Princeton, 1956). TR's address to the American Historical Association is in *The Works,* Vol. XII. His disparaging remarks to Trevelyan about history professors should be weighed, perhaps, against his several deferential letters to Frederick Jackson Turner printed in *The Letters,* Vol. I. I have drawn on the brief and interesting account of TR's South American expedition in Cutright, *Theodore Roosevelt the Naturalist.* The record of the libel suit is in *Roosevelt* vs. *Newett: A Transcript of the Testimony Taken at Depositions Read at Marquette, Michigan* (Privately printed, 1914). TR's review of the Armory Show is in *The Works,* Vol. XII. Sam Hunter, *Modern American Painting and Sculpture* (New York, 1959) gives a good account of the Armory Show's critical reception. He recognizes the force of TR's affirmation, but emphasizes more his negative views.

As I said in the text, Wagenknecht, *The Seven Worlds,* offers the most inclusive appreciation of TR's feeling for the arts I have read. Wagenknecht is not as penetrating as many of Roosevelt's negative critics, but TR himself never professed to be a critic. If Roosevelt's sophistication was less than that of the critics and academicians, it was greater, certainly, than that of the average college graduate and incomparably superior to that of most politicians. At the risk of being didactic I repeat the judgments implied in my text: It is a good thing to have a President or former President interested in the arts; TR did more to advance them than any President between Jefferson and Franklin Roosevelt, whose great service was performed through the WPA.

I have also used Homer Saint-Gaudens, "Roosevelt and Our Coin Designs," *Century*, XCIV (1920); Glenn Brown, "Roosevelt and the Fine Arts," *American Architect*, CXVI (1919); and Carl J. Weber, "Poet and President," *New England Quarterly*, XVI (1943). I have also drawn on Owen Wister, *Story of a Friendship;* Henry Adams, *The Education of Henry Adams* (Boston, 1918); and Hermann Hagedorn and Sidney Wallach, *A Theodore Roosevelt Round-Up* (New York, 1958), wherein are printed the statements by Robert Frost, *et al.* These have the ring of the memoria —they were written after TR's death—but they are surely of value. Hamlin Garland's affection for and appreciation of TR is also brought out in Jean Holloway, *Hamlin Garland, A Biography* (Austin, Texas, 1960). The most recent criticism of TR's literary values is Don D. Walker, "Wister, Roosevelt and James: A Note on the Western," *American Quarterly*, XII (1960). Walker describes how TR prevailed on Wister to eliminate the gory details from an episode in *The Virginian* and suggests that TR may have been responsible for Wister's subsequent failure to realize his potential. In the same article, however, Walker quotes W. D. Howells, the then dean of realism, as advising Wister that he not show his first novel to a publisher because "it was certain to shock the public gravely" and because "a whole fig tree would not cover the Widow Taylor." Many of TR's letters to Wister and numerous other writers are in the eight volumes of *The Letters.* I have formed my conclusions on the whole body of them.

Chapter 29. THE BUGLE THAT WOKE AMERICA

The title for this chapter is taken from Hermann Hagedorn, *The Bugle That Woke America: The Saga of Theodore Roosevelt's Last Battle for His Country* (New York, 1940). The chapter as a whole is a condensation of part of my doctoral dissertation, "Wilson, Roosevelt, and Interventionism, 1914–1917" (Northwestern University, 1954). Readers interested in published works covering the same period might consult Link, *Woodrow Wilson and the Progressive Era,* or William E. Leuchtenberg, *The Perils of Prosperity* (Chicago, 1958); also most of the works cited in the notes for Chapter 31. For a revealing insight into Roosevelt's matured views on the need to extend popular control of the government, his continued contempt for legalism, his belief "that strong labor unions are indispensable to progress," and his reaffirmation of Charles Van Hise's theories on the regulation of trusts—all of which positions, as I have tried to show, he had come to during the last years of his presidency—see his *Outlook* review (November 18, 1914) of Herbert Croly's *Progressive Democracy* and Walter Lippmann's

Drift and Mastery. It is republished in *The Works,* Vol. XII under the title "Progressive Democracy." The letter by TR describing his meeting with the German emissary is in Mrs. Theodore Roosevelt, Jr., *Day Before Yesterday* (Garden City, 1958).

Chapter 30. THE CAMPAIGN FOR AMERICAN RIGHTS

This chapter is also a condensation of a part of my dissertation as cited under the preceding heading. The report of the telephone conversations at the convention was originally taken from John A. Garraty (ed.), "TR on the Telephone," *American Heritage,* IX (1957). I have since used the original. It is in the Perkins Papers in the Special Collections Room of the Butler Library at Columbia University. I am impressed by the evidences of TR's hope, expressed over the phone to Lodge and others, that a militant nominating speech by Senator Albert Fall on the Mexican situation might swing the Republican convention behind him. It tends to confirm, regrettably, my speculation that TR would have been as ready to go to war against Mexico as against Germany had there been no conflagration in Europe. The report of President Wilson's conversation with Cobb is taken from John L. Heaton, *Cobb of "The World"* (New York, 1924).

Chapter 31. THE LAST BATTLE

I have based this chapter partly on the collections of the Papers of Theodore Roosevelt, Woodrow Wilson, Newton D. Baker, John J. Pershing, and Hugh S. Scott, all on deposit in the Manuscripts Division of the Library of Congress. I have also drawn liberally from TR's wartime writings as published in Ralph Stout (ed.), *Roosevelt in the Kansas City Star* (Boston, 1921). My views on the excesses of the war years have been formed, if they needed to be formed, by such works as H. C. Peterson and G. C. Fite, *Opponents of War, 1917–1918* (Madison, Wis., 1957); Carl Wittke, *The German-Language Press in America* (Lexington, 1957); Zechariah Chafee, *Free Speech in the United States* (Cambridge, 1941); J. Weinstein, "Anti-War Sentiment and the Socialist Party, 1917–1918," *Political Science Quarterly,* LXXIV (1959); Robert K. Murray, *Red Scare: A Study in National Hysteria, 1919–1920* (Minneapolis, 1955); John Blum, "Nativism, Anti-Radicalism, and the Foreign Scare, 1917–1920," *Midwest Journal,* III (1950–51); and Arthur Ekirch, *Civilian and the Military* (New York, 1956). I have also read with interest, but not used, Harry N. Scheiber, *The Wilson Administration and Civil Liberties, 1917–1921* (Ithaca, N.Y., 1960). Scheiber places a heavy burden of blame on President Wilson.

I have drawn most of my personal anecdotes from Hagedorn, *The Bugle That Woke America;* Oscar K. Davis, *Released for Publication* (New York, 1925); Frederick S. Wood (ed.), *Roosevelt As We Knew Him* (Philadelphia, 1927); Charles Willis

Thompson, *Presidents I Have Known* (Indianapolis, 1929); Leary, *Talks With T.R.;* Bishop, *Life and Times;* James Amos, *Theodore Roosevelt* (New York, 1927). The description of Taft at the grave is from a letter by Kent B. Stiles to Hermann Hagedorn, December 24, 1955. Mr. Stiles, who was in 1919 a reporter for the Associated Press, writes that the "scene was too sacred" for him to report at the time.

I am aware, of course, that the reports of TR's various sayings as recorded in the above cited memoirs and reproduced in my text may not be literally accurate in all cases. Yet every one of them seems to be in character with TR's personality and the historical situation. Most of them were recorded, moreover, by trained newspapermen accustomed to taking down verbatim accounts of conversations. On the theory that the historian's charge to recreate the past is more nearly, if still imperfectly, achieved by using such materials with discrimination rather than by dismissing them in the interest of what may become a sterile literalism, I have chosen to include them.

Scholarly support for the speculations that TR would have been the leading contender for the Republican nomination in 1920 may be found in Howard Scott Greenlee, "The Republican Party in Division and Reunion, 1913–1920," (Doctoral dissertation, University of Chicago, 1950). My generalizations about the nature of the Republican party in the post-war era are substantiated by the facts, if not always the interpretations, set forth in almost any textbook on the period. Also see Arthur S. Link, "What Happened to the Progressive Movement in the 1920's?" *American Historical Review,* LXIV (1959). Link recounts the persistence of progressivism in Congress, but also speculates that neither Wilson nor Roosevelt could have formed a viable progressive government. The most dispassionate account I have read of the wellsprings of Lodge's opposition to Wilson's conception of the League of Nations is in Garraty's *Henry Cabot Lodge.* Although Garraty does not discount the personal equation, he succeeds in showing that Lodge's position was consistent with the one he (and Roosevelt) had always taken on national sovereignty. Thus he writes of the Lodge reservations: "Though some of them were unnecessary and others plainly motivated by political considerations, the chief purpose of most of them was to define the obligations of the United States more specifically and to make clear the right of Congress to control American performance of these duties."

Elting E. Morison and John M. Blum (eds.), *The Letters of Theodore Roosevelt,* from Vol. VIII of which is taken Clemenceau's editorial, have been to the end of inestimable value.

Index

Index